THE FUTURE OF COMMERCIAL LAW

The reform of commercial law through harmonisation, unification, codification and other means remains one of the most important projects in developing the institutional architecture for the global economy. This edited collection engages with the challenges and contributes to a greater understanding of the problems faced by states, international organisations, and private sector actors in this ongoing reform project for commercial law. The volume takes stock of the project to date and looks towards a restructuring of the agenda to deal with new challenges. The primary aim of the collection is to understand the future of commercial law reform in a way that offers ideas and strategies for innovation as well as in methodologies for project selection and evaluation. In so doing, the collection informs the debate on the global reform of commercial law and will be of interest not only to academics, but also to those involved in the reform of commercial law around the world. The volume collects papers presented at the UK Society of Legal Scholars Annual Seminar 2017.

Hart Studies in Commercial and Financial Law: Volume 4

Hart Studies in Commercial and Financial Law

Series Editor: John Linarelli

This series offers a venue for publishing works on commercial law as well as on the regulation of banking and finance and the law on insolvency and bankruptcy. It publishes works on the law on secured credit, the regulatory and transactional aspects of banking and finance, the transactional and regulatory institutions for financial markets, legal and policy aspects associated with access to commercial and consumer credit, new generation subjects having to do with the institutional architecture associated with innovation and the digital economy including works on blockchain technology, work on the relationship of law to economic growth, the harmonisation or unification of commercial law, transnational commercial law, and the global financial order. The series promotes interdisciplinary work. It publishes research on the law using the methods of empirical legal studies, behavioural economics, political economy, normative welfare economics, law and society inquiry, socio-legal studies, political theory, and historical methods. Its coverage includes international and comparative investigations of areas of law within its remit.

Volume 1: The Financialisation of the Citizen: Social and Financial Inclusion through European Private Law
Guido Comparato

Volume 2: MiFID II and Private Law: Enforcing EU Conduct of Business Rules
Federico Della Negra

Volume 3: Reforming Corporate Retail Investor Protection: Regulating to Avert Mis-Selling
Diane Bugeja

Volume 4: The Future of Commercial Law: Ways Forward for Change and Reform
Edited by Orkun Akseli and John Linarelli

The Future of Commercial Law

Ways Forward for Change and Reform

Edited by
Orkun Akseli
and
John Linarelli

•HART•
OXFORD • LONDON • NEW YORK • NEW DELHI • SYDNEY

HART PUBLISHING
Bloomsbury Publishing Plc
Kemp House, Chawley Park, Cumnor Hill, Oxford, OX2 9PH, UK
1385 Broadway, New York, NY 10018, USA

HART PUBLISHING, the Hart/Stag logo, BLOOMSBURY and the Diana logo are trademarks of Bloomsbury Publishing Plc

First published in Great Britain 2020

A catalogue record for this book is available from the British Library.

Library of Congress Cataloging-in-Publication data

Names: Future of commercial law (Conference) (2017 : University of Durham). | Akseli, Nazmi Orkun, editor. | Linarelli, John, editor. | Society of Legal Scholars, sponsoring body. | Durham Law School, host institution, sponsoring body.

Title: The future of commercial law : ways forward for change and reform / edited by Orkun Akseli and John Linarelli.

Description: Oxford ; New York : Hart, 2020. | Series: Hart studies in commercial and financial law; vol 4 | "The papers collected in this volume derive from a Society of Legal Scholars (SLS) seminar held at the College of St Hilde and St Bede at Durham University on 27–28 February 2017. The seminar was convened under the auspices of Durham Law School's Institute for Commercial and Corporate Law"—ECIP Introduction. | Includes bibliographical references and index.

Identifiers: LCCN 2019051887 (print) | LCCN 2019051888 (ebook) | ISBN 9781509914692 (hardback) | ISBN 9781509914715 (Epub)

Subjects: LCSH: Commercial law—International unification—Congresses.

Classification: LCC K1004.8 .F88 2020 (print) | LCC K1004.8 (ebook) | DDC 346.07—dc23

LC record available at https://lccn.loc.gov/2019051887

LC ebook record available at https://lccn.loc.gov/2019051888

ISBN: HB: 978-1-50991-469-2
ePDF: 978-1-50991-470-8
ePub: 978-1-50991-471-5

Typeset by Compuscript Ltd, Shannon
Printed and bound in Great Britain by CPI Group (UK) Ltd, Croydon CR0 4YY

MIX
Paper from responsible sources
FSC www.fsc.org FSC® C013604

TABLE OF CONTENTS

PART IV
TENSIONS FOR SALE OF GOODS LAW

PART V
LAW FOR ACCESS TO FINANCE

PART VI
SECURED TRANSACTIONS: GLOBAL AND NATIONAL MOVEMENTS

PART VII
PUBLIC–PRIVATE PARTNERSHIPS: AN AREA FOR FUTURE REFORM?

LIST OF CONTRIBUTORS

Orkun Akseli, Associate Professor of Commercial Law, Durham University Law School

Teresa Rodríguez de las Heras Ballell, Associate Professor of Commercial Law, Universidad Carlos III of Madrid, Spain

Anca Chirita, Assistant Professor of Competition Law, Durham University Law School, Non-Governmental advisor to the International Competition Network for the European Commission Directorate-General for Competition

Richard Craven, Senior Lecturer in Law, University of Sheffield

Henry Gabriel, Professor of Law, Elon University

Louise Gullifer QC (hon) FBA, Rouse Ball Professor of English Law, University of Cambridge; Fellow of Gonville & Caius College, Cambridge

Richard M Koln, Principal, Goldberg Koln Ltd.,

Souichirou Kozuka, Professor, Faculty of Law, Gakushuin University

John Linarelli, Professor of Commercial Law, Durham University Law School (on leave), Visiting Professor of Law, Touro College Jacob D Fuchsberg Law Center

Caroline Nicholas, Head, Technical Assistance Section, Senior Legal Officer, International Trade Law Division, UNCITRAL Secretariat, United Nations Office of Legal Affairs

Julian Ranetunge, Associate, King & Spalding

Chris Reed, Professor of Electronic Commerce Law, Centre for Commercial Law Studies, School of Law, Queen Mary University of London

Ingeborg Schwenzer, Dean, Swiss International Law School, Professor emirita of Private Law, University of Basel

Dr Andrew JM Steven, Senior Lecturer in law, University of Edinburgh

Fernando Tafur, MLaw, University of Basel

Dr Sean Thomas, Reader, The York Law School, University of York

Jenifer Varzaly, Director of Studies, Downing College, Academic Member of the Faculty of Law, University of Cambridge

Dr Ping Wang, Assistant Professor of Law, Deputy Director of the Public Procurement Research Group, School of Law, University of Nottingham

LIST OF CONTRIBUTORS

[illegible]

Introduction

The papers collected in this volume derive from a Society of Legal Scholars (SLS) seminar held at the College of St Hild and St Bede at Durham University on 27–28 February 2017. The seminar was convened under the auspices of Durham Law School's Institute for Commercial and Corporate Law. The seminar benefitted from SLS funding and from funding from the law firm of Womble Bond Dickinson. The editors and contributors express their sincerest appreciation for this funding.

The editors and contributors were most honoured that Sir Roy Goode gave the keynote address for the seminar. Sir Roy has our sincerest gratitude for his participation.

When the editors were putting together the funding proposal for the SLS, we shared a view that for global commercial law-making in whatever form or with whatever label one may wish to put on it – harmonisation, unification, codification, law reform, modernisation and so on – we began by asking what needed to be done next. We saw the seminar as an academic complement to an UNCITRAL Congress, scheduled for 4–6 July 2017 at UNCITRAL headquarters in Vienna, to celebrate UNCITRAL's 50th anniversary and explore new directions in the law relevant to cross-border commerce. We had an idea that global commercial law-making probably should follow and not lead – in other words, follow and be of service to transactors in markets. We believe the contributions in this volume reflect this logic, though some also test the boundaries.

States have sought to harmonise commercial law across their borders at least since the era of economic globalisation of the nineteenth century. With the global economy creating an interdependent world, the law governing market transactions has taken on an ever more vital importance. Three intergovernmental organisations, the United Nations Commission on International Trade Law (UNCITRAL), the International Institute for the Unification of Private Law (UNIDROIT) and the Hague Conference on Private International Law, all established in different times when the global economic order was in a different configuration, have played important roles, as do international financial institutions such as the World Bank. Representatives of both UNCITRAL and UNIDROIT participated in the seminar, as well as a representative of the World Bank.

The current era of economic globalisation is more interconnected than ever before. Trade and investment are the main drivers, which are in themselves not new phenomena, but what is new is how these economic activities are accomplished. The character of economic globalisation has changed, and these changes have increased interdependence and linkages between states.[1] Global value chains have become much

[1] See eg, J Linarelli, 'How Trade Law Changed: Why it Should Change Again' (2014) 65 *Mercer Law Review* 621; NO Akseli, *International Secured Transactions Law: Facilitation of Credit and International Conventions and Instruments* (Abingdon, Routledge, 2011).

more prominent and production processes have become increasingly fragmented across state borders. Outsourcing and offshoring have risen dramatically as preferred methods of operation for many multinational enterprises. The services trade has increased. The lines between goods and services are blurred. New forms of financing are coming into play. Cross-border technology flows have increased substantially, and require not only fair and effective intellectual property protection but also a substantial architecture for contract and finance, as well as for facilitating transactions in cyberspace. What is the most valuable about goods are not the tangible aspects of the good, but the technology and branding embedded in the good. It is not the plastic surrounding the mobile phone but the design and the technology which provides for most of its value. Cross-border financial flows have been on a steady rise with the demise of the old Bretton Woods order in the 1980s and the rise of global capital markets. Finally, the need for government engagement in both old-style 'hard' infrastructure and in the development of 'soft' infrastructure for markets seems ever more paramount. The rules for markets are constitutive of markets themselves and that the terms and conditions for contracting need to be set in a way that is fair to contract parties as well as to stakeholders more generally. Fairness in the rules applies both to business-to-business commerce as well as to terms and conditions for public private partnerships.

The changing configurations of economic globalisation prompt us to ask whether fundamental changes need to be made to the way that reform of transactional law should proceed. Intergovernmental law-making organisations have reached an important tipping point. New techniques, methods and technologies are on offer and these organisations are absorbing the message.

The issues facing reform efforts are both technical and political. Economic globalisation is a driver of harmonisation of law across borders, but law at its core is a state-driven phenomenon, linking closely to sovereignty, self-determination and government accountability to citizens. An inevitable tension is present in any international harmonisation project, with self-determination driving the need to make law at the lowest level practical for reasons having to do with popular consent and accountability, whilst recognising the need for uniform law to be at work in the global economy to reduce transaction costs, make enforceable agreements in circumstances in which transactors want them to be enforced, to establish clear rules for property and contract across borders, and to provide institutions of a contemporary nature for the creation and facilitation of credit.

Commercial law reform brings out various stakeholder interests. Governments, intergovernmental organisations, and industry have interests in reform efforts while reform efforts bring out regulatory competition among rule-producing stakeholders. International organisations have an interest in efficacious and relevant harmonisation within their mandates. Regulators and governments have an interest in facilitating successful and effective product, technology and capital markets through appropriate legal institutions. Of course, harmonised commercial law is important to citizens and communities; it really does not do the job if it does not improve the lives of citizens in communities within states.

Apart from the political considerations, harmonisation must work, and these are issues of a technical nature. Harmonising bodies need to prepare instruments that both facilitate economic exchange and foster development for low and middle-income countries. A principal aim of the seminar was to foster greater understanding of the problems faced by states, international organisations, and private sector actors in the reform of commercial law in the global economy.

The contributions in this volume may profitably be seen as offering at least a partial roadmap of new subjects for commercial law reform, as identifying tensions in existing global commercial law reform projects in need of addressing for a more robust match for the twenty-first-century global economy, and as a serious set of methodological questions and insights on how organisations engaged in global commercial law reform should proceed in project selection and evaluation.

The contributions in Part I of this volume offer foundations for the all the contributions in the volume. Caroline Nicholas's contribution set forth in chapter one, 'UNCITRAL's Role in Commercial Law Reform: History and Future Prospects', offers a much-needed exploration of UNCITRAL's history and its role in global commercial law-making. It lays essential groundwork for the rest of the chapters. The history and structure of the institutions at work in global commercial law-making are sometimes overlooked, but it is that history and structure that has an important role in determining what law reform projects can feasibly move forward. To refer to by now what may be dogma in the study of the relationship of law to economic development, 'institutions matter'.[2] UNCITRAL has played an essential role in any such developments. Henry Gabriel's contribution in chapter two, 'The Harmonisation of Laws in the United States of America', provides a much-needed historical account. The study of how American federalism has affected the production of private and commercial law is often misunderstood. A great deal can be learned from the study of the history of the American Law Institute and the National Conference of Commissioners on Uniform State Laws (now known as the Uniform Law Commission) in the production of a common commercial law to span great distances in a large and complex economy. These institutions produced what may be the most successful commercial law reform project in the modern history of such projects, the American Uniform Commercial Code (UCC), which includes what is likely a global standard for the law on secured transactions, UCC Article 9.

Part II transitions from the foundational chapters offered by Nicholas and Gabriel into constructive and critical interventions. Souichirou Kozuka's contribution, 'Do We Need Harmonisation for Everything? The Possibilities and Limits of Harmonising Financial Law', set forth as chapter three, advocates a case for pragmatism in commercial law reform projects. According to Kozuka, not all commercial law is an area for harmonisation. Kozuka explains that not all of commercial law harmonisation has been widely accepted and that this phenomenon has to be more fully understood. Kozuka addresses the complex question of why this is so. He addresses three questions: (1) what the benefits of 'selective' or partial harmonisation might be; (2) what the constitutes the character of the domestic law in issue; and (3) what factors determine when harmonisation will be successful. Kozuka offers a probing examination of the costs and benefits of reform towards harmonisation, and explores the reasons for divergence or legal diversity.

[2] A recent survey of institutional economics can be found in Stefan Voigt, *Institutional Economics: An Introduction* (Cambridge, Cambridge University Press, 2019).

John Linarelli's contribution in chapter four, 'Behavioural Comparative Law: Its Relevance to Global Commercial Law-making', develops a framework by which to evaluate the making of commercial law at the global level. Linarelli's approach grounds in both behavioural science and comparative law. He identifies an emerging school of comparative law, which he calls behavioural comparative law (BCL). BCL has the potential to advance substantially the ability to explain why commercial law is produced the way it is at the global level. Linarelli's analysis leads to findings about the methods that global commercial law-makers use, how they choose areas of law to work on, and how they go about doing their work. Linarelli finds that because of the cognitive limitations on the participants in the global commercial law-making process, when feasible, global commercial law-makers should use methods of cost–benefit analysis when evaluating project selection or get as close to they can in doing so when cost–benefit analysis is not feasible, though it may not usually be feasible, due to methodological constraints and the lack of data. Jennifer Varzalay's contribution in chapter five, 'Towards a Unified Approach to Economic Assessment in International Commercial Law Reform', takes the position that economic assessment is critical to global commercial law reform, to ensure law reform efforts are evidence-based and result in economic benefit. Varzalay finds that such assessment is seldom undertaken and, when undertaken, is not uniform in its scope or methodology, nor subject to systematic review. Varzalay proposes guidelines to address this challenge. Her chapter aims to provide a first step forward towards creating a unified approach, by proposing guidelines on five key components of any economic assessment, with a focus on quantitative analysis, replicability, transparency and continuous improvement.

Part III deals with a set of critical issues facing the ability of existing institutions of harmonisation and reform to be able to achieve effective outcomes. Chris Reed's contribution, 'Cyberspace Institutions, Community and Legitimate Authority, set forth as chapter six, offers a compelling account of the challenges that international organisations and even states face in possessing and exercising the requisite authority needed to regulate cyberspace. Reed explores how many existing organisations have at most charismatic or persuasive authority to regulate but they lack even this kind of weaker authority when it comes to regulating cyberspace. According to Reed, further harmonisation of the norms regulating cyberspace is unlikely to come from the traditional sources of transnational law. Even reliance on traditional state law is problematic for governing cyberspace. Reed provides a set of criteria for evaluating the authority to make rules for cyberspace and identifies institutions that have this authority, though they are not the traditional institutions one would think for reform of the law. Anca Chirita's contribution is chapter seven, 'Data-driven Mergers Under EU Competition Law', which reminds us of the complexities associated with the harmonisation of competition law and policy in the EU. The EU may be the only source of competition law and policy harmonised among nation-states. Competition law and policy involves regulation and public law, areas that have been traditionally resistant to transnational law reform. Like Reed's contribution, Chirita's contribution suggests fresh difficulties when it comes to reforming the law associated with online platforms. Chirita examines data-driven mergers subject to EU regulation, which are mergers of firms that involve large-scale individual user data. Firms engage in these mergers partly to access and accumulate big data about individuals. Chirita argues that data-driven merger activity must be regulated to go beyond conventional market questions and into privacy concerns for individuals. Part III informs us that transnational law reformers will have challenges in attempting to propose rules for new normative terrain brought about by new technologies.

Part IV continues with the challenges of new normative terrains but with a focus on what has traditionally been characterised as 'sale of goods' law. Sean Thomas's contribution in chapter eight, 'Circular Economy, Title and Harmonisation of Commercial Law', considers the implications of law and the circular economy on commercial law reform in light of the necessarily cross-jurisdictional nature of circular economies and the recognised role for English law in global reform debates. Some of the more profound effects are, most importantly, the shift from 'ownership' to 'use' of goods as a guiding principle. The foundation of Thomas's analysis is on an illustration of the shift to governance of circular economic practices through contract rather than title, as better able to control use of goods. Thomas also considers the implications for harmonisation as a mechanism for regulating the circular economy, exploring how aspects of commercial law may be harmonised and reformed through various means to effectively implement the contractual focus of circular economy. In chapter nine, 'Service Contracts and the CISG', Ingeborg Schwenzer, Julian Ranetunge and Fernando Tafur explore the tensions in the traditional conceptual distinctions between goods and services in sale of goods law and in particular, in the United Nations Convention for the International Sale of Goods (CISG). This tension is largely the result of the changing nature of products which are the subject of sales contracts. The distinction between goods and services, they contend, will not continue to hold into the future. But the prognosis they offer is positive. They examine the reasons why the CISG excludes service contracts from its scope by undertaking a comparative examination of domestic laws dealing with the distinction between goods and services and offer an approach to handling the more challenging CISG provisions on how they apply to service contracts.

Part V covers the important subject of law and finance for businesses. Small and medium enterprises (SMEs) account for the vast majority of firms worldwide. SMEs play an important role in national economies and in the global economy. They are significant contributors to employment. They face, nevertheless, more significant financial obstacles than larger firms. They generally have less access to external finance and encounter higher transaction costs and risk premiums for external finance. Policymakers have identified access to finance as one of the most significant constraints on SME growth. Unsurprisingly, the availability of external finance is critical for the promotion of entrepreneurship and innovation. Louise Gullifer's contribution, chapter ten, 'The Financing of Micro-Businesses in the United Kingdom: The Current Position and the Way Forward', sets forth important groundwork for understanding both how external finance actually works for the very smallest businesses in the UK and how the UK has developed legal and institutional responses. Gullifer works out a detailed financial picture and constraints for typical micro-businesses and identifies the sorts of legal frameworks that support various forms of external finance for these businesses. Teresa Rodriguez de las Heras Ballell's contribution in chapter eleven, 'Equity Crowdfunding to Facilitate Access to Finance for Small Business: The Regulatory Response and the Indirect Impact on Company Law', offers substantial insights on one of the newest and most innovative forms of financing for small businesses: equity crowdfunding.

Ballel offers important research on a new source of funding for innovative firms and entrepreneurship. She sets forth a foundational discussion of the nature and features of equity crowdfunding and offers a comparative analysis of the regulation of equity crowdfunding in the US and the EU. Ballel offers an important finding in her chapter: the way equity crowdfunding is regulated produces a problem for corporate governance in that regulation effectively imposes a corporate governance model for public companies on private companies. She calls this phenomenon the indirect effect. Ballel discusses the problems the indirect effect causes for small privately held businesses.

Part VI drills down into law and finance issues with a focus on the law on secured transactions and its reform. It starts with Orkun Akseli's contribution in chapter twelve, 'Global Secured Transactions Law-Making and National Law Reforms: Quo Vadis Secured Transactions Law?'. Akseli focuses on lessons learned from the development of texts and instruments on the law on secured transactions and how those texts and instruments have influenced national law reform. The ability to give security influences not only the cost of credit but also, in some cases, whether credit will be available at all. The difficulties posed by poor secured credit laws are felt acutely in countries which are most in need of finance: emerging market countries which, for various reasons, tend to have laws falling below the expectations of international banks and lenders. Akseli examines the role of UNCITRAL and international financial institutions, notably the World Bank and the European Bank for Reconstruction and Development (EBRD), in setting standards on secured transactions and insolvency laws. These organisations have taken an active part in reforming secured transactions laws since the 1990s.

Richard Koln's contribution in chapter thirteen, 'The Role of Innovation in Cross-Border Business Lending', explains how the move of US middle market companies in economic globalisation have driven the move to cross-border lending by American financial institutions. According to Koln, these middle market companies have taken part in economic globalisation and have incentivised American lenders to engage in cross-border lending, which Koln characterises as a sea change in lending practices. These American lenders have identified lender-friendly jurisdictions that can offer the functional equivalent of American-style creditor protection. The focus, according to Koln, has been on the quality of secured transactions law and on institutional quality more generally. Koln offers innovative examples of how lawyers and lenders have engaged in creative transaction structuring to bridge gaps between the demand for lending and the supply of adequate legal protections for creditors. An important factor influencing cross-border lending, according to Koln, has been the reform of secured transactions law by countries, on a global scale. Since the 1970s the normative structure of secured transactions law has been embodied in an increasing variety of international conventions and instruments, many of which draw on the notion that a harmonised law of credit and security lowers the cost of credit. Domestic law reform in this field has taken diverse routes. Some jurisdictions have followed the UCC Article 9, while others seek to evolve from existing practice through codification which enables a transparent and simplified access to rules and principles.

Andrew Steven's contribution in chapter fourteen, 'Reform of Moveable Transactions Law in Scotland', discusses the completed long-term project of the Scottish Law Commission to study and reform the law of secured transactions in Scotland. The Commission's work resulted in the publication of a report and the preparation of draft legislation for consideration by the Scottish Government. Steven's chapter offers an overview of the draft law and the process by which it was made and puts it in the general context of commercial law reform. Steven's contribution highlights the diversity of views on how a law on secured transactions should be constructed and how some American UCC Article 9 type influences must be tempered with how those changes might be received within the longstanding conceptualisation of the law in various jurisdictions.

With UNCITRAL's conclusion of its work on its Model Law on Procurement of Goods, Construction, and Services in 2011 and the influence of its Legislative Guide on Privately Financed Infrastructure Projects published in 2000, the seminar organisers pondered whether there might be other fruitful areas of follow-on reform work that is broadly related to public procurement. This led us to think about infrastructure issues and public private partnerships. Part VII deals with these issues. Richard Craven's contribution, chapter fifteen, 'Public Private Partnerships and Harmonisation: The UK Public Private Partnership Act', begins with an exploration of the growth of public private partnerships, the globalisation of its regulation, and the need for harmonisation. Craven then proceeds to discuss key issues that UNCITRAL would need to address in any model law on public–private partnerships, when they may be used, the possible need for developing policy and standardised documents, and whether a special procurement process might be needed such as the EU's competitive dialogue. Craven concludes his chapter with a plea for caution, warning that there may be a need for flexibility, for example, so as not to constrain the advancement of innovation in public–private partnership structures. Craven acknowledges that a need for some legal diversity may be evident, which may also relate to the need for capacity-building in government. Finally, Ping Wang's contribution, chapter sixteen, 'Regulation of Public Private Partnerships in China: The Search for Coherence, Consistency, and Clarity', offers a systematic analysis of the current state of Chinese law on public–private partnerships. Wang explains that while China has long been engaged in the use of private finance in major projects, such as in the use of build–operate–transfer contracts in the 1980s, the current diversity of law across the country, and the segregated framework that results, has lead to the need for new legislation at the national level. There is some lack of clarity in China as to what public–private partnerships might entail. Wang provides an exhaustive treatment of existing Chinese law and the road to reform. We can learn much from the Chinese experience, given the Chinese focus on infrastructure development both within its national borders and globally.

To conclude, we hope this volume will be seen as offering a rich set of insights on what might be some of the elements of a future for commercial law reform, broadly conceived in terms of both subject coverage and methodology. The law regulating markets at the transactional level has become a wide-open field, with new areas evolving at a very fast pace. Our coverage could only be very selective in this volume. We look forward to seeing more volumes on the future of commercial law.

PART I

Foundations and Fundamentals of Commercial Law Reform

1

UNCITRAL's Role in Commercial Law Reform: History and Future Prospects

CAROLINE NICHOLAS*

UNCITRAL (the United Nations Commission on International Trade Law) has held three 'Congresses' in its 50 years of existence, celebrating its 25th, 40th and 50th anniversaries respectively. It has also celebrated milestones, such as the 1998 New York Convention Day,[1] on the 40th anniversary of the Convention on the Recognition and Enforcement of Foreign Arbitral Awards (1958),[2] and a High Level Panel in 2015 on 'Thirty-five Years of Uniform Sales Law: Trends and Perspectives'.[3] Each of these events has looked at topical aspects of the law of international commerce and United Nations activities, as well as what have been termed the 'recurring themes' arising in harmonisation and unification of international trade law.[4] While each of these events has welcomed the pivotal role that UNCITRAL has played in reform of the law of international trade, the discussions have considered lessons learned and challenges in meeting its objectives. These issues will be the focus of this chapter, and considering them indicates that those involved in setting up UNCITRAL were remarkably prescient as regards both the likely successes of and challenges for UNCITRAL.

* Many thanks to Jae Hyuk Lee, an UNCITRAL intern, for his substantial assistance in the research of this chapter.

[1] See 'Possible future work in the area of international commercial arbitration: Note by the Secretariat' UNCITRAL, Thirty-second session, Vienna, 17 May–4 June 1999 (A/CN.9/460), available at https://uncitral.un.org/en/commission. For the texts of the 1958 New York Convention Day speeches, see 'Enforcing Arbitration Awards under the New York Convention: Experience and Prospects' (United Nations Publication), available at https://uncitral.un.org/sites/uncitral.un.org/files/media-documents/uncitral/en/nycday-e.pdf.

[2] 'Enforcing Arbitration Awards under the New York Convention' (ibid).

[3] 'Thirty-five Years of Uniform Sales Law: Trends and Perspectives, Proceedings of the High Level Panel held during the Forty-eighth Session of the United Nations Commission on International Trade Law', Vienna, 6 July 2015, available at https://uncitral.un.org/en/library/publications.

[4] See sections II through IV below.

I. The Establishment of UNCITRAL

A. Mandate

UNCITRAL's mandate is based on 'the promotion of the progressive harmonisation and unification of the law of international trade', and was designed to address concerns that 'conflicts and divergences arising from the laws of different States in matters relating to international trade constitute an obstacle to the development of world trade'.[5] Hungary, in 1964, had proposed that the General Assembly consider steps to be taken for progressive development of the law of international trade.

It is worth pausing briefly to consider what the drafters of the mandate intended: what did they mean by 'progressive', 'harmonisation', 'unification' and the 'law of international trade'?

UNCITRAL does not handle the state-to-state relationships the World Trade Organization does, but addresses cross-border transactions (sales, transport, financing investment), and disputes arising from those transactions. UNCITRAL parties are two commercial entities (eg buyers and sellers, transport companies, e-commerce operators, secured lenders and borrowers, and claimants and insolvent companies), or a commercial entity and a government (eg in public procurement transactions and in investor-state disputes).

UNCITRAL has adopted flexible and functional techniques in fulfilment of its mandate, issuing legislative, contractual and explanatory texts.[6] These techniques involve different types of compromise. There are two main types of text: first, 'unification' texts, which are legislative texts involving 'the adoption by States of a common legal standard governing particular aspects of international business transactions'.[7] A common example is an international Convention, such as the United Nations Convention on Contracts for the International Sale of Goods (CISG). Another form of unification is a text that states enact domestically in the form in which it was issued (the only UNCITRAL example is the Uniform Rules on Contract Clauses for an Agreed Sum Due upon Failure of Performance (1983) – though it should be noted that this text is not treated as one of UNCITRAL's major works). As the Chinese representative to the General Assembly's Legal Committee observed, the effect of a uniform law is to 'replace the municipal laws that would otherwise apply with a universally-accepted regulation of a particular transaction'.[8]

[5] See General Assembly resolution 2205 (XXI), Establishment of the United Nations Commission on International Trade Law, A/RES/2205 (XXI) (17 December 1966), available at https://uncitral.un.org/e-n/commission/archivaldocs.

[6] 'A Guide to UNCITRAL: Basic Facts About the United Nations Commission on International Trade Law' (2013) 11–20, available at https://uncitral.un.org/sites/uncitral.un.org/files/media-documents/uncitral/en/12-57491-guide-to-uncitral-e.pdf.

[7] 'FAQ – Origin, Mandate and Composition of UNCITRAL', available at https://uncitral.un.org/en/a-bout/faq.

[8] Statement of the representative of China when discussing the proposal that ultimately led to the creation of UNCITRAL. See Official Records of the General Assembly, Twenty-first Session, Report to the Secretary General ('The Schmitthoff Study') (A/6396 and Adds 1 and 2) n 5, citing Official Records of the General Assembly, Twentieth Session, Sixth Committee, 895th meeting, paras 13 and 15, available at https://uncitral.un.org/en/commission/archivaldocs.

Secondly, 'harmonisation' texts such as Model Laws, legislative guides and non-legislative texts, seek to limit divergence in the rules that apply in different states: as the United Nations Legal Counsel has observed, they are designed to 'alleviate the challenges of confronting dense and unfamiliar regimes that otherwise contrive to keep businesses out of international markets'.[9] Harmonisation has been described as 'a process whereby the effects of a type of transaction in one legal system are brought as close as possible to the effects of similar transactions under the laws of other countries'.[10] Harmonisation texts are designed to allow states to adopt an UNCITRAL norm in their domestic legal framework, adapted to local circumstances as the state sees fit. Consequently, these norms are texts 'through which domestic laws may be modified to enhance predictability in cross-border commercial transactions.' In addition, the incoming commercial legal environment must be certain and predictable – business-friendly and investor-ready – as a lack of predictability and quality in the domestic regime could raise barriers to international commerce.[11] From this perspective, and as was explained at the 2017 UNCITRAL Congress, the scope of UNCITRAL's activities run through establishment of a corporation, financing of the business, international sales (online as well as traditional person-to-person), disputes and – in some cases – the winding up of the business.[12]

Both unification and harmonisation approaches have been described as 'preventive', meaning that they avoid conflicts-of-law issues by providing single solutions to replace the different substantive rules that would otherwise apply to a transaction, though the extent of flexibility and so degree of convergence therefore varies. In consequence, all UNCITRAL texts require domestic implementation, such as ratification of a Convention, domestic enactment based on a Model Law or Legislative Guide or use in practice of a non-legislative text.

The notion of 'progressive' legal reform has its roots in the development of the United Nations Charter. Debates on how to refer to the desired codification of international law raised objections to the use of the word 'revision', which was considered to place too much emphasis on change. Consequently, it was decided to refer to the 'progressive development' of international law in Article 13(1)(a) of the Charter, to balance stability and change in the law. This approach was followed in the statute of the International Law Commission and in the UNCITRAL mandate.

[9] M de Serpa Soares at Congress on 'Modernizing International Trade Law to Support Innovation and Sustainable Development' hosted by the United Nations Commission on International Trade Law, 4–6 July 2017, available at http://legal.un.org/ola/media/info_from_lc/mss/speeches/MSS_Congress_UNCITRAL_4-July-2017.pdf.

[10] J Goldring, 'Unification and Harmonisation of the Rules of Law' (1978) 9 *Federal Law Review* 284, 289, as cited by PJ Osborne, 'Unification or Harmonisation: A Critical Analysis of the United Nations Convention on Contracts for the International Sale of Goods 1980' (2006), available at www.cisg.law.pace.edu/cisg/biblio/osborne.html.

[11] As the then Secretary-General explained at the first Congress, 'Differences in law can, as you well know, create an impenetrable thicket of norms in which only the most powerful can find their way – and all this to the detriment of those who are comparatively weak'. 'Uniform Commercial Law in the Twenty-First Century: Proceedings of the Congress of the United Nations Commission on International Trade Law', New York, 18–22 May 1992, 1, available at https://uncitral.un.org/sites/uncitral.un.org/files/media-documents/EN/Colloquia/uniform_commercial_law_congress_1992_e.pdf.

[12] Remarks by Mr Choong-hee Hahn, Former Chairman of UNCITRAL, Republic of Korea, 'Modernizing International Trade Law to Support Innovation and Sustainable Development: Proceedings of the Congress of the United Nations Commission on International Trade Law', Vienna, 4–6 July 2017, Vol 1 (forthcoming).

This 'progressive' approach is another feature of the UNCITRAL mandate that is not often discussed but provides a crucial explanation as to why the United Nations considered that harmonisation and unification of international trade law were desirable and feasible. The General Assembly noted three characteristics of international trade law that would support convergence (used in this context to refer to unification and/or harmonisation: (1) the notion of party autonomy (subject to any restrictions from domestic law, parties they could contract as they pleased); (2) the concept of *pacta sunt servanda* (the contract must be faithfully fulfilled), subject to force majeure or similar exceptions; and (3) the recognised use of arbitration rather than domestic dispute settlement, with decisions capable of international enforcement.[13] As the General Assembly also heard, the law of international trade was consistent in practice, and it had its roots in the mediaeval *lex mercatoria*, whose own sources included trade usages and practices, international conventions and model laws, and, in the eyes of some, uniform rules, standard contract forms and clauses, codes of conduct and arbitral awards.[14] Indeed, the *lex mercatoria* had been incorporated into domestic systems (such as the commercial codes in France and Germany), and its principles were applied not as a matter of external imposition, but freely at the national level.[15] Combined with developed commercial custom and accepted trade terms (fob, cif, among others), the result was that there was already a high degree of unification in some aspects of international trade – chiefly, in transport, bankers' commercial credits and in arbitration.[16] In addition, the formulating agencies were furthering the use of standardised terms and practices in international trade, and countries had 'found without difficulty that they [spoke] a common language'.[17]

Given these features of the law of international trade, it might be queried why the UNCITRAL mandate focused on the progressive unification and harmonisation of the law of international trade rather than on its codification. The answer may be that convergence was considered to be 'more easily achieved in technical branches of the law than in subjects closely connected with national traditions and basic principles of domestic law'.[18] In the General Assembly debate, 'international trade terms, provisions,

[13] *Yearbook of the United Nations Commission on International Trade Law*, vol I: 1968–70 (United Nations) 22, para 23.

[14] See T Ayoğlu, 'Some Reflections on the Sources of Lex Mercatoria' in A Cemil Yıldırım and S Eskiyörük (eds), *International Commercial Law and the New Lex Mercatoria* (İstanbul, Oniki Levha Yayınları, 2014) 27–36. One of the main advocates of the 'restrictive' definition was Clive Schmitthoff, who authored a General Report on a Colloquium held in London on the Law of International Trade, its Growth, Formulation and Operation in 1962. See CM Schmitthoff (ed), *The Sources of the Law of International Trade: With Special Reference to East-West Trade* (New York, Praeger, 1964) 3–38. His report led the United Nations Secretary General to request a further report for the General Assembly at its 21st session, A/6396, and which ultimately led to the foundation of UNCITRAL. See A/6396 and Adds 1 and 2 (n 8).

[15] *UNCITRAL Yearbook 1968–70* (n 13) 22, para 24.

[16] Other topics considered potentially relevant: insurance, elimination of discrimination in laws affecting international trade, agency and legalization of documents, general law of contract, remain untouched (at least in UNCITRAL). See 'A strategic direction for UNCITRAL', para 6, Note by the Secretariat, UNCITRAL, Forty-fifth session, New York, 25 June–6 July 2012 (A/CN.9/752), available at https://uncitral.un.org/en/commission.

[17] The General Assembly noted that the 'formulation of the rules of international trade by international 'formulating agencies' is the outstanding characteristic of the modern development of international trade law': *UNCITRAL Yearbook 1968–70* (n 13) 22, para 25 and 22, para 22, citing Henryk Trammer, 'The Law of Foreign Trade in the Legal Systems of the Countries of Planned Economy' in A/6396 and Adds 1 and 2 (n 8).

[18] *UNCITRAL Yearbook 1968–70* (n 13) 41, para 203.

customs and practices' were among the most technical of the items under discussion, and these are the areas specifically referenced in terms of codification in the mandate. (In fact, the private sector has taken the lead in codification of these standards – an example is the International Chamber of Commerce's Incoterms – and UNCITRAL has consistently endorsed and promoted the wider acceptance of that work.[19])

In other words, it was precisely because further harmonisation or unification of international trade rules and practices would involve 'progressive' development rather than the external imposition of major revisions, and bilateral commitment would not be required, that the General Assembly saw the potential for what became UNCITRAL.[20] The General Assembly concluded that international trade law as regards industrial property, transport (land, sea and air), international sale of goods, supply and erection of plant and machinery abroad, bills of exchange and bankers' commercial credits and commercial arbitration were already subject to a high degree of convergence and thus could be reflected in uniform or harmonisation texts. It identified others in which convergence would be feasible: agency law, cross-border joint ventures, rules governing companies entering into 'foreign trade relations', and the general law of contract as it applied to international trade.[21]

It was recognised, however, that progressive development and codification were linked, and should take account of gaps and developments in the existing law. Consequently UNCITRAL, as the International Law Commission, should consider reform in fields 'which have not yet been regulated by international law or in regard to which the law has not yet been sufficiently developed in the practice of States'.[22] The General Assembly's discussion of shortcomings in harmonisation and unification of international trade law, and steps to remedy those shortcomings, expressly included modernisation on a par with harmonisation and unification, especially where developing countries were concerned,[23] and modernisation is clearly implicit, though not directly stated, in the mandate. UNCITRAL's website accurately describes its work, therefore, as the 'the modernisation and harmonisation of rules on international business'.[24]

The above, admittedly detailed, review of the rationale for providing UNCITRAL with a 'rule-formulating' mandate explains clearly that UNCITRAL was not intended to be what would now be called a disruptive body, but one that would unify or harmonise existing practice and supplement it as necessary. Indeed, the General Assembly was reminded that new rules were not the only, or even main need: encouraging wider participation in the existing conventions and adoption of other codified commercial practices would also make progress towards convergence. Hence the second element of the UNCITRAL mandate is to promote 'wider participation in existing international conventions and wider acceptance of existing model and uniform laws'.[25] In this regard,

[19] See the Texts of Other Organisations endorsed by UNCITRAL, available at https://uncitral.un.org/en/texts/endorsed.

[20] *UNCITRAL Yearbook 1968–70* (n 13) p 22, para 24.

[21] See A Guide to UNCITRAL' (n 6).

[22] Borrowing from Statute of the International Law Commission Art 15, available at http://legal.un.org/ilc/texts/instruments/english/statute/statute.pdf. The International Law Commission has a remit over progressive development of public international law.

[23] *UNCITRAL Yearbook 1968–70* (n 13) 41, para 210(b) and 42, para 212.

[24] About UNCITRAL, https://uncitral.un.org/en/about. See also 'A Guide to UNCITRAL' (n 6).

[25] ibid.

the related promotion of UNCITRAL texts as another core feature of the mandate[26] includes facilitating the enactment and use of UNCITRAL texts rather than just marketing.[27]

The remaining elements of the UNCITRAL mandate, now generally viewed as 'secondary' to the rule-formulating function, were in fact tasks that the General Assembly considered should take priority over rule-formulation. First among them is to 'coordinate the work of organisations active in the field of international trade law and to encourage cooperation among them, as a former Legal Counsel of the United Nations, Hans Corell, recalled in 2000'.[28]

The intention was for UNCITRAL to act as a 'kind of international clearing-house to coordinate and supervise'[29] the work of other rule-formulating agencies which were regional or aimed at developed countries, or at least not universal in coverage, and this function was considered to be a key one in justifying the establishment of UNCITRAL. So in addition to the general coordination mandate, UNCITRAL should 'establish [...] and maintain [...] a close collaboration with the United Nations Conference on Trade and Development' and maintain 'liaison with other United Nations organs and specialized agencies concerned with international trade'.[30]

B. Challenges in Meeting the Objectives of the UNCITRAL Mandate

Having surveyed developments in world trade and the legal rules governing it, the General Assembly recognised the following main shortcomings in the reform of international trade law:

(a) There had been slow progress in reform, especially given the time and effort expended.
(b) Developing countries had not been as able to participate as fully as developed countries, despite a recognition that they were most in need of adequate and modern laws to support development, and that existing laws were in many cases unsuitable for their needs.
(c) None of the then relevant agencies included universal membership and none commanded worldwide acceptance.
(d) There was a lack of coordination among the formulating agencies.[31]

[26] The third element of the mandate is 'Preparing or promoting the adoption of new international conventions, model laws and uniform laws and promoting the codification and wider acceptance of international trade terms, provisions, customs and practices, in collaboration, where appropriate, with the organizations operating in this field': ibid.

[27] See 'A strategic direction for UNCITRAL: Note by the Secretariat', UNCITRAL, Forty-fifth session, New York, 25 June–6 July 2012 (A/CN.9/752), available at https://uncitral.un.org/en/commission.

[28] Opening Speech at UNCITRAL's 33rd session, by Mr Hans Corell, Under-Secretary-General for Legal Affairs, The Legal Counsel, New York, 12 June 2000, available at www.un.org/law/counsel/uncitral.htm.

[29] A/6396 (n 8), para 210(d), citing HC Gutteridge, Comparative Law, 2nd edn (Cambridge, Cambridge University Press, 1949) 183–84.

[30] A/RES/2205 (XXI) (n 5) paras 8(e) and (f).

[31] A/6396 (n 8), para 210. These international and non-governmental 'formulating' agencies include UNIDROIT, the Hague Conference on Private International Law, various UN Economic Commissions, the forerunner to the World Intellectual Property Organisation, and private sector organisations.

The UNCITRAL mandate was expressly designed to meet these shortcomings, as we have seen.

The General Assembly required UNCITRAL to 'bear in mind the interests of all peoples, and particularly those of developing countries, in the extensive development of international trade'.[32] Speakers also emphasised the need for justice and fairness in the process: 'It was particularly important for [the developing countries] that the law of international trade should be updated and guarantee the highest security so that they would not be at the mercy of more experienced trade partners',[33] and the importance of developing country participation was repeatedly emphasised. It was suggested that participation in UNCITRAL could lessen the need for participation in the numerous other agencies engaged in commercial law reform.[34] Developing country representatives 'expressed the hope that the Commission would be instrumental in establishing equitable conditions for international trade by eliminating from existing international instruments provisions which failed to give fair recognition to their interests.'[35]

To address the question of universal membership, UNCITRAL was established with 29 United Nations Member States, and the membership was expanded by the General Assembly to 36 states in 1973[36] and again to 60 states in 2002.[37] The Member States are elected from United Nations Member States for a six-year, renewable term, and numbers are allocated to ensure appropriate balance between the United Nations' regional groups.[38] UNCITRAL sessions are therefore designed to ensure that all regions, and the principal economic and legal systems of the world are fairly represented. The two expansions of the Member States reflected more states' wishes to participate and contribute and a wish to stimulate interest in the expanding work programme,[39] and reflected the increasing numbers of sovereign states.[40]

On the question of coordination, the General Assembly recalled the extent of 'waste of effort and confusion that has, at times, been caused by the existence of competing

[32] A/RES/2205 (XXI) (n 5) para 9.

[33] Statement from the representative of Hungary, when submitting the proposal that ultimately led to the establishment of UNCITRAL. See A/6396 (n 8) n 85, citing Official Records of the General Assembly, Twentieth Session, Sixth Committee, 894th meeting, para 8.

[34] *UNCITRAL Yearbook 1968–70* (n 13) 62, para 17; A/6396 (n 8) para 201.

[35] *UNCITRAL Yearbook 1968–70* (n 13) 123, para 9.

[36] 'Report of the United Nations Commission on International Trade Law on the work of the Seventh Session' (New York, 13–17 May 1974) (A/9617), para 2 reproduced in *Yearbook of the United Nations Commission on International Trade Law*, vol V: 1974 (United Nations) 13–25.

[37] General Assembly Resolution A/RES/57/20, Enlargement of the membership of the United Nations Commission on International Trade Law (19 November 2002) para 2 reproduced in *Yearbook of the United Nations Commission on International Trade Law*, vol XXXIII: 2002 (United Nations publication, Sales No E.05.V.13) 45–50.

[38] The members comprise 14 African states, fourteen Asian states, eight Eastern European states, 10 Latin American and Caribbean States and 14 Western European and other states. See United Nations, Department for General Assembly and Conference Management, United Nations Regional Groups of Member States, available at www.un.org/depts/DGACM/RegionalGroups.shtml.

[39] JA Estrella Faria, 'Legal Harmonization Through Model Laws: The Experience of the United Nations Commission on International Trade Law (UNCITRAL)' 5–8, available at www.justice.gov.za/alraesa/conferences/2005sa/papers/s5_faria2.pdf.

[40] The number of which had nearly trebled between the 1920s and 1960, and which continues to increase. L Réczei, 'Process and Value of the Unification of Commercial Law: Lessons for the Future Drawn from the Past 25 Years' in 'Uniform Commercial Law in the Twenty-First Century' (n 11) 5–7.

agencies engaged in the work of unification',[41] echoed by speakers at the first session in 1968, and emphasised by another formulating agency, the Hague Conference.[42] However, views differed on the appropriate remedy: some considered that the commission should be a 'rallying-ground for unificationary (sic) activities' and should coordinate and supervise such activities; others that the Commission's work should complement other agencies' work, so that 'stimulating wider interest in, and particular work by, existing institutions was among the significant contributions that the Commission could make'.[43] This divergence of views, and the lack of authority in UNCITRAL to coordinate others' activities, may have contributed to what Hans Corell in 2000 pithily expressed as a continuing 'multilaterally-funded dis-unification of law'.[44]

Under the heading 'Is there a realistic chance of success or is the task too difficult for tangible results?', the General Assembly noted that the challenges of unifying international trade law should not be underestimated. Nonetheless, it added that, as such law raised issues primarily of a technical nature, the task should be easier than in family law, succession, personal status and other subjects deeply rooted in national or religious traditions.'[45]

The following sections will examine the challenges and how each of the UNCITRAL Congresses has considered them.

II. The First UNCITRAL Congress

The first Congress, held in 1992 during the 25th session of UNCITRAL,[46] was entitled Uniform Commercial Law in the Twenty-First Century and was held in the context of the United Nations Decade of International Law.[47] The aim of the Congress was to

> provide to practising lawyers, corporate counsel, ministry officials, judges, arbitrators, teachers of law and other users of uniform legal texts: (a) up-to-date information and practical guidance concerning principal legal texts of universal relevance; (b) an opportunity to express their opinion on the current state of the unification of the laws and rules governing world commerce; and (c) a forum in which to voice their practical needs as a basis for future work by the Commission and other formulating agencies.[48]

The opening address, given by the then Secretary-General of the United Nations, Boutros Boutros-Ghali, entitled 'Process and value of the unification of

[41] A/6396 (n 8) para 210.
[42] A/6396/Add 1 (n 8) section B, para 4.
[43] *UNCITRAL Yearbook 1968–70* (n 13) 91, para 20.
[44] See Corell (n 28).
[45] A/6396 (n 8) para 222.
[46] UNCITRAL meets in plenary session once annually, and these meetings are referred to as the 'Commission sessions'. Consequently, the 25th session was held 25 years after UNCITRAL was established in 1966.
[47] For the report of the Congress proceedings, see 'Uniform Commercial Law in the Twenty-first Century' (n 11).
[48] 'Report of the United Nations Commission on International Trade Law on the work of its 25th session', 4–22 May 1992, General Assembly Official Records, Forty-seventh Session, Supplement No 17 (A/47/17), available at https://uncitral.un.org/en/commission.

commercial law: lessons for the future drawn from the past 25 years', focused on the 'recurring' themes mentioned in the Introduction. These include the different techniques of harmonisation and unification, the application and interpretation of UNCITRAL texts, the value of universal application for regional integration and development and the methods of improving coordination between the rule-formulating agencies.[49] Further details of the points discussed are set out in the thematic sections below, but some key highlights are noted here.

First, a particular benefit of UNCITRAL techniques in rule-formulation was highlighted by John Honnold, Secretary of UNCITRAL from 1969 to 1974. He observed that

> delegates found that the best approach to seemingly intractable problems was to focus on concrete factual examples at the crossroads of crucial choices (there seem to be words in most languages for 'facts', as contrasted with disembodied legal concepts). Addressing these concrete facts, the group could usually agree on what result was best for international trade. Then, with agreed results as the target, it was usually possible (although not easy) to reflect the agreed results in earthy language cleansed of untranslatable local legal idioms.[50]

This approach had surmounted the early experience that 'delegates nurtured in their domestic legal systems would come to UNCITRAL with a mission to get as much as possible of their cherished domestic legal culture into the uniform international text'.[51]

Secondly, it is interesting to note UNCITRAL's initial focus on unification texts, and their technical subjects. The main UNCITRAL texts issued up to 1992 included the United Nations Convention on Contracts for the International Sale of Goods, the 'CISG' (1980), the UNCITRAL Legal Guide on Drawing up International Contracts for the Construction of Industrial Works (1987), the United Nations Convention on International Bills of Exchange and International Promissory Notes (1988), the United Nations Convention on the Carriage of Goods by Sea, the 'Hamburg Rules' (1978), the United Nations Convention on the Liability of Operators of Transport Terminals in International Trade (1991) and the UNCITRAL Model Law on International Commercial Arbitration (1985). These texts indeed reflected those areas noted in 1966 as most amenable to unification or harmonisation.

The Congress also considered future work under the headings 'From goods to services' and 'From traditional payments to electronic messages', and proposals for study and possible future legislative development on general contracting, on specific types of contracts, on payments and security interests, on electronic data interchange, on dispute settlement, and for a uniform anti-monopoly law, transnational tax laws, environmental labelling for products or services, and consumer protection law.[52] It is interesting to note that, among these topics, UNCITRAL has since been most active

[49] See 'Uniform Commercial Law in the Twenty-First Century' (n 11).

[50] J Honnold, '3. Goals of unification' in 'Uniform Commercial Law in the Twenty-first Century' (n 11) 11.

[51] ibid.

[52] See 'Possible future work: proposals for possible future work made at the UNCITRAL Congress: Note by the Secretariat', UNCITRAL, Twenty-sixth session, Vienna, 5–23 July 1993 (A/CN.9/378), available at https://uncitral.un.org/en/commission.

in payments and security interests, e-commerce and dispute settlement – considered, by some, to reflect an increase in common over civil law influences in UNCITRAL.[53]

In addition, a series of proposals were made on enhancing coordination and uniform interpretation. As a note by the Secretariat explained, most were aimed at enhancing coordination with other rule-formulating and international agencies, both on substantive legal development and on promoting the understanding and uniformity in interpretation of UNCITRAL texts. Tellingly, the Secretariat noted explained that it would consider them and, as appropriate, 'implement them within available resources'[54] – a constraint that has proved ever-present. Indeed, the Note to the Commission by the Secretariat focused on prospective legislative development.

III. The Second UNCITRAL Congress

The second Congress,[55] held in 2007 during the 40th session of UNCITRAL, was entitled 'Modern Law for Global Commerce'.[56] It took the opportunity to review the working methods and achievements of UNCITRAL and related work of other organisations active in the field of international trade law, and assessed of ongoing work and an evaluation of topics for future work programmes. The first day of the Conference focused on the process and methods of international rule-making and harmonisation of commercial law. The second day considered economic and social development through enhanced access to credit and developing effective and efficient insolvency regimes. The third day placed the future of contract harmonisation on the agenda, also analysing electronic commerce. The final day was dedicated to procurement-related issues and commercial dispute settlement. Speakers from all regions and legal system reported on practical aspects and recent developments relating to areas where uniform law instruments already existed, as well as new areas in need of harmonisation. Commenting on the results of the Congress and progress in UNCITRAL at that time, the Nordic countries noted that extended cooperation and awareness in the field of international trade law was a key to success in global trade and economic development.[57] The Chinese delegation also welcomed the event, and recommended regular such Congresses, to

> facilitate the exchange of views on the current status of international rules formulated by international organisations and on national commercial legislation and its implementation. Such meetings will also improve the understanding and enhance implementation by countries of the legal instruments on international commerce.[58]

[53] ibid.

[54] ibid, para 3.

[55] See 'Modern Law for Global Commerce: Proceedings of the Congress of the United Nations Commission on International Trade Law held on the Occasion of the Fortieth Session of the Commission', Vienna, 9–12 July 2007, available at https://uncitral.un.org/sites/uncitral.un.org/files/media-documents/EN/Colloquia/09-83930_ebook.pdf.

[56] ibid.

[57] That is, the speakers for Denmark, Sweden, Finland and Iceland. See www.un.org/press/en-/2007/gal3324.doc.htm.

[58] Statement by Mr WANG Chen, Chinese Delegate, at the Sixth Committee of the 62nd Session of the UN General Assembly, on Item 81 'Report of the United Nations Commission on International Trade Law

Although the Congress was organised during the 40th session of the Commission, attendance was open to individuals interested in UNCITRAL activities, in contrast to formal UNCITRAL sessions, at which only representatives of states, international organisations and international NGOs may participate.

The Congress also noted developments in commercial law that indicated, in the words of a former Secretary of UNCITRAL, a 'shift from the traditional orientation of UNCITRAL to limit its work to legal relations that are international'. States, he continued, were 'increasingly interested in legislative texts that govern transactions irrespective of whether they are domestic or international', and in modernisation more generally. The implication was, surprisingly, that differences among legal systems were less of an obstacle than 'effective and efficient enforceability of contractual obligations and … accommodating modern contract practices', and a major need for developing countries in particular was for 'mechanisms to support long-term and long-distance transactions', the absence of which constituted less visible obstacles to international trade. The rise of dispute settlement activity in UNCITRAL – now represented by two Working Groups and which has seen the issue of six UNCITRAL texts since 2007 – may be attributed to meeting that need.[59]

The Commission had agreed in 2004 to adopt a more proactive approach to coordination, with the Secretariat seeking greater dialogue with partner organisations.[60] Speakers from UNIDROIT and the Hague Conference, two organisations active in international commercial law with which UNCITRAL has in-depth and long-standing cooperation, at the second Congress considered various methods of enhancing coordination in practice, and, indeed, these organisations and UNCITRAL issued a joint publication, the UNCITRAL, Hague Conference and UNIDROIT Texts on Security Interests: Comparison and analysis of major features of international instruments relating to secured transactions, in 2012.[61] Nonetheless, participants were cautioned that there remained room for improvement, to reduce the further perpetuation of an 'existing international patchwork of treaties … [called] the "spaghetti bowl" of international

on the Work of Its Fortieth Session', New York, 22 October 2007, available at www.china-un.org/eng/hyyfy/t374537.htm.

[59] UNCITRAL Working Group II developed the United Nations Convention on Transparency in Treaty-based Investor-State Arbitration (New York, 2014) (the 'Mauritius Convention on Transparency'); the amended UNCITRAL Model Law on International Commercial Arbitration (2006); UNCITRAL Rules on Transparency in Treaty-based Investor-State Arbitration (effective date: 1 April 2014); UNCITRAL Secretariat Guide on the Convention on the Recognition and Enforcement of Foreign Arbitral Awards (2016); UNCITRAL Notes on Organizing Arbitral Proceedings (2016); and the Recommendations to assist arbitral institutions and other interested bodies with regard to arbitration under the UNCITRAL Arbitration Rules (as revised in 2010) (see https://uncitral.un.org/en/texts/arbitration). UNCITRAL Working Group III developed the Technical Notes on Online Dispute Resolution (2016, available at https://uncitral.un.org/sites/uncitral.un.org/files/media-documents/uncitral/en/v1700382_english_technical_notes_on_odr.pdf), and is currently tasked with Investor-State Dispute Settlement Reform (see https://uncitral.un.org/en/working_groups/3/investor-state).

[60] Report of the United Nations Commission on International Trade Law of its thirty-seventh session, 14–25 June 2004, General Assembly Official Records, Fifty-ninth session, Supplement No 17 (A/59/17), available at https://uncitral.un.org/en/commission.

[61] 'Comparison and analysis of major features of international instruments relating to secured transactions: Note by the Secretariat', UNCITRAL, Forty-fourth session, Vienna, 27 June–8 July 2011 (A/CN.9/720), available at https://uncitral.un.org/en/commission.

rule-making', and increasing bilateralism and regionalism, considered to be the opposite of a harmonised, collective approach.[62]

Speakers also emphasised the contribution of unification and harmonisation to reducing the transaction costs of international commerce, and so removing practical obstacles to the further development of trade. However, speakers also referred to the possibility that different regional bodies might formulate different solutions to a common problem, and then promote their solutions to different groups of states, resulting in 'dis-harmonisation'. In other words, uncoordinated law reform was leading to exactly the same problems that UNCITRAL sought to mitigate: 'confusion over applicable legal rules, increased cost and more obstacles to the expansion of world trade'.[63] Echoing the remarks in 1966, the solution required clearer delineations of work between different agencies, better and more efficient use of human and other resources, and requiring the leadership of the United Nations.[64] Once again, the coordination question was identified as a key challenge.

IV. The Third UNCITRAL Congress

The third Congress,[65] held in 2017 during the 50th session of UNCITRAL, was entitled 'Modernizing International Trade Law to Support Innovation and Sustainable Development', setting it squarely in the context of the United Nations programme, particularly the Sustainable Development Goals and the Agenda 2030 (including economic growth, development and institution-building).[66] In this regard, it followed the earlier events in considering the effectiveness of UNCITRAL on the ground as well as in terms of its legislative and other texts.

High-level speakers gave examples of how UNCITRAL texts had improved international commerce from international, regional and national perspectives, and had contributed to the rule of law and sustainable development through linking trade, development and law. Developing and transition states, in particular, expressed their willingness to get involved and share their experiences to support UNCITRAL in new norm-setting.

In terms of possible future work areas, an expected area of focus was digital commerce. Legal issues highlighted as in need of detailed study arose in digital contracts and in digital property. They included smart goods, whose software component, including

[62] Remarks of Khalil Hamdani, 'Modern Law for Global Commerce' (n 55) 25–27.

[63] J Chan Wah-Teck, '3. Allocation of work among formulating agencies' in 'Modern Law for Global Commerce' (n 55) 29–34.

[64] ibid.

[65] The papers presented to the Congress are available in 'Modernizing International Trade Law to Support Innovation and Sustainable Development: Proceedings of the Congress of the United Nations Commission on International Trade Law', Vol 4, Vienna, 4–6 July 2017, available at https://uncitral.un.org/en/colloquia/general. A transcript of the Congress (the 'Proceedings') will be made available at the same location in due course.

[66] Participants submitted additional policy and proposed research papers that are available at https://uncitral.un.org/en/colloquia/general and a multi-volume set of publications from the proceedings of the Congress will be added in the course of 2019.

periodic access to updates, was essential for proper use, and electronic enforcement of contracts. Business practices in transport, trade facilitation and payments had changed markedly, requiring additions to the existing rules to allow for dematerialised bills of lading and similar commercial documents, and to support regulatory mechanisms, financial inclusion and stability and the implementation of monetary policies more effectively. On the other hand, innovations such as distributed ledgers based on blockchain technology, including cryptocurrencies and smart contracts, were considered less challenging from a legal perspective. Many issues could be addressed in existing legislative texts based on the UNCITRAL Model Law on Electronic Transferable Records (2017), the United Nations Convention on the Use of Electronic Communications in International Contracts (2005), the UNCITRAL Model Law on Electronic Signatures (2001) and even the UNCITRAL Model Law on Electronic Commerce (1996), in that all these texts reflected the notions of functional equivalence and technological neutrality. Another suggestion was that the rules of the UNCITRAL Model Law on Secured Transactions that apply to equity securities should also apply to crypto-currencies and tokens. Participants were encouraged to engage in a digital 'fitness check', which could well indicate that their legal systems were better able to accommodate modern tools than was in fact appreciated.

Success criteria for unification and harmonisation texts – both in terms of development and use – featured highly. On development, it was observed that a harmonised solution must be good law, in the sense that the interests of the parties are taken into account and are properly balanced, and the law should be as coherent, clear and concise as possible, avoiding legal jargon (or 'untranslatable local legal idioms', as John Honnold had put it 25 years earlier). Among the range of soft-law instruments that UNCITRAL issues, the benefits of flexibility in legislative and practice guides should be set against the risk of unintended or incoherent results, which a model law might better mitigate. The comments again echoed those of 1966, to the effect that convergence was easier to achieve in a technical narrow field that specialists could explain.

In a panel on working methods and another providing reflections of former Chairmen and Secretaries of UNCITRAL, cooperation and competition in the UNCITRAL context were discussed. Competition between UNCITRAL and other agencies, and among ministries and departments in the national context, was acknowledged as a fact of life. UNCITRAL was urged to bear in mind that the taxpayer would question why it was funding international organisations competing among themselves, an issue that leaders should bear in mind when deciding whether to co-operate, whether to put something on the agenda, and whether to assert their positions or not. Other panels gave practical examples of the need for coordination, such as between organisations providing secured transactions law and those tasked with prudential regulation. Current capital requirements rules did not allow for the use of non-financial assets to reduce risk, to some extent explaining the rise of asset-based lending outside regulated banking activities and reducing inclusiveness by adding barriers to SMEs. UNCITRAL should therefore cooperate with the Basel Committee on Banking Supervision, among others, it was noted, to allow secured transactions and support access to credit and thereby financial stability.

The Congress also heard of the move from unification texts to harmonisation texts that had become evident over the 25 years since the first Congress. It was said that, in the past 10 years, the word 'unification' had not been uttered in meetings of UNCITRAL. The preference was for harmonisation, which allowed a better understanding of the results of UNCITRAL. The World Bank and European Bank for Reconstruction and Development had spoken about setting their standards based on UNCITRAL texts, which was considered to be a prime example of how UNCITRAL had worked and should continue to work. Given that UNCITRAL had no financial leverage or other means to compel the use of its texts, the development banks and other agencies were in many ways proxies for implementation. Another example of a very successful text was given: the Model Law on International Credit Transfers. It is a forgotten text, and perhaps half of the participants at the Congress might not have heard of it, but the participants were informed that the law of inter-bank transactions and transfers of money worldwide, EU law and banks in practice, operated under the principles of this law, which was, at the time it was adopted, revolutionary. The European Commission, too, emphasised the importance of coherence between regional and global solutions, which could be supported through participation in both levels of reform and 'mutual influence', based on a mutual recognition of each other's values.

The Congress considered the importance to the success of UNCITRAL texts of ensuring that those texts are well understood and implemented in the manner that the drafting Working Group and Commission anticipated. The need to balance national and international elements of interpretation was highlighted: a model law, from a national perspective, could not operate as a self-contained system of law, disconnected with other elements of the legal order in which the model law has been implemented. On the other hand, taking into account foreign legal decisions, case law or legal writings is more difficult than it usually is for national sources. A panel on the CISG took up these questions further, noting that the issues encountered in the CISG might have implications for UNCITRAL texts more generally. One speaker considered the manner in which law schools in the UK addressed international trade law, observing that while half covered Incoterms and similar standards, only 15 per cent covered the CISG, and that, broadly speaking, international conventions were treated as an academic subject rather than a potentially applicable source of law. In the court system, international rules of interpretation in practice tended to be used only to the extent they did not compromise the domestic law. The overall result was an outward sense of internationality but an internal approach that sought to better fit English law to international contracts. Other speakers referred to low numbers of citations of the CISG in domestic judgments. It was suggested that a new *lex mercatoria* might overcome cultural resistance to an externally derived international trade law at the national level and perhaps misunderstanding of legal concepts (eg a fundamental breach of contract, which was completely unknown in the Hungarian national system). Some speakers also provided positive examples of references to international concepts applied domestically, such as CISG-based good faith considerations, and UNCITRAL's role in promoting consistency in terminology as an aid to understanding.

Speakers also drew attention to empirical research indicating a lack of awareness of international case law among judges as well as students of law. Part of the problem was attributed to a language issue – the main language in international trade and law was English. Hungary was cited as but one example of a country without a multilingual tradition, whose citizens would struggle to access that case law. Speakers noted the benefits of the Case Law on UNCITRAL Texts (CLOUT) system, which provided abstracts of decisions and awards in all of the official languages of the United Nations (Arabic, Chinese, English, French, Russian and Spanish) for use by judges, arbitrators, lawyers, parties to commercial transactions, academics, students and other interested persons.[67] However, those abstracts, and texts of decisions and awards in the original language that the Secretariat can also provide, are available in relatively few languages. The Congress heard that, in 2016, the Széchenyi István University and the Ministry of Justice in Hungary had started a programme to support uniform interpretation with Hungarian-language materials. This programme is focussing on remedies, interest, fundamental breach and notification in time, and the goal is to work as a model for countries that are facing similar challenges. Other examples given was the Asia Pacific Judicial Summit on enforcement of arbitral awards, which first started in 2015 as a result of joint efforts between the UNCITRAL Regional Centre for Asia and the Pacific and the Department of Justice of the Hong Kong Special Administrative Region of China, and the OHADA Common Court of Justice and Arbitration (CCJA), which has supranational authority and ensures the uniformity of interpretation and application of OHADA Uniform Acts.

Such activities facilitate sharing of experience among judges of different jurisdictions, and contribute to consistency in interpretation, notwithstanding differences in legal culture. They are supported by UNCITRAL's published bibliography of academic writings, historical documents, preparatory work, foreign case law, the UNCITRAL Digest of Case Law on the Model Law on International Commercial Arbitration, the New York Convention Guide, the Toolbox of the Swiss Arbitration Association covering the Notes on Organising Arbitral Proceedings (in addition to CLOUT noted above). These tools are expected to become increasingly useful given the increase in harmonisation and the use of options and guidance as well as legislative text.

Nonetheless, the idea of a *jurisconsultorium* (the harmonisation of court and arbitral decisions with foreign precedents) remains a work in progress. In addition, as Eric Bergsten recalled, the CISG 'is excluded as the governing law in a significant number of contracts to which it would otherwise apply. The evidence suggests that the reason is largely that the lawyers negotiating the contract or preparing the standard conditions prefer to deal with the domestic law that they learned in law school and which they use regularly in domestic sales contracts', though he considered that the growing familiarity with its provisions (through the Moot and otherwise) could be reducing the exclusions.

A common theme running throughout the Congress was the need for collaboration and cooperation in support of these activities, as a support for the more traditional coordination function of UNCITRAL. Many speakers also agreed that UNCITRAL's 'power to convene', a phrase repeated throughout the Congress, which was considered vital to success in such vital cooperation efforts. Panellists also discussed the challenges of keeping UNCITRAL texts up to date. Working in dynamic areas of the law, common to many UNCITRAL projects, necessitates modernisation of complicated texts.

[67] The CLOUT system is also available free of charge on the UNCITRAL website at https://uncitral.un.org/en/library.

V. Four Key Lessons from the Three UNCITRAL Congresses

As we have seen, the Congresses recognised and celebrated the success of UNCITRAL in issuing its texts, and the extent of their use in national enactments and by other organisations in developing their own standards. As might be expected, the events also looked at lessons to be learned from the process to develop and implement those texts. Four of the most common themes are discussed below.

A. Broad and Representative Participation in UNCITRAL

In order to be effective in distilling best international practice, the UNCITRAL process requires the participation of 'member States of UNCITRAL, which represent different legal traditions and levels of economic development; non-member States; intergovernmental organisations; and non-governmental organisations'.[68] 'Participation' in this sense refers to attendance at one of the Working Groups that drafts UNCITRAL's legislative texts.

As we have seen, UNCITRAL has 60 Member States distributed among the United Nation's regional groups, so that the principal economic and legal systems of the world are fairly represented at its sessions. All other United Nations Member States may also attend UNCITRAL sessions as observers, at which they may participate in discussions to the same extent as members and may submit papers for consideration. Interested international organisations and invited NGOs also take part as observers. The objective is two-fold: first, to ensure that UNCITRAL texts are 'widely accepted as offering solutions appropriate to different legal traditions and to countries at different stages of economic development'[69] and, secondly, that no major economy can consider itself as having the power of veto over a solution. While UNCITRAL Member States alone take decisions, on those all substantive matters have always been reached by consensus (that is, without a vote),[70] so members and observers alike can influence the process through sharing relevant experience and expertise.

Although UNCITRAL does not routinely survey participation at its sessions, there are fairly regular reports to the effect that participation is not as broad and as representative as it could be. In 2007, for example, states noted a 'perception that the working methods of the Commission and its working groups might not sufficiently encourage effective participation in the creation of UNCITRAL standards or the subsequent enactment of those standards by a broad range of States'.[71] Indeed, an analysis of some working groups had indicated that only 12–15 individuals were present 75 per cent or more of the time.

[68] 'A Guide to UNCITRAL' (n 6) 1, para 1.

[69] ibid.

[70] There have been two votes on procedural matters: the first on moving the UNCITRAL Secretariat from New York to Vienna in 1979, and the appointment of the Chairman to Working Group III in 2017.

[71] Report of the United Nations Commission on International Trade Law on the work of its fortieth session, 25 June–12 July 2007, General Assembly Official Records, Sixty-second session, Supplement No 17(A/62/17 (Part 1)), para 234, available at https://uncitral.un.org/en/commission.

As a discussion on UNCITRAL's working methods in 2007 highlighted, UNCITRAL session participants must generally be self-funded,[72] though UNCITRAL has a small Trust Fund for Travel Assistance to assist delegates from developing countries to attend its Commission sessions in Vienna.[73] The resources required are not limited to the costs of travel to New York and Vienna to attend week-long UNCITRAL meetings: a main need is for in-depth preparation for discussion of highly technical issues.

One state has set out in some detail how it prepares for UNCITRAL meetings are indeed significant. It has established a dedicated government advisory committee, which 'obtains the requisite expertise and guidance on both the general direction the [State] should take in its efforts, and the specific positions [it] should pursue in specific pending projects'.[74] The Committee consults with groups of experts known as Study Groups, which themselves hold regular meetings, open to the public and publicly announced in advance, and issues consultation papers seeking input. The aim is to 'ensure that the views expressed [...] in international negotiations represent a balanced position that is the product of the suggestions and concerns of many, sometimes competing, private sector stakeholders and responsible government agencies'.[75] The delegates to UNCITRAL, generally chosen from the Study Group, are led by specialist international trade lawyers, and usually include

> officials from the relevant federal or other government agencies, academics, lawyers representing the various industry sectors, and non-lawyer industry representatives. The goal of this very inclusive process is to include every interest group in the process of developing the [...] position on the various legal and policy issues that arise in each international project.[76]

At the second session of the Commission, in 1969, several representatives 'noted that the success of the Commission's work depended on the selection by Member States of skilled experts for the sessions of the Commission and the meetings of its working groups'.[77] Prior to the establishment of UNCITRAL, the delegates to the General Assembly noted that there were even then insufficient qualified personnel in government institutions able 'to keep abreast of fast-moving developments at the international level'.[78] The observation continued that 'If participating Governments seriously wish to make greater headway ... it is felt that they should endeavour to obtain from their respective parliaments sufficient funds'.[79] Debate in UNCITRAL has noted the challenge in

[72] 'France's Observations on UNCITRAL's working methods: Note by the Secretariat', UNCITRAL, Fortieth session, Vienna, 25 June–12 July 2007 (A/CN.9/635), available at https://uncitral.un.org/en/commission. See also Claire R Kelly, 'The Politics of Legitimacy in the UNCITRAL Working Methods' in Tomer Broude, Marc L Busch and Amelia Porges, *The Politics of International Economic Law* (Cambridge, Cambridge University Press 2016) 109–32.

[73] See Speech of Austria to the Sixth Committee, 2008, available at www.un.org/press/en/2008-/gal3346.doc.htm. The small size of the fund means that its potential for support should not be overstated, as the annual requests for contributions made to the Commission emphasise.

[74] MH Carlson, 'U.S. Participation in the International Unification of Private Law: The Making of the UNCITRAL Draft Carriage of goods by Sea Convention' (2007) 31 *Tulane Maritime Law Journal* 615.

[75] ibid 622.

[76] ibid.

[77] 'Programme of Work through 1973: Note by the Secretary-General', UNCITRAL, Third Session, New York 6 April 1970 (A/CN.9/46), para 12, available at https://uncitral.un.org/en/commission.

[78] A/6396/Add.1 (n 8) section B, para 9.

[79] ibid.

this regard, as we have seen. In a discussion of participation and funding issues in 2008, and another on proposed reduction of costs through hosting all meetings in Vienna (rather than alternating between New York and Vienna) in 2011, the burden on developing countries of participating and proportionate distribution of travel costs between delegations were highlighted.[80] While Working Group sessions are now generally of one rather than two weeks' duration, time away from the home base remains considerable in the context of modern commercial practice, and that developing countries in particular may not have the resources available to divert from immediate in-country needs to participate in UNCITRAL meetings.

It may therefore not be surprising that the above study's authors concluded that, 'most developing nations did not have the resources to mount consistent, well-staffed delegations, nor the legal capacity effectively to engage specialists from the Global North on their own grounds (reference omitted)'.[81] Participation at the level of the most effective delegations – which have 'high attendance of delegations; high consistency of delegations; high density of delegations [meaning expert and well-informed delegates]; high diversity of delegations; high consistency of delegates',[82] will remain beyond many states, developed and developing alike.

In 2000, the then UN Secretary-General Kofi Annan discussed an emerging concept of 'inclusive globalisation', explaining that globalisation's potential was not only to open markets across borders, but also to expand opportunity and to promote cooperation.[83] The risks of focusing on growth without inclusion, he noted, were grave and could even threaten peace and security. Opening the 2017 Congress, the Legal Counsel acknowledged the transparent, inclusive and multilingual process through which UNCITRAL texts are developed, and welcomed the opportunity it provided for developing countries to have a voice in that process, echoing the overarching goal in the sustainable development goals to 'leave no one behind'.[84] The Sixth Committee of the General Assembly[85] has also welcomed UNCITRAL's efforts to avoid 'politicisation and entrenched disagreement, remain […] technically focused, and establish […] itself as an effective standard setting organisation. This method of work has benefited countries in all

[80] Austria's delegate, speaking on UNCITRAL to the Sixth Committee (Legal) of the General Assembly, in 2008, regretted 'that during the last year several members of UNCITRAL were not represented at its sessions and working groups', an absence largely attributed to the financial burden concerned. See www.un.org/press/en/2008/gal3346.doc.htm. For the 2011 discussion, see Report of the United Nations Commission on International Trade law of its forty-fourth session, 27 June–8 July 2011, General Assembly Official Records, Sixty-sixth session, Supplement No 17 (A/66/17), para 336.

[81] The study (Susan Block-Lieb and Terence Halliday, 'Harmonization and Modernization in UNCITRAL's Legislative Guide on Insolvency Law' (2007) 42 *Texas International Law Journal* 3 475–514) also considered the influence of NGOs, a topic beyond the scope of this chapter, and one that has received considerable ventilation in the literature. See, for example, Claire Kelly, 'The Politics of International Economic Law: Legitimacy and the UNCITRAL Working Methods' (2009) Brooklyn Law School, Legal Studies Paper No 140. UNCITRAL set out its working methods and the roles of NGOs, highlighting its state-led process, after discussion in the Commission. See https://uncitral.un.org/en/ab-out/methods.

[82] Block-Lieb and Halliday, 'Harmonization and Modernization' (ibid) 477.

[83] KA Annan, 'We the Peoples: The Role of the United Nations in the 21st Century' (New York, United Nations, 2000) 6.

[84] M de Serpa Soares (n 9).

[85] The Legal Committee, to which UNCITRAL reports annually.

economic stages, especially developing and emerging states',[86] as external commentators have also noted.[87]

The challenges of securing broad participation were recognised at the 2017 Congress, as noted above, and the then Secretary acknowledged acknowledged the need

> to make sure that ownership is taken by more countries and more stakeholders of the texts prepared by UNCITRAL. The way to do that is increased participation, which would also allow us to tailor or refine the type of instruments we may think of.

Some speakers suggested that a more proactive approach to the use of informal experts' meetings at much lower costs, host country or host business funding assistance, and outreach to the regions would help meet the challenge. The risks of such an approach – including 'bloc activities' based on regional allegiances and ensuring meaningful transparency – would need to be brought into the equation. Discussions in the Commission at its 50th session on a mandate to reform investor–state dispute settlement highlighted the importance of 'benefiting from the widest possible breadth of available expertise from all stakeholders', in a process that was 'government-led with high-level input from all governments'.[88]

On the other hand, broader participation can increase the time taken to issue a text, and the need for compromise. While most commentators have welcomed the increase in UNCITRAL membership as recognising its importance, a note of caution was recorded when UNCITRAL was established: 'because the work of the commission would be of an essentially technical nature, including a certain amount of legal drafting, it would seem desirable to have a membership of eighteen, and in any event not more than twenty-four'.[89] Willem Vis, Secretary of UNCITRAL from 1974 to 1980, speaking at the first Congress, observed that 'the consideration of draft texts by larger groupings at successive stages of the process' was a contributory factor to an overly lengthy process' (a comment that has been voiced about the time taken by UNCITRAL to develop its texts since the early days of UNCITRAL). While increasing the number of Member States might 'be the answer to the need for greater acceptability of texts, … some may ask the question whether it is feasible to formulate the best possible legal texts in large groupings,' he added.[90] In particular, he suggested that compromises and

[86] 'UNCITRAL Rules of Procedure and Methods of Work: Note by the Secretariat, Observations of the United States', UNCITRAL, Resumed fortieth session, Vienna, 10–14 December 2007 (A/CN.9/639), citing General Assembly resolutions 43/166, 42/152, 41/77, 40/71, 39/82, and 38/134, available at https://uncitral.un.org/en/commission.

[87] See K Mondheim, 'The "Power of Process": The Impact of Process Management on Multilateral Negotiations', available at http://etheses.lse.ac.uk/673/1/Monheim_Power_of_process.pdf (2013) 65. See, as cited in that paper, a case study of WTO negotiations in Cancun and Geneva in 2003 and 2004, which found that transparency, fair representation and fair treatment (that is, inclusion in deliberations by the organisers) significantly contributed towards consensus-building and success. See also C Albin and A Young, 'Setting the Table for Success – or Failure? Agenda Management in the WTO' (2012) 17 *International Negotiation* 37.

[88] Report of the United Nations Commission on International Trade Law, Fiftieth session, 3–21 July 2017, General Assembly Official Records, Seventy-second session, Supplement No 17 (A/72/17), para 264, available at https://uncitral.un.org/en/commission.

[89] A/6396 (n 8) para 229.

[90] W Vis, '4. Process of preparing universally acceptable uniform legal rules' in 'Uniform Commercial Law in the Twenty-first Century' (n 11) 15.

on-the-spot redrafting to secure consensus could compromise quality, with the risk, as another commentator has put it, that UNCITRAL texts are 'drafted as multi-cultural compromises between different schemes of law',[91] and producing '"sub-optimal", vaguely drafted rules for the purpose of achieving political compromise.'[92]

How, then, might UNCITRAL meet these possibly competing considerations? The solutions may be found in the early discussions of UNCITRAL as well as more recent comments on the process of convergence. The aim of broad participation is to identify the objectives that UNCITRAL participants agree will meet the technical needs concerned and will be acceptable to all regions and levels of development – as John Honnold put it, to agree on 'concrete factual examples' when making significant choices. It is also important to bear in mind the development of legal thinking since 1966: at that time, there was a greater expectation that the so-called 'big' topics would be unified through the adoption of 'law-making' treaties. Convergence through harmonisation is preferred, as we have seen. The process in reality relies to a great extent on the elucidation and crystallisation of agreed and good practice being translated into acceptable rules.

Once broad agreement on substance is achieved, a more limited group might be better able to express the policy choices in legal language: UNCITRAL Working Group reports allow for this by recording instructions of the Working Groups to the Secretariat to do precisely that in a Working Paper for the Working Group to consider at its next session. The Commission has also suggested that there should be a limit to the length of time that a project should be with a working groups.[93] Nonetheless, as Eric Bergsten, former Secretary of UNCITRAL, observed in 2015, convergence 'is a slow process. There are many steps along the way. That can be true of domestic legislation as well, but it is particularly true when it is a question of unifying the law amongst nation States.'[94]

Harmonisation is not complete when UNCITRAL adopts a text, so the overall timeframe should take into consideration the time until it is implemented and used in practice. It is commonly assumed that there will inevitably be a significant time-lag between the issue of an UNCITRAL text and its use, but this is not inevitable. Where commercial interests recognise the usefulness and value of a harmonised text, they may use the norm on a voluntary basis. For example, Exxon Mobil (the largest oil company in the US and the world's fifth largest company by revenue) in its 'Tanker Voyage Charter Party' standard form (VOY2012) made the Rotterdam Rules[95] the

[91] ibid; Faria, 'Legal Harmonization Through Model Laws' (n 39), quoting JS Hobhouse, 'International Conventions and Commercial Law: The Pursuit of Uniformity' (1990) 106 *Law Quarterly Review* 530–35, 533.

[92] S Walt, 'Novelty and the Risks of Uniform Sales Law,' (1999) 39 *Virginia Journal of International Law* 671–705, cited in Faria (n 39) 10.

[93] Report of the United Nations Commission on International Trade Law, Forty-sixth session, 8–26 July 2013, General Assembly Official records, Sixty-eighth session, Supplement No 17 (A/68/17), para 299, available at https://uncitral.un.org/en/commission.

[94] EE Bergsten. 'Thirty-Five Years of the United Nations Convention on Contracts for the International Sale of Goods: Expectations and Deliveries' in 'Thirty-five Years of Uniform Sales Law: Trends and Perspectives,' 6 July 2015, 7–12.

[95] Web Alert: ExxonMobilvoy 2012 form of charter party, 16 April 2013, available at http://www.standard-club.com/news-and-knowledge/news/2013/04/exxonmobilvoy-2012-form-of-charter-party.aspx.

default regime, without waiting for the Convention to come into force. This situation also provides a modern example of what was called the 'radiation' effect of unification or harmonisation texts:

> when, for example, a State which is not a party to an international convention decides to apply the principle on which the convention is founded, or when a unifying technique used in one international instrument is subsequently made part of another.[96]

The Commission has itself recognised the link between its process and the 'universal applicability and hence acceptance of UNCITRAL texts, the importance of the transparency that [the] process conferred, and the need to continue the inclusive working methods of UNCITRAL'.[97] Intergovernmental control over the text at all stages in the elaboration process is preserved through this approach, in which developing countries arguably have better visibility and control than in any other comparable organisation.[98]

Nonetheless, how UNCITRAL balances the ongoing participation challenges and demands for faster results will be an issue of considerable interest in coming years.

B. The Importance of Coordination with Other Formulating Agencies

The importance of coordination in UNCITRAL is reflected in its mandate (being the first and presumably therefore the most important of the tasks entrusted to UNCITRAL). The General Assembly has repeatedly emphasised the importance it attaches to this coordination function. Its standard reference to UNCITRAL is 'as the core legal body in the United Nations system in the field of international trade law'.[99] However, as a former Secretary of UNCITRAL has explained, 'Unfortunately, the General Assembly did not give the Commission institutional resources to carry out the coordination role it had been assigned', UNCITRAL has come to consider itself as a core legal body 'in respect of its formulating role and not in respect of its coordination role', and its success in that role may have interfered with its coordination function, not least in introducing an element of competition among the formulating agencies.[100]

UNCITRAL continues to debate the need for and challenges in coordination from various perspectives. It has noted the growing number of bodies, both international

[96] *UNCITRAL Yearbook 1968–70* (n 13) 41, para 205, citing A Tunc, 'English and Continental Commercial Law' (1961) *Journal of Business Law* 246.

[97] A/68/17 (n 93) para 300.

[98] See Commission statement that all UNCITRAL legislative texts should be considered by the Commission prior to adoption, ibid, para 301.

[99] See, for example, General Assembly resolution 45/42, Report of the United Nations Commission on International Trade Law on the work of its twenty-third session, A/RES/45/42 (29 January 1991), para 2, 'Reaffirms the mandate of the Commission, as the core legal body within the United Nations system in the field of international trade law …' available at https://documents-dds-ny.un.org/doc/UNDOC/GEN/N91/028/6-7/img/N9102867.pdf?OpenElement.

[100] E Bergsten, 'Methods of improved coordination between formulating agencies' in 'Uniform Commercial Law in the Twenty-First Century' (n 11) 18.

and regional, developing texts in international commercial law, making the task at the same time ever more necessary and difficult.[101] UNCITRAL is not routinely informed about other agencies' activities, and increasing regionalism and bilateralism may facilitate cooperation and coordination between the countries of the region at the expense of cooperation and coordination on a global scale. The discussions at the 2007 Congress agreed that reducing the transaction costs of international commerce would remove obstacles to the further development of trade. However, different bodies might formulate different solutions to a common problem, and then promote their solutions to different groups of states, resulting in 'dis-harmonisation' and 'confusion over applicable legal rules, increased cost and more obstacles to the expansion of world trade'.[102] Echoing remarks in 1966, the solution posed in 2007 would be clearer delineation of work between different agencies, to improve utilisation of resources, and leadership on the part of the United Nations.[103]

To try to meet this challenge, the Secretariat is increasing activities to promote UNCITRAL texts not only for adoption and enactment by states, but also for use in regional contexts, with some successes. As reported at the 2017 Congress, UNCITRAL has supported enactment in OHADA (the acronym for the French *Organisation pour l'harmonisation en Afrique du droit des affaires*, in English Organisation for the Harmonisation of Corporate Law in Africa). The OHADA Uniform Act relating to General Commercial Law (2010) uses many, though not all, CISG solutions; the *Acte uniforme portant organisaiton des procédures collectives d'apurement du passif* (in English, Uniform Act Organizing Collective Proceedings for Wiping off Debts) (2015) is very largely inspired by the UNCITRAL Legislative Guide on Insolvency Law, and the Uniform Act on Insolvency includes enactment of the UNCITRAL Model Law on Cross-Border Insolvency. Finally, the influence of the work of UNCITRAL on international commercial arbitration is clear in ongoing efforts to reform arbitration law within OHADA.

Another coordination challenge arises at the national level: government organisation varies among states, so that the allocation of responsibility for any given organisation varies from one state to another, so there is no natural counterpart for UNCITRAL. A consequence was noted at the 2017 Congress: this feature, 'combined with overlapping, but not identical, mandates in the various international organisations, and in many cases a perennial lack of resources, one can understand how inadequate information-sharing can result'.[104] Again, echoes from 1996 were heard on the resource question, reflected in the 'scarcity of qualified personnel within the national administrations and parliaments able to devote their limited amount of time to the preparation of laws approving international conventions'.[105]

[101] 'A Guide to UNCITRAL' (n 6) 5, para 10.
[102] Wah-Teck (n 55) 32.
[103] ibid 33–35.
[104] Remarks of Kathryn Sabo, General Counsel, Department of Justice, Canada, 'Modernizing International Trade Law to Support Innovation and Sustainable Development' (n 12).
[105] A/6396/Add.1 (n 8) para 9.

C. Uniform Interpretation of UNCITRAL Texts

As noted above, a number of UNCITRAL's legislative texts include an article promoting uniform interpretation (see, for example, Article 7(1) of the CISG). Disseminating knowledge of and information about the decisions rendered in foreign jurisdictions on the interpretation of these instruments is key in achieving that uniform interpretation, particularly in the absence of an international civil jurisdiction.

The extent of the challenge varies among UNCITRAL texts. To take some examples of harmonisation texts, the UNCITRAL Model Law on International Commercial Arbitration (1985/2006), the UNCITRAL Model Law on Electronic Commerce (1996) and the UNCITRAL Model Law on Public Procurement (2011), the former provides a discrete set of interdependent articles. UNCITRAL recommends that, in adopting this Model Law, very few amendments or changes should be made. In practice, states adopting enacting legislation have largely followed that recommendation, suggesting that the procedures it establishes are widely accepted. Consequently, international decisions on the procedures can lead to a coherent body of interpretation. The Model Laws on Electronic Commerce and Public Procurement, on the other hand, are more conceptual texts with options for enacting states. Legislation based on them reflect both departures in terms not only of drafting, and the combination of provisions adopted also varies. The CLOUT system, Digest of case law and other tools mentioned in section IV above would inevitably be less helpful as interpretative tools across jurisdictions and, to date, do not address those texts.

At the 1992 Congress, UNCITRAL was encouraged to publish differing interpretations and contradictory judgements, and to discuss them, to achieve uniform interpretation not by power and authority of a court, but by scientific arguments. This approach has been followed through making all UNCITRAL documents used for the preparation of a text publicly available on its website, and through the other tools referred to in section V.A. above, and through UNCITRAL's now standard practice of issuing a detailed Guide to Enactment on its Model Laws (whose names are somewhat of a misnomer, as detailed policy and implementation discussions are included). They have more recently been complemented by the Transparency Registry – a repository for the publication of information and documents in treaty-based investor-state arbitration.[106] As regards the more 'conceptual' texts, in particular, academic writings are a useful complement.

The 1992 Congress also established a key educational tool: the Willem C Vis International Commercial Arbitration Moot.[107] The Moot was set up to study international commercial law, arbitration practice and the CISG, and to educate future dispute resolution professionals. (It was named for Willem Vis, the then Secretary of UNCITRAL, and who sadly died in late 1993 before the Inaugural Vis Moot took place.) It takes place annually, in Vienna, and involves a hypothetical commercial

[106] Available at https://uncitral.un.org/en/library.

[107] The sister Willem C Vis (East) International Commercial Arbitration Moot was founded in 2003. There are many other preparatory moots in all regions. A Spanish language moot operates in Latin America.

dispute, raising challenging issues of law and fact, between private parties from two different states, of which at least one is a party to the CISG. The dispute is 'referred' to arbitration in Danubia, a state that has enacted the UNCITRAL Model Law on International Commercial Arbitration and is a party to the New York Convention on the Recognition and Enforcement of Foreign Arbitral Awards. The (several hundred) teams of participants submit pleadings and engage in oral argument. Co-sponsored by UNCITRAL, the arbitration rules applied alternate among the sponsors.[108]

The visiting arbitrators (who hear the disputes) include the world's most eminent, the participating teams are drawn from all regions so that the event is multi-cultural (even if developed country participants may be over-represented), and the Moot Alumni Association is a leading provider of resources in international commercial law and arbitration. As Eric Bergsten, former Secretary of UNCITRAL and Director of the Moot until his retirement in 2013 noted, the VIS Moot is a 'pedagogical tool *par excellence* in teaching international commercial law and arbitration, and a platform for making significant contributions to the development of the rule of law'.[109] In the context of the CISG, which is founded on international rather than national interpretation of its provisions, the potential benefits towards promoting uniform interpretation of the CISG and arbitral decisions in commercial disputes are clear (and in consequence, fulfilling the objective of the CISG, expressed in its Preamble as to 'contribute to the removal of legal barriers in international trade and promote the development of international trade').[110] The 2017 Congress agreed that the Moot was an initiative that had 'gone a very long way in creating a generation of lawyers that is familiar with uniform law'.[111]

[108] The sponsors are Pace University Law School, the International Centre for Dispute Resolution (ICDR)/ The American Arbitration Association (AAA), the International Arbitral Centre of the Austrian Federal Economic Chamber, the Australian Centre for International Commercial Arbitration (ACICA), CEPANI (Belgium), the Chartered Institute of Arbitrators, Chicago International Dispute Resolution Association (CIDRA), the Chinese-European Arbitration Centre (CEAC), German Institution of Arbitration (DIS), the Hong Kong International Arbitration Centre (HKIAC), the International Chamber of Commerce, JAMS, the London Court of International Arbitration (LCIA), the Moot Alumni Association (MAA), the Singapore International Arbitration Centre (SIAC), Swiss Arbitration Association (ASA), Swiss Chambers' Arbitration, UNCITRAL, and the University of Vienna Faculty of Law.

[109] S Kröll, LA Mistelis, P Perales Viscasillas and V Rogers (eds), *International Arbitration and International Commercial Law: Synergy, Convergence, and Evolution: Liber Amicorum Eric Bergsten.* (The Hague, Kluwer Law International, 2011) 694. See also E Bergsten. 'The Willem C. Vis international Commercial Arbitration Moot and the Teaching of International Commercial Arbitration' (2006) 22 *Arbitration International* 309–14; E Bergsten, 'Teaching about International Commercial Law and Arbitration: The Eights Annual Willem C. Vis International Commercial Arbitration Moot' (2003) 18 *Journal of International Arbitration* 481; E Bergsten, 'Ten Years of the Willem C. Vis International Commercial Arbitration Moot' (1999) 6 *International Arbitration Law Review* 37; E Bergsten. 'The Willem C. Vis International Commercial Arbitration Moot: The Perspective of the Organizer' (1999) 6 *Croatian Arbitration Yearbook* 167.

[110] See also MR Shulman and L Singh, 'China's Implementation of the UN Sales Convention Through Arbitral Tribunals' (2010) 48 *Columbia Journal of Transnational Law* 242, 286, in which the authors submit that international commercial arbitration raised expectations of professionalism and skills among the legal profession in China.

[111] 'Modernizing International Trade Law to Support Innovation and Sustainable Development' (n 12).

D. Challenges in Modernisation

During the discussions leading up to the establishment of UNCITRAL, the challenges in rising 'lowest common denominator' approach were noted,[112] and UNCITRAL was encouraged to face the challenges in seeking to 'create legislation more responsive to the needs',[113] and in filling in the gaps in the existing legal order.[114] It was also suggested that UNCITRAL should seek to simplify laws where possible, for the benefit of those other than 'academic jurists or professional lawyers', and emerging commercial actors in developing countries.[115] Recalling the 'progressive' nature of UNCITRAL's mandate, which commentators have expressed as 'unification over time',[116] modernisation, as we have seen, is at least implicit in the mandate.

Modernisation will be appropriate 'where national law exists on a topic, but is viewed by the international community as out-of-date', or 'where technical or market developments have outstripped existing law and the lack of suitable regulation is viewed by the international community to stall commercial development'.[117] Modernisation, however, brings with it a considerable degree of challenge – especially as it may 'speak authoritatively to national legislatures both about the need and the content of law'.[118] And as commentators concerned have noted, 'frequently … "modernization" is a euphemism for adaptation of a weaker country's laws in the direction of a powerful sovereign state or international organisation which has the cultural authority to define the meaning of "modern"'.[119] This implies that 'modernisation might either take the form of a functional adaptation of law to new circumstances, or the form of cultural conformity with a powerful symbolic standard promulgated by a 'modernising' global institution, or both'.[120] The potential link between moving towards more obviously 'modernising' texts may impede developing country participation: commentators report that

> some developing and transitional countries did not believe their interests were being sufficiently addressed. And it is doubtful that if developing and transitional nations had wanted to alter significantly the terms of [a text under consideration] they could have done so given the relative weakness of their delegations.[121]

Moreover, modernisation might in fact impede unification, unless there is broad agreement on a policy solution suitable for divergent countries and systems, by requiring compromise at the level of the 'lowest common denominator' solution. On the other

[112] Including that 'excessive zeal might lead to unification at the lowest common denominator', ie at the level of the least progressive systems. *UNCITRAL Yearbook 1968–70* (n 13) 43–44, para 223.
[113] ibid 15, para 11.
[114] ibid 12, para 73, emphasising the need for creativity in addition to finding a common denominator.
[115] ibid 48, para 10.
[116] Block-Lieb and Halliday, 'Harmonization and Modernization' (2017) 494.
[117] ibid 477.
[118] ibid.
[119] ibid.
[120] ibid.
[121] S Block-Lieb, TC Halliday and J Pacewicz, 'Who Governs? Delegations in Global Trade Lawmaking' (2013) 7 *Regulation & Governance* 279, 295, available at http://ir.lawnet.fordham.ed-u/faculty_scholarship/614.

hand, model laws – which can include options that can be adapted to suit an enacting state's level of maturity – now have a higher implementation rate than conventions.[122] They may in fact be promoting harmonisation in practice at a faster rate than unification texts, operating as a stepping stone towards agreed solutions.

In addition, as states negotiating in UNCITRAL are not committing themselves to domestic adoption of a uniform text, they may agree to higher (or more modern) standards, they may agree to go along with an emerging consensus that they would not accept in a convention. The 2017 Congress noted that, over time, resistance to some elements in the CISG has fallen away, and monitoring use and implementation of UNCITRAL texts (particularly model laws) indicates that once-controversial Articles become quite acceptable. For example, UNCITRAL's 1994 Model Law on Procurement of Goods, Construction and Services contained 'optional' provisions enabling allegedly wronged suppliers to the Government to challenge the wrong concerned – a footnote to the relevant part of the Model Law provided that enacting states might choose not to incorporate some or all of the Articles.[123] The reason for this gentle approach was a historic concern that the remedies issue raised the legality of government acts, could affect the separation of powers between the executive and the judicial branches of a particular state, and choice should not be made among the broad range of approaches to the topic in different legal systems.[124] A decade later, when revising that Model Law, it was agreed that, although divergent approaches remained, there was consensus that remedies provisions should be mandatory. This consensus was based on identified good practice and on the requirements of the mandatory language of Article 9(1)(e) of the United Nations Convention against Corruption, which required an effective system of review and appeal in procurement proceedings.[125] Behind the Working Group's reasoning was that most procurement laws enacted at that time indeed included remedies provisions, and the policy debate had simply moved on.

The UNIDROIT representative to the General Assembly in 1996 emphasised that international commercial law had moved beyond governing solely the transaction parties, but also that 'account is more and more taken of the direct and indirect interest of third persons, eg of users or consumers', and we have seen that the General Assembly agreed that convergence would be more likely to be successful where the issues were technical, rather than policy-sensitive in the domestic context. UNIDROIT added that

[122] Data from the annual reports by the UNCITRAL Secretariat, entitled 'Status of conventions and model laws', the latest example of which is 'Status of conventions and model laws: Note by the Secretariat', UNCITRAL, Fifty-first session, New York, 25 June–13 July 2018 (A/CN.9/950), available at https://uncitral.un.org/en/commission. UNCITRAL also publishes a status report for each text. See, for example, the status of the UNCITRAL Model Law on International Commercial Arbitration (1985), with amendments as adopted in 2006, available at https://uncitral.un.org/en/texts/arbitration/modellaw/commercial_arbitration/status.

[123] Footnote attached to Chapter VI, 'Review' in UNCITRAL Model Law on Procurement of Goods, Construction and Services with Guide to Enactment, available at https://uncitral.un.org/sites/uncitral.un.org/files/media-documents/uncitral/en/ml-procure.pdf.

[124] See Report of Working Group I (Procurement) on the work of its sixth session (Vienna, 30 August–3 September 2004), UNCITRAL, Thirty-eighth session, Vienna, 4–22 July 2005 (A/CN.9/568), available at https://uncitral.un.org/en/commission.

[125] See Report of Working Group I (Procurement) on the work of its fourteenth session (Vienna, 8–12 September 2008), UNCITRAL, Forty-second session, Vienna, 29 June–17 July 2009 (A/CN.9/664), available at https://uncitral.un.org/en/commission.

a main challenge for formulating agencies was to reconcile the needs of states to regulate and yet to 'maintain a certain flexibility and the adaptability necessary for commercial transactions'.[126]

These points have recently emerged in UNCITRAL's Working Group III, in the first instance on Online Dispute Resolution. A considerable stumbling block in the process of developing what became UNCITRAL's Technical Notes on the topic[127] were divergent views between two blocs of states on appropriate consumer protection (demonstrating the far-sightedness of the UNIDROIT representative in 1966). As the relevant reports of the Working Group made clear, the divergent views on the matter were irreconcilable and consensus on the final stage of an online dispute resolution process proved impossible as a result.[128] The Technical Notes do not therefore address that final stage. However, commentators have recognised that states were simply unable at that time to agree on the appropriate factual solution on this area of considerable national policy significance, and that the significance of the work was that UNCITRAL remained engaged on this emerging topic. Once again, the predictions in 1966 were accurate: success is much harder in policy-sensitive areas.

In 2010, UNCITRAL commenced work on transparency in international investment arbitration involving states (a process previously treated as confidential), and the United Nations Convention on Transparency in Treaty-based Investor-State Arbitration ('The Mauritius Convention') was adopted in 2014.[129] The expansion of this work to investor-state dispute settlement reform (again in Working Group III) raises the need to balance the interests of private (investors) and public sectors (citizens): disputes may involve regulations with public policy implications, such as tax laws, environmental laws, health regulations and natural resources laws, and as the defence of a claim and the payment of any award will ultimately come from public funds.[130] The Commission

[126] A/6396 and Add 1 (n 8) section A, paras 5–6.

[127] UNCITRAL decided to draft procedural rules to apply to both business-to-consumer and business-to-business online transactions. See 'Online dispute resolution for cross-border electronic commerce transactions: Note by the Secretariat', UNCITRAL Working Group III (Online Dispute Resolution), Twenty-second session, Vienna, 13–17 December 2010, A/CN.9/WG.III/WP.105, para 2.

[128] The Working Group envisaged a three-tiered ODR procedure, involving party negotiation, mediation and a final phase (arbitration or a non-binding recommendation). Pre-dispute consumer agreements to arbitrate disputes can be legally binding in, for example, the US, but not in, for example, the EU. The Working Group proposed two tracks for the final phase to deal with this difference, one ending in a binding arbitration phase (Track I) and the other one concluding with a non-binding recommendation by a neutral (Track II) – see Report of the United Nations Commission on International Trade Law, forty-fifth session (25 June–6 July 2012), A/67/17, para 74 and Report of the United Nations Commission on International Trade Law, forty-seventh session (7–18 July 2014), A/69/17, paras 137 and 138. However, in light of the consumer protection question, consensus on the nature of and default procedure for the final determination was not possible, and the Technical Notes excluded that final phase. See, further, Report of the United Nations Commission on International Trade Law, forty-fourth session (27 June – 8 July 2011), A/66/17, para 218; A/67/17, supra, paras 74–79; Report of the United Nations Commission on International Trade Law, forty-sixth session (8–26 July 2013), A/68/17, para 222; A/CN.9/833, paras 23–34, and Report of the United Nations Commission on International Trade Law, forty-eighth session (29 June–16 July 2015), A/70/17, paras 342–52.

[129] There are three mains instruments to be considered as part of the transparency standards developed by UNCITRAL: the UNCITRAL Transparency Rules, the Mauritius Convention and the UNCITRAL Transparency Registry.

[130] 'Settlement of commercial disputes, Revision of the UNCITRAL Arbitration Rules, Observations by the Government of Canada: Note by the Secretariat', UNCITRAL, Forty-first session, New York, 16 June–3 July 2008 (A/CN.9/662), para 9, available at https://uncitral.un.org/en/commission.

required the Working Group to 'ensure that the deliberations, while benefiting from the widest possible breadth of available expertise from all stakeholders, would be government-led with high-level input from all governments, consensus-based and be fully transparent'.[131]

These topics provide examples of modernisation efforts raising issues of public law in the traditionally commercial sphere. Working Group III started its work in November 2017, and its progress will be an area to watch.

VI. Conclusions

The three Congresses over the course of UNCITRAL's 50 years of existence demonstrate that UNCITRAL can adapt successfully to changing economic circumstances and ways of doing business. At the 2017 Congress, the phrase 'convening power of UNCITRAL' was repeated throughout the Congress, and it was identified as the key factor in its success. The intellectual leadership of UNCITRAL and its transparent, inclusive and multilingual working methods were among the factors that had contributed to this convening power – which, in turn, allowed for the empirically based solution-seeking that underpinned its success. Indeed, the notion of 'competitive cooperation' was highlighted – meaning that organisations that might be considered as in competition with each other, had decided in the UNCITRAL sphere to sit down and work together to find a solution fit for all.

The Congresses, too, noted that UNCITRAL provides a learning space in which people can gain an understanding of the questions that delegates should ask of themselves, and in which they can listen to others, to develop the law of international trade in a way that would, to coin a phrase, be fit for purpose. Making the Congresses open to the public, and publishing their proceedings and materials, further encourages practitioners, academics and others to consider UNCITRAL's activities, encourages others to host conferences and provide commentary on UNCITRAL documents beyond government circles, and in turn inspire international best practice.[132]

This chapter has demonstrated that UNCITRAL's successes cannot be taken for granted, but its members – who are, in fact, UNCITRAL – are constantly striving to find ways to continue them – in the words of the 2017 Congress, engaging in positive creative law-making for the benefit of all, exactly as the designers of the United Nations Agenda 2030 have encouraged its members to do.

[131] 'Official Records of the General Assembly, Seventy-second Session, Supplement No 17' (A/72/17), para 264 (Commission Report, 2017).

[132] Opening address by Nicolas Michel, Legal Counsel, Modernizing International Trade Law to Support Innovation and Sustainable Development' (n 12).

2

The Harmonisation of Laws in the United States of America

HENRY GABRIEL

I. The Need for Harmonisation

Legal life in the US would be simpler if there were one set of laws to regulate matters throughout the entire nation. Instead, the US has separate laws for each of the 50 states and the District of Columbia as well as innumerable federal laws that govern alongside the state laws. A person or goods travelling across the country may be governed by a dozen set of laws. In the early days of the country, this was less a problem than today as most legal issues were local and therefore people and transactions for the most part were not subjected to the possibility of multiple state laws.

The need for harmonisation[1] of laws in the US has been evident from the time the country came into existence. This need arose from the country's federal system of government and laws; a system that divides the legal jurisdiction between national and state governments. Within this federal system, a substantial amount of law is reserved for the states,[2] and this created the potential for and the continued existence of dis-harmonisation among the laws of the respective states in a country where economic and social ties are often national.[3]

Under the US Constitution, federal law in US has supremacy over state law,[4] and to the extent that there is a conflict between federal and state law, the federal law prevails.

[1] The terms 'harmonisation' and 'unification' are closely interrelated. I view 'harmonisation' as the process through which domestic laws may be modified to enhance predictability. in cross-border commercial transactions; and 'unification' may be seen as the adoption by states of a common legal standard governing aspects of international business transactions. A model law or a legislative guide is an example of a text which is drafted to harmonise domestic law, while a convention is an international instrument which is adopted by states for the unification of the law at an international level. Texts resulting from the work of UNCITRAL include conventions, model laws, legal guides, legislative guides, rules and practice notes.

[2] The Tenth Amendment to the United States Constitution provides that:, 'The powers not delegated to the united States by the Constitution, nor prohibited to it by the States, are reserved to the States respectively, or to the people.'

[3] The country started with 13 states, each with their individual laws. The country now has individual laws for 50 states and the District of Columbia.

[4] United States Constitution (Article VI, Clause 2) provides that in case of a conflict between federal and state law, the federal law must be applied.

Thus, with few exceptions, there has not been a significant need to harmonise state and federal law in the US.

This has not been the case among the states. Not only has each state developed its own law, but as a common law country, for substantial part of the country's history, the individual state law was judge made case law with each state developing its laws independent of one another.[5] Moreover, although loosely based on the English common law,[6] the states varied greatly on what the respective states understood to be the common law.[7]

It is worth noting that in the early years of the nation, harmonisation of laws among the states was probably less a problem than was the ability of courts and lawyers within the respective states to know the local law. Only a few states had published reports of the state court decisions,[8] and local practice varied from court to court.[9]

Interestingly, the paucity of published court reports and other legal materials[10] may have provided some basis of harmonisation of the laws among the states because one of the few, but somewhat universal legal sources relied upon by American lawyers and courts was William Blackstone's *Commentaries on the Laws of England*.[11] This ubiquitous

[5] See, eg, A-H Chroust, *The Rise of the Legal Profession in America, Vol 1* (Norman, University of Oklahoma Press, 1965) 5–29.

[6] It is fair to say that this very loosely based. With the possible exception of New Jersey, New York, Virginia and Georgia, the colonies as a rule did not recognise the common law as binding. See, eg, Chroust, *Rise of the Legal Profession* (ibid) 11. And this recognition did not necessarily survive the American Revolution. A New Jersey Act of 1799 prohibited lawyers from citing in court any legal decision, opinion, commentary, digest or lecture made or written in Great Britain since 4 July 1776. JH Langbein, 'Chancellor Kent and the History of Legal Literature' (1993) 93 *Columbia Law Review* 547. Moreover, to the extent that the early colonies and states espoused the English common law, they often used it for purposes diametrically opposed to its usage in the British courts. See, eg, MNS Sellers, 'Legal history and Legal Theory: The Doctrine of Precedent in the United States of America' (2006) 54 *American Journal of Comparative Law* 67.

[7] Thus, for example, when Arkansas became part of the US in 1836, it adopted the common law of England as it existed in 1607. The Statute providing for this read: 'The common law of England, so far as the same is applicable and of a general nature, and all of the statutes of the British Parliament in aid of or to supply the defects of the common law made prior to the fourth year of James the First (that are applicable to our own form of government), of a general nature and not local to that kingdom, and not inconsistent with the Constitution and laws of the United States or the Constitution and laws of this state, shall be the rule of decision in this State unless altered or repealed by the general Assembly of this State.' Each state had a similarly vague reception of the common law. Maryland, for example, provided: 'That the inhabitants of Maryland are entitled to the common law of England, and the trial by jury, according to that law, and to the benefit of such of the English statutes as existed at the time of the first emigration, and which, by experience, have been found applicable to their local and other circumstances, and of such others as have been since made in England, or Great Britain, and have been introduced, used and practiced by the courts of law or equity ….' A Declaration of Rights, and Constitution and Form of Government agreed to by the Delegates of Maryland, 11 November 1776 at III.

[8] A-H Chroust, *The Rise of the Legal Profession in America, Vol 2* (Norman, University of Oklahoma Press 1965) 74–75.

[9] 'Judges literally brought the law to the people – a task filled with physical and intellectual obstacles. Circuit riding to country courthouses in back-country settlements was a lonely and arduous practice: time in transit – if the circuit was extensive – often matched time in court. The judge carried his law books with him as there were no public law libraries.' GE White, *The American Judicial Tradition* (Oxford, Oxford University Press, 1976) 43.

[10] Until 1775 only 48 legal texts had been published in America. R Pound, *The Formative Era of American Law* (New York, Little Brown, 1938) 8.

[11] W Blackstone, *Commentaries on the Laws of England* (Oxford, Oxford University Press, 1765).

text provided a common source of private law rules for lawyers practising in the US in the late eighteenth and early nineteenth century, and its use as a source of legal rules was common in all the states.

This tradition of a strong reliance on a single legal source continued in America with the publication of Kent's *Commentaries on American Law* between 1826 and 1830.[12] The Commentaries treated state, federal and international law, and the law of personal rights and of property, and went through six editions in Kent's lifetime. Modelled on *Blackstone's Commentaries*, *Kent's Commentaries* provided a single and well-used source of principles common to most American jurisdictions, and as such provided significant harmonisation among the states of basic private law principles.[13]

As the country and its economy grew, though, it was clear that there would be diverse state cases and statutes, 'leading to confusion and difficulty in areas common to all jurisdictions'.[14]

To address this problem, there were suggestions by the mid-nineteenth century for codification of the common law. For example, in 1837, US Supreme Court Justice Joseph Story wrote a report for the Commission to Codify the Common Law of Massachusetts where he emphasised that:

> One great advantage, therefore, of a Code, an advantage, which in a practical view, can scarcely be over-estimated, is, that it supersedes the necessity, in ordinary cases at least, of very elaborate researches into other books: and, indeed, it often supersedes in all cases, but those rare and extraordinary occurrence, the necessity of consulting an immense mass of learned collections and digests of antecedent decisions.[15]

The first major attempt at codification for harmonising American laws was undertaken by David Dudley Field, a lawyer from New York. Field drafted a civil, penal and procedural code that were collectively known as the 'Field Codes'.[16] New York adopted the penal and procedural code, and the procedural code was subsequently adopted by another 29 states.[17]

The usefulness of harmonisation among the laws of the states existed from the founding of the country, and as we have seen there were attempts to provide for harmonisation. But for many years in the earlier history of the nation, because legal relationships in commercial as well as family matters were mostly local, the diverse and individual laws of the various states did not create insurmountable problems.

It should also be noted that regardless of the desire for national harmonisation of the laws among the states, this was not going to happen until there was some recognition

[12] J Kent, *Commentaries on American Law* (New York, O Halsted, 1826–30).

[13] JH Langbein, 'Chancellor Kent and the History of Legal Literature' (1993) 93 *Columbia Law Review* 547.

[14] WP Armstrong, Jr, *A Century of Service: A Centennial History of the National Conference of Commissioners on Uniform Laws* (St Paul, West, 1991) 13.

[15] J Story and Massachusetts, Commissioners on Codification of the Common Law, 'Report of the Commission Appointed to Consider and Report upon the Practicability and Expediency of Reducing to a Written and Systematic Code of the Common Law of Massachusetts or Any Part Thereof' (1837) 17 *American Jurist and Law Magazine* 17, 41.

[16] AP Morriss, SJ Burnham and JG Nelson, 'Debating the Field Code 105 years Late' (2000) 61 *Montana Law Review* 371.

[17] T Shaw, Jr, 'Procedural Reform and the Rule-Making Power in New York' (1955) 24 *Fordham Law Review* 338, 339 n 4.

and recordation of what the actual law was in the individual states. Fifty years after the American Revolution, the number of reported cases in the US remained small. Only the states of New York and Pennsylvania and the US Supreme Court had consistently reported their respective cases.[18]

In the latter part of the nineteenth century, however, with increased industrialisation and the rapid development of a national economy and the rapid rise in the number of people and goods moving across the country, the system of state laws within a federal system began to cause significant strain on the American legal system.

There were obviously two possible responses to this problem. First, areas of the law necessary for the regulation of a national economy could be federalised, and therefore, with a single national law harmonisation would have been achieved. The second possibility, and the one taken, was to harmonise the state laws such that each state retained jurisdiction and control over those areas of the law that were traditionally state law, but to harmonise these areas of the law among the states.

This second approach has been significantly achieved in the US primarily through two organisations, the National Conference of Commissioners on Uniform State Laws (NCCUSL) and the American Law Institute (ALI). As will be discussed below, the approach by the NCCUSL has been primarily harmonisation by statute and the work of the ALI has been primarily by Restatements of the law that attempt to harmonise case law principles.

It is important to appreciate that the work of both organisations has been not only to harmonise the state laws in the US but also to improve the laws as well. These two goals have always operated together, and it would be difficult to separate the two in the work of these respective organisations.

II. The National Conference of Commissioners on Uniform State Laws

A. Founding and Early Work of NCCUSL

By the late nineteenth century the need for uniform and predictable state laws intensified as industrialisation increased the commercial relations among the states.[19] The movement for uniform state laws was one of the justifications for the creation

[18] GE White, *Law in American History: Vol 1* (Oxford, Oxford University Press, 2012).

[19] What would have been an obvious solution would have been a series of federal laws that would govern national commercial law and other areas of the law that could use uniformity across the country as the country dealt with an increasingly mobile population and national commerce. However, in the decades follow the American Civil War the US Supreme Court issued a series of opinions that put into doubt the scope of the Federal Government to regulate interstate and state commerce. In response, the bar, in cooperation of the states, created the National Conference of Commissioners on Uniform State Laws to provide for a national commercial law without having to run the risk that a federalised approach would be invalidated by the US Supreme Court. See WM Wiecek, *The Lost World of Classical Legal Thought* (Oxford, Oxford University Press, 1998) 149.

of the American Bar Association (ABA) in 1878,[20] and in 1889, the ABA on its own initiative,[21] as well as at the instigation of individual state bar associations,[22] passed a resolution to look into the possibility of the individual states appointing commissions on uniform laws. By 1891, six states had done so,[23] and in 1892, the newly formed Conference of State Uniform Law Commissioners[24] met in Saratoga, New York with representatives from seven states. Attendance grew over the years; a second meeting in 1892 had representatives from eight states, and a meeting in 1893 had representatives from 20 states. By 1894 27 states were represented, and by 1900, 35 states and territories were represented. NCCUSL has met every year since 1892, except for 1945, and membership now includes all of states in the US as well as the District of Columbia.

By 1893, NCCUSL had established several committees to explore areas of the law for harmonisation. These included wills, marriage and divorce, commercial law, descent and distribution, and deeds and conveyances. Early on it was established that NCCUSL would concentrate on the harmonisation of commercial and family law matters; and penal and tax matters were best left to the individual states.

To ensure uniformity among state laws, it has always been the policy of NCCUSL to draft statutes for adoption by the states. As we shall see, the ALI has taken a different path and has usually drafted Restatements of the Law that are synthesis of case law and are primarily used by courts as a basis for creating and stating judicially made rules.

In 1896, the first uniform act, the Uniform Negotiable Instruments Law, was adopted by NCCUSL. It was widely adopted, and by 1916 it had been enacted by every state.[25] Future uniform acts have rarely been as successful.

During the rest of the nineteenth and the early part of the twentieth century NCCUSL produced several uniform acts dealing with family and inheritance laws, but these were not widely adopted.[26]

Beginning in the early part of the twentieth century, following up on its success of the Uniform Negotiable Instruments Law, NCCUSL undertook a series of uniform laws dealing with commercial law. This included the Uniform Sales Act[27] and the

[20] SE Baldwin, 'The Founding of the American Bar Association' (1917) 3 *American Bar Association Journal* 658.

[21] Armstrong, *A Century of Service* (1991) 18.

[22] See, eg, 'Uniformity in Laws in the Several States' (1889) 23 *American Law Review* 819.

[23] The states were New York, Pennsylvania, Michigan, Massachusetts, New Jersey and Delaware. See, JW Day, 'The National Conference of Commissioners on Uniform State Laws' (1955) 8 *University of Florida Law Review* 276, 277.

[24] The current name, the National Conference of Commissioners on Uniform State Laws, was adopted in 1915. RA Stein, *Forming a Perfect Union: A History of the Uniform Law Commission* (New York, LexisNexis, 2013) 20.

[25] C Thaddeus Terry, *Uniform State Laws in the United States* (New York, Baker, Voorhis & Company, 1920) 17.

[26] In 1892, NCCUSL adopted what may be the shortest uniform Act it has ever produced: The Uniform Act Relating to Wills Executed Without the State. The Act provided: 'That a last will and testament, executed without this state in the mode prescribed by the law, either of the place executor of the testator's domicile, shall be deemed to be legally executed, and shall be of the same force and effect as if executed in the mode prescribed by the laws of this state, provided, said last will and testament is in writing and be subscribed by the testator.' The Act was adopted by six states.

[27] This Act was fairly successful and was adopted by 34 states between 1906 and 1947.

Uniform Warehouse Receipts Acts in 1906, the Uniform Bill of Lading Act in 1909,[28] the Uniform Conditional Sales Act in 1918, the Uniform Chattel Mortgages Act in 1926, and the Uniform Trust Receipts Act in 1933. Some of these acts were more successful than others. The bill of lading act had 24 adoptions, but only seven states adopted the Uniform Conditional Sales Act.

Some of these acts served primarily to unify the law across the nation, as such, did not necessarily create any new fundamental changes to the law.[29] On the other hand, some of the uniform acts were responses to commercial practices in areas where the existing law was inadequate.[30]

These acts made significant progress in the harmonisation of commercial law in the US, but they suffered from two drawbacks. The first was, obviously, the lack of universal enactment, and the second problem was the question of uniform interpretation.

Not surprisingly, the two areas that NCCUSL has done the most work in harmonisation is commercial and family law, as these two areas of the law create the largest amount of interstate legal conflicts. The best known and most successful harmonisation of American state law is the Uniform Commercial Code (UCC).

B. Further Work by NCCUSL in Commercial and Corporate Law

Over the years the conference has drafted several significant uniform commercial and corporate laws. The most notable uniform acts have been in partnership law, limited partnership laws[31] and limited liability corporations.[32]

It is interesting to note that some of the early work by the Conference in partnership law looked to the then current English law as a model. Sir Mackenzie Dalzell Chalmers, who had drafted both the English Bills of Exchange Act and the Sale of Goods Act, spoke at the annual NCCULS Conference in 1902 and advocated the adoption of the English model.[33] This was also advocated by Sir Frederick Pollock, the English jurist

[28] In an attempt to push forward national harmonization, a Federal Bills of Lading Act was promulgated in 1916.

[29] This was, for example, the case with Uniform Sales Act. Although it was widely adopted by the states, it did little more than replicate the English Sale of Goods Act of 1893.

[30] This was, for example, the impetus behind the Uniform Trust Receipts Act. With the rise of mass-produced automobiles that were being distributed nationwide from a small number of manufacturers to retail dealers in all states, the trust receipt provided a means for the dealers to acquire the inventory. With the trust receipt, the cars would move, but the dealer would never own the cars. The title would pass from the manufacturer to the finance company that paid for the cars, and then in the end, to the consumer buyers. The finance company would pay the manufacturers and take the title to the cars in trust, with the dealer having only beneficial ownership.

[31] Uniform Limited Partnership Act, completed in 2001 and last amended in 2013, and adopted in Alabama, Arkansas, California, District of Columbia, Florida, Hawaii, Idaho, Illinois, Iowa, Kentucky, Maine, Minnesota, Mississippi, Montana, Nevada, New Mexico, North Dakota, Oklahoma, Pennsylvania, Tennessee, Utah and Washington.

[32] Completed by the Uniform Law Commission in 2006, amended in 2011 and 2013, and adopted by Alabama, California, Connecticut, District of Columbia, Florida, Idaho, Illinois, Iowa, Minnesota, Nebraska, New Jersey, North Dakota, Pennsylvania, South Dakota, Utah, Vermont, Washington and Wyoming.

[33] P Winship, 'The National Conference of Commissioners on Uniform State Laws and the Unification of Private Law' (1992) 13 *University of Pennsylvania International Business Law Review* 227.

and drafter of the English Partnership Act.[34] Although there was much discussion and disagreement over several years, the English model was adopted as the Uniform Partnership Act in 1914.

It is interesting that the core debate in the drafting of the original Partnership Act was whether to adopt the 'entity' theory or the English 'aggregate' theory. Although the aggregate theory originally won out, the Uniform Partnership Act was revised in 1997, and that version adopts the 'entity' theory.[35] The revised Act has been adopted by 40 jurisdictions, and hence has been quite successful in harmonising this branch of the law.

Corporations law has been mostly harmonised among the states, not by the Uniform Law Commission (ULC), but by the Model Business Corporation Act that was drafted by the ABA.[36] First promulgated in 1950 and most recently revised in 2016, this model law has been adopted by 24 states.

C. Unification of Family and Probate Law

Areas of family law that have been identified where interstate uniformity is desirable include interstate child support and family maintenance. Although it was recognised early that a court only need to have jurisdiction on one party for a divorce, a court needs to have jurisdiction over both parties in child support proceedings.[37] In response to these needs, over the years NCCUSL has adopted a series of uniform acts that have been progressively more widely accepted by the states. In 1910, the Conference promulgated the Uniform Desertion and non-Support Act. Although it had 26 adoptions, its effectiveness was limited as it did not provide for interstate enforcement.[38] This was replaced in 1948 by the Uniform Support of Dependents Law. Although it provided for interstate enforcement, it only had eleven adoptions and therefore was also fairly unsuccessful. After several other attempts to address the problem of interstate family support, the Conference adopted the Uniform Interstate Family Support Act in 1996. This Act has been adopted by all states and therefore child support orders from any state are enforceable in any other state.

It is worth noting that many of the uniform laws in family law serve not only the goal of harmonisation, but in many respects the primary purpose is to provide interstate enforcement. Harmonisation of these laws is, therefore only one of the policies behind uniform state laws.

[34] ibid.

[35] Stein, *Forming a Perfect Union* (2013) 41.

[36] The ABA is a national voluntary professional organisation of lawyers that was founded in 1878. With over 400,000 members, it is one of the largest voluntary professional organisations in the US.

[37] The United States Constitutional mandate that a state recognise the judgements of another state does not extend to child support. The Full Faith and Credit Clause of the United States Constitution provides that 'Full Faith and Credit shall be given in each state to the public Act, Records, and judicial proceedings of every other state'. United States Constitution Art IV, § 1. This mandate, however, only applies to final orders, and support orders are almost always modifiable.

[38] Stein (n 24) 136.

These multi-goals of harmonisation are also evident in the Conference's many uniform laws in probate and trusts and estates.[39] This began in 1895 with the Act Relating to the Execution of Wills and an Act Relative to the Probate in this State of Foreign Wills. Since those first acts, the Conference has adopted the Uniform Principal and Income Act in 1931, Uniform Trustees Accounting Act in 1936, and the Uniform Trust Act in 1937. In 1938, the Uniform Estates Act and the Uniform Common Trust Fund Act were adopted. In 1956, the Conference adopted the Uniform Gift to Minors Act and the Uniform Estate Tax Apportionment Act.

It is clear that all these uniform acts were designed to harmonise the laws among the states to accommodate both the widespread movement of people from one state to another as well as the common situation where people owned assets both real and personal in multiple states. But other goals were desired and achieved by these uniform acts. For example, by having harmonised language in the various state statutes, uniformity of interpretation has been encouraged and often achieved thereby providing a basis for reliance in legal instruments that may have enforceability in more than one jurisdiction. It is also clear that, as with the Restatements of Law discussed below, a significant drive toward nationwide uniform, and therefore harmonised laws, is to improve the laws themselves.

Thus, for example by the 1960s it was clear that the probate laws among the states not only were not harmonised but were seriously out of date.[40] In response to this, in a process spanning from 1962 until 1969, the Conference drafted the Uniform Probate Code. This harmonisation of probate law has not been very successful. Having gone through multiple revisions over the years,[41] it has still only been adopted in 18 jurisdictions.[42] This low number of adoptions has been more the rule than the exception among the various uniform laws promulgated. In this respect, except for a small number of widely adopted uniform laws such as the Uniform Commercial Code, harmonisation of state laws by statute in the US has not been particularly successful.

D. How NCCUSL Works

The NCCUSL is an interstate governmental organisation that is made up of Commissioners appointed by their respective states. NCCUSL Commissioners are appointed by the states independently of one another and are typically chosen by the Governors of each state, although some are chosen by legislative directive.

The working methods of the NCCUSL have been fairly consistent over the last century. First, NCCUSL forms a Study Committee of Commissioners to examine a suggestion for a new uniform statute or the need to revise an existing uniform statute.[43]

[39] Stein (n 24) 119–36.

[40] See, eg, LW Averill, 'An Eclectic History and Analysis of the 1990 Uniform Probate Code' (1992) 55 *Alabama Law Review* 891.

[41] 1975, 1982, 1987, 1989, 1990, 1991, 1997, 1998, 2002, 2003, 2008 and 2010.

[42] Alaska, Arizona, Colorado, Hawaii, Idaho, Maine, Massachusetts, Michigan, Minnesota, Montana, Nebraska, New Jersey, New Mexico, North Dakota, Pennsylvania, South Carolina, South Dakota and Utah.

[43] As will be discussed below, with the UCC, this step is often performed instead by the Permanent Editorial Board for the UCC (PEB) or a body of ALI members and Commissioners acting on behalf of the PEB, or, in some cases, by the ABA or the ALI.

If the study group recommends that a statute be prepared, before any drafting begins, then the recommendation must be approved by the Scope and Program Committee of NCCUSL, as well as the Executive Committee of NCCUSL. Once the decision to prepare a proposed statute is reached, a Drafting Committee composed of six to 10 Commissioners is appointed. In addition, under an agreement with the ABA, each Drafting Committee has an ABA advisor appointed to work with it.

Each Drafting Committee has a reporter. The reporter presents the information with policy choices in alternative draft language. The reporter in this process does not decide what goes into the statute, but simply drafts the statute consistent with the decisions of the members of the Drafting Committee. The Drafting Committee determines the policy and provisions of the proposed statute based on the work of the reporter, on advice received from various relevant constituencies concerning those policies and provisions, and on the experience of the members in their practice in the various states.

The proposed statute is then discussed and debated at the annual meetings of NCCUSL during each of at least two years and, in the case of the UCC, at least at one annual meeting of the ALI. The Act is approved only by a majority of the of the states. The adoption of a uniform act by NCCUSL creates no binding law. It is up to the individual states to adopt the uniform act.

III. The American Law Institute

In the early part of the twentieth century, judicial decisions (case law) provided a significant body of the law among the states. As we have seen, primarily through the ULC, there was great push to harmonise the law among the states by statute. As a common law country, however, the US was not inclined to move toward a more legislative and statutory legal system. Within the legal establishment, though, there was a clear recognition that case law throughout the various states was not keeping pace with economic, social and business conditions.

This concern by the practising bar was complemented by the rise in the US of a new type of legal education which was begun at Harvard Law School under the deanship of Christopher Columbus Langdell. Langdell instituted the 'case method' where law students primarily studied and discussed reported cases with the goal of extracting the underlying legal principles.[44] Although the 'case method' of legal education was initially quite controversial at Harvard and other American law schools,[45] by the second decade of the twentieth century it had effectively become the standard mode of teaching in American legal education.[46]

The case method brought forth the need for textbooks containing the relevant cases so that students could extract the 'legal principles' that supposedly

[44] BA Kimball, *The Inception of Modern Professional Education: C. C. Langdell, 1826–1906* (Chapel Hill, University of North Carolina Press, 2009).

[45] See, eg, J Redlich, *The Common Law and The Case Method in American University Law Schools: A Report to the Carnegie Foundation for the Advancement of Teaching* (New York, Carnegie Foundation, 1914).

[46] R Stevens, *Law School: Legal Education in America from the 1850s to the 1980s* (Chapel Hill, University of North Carolina Press, 1983) 51–72.

encompassed the law.[47] The rise of casebooks introduced the need for systematic treatises in the various areas of the law – texts that were produced by the same academics who were producing the casebooks. Thus arose in the last two decades of the nineteenth century a major attempt to systematise a national American law that could be used to teach students, and guide practitioners and judges.[48] These two activities – the academic project of classifying and systematising a general American common law and the desire of the practising bar and the judiciary for a non-local, national legal regime that transcended the gap between the often archaic and parochial case law with contemporary social and economic conditions – began to merge.

Beginning in 1888, the ABA appointed various committees to study the possibility of classifying American law and these committees compiled elaborate reports in 1891, 1902 and 1910. After a pause for the First World War the ABA restarted this project, this time with the cooperation of the Association of American Law Schools.[49] The two organisations produced a study conducted by a group of prominent American judges, lawyers, and teachers known as The Committee on the Establishment of a Permanent Organisation for the Improvement of the Law. The Committee reported that the two chief defects in American law, its uncertainty and its complexity, had produced a 'general dissatisfaction with the administration of justice'.[50] The Committee recommended that an organisation be formed to improve the law and its administration. This led to the creation in 1923 of the ALI.

The ALI is a self-perpetuating voluntary organisation, and under its bylaws it limits the elected membership to 3,000, which is about one-third of one per cent of the lawyers in America. This membership consists of judges, lawyers and law teachers from all areas of the US as well as some foreign countries, selected based on professional achievement and demonstrated interest in the improvement of the law.

The stated purpose of the Institute is 'to promote the clarification and simplification of the law and its better adaptation to social needs, to secure the better administration of justice, and to encourage and carry on scholarly and scientific legal work'.[51] From its inception, the ALI has defined its purpose as addressing the uncertainty in American law through a series of restatements of the basic legal subjects to allow judges and lawyers to know the law. The objectives of the ALI are not put in terms of the harmonisation of American law, but of improving the law. Harmonisation of American law among the states, though, has been one of the significant by-products of the work of the ALI because of the significant influence and reliance of the restatements by courts nationwide.

[47] See, eg, DR Coquillette and BA Kimball, *On the Battlefield of Merit: Harvard Law School, The First Century* (Cambridge, MA, Harvard University Press, 2015) 304–34.

[48] G Gilmore, *The Ages of American Law* (New Haven, Yale University Press, 1977) 41–67.

[49] WP LaPiana, *Logic & Experience: The Origin of Modern American Legal Education* (Oxford, Oxford University Press, 1994) 158–64.

[50] Committee on the Establishment of a Permanent Organization for the Improvement of the Law, Report Proposing the Establishment of an American Law Institute 11 (1923), reprinted in American Law Institute 50th Anniversary, 2nd edn (1973).

[51] ALI By-Laws Art 1, reprinted in (1923) 2 *ALI Proceedings* 429.

Between 1923 and 1944, Restatements of the Law were written on Agency, Conflict of Laws, Contracts, Judgments, Property, Restitution, Security, Torts and Trusts. In 1952, the Institute began the drafting of the Restatements (Second). These were updated editions of the original Restatements, which reflected new analyses and concepts, as well as expanded use of authorities. Restatements (Second) also covered subjects not included in the first series of Restatements. In 1987, a third series of Restatements was inaugurated. Work on that series continues today. In addition to the initial subjects, the Restatements now include Foreign Relations Law of the US, The Law Governing Lawyers, Suretyship and Guaranty and Unfair Competition.

The Restatements are not drafted as statutes and have no legal authority as positive law unless adopted by a court. However, their influence on the law has been extraordinary. The Restatement of Contracts (and for the last 30 years, the Second Restatement of Contracts) has effectively defined the common law of contract in America. For this reason, as for basic contract law, one can accurately state that there is harmonised contract law in the US, and the law is what is stated in the Restatement.

In some cases, the Restatements have provided rules and principles that did not exist in the case law but were aspirational goals for where the law should develop. This, for example, was the case for section 402A of the Second Restatement of Torts, which provides for strict products liability as a basis for tort liability. This novel concept, quickly adopted by the California Supreme Court,[52] has now been adopted by most of the states.

IV. Harmonisation of Commercial Law in America

Commercial law is one area where harmonisation has been conspicuously effective in the US in the last century. This is not surprising given that commercial law has always involved a significant number of interstate transactions as well as being an area of the law where parties and interests could provide the financial resources for law revision and harmonisation.[53]

As we have seen, the need for harmonisation (and therefore predictability) in commercial law arose early in American law. Some inroads toward this was made in the nineteenth century. For example, in 1842, The US Supreme Court decided in *Swift v Tyson*,[54] in which the court determined that the federal courts could, in some circumstances, enforce a 'general commercial law'. This provided federal courts a basis for the development of a national commercial law which was clearly needed in areas such as negotiable instruments that had become the basis of a significant part of interstate payments.

However, it was not until the late nineteenth century after the founding of the ULC that the harmonisation of commercial law was seriously undertaken by statutory

[52] *Greenman v Yuba Power Products, Inc*, 59 Cal 2d 57, 377 P 2d 897, 27 Cal Rptr 697, 1963 Cal LEXIS 140, 13 ALR 3d 1049 (Cal 1963).

[53] 'Subsidization of Economic Growth through the Legal System' in MJ Horowitz, *The Transformation of American Law:1780–1860* (Cambridge, MA, Harvard University Press, 1977) 63–108.

[54] *Swift v Tyson*, 41 US 1 (1842).

uniform laws.[55] As we have seen, though, these attempts to have harmonised state commercial law had limited success. Moreover, in 1938, the United State Supreme Court overruled *Swift v Tyson*,[56] and therefore put into doubt the question of whether the US might have a national commercial common law, at least in the federal courts.

There was some push for a national sales act to replace the Uniform Sales Act that had been adopted by many states.[57] Federal legislation was drafted and submitted to the US Congress twice but was not successful.[58] After the failure of the federal legislation, the NCCUSL decided to revise the various commercial uniform laws to make them more acceptable.[59] By 1940 the NCCUSL was revising the Uniform Sales Act and the Uniform Negotiable Instruments Act.[60]

In what proved to be stroke of great insight, the President of the NCCUSL proposed to have one unified Uniform Commercial Code instead of a piecemeal revision of the existing uniform acts that would have to be individually introduced and adopted by the various states.[61] Given the size of the project, the NCCUSL arranged to have the ALI co-sponsor the project with the ALI a full partner both in terms of drafting and funding,[62] and in 1944 work began on the Uniform Commercial Code. As with other uniform acts promulgated by the NCCUSL, the UCC is not the law in a state until it is adopted by a state's legislature.

The first official UCC text was published in 1952. The Code was divided into nine substantive articles: Article One: General Provisions; Article Two: Sales;[63] Article Three: Commercial Paper;[64] Article Four: Bank Deposits and Collections; Article Five: Letters of Credit; Article 6: Bulk Transfers; Article Seven: Documents of Title;[65] Article Eight: Investment Securities;[66] and Article Nine: Secured Transactions.[67]

In 1953, Pennsylvania was the first state to enact the UCC. Massachusetts adopted the UCC in 1957. In 1960, Kentucky, Connecticut and New Hampshire also followed suit. By 1968, 49 of the 50 states as well as the District of Columbia had adopted the UCC. In 1974, Louisiana, the 50th state, adopted the all of the UCC except Articles Two[68] and Nine.[69] In 1987, Article 2A: Leases, and in 1989, Article 4A: Electronic Funds Transfers were added to the UCC. As with the rest of the UCC, these additional articles have been adopted by all states[70] and the District of Columbia.

[55] See nn 25–27 and accompanying text.

[56] *Swift* was overruled by the US Supreme Court in *Erie Railroad Co v Tompkins*, 304 US 64 in 1938.

[57] HK Patchel, 'Interest Group Politics, Federalism and the Uniform Law Process: Some Lesson from the Uniform Commercial Code' (1993) 78 *Minnesota Law Review* 83, 93.

[58] ibid at 95–96.

[59] W Schnader, 'A Short History of the Preparation and Enactment of the Uniform Commercial Code' (1967) 22 *University of Miami Law Review* 1.

[60] WD Malcolm, 'The Uniform Commercial Code in the United States' (1963) 12 *International and Comparative Law Quarterly* 226, 229.

[61] S Mentschikoff, 'Reflections of a Drafter: Soia Mentschikoff' (1982) 43 *Ohio State Law Journal* 537.

[62] Stein (n 24) 81.

[63] Revision of the Uniform Sales Act (1906).

[64] Revision of the Uniform Negotiable Instrument Act (1896).

[65] Revisions of the Uniform Warehouse Act (1906) and the Uniform Bills of Lading Act (1909).

[66] Revision of the Uniform Stock Transfer Act (1909).

[67] Revisions of the Uniform Conditional Sales Act (1918) and the Uniform Trust Receipts Act (1933).

[68] Louisiana is a civil law jurisdiction and Art 2 is based on the common law of contracts.

[69] Louisiana adopted Art 9 in 1988.

[70] Except for Art 2A, which has not been adopted by Louisiana.

Individual Articles have been revised over the years, but mostly these revisions have been adopted by the states so that the UCC, as it has evolved over the last 70 years, has mostly remained uniform among the states. Thus, today a party in California, for example, can have some idea of what to expect while engaged in a commercial transaction with a party in Florida.

Although the UCC is probably the most successful harmonisation of state laws in the US, there is less than full uniformity. Because the individual states have the power to adopt whatever version or modifications the state pleases, there is some non-uniformity of the UCC among them. This has not, however, been a significant problem, and there is general uniformity of commercial law in the US that parties rely on for millions of transactions yearly.

V. Conclusion

There is no comprehensive harmonisation of the laws in the US. There is no way to measure how much this affects the domestic and commercial lives of Americans; however, this had led to one of the most complex and convoluted set of conflict of laws rules in the world, with at least six major theories spread among the states.[71]

The two sources of legal harmonisation in the US – the ULC, an organisation that has been working on hermitisation of state statutes for 120 years, and the ALI, an organisation that has been through its Restatements harmonising common law principles for the last century – have made significant progress in the harmonisation of American Law. Both organisations continue to work on a large variety of laws for further harmonisation, but it is unlike that American law will ever be wholly harmonious among the states.

[71] If there is any place in American law that lacks harmonisation, it is conflict of laws. See P Hay, PJ Borchers and SC Symeonides, *Conflict of Laws*, 5th edn (St Paul, West, 2010).

PART II

New Techniques for Choosing and Evaluating Commercial Law Projects

3

Do We Need Harmonisation for Everything? The Possibilities and Limits of Harmonising Financial Law*

SOUICHIROU KOZUKA

I. The Truth about Harmonisation of Law

When the economy started to go global in the nineteenth century, the uniform law movements were initiated to fill the gap between globalising trade and nationally monopolised law-making power. In those days, the goal was to establish the 'World law (Weltrecht).'[1] The assumption was that the elimination of differences in legal rules is itself the value. If the uniform laws took the form of international conventions each addressing a specific issue, rather than the comprehensive uniform code, it was simply because the work had to make progress step by step.

By now the economic relationship across the borders has proceeded to the new stage. Not only the cross-border trade of goods has become the norm, but cross-border production networks have emerged.[2] On the legal side, we now have a good number of uniform law instruments, covering a large variety of legal issues related to these developments. Still, it is apparent that the harmonisation does not cover each and every subject of commercial law, and a unified (commercial) code is unlikely to appear. Furthermore, only some of the uniform law instruments have been widely accepted.[3] Not a few uniform law instruments failed to attract a substantial number of contracting

* The author's research for this chapter is funded by the Japan Society for the Promotion of Science (JSPS), grant identifier 15H01917.

[1] On the history of the uniform law movements, see R David, 'The International Unification of Private Law' in R David, H Egawa, R Graveson, A T von Mehren, Y Noda, S Rozmaryn, VM Tschchikvadze, H Valladão, H Yntema, K Zeigert and U Drobnig (eds), *International Encyclopedia of Comparative Law* vol II (Tübingen, JCB Mohr, 1971) ch 5, paras 327ff.

[2] J Linarelli, 'How Trade Law Changed: Why It Should Change Again' (2014) 65 *Mercer Law Review* 621, 663–64.

[3] The author recently reviewed the status of what are usually considered as uniform law instruments, based on the public information. The result is on the website of the Japanese Branch of International Law Association. www.ilajapan.org/jyil/components/archive/vol60/table_kozuka.pdf.

states, and many of them have not even entered in force. These facts reveal the honest truth that the harmonisation takes place only selectively.

From a theoretical perspective, the question that must ultimately be answered is why the past ideal of comprehensively unifying private law has failed to come true. Apparently, however, this is not an easy question. Some may argue that the ideal was too ambitious and did not match the reality of the international system.[4] Others raise the issue that the early concentration on treaties as the modality for unification was too narrow and point to the fact that the modern harmonisation efforts know a wider variety of types of instruments, such as the model law, legal guide and model contract clauses.[5] A recent treatise has gone beyond the instruments produced as a result of unification or harmonisation and claims that there exists a body of 'transnational commercial law', which denotes 'that set of principles and rules, from whatever source, which governs international commercial transactions and is common to legal systems generally or to a significant number of legal systems'.[6] Thus, instead of trying to answer the ultimate question directly, this paper examines three sub-questions that may be useful to consider the former question. The first of these sub-questions is what are the benefits of selective harmonisation of the law, if the unification of comprehensive set of laws is no longer the goal. The second sub-question is what are the domestic laws like on the subjects for which harmonisation does not take place. Convergence without institutional harmonisation is discussed here. The final sub-question is what are the determinants as to whether the domestic laws are successfully harmonised or converged or end up in being neither harmonised nor converged.

The following sections of this chapter discuss these sub-questions in order. The subjects discussed are limited to the law related to financing, though the implications may be general and relevant to any sector of law, such as sales law or transport law. This chapter is mainly theoretical, only referring to anecdotes here and there. Empirical examination of the validity of the theory is left for future work.

II. The Harmonisation of Law as Measure of Reform

A. The Normative and Non-normative Benefits of Harmonisation

One of the classic arguments for unification of laws assumed that the states will benefit from eliminating the divergence among various state laws, as such divergence could hinder the international trade. Employing the principles of modern economics, divergence among laws creates transaction costs, reduction of which (through harmonisation) can enhance the social welfare.[7] A recent study measured the

[4] David et al, *International Encyclopedia* (1971) para 7.

[5] H Kronke, 'International Uniform Commercial Law Conventions: Advantages, Disadvantages, Criteria for Choice' (2000) *Uniform Law Review* 13, 20–21.

[6] R Goode, H Kronke and E McKendrick (eds), *Transnational Commercial Law: Texts, Cases and Materials* (Oxford, Oxford University Press, 2015) para.1.03.

[7] ibid para.5.03.

economic benefit of unifying the law among OECD states by the increase in international trade, predicted to be 50 to 80 percent.[8] If, however, harmonisation takes place only selectively, that fact implies that the elimination of divergence is not the (sole or primary) goal.

By citing the metaphor of the 'islands' and the 'ocean',[9] which refer to the policy-oriented regulation and general principles of law, respectively, this author recently argued that what are recognised as uniform law instruments actually include both the unified rules of the 'islands'-type regulations and the common principles found for the 'ocean'-type law.[10] The former type of uniform law is policy-oriented and based on instrumentalism. It is a policy tool to 'improve' the domestic law, and its usefulness is measured by the benefits that it brings about to the state that accepts it. The most typical and most successful of such uniform law is the Cape Town Convention.[11] The Cape Town Convention is a carefully drafted instrument with the aim of establishing a legal framework conducive to asset-based financing.[12] Its benefit was tested by the methods of economics: how much finance cost the debtor can save by making use of the international interests under the Convention, which will benefit the users of the financed asset (aircraft) through reduction in costs of operation, and ultimately the society in general.[13]

It is thus indicated that the most recent harmonisation instrument, despite its label, does not aim at eliminating the differences among the domestic laws. By using the taxonomy of one commentator, one can identify normative and non-normative benefits in harmonisation.[14] The non-normative benefit denotes that of reducing the abovementioned transaction cost that arises from the differences, while the normative benefit means that of improving the existing (domestic) law by way of accepting the rules of harmonised instrument. One of the key drafters of the Cape Town Convention is now working on how to quantify these normative and non-normative components of harmonisation's benefit.[15]

[8] A Turrini and T van Ypersele, 'Legal Costs as Barriers to Trade', Discussion Paper Series No 5751, Centre for Economic Policy Research (2006).

[9] The metaphor originates in the writing of a famous legal historian, Hein Kötz, but more directly related to this chapter is the argument by R Michaels, 'Of Islands and the Ocean: The Two Rationalities of European Private Law' in R Brownsword, H-W Micklitz, L Niglia and S Weatherill (eds), *The Foundations of European Private Law* (Oxford, Hart, 2011) 139.

[10] S Kozuka, 'The Bifurcated World of Uniform Law: The Uniform Law of "Islands" and of "The Ocean"' in UNIDROIT (ed), *Eppur si muove: The Age of Uniform Law*, vol 1 (Rome, UNIDROIT, 2016) 333.

[11] For the detailed analysis of the Cape Town Convention, including its unique approach to drafting, see S Kozuka, 'The Cape Town Convention and Its Implementation in Domestic Law: Between Tradition and Innovation' in S Kozuka (ed), *Implementing the Cape Town Convention and the Domestic Laws of Secured Transactions* (Cham, Springer, 2017) 15.

[12] The drafting approach was chosen with full awareness by the group of drafters. See R Goode, 'From Acorn to Oak Tree: The Development of the Cape Town Convention and Protocols' (2012) 17 *Uniform Law Review* 599; J Wool, 'The Case for a Commercial Orientation to the Proposed UNIDROIT Convention as Applied to Aircraft Equipment' (1999) 4 *Uniform Law Review* 289.

[13] A Saunders, A Srinivasan, I Walter and J Wool, 'The Economic Implications of International Secured Transactions Law Reform: A Case Study' (1999) 20 *The University of Pennsylvania Journal of International Economic Law* 309.

[14] DW Leebron, 'Claims for Harmonization: A theoretical Framework' (1996) 27 *Canadian Business Law Journal* 63. The argument here is elaborated by using a simple game theory in S Kozuka, 'The Economic Implications of Uniformity in Law' in J Basedow and T Kono (eds), *An Economic Analysis of Private International Law* (Heidelberg, Mohr Siebeck, 2006) 73, reprinted in (2007) 12 *Uniform Law Review* 683.

[15] See Cape Town Convention Academic Project, Economic Assessment, available at www.ctcap.org.

B. Harmonisation as Part of the Reform Programme

The normative benefit of harmonisation is equivalent to the benefit of legal transplant, as the accepted harmonisation instrument is transplanted into, and implemented under, the domestic legal system.[16] In this context, it is important to define what exactly the 'improvement' of the law through harmonisation or legal transplant means. An article by Mathias Siems distinguishes three categories of improvements that a legal transplant can bring about:[17] technically improved law without any implications on the aim of the law; the reform of law to meet a particular aim more effectively; and law that promotes a socially new aim. While the non-normative benefit of harmonisation (eliminating the divergence) is a kind of the technical improvements in that there are no implications of the aim of the law, most of the modern harmonisation whose true target lies in the improvement of the existing law may be either the law reform to meet more effectively a policy goal that is not itself controversial or the law that reforms the policy goal by bringing in the new goal. The Cape Town Convention may fall under the third category, because the idea of facilitating the asset-based financing, which the drafters aimed at, has not been a commonly shared policy goal of secured transactions law. In fact, opening up the access to the capital market by enabling the operators of aircraft to issue EETC (enhanced equipment trust certificates) was one of the intended achievements of the Aircraft Protocol to the Cape Town Convention. The harmonisation instrument on more general law of secured transactions, such as the UNCITRAL Model Law on Secured Transactions, may belong to the second category. Its policy goal is ameliorating the access to finance, which is not controversial. The issues addressed by the Model Law is how this goal is better served.[18]

As explained above, in modern times, the harmonisation of private law has become a part of the reform programme. It appears that the international organisations dedicated for unification and harmonisation of private law are now taking this path by turning their attention to the subject of 'law and development'. Unidroit includes in its recent work programme the item 'private law and development',[19] while UNCITRAL mentions 'modernisation' of laws, besides their 'harmonisation', when describing its role.[20] The latter organisation also makes it clear that it has a role to play in achieving the sustainable development goals.[21] On the other hand, if the question is

[16] This implies that how precisely the accepted harmonisation instrument is implemented and enforced becomes the issue, which is discussed in detail in J Wool, 'Compliance with Transnational Commercial Law Treaties – A Framework as Applied to the Cape Town Convention' (2013) 3 *The Cape Town Convention Journal* 5.

[17] M Siems, 'Bringing in Foreign Ideas: The Quest for "Better Law" in Implicit Comparative Law' (2014) 9 *Journal of Comparative Law* 119.

[18] SV Bazinas, 'The UNCITRAL Model Law on Secured Transactions' in SV Bazinas and N Orkun Akseli (eds), *International and Comparative Secured Transactions Law* (Oxford, Hart, 2017) 55.

[19] See UNIDROIT's website: www.unidroit.org/about-unidroit/work-programme.

[20] 'A Guide to UNCITRAL: Basic fact about the United Nations Commission on International Trade Law' (2013) 1. On this point, see G McCormack, *Secured Credit and the Harmonisation of Law* (Cheltenham, Edward Elgar, 2011) 17.

[21] See UNCITRAL's website: www.uncitral.org/uncitral/en/about/SDGs/Sustainable_Development_Goals.html.

reform of the law to facilitate development, the instrument to be used for that purpose does not have to be the harmonised law. It can be a single state's law that has been successful, which the legislator of the reforming state may copy. In other words, the harmonised law is exposed to the competition in the law market and its effectiveness is compared with other models for reform, whether international instrument or a single state's domestic law. It is in fact reported that, when the European transition economies reformed their secured transactions law during the 1990s, some states used the Model Law of the European Bank for Reconstruction and Development (EBRD), which is a regionally harmonised instrument, but others took the United States' Article 9 of the Uniform Commercial Code (UCC) as the model for reform.[22]

III. Harmonisation versus Regulatory Competition

A. Secured Transactions Law as a Subject of Harmonisation

Few people will disagree that the secured transactions law is one of the subjects for which the harmonisation efforts have been most actively made. Earlier in time, uniform law treaties on the secured transactions in a specific industry sector were adopted, such as the conventions on maritime liens and aircraft mortgages. More recently, the general secured transactions law, applicable to any industry sector, have become the subject of harmonisation. The resulting uniform law instruments count more than 20, as shown in Table 3.1.

Table 3.1 Instruments for harmonisation of the secured transactions law (both global and regional)

	Year	Name of the instrument
A	1926	International Convention for the Unification of Certain Rules Relating to Maritime Liens and Mortgages
B	1948	Convention on the International Recognition of Rights in Aircraft (Geneva Convention)
C	1967	International Convention for the Unification of Certain Rules Relating to Maritime Liens and Mortgage
D	1967	International Convention relating to the Registration of Rights in respect of Vessels under Construction
E	1988	Unidroit Convention on International Financial Leasing
F	1988	Unidroit Convention on International Factoring
G	1993	International Convention on Maritime Liens and Mortgages
H	1994	EBRD Model Law on Secured Transactions

(continued)

[22] J-H Röver, 'The EBRD's Model Law on Secured Transactions and its Implications for an UNCITRAL Model Law on Secured Transactions' (2010) 15 *Uniform Law Review* 479, 501.

Table 3.1 ***(Continued)***

	Year	Name of the instrument
I	1997	EBRD Core Principles for a secured transactions law
J	1997	OHADA Uniform Act on organizing securities
K	2001	The World Bank principles and guidelines for effective insolvency and creditor rights systems
L	2001	United Nations Convention on the Assignment of Receivables in International Trade
M	2001	Cape Town Convention on International Interests in Mobile Equipment
N	2001	Protocol to the Convention on International Interests in Mobile Equipment on Matters Specific to Aircraft Equipment
O	2002	OAS Model Inter-American Law on Secured Transactions
P	2006	Convention of 5 July 2006 on the Law Applicable to Certain Rights in Respect of Securities held with an Intermediary
Q	2007	Luxembourg Protocol to the Convention on International Interests in Mobile Equipment on Matters Specific to Railway Rolling Stock
R	2007	UNCITRAL Legislative Guide on Secured Transactions
S	2008	Unidroit Model Law on Leasing
T	2009	Unidroit Convention on Substantive Rules for Intermediated Securities
U	2009	OAS Model Registry Regulations under the Model Inter-American Law on Secured Transactions
V	2010	UNCITRAL Legislative Guide on Secured Transactions: Supplement on Security Rights in Intellectual Property
W	2010	Revised OHADA Uniform Act on organizing securities
X	2012	Protocol to the Convention on International Interests in Mobile Equipment on Matters Specific to Space Assets
Y	2013	UNCITRAL Guide on the Implementation of a Security Rights Registry
Z	2015	The World Bank Principles for Effective Insolvency and Creditor/Debtor Regimes
AA	2016	UNCITRAL Model Law on Secured Transactions

The recent focus on harmonisation of the general secured transactions law is justified by the assumption that the efficient law on secured transactions will encourage financiers to extend credit to the businesses in the jurisdiction, which, in turn, will bring about the growth of the local economy. When transition to market economy became the reform agenda of many countries in the 1990s, economists argued that the legal environment was part of the determinants of economic growth.[23]

[23] R La Porta, F Lopez-de-Silanes, A Shleifer and R Vishny, 'Legal Determinants of External Finance' (1997) 52 *Journal of Finance* 1131; R La Porta, F Lopez-de-Silanes, A Shleifer and R Vishny, 'Law and Finance' (1998) 106 *Journal of Political Economy* 40.

Some harmonisation instruments were drafted to be used in such a reform.[24] Other instruments have a more general aim, but the thoughts behind may, after all, boil down to a similar idea.[25]

B. The Convergence of Corporate Law

However, the source of finance that will contribute to the local economic growth is not limited to bank finance. In fact, the same group of economists also analysed the effects of corporate law on the economic growth.[26] While the laws relevant to debt finance include the law on secured transactions, execution and foreclosure as well as insolvency, the legal environment for equity finance requires that the attention be paid to the corporate law and securities regulation.

Interestingly, the harmonisation of law has been least successful on the corporate law. Even the attempts for harmonisation has been exceptional.[27] None of the instruments produced by UNIDROIT or UNCITRAL deals with the issue of corporate law, though UNCITRAL is currently working on the legal guide for micro, small and medium-sized enterprises. Among the 38 conventions adopted by the Hague Conference on international private law, only one of them concerns corporations.[28] Thus the potential economic benefit of the law alone does not imply that efforts toward the harmonisation will be made.

Still, such a fact does not mean that the corporate law in the world remains entirely diverged. To the contrary, the convergence of corporate law has been argued for more than a decade. The argument anticipates that the shareholder-centric model of corporate law will dominate the world because of its superiority.[29] Such convergence may occur as a result of the competitive pressure. It is correctly pointed out that this is

[24] On the Model Law of EBRD, see F Dahan and J Simpson, 'The European Bank for Reconstruction and Development's Secured Transactions Project: A Model Law and Ten Core Principles for a Modern Transactions Law in Countries of Central and Eastern Europe (and elsewhere!)' in E-M Kieninger (ed), *Security Rights in Movable Property in European Private Law* (Cambridge, Cambridge University Press, 2004) 98. On the Model Law of the Organization of American States (OAS), see AM Garro, 'The OAS-Sponsored Model Law on Secured Transactions: Gestation and Implementation' (2010) 15 *Uniform Law Review* 391.

[25] UNCITRAL's Model Law and Legal Guide on Secured Transaction claim that the modernisation of secured transactions law will improve access to finance, but neither of them elaborates how the instruments can bring about that outcome. According to economic theory, security is useful to control the opportunistic behaviour of the debtor, which will solve the problem of information asymmetry between the debtor and creditor. See RM Stulz and H Johnson, 'An Analysis of Secured Debt' (1985) 14 *Journal of Financial Economics* 501; AWA Boot, AV Thakor and GF Udell, 'Secured Lending and Default Risk: Equilibrium Analysis, Policy Implications and Empirical Results' (1991) 101 *Economic Journal* 458.

[26] R La Porta, F Lopez-de-Silanes, A Shleifer and R Vishny, 'Investor Protection and Corporate Valuation' (2002) 42 *Journal of Finance* 1147. Note, however, that the result of this analysis is criticised by H Spamann, 'The "Antidirector Rights Index" Revisited' (2010) 23 *Review of Financial Studies* 467.

[27] It is to be noted that, on the regional level, the OAS recently adopted the Model Simplified Corporations Law.

[28] The Convention of 1 June 1956 concerning the recognition of the legal personality of foreign companies, associations and institutions.

[29] H Hansmann and R Kraakman, 'The End of History for Corporate Law' (2001) 89 *Georgetown Law Journal* 439.

different from 'the competition for charter' in the narrow sense. The competition for charter, which means the competition among legislators to attract incorporation by making their corporate law more attractive, presumes the freedom of choosing the place of incorporation. Therefore, it is unlikely to take place outside the US.[30] However, in the broader sense, jurisdictions compete with each other in drawing the money of global investors to their corporations rather their neighbours'. The prediction has proven to be true, for example, with regards to the now widespread acceptance of independent directors.[31] Starting from the recommendation in the UK as means for the reform of corporate governance, the requirement of independent members in the boardroom, in most cases not as mandatory rule but as 'comply or explain' scheme, has become common, first in Europe and then quickly in Asia and Pacific.[32] Regulators compete with each other in the 'law market' (or regulatory market), motivated to keep their jurisdictions up with the globally accepted standards.[33]

C. When Neither Harmonisation nor Convergence Takes Place

The argument for convergence of corporate law may still be exaggerated, as one observes that the convergence takes place with only some aspects of the corporate law, but not with others.[34] The well-known comparative analysis of corporate law argues that there are several strategies to address the agency problem of corporations.[35] The argument distinguishes the regulatory (prescriptive) strategies from governance (controlling power) strategies, the former strategies further sub-divide into constraints on and affiliation with the agent, while the latter sub-divide into the incentives for, appointment of, and distribution of powers with, the agent. Each of these strategies can be designed as mechanism valid ex ante or ex post. Among the strategies thus identified, the convergence of the rules on independent directors concerns only one of them, namely the incentive structure. Independent directors are not involved in day-to-day management and are expected to evaluate the management from a broad and long-term perspective.[36] The indirect implications of independent directors might be relevant to some other strategies, such as the selection and removal of agents (managers/executive officers), the exercise of the decision rights shared with agents and reward for agents,

[30] ibid 454. On the competition for charter in the US, see R Romano, *The Genius of American Corporate Law* (Washington DC, AEI Press, 1993), which reversed the negative evaluation of such a competition as 'race to the bottom' most typically by WL Cary, 'Federalism and Corporate Law: Reflections Upon Delaware' (1974) 83 *Yale Law Journal* 663.

[31] See generally, C Jordan, 'Cadbury Twenty Years On' (2013) 28 *Villanova Law Review* 1.

[32] DW Puchniak, H Baum and L Nottage (eds), *Independent Directors in Asia* (Cambridge, Cambridge University Press, 2017).

[33] CJ Milhaupt and K Pistor, *Law & Capitalism* (Chicago, University of Chicago Press, 2008).

[34] For a critical examination of the regulatory competition claim, see M Siems, *Comparative Law* (Cambridge, Cambridge University Press 2014) 229–30.

[35] R Kraakman, J Armour, P Davies, L Enriques, H Hansmann, G Hertig, K Hopt, H Kanda, M Pargendler, W-G Ringe and E Rock, *The Anatomy of Corporate Law*, 3rd edn (Oxford, Oxford University Press, 2017) 31ff. The 'agency problem' is an economic term to denote the situation where one party's benefit or loss depends on another party's behaviour.

[36] ibid 62.

because these are the subjects that the independent directors will decide (or take the lead in the board's decision). Other important strategies, such as the rules and standards of an agent's action in case of a takeover, have not converged, ranging from the wide discretion of the management to take defensive measures to strict requirement of neutrality and subjecting the decision to third-party institutions (such as the Takeover Panel in the UK or Australia).[37]

The focus of the convergence claim, if read carefully, was on the 'model'. On the convergence of formal rules, the argument accompanies many reservations about the extent to which the convergence occurs. However, in the context of harmonisation, the formal rules are the issue. One commentator emphasises this point and argues that the convergence of corporate law may take place with regard to its function, but not to the rules.[38]

A similar observation may be made with the debt finance. The past efforts on harmonisation have not paid much attention to the credit extended by trade partners. It is even doubtful that the trade credit is recognised as a single subject of law. The trade credit is often unsecured (though sometimes the trade creditor reserves title to the traded goods until payment) and various laws, including the rules on insolvency, fraudulent conveyance, law on corporate creditors in general, or even regulations on payment conditions, such as the prohibition of price discrimination, are relevant.[39] These laws are seldom discussed as a single subject, not to mention as a single agenda for harmonisation.

The above observations reveal that when harmonisation does not take place, the law may still converge as a result of the regulatory competition or may remain divergent at all. It must be identified, therefore, under which conditions the harmonisation or convergence fails to take place. This is the question that we turn to in the next section.

IV. Reasons for Divergence of Laws: Failure of Harmonisation or Optimisation?

If it is assumed that eliminating all the differences among domestic laws is the ultimate goal, the remaining divergence is the 'failure'. Such assumption is often argued against by a claim that 'one size does not fit all'.[40] It is true that in some cases states have reasons not to conform to the harmonised law. However, there are some varieties in the reasons for not harmonising, and each of them has a different implication for harmonisation projects.

[37] See J Armour, J Jacobs and C Milhaupt, 'The Evolution of Hostile Takeover Regimes in Developed and Emerging Markets: An Analytical Framework' (2011) 52 *Harvard International Law Journal* 219; L Nottage, 'Perspectives and Approaches: A Framework for Comparing Japanese Corporate Governance' in L Nottage, L Wolff and K Anderson (eds), *Corporate Governance in the 21st Century* (Cheltenham, Edward Elgar, 2008) 21.

[38] RJ Gilson, 'Globalizing Corporate Governance: Convergence of Form or Function' (2001) 49 *American Journal of Comparative Law* 329.

[39] This author once attempted to describe the relevant rules together for his own jurisdiction. See H Uchida, A Ono, S Kozuka, M Hazama and I Uesugi, *Interfirm Relationships and Trade Credit in Japan: Evidence from Micro-Data* (Berlin, Springer, 2015) 76–78.

[40] See, eg, P Legrand, 'Antivonbar' (2006) 1 *Journal of Comparative Law* 13; B Fauvarque-Cosson and A-J Kerhuel, 'Is Law an Economic Contest? French Reactions to the *Doing Business* World Bank Reports and Economic Analysis of the Law' (2009) 57 *American Journal of Comparative Law* 811.

A. Fitness to the Local Circumstances

First, local conditions may demand the local law to be adapted. In other words, the most effective rules to achieve a certain policy goal under the conditions in one state differ from those effective in another state. As an example, when American states negotiated the harmonised rules on road transport at the sixth International Conference for the Private International Law (CIDIP-VI), the North American delegates preferred to concentrate on the non-negotiable transport document, while the South American delegates wished to work on the negotiable document. In South America, international road transport connecting contiguous states plays a significant role, while in North America much of the road transport finishes without crossing a border, which makes a negotiable document less useful.[41] The different attitudes of delegates reflected that the different rules are optimal under the different conditions.

In the field of finance law, it has been claimed that secured transactions law must be designed to satisfy the 'fitness' to the local context.[42] The structure of the relevant industry could constitute the local context here. For example, there is an argument about whether the rules on secured transactions proper and those on title finance to secure the payment of the credit should be unitary. The unitary rule can provide for the fair conditions of competition (the level playing field) for traditional banks and financiers of title finance, such as leasing companies.[43] However, even if the unitary rules become the globally harmonised law, a state will find only limited benefit if there are few leasing companies or other non-traditional financiers that will utilise the title finance.

B. Differences in the Policy Goal

Secondly, a state may have a policy goal different from that of another state. In the case of the reform of secured transactions law, to the extent that its reform improves the access to finance by some sector of the industry, other sectors may be adversely affected if the total amount of available finance does not change. Such an 'allocation effect' of the reform was observed when many former socialist states reformed the secured transactions law in 1990s to facilitate the transition to the market economy.[44] The focus of those reforms was to introduce non-possessory security over moveables that the laws of these states, often under the influence of the civil law, had not been familiar with. The reform helped the new start-ups that did not own much real property to be mortgaged to have access to finance by using their products and equipment as security for credit. The net result in the economy could have been the shift of finance from the state-owned companies (or former state-owned companies after privatisation), which often retained

[41] C Fresnedo de Aguirre, 'Unifying the Law on Carriage of Goods: A View from MERCOSUR' (2003) *Uniform Law Review* 241, 246–47.

[42] F Dahan and J Simpson, 'Legal Efficiency of Secured Transactions Reform: Bridging the Gap between eEonomic Analysis and Legal Reasoning' in F Dahan and J Simpson (eds), *Secured Transactions Reform and Access to Credit* (Cheltenham, Edward Elgar, 2008) 136.

[43] *UNCITRAL Legislative Guide on Secured Transactions*, Introduction, para 52; ch I, para 106.

[44] Röver, 'The EBRD's Model Law' (2010) 491.

the real property from the former regime, to new start-ups. In the context of transition from the inefficient former socialist system to market economy, the policy made sense.[45] However, the policy goal may be different in other states under a different political or economic situation, which can affect the design of secured transactions law that the states may wish to adopt.

A similar problem could arise with regards to the draft MAC Protocol to the Cape Town Convention that is now being negotiated. The aim of the MAC Protocol is to provide an easy access to finance to the relevant sectors of industry, namely mining, agriculture and construction industries. If the source of financing for one economy (ie economy of a contracting state) is limited, the outcome would be to disadvantage other industry sectors (such as retail merchants), depriving the latter of availability to get finance, as the financial resources will now be channelled to the MAC sector. This will give rise to the policy question when a state considers ratifying the MAC Protocol.

C. Nature of the Subject: The Case of Debt versus Equity

The third element that may detract states from harmonising the laws is the nature of the subject. As examined in the previous section, much of the corporate law has not been harmonised, with some issues converged through the regulatory competition and others being left diversified. This may be explained by the fact that the corporate law mainly concerns the interests of shareholders. According to the theory of corporate finance, the interests of the shareholders (equity-holders) are the opposite of that of the debt-holders. The debtholders of a corporation with limited liability suffer when the debtor corporation is insolvent but do not benefit even if the corporate value grows beyond the face value of the debt. In contrast, the larger the corporate value becomes the happier equity-holders are.[46] As a result, equity-holders (shareholders) appreciate rules that give incentives to corporate managers to maximise the corporate value. It is obvious that there is no single answer as to how the corporate value can be maximised or how best managers can be incentivised. This is contrary to that the rules to preserve the creditors' interests in the case of the debtor's insolvency are far easier to standardise and harmonise, as the latter focuses on excluding the risk. Thus, the extensive achievements of harmonisation in the secured transactions law and the absence of harmonisation in a large part of the corporate law is no coincidence. It can be explained by the nature of the subjects.

[45] A reform with a similar goal was conducted in Taiwan in the 1960s. Taiwan is a jurisdiction that has traditionally been influenced by the German law, but it introduced a law that enables security interests in moveables, modelled after the US law. The aim was to facilitate finance to small and medium-sized companies without much land to be mortgaged. See T-F Chen, 'Transplant of Civil Code in Japan, Taiwan, and China: With the Focus of Legal Evolution' (2011) 6 *National Taiwan University Law Review* 389, 405; J Kaufman Winn, 'Security Interests Under the Laws of the Republic of China on Taiwan: An Introductory Guide' (1988) 23 *Texas International Law Journal* 395, 404ff.

[46] For a concise discussion on capital structure, see RA Brealey, SC Myers and F Allen, *Principles of Corporate Finance*, 12th edn (New York, McGraw-Hill International, 2017) ch 18; L Gullifer and J Payne, *Corporate Finance Law*, 2nd edn (Oxford, Hart, 2015) 55–58; H Kanda, 'Debtholders and Equityholders' (1992) 21 *Journal of Legal Studies* 431.

In the case of trade credit, which is scarcely recognised as a unitary subject, the efficient rules may vary, depending on the situation. Economists argue that there may be some cases where trade creditors are in a better position to monitor the debtor than financial institutions, in which case the trade credit improves economic efficiency.[47] However, the reason why the trade creditor is in such a position has a large variety: the trade creditor may be able to monitor the debtor through their transactions,[48] or may have advantage in monitoring (and foreclosing, if necessary) the debtor's merchandise, which the trade partner is familiar with.[49] Or they may make use of the opportunity to scrutinise the credible debtor through pricing of the traded goods.[50] Each of these situations requires a different legal solution, which is the reason why the harmonisation of trade credit law has not even been recognised as a single agenda. Here again, the nature of the subject matters.

D. The Relevance of Private Law

Fourthly, there is what one might call a cultural reason for not conforming to harmonisation: the relevance of private law in the society. Even when the applicable black letter rules are identical, the scope of social relationship that are subjected to the private law may be different from one society to another.

The relevance of law has been a favourite subject of some comparative law researchers, such as specialists in Japanese law. It has long been debated whether, and to what extent, the Japanese are 'litigious'.[51] To explain Japan's low rate of litigation per population, some argue that the Japanese do not like resorting to the law and judiciary, while others point to the possible institutional causes, such as the relatively small number of lawyers, as well as the mechanisms that makes it a rational choice not to bring the dispute before the judiciary, such as the widely accepted standards for identifying the ratio of negligence in case of traffic accidents.[52] Setting aside the question about which of these arguments best explains the reality, the arguments connote that in some society people may not rely on the law to govern some aspects of life. Contrary to the possible impression, the question is not necessarily a cultural one. A well-known book about the developments of digital technology argues that the technological design can

[47] MA Petersen and RG Rajan, 'Trade Credit: Theory and Evidence' (1997) 10 *Review of Financial Studies* 661.

[48] ibid.

[49] SD Longhofer and JAC Santos. 'The Paradox of Priority' (2003) 32 *Financial Management* 69; D Fabbri and AMC Menichini, 'Trade Credit, Collateral Liquidation, and Borrowing Constraints' (2010) 96 *Journal of Financial Economics* 413.

[50] RA Schwartz and DK Whitcomb, 'The Trade Credit Decision' in JL Bicksler (ed), *Handbook of Financial Economics* (Amsterdam, North Holland, 1979); MJ Brennan, V Maksimovic and J Zechner, 'Vendor Financing' (1988) 43 *Journal of Finance* 1127.

[51] For the overview of the discourse, see L Nottage, 'The Development of Comparative Law in and for Japan' in R Zimmerman and M Reiman (eds), *Oxford Handbook of Comparative Law*, 2nd edn (Oxford, Oxford University Press, 2019).

[52] See JM Ramseyer and M Nakazoto, *Japanese Law: An Economic Approach* (Chicago, University of Chicago Press, 1999) 90–99; JM Ramseyer, *Second Best Justice: The Virtues of Japanese Private Law* (Chicago, University of Chicago Press, 2015) 10–34.

determine what otherwise should have been the subject of legal rules, in which case the 'code' replaces the law.[53] This is another example that the relevance of law becomes a question.

The relevance of law in the society may affect the state's attitude towards the international legal rules. A recent article finds that Asian states have had smaller engagements in international law for their size and economic significance.[54] Though the article looks only at public international law treaties, it is also empirically revealed that Asian states have made reception of uniform private law instruments only selectively.[55] There can be a variety of interpretations for this observation, but one possible explanation is that Asian states can fare sufficiently well without relying much on international instruments. In the international economic relationship, this is evidenced by the historical experience that the inter-regional trade developed during the first half of the twentieth century without harmonising the common law and civil law that coexisted in the region. Recently, again, the supply networks for high-technology products has emerged across the borders of China, Korea, Japan and Taiwan, but it has accompanied no harmonisation in law.[56] Even the market integration of ASEAN has not urged the Member States to discuss harmonisation of private law within the region, in a sharp contrast to the market integration in Europe.[57]

V. Conclusions

This chapter has given a very cursory review about the harmonisation of finance law. Contrary to the aspirations held when the uniform law movements initiated, it is now clear that the harmonisation takes place only selectively. This fact is no longer considered as a problem, as the focus of the harmonisation (unification) has shifted from the elimination of divergences itself, which may be labelled 'non-normative benefits' of harmonisation, to the achievement of some goal through the harmonised law, or what may be labelled 'normative benefits' of harmonisation. In this sense, the harmonisation of law today means the reform through the modernisation of law.

Even admitting that the harmonisation is now a measure of reform, it may still appear puzzling that the harmonisation does not take place on all the subjects. In the

[53] L Lessig, *Code: Version 2.0* (New York, Basic Books, 2006).

[54] S Chesterman, 'Asia's Ambivalence about International Law and Institutions: Past, Present and Futures' (2017) 27 *European Journal of International Law* 945.

[55] S Kozuka, 'The Selective Reception of Uniform Law in Asia' (2018) 60 *Japanese Yearbook of International Law* 86.

[56] See I Han, K Oh and J Yoo, 'Changes in Competitiveness of LCD Industry of East Asia: from Bamboo Capitalis to Water Lily' (2012) 19 *International Telecommunications Policy Review* 15; M Ando and F Kimura, 'Expanding Fragmentation of Production in East Asia and Domestic Operations: Further Evidence from Japanese Manufacturing Firms' (2013) 4 *Journal of International Commerce, Economics and Policy* 1; W Thorbeke, 'Understanding the Flow of Electronic Parts and Components in East Asia' *RIETI Discussion Paper Series* 16-E-072 (2016).

[57] B Jaluzot, 'Quelle intégration juridique pour l'ASEAN?' in F Osman (ed), *Vers une lex mercatoria mediterranea: Harmonisation, unification, codification du droit dans l'Union pour la méditerranée* (Brussels, Bruylant, 2012) 151.

absence of harmonisation, the law could still converge through regulatory competition. Again, however, the convergence through regulatory competition does not cover all the areas that falls outside the harmonisation projects. A variety of laws still remain divergent, or not even recognised as a single subject, though the latter subjects are no less important as institutions to facilitate financing for business.

These facts require examination about when a state has a reason not to conform to the harmonised law. There are a few possibilities: the local conditions may require a different solution; the policy goal of the state may be different from that assumed by the harmonised law; or the harmonisation may not be effective due to the nature of the subject. Finally, there is a possibility that the relevance of the private law may differ in some society from others, or in some sector from others. The reality that the harmonisation takes place only selectively does not mean a simple failure or the result of coincidence. There are serious reasons for it, which needs further examination.

4

Behavioural Comparative Law: Its Relevance to Global Commercial Law-making

JOHN LINARELLI

This chapter develops a new framework by which to evaluate the making of commercial law on the global level. It offers a new approach to evaluating the process by which primarily intergovernmental organisations produce commercial law. This approach grounds in both behavioural science and comparative law. The focus is mainly but not exclusively on global rule-makers such as the United Nations Commission on International Trade Law (UNCITRAL) and the International Institute for the Unification of Private Law (UNIDROIT). It articulates what appears to be an emerging school of comparative law, labelled behavioural comparative law or BCL for short, which has the potential to advance substantially the ability to explain why commercial law is produced the way it is at the global level. The discussion will lead us to findings about the methods that global commercial law-makers use, how they choose areas of law to work on, and how they go about doing their work. This chapter finds that because of the cognitive limitations on the participants in the global commercial law-making process, when feasible, global commercial law-makers should use methods of cost–benefit analysis when evaluating project selection or get as close to they can in doing so when cost–benefit analysis is not feasible. It will not usually be feasible, due to the lack of data and methodological constraints. Other methods of evaluation, designed to de-bias and around the statistical evaluation of evidence, should be used as much as is practical when cost–benefit analysis is not practical.

Section I of this chapter explains that the current approach to global commercial law-making is based in the expert judgment of traditional legal analysis. It examines how expert legal judgment has its origins in a prior era of codification and suffers from limitations imposed on it by what is now an antiquated nineteenth-century historical school of jurisprudence. Nineteenth-century approaches to commercial legislation imposed strict limits on the avowed aim of any reform project as mainly to memorialise pre-existing rules that have evolved in a society. Prior commercial law reform projects were, moreover, strictly national in scope. With these limited aims the expert judgment of the lawyer may have been enough. Present-day projects, however, go well beyond this limited 'memorialisation' remit and into improving the law, substantial reform and modernisation, and facilitating cooperation among states. They are primarily normative projects. Expert judgment will remain indispensable in the production of global commercial law, but it will likely be insufficient on its own in many cases.

Section II offers skeletal accounts of two dissenting or 'external' critiques of global commercial law-making, one grounded in rational choice theory in the American political economy school of thought and the other in a law and society approach. 'External' refers to approaches to the study of global commercial law-making that are not based in the discipline or social practices of law. These external critiques offer significant insights. They are the most influential investigations of global commercial law-making based in the social sciences to date. The political economy approach is now dated, and fresh inquiries seem required that relax its rational choice assumption, to explore the psychology of expert judgment in the global commercial law-making context. Law and society approaches offer detailed or 'thick' descriptions focusing predominantly on institutional structure, an approach that is illuminating but which investigates different questions from those investigated in behavioural science.

Section III outlines an emerging school of thought known as behavioural comparative law (BCL). It explains why BCL offers substantial promise for improving our understanding of how global commercial law-making operates. BCL gets us closer to examining the behaviour of the participants in the law-making process and the mental processes that reliably predict that behaviour. It also informs us how to make better commercial law.

Section IV applies BCL insights to global commercial law-making. It explores how cognitive biases and motivated reasoning are likely in play in global commercial law-making, resulting in obstacles in the selection of superior or improved legal norms for the legal products produced in these processes. It also offers examples of how biases and motivated reasoning can impede implementation of legal products produced in global commercial law-making. Given the cognitive constraints likely at work in global commercial law-making, Section IV recommends the use cost–benefit analysis when feasible, and other complementary methods, as tools to de-bias the global commercial law-making process.

This chapter puts the discussion within the frame of comparative law for two complementary reasons. First, one of the aims of this chapter is to make clear a school of thought known as BCL. This work needs to be done for its own sake, independent of its application to commercial law-making. Second, incorporating the methods and insights of behavioural science into comparative law should lead to improvements in understanding how law is produced at the global level. Comparative law helps us to understand how to reform commercial law at the global level.[1] With its substantial corpus on legal transplants, law reform, harmonisation, unification, comparison, legal culture, and legal families, comparative law offers an excellent framework for the study of global commercial law-making.

Before moving on, let us get clear on terminology. I use the term 'law-making' as an umbrella concept to refer to a variety of rule-producing activities occurring

[1] See M Siems, *Comparative Law* (Cambridge, Cambridge University Press, 2014) 4–5.

at the global level. I spend little effort in parsing the intricacies of the meanings of terms such as 'codification,' 'harmonisation', 'unification', 'reform' and 'modernisation' of law.[2] There are some shorthand definitions if the reader feels the need to consult them. One of the very first documents UNCITRAL produced, 'Unification of the Law of International Trade: Note by the Secretariat' defines 'unification' of international trade law as 'the process by which conflicting rules of two or more systems of national laws applicable to the same international legal transaction is replaced by a single rule'.[3] Harmonisation, in contrast, is generally understood to refer to an approximation or coordination of legal rules and policies in different jurisdictions by eliminating or minimising major differences and creating minimum standards.[4] 'Codification' can be understood as unification in the form of a code, but this definition just pushes the discussion down to the question of what is a 'code'. 'Reform' is an ambiguous concept, but it is often at work whenever any organisation, domestic or international, formulates legal rules in some instrument. UNCITRAL's mission, as stated in its founding documents, is the 'progressive harmonisation and unification of law', with 'progressive' signalling 'reform'.[5] At UNCITRAL's founding, debate ensued in the United Nations as to whether UNCITRAL could 'formulate' law.[6] UNCITRAL's mission, moreover, includes the 'modernisation' of law.[7] 'Modernisation' is yet another ambiguous concept, which carries particular connotations about the role of law in economic development.[8] UNIDROIT engages in similar aims.[9] The distinctions between these concepts can have political or rhetorical value to the agents who use them, but from an analytical standpoint, whatever these organisations do can be described using a simple rubric of global law-making. As we shall see later when the chapter turns to discussion of the relationship of historical jurisprudence to the development of commercial law, it is of limited usefulness to conceptualise developments of commercial law at the global level to simple memorialisation of formal law already in existence through some pre-existing approach to law formation, such as case law or customary evolution. Global commercial law-making tends to be normative in its approach because decisions have to be made about the 'right' rules.

[2] For an attempt at an explanation of the differences between 'unification' and 'harmonisation', see P de Cruz, 'Comparative Law: Functions and Methods, *Max Planck Encyclopedia of Public International Law*, available at http://opil.ouplaw.com/home/EPIL.

[3] UN Document A/C.6/L.72, *Yearbook of the United Nations Commission on International Trade Law*, 1970, Vol 1, 13–17.

[4] See WJ Kamba, 'Comparative Law: A Theoretical Framework' (1974) 23 *International and Comparative Law Quarterly* 485.

[5] Establishment of the United Nations Commission on International Trade Law, GA Res 2205 (XXI), UN GAOR, 21st Session, Supp No 16, UN Doc A/6594 (17 December 1966), available at www.un.org/documents/ga/res/21/ares21.htm.

[6] S Block-Lieb and TC Halliday, *Global Lawmakers: International Organisations in the Crafting of World Markets* (Cambridge, Cambridge University Press, 2017) 62–64.

[7] See section I B below.

[8] See J Linarelli, 'Law, Rights, and Development' in John Linarelli (ed), *Research Handbook on Global Justice and International Economic Law* (Cheltenham, Edward Elgar, 2013) 301.

[9] Statute of UNIDROIT, art 1, available at www.unidroit.org/about-unidroit/institutional-documents/statute.

I. Global Commercial Law-making: The Status Quo

This section reflects on what lawyers do when they engage in the making of commercial law in the form of a legal product in the usual form of a convention or model law or in the production of a guide for national legislatures. The tool used almost exclusively in the relevant fora are those of the traditional lawyer. This section explores what the use of expert legal judgment entails and how it became firmly entrenched as the only method in play in global commercial law-making.

A. Expert Judgment: The Official Story

Lawyers rule global commercial law-making. The expert judgment of the lawyer is by far the most common method for project selection and development in international organisations with responsibilities in global commercial law-making. Clive Schmitthoff, characterised by Susan Block-Lieb and Terence Halliday as UNCITRAL's 'founding institutional entrepreneur',[10] wrote a report in 1966 for the United Nations, which became one of the founding documents for UNCITRAL. In his report, Schmitthoff recommended that project identification requires 'a thorough search for the right and ripe topics' involving 'close collaboration between legal experts and trade experts'.[11] The 1970 UNCITRAL document, 'Unification of the Law of International Trade: Note by the Secretariat', one of the first documents produced by UNCITRAL, captures the essence of using expert judgment in project selection.[12] The Secretariat noted that procedures have varied among organisations and according to the complexity and technical aspects of the subject, but invariably three steps are followed. The first step is the 'selection of a subject appropriate for study and drafting'. The Secretariat continues:

> In some cases selection of subjects has been made by bodies of legal experts which have been requested by Governments concerned to consider appropriate projects for unification, while in other cases the topics were chosen by organs concerned with economic or technical matters in the light of the problems facing these bodies.[13]

The second stage following selection of a subject is the preparation of the problem, which includes 'an analysis of the various laws and a consideration of the extent to which these laws fulfil certain economic or other practical ends'.[14] The third stage is the drafting stage.[15]

This three-stage procedure specified here might not reflect the complexity of actual practice over the course of UNCITRAL's history and we could explore much more institutional detail, but UNCITRAL probably still approximately adheres to the essential aspects of these three steps. The procedure is an exercise in using the expert judgment

[10] Block-Lieb and Halliday, *Global Lawmakers* (2017) 59.
[11] ibid 60.
[12] See n 3.
[13] Note of the Secretariat (n 3).
[14] ibid.
[15] ibid.

of the lawyer along with intuition about the relevant economic conditions to be affected. John Spanogle, a former US delegate to several UNCITRAL Working Groups, including the Working Group that produced the UN Convention on the International Sale of Goods (CISG), described UNCITRAL's process for project selection as often starting with

> the convening of a 'group of experts' which meets over a long period of time in a Study Group to do initial investigation of issues. Then, representatives of States meet in a Working Group to draft the proposed convention – again over a long period of time.[16]

Debates about whether cost–benefit analysis is feasible or desirable to evaluate financial regulation include a focus on whether expert judgment is a sufficient or superior alternative.[17] Global commercial law-makers such as UNCITRAL and UNIDROIT lack remits over financial regulation, because of limitations formally imposed in their charters or informally imposed through a low-level politics among intergovernmental organisations and member governments, or simply because of historical trajectories as to which rule-making body does what.[18] To further our understanding of the role of expert judgment, it nevertheless will be helpful to examine the role of expert judgment in the creation and evaluation of financial regulation. John Coates, a proponent of the use of expert judgment in the making of financial regulation, explains:

> In the context of financial regulation, the judgment of regulatory staff is expert because the appointees of the financial agencies have generally spent their careers in and have developed specialized knowledge of finance, financial institutions, and financial markets. They have sharpened their intuitive sense of what kinds of regulations work and why – particularly relative to non-experts, such as generalist judges. Such intuitions can be disciplined and informed in ways other than through CBA, such as through discussions with other experts (within or outside the agency); case studies, surveys, and polls; retrospective evaluations; regulatory experiments that are deliberately adopted without specific predictions about how they will turn out; and other forms of assessment that are not part of quantified [cost–benefit analysis of financial regulation].[19]

Similar considerations are relevant for commercial law-making.

The US Office of Management and Budget (OMB) Circular A-4, on 'Regulatory Analysis' provides some clarification of the concept of expert judgment, though it

[16] JA Spanogle, Jr, 'The Arrival of International Private Law' (1991) 25 *George Washington Journal of International Law and Economics* 477, as quoted in PB Stephen, 'Accountability and International Lawmaking: Rules, Rents and Legitimacy (1997) 17 *Northwestern Journal of International Law and Business* 682, 713–14. See also JO Honnold, 'The United Nations Commission on International Trade Law: Mission and Methods' (1979) 27 *American Journal of Comparative Law* 201.

[17] JC Coates IV, 'Cost–benefit Analysis of Financial Regulation: Case Studies and Implications' (2015) 124 *Yale Law Journal* 882; EA Posner and EG Weyl, 'Cost–benefit Analysis of Financial Regulations: A Response to Criticisms' (2015) *Yale Law Journal Forum*, 246; JC Coates IV, 'Cost–benefit Analysis of Financial Regulation: A Reply' (2015) *Yale Law Journal Forum* 305.

[18] Other global law-makers, such as the Basel Committee on Banking Supervision, promulgate norms in the form of soft law or guidance for domestic regulatory agencies, which does involve the regulation of finance. C Brummer, *Soft Law and the Global Financial System*, 2nd edn (Cambridge, Cambridge University Press, 2015).

[19] Coates, 'Cost–benefit Analysis of Financial Regulation' (2015) 904 (footnotes omitted).

makes the case that it cannot be deployed without cost–benefit analysis.[20] It states in a number of places that professional judgment has to be exercised when quantification is not realistic and to temper the use of quantified methods to avoid formulaic approaches to regulation.

What *is* expert judgment? The standard answer would seem to be: reliance on the traditional tools of the lawyer, including reliance on the lawyer's sense of what areas of law need improvement. Schmitthoff also mentioned the need for 'trade experts' in his report on the need for a UN organisation but really his emphasis was on legal expertise to lead what was to be an organisation dedicated to law-making. Expert judgment for global commercial law-making of the kind Schmitthoff (and others) envisioned amounts to what Philip Bobbitt calls the 'modalities of legal argument' to determine the truth of propositions about law.[21] It is a focus on the distinctive internal logic and integrity of the actual social practice of legal argument. It is what Richard Posner characterises as law as an 'autonomous discipline',[22] with no need for help from economics of any other social science.[23]

The expert judgment of the lawyer maintains a preclusive domination over global commercial law-making. Global commercial law-making is almost exclusively the realm of the traditional legal conceptualist. Normative welfare economics and its allied field, law and economics, which offer the most efficacious and pragmatic methods for evaluation of large-scale legal reform, which global commercial law-making projects constitute, are almost entirely absent from the process. Law and economics scholars are noticeably absent, no doubt at least partly the result of the critical literature on the work of so-called private legislatures, discussed in section II A below. A significant law and economics literature, moreover, advocates piecemeal evolution of the law and contends that the US Uniform Commercial Code (UCC) is a misguided project.[24] Two diametrically opposed positions have ignored each other for quite some time: legal conceptualists hail the UCC as a success while lawyer-economists critique it as resting on dubious empirical grounds and find its amending processes prone to capture by interest groups.

B. The Persistent Influence of the Historical School

The almost exclusive reliance on the expert judgment of the lawyer may be a relic of a bygone era. Here we consider the question whether we rely too much on methods of

[20] Office of Management and Budget (OMB) Circular A-4, 17 September 2003, available at https://georgewbush-whitehouse.archives.gov/omb/circulars/a004/a-4.html. OMB Circular A-4, continues the work of the Reagan Administration, which in the early 1980s issued Executive Order 12,291 mandating the use of cost–benefit analysis on all major US federal proposed regulation. MD Adler and EA Posner, *New Foundations of Cost–benefit Analysis* (Cambridge MA, Harvard University Press, 2006) 3.

[21] P Bobbitt, *Constitutional Fate: Theory of the Constitution* (Oxford, Oxford University Press, 1981).

[22] R Posner 'The Decline of Law as an Autonomous Discipline: 1962–1987' (1987) 100 *Harvard Law Review* 761.

[23] Perhaps expert judgment shares affinities with Henry Richardson's notion of 'intelligent deliberation'. H Richardson, *Democratic Autonomy* (Oxford, Oxford University Press, 2002) ch 9.

[24] See eg, RE Scott, 'The Rise and Fall of Article 2' (2002) 62 *Louisiana Law Review* 1009; L Bernstein, 'An (Un)Common Frame of Reference: An American Perspective on the Jurisprudence of the CESL' (2013) 50 *Common Market Law Review* 169.

the past when the mission of legal change has moved from codification of what was understood to be existing law, to improving and modernising the law, sometimes in dramatic ways, or in creating new law. Of course, one of the basic lessons in the application of social science methods to law is that what participants in any law-making process might say they are doing can differ substantially from what they actually do. Nevertheless, it is important to understand how a school of jurisprudence well-understood by prominent lawyers in the nineteenth century, the so-called historical school of jurisprudence, came to influence lawyers in the past and how its methods carried on well beyond the sell-by date of this particular school of jurisprudence.

A substantial movement to legislate commercial law on a national scale began in the late nineteenth century. The movement involved codification, a form of nationalising commercial law and putting it in the form of a set of positive declarations, away from a conception of law held by many lawyers and judges of the time that commercial law either evolved from or was custom, in the form of a law merchant. This move to legislate turned what was known as mercantile law or the law of merchants into what we call commercial law today. Whether or not a law merchant transcending the state's control existed or not is beside the point; it was a notion accepted by many in centuries past but was the subject of some tension in the nineteenth century, in an era of the modern state in which positive law became an important source of law.[25]

The period in which this legislative innovation occurred was an era of economic globalisation, from about the mid-nineteenth century until World War I. The next great era of economic globalisation began in the 1990s and continues today, rising from the end of the Cold War with the liberalisation of global capital movements in the aftermath of the erosion of the Bretton Woods financial system.[26]

As a national movement, codification had a political aim. In that prior era of economic globalisation, the push to nationalise commercial law was a means by which to consolidate state power, either to establish a common market within the state or to put the state firmly in control of all normative orders that could be considered legal in pedigree.[27] To consolidate state power, it was considered necessary to liberalise national markets and make them more compatible for the industrial economy. Nineteenth-century nationalism in commercial law reform occurred at a time before there were intergovernmental organisations such as UNCITRAL and UNIDROIT. The first German code was the *Allgemeines Deutsches Handelsgesetzbuch*, a commercial code for what was then the German Confederation.[28] The German Civil Code was the product of Imperial Germany and came later.[29] In the US, the first uniform commercial legislation came into existence in the latter nineteenth and early twentieth centuries,

[25] For a survey of contested theories about the law merchant, see J Linarelli, 'Commercial Law and Global Legal Pluralism' in Paul Schiff Berman (ed), *Oxford Handbook on Global Legal Pluralism* (Oxford, Oxford University Press, forthcoming, 2019), available at https://papers.ssrn.com/sol3/papers.cfm?abstract_id=3285315.

[26] For a brief outline of this history, see J Linarelli, ME Salomon and M Sornarajah, *The Misery of International Law: Confrontations with Injustice in the Global Economy* (Oxford, Oxford University Press, 2018).

[27] See M John, *Politics and the Law in Late Nineteenth Century Germany: The Origins of the Civil Code* (Oxford, Oxford University Press, 1989).

[28] See DM Rabban, *Law's History: American Legal Thought and the Transatlantic Turn to History* (Cambridge, Cambridge University Press, 2013).

[29] John, *Late Nineteenth Century Germany* (1989).

largely modelled on English legislation.[30] This first US legislative effort was largely driven by the need for uniformity of commercial law across a geographically dispersed common market.[31] In England and Wales, legislation was the final step in getting mercantile law firmly into the category of state law, if there ever was a doubt by the nineteenth century.

It is reasonable to say that nineteenth-century legislative reformers relied on expert legal judgment on how commercial legislation should be drafted but we must put their use of this judgment in historical context. We need to understand how lawyers of the time conceptualised law and legislation. Many lawyers of this era believed that legislative enactments of commercial law should go no further than codifications or legislative enactments of pre-existing law. Progressive development, formulation of new legal rules, or modernisation were not practices that a nineteenth-century lawyer involved in this work could endorse, at least not officially, though what they said they were doing and what they actually did could diverge.[32] Sir MacKenzie Chalmers' address to the American Bar Association in 1902 illustrates the approach. Chalmers was the principal author of two of the most often copied pieces of commercial legislation in the common law tradition, the Bills of Exchange Act 1883 and the Sale of Goods Act 1893. Chalmers explained his approach to legislating commercial law in his American Bar Association address: 'When the principles of the law are well settled, and when the decided cases that accumulate are mere illustrations of accepted general rules, then the law is ripe for codification.'[33] He also explained:

> The province of a code, I venture to think, is to set out, in concise language and logical form, those principles of the law which have already stood the test of time. It co-ordinates and methodizes, but does not invent, principles.[34]

To get to the point of being able to write such legislation, Chalmers recommended doing a digest of the law first, to synthesise the law as it is found in the existing case law. Something like this practice continues to this day in the production of American

[30] See, eg, S Williston, 'The Law of Sales in the Proposed Uniform Commercial Code' (1950) 63 *Harvard Law Review* 561, 564. Williston said in favour of the US Uniform Sale of Goods Act over Uniform Commercial Code Article 2: 'Moreover, the extensive commerce of and elsewhere has made the English Sale of Goods Act the recognized statement of the common law, as distinguished from the civil law. The wide enactment in the US of the Uniform Sales Act, identical in most respects with the British Act, has strengthened this assumption. The British statute was intended to be a codification of the English common law, which had been largely formulated in the treatises of Blackburn and of Benjamin. There is no indication that the English Sale of Goods Act will be repealed or materially amended. Except in a few respects the American Sales Act followed the English statute both in substance and in the use of identical words. When the American Act was drafted it was thought to be of considerable advantage that the statute so closely resembled the English statute. This advantage has subsequently been increased by the wide adoption of the English statute, especially in the provinces of Canada.' (footnotes omitted)

[31] The usual argument is that the US Supreme Court decision of *Swift v Tyson*, 41 US 916 Pet 1 (1842) failed to achieve uniformity through the judiciary and that uniform legislation was needed. See, eg, G Gilmore, 'On the Difficulties of Codifying Commercial Law' (1948) 57 *Yale Law Journal* 1541.

[32] See R Goode and E McKendrick, *Goode on Commercial Law*, 5th edn (London, Penguin, 2016) 209 (the Sale of Goods Act 1893 was partly a restatement of existing common law on sales and partly a departure).

[33] MD Chalmers, 'Codification of Mercantile Law' (1902) 25 *Annual Reports of the American Bar Association* 282, 283.

[34] ibid.

restatements, though restatements have different aims than the projects of relevance to this chapter.[35]

This was a time when the school of historical jurisprudence, now almost entirely forgotten except by historians of legal thought, competed with positivist approaches to the law.[36] Legal historians are now reassessing the significance of historical jurisprudence and finding that it may have had more influence than previously thought, at least in the US where commercial law codification was ever on the forefront of legal developments of the time.[37] This is not the place for a detailed exposition of the historical school, assuming that it even formed a coherent school of thought, but suffice to say that historical jurisprudence offered a dim view of legislation. The historical jurisprude saw legislation as not really law but politics, as an interference with the evolution of law, unless it was undertaken after serious study of the law as a historical science and then undertaking of codification of existing law.[38] So, if legal entrepreneurs of the time were to get their legislative efforts to be accepted, it was imperative that they stylise any legislative interventions as merely codifications of pre-existing law. They could then be seen to have accommodated the competing interests of the *status quo*, supported by historical jurisprudence, and reform, supported by the competing school of thought, analytical jurisprudence. Whether the national legislative achievements of the late nineteenth century only codified pre-existing law is an empirical question beyond our scope here. The point for our purposes is only that for a good many prominent lawyers of the time, this was at least in their 'legal consciousness' as the proper way to proceed.[39]

That legal entrepreneurs influenced by the ascendant schools of jurisprudence of the time sought only to codify existing law did not mean they were provincial in outlook. Chalmers (and his contemporaries) still looked to a law merchant transcending the state for settled principles. Roscoe Pound characterised commercial lawyers of his day as cosmopolitan in outlook while contrasting private lawyers of the time as tribal in clinging to national traditions.[40] Pound was prescient, advocating a uniform

[35] See *Capturing the Voice of The American Law Institute: A Handbook for ALI Reporters and Those Who Review Their Work* (Washington DC, American Law Institute, 2015) 6. The Harvard Law School Library website guidance on sources offers the following description: 'Restatements are highly regarded distillations of common law. They are prepared by the American Law Institute (ALI), a prestigious organization comprising judges, professors, and lawyers. The ALI's aim is to distill the "black letter law" from cases to indicate trends in common law, and occasionally to recommend what a rule of law should be. In essence, they restate existing common law into a series of principles or rules.' Available at https://guides.library.harvard.edu/c.php?g=309942&p=2070280.

[36] Rabban, *Law's History* (2013).

[37] ibid.

[38] ibid 14.

[39] See D Kennedy, 'Toward an Historical Understanding of Legal Consciousness: The Case of Classical Legal Thought in America, 1850–1940' (1980) 3 *Research in Law and Sociology* 3.

[40] R Pound, 'Uniformity of Commercial Law on the American Continent' (1909) 8 *Michigan Law Review* 91. It is difficult to say whether Pound's views were more or less universally held, but a perusal of the commentary of the time suggests he was not an outlier on these points. Pound was one of the founders of the school of thought known as sociological jurisprudence, a middle way between analytical and historical schools of jurisprudence of the nineteenth century and presaging American Legal Realism, which brought us the American Uniform Commercial Code. See D Wigdor, *Roscoe Pound, Philosopher of Law* (Westport, Greenwood Press, 1974); NEH Hull, *Roscoe Pound and Karl Llewellyn: Searching for an American Jurisprudence* (Chicago, University of Chicago Press, 1997).

commercial law produced 'through the adoption in different states of uniform statutes worked out by international conferences'.[41] He said this at a time when the first wave of uniform legislation was working itself through the state legislatures of his home country the US and when substantial interaction between British and American lawyers on how uniform legislative efforts should proceed was frequent.[42]

In contrast to the resistance to legislative and non-evolutionary change of the historical school, modernisation of law was an ascendant idea when UNCITRAL was formed. It is embedded in UNCITRAL's constitutional framework.[43] Modernisation theory, employed principally by political scientists and political economists, is formed around the claim that economic development links casually to social and political change, usually in the form of a change toward liberal democracy.[44] When modernisation theory first came to prominence in political science in the 1950s and 1960s, the field of law and development also began to form as area of inquiry and as consulting on law reform and legal education in developing countries. Its rise tracked closely with the rise of modernisation theory in political science. A functioning, modern legal system was seen as essential for a modern, then industrial, economy.[45] A modern legal system was seen as essential for political and social development, with the idea being that a modern legal system would help to catalyse a move towards liberal democracy in which pluralism would flourish and rule of law would curtail arbitrary state action

[41] Pound (ibid) 98.

[42] One only needs to read the scholarship of MD Chalmers to get this point. See, eg, Chalmers, 'Codification' (1902); MD Chalmers, 'Codification of Commercial Law' (1902–03) 2 *Canadian Law Review* 146; MD Chalmers, 'Experiment in Codification' (1886) 2 *Law Quarterly Review* 125.

[43] On the earliest documents of a constitutional nature for UNCITRAL is 'Progressive Development of the Law of International Trade: Report of the Secretary-General of the United Nations' (1966). The Report states: 'The developing countries of recent independence have had the opportunity to participate only to a small degree in the activities carried out up to now in the field of harmonization, unification, and modernization of the law of international trade. Yet those are the countries that especially need adequate and modern laws, which are indispensable to gaining equality in their international trade. In many of these States the prevailing legal system was introduced before their independence by the metropolitan countries; often the provisions thus received are unsuitable to their present stage of economic development or to the requirements of newly independent states. The unification process in the field of international trade law would be a step in the direction of remedying this situation.' (footnotes omitted) The Report also states: 'To remedy the shortcomings described above, several measures such as the following should be taken. The process of harmonization and unification of the law of international trade should be substantially systematized and accelerated. This would entail a concerted effort to secure a wider participation in existing international conventions and a wider adoption of uniform legislation, where such conventions and uniform laws reflect the present requirements of world trade, as well as a wider use of standard trade terms, provisions and practices. It would also entail action towards further unification and modernization of legal techniques in this area, such as the adoption of new international conventions and uniform laws, codification of existing rules and trade practices and the dissemination of information on up-to-date methods and solutions. In addition, it would be desirable to secure a broad participation of the developing countries of recent independence in the progressive development and codification of the law of international trade; this would facilitate the adoption by those countries of laws and other measures adequate for the protection of the interests of their international trade transactions. Finally, it would be appropriate to bring about a close co-ordination of the activities of the existing formulating agencies, regardless of whether their members belong to one or another economic or legal system.'

[44] S Berman, 'What to Read in Modernization Theory (2009) *Foreign Affairs*, 12 March, available at www.foreignaffairs.com/articles/2009-03-12/what-read-modernization-theory.

[45] DM Trubek, 'The "Rule of Law" in Development Assistance: Past, Present and Future' in DM Trubek and A Santos (eds), *The New Law and Development: A Critical Appraisal* (Cambridge, Cambridge University Press, 2006) 74–94.

and help to bring about social change.[46] UNCITRAL was formed at a time when post-war decolonisation and the development of the state was very much on the agenda of international organisations. Reliance on modernisation by the United Nations of the time is analogous to reliance on governance later when the World Bank sought to work around the restrictions in its Articles of Agreement prohibiting it from promoting human rights.[47] Modernisation as an ideal may have changed meaning over the years to refer not so much to bringing democracy to former colonies but to promoting liberal global market orders. For our limited purposes, we can conclude with some certainty that: (i) modernisation of law as it is understood in the mid-twentieth century differs in substantial respects from any modernisation by nineteenth century legal codifiers; and (ii) modernisation as an aim of current law-making bodies entails something more than simple 'memorialisation' or codification of pre-existing legal norms.

We come to the problem: lawyers reforming, progressively developing, formulating, and modernising law still seem to adhere to the methods of Chalmers and others who needed to accommodate competing jurisprudential tensions in the prior era of economic globalisation, but their developing, formulating and modernising tasks far outreach the ambitions of nineteenth-century drafters and are now robustly global in scope.[48] If all we are doing is codifying pre-existing domestic law that already existed in the form of case law or fragmentary legislation, then reliance on expert judgment in the law is probably enough. In fact, that is what historical jurisprudes advocated – a deep, rich historical scholarship.[49] In these codifications, we would only be seeking the expert's opinion on the state of the law and how to draft it into legislative form. These are the skills of the lawyer. The only concern in comparing the *status quo* to the proposed situation would be in evaluating the advantages and disadvantages of legislative intervention. But if law-reformers seek to improve the law and need to cross borders where there may be no settled precedent or legal rules to codify, or where legal rules are not entirely compatible or even conflict across jurisdictions, will the expert judgment of the lawyer alone suffice? In the present day, no intellectual movement of global scope pulls lawyers towards simple legislative restatements of pre-existing law. Consistent with modernisation arguments, global commercial law-making now in many forms produces change, often substantial, and is indeed designed to promote change,[50] to improve the law, to fill gaps, to produce whole-cloth a new uniform law or international convention, or to produce cooperation among states in areas in which externalities are present.[51]

[46] DM Trubek and M Galanter, 'Scholars in Self-Estrangement: Some Reflections on the Crisis in Law and Development Studies in the United States' (1974) *Wisconsin Law Review* 1062, 1073–74.

[47] IFI Shihata, *The World Bank in a Changing World* (Leiden, Martinus Nijhoff, 1991) ch 18.

[48] For an account based in law and sociology, see Block-Lieb and Halliday (n 6) explored in section D below.

[49] Rabban (n 28) 12–14.

[50] There are many examples. The UNCITRAL Model Law on Procurement of Goods, Construction and Services is an example of a model law that seeks to promote substantial change in domestic law. Much has changed since the first book on comparative and international public procurement law was published. See S Arrowsmith, J Linarelli and D Wallace Jr, *Regulating Public Procurement: National and International Perspectives* (Alphen aan den Rijn, Kluwer/Aspen, 2000). Another is the UNCITRAL Model Law on Secured Transactions, which promotes significant change in secured lending based on the US UCC Article 9.

[51] The UNCITRAL Model Law on Cross-Border Insolvency is an example of a cooperation-facilitating instrument. UNCITRAL Model Law on Cross-Border Insolvency with Guide to Enactment, UNCITRAL, 30th Session, at 3, UN Doc A/CN.9/442 (1997), reprinted in (1997) 28 *UNCITRAL Yearbook* 305.

That their texts promote these aims, however, does not mean that actual legal change necessarily results.[52] The limited point here is that a memorialisation or 'sticking to existing law' constraint do not exist when the drafters of these instruments do their work.

Why are the current operating methods for global commercial law-making largely continuous with methods made prominent in the prior era of economic globalisation? It is difficult to say without further empirical or experimental investigation. The behaviour of those involved in commercial law reform, however, is plausibly consistent with a form of path dependence characterised as 'behavioural lock-in', which can produce difficulties in reversing situations because of learning and habituation.[53] It occurs when an agent's behaviour is 'stuck' in a particular and sometimes sub-optimal position 'due to habit, organisational learning, or culture'.[54] Behavioural lock-in can result when professionals reject new standards when these standards could reduce their power or autonomy. Training can facilitate path dependence. Lawyers may have a professional concern from being asked to accept a situation beyond their training.[55] Training is a form of organisational learning within groups and among professionals and becomes a source of power. Once a behaviour embeds, then *status quo* bias makes change ever more difficult. A plausible argument can be made that the prior more traditional methods of law-making have a grip on our beliefs and attitudes as lawyers engaged in global commercial law-making.

II. The Dissenters: Prevailing External Points of View

More international collaboration to improve commercial law always results in better law because experts gather to make it so. How can making the law better be a bad thing? Such arguments beg many questions. External observers of global commercial law-making question the unexamined premises of such positions. 'External' refers to methods of inquiry about global commercial law-making that do not depend on the discipline or the social practice of law-making itself. This section offers skeletal surveys of the two most influential social science critiques of global commercial law-making, one grounded in the American political economy school and the other in law and sociology. Inquiry about law-making processes using theory, methods, and evidence of the

[52] To appreciate the distinction, see, eg JF Coyle, 'The Role of the CISG in US Contract Practice: An Empirical Study' (2016) 38 *University of Pennsylvania Journal of International Law* 195 (on how practitioners have excluded the CISG from contract practice or thought they were doing so in a choice of law clause).

[53] W Barnes, M Gartland and M Stack, 'Old Habits Die Hard: Path Dependency and Behavioural Lock-In' (2004) 38 *Journal of Economic Issues* 371; OA Hathaway, 'Path Dependence in the Law: The Course and Pattern of Legal Change in a Common Law System' (2001) 86 *Iowa Law Review* 601. For applications to corporate law, see RH Schmidt and G Spindler, 'Path Dependence, Corporate Governance and Complementarity' (2002) 5 *International Finance* 311; LA Bebchuk and MJ Roe, 'A Theory of Path Dependence in Corporate Ownership and Governance' (1999) 52 *Stanford Law Review* 127.

[54] Barnes, Gartland and Stack (ibid).

[55] See L Spagnolo, 'Green Eggs and Ham: The CISG, Path Dependence, and the Behavioural Economics of Lawyers' Choices of Law in International Sales Contracts' (2010) 6 *Journal of Private International Law* 417; J Linarelli, 'The Economics of Uniform Laws and Uniform Law Making' (2003) 48 *Wayne Law Review* 1387.

social sciences has produced scepticism about the efficacy of global commercial law-making. The limits of these approaches are also briefly explored.

A. Dissenters I: Political Economy

Anyone who has read into the law and economics literature on so-called private legislatures will discover disagreement between those who hold positive views of the work of domestic and global commercial law-makers and those who do not.[56] The disagreement is sharp, with some going so far as to critique the American UCC project, widely considered by many lawyers in the US and beyond as a huge success.[57] It reflects a longstanding fault line between legal doctrinalists and law and economics scholars.

The critique comes in particular from the American political economy school of thought, with its foundations in positive political theory and public choice theory. In summary, the argument, developed primarily by Alan Schwartz and Robert Scott, is that private legislatures produce two kinds of legal rules, depending on the structure of their decision-making process and the incentives the participants in the law-making process have.[58] Model I rules are specific rules, usually 'bright line' in the sense that they require the application of objective facts to determine whether the rule criteria are met. Model II rules are more abstract and general, tending to rely more on the concepts like reasonableness and leaving it to the discretion of the decision-maker on the application of the rule.[59] The predictions of this research proceeds as follows. A law-making organisation will produce Model II rules when the incentives of the delegates are to promote getting something done and widespread adoption. This is often the case, so the research concludes, because of the reputational benefits, prestige and future work associated with a successful law-making project.[60] The usual example offered for Model II rules is the CISG.[61] Because of the emphasis on widespread adoption and getting something done

[56] CP Gillette and RE Scott, 'The Political Economy of International Sales Law' (2005) 25 *International Review of Law and Economics* 446; PB Stephan, 'The Futility of Unification and Harmonization in International Commercial Law' (1999) 39 *Virginia Journal of International Law* 743; EJ Kanger, 'Predicting When the Uniform Law Process Will Fail: Article 9, Capture, and the Race to the Bottom' (1998) 83 *Iowa Law Review* 569; PB Stephan, 'Accountability and International Lawmaking: Rules, Rents and Legitimacy' (1997) 17 *Northwestern Journal of International Law and Business* 681; LE Ribstein and BH Kobayashi, 'An Economic Analysis of Uniform State Laws' (1996) 25 *Journal of Legal Studies* 131; A Schwartz and RE Scott, 'The Political Economy of Private Legislatures' (1995) 143 *University of Pennsylvania Law Review* 595; SL Schwarcz, 'A Fundamental Inquiry into the Statutory Rulemaking Process of Private Legislature' (1995) 29 *Georgia Law Review* 909; RE Scott, 'The Politics of Article 9' (1994) 80 *Virginia Law Review* 1783; Kathleen Patchel, 'Interest Group Politics, Federalism, and the Uniform Laws Process: Some Lessons from the Uniform Commercial Code' (1993) 78 *Minnesota Law Review* 83. For a rebuttal of some of the arguments, see Linarelli (ibid).

[57] It is worth reading Scott, 'The Rise and Fall' (2002) to appreciate at least some of the native critiques of the UCC.

[58] Schwartz and Scott, 'Private Legislatures' (1995).

[59] ibid; Schwartz and Scott also explicate a Model III rule, which combines elements of Model I and Model II rules, but lumps Model III rules into Model II for purposes of analysis.

[60] See Gillette and Scott (n 56).

[61] ibid; Stephan, 'Accountability and International Lawmaking' (1997).

upon which one can affix one's name, most products that private legislatures produce are substantially based in Model II rules.[62] A global law-maker will produce a product with Model I rules when delegates are overwhelmingly from a single industry and the rules are designed to favour that industry. Paul Stephan offers the example of the Uniform Customs and Practices for Documentary Credits, produced by the International Chamber of Commerce, an industry group, as an example of a product with Model I rules.[63] These critiques are more widely replicated in the study of experts in regulatory contexts, though not specifically around Model I and II rules.[64]

The political economy research on private legislatures provides important insights but has several limitations. Its rational choice assumptions should be revisited. Its predictive or explanatory power is ready for re-examination based on advances in behavioural economics and the behavioural sciences more generally. A focus on behaviour would remove the need to focus on misaligned incentives.[65] Moreover, how global commercial law-making has proceeded does not fit well in these models. On the global level this literature has focused on international conventions, but global commercial law-makers now produce relatively few of these. The move has been well underway for quite some time towards soft law in the form of model laws and guides, reflecting a shift from unification or harmonisation to modernisation. While no empirical work exists on this subject, it appears, based on a tentative look at the evidence, that global commercial law-making now produces products that contain an appreciable number of Model I rules, even with the participation in the process of diverse interests. Finally, the rational choice literature has remained an outlier in the discussion of global commercial law-making because it does not deal with questions that legal comparativists explore, such as the role of culture. These limitations put into question whether the existing models are sufficiently predictive.

B. Dissenters II: The Other Chicago School

Another 'external' approach to the study of global commercial law-making is the 'other' Chicago School, to distinguish it from the Chicago School of Economics.[66] This Chicago School is one in sociology. It is best known for its work in the study of urban communities in Chicago though its research methods are generalisable. One of its most well-developed approaches is one of social ecologies, in which the research digs deep

[62] Schwartz and Scott (n 56); Gillette and Scott (n 56).

[63] Stephan (n 56).

[64] See O Perez, 'Can Experts be Trusted and What Can be Done About It? Insights from the Biases and Heuristics Literature' in A Alemanno and A-L Sibony (eds), *Nudge and the Law: A European Perspective* (Oxford, Hart, 2015) 115.

[65] ibid.

[66] Block-Lieb and Halliday (n 6). I cannot cover all methods of evaluating global commercial law-making. At least two other approaches need to be taken seriously. One is grounded in critical theory and asks questions about the increasing role of private power in making of transnational commercial law. Critical approaches ground in the idea that the contemporary law merchant is political, essential to the juridical foundations of global capitalism. This critical work is in the main designed to expose the influence of private power over the state. It is perhaps best known though the work of A Claire Cutler. AC Cutler, *Private Power and Global Authority* (Cambridge, Cambridge University Press, 2003).

into qualitative fieldwork to study relevant actors and institutions. Recent work by Susan Block-Lieb and Terence Halliday offers insights into the law-making processes of UNCITRAL, with a focus on the UNCITRAL Model Law on Cross-Border Insolvency.[67]

An ecological method, quite simply, focuses on the interactions of actors in an environment. It offers a rich account of institutional detail. It is ethnographic in approach, offering thick descriptions of actors and organisations. As its proponents say, it opens the 'black box' of the making of transnational commercial law, or at least one such black box.[68] It has offered important insights on the ecologies of expert judgment at UNCITRAL. The focus on ecologies holds promise for a complementary relationship between law and society approaches and behavioural sciences approaches in the study of global commercial law-making. Law and society approaches may be able to assist in identifying socio-cultural variables at work in affecting the psychology of decision-making in law-making processes. But as we shall see, the cognitive focus advocated in this chapter opens not the black box of the environment for law-making but that of the psychology of law-making.

C. The Cognitive Turn

This chapter advocates an approach to evaluating global commercial law-making differing for our purposes in at least one fundamental respect from the above political economy and sociological approaches: the approach based in the behavioural sciences advocated in this chapter looks neither to institutions nor to structure to explain the actions of legal entrepreneurs in global commercial law-making. Rather, the focus is *cognitive*. It renders inessential to its task a focus on institutions but gets right into examining the psychology of expert judgment. It starts and ends with what is 'in the head': mental processes identified from repeat experiments in controlled laboratory settings, which tell us what motivates legal entrepreneurs to take positions and actions in global commercial law-making processes. In barest of terms and risking oversimplification, mental events are causes: our beliefs and attitudes cause us to behave in particular ways and this behaviour can be predicted from these beliefs and attitudes. As we shall see below, the behavioural sciences hold promise for discovering why actors in the law-making processes behave in particular ways and how this behaviour influences the law-making process.

III. Behavioural Comparative Law as a Field

To date there has been little published work deploying behavioural science in comparative law. Early work provides important insights.[69] There is now a growing literature.

[67] Block-Lieb and Halliday (n 6).

[68] ibid 4, 11.

[69] J De Conink, 'Reinvigorating Comparative Law through Behavioural Economics? A Cautiously Optimistic View' (2011) 7 *Review of Law and Economics* 711; J De Coninck, 'The Functional Method of Comparative Law: *Quo Vadis?*' (2010) 74 *Rabels Zeitschrift für ausländisches und internationales Privatrecht* 318; R Michaels,

A psychological intervention seems apt for comparative law. Ralf Michaels explains that 'the problem among traditional comparative lawyers is that each of us tends to adopt the perspective of our own legal system'.[70] Legal comparativists are humans too. They make decisions and take positions that will be subject to heuristics and biases well known in the behavioural sciences, even though they are inclined by the field in which they operate to compare law and legal systems across borders. But for comparative law to be even more robust in its use of the behavioural sciences to explain difference across legal systems, comparativists will have to go further and inquire into the psychology of the actors in the legal systems they study and, for purposes of this chapter, those involved in reforming, harmonising, unifying, or otherwise making law meant to have authority across a significant number of states. Putting a group of lawyers from different jurisdictions in a deliberative process in an intergovernmental organisation to produce a legal instrument that will be widely accepted across a large number of jurisdictions could be understood as the setting for a natural experiment for comparativists.

BCL may be understood as aligned with law and economics, if we understand behavioural science about the law to be the use of behavioural economics to study the law. Putting it into economics, however, may be an exercise in reductionism. BCL may align in some respects with behavioural economics but it is broader in conception, relying on the full panoply of the behavioural sciences, including psychology and cognitive science, to inquire about differences in the law across jurisdictions. The approach of behavioural economics, on the other hand, is to look for exceptions to well-established theories in economics, and hence to see the move as one of relaxing the rationality assumption in economics,[71] to look for 'behavioural market failure', or to replace expected utility theory with prospect theory.[72] Still, given the importance of law and economics, and its dominance in private and transactional law research in North America, some placement of BCL in the context of law and economics seems necessary.

The rational choice economics of comparative law is an established field, though its beginnings were halting. In his 2002 article, 'The Progress and Failure of Comparative Law in the Second Half of the Twentieth Century', Mathias Reimann states that interdisciplinary work in comparative law is the 'rare exception' and comparative law 'has still not acquired a solid empirical basis'.[73] Ralf Michaels, in his article, 'The Second Wave

'Explanation and Interpretation in Functionalist Comparative Law – A Response to Julie de Coninck' (2010) 74 *Rabels Zeitschrift für ausländisches und internationales Privatrecht* 351; J De Coninck, Overcoming the Mere Heuristic Aspirations of (Functional) Comparative Legal Research? An Exploration into the Possibilities and Limits of Behavioural Economics' (2009) 9 *Global Jurist*, Issue, Article 3; J De Coninck and B Du Laing, 'Comparative Law, Behavioural Economics and Contemporary Evolutionary Functionalism' (2009) 26 *Abstracts Annual Conference European Association of Law and Economics* 10. See also R Caterina, *I Fondamenti Cognitivi del Diritto* (Rome, Mondadori Bruno, 2008); R Caterina, 'Comparative Law and the Cognitive Revolution' (2004) 78 *Tulane Law Review* 1501.

[70] R Michaels, 'The Second Wave of Comparative Law and Economics' (2009) 59 *University of Toronto Law Journal* 197, 204.

[71] See RB Korobkin and TS Ulen, 'Law and Behavioral Science: Removing the Rationality Assumption from Law and Economics' (2000) 88 *California Law Review* 1051.

[72] See M Rabin, 'A Perspective on Psychology and Economics' (2002) *European Economic Review* 657; C Camerer, 'Behavioral Economics: Reunifying Psychology and Economics' (1999) 96 *Proceedings of the National Academy of Sciences of the United States of America* 10575.

[73] M Reiman, 'The Progress and Failure of Comparative Law in the Second Half of the Twentieth Century' (2002) 50 *The American Journal of Comparative Law*, 671, 686.

of Comparative Law and Economics', argues that law and economics is 'almost never used in comparative law'.[74] Ugo Mattei, who wrote *Comparative Law and Economics*,[75] advocated that comparative law has no future, at least in the US, unless it links to the analytical social sciences tradition that is so robustly represented in the American legal academy.[76]

The linkage with rational choice economics is now well established. The *Oxford Handbook on Comparative Law* offers a chapter by Florian Faust, 'Comparative Law and the Economic Analysis of Law'.[77] The *Cambridge Companion to Comparative Law* deals with the economics of comparative law in two chapters, very briefly by Mathias Reimann in 'Comparative Law and Neighbouring Disciplines'[78] and in another by Nuno Garoupa and Tom Ginsburg, 'Economic Analysis and Comparative Law'.[79] The collection of previously published articles reprinted in Geest's and Van den Bergh's *Comparative Law and Economics* are mainly on legal origins, the economics of legal transplants, the relevance of new institutional economics to law, and articles by legal scholars about law and economics research in a particular country. A research handbook, *Comparative Law and Economics*, was published in 2016.[80] None of the major handbooks on comparative law, however, offer a chapter on comparative law and behavioural science.

Empirical comparative law has met with success as well, though distinguishing it from the economics of comparative law can be difficult. Holger Spamann's article, 'Empirical Comparative Law', surveys quantitative work that might be classified as empirical comparative law.[81] He surveys the comparative empirical literature on constitutions in comparative politics and political economy, the areas of law and finance, doing business and legal origins, and empirical work in diffusion and legal transplants.[82] Work by Tom Ginsburg, Nuno Garoupa, Holger Spamann and others offer a clear case for the existence of a substantial corpus in empirical and comparative law and economics.[83]

Several directions for BCL are evident when it comes to the study of law reform. The discussion to follow outlines three areas for BCL that seem to require further exploration, and which include but go beyond the standard behavioural law and economics paradigm. First, behavioural science offers tools to aid in comparing legal rules

[74] Michaels, 'Second Wave' (2009) 199. Michaels explains that the exception is Ugo Mattei's *Comparative Law and Economics* (Ann Arbor, Michigan, 1997) and he notes that Hein Kötz 'strongly endorsed' law and economics.

[75] U Mattei, *Comparative Law and Economics* (Ann Arbor, University of Michigan Press, 1999).

[76] U Mattei, 'An Opportunity Not to Be Missed: The Future of Comparative Law in the United States' (1998) 46 *American Journal of Comparative Law* 709.

[77] F Faust, 'Comparative Law and the Economic Analysis of Law in M Reimann and R Zimmerman (eds), *The Oxford Handbook on Comparative Law* (Oxford, Oxford University Press 2008) 837.

[78] M Reimann, 'Comparative Law and Neighbouring Disciplines' in M Bussani (ed), *Cambridge Companion to Comparative Law* (Cambridge, Cambridge University Press, 2012).

[79] G de Geest and RJ Van den Bergh, *Comparative Law and Economics* (Cheltenham, Edward Elgar, 2004).

[80] T Eisenberg and GB Ramello (eds), *Comparative Law and Economics* (Cheltenham, Edward Elgar, 2016).

[81] H Spamann, 'Empirical Comparative Law' (2015) 11 *Annual Review of Law and Social Science* 131.

[82] Spamann and Geest and Van den Bergh invite a boundary problem. If you are going to study the economics of a field of law, you can just as easily do that using law and data from a variety of jurisdictions. Comparing is simply subsumed within the social science methodology being used.

[83] This phenomenon may be primarily American in origin. See N Goroupa and TS Ulen, 'The Market for Legal Innovation: Law and Economics in Europe and the United States' in Eisenberg and Ramello, *Comparative Law* (2016) 78.

across jurisdictions. Second, behavioural science offers tools to evaluate legal transplants that will help us to understand how to make transplants more likely to succeed. Third, behavioural science helps us to get around the epistemological obstacles that 'legal culture' has presented in comparative law. A caveat: this three-part categorisation works for comparative law because it is based in the way comparative law is organised as a subject, but it is arbitrary for behavioural science as some of the insights of behavioural science are relevant across these categories. Research can either rely on original experiments or on settled findings from behavioural research. The discussion to follow will demonstrate the relevance of these areas to global commercial law-making.

A. BCL and Comparing Legal Rules

Comparing legal rules is a routine occurrence in global commercial law-making. The actors in the institutions and processes of global commercial law-making often work from a few or several models from domestic legal systems. For example, the American UCC Article 9 has been widely influential in proposals for reform of the law on secured credit.[84] To understand the effects of the American approach to secured credit and how it might affect lending is a comparative task. Other products, such as the CISG, are often characterised as hybrids between civil and common law.[85] To characterise a law as a hybrid means that one must be able to know something of the difference between the two approaches being combined. Other global commercial law-making products, such as the UNCITRAL Model Law on Cross-Border Insolvency, facilitate cooperation and coordination between jurisdictions but does not purport to unify insolvency law of different states.[86] To know how this cooperation might work in practice requires comparing insolvency systems across different countries. The actors in the institutional environment set by organisations such as UNCITRAL and UNIDROIT engage in frequent rule comparing and in negotiating rule formulations in their deliberations.

Behavioural science research can inform research on comparing legal rules in at least three ways, though the distinctions to follow may be artificial. First, behavioural science can inform law-making. In Eyal Zamir's scheme of classification, this is using behavioural science as an input into law-making.[87] Legal experts are subject to heuristics

[84] NO Akseli, 'International Harmonisation of Credit and Security Laws: the way forward' in M Andenas and C Baasch Andersen (eds), *Theory and Practice of Harmonisation* (Cheltenham, Edward Elgar, 2012) 551; RCC Cuming, 'The Internationalization of Secured Financing Law: The Spreading Influence of the Concepts of UCC, Article 9 and its Progeny' in R Cranston (ed), *Making Commercial Law Essays in Honour of Roy Goode* (Oxford, Oxford University Press, 1997) 499.

[85] A Janssen and NG Ahuja, 'Legal Laboratory CISG: "Bridging the Gap: The CISG as a Successful Legal Hybrid between Common Law and Civil Law?"' (2017) 21 *Vindobona Journal of International Commercial Law and Arbitration* 129; U Magnus, 'The Vienna Sales Convention (CISG) between Civil and Common Law – Best of all Worlds?' (2010) 3 *Journal of Civil Law Studies* 67.

[86] JL Westbrook, 'Chapter 15 at Last' (2005) 79 *American Bankruptcy Law Journal* 713; J Clifft, 'The UNCITRAL Model Law on Cross-Border Insolvency – A Legislative Framework to Facilitate Cooperation and Coordination' (2004) 12 *Tulane Journal of International and Comparative Law* 307.

[87] E Zamir, *Law, Psychology, and Morality* (Oxford, Oxford University Press, 2015) 99.

and biases. An example of such a use of behavioural science is in the development of consumer protection legislation or regulation.[88] Global commercial law-makers can use behavioural science as a toolkit for understanding the effects of alternative sets of legal rules on behaviour. Second, legal rules can be examined to understand how they act on cognition. Loss aversion, for example, can in Zamir's classification, be an output of legal rules. The first and second uses of behavioural science are two sides of the same coin and are conceptually difficult to disentangle. Think of the first use as *ex ante,* related to the design of law, and the second as ex post, related to the evaluation of law. A third use of behavioural science in comparative law research is in the evaluation of expert judgment in global law-making. This third use is relevant for global commercial law-making, when experts of different national traditions come together to produce law. Another way to understand this conceptual scheme is that there are producers and consumers of law, or experts and users, though producers and consumers, or experts and users, are sometimes the same people.

As for the third use of behavioural science, two not entirely distinct ways to evaluate expert legal judgment are relevant. One is to focus on heuristics and biases, an approach associated with behavioural economics and the work of Dan Kahneman and Amos Tversky. In this approach, experts will likely be subject to heuristics and biases when making law.[89] The other is to focus on identity-protective cognition, an approach associated with the work of Dan Kahan and collaborators. In this second approach, we will explore how experts may (or may not) engage in motivated reasoning caused by their affiliations with their legal systems or countries. This second approach is known as the study of cultural cognition.

i. Heuristics and Biases

Several well-understood biases may be at work in the above three contexts. We will focus on the third context, that of the exercise of expert judgment, given the almost exclusive use of expert judgment in commercial law-making. Confirmation bias will predictably be at work in the exercise of expert judgment. Confirmation bias is the use of evidence and argument in ways partial to beliefs a person already holds.[90] People are unable to ignore pre-existing beliefs when evaluating evidence and argument that their pre-existing beliefs cannot validate. So, a lawyer will tend to weigh evidence and argument more favourably that the rules of her particular legal system solve a legal problem in a superior fashion than legal rules from another legal system.

[88] O Bar-Gill, *Seduction by Contract: Law, Economics, And Psychology in Consumer Markets* (Oxford, Oxford University Press, 2013). On the notion of behaviourally informed regulation generally, see CR Sunstein, 'Nudges.gov: Behaviorally Informed Regulation' in E Zamir and D Teichman (eds), *Oxford Handbook of Behavioural Economics and the Law* (Oxford, Oxford University Press, 2014); MS Barr, S Mullainathan and E Shafir, 'Behaviorally Informed Regulation' in E Shafir (ed), *Behavioral Foundations of Public Policy* (Princeton, Princeton University Press, 2012) 440.

[89] Perez, 'Can Experts be Trusted' (2015). On expert judgment in political contexts, see PE Tetlock, Expert Political Judgment: How Good is it? How Can We Know? (Princeton, Princeton University Press, 2017).

[90] D Kahneman, *Thinking Fast and Slow* (Princeton, Princeton University Press, 2011); J Baron (2000), *Thinking and Deciding*, 3rd edn (Cambridge, Cambridge University Press, 2000); RS Nickerson, 'Confirmation Bias: A Ubiquitous Phenomenon in Many Guises' (1998) 2 *Review of General Psychology* 175.

She will tend to discount the evidence offered about the efficacy of rules of other legal systems.

Confirmation bias is part of a more general set of mental processes having to do with associative memory, the unconscious linking of ideas in our minds into categories and sequences. We cannot help ourselves but substitute association and familiarity for logic, truth conditionality and the use of evidence. Familiarity is not easily distinguishable from truth. A reliable way to make people believe something is true is to repeat it and make it familiar. Frequent use of one's own domestic law or legal practices biases us towards our own legal systems. Placing the discussion in the dual mental processing framework, we can use system 2 but we experience cognitive strain in doing so in contrast with the cognitive ease of association. We need system 2 deliberation-forcing tools to counteract these mental processes, such as cost–benefit analysis, as covered in section IV below. Figure 4.1 is a rough illustration of how associative memory works in the context of expert legal judgment. It is a predictable tendency of humans to think they are starting with reason and evidence, which then affects their legal judgment, and that familiarity and pre-existing beliefs have nothing or at least very little to do with reaching a conclusion. But mental processes work in the opposite direction, starting with the cognitive ease of familiarity and pre-existing beliefs, which determine how we exercise our legal judgment, and from there we deploy deliberation and evidence to justify or rationalise legal concepts we are already familiar with. Reasons become rationalisations for familiarity and pre-existing beliefs.

Figure 4.1 The Sequence of Comparative Legal Analysis

Another well-understood bias affecting expert judgment is *status quo* bias: people tend to prefer the present to alternative states, all things being equal. *Status quo* bias relates to two related and well-understood mental processes: the endowment effect and loss aversion. Humans exhibit what Kahneman calls 'asymmetric intensity' to avoid losses and achieve gains.[91] When it comes to legal reform, there will be a bias favouring the law as it is to the delegate. The *status quo* in a comparative law context is the law as it is to the agent in question. For the English lawyer, for example, the *status quo* is English law. Lawyers feel the loss intensely if law reform moves away from 'their' law. Their law is a reference point in the reform process.

Finally, research on how anchors influence the interpretation of vague legal standards is relevant to evaluating expert judgment in the form of global commercial law-making. Anchoring occurs when a subject is exposed to a reference point, which then influences

[91] Kahneman, *Thinking Fast and Slow* (2011) 80–81.

subsequent judgments.[92] Yuval Feldman, Amos Schurr and Doran Teichman have conducted experimental research showing that anchors influence the interpretation by legal experts of vague legal norms.[93] This work offers methodological insights on how to conduct further experimental research on how anchoring might affect legal experts in law-reform projects. For example, experimental design could encompass giving subjects different legal standards and asking them to recommend standards for incorporation into a new legal product.

ii. Identity-protective Cognition

The heuristics and biases approach developed in the preceding section is well developed in the law and behavioural economics literature. Another strand of research holds promise for research in comparative law on motivated reasoning, the tendency of individuals to conform their evaluation of evidence and use of reasons, as well as their sense of the matter and their intuitions, to some aim distinct and extrinsic to reaching a conclusion based only on reasons and evidence.[94] Identity-protective cognition is a form of motivated reasoning, occurring when individuals selectively credit evidence and reasoning aligning with the group to which they belong.[95] The insight at work here is not that we can override our biases in the fast and automatic system 1 mental processes with slow and deliberative system 2 processes, but instead, all our mental processes operate together to protect our identities. Evidence-driven, deliberative system 2 mental processes magnify biases and do not defeat them.[96]

Howard Margolis offers an influential psychological account of expert judgment.[97] He offers and integrated and reciprocal relationship between automatic system 1-type cognition and deliberative system 2-type cognition in experts.[98] For Margolis, expert judgement consists of habits of mind based in pattern recognition, the fast and automatic assimilation of evidence to a mental inventory of prototypes. A legal expert applies these prototypes to facts and evidence in legal decision-making. System 2 does not override system 1, but rather these dual modes of though work together. Expert assessment needs a reliable system 1 or 'preconscious' apprehension to help the expert decide what requires more deliberative and evidence-driven mental processing. Once intuitive judgment is applied, the use of evidence and argument – the deployment of system 2 – will depend on the expert's 'assimilation of such evidence to an inventory of

[92] ibid 119–28; A Furnham and H Chu Boo, 'A Literature Review of the Anchoring Effect' (2011) 40 *Journal of Socio-Economics* 35.

[93] Y Feldman, A Schurr and D Teichman, 'Anchoring Legal Standards' (2016) 13 *Journal of Empirical Legal Studies* 298.

[94] DM Kahan, 'Laws of Cognition and the Cognition of Law' (2015) 135 *Cognition* 56.

[95] ibid; A Mehta Sood, 'Motivated Cognition in Legal Judgments – An Analytic Review' (2012) 9 *Annual Review of Law and Social Science* 307.

[96] DM Kahan, 'Ideology, Motivated Reasoning, and Cognitive Reflection' (2013) 8 *Judgment and Decision Making* 407.

[97] ibid.

[98] H Margolis, *Dealing with Risk: Why the Public and The Experts Disagree on Environmental Issues* (Chicago, University of Chicago Press, 1997); H Margolis, *Patterns, Thinking and Cognition: A Theory of Judgment* (Chicago, University of Chicago Press, 1990).

patterns that consist in prototypical representations of cases that give proper effect to data of that sort'.[99] In short, system 1 must reliably activate system 2.[100]

Dan Kahan contends that Margolis's account of professional judgment is like Karl Llewellyn's account of the 'situation sense' of the judge.[101] For Llewellyn, situation sense is a perceptive faculty that lawyers and judges develop through professional experience, enabling them to reliably connect legal controversies to 'situation types' to suggest appropriate legal resolution. Llewellyn saw legal reasoning as psychological not logical. For Llewellyn, formal legal reasoning primes or activates the situation sense of the legal expert.

In a recent experimental study on whether political predispositions influence judicial decision making, Kahan and colleagues found that professional judgment imparted by legal training and experience produces resistance to identity-protective cognition.[102] Judges and experienced lawyers (but not law students) who were on the opposing sides of the US political spectrum did not engage in biased *legal* decision-making. This study tested legal reasoning in a single country against *political* (non-legal) predispositions in that country.

There is currently no answer to the question whether expert legal judgement would resist identity-protective cognition in a comparative legal context. It may be that we find identity-protective cognition in a comparative legal context for at least two reasons. First, the political and the legal are somewhat indistinct in the comparative realm, in the sense that one's legal system may be perceived as part of one's politics and associatively relevant to one's political allegiances. In the Kahan *et al* study, the subjects were judges and lawyers in the *same* national legal system. Law in that study was a clearly distinct variable from political allegiance or culture, which may not be the case in a comparative legal context. Second, reputational motivations about promoting one's own law as a global standard may be in play. The experimental work has yet to be done.

B. Cognitive Constraints and Legal Transplants

Much of global commercial law-making can be understood as some form of legal transplant. In the global commercial law-making process, one or a few influential

[99] DM Kahan, D Hoffman, D Evans, N Devins, E Lucci and K Cheng, '"Ideology" or "Situation Sense"? An Experimental Investigation of Motivated Reasoning and Professional Judgment' (2016) 64 *University of Pennsylvania Law Review* 349, 373.

[100] ibid. Another way to understand identity-protective cognition is through Gerd Gigerenzer's concept of expressive utility. Identity-motivated reasoning is expressively rational because it conveys and supports a person's membership in a group. G Gigerenzer, *Adaptive Thinking: Rationality in the Real World* (Oxford, Oxford University Press, 2002). Another complementary approach is Nancy Pennington and Reid Hastie's story-based model, positing that decision-makers are endowed with a stock of story schema, which form templates for shaping the evidence presented in a legal case. Kahan et al (ibid) collect the research. The Pennington–Hastie research appears to be more relevant for juries than judges, though judges are factfinders too.

[101] Kahan et al, '"Ideology" or "Situation Sense"?' (2016); K Llewellyn, *The Common Law Tradition: Deciding Appeals* (New York, Little Brown, 1960).

[102] Kahan et al (n 99).

national models often arise, upon which to base the law-making process. Usually in the process the legal systems of the participants play an influential role. Transplants are either piecemeal or wholesale. Borrowing can be explicit. In some cases, the law of a particular jurisdiction becomes a global standard, as is the case for the law on secured transactions and American UCC Article 9. Borrowing can also be implicit or unintended, such as a result of the biases of the participants for their own law.

Suppose the working group of an international organisation is in the early stages of preparing a model law. The process entails substantial negotiations among delegates. Assume that organisation officials and Member State delegates have several national codes under consideration for the potential borrowing of rules that seem to promote economic activities that international financial institutions like the World Bank have found to promote economic growth. Behavioural science can assist us in predicting how Member State delegates will deliberate on the borrowing. It can also assist in understanding how transplanted rules will be received in the borrowing country.

As for the process of producing, for example, a model law based on transplanting a national law or approach to the law from a particular state or group of states, Kahneman states that loss aversion may generally be an 'ever present feature of negotiations'.[103] Along these lines. Tomer Broude has extended to treaty negotiations theories about the effects of *status quo* bias on contract default rules.[104] We can extend Kahneman's thinking about trade and arms control negotiations to deliberations about the contents of a model law.[105] The domestic law of the Member State delegates are reference points for the deliberation. Any proposed move away from the existing domestic law of a delegate will inevitably be viewed as a concession by that delegate. One's own law primes one to think about what is appropriate for transplanting to a model law. You might think system 2 is guiding you, but really you are simply primed by your legal tradition. As we know, losses are felt more intensely than gains. We can thus predict significant negotiations over the contents of model laws, rationalised in the language of reason and doctrine, but what in fact is likely going on is delegates have a *status quo* bias for their own law.

The heuristics and biases literature can also inform us how transplants will be received by states. Here we might see local experts, domestic lawyers of the importing country and judges who must interpret the new law once it is in force, experiencing loss aversion and resisting the importation. Until they are trained in the new law and accept it as their own, they may feel they are losing expertise and prestige while the exporters – the international organisation producing the model law and its experts – receive gains from reputational effects associated with the number of adoptions, but no real losses. An outside expert has no 'dog in the hunt' other than perhaps her reputation as an expert, but she is unaffected by the reform of the law itself. The behaviour of those who favour the *status quo* is like that of territorial animals who rigorously and swiftly protect against threats to territory.[106] If *status quo* losers have political power or

[103] Kahneman (n 90) 304.
[104] T Broude, 'Behavioural International Law' (2015) 163 *Georgetown Law Journal* 1099.
[105] Kahneman (n 90) 304–05.
[106] Kahneman (n 90) 305.

influence, they will use it. The actual outcome will likely be biased against real reform unless countermeasures are in place. As Kahneman explains, loss aversion is a 'powerful conservative force' favouring 'minimal changes from the *status quo* in the lives of both institutions and individuals'.[107] The World Bank and other law-reformers do put some counter-measures in place, such as training and the use of local consultants (and not just outsiders) in law-reform projects.

Finally, identity-protective cognition might have a role in the drafting of the law, its implementation in-country, and its application by judges and lawyers. There has been empirical work by Daniel Berkowitz, Katherina Pistor and Jean Francois Richard on the 'transplant effect': they find that what matters more for the success of a legal transplant is its acceptance in the borrowing country than the association of the transplant with a legal family.[108] This literature, grounded in rational choice, finds that for a successful transplant, the imported law must be 'meaningful' to the citizens who use it who will then demand institutions to make it work, and judges, lawyers and other legal intermediaries must be in a position to respond to this demand. Receptivity, a country's 'ability to give meaning to the imported law', requires significant adaptation of the foreign legal rules to pre-existing conditions. Research on motivated reasoning and identity-protective cognition holds the promise of shedding significant new light on what makes transplants viable and subject to reception and meaningfulness to end-users.

C. Demystifying Culture Arguments

One of the more casually and often repeated statements one hears in both global law-making processes and in the comparative law community is that law is about culture. The invocation of culture can at times seem to be a strategy to censor discussion of difference. Culture has been one of the most discussed areas in comparative law and we cannot cover all the approaches to studying it here.[109] Given the focus of this chapter on behavioural science, at least three strands of thinking about culture are relevant to our discussion.

First, let us look at culture from the standpoint of rational choice theory as it has been deployed in traditional versions of law and economics. Rational choice economics can be understood as the predecessor to behavioural economics. Rational choice theorists have tended to ignore culture in comparative work. Chicago School rationalists take a hard line against culture as having any real explanatory power, taking the standard position in favour of parsimonious economic models. J Mark Ramseyer and Minoru Nakazato, for example, explain in their book, *Japanese Law: An Economic Approach*:

> We do not use economics because we think everyone (or anyone) always rationally maximizes. We all know no one does. We use economics because we think classical Chicago-school

[107] ibid.

[108] D Berkowitz, K Pistor and J-F Richard, 'The Transplant Effect' (2003) 51 *American Journal of Comparative Law* 163; D Berkowitz, K Pistor and J-F Richard, 'Economic Development, Legality, and the Transplant Effect' (2003) 47 *European Economic Review* 165.

[109] For an extensive discussion, see Siems, *Comparative Law* (2014) 101–04, 119–35.

> economic intuition (taken alone and simply, without much elaboration) goes far toward explaining much (not all) law-related behaviour in Japan. Surely, many readers will protest, Japan is a complex place, a multifaceted universe where every phenomenon results from the subtle interplay of myriad disparate and interconnected causes. … But unless our critics tell us which of the myriad causes has what relative impact (they rarely do), the complexity is not much of an improvement.
>
> The same readers will probably insist that we could explain more if we added culture to our spare model. What we would gain in explanatory breadth, however, we believe we would lose in theoretical parsimony. … Consider [this book] an attempt to show just how far extremely spare economic models go toward explaining the world of law-related behaviour.[110]

Of course, the law and economics of social norms literature could be said to be addressing cultural norms, but these approaches focus not on culture but on the incentive effects of norms that are not official legal rules.[111]

There are at least two problems with the rational choice approach. First, it is not predictive, as advances in behavioural science have shown in repeated experiments. Rational choice assumptions have been shown to matter greatly when it comes to individual decision-making and behaviour. Moreover, rational choice theory cannot explain why the law differs across jurisdictions.[112] It is *too* parsimonious, risking falsification.

Second, work in empirical comparative law could be said to be seeking some reliability in causal inferences relating to culture, though the gains are debatable and the researchers in the field do not make direct claims or findings about culture. This literature is responsive to Ramseyer's and Nakazoto's plea for evidence of causation. Culture itself is not an independent variable and so this work, located primarily in the 'law and finance' literature, develops proxies such as variables for legal origins, tenure of Supreme Court judges, the power of judicial review, and so on.[113] Legal origins variables are set up in the multiple regression models used in the 'law and finance' literature based on whether the origin of the legal system is England and Wales, France or Germany. The problems with these variables in accounting for culture in statistical models is that we really do not know what is being tested. They may capture some element of culture, or they may simply be controlling for something else. The decision of what proxy variables might be testing for culture are in the heads of the modellers. Behavioural scientists might look at this as potentially a problem of artefacts, a situation in which the views or biases of the researchers unintentionally interfere with the validity of the research.[114] Mathias Siems has offered an alternative

[110] JM Ramseyer and M Nakazoto, *Japanese Law: An Economic Approach* (Cambridge MA, Harvard University Press, 1999) xii–xiii.

[111] The norm theory literature in law and economics is substantial. A good place to start is with RC Ellickson, *Order without Law: How Neighbours Settle Disputes*, new edn (Cambridge MA, Harvard University Press, 1994). For another book-length treatment, see EA Posner, *Law and Social Norms* (Cambridge MA, Harvard University Press, 2002).

[112] Michaels (n 70) 352.

[113] The law and finance or legal origins literature is vast. For a survey, see Siems (n 1) 146–87.

[114] R Rosenthal and RL Rosnow, *Artifacts in Behavioral Research* (Oxford, Oxford University Press, 2009).

set of variables.[115] Culture, or some aspects of it, may be reflected in the error term in the law and finance multiple regressions.[116] It is probably better just to say that a variable that tests for, say, legal origins, tests for legal origins as understood by the modellers, and probably nothing more.

Third, postmodernists assert that culture is an overriding factor in the evaluation of legal systems.[117] The focus of the critique here is on a mistake that legal postmodernists make in relying on an outdated distinction between explanation and understanding.[118] An empirical or analytical social scientist seeking to explain a phenomenon will cite causes, general principles, and evidence of actual behaviour. The task of explanation complies with norms of empirical science – third-party objectivity, nomological principles, the construction of general theories – all to promote the nomothetic ideal of causal adequacy. An explanation arising from this kind of social science might be unrecognisable to those immersed in the practice being studied. A social theorist focusing on understanding studies the world of those participating in a phenomenon by seeking meaning for the participants of the social practice under investigation, examining the qualities of lived experience. The task of understanding complies with the norms of hermeneutics: first-person perspective, interpretive principles, phenomenological approaches and an emphasis on the particular, all to promote the hermeneutic ideal of meaning adequacy. An understanding arising from this kind of account would be recognisable to those immersed in the practice being studied. We see these distinctions between the empirical and postmodern wings of comparative law.

Behavioural science has the potential to dissolve these distinctions or at least make them less important. It offers methods to explain causation in mental processes and events that are sufficiently replicable to be predictive of behaviour, but which also account for meaning and the lived experiences of those immersed in the social practice of law. It does not accept without further investigation the self-narratives of persons as authoritative concerning meanings, but is by its very conception mentalist in seeking to account empirically for people's actual beliefs. While not a perfect substitute for humanities-oriented approaches to comparative law inquiry, culture can no longer be used as a blockage of comparative legal analysis, because psychology offers ways of explaining why actors think the way they do about 'their' law.

So how would we investigate culture using the behavioural sciences? A place to start would be in the evolutionary wing of behavioural science suggesting that the scientific project should be more fully understood in a larger frame of culture-gene

[115] MM Siems, 'Legal Origins: Reconciling Law and Finance and Comparative Law' (2006) 52 *McGill Law Journal* 55.

[116] This point is suggested by AE Roth, V Prasnikar, M Okuno-Fujiwara and S Zamir, 'Bargaining and Market Behaviour in Jerusalem, Ljubljana, Pittsburgh, and Tokyo; An Experimental Study' (1991) 81 *American Economic Review* 1068, one of the first studies of cross-country variation in behaviour in bargaining contexts.

[117] For a survey, see Siems (n 1) 101–08, 119–45.

[118] The distinction between explanation and understanding is a longstanding topic in epistemology and philosophy of science. For an analogous discussion about ethics, see P Railton, 'Toward an Ethics that Inhabits the World' in B Leiter (ed), *The Future for Philosophy* (Oxford, Oxford University Press, 2004) 265.

co-evolution.[119] In this research, culture is understood as a form of social learning to acquire behaviours that adapt to local conditions. Humans are endowed with learning capacities allowing us to acquire the beliefs and attitudes relevant and necessary for the given local social environment. Social learning accumulates over generations and can create multiple stable equilibria in and across societies. Over time, humans would have culturally evolved different social organisations and institutions to adapt to diversity. While cultural capacities develop over a much shorter time span than genetic evolution, they, so the theory holds, influence the human genotype.[120] This theory predicts that humans can learn in a way that accurately and efficiently acquires the motivations and preferences relevant to a local and culturally evolved social equilibria. Social equilibria are the various forms of social organisation and institutions found in societies, which includes law. Our beliefs and attitudes become part of our preference functions.

The research to date in this evolutionary wing is normal science in a Kuhnian sense: it does not challenge the basic teachings of behavioural science. It offers evidence that mental states and processes have an evolutionary origin. Repeat experiments have shown people universally not to be self-maximising but to exhibit variability in altruistic and prosocial behaviours based on factors such as market integration, the publicity of cooperation, and the industrialisation and scale of societies. Differences in economic and social organisation, the complexity of social organisation, the need for cooperation in everyday life, and market integration affect results. This research is so far almost entirely limited to cross-cultural variations on fairness and reciprocity norms in experiments using ultimatum, dictator and public goods games in small-scale societies.[121]

[119] J Henrich, R Boyd, S Bowles, C Camerer, E Fahr, H Gintis, R McElreath, M Alvard, A Barr, J Ensminger, N Smith Henrich, K Hill, F Gil-White, M Gurven, FW Marlowe, JQ Patton and D Tracer, '"Economic Man" in Cross-Cultural Perspective: Behavioural Experiments in 15 Small-Scale Societies' (2005) 28 *Behavioural and Brain Sciences* 795.

[120] PJ Richerson and R Boyd, *Not by Genes Alone: How Culture Transformed Human Evolution* (Chicago, University of Chicago Press, 2004); R Boyd, *Culture and the Evolutionary Process* (Chicago, University of Chicago Press, 1988).

[121] Henrich et al, '"Economic Man"' (2005); J Ensminger and J Henrich (eds), *Experimenting with Social Norms: Fairness and Punishment in Cross-Cultural Perspective* (Los Angeles, Sage, 2014); J Henrich, SK Heine and A Norenzayan, 'The Weirdest People in the World?' (2010) 33 *Behavioural and Brain Sciences* 61; K Chen and F-F Tang, 'Cultural Differences Between Tibetans and Ethnic Han Chinese in Ultimatum Bargaining Experiments' (2009) 25 *European Journal of Political Economy* 78; M Gurven, A Zanolini and E Schniter, 'Culture Sometimes Matters: Intra-Cultural Variation in Pro-Social Behaviour Among Tisimane Amerindians' (2008) 67 *Journal of Economic Behaviour and Organization* 587; J Henrich and N Henrich (eds), *Why Humans Cooperate Across Societies: A Cultural and Evolutionary Perspective* (Oxford, Oxford University Press, 2007); L Cronk, 'The Influence of Cultural Framing on Play in the Trust Game: A Maasai Example' (2007) 28 *Evolution and Human Behaviour* 352; J Henrich, Richard McElreath, A Barr, J Ensminger, C Barrett, A Bolynatz, J Camilo Cardenas, M Gurven, E Gwako, N Henrich, C Lesorogol, F Marlowe, D Tracer and J Ziker, 'Costly Punishment Across Human Societies' (2006) 312 *Science* 1767; J Henrich, R Boyd, S Bowles, C Camerer, E Fehr and H Gintis (eds), *Foundations of Human Sociality: Economic Experiments and Ethnographic Evidence from Fifteen Small-Scale Societies* (Oxford, Oxford University Press, 2004); M Gurven, 'Economic Games Among the Amazonian Tsimane: Exploring the Roles of Market Access, Costs of Giving, and Cooperation on Pro-Social Game Behaviour' (2004) 7 *Experimental Economics* 5; ME Price, 'Punitive Settlement Among the Shuar and in Industrialized Societies: Cross-Cultural Similarities' (2004) 26 *Evolution and Human Behaviour* 279; A Barr, 'Trust and Trustworthiness: Experimental Evidence from Zimbabwean Villages' (2003) 113 *Economic Journal* 614; J Henrich, W Abers, R Boyd, G Gigerenzer, KA McCabe, A Ockenfels and HP Young, 'Group Report: What is the Role of Culture in Bounded Rationality?' in

The basic finding is that the values that are rejected or not by the players in these games can differ when one changes the sample from that of university students that are WEIRD (Western, educated, industrialised, rich and democratic) to samples from different subpopulations. One study has found no endowment effect in a small-scale traditional society not exposed to markets and modern society.[122]

The science sketched above may be relevant for comparative law. Because of adaptive social learning processes, societies populated by people who historically adapted to divergent ecologies and historical circumstances may arrive at differing stable social equilibria. The result just might be that legal actors across societies may develop different forms of social organisation and institutions – different law – based on the psychology of legal decision-making in different historical trajectories. If properly developed, BCL could be at the vanguard of law-related behavioural science in attempting to replicate single-country experiments in different countries. For example, one BCL project could be the study the loss aversion of contract default rules across several countries using samples from each country. Notably, this means that claims about the effects of culture will be subjected to the demands of empirical validation.

But the above cross-cultural research about small-scale societies may be of limited relevance to comparative law for at least two reasons. First, comparative law research tends to be about large-scale societies with substantial market integration, dealing with people who have experienced substantial exchange-type interactions with a variety of people. The above research may support the position that we should not worry too much about culture in comparative law research. Law tends to be a large project of mass societies to solve large-scale problems of coordination and cooperation. Law just might be less important than social norms in smaller-scale societies. Second, the above literature is limited in its focus mainly on reciprocity and fairness. A more promising line of research into legal culture might be a focus on identity as it is understood cognitively, as in the identity-protective cognition work outlined above.

Extending the discussion to global commercial law-making, culture seems of dubious relevance. When it comes to the making of transnational commercial law, we are dealing with the regulation of people and firms – 'merchants' in the usual parlance – usually multinational enterprises, operating in explicit markets within a vast network of market integration comprising global supply chains. There will likely be little variation in the behaviour of these users of the law. But, as we have discussed, there remains the possibility that the experts who will be making the law are subject to biases in favour of their own law and institutions. The origins of those biases may (or may not) be evolutionary, but that they are likely to exist is the more important question for us here.

G Gigerenzer and R Selten (eds), *Bounded Rationality: The Adaptive Toolbox* (Cambridge MA, MIT Press, 2001); J Henrich, 'Does Culture Matter in Economic Behaviour? Ultimatum Game Bargaining Among the Machiguenga of the Peruvian Amazon' (2000) 90 *American Economic Review* 973. There is some experimental evidence of cross-cultural differences across large-scale market societies, though, at least along the discplinary lines explored here, is relatively less well-developed and is not clearly grounded in evolutionary explanations. See, eg, S-H Chuah, R Hoffman, M Jones and G Williams (2007) 64 *Journal of Economic Behaviour and Organization* 35.

[122] CL Apicella, EM Azevado, NA Christakis and JH Fowler, 'Evolutionary Origins of the Endowment Effect: Evidence from Hunter-Gatherers' (2014) 104 *American Economic Review* 1793.

IV. Improving Global Commercial Law-making

This section of the chapter moves on to applying the insights developed above to global commercial law-making. It focuses on two points: (i) how biases and motivated reasoning might interfere with the making of global commercial law and its operation and implementation in practice; and (ii) how to de-bias and render less influential the cognitive constraints on expert judgment in global law-making. The focus in this second section is on the use of cost–benefit analysis when feasible.

A. Cognitive Imperialism

Your own legal system dominates your thinking. Call this *cognitive imperialism*: the domination of a lawyer's reasoning about what is good and right about the law, based on what they sense or know about their own law. 'Domination' connotes that a lawyer has no or few cognitive mechanisms by which to defeat this imperialism.

Applying these insights to global commercial law-making, lawyers involved in global commercial law-making will prefer their own law, regardless of any Pareto improvements for the prospective users of the law. The same holds for the implementation of the new law: all things being equal, lawyers and judges will subvert reform in favour of their own law. They will predictably substitute one question – 'What is a good rule?' – for another – 'What is the rule I am familiar with?' – which will inevitably be the rule in their own jurisdiction.

The argument in this form is at a stage of a rudimentary working hypothesis, based simply on what we know about the psychology of expert legal judgment. It would take significant refinement of the question and experimental research to explain these insights in actual operation. The first step in developing a theory or model in the social sciences is to rely on one's intuition based on what we see anecdotally.[123] That is what I do here.

i. Cognitive Imperialism in Law-making

Examples of potential loss aversion or identity-protective cognition in global commercial law-making processes seem apparent. I will focus on one: the debate in UNCITRAL Working Group 1 about whether minimum legal capital requirements should be recommended as a requirement for incorporation in the draft Legislative Guide on an UNCITRAL Limited Liability Organization (UNLLO) and in the UNCITRAL Draft Legislative Guide on Key Principles of a Business Registry.[124]

[123] See HR Varian, 'How to Build an Economic Model in Your Spare Time' (2016) 61 *The American Economist* 81.

[124] For the UNCITRAL history on the development of these guides, see https://uncitral.un.org/en/working_groups/1/msmes.

American corporate law eliminated minimum capital requirements as a requirement for registering a corporation long ago. This abolition applies equally to publicly and privately held corporations. Other countries have also eliminated these requirements. The modern trend in corporate law appears to be for corporate enabling statutes not to contain minimum capital requirements for corporate formation. Minimum capital requirements are likely to be widely perceived by experienced American business lawyers as provisions left over in an antiquated state corporate legislation in need of updating, but which a state legislature has ignored. Younger American lawyers may not even know of their prior existence. If you attended law school in the US in 1970s or the early 1980s, you may have been instructed from a slim paperback by Bayless Manning, *A Concise Textbook on Legal Capital*, first published in 1977.[125] By the late 1980s the book became widely viewed as an anachronism in American legal education. The absence of minimum capital requirements in the US can be widely seen as a move from a paternalistic view of corporate law as a matter of regulation to an autonomy-based view of corporate law comprised mainly of default rules.[126] Minimum legal capital rules are widely understood as obsolete in the US. Any lawyer working in the American tradition of corporate law will probably have a reference point that will be strongly against minimum capital requirements as needless obstacles to corporate formation.

The EU is not so far from the US in terms of the letter of the law, though the move came much later and Europe remains an outlier on requiring minimum capital for some companies. Article 6 of the Second Company Law Directive (77/91/EEC) requires that publicly held companies have at least 25,000 euros in legal capital to incorporate, but there seems to be a trend in Europe away from minimum capital requirements for closely held firms, represented by such entities as the *Unternehmergesellschaft* (UG) in Germany and the *société à responsabilité limitée* (SARL) in France.[127]

The focus on the work of UNCITRAL Working Group 1 under consideration here is on micro, small and medium-sized enterprises (MSMEs). Its work on the LLO seems to connect to the advent of the American limited liability company and similar forms of organisation found in other countries. Why would some UNCITRAL delegates focus on minimum capital requirements? UNCITRAL started out in its early deliberations taking the position that 'Importantly, simplified corporate forms do not typically include a minimum capital requirement, or require only a nominal amount, thus allowing greater

[125] B Manning, *A Concise Legal Textbook on Legal Capital* (New York, Little Brown, 1977). This book, however, has more to do with legal capital requirements post-formation, which can affect distributions to shareholders.

[126] See LA Hamermesh, 'The Policy Foundations for Delaware Corporate Law' (2006) 106 *Columbia Law Review* 1749.

[127] See Note by the Secretariat, Observations by the Government of the French Republic, 12 August 2015, A/CN.9/WG.1/WP.94; Note by the Secretariat, Micro, Small and Medium-Sized Enterprises, Features of Simplified Business Incorporation Regimes, 10 December 2013, A/CN.9/WG.1/WP.82, at p 6 (discussing the UG in Germany).It is doubtful a 25,000 euro requirement has any real significance for publicly held corporations. J Armour, G Hertig and H Kanda, 'Transactions with Creditors' in R Kraakman, J Armour, P Davies, L Enriques, H Hansmann, G Hertig, K Hopt, H Kanda, M Pargendler, W-G Ringe and E Rock, *The Anatomy of Corporate Law: A Comparative and Functional Approach*, 3rd edn (Oxford, Oxford University Press, 2017) 109.

access to formalization for much smaller entrepreneurs and enterprises'.[128] There apparently was resistance to this position, with the position taken being the standard European arguments in favour of minimum capital requirements.[129] These included the argument that minimum capital requirements are necessary to offset the effects of limited liability.[130] The dividing lines apparently having been drawn, the World Bank, which as a matter of practice participates in UNCITRAL working groups, offered substantial evidence on why minimum capital requirements are poor corporate policy. Its expertise in corporate registration derives from its Ease of Doing Business Index and Doing Business Reports.[131] While the World Bank's work in these areas has generated controversy, for our limited purposes here, the World Bank, an intergovernmental organisation with a broad membership of most countries in the world, has no national law of its own to promote. It is worth quoting UNCITRAL's summary at length of the World Bank evidence, in a document UNCITRAL styled as 'Best Practices in Business Registration':

> Several reforms in recent years have questioned the function of the minimum capital requirement, which is said to considerably slow the registration of new businesses. Although supporters of the minimum capital requirement insist that it is necessary to protect creditors and investors, it has increasingly been observed that the requirement does not fulfil any regulatory function by protecting creditors, customers or the business itself against poor performance of the business. For instance, the requirement does not shield the business from insolvency: in several countries the minimum capital can be paid in kind or withdrawn immediately after registration. Furthermore, recovery rates in bankruptcy are not higher in countries with minimum capital requirements when compared with those with no such requirements. Minimum capital requirements do not protect investors and consumers from new firms that are carelessly set up or might not be financially viable, since the minimum capital is often a fixed amount that does not take into account the firms' economic activities, size or risks. In some cases the amount of the capital requirement is the same even when the companies are of a different type. In one State, for instance, a small company in the services industry with a low start-up capital has to pay the same amount as a large manufacturing company with high initial capital. Research shows that States protect investors and creditors, particularly in the case of limited liability companies, through means other than the minimum capital requirements. Some economies adopt provisions on solvency safeguards in their legislation, others conduct solvency tests or require an audit report showing that the amount a company has invested is enough to cover its establishment cost.
>
> Of the 189 economies reviewed in *Doing Business 2014*, 99 have no minimum capital requirement. Some economies never required businesses to deposit money for incorporation, while others have eliminated minimum capital requirements in the recent past. In other cases new forms of limited liability companies with lower minimum capital requirements and simplified

[128] Note by the Secretariat, Micro, Small and Medium-Sized Enterprises Features of Simplified Business Incorporation Regimes, 10 December 2013, A/CN.9/WG.1/WP.82, 6.

[129] See L Enriques and JR Macy, 'Creditors Versus Capital Formation: The Case Against the European Legal Capital Rules' (2001) 86 *Cornell Law Review* 1165.

[130] Report of Working Group 1 (MSMEs) on the Work of its Twenty-Second Session (New York, 10–14 February 2014), 28 February 2014, A/CN.9/800.

[131] See www.doingbusiness.org.

incorporation procedures have been introduced. Some States allow initial incorporation of a simplified limited liability company for only 1 euro, provided that progressive capitalization occurs, for example, the company must set aside a certain percentage of its annual profits until its reserves and the share capital jointly total the required amount. In another State, the introduction of a lower capital requirement resulted in a 40 per cent increase in registration in the year following the reform.

According to a study of selected European Union (EU) States, lowering or abolishing the minimum capital requirement has led to a marked increase in the number of registered business in four of the States considered: in the year after the reform, average daily incorporations in those States increased by as much as 85 per cent.[132]

Despite the substantial evidence against minimum capital requirements, resistance among some delegates seems to have continued, with the more prominent argument that without a minimum capital requirement, creditor protections would be all ex post and not *ex ante*.[133] There appeared to be some consensus with the World Bank view along with some dissension, though delegate views are sometimes difficult to discern in official documents. The Working Group agreed that 'the issues of minimum capital requirement and protection of third parties should be treated under the general category of protection of creditors and other third parties'.[134] The delegates did not agree on standards for protection but that the legal text should ensure 'sufficient flexibility for a State to choose its own criteria as it saw fit'.[135]

Some of the disagreement appears to have come from the German delegation. UNCITRAL published a note on the German position that appears to advocate minimum capital requirements and more regulatory burdens for SMSEs, arguing for 'ex ante preventive measures of justice', but also making some pro-SMSE statements.[136] One argument was that 'it has become apparent' through the Working Group 1 sessions 'that a business cannot be separated from its national economic and cultural context' and that the aim should be to 'bridge gaps between different legal traditions in terms of business incorporation'.[137] These arguments seem to contradict a well-settled claim that corporate law is substantially similar across nations, probably more so than other areas of law. As explained in the first paragraph of probably the most influential comparative work in the field,

despite the very real differences across jurisdictions … the underlying uniformity of the corporate form is at least as impressive. Business corporations have a fundamentally similar set of legal characteristics – and face a fundamentally similar set of legal problems – in all jurisdictions.[138]

[132] Note by the Secretariat, Best Practices in Business Registration, 5 September 2014, A/CN.9/WG.1/WP.85 (citations omitted). The Note by the Secretariat, Micro, Small and Medium-Sized Enterprises, Legal Questions Surrounding the Simplification of Incorporation, 8 September 2014, A/CN.9/WG.1/WP.86, reiterated the focus on the World Bank evidence.

[133] Report of Working Group I (MSMEs) on the Work of its Twenty-Third Session (Vienna, 17–21 November 2014), 2 December 2014, A/CN.9/825, 77.

[134] ibid.

[135] ibid 78.

[136] Note by the Secretariat, Observations by the Government of the Federal Republic of Germany, 19 February 2015, A/CN.9/WG.1/WP.90.

[137] ibid.

[138] J Armour, H Hansmann, R Kraakman and M Pargendler, 'What is Corporate Law' in Kraakman et al, *The Anatomy of Corporate Law* (2017) 1.

The culture argument, moreover, appears to be an attempt to censor discussion of the evidence. The German position was also that 'Extensive contractual freedom might be problematic in countries where founders of business entities lack the education or access to legal counsel to make best use of such freedom'.[139] This argument appears to be a critique of the approach to corporate law that focuses on autonomy rather than paternalism. Finally, the note contains a section that is entitled 'honouring what is already there', which seems to offer an example of *status quo* bias.[140]

The minimum capital requirement eventually receded in importance in UNCITRAL deliberations. UNCITRAL reported that that no consensus existed on whether minimum capital requirements should be required to offset limited liability, but that 'there was broad agreement that the modern trend in legal reform in this area was to move away from minimum capital requirements'.[141] UNCITRAL began preparation of a draft model law on a simplified business entity that did not contain a minimum capital requirement, but consistently with the 'modern trend' was 'sufficiently flexible' to allow states to include such a requirement, but advocating restriction to a 'nominal sum'.[142] How a nominal sum would serve any purpose other than to respond to loss aversion or identity-protective cognition by some of the members of Working Group 1 is unclear.

The current state of affairs as of the date of this writing is that UNCITRAL deliberations are ongoing on parallel tracks on a draft Legislative Guide on an UNCITRAL Limited Liability Organization and a draft Legislative Guide on Key Principles of a Business Registry. The draft Legislative Guide on an UNCITRAL Limited Liability Organization sets forth a recommendation 5: 'The law should not contain a minimum capital requirement for the formation of an UNLLO'.[143] The draft Legislative Guide on Key Principles of a Business Registry discourages countries from adopting minimum capital requirements offering rationales consistent with the evidence-based World Bank position.[144]

The point of this example is not to debate the merits of legal capital requirements but to illustrate how various biases or motivated reasoning might be in play in global commercial law-making. Of course, the above narrative is not proof, but merely a set of observations that reasonably could lead us to believe that biases and motivated reasoning are at work. The next step would be in developing a set of clearly specified hypotheses and to conduct a set of experiments by which to test the hypothesis.

[139] Note by the Secretariat, Observations by the Government of the Federal Republic of Germany, 19 February 2015, A/CN.9/WG.1/WP.90.

[140] ibid.

[141] Note by the Secretariat, Micro, Small and Medium-Sized Enterprises, Draft Model Law on Simplified Business Entity, 28 January 2018, 15.

[142] ibid 16.

[143] Note by the Secretariat, Draft Legislative Guide on an UNCITRAL Limited Liability Organization, 25 July 2016, A/CN.9/WG.1/WP.99/Add.1; Note by the Secretariat, Draft Legislative Guide on an UNCITRAL Limited Liability Organization, 24 July 2018, A/CN.9/WG.1/WP.112.

[144] Note by the Secretariat, Draft Legislative Guide on Key Principles of a Business Registry, 10 February 2017, A/CN.9/WG.1/WP.101; Note by the Secretariat, Draft Legislative Guide on Key Principles of a Business Registry, 81–82; Note by the Secretariat, Draft Legislative Guide on Key Principles of a Business Registry, 2 Jan 2018, A/CN.9/WG.1/WP.109, 74.

B. Cognitive Imperialism in Implementation

There is space in this chapter to only briefly explore a few illustrations in which biases and motivated reasoning may be at work in the implementation of global commercial law at the national level. The illustration is that of the non-use of the UN Convention on the International Sale of Goods (CISG) by contract parties. The discussion to follow is by no means exhaustive.

Commentators have expressed a longstanding concern about a 'homeward trend' in judicial interpretations of the CISG.[145] The problem goes further: there seems to be attempts at wholesale exclusion of the CISG by lawyers across several countries. Several empirical studies offer evidence of very low reliance on the CISG in the US, for example.[146] This homeward trend might be explained with behavioural science. John Coyle's work on the non-use of the CISG by American contract parties offers clues. Coyle developed a dataset of over 5,000 contracts and interviewed several lawyers involved in contract drafting. His research revealed that many US contracting parties (or their lawyers) 'reflexively exclude' the CISG, which means that they excluded the CISG from contracts even when it would clearly not apply. His research also revealed that US contracting parties almost never explicitly choose the CISG and they are often unaware that selecting the law of a US state can result in the application of the CISG.

Experimental research on how lawyers make decisions about the drafting of choice of law clauses would be the next step. Statutory interpretation problems have been the subject of experiments and there is no reason to believe that a valid experiment could not be developed to test expert legal judgment about choosing an international convention or foreign law in the drafting of a choice of law clause. There is some indication in this research that lawyers react to law nationalistically, as in choosing 'New York', though any such experiment will have to control for the location of the client, among other things.

Other illustrations can be offered. The thwarting of the universalism of the United Nations Model Law on Cross-Border Insolvency in the UK Supreme Court decision in *Rubin v Eurofinance SA*[147] just might offer another illustration. In *Rubin*, the UK Supreme Court took a sharp break from precedent by rejecting the UK enforcement of default judgments entered by the Southern District of New York and the New South

[145] The phrase is attributable to John Honnold, but the phenomena has been examined in many articles too numerous to cite here. See, eg, 'The Sales Convention in Action – Uniform International Words: Uniform Application? (1988) 8 *Journal of Law and Commerce* 207.

[146] Coyle, 'The Role of the CISG in US Contract Practice' (2016); Spagnolo, 'Green Eggs and Ham' (2010); PL Fitzgerald, 'The International Contracting Practices Survey Project: An Empirical Study of the Value and Utility of the United Nations Convention on the International Sale of Goods (CISG) and the Unidroit Principles of International Commercial Contracts to Practitioners, Jurists, and Legal Academics in the United States' (2008) 27 *Journal of Law and Commerce* 1; MF Koehler, 'Survey regarding the relevance of the United Nations Convention for the International Sale of Goods (CISG) in Legal Practice and the Exclusion of its Application', available at www.cisg.law.pace.edu/cisg/biblio/koehler.html; GV Philippopoulos, 'Awareness of the CISC Among American Attorneys' (2008) 40 *Uniform Commercial Code Law Journal* 357.

[147] [2012] UKSC 46.

Wales Supreme Court, even though the centre of main interests (COMI) of the bankrupt estates were in the US and Australia. The *Rubin* judgment is likely an example of motivated reasoning. Again, and more generally beyond *Rubin* or any single case, experiments testing the 'nationalism' of judging can be designed. It appears to reflect a similar homeward trend-type problem found in many CISG cases decided in many national courts.

C. De-biasing: Moving to System 2

Given what behavioural science tells us, an important aim of any global commercial law-making process should be to de-bias the process. The process should move away from reliance only on expert legal judgment of the traditional sort. Some form of 'third-party' neutrality is warranted. Even an attempt at system 2 reasoning by experts is problematic. Even experts trained to use evidence and reasoning may deploy evidence and reasoning in identity-protecting ways. The job of evaluation of new law should therefore be outsourced and cost–benefit analysis should be employed when feasible.

The 'when feasible' proviso is an important qualification. De-biasing should make the process better and not worse off. Feasibility has to do with both identifying what can be measured and measuring itself – both conceptual and empirical considerations are relevant. There will be many cases in which cost–benefit analysis is not feasible. So far there have been few advances in employing cost–benefit analysis to evaluate private or transactional law.[148] There is a considerable movement towards using cost–benefit analysis in the analysis of protocols to the Capetown Convention.[149] For the Aircraft Protocol of that Convention, it can be demonstrated that secured financing of aircraft lowers the cost of credit for purchasers. How these lower private costs translate into lower social costs and increased social benefits is the more central question, about which it may be impractical to say much. Cost–benefit analysis probably did not come to be understood as a tool for evaluating proposed regulation until the early 1980s, when US President Ronald Reagan issued Executive Order 12,291 mandating the use of cost–benefit analysis on all major US federal proposed regulation.[150] We should not have expected any global law-making body to have adopted cost–benefit analysis at the time to evaluate private or transactional law.

[148] There has been considerable discussion on the use of cost–benefit analysis to evaluate financial regulation. See, eg n 17 and two symposium issues at (2014) 43 *Journal of Legal Studies* No S2 and (2000) 29 *Journal of Legal Studies* S2. A significant difference exists, however, between conducting cost–benefit analysis of financial regulation and commercial law. UNCITRAL's remit, moreover, at least informally, excludes regulation.

[149] J Wool, 'Treaty Design, Implementation, and Compliance Benchmarking Economic Benefit – A Framework as Applied to the Capetown Convention' (2012) 17 *Uniform Law Review* 633; J Wool, 'Economic Analysis and Harmonised Modernization of Private Law' (2003) 8 *Uniform Law Review* 389; A Sanders, A Srinivasan, I Walter and J Wool, 'The Economic Implications of International Secured Transactions Law Reform: A Case Study' (1999) 20 *University of Pennsylvania Journal of International Economic Law* 309; J Wool, 'Rethinking the Notion of Uniformity in the Drafting of International Commercial Law: A Preliminary Proposal for the Development of a Policy-Based Unification Model' (1997) 2 *Uniform Law Review* 46.

[150] Adler and Posner, *New Foundations* (2006).

One potentially formidable feasibility constraint might be on the use of cost–benefit analysis at the international level: how to measure costs and benefits when it is unknown who will adopt a model law, ratify a convention, or follow a legislative guide. It is all too often the case that what is in force globally is a diversity of international conventions governing a particular area of commerce. Model laws are meant to be national laws and costs and benefits may be impractical to quantify unless tied to a national evaluation. Still we want to be able to use cost–benefit analysis or come as close as possible to using it at the more abstract global level if we want it to de-bias global commercial law-making.

When cost–benefit analysis is not feasible, a solution might be to look for an alternative methodology.[151] In 2003, attempting to repair the above political economy critique of private law harmonisation, I recommended as follows:

> Model laws and international conventions tend to be accompanied by official commentary. States could require demonstrations in the commentary of efficiency improvements in the law. It would be naive to suggest that because the commentary says that the law is an efficiency improvement, that the law makers actually took efficiency into account in producing the law. That they are required to provide such an analysis, however, does at least five things to improve upon the status quo. First, it signals that unifying bodies are amenable to efficiency-oriented approaches. Second, it produces information about the content of the law. Third, it has the potential to focus the drafting of law on improvements in the law rather than on legal change by itself as a goal. Fourth, it assists in getting law and economics scholars to review proposed laws. Fifth, it is difficult to 'fake' efficiency. The public choice-oriented explanations for unification will remain relevant, and actors involved in unification projects will not somehow miraculously begin to act only in the public interest. There are no panaceas. And, uncertainty will remain for some laws as to whether they actually will be efficient when implemented by courts. But still, drawing attention to efficiency should channel some law-unifying behaviour towards the production of better or at least more efficient law.[152]

Any such work would have to be done by 'experts' who are independent of the law-making process and with the appropriate expertise and should be as quantitative as is sensible to the production of reliable results. Moreover, regardless of the methodology employed, the work should be conducted under conditions of transparency, in which interested parties have access to the data and are in a position to evaluate the results.[153]

V. Conclusion

In this chapter I have strived to identify two innovations. One is the development of a new field of behavioural comparative law or BCL. The other is in the application of behavioural science insights to global commercial law-making. Scholars have paid scant attention to the potential for behavioural science to contribute to comparative law

[151] Coates makes this same point about cost–benefit analysis of financial regulation (n 17).

[152] Linarelli, 'Economics of Uniform Laws' (2003) at 1445–46.

[153] See G Klass, 'Empiricism and Privacy Policies in the Restatement of Consumer Contract Law' (2019) 36 *Yale Journal on Regulation* 45, 97–101 (on transparency and the American Law Institute restatement process).

research, though work in behavioural law and economics, a major field in behavioural science, has emerged. Nothing to date has been written about the application of behavioural science to global commercial law-making.

There appear to be promising lines of research still be done in both areas. Intuition informs us that heuristics and biases, as well as other cognitive insights associated with culture and national identity, are in play in global law-making. More generally, behavioural science seems to hold significant potential for understanding how legal problems are solved in different states. Future work would seem to require data-driven and experimental investigation. It is my hope that this chapter serves as a catalyst to instigate further work in the use of behavioural comparative law methods to study global commercial law-making.

5

Towards a Unified Approach to Economic Assessment in International Commercial Law Reform

JENIFER VARZALY*

The process of economic assessment (EA) is described using varied terminology across international organisations, governments and regulatory agencies. The use of disparate terminology leads to unnecessary complexity and costs, despite the uniform aims of the process at both international and national levels.[1] EA can be simply defined as a systematic approach to analysing and assessing regulations, both proposed and existing, for the purpose of measuring net economic benefit (EB) or cost. EA is critical to international commercial law reform (ICLR) given that it is the only uniform means by which to ensure law reform efforts are evidence-based and result in a net economic benefit capable of justifying the costs incurred by international organisations in promoting such reform. Yet, such assessment is seldom undertaken and, when done so, is not uniform in its scope or methodology, nor is it subject to systematic review.[2] In order to address this challenge, this chapter proposes a unified set of guidelines for use in the EA of ICLR. Thus far, there is an absence at the international level of such guidelines which can inform international organisations, and at the national level there are no harmonised

* The author is grateful to Professor Jeffrey Wool, Professor Louise Gullifer, Professor Teresa Rodríguez de las Heras Ballell and Dr Kristin van Zwieten for their comments on earlier drafts of this chapter.

[1] Terminology relating to EA is non-uniform. Terms such as 'cost–benefit analysis', 'regulatory impact analysis', 'regulatory impact assessment', 'economic impact analysis' and 'quantitative impact assessment' have been used. For clarity, EA will be used throughout this paper as subsuming the different terminology in this area.

[2] MM Johns and V Saltane, 'Citizen engagement in rulemaking – evidence on regulatory practices in 185 countries' (2016) Policy Research working paper WPS 7840, World Bank Group 16: 'In 98 of the 185 countries surveyed for this paper, ministries and regulatory agencies do not conduct impact assessments of proposed regulations. In those where they do, the impact assessments vary in scope.' Likewise at 17: 'Among the countries where impact assessments are conducted, only slightly over half have guidelines on how to conduct them … Another 28 percent (24) of the countries with impact assessments have developed no guidelines for conducting them. These countries fall in all income groups and regions.'

guidelines which exist across countries.[3] While there are both political and technical challenges to international law reform efforts and the implementation of a clear framework for assessment, this chapter aims to provide a first step forward towards creating a unified approach. It does so by proposing a series of guidelines which traverse five key components of any EA undertaking, drawing on international and within-country data regarding EA processes in setting guidelines, presenting comparison points and providing recommendations. More specifically, section I deals with the role and components of EA, part A providing guidelines in relation to undertaking quantitative analysis, part B covering choice of instrument and multiple benefit analysis, part C presenting EA structural recommendations, and part D focusing on ex-post evaluation and continuous EA improvement. Section II concludes. These guidelines aim to inform law reform at the international level, whether directed towards modernising, harmonising, or coordinating commercial law.

I. The Role of Economic Assessment in International Commercial Law Reform

ICLR can be defined as the development of commercial laws designed to facilitate transactions through the use of international conventions, treaties, rules, norms and practices.[4] This reform process aims to enhance legal certainty and predictability, so that transaction costs will be reduced, and international business will be facilitated, which will ultimately result in economic growth.[5] ICLR further aims to facilitate improvements in the performance of national economies and enables countries to adapt to economic uncertainty and change.[6] In this way, ICLR is a complement to progressive fiscal and economic policy and should be viewed as a dynamic, continual and multidisciplinary process.[7]

As such, the proposition that some measurable form of EB will be achieved through ICLR is viewed as paramount to motivating nations, intergovernmental organisations and industry stakeholders to engage in this process at the outset.[8] Therefore, it is important to quantify EB for the purpose of fulfilling ICLR objectives.[9] While specific

[3] See eg The World Bank Global Database for Regulatory Impact Assessment (RIA), collating 303 varying approaches to within country impact assessment of proposed regulation, available at http://rulemaking.worldbank.org/ria-documents.

[4] J Wool, 'Treaty Design, Implementation, and Compliance Benchmarking Economic Benefit – a Framework as Applied to the Cape Town Convention' (2012) 17 *Uniform Law Review* 633, 633.

[5] JA Estrella Faria, 'Future Directions of Legal Harmonisation and Law Reform: Stormy Seas or Prosperous Voyage?' (2009) 14 *Uniform Law Review* 5, 5; APEC-OECD Integrated Checklist on Regulatory Reform (2005) 4.

[6] OECD, 'Guiding Principles for Regulatory Quality and Performance' (2005) 1; OECD, 'Recommendation of the Council of the OECD on Regulatory Policy and Governance' (2012) 1.

[7] OECD, 'Guiding Principles for Regulatory Quality and Performance' (ibid) 1.

[8] Wool, 'Treaty Design' (2012) 634.

[9] Wool has usefully described EB as falling into the following categories: microeconomic, macroeconomic and developmental (assuming effective implementation and compliance). Microeconomic benefits may include reducing transaction costs, increasing the practical efficiency of entering into a transaction, or reducing the risk associated with entering a deal. Macroeconomic benefits can be understood as the aggregate benefits which may flow to consumers at a national or regional level, increase trade and investment, or

requirements and methodologies vary, best practice EA should include the following key elements:

(1) a choice amongst alternative regulatory options;
(2) the identification and quantification of impacts;
(3) a process of data collection and assessment;
(4) transparency and accountability;
(5) effectiveness and policy coherence;
(6) the use of a threshold test; and
(7) the application of a risk assessment metric.[10]

Such an analysis must also determine that any economic benefit (EB) or efficiency which is expected to accrue will outweigh the identified costs. More specifically, within country effects should be analysed at first instance, with international impacts considered as a secondary step. In this manner, EA will improve the evidence basis for regulation, so that implementation only occurs when there will be EB.[11] Disciplined EA procedures must be incorporated into all regulatory processes, to ensure that proposed rules or standards are both optimal and effective.[12]

Therefore, it is proposed that EA should form a permanent part of any ICLR process, and that there should be one global framework applied by international organisations in their efforts to sponsor, fund or support law reform. EA should be integrated into an overall decision-making system and utilised as a structured, functional framework to support consultation, policy development and rule-making in order to consider the likely effects of regulatory reform.[13] In practice, this should involve the exploration of potential impacts by analysing costs and benefits; modelling how effective the intended action will be in achieving economic and policy goals; and identifying any superior alternate approaches which may be pursued.[14]

International organisations are well placed to initiate the EA, and may usefully engage experts to assist in conducting the analysis.[15] It is apparent that there are costs related to regulatory heterogeneity and the multiplicity of ICLR efforts, which can be addressed by this process. Additionally, there are unilateral, bilateral, plurilateral and multilateral approaches to ICLR, as well as the involvement of a diversity of

decrease unemployment. Lastly, developmental economic benefits deal with broader international objectives relating to infrastructure enhancement, the establishment and strengthening of trade systems and external debt reduction: Wool (n 4) 634–35.

[10] See eg MM Johns and V Saltane, 'Citizen engagement in rulemaking' (2016); HM Treasury, 'The Green book: Appraisal and evaluation in central government: Treasury guidance' (2003); N Malyshev, 'Regulatory Impact Assessment: State of Play in OECD Countries' (2017) Regulatory Scrutiny in the EU RSB Brussels Conference; C Kirkpatrick and D Parker (eds), Regulatory Impact Assessment: Towards Better Regulation? (Cheltenham, Edward Elgar, 2007).

[11] ibid.

[12] J McCabe, 'The Need for Improved Cost–Benefit Analysis of Dodd-Frank Rulemaking' (2012) Harvard Law School Forum on Corporate Governance and Financial Regulation.

[13] OECD, 'Regulatory Impact Analysis: A Tool for Policy Coherence' (2009) 12; Johns and Saltane (n 2).

[14] OECD, 'Regulatory Impact Analysis' (2009), 12; Kirkpatrick and Parker (eds), 'Regulatory Impact Assessment' (2007); HM Treasury, 'The Green book' (2003).

[15] For example, the OECD and the World Bank Group have prepared numerous reports and case studies which can inform this process.

organisations which increases complexity when it comes to setting or reforming international rules.[16] A unified, data-driven, EA process can assist in reducing such costs and overlapping regulation.

In addition to the production of EB, it is recognised that such reform should create 'better' regulation. In distilling generally agreed-upon concepts from existing practice and literature, it is proposed that ICLR should be measured against the following 10 criteria:

(1) having a logical rationale and clearly defined objectives supported by policy goals;
(2) having a sound legal and empirical basis;
(3) directly targeting what has been identified as the source of a problem, or facilitating what is recognised as creating EB;
(4) the production of EB that justifies the costs involved;
(5) proportionality to the scale of the problem or the risk involved;
(6) avoiding excessive prescription and/or the curtailment of private ordering;
(7) complementing existing regulation and policies (where such regulation is viewed as progressive);
(8) is understandable, simple and practical for commercial parties to implement;
(9) can be effectively administered and reviewed (to ensure that it remains fit for purpose); and
(10) avoiding overlapping responsibilities among regulatory and government authorities.[17]

Once the purpose and key components of EA are understood, it is critical that quantitative analysis is undertaken in order to provide a data-driven assessment of any regulatory proposal.

A. Quantitative Analysis should be Utilised wherever Possible

While data will be limited (and sometimes non-existent) prior to ICLR implementation, the most statistically powerful methodologies should be applied in the EA, inclusive of critical assumptions to provide guidance. In cases where there simply is no data, analogous ICLR projects and data can be drawn upon, and a qualitative assessment should be used at the initial stage, which outlines expected effects. This can then be populated with data as the project continues. Indeed, the challenges identified in measuring and quantifying the costs and benefits when considering new regulatory proposals are commonly noted in EA materials.[18] In order to maximise the contribution of EA to policy decision-making, efforts should be made to incorporate quantification at

[16] N Malyshev, 'The Role of International Organisations in Fostering Better Rules of Globalisation' (2017), Workshop on the Economic Assessment of International Commercial Law Reform, Oxford University, UK.

[17] See eg, OECD, 'Guiding Principles' (n 6) 3; Kirkpatrick and Parker (n 10); HM Treasury (n 10); OECD, 'Recommendation of the Council on Improving the Quality of Government Regulation' (1995); OECD, 'Recommendation of the Council' (n 6) 10.

[18] OECD, 'International Regulatory Co-operation and International Organisations: The Cases of the OECD and the IMO' (2014) 81.

whichever stage possible – regardless of the degree of uncertainty – as long as the fundamental assumptions and evaluation criteria are clearly stated.[19] Moreover, suitable sensitivity analysis must also be undertaken to reflect data ambiguities which are encountered (as detailed below).[20]

From a practical perspective, decision-makers must be equipped with suitable information about the potential costs and benefits as well as any inadvertent impacts which may be expected to occur in other areas of policy.[21] In this regard, there are questions which arise regarding the feasibility of accurately quantifying or evincing potential costs and benefits. Recent academic debate has focused on the areas of financial and corporate regulation.[22] While current scholarship does not solve the challenges associated with this process, many commentators argue that EA quantification must be expanded, particularly in relation to financial and corporate regulation.[23]

When data is limited, particularly ex ante, comparable ICLR examples and economic theory can assist in the assessment process. The initial EA will then be reviewed after implementation as part of the two-stage process (detailed in part B below). Due to the technical challenges inherent in conducting EA, international organisations and countries should additionally supply practitioners with simple, yet practical, methodological guidance to aid in the achievement of process aims. Recommendations, based on the ICLR subject matter, include: setting a suitable threshold test to validate the EA so it is clear when a regulatory proposal should pass the EA or be sent back for refinement; identifying suitable analytical measures, such as break-even analysis and cost–benefit analysis; the use of multifactorial risk-assessment tools; and the application of suitable criteria weightings and valuation methods.[24]

The need for EA to analyse impacts on specific macroeconomic variables such as poverty or innovation on conceptual grounds has been disputed by some analysts, particularly in the context of more limited regulatory reforms.[25] However, these views have more recently been challenged, as progress has been made regarding macroeconomic modelling and assessment.[26] Therefore, where data is available and advanced

[19] ibid; HM Treasury (n 10).

[20] ibid.

[21] OECD (n 13) 13.

[22] RL Revesz, 'Cost–Benefit Analysis and the Structure of the Administrative State: The Case of Financial Services Regulation' (2017) 34 *Yale Journal on Regulation* 545; JC Coates, 'Cost–Benefit Analysis of Financial Regulation: Case Studies and Implications' (2015) 124 *Yale Law Journal* 882, 1011; EA Posner and EG Weyl, 'Cost–benefit Analysis of Financial Regulations: A Response to Criticisms' (2015) 124 *Yale Law Journal* 246, 247–57; CR Sunstein, 'Financial Regulation and Cost–Benefit Analysis' (2015) 124 *Yale Law Journal* 263, 270, 274–75.

[23] Revesz, 'Cost–Benefit Analysis' (2017).

[24] OECD, 'Regulatory Impact Analysis' (2009) 20.

[25] S Jacobs 'Regulatory Impact Analysis in Regulatory Process, Method and Cooperation: Lessons for Canada from International Trends' (2006) Government of Canada Policy Research Initiative, Working Paper 26, 82–83; OECD (n 21) 33. For example, Jacobs posits that macroeconomic variables such as poverty and innovation 'are not the result of a single government intervention or regulation, and there is no analytical technique for assessing these impacts in an EIA'.

[26] Revesz (n 22) 545; Posner Weyl, 'Cost–benefit Analysis of Financial Regulations' (2015) 246. However, it should be noted that the inclusion of more complex economic methodologies with respect to EA will result in greater demands being placed on analysts undertaking EA. This raises questions regarding the ability to justify costs associated with EA procedures, which will be linked to the accuracy of assessments upon future review.

quantitative methodologies are used, microeconomic as well as macroeconomic impacts should be examined.

The array of available methods which may be employed in the EA analytical process, which are well documented in the economics literature, include the following: discounting; the application of a risk premium; net present value and internal rate of return calculations; and sensitivity analysis.[27] Moreover, developments continue to be made in the field of empirical assessment, with powerful methods such as difference in difference regression techniques and Computable General Equilibrium (CGE) modelling now available to those undertaking EA.[28]

Further to the above, sensitivity analysis should be undertaken as a matter of course wherever there is substantial uncertainty regarding the value assigned to a variable. Sensitivity analysis allows for the exploration of the impacts of potential uncertainty around key EA assumptions. This will particularly be the case where the EA is conducted ex ante and the variable(s) in question is likely to have a large impact on the outcome. From a practical perspective, assessing two to three sensitivity scenarios should allow those undertaking the EA to observe whether threshold tests will be met at all or fewer sensitivity scenarios.[29]

Additionally, central to EA methodology is the concept of discounting; however, disagreement persists across organisations and countries in relation to its application.[30] This difference of opinion is apparent in both the specific rates recommended and the theoretical reasoning provided for the selection of discount rates.[31] The divergent use of discount rates in EA calculations should be harmonised at the international organisation level and, ultimately, across countries to allow for more meaningful comparisons and EA replicability. However, a single agreed-upon discount rate will require lengthy negotiation and regular ex-post evaluations to take place based on ensuing interest rate and market conditions across states. Therefore, a more readily implementable solution is for the EA to ultilise different discount rates within calculations to take into account uncertainties surrounding the time value of money and any associated risk. While there is no hard and fast rule regarding the selection of a discount rate, it is logical to utilise at least two different rates. For example, the EPA selected three per cent and seven per cent

[27] OECD, 'International Regulatory Co-operation' 82; HM Treasury (n 10).

[28] D Roland-Holst, 'California's Energy Future Scenarios for Economic Growth and Sustainability from the BEAR Model of the California Economy' (2005), Second Annual CEC-PIER Climate Change Conference, Sacramento; D Roland-Holst, 'Empirical Methods for Integrating Regional and National Economic Policy Analysis' (2006) Development Research Center, State Council of the PRC, Beijing; D Roland-Holst and S Evans 'An Introduction to General Equilibrium Policy Modeling' (2015), UC Berkeley Computable General Equilibrium (CGE) Model Training Workshop, CAREC Institute, Urumqi, PRC.

[29] For example, six total scenarios were computed as a part of the Standardized Regulatory Impact Assessment Prepared for the California Energy Commission by David Roland-Holst, Samuel Evans, Cecilia Han Springer and Tessa Emmer (University of California Berkeley) in June 2016. This was made publicly available so that data and assumptions could be independently verified. Sensitivity scenarios were high and low around: different regulatory options, projected prices, anticipated compliance costs and alternative market growth rates. In this CGE model, all sensitivity scenarios had a negligible impact on results.

[30] OECD, 'International Regulatory Co-operation and International Organisations' (2014) 85; HM Treasury (n 10).

[31] ibid.

in their RIA calculations, and a third rate based on prevailing market conditions may also be used for comparison.[32]

In terms of the EA data used, while it is not possible to provide an exhaustive list of credible sources given the breadth of ICLR, the following core guidelines are instructive at the practical level (Figure 5.1 below):

(1) Data should be publicly available, or made so post publication of the EA;
(2) The EA itself should be replicable;
(3) The data sources should be transparent.

Figure 5.1 Appropriate data for use in EA

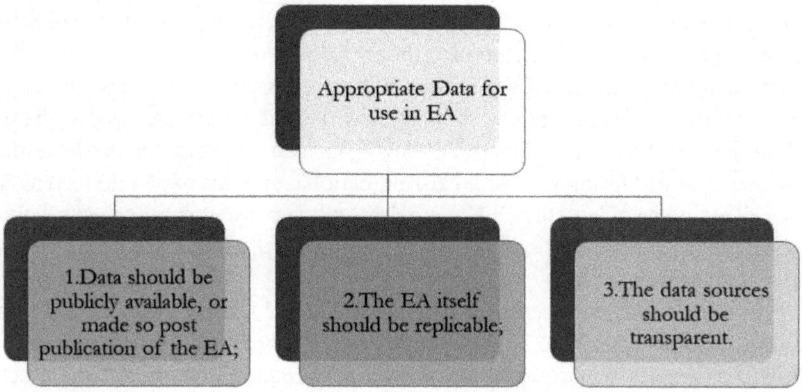

In this manner, a number of challenges with the EA process can be overcome given that interest groups, countries and stakeholders will be able to independently verify the data, process and results.

Further to the economic research in this area, an additional aim should be the development of a database and modelling software which can be used at the international level by those undertaking the EA.[33] This platform can then include a gradually developed set of verified data sources which are made publicly available.

In addition to the use of rigorous quantitative methodologies and the need to ensure publicly available data sources and EA replicability, at the international level it is also critical to analyse the best choice of instrument in any ICLR process and ensure that EB is not restrictively defined.

[32] See eg US Environmental Protection Agency Regulatory Impact Analysis, 'Final New Source Performance Standards and Amendments to the National Emissions Standards for Hazardous Air Pollutants for the Oil and Natural Gas Industry' (2012). They are recognised as international leaders in RIA, based on practical assessment and accuracy.

[33] See eg M Horridge and K Pearson, 'Solution Software for CGE Modeling' (2011) Centre of Policy Studies, Monash University. Describing the progress in CGE and the main systems used today: GAMS, MPSGE, and GEMPACK. The development of these modelling systems has underpinned rapid growth in the use of CGE models and allowed for their results to be replicated.

B. EA should Analyse Choice of Instrument and take into Account Multiple Forms of EB

There must additionally be an analysis of the best choice of instrument to use in the law reform process. That is, there will be a need to consider alternative courses of action, for example, hard law versus soft law. This analysis should include relevant data constraints and take into account the inability to assume compliance in the case of soft law.

As such, a clear challenge to the aim of accurately measuring EB is the increasing use of soft law in the ICLR field. For example, UNIDROIT has drafted numerous instruments which are not binding on Member States, and thus do not strictly require the involvement of Member State governments.[34] These soft law instruments may take the form of model laws, codifications of custom or usage, general principles, international trade terms or legislative guides, among other things.[35]

When soft law instruments are utilised in harmonisation efforts, this indicates an avoidance of the use of conventions concluded by nations, which is viewed as the traditional mechanism for harmonising private law.[36] Such an approach has also be criticised by Vogenauer as not fitting well with existing national systems of private international law as well as choice of law rules.[37] Nonetheless, soft law instruments can subsequently lead to law reform at both national and international levels, and therefore are viewed as valuable in their own right.[38]

While conventions have served as the main method for international law reform, numerous scholars have been vocal in explicating the limitations of this process. For example, Faria notes that country ratification may require additional formal action, involve various agencies and take years to be completed, resulting in delayed domestic implementation and lost economic benefits.[39] A second issue is the difficulty faced in amending international conventions in light of a revised economic analysis; further, there is a risk that revisions will not be ratified by all nations, or will be completed in a piecemeal manner.[40] Third, the lack of flexibility inherent in international conventions serves as a disincentive to nations in adopting, implementing and/or complying with binding instruments.[41] Finally, the utilisation of hard law has been criticised for resulting in the drafting of suboptimal and inefficient provisions in order to successfully negotiate a political compromise.[42]

[34] S Vogenauer, 'The Unidroit Principles of International Commercial Contracts at twenty: experiences to date, the 2010 edition, and future prospects' (2014) 19 *Uniform Law Review* 481, 483.

[35] ibid; H Gabriel, 'Toward Universal Principles: The Use of Non-Binding Principles in International Commercial Law' (2014) 17 *International Trade and Business Law Review* 241; MJ Bonell, 'Soft Law and Party Autonomy: The Case of the UNIDROIT Principles' (2005) 51 *Loyola Law Review* 229.

[36] Vogenauer, 'The Unidroit Principles of International Commercial Contracts at twenty' (2014) 481.

[37] ibid.

[38] ibid 488; Gabriel, 'Toward Universal Principles' (2014) 241.

[39] E Faria, 'Future Directions of Legal Harmonisation and Law Reform' (2009) 8.

[40] ibid 8–9.

[41] ibid 9; A Rose, 'The Challenges for Uniform Law in the Twenty-First Century' (1996) 1 *Uniform Law Review* 9.

[42] E Faria (n 5) 10; Steven Walt, 'Novelty and the Risks of Uniform Sales Law' (1999) 39 *Virginia Journal of International Law Association* 671.

In relation to soft law, it has been argued that one of the major advantages of the use of soft law in the area of ICLR is the achievement of a degree of flexibility which is not possible when hard law is used.[43] However, the use of soft law undoubtedly poses a challenge to the measurement of EB, given the flexible, non-binding nature of such instruments. Nonetheless, relevant costs and benefits should be quantified wherever possible, taking into account political and institutional risk. These results should be supported by qualitative analysis, to reduce the inherent uncertainty.

In practice, soft law benefits have been approximated by the OECD. For example, standards have been measured as increasing social welfare through improving economic efficiency, establishing network effects (positive externalities), reducing market failure, decreasing information asymmetries, promoting trade, facilitating access to new markets and reducing transaction costs.[44] Research in this area has shown a positive correlation between the implementation of standards and the productivity and GDP growth of countries.[45] Further, case studies have consistently indicated that the contribution of new standards to the gross profit of companies ranges between 0.15 per cent and five per cent of reported annual sales revenues.[46]

In recognition of such positive correlations, the scope of the EA should be broad enough to take into account multiple risks and multiple forms of EB. This should look beyond cutting administrative costs and avoid unnecessary simplification. In relation to the inclusion of non-economic factors, the key question in undertaking the analysis will be whether a given issue is reliably and efficiently quantifiable. If not, such factors should only be included from a qualitative perspective, if at all. Inclusions will obviously be determined on a case-by-case and ICLR project basis.

Policy analysts undertaking EA have been specifically criticised for failing to calculate the monetary impacts of regulatory reform, and for not placing initial proposals under sufficient scrutiny.[47] Many EAs simply include a quantitative examination of the expected costs and benefits associated with regulation, in spite of additional procedural requirements.[48] As a result, an assessment undertaken to determine if regulations should pass a qualitative test may be subject to an undue degree of rationalisation.[49] Conversely, if the EA is not required to include a cost–benefit analysis and principles under which it is formulated are too general, the EA may become subject to manipulation and may simply be put together to justify a predetermined position, rather than to facilitate the rigorous exploration of possible alternatives.[50]

Further, a propensity among officials to perform insufficient analysis of the economic costs and benefits of regulatory proposals has been consistently identified by research on the effectiveness of EA.[51] This may indicate that officials have not been suitably

[43] Gabriel (n 35) 245.

[44] OECD and ISO, 'International Regulatory Co-operation and International Organisations: The Case of the International Organization for Standardization (ISO)' (2016) 57–58.

[45] ibid 59.

[46] ibid 61.

[47] Coates, 'Cost–Benefit Analysis of Financial Regulation' (2015) 1011; OECD (n 21) 17.

[48] ibid.

[49] ibid.

[50] OECD (n 21) 17; HM Treasury (n 10); Johns and Saltane (n 2).

[51] OECD (n 21) 17; RW Hahn and PC Tetlock, 'Has Economic Analysis Improved Regulatory Decisions?' (2008) 22 *Journal of Economic Perspectives* 67, 71; RW Hahn and PM Dudley, 'How Well Does the

trained in cost–benefit analysis, or it may suggest there is an underlying belief that the analysis will not result in any material change in regulatory policy.[52]

The big challenge therefore is in ensuring that EA is incorporated in the culture of policy making and that decision-makers see the benefits of the analytical approach of EA.[53] This is what Weiner describes as 'embodying serious analysis of the full variety of impacts and trade-offs, some quantitative and some qualitative, with compassion for those who incur risks and those who incur abatement costs'.[54] Weiner contrasts this to what he terms a 'cold' analysis, which would alternatively focus solely on monetised benefits and costs to determine policy outcomes.[55]

Notably, a growing number of oversight bodies are now assessing data regarding how many initial regulatory proposals have improved as a result of EA, including the projected marginal increase in anticipated benefits. This data supports the hypothesis that the EA process is a reliable screener of weak regulatory proposals and encourages analytical rigour.[56] However, this type of empirical data is in short supply and is challenging to aggregate across nations. Nonetheless, there is likely to be improved information about the quantifiable benefits of EA as its scope is expanded moving into the future.

The following section deals with the important question of how to structure the EA process in order to ensure that any assessment is as independent and free from political influence as possible.

C. A Two-stage EA Process should be Implemented Requiring Expert Oversight

It is proposed that a two-stage EA process should be implemented, requiring *ex-ante* and ex-post review of regulation which will better align agent incentives with the purposes of EA. In this manner, both analysts and decision-makers will know that implementation results will be reviewed.

The ideal timing for conducting an EA is at the start of a project, that is, on an *ex-ante* basis.[57] To implement a robust procedure at this stage, rigorous empirical and analytical processes must be in place, and the provision of information must occur in a timely manner in order to effect regulatory decisions *ex ante*.[58] Further, it is desirable for this initial assessment to be revisited at the time nations are deciding whether to ratify

US Government Do Benefit–Cost Analysis?' (2007) *1 Review of Environmental Economics and Policy* 192; A Sinden, 'The Problem of Unquantified Benefits' (2018) Temple University Legal Studies Research Paper No 2018-09.

[52] ibid. That is, insufficient analysis of costs and benefits may occur because of a lack of available data, or a lack of technical knowledge on the part of those conducting the analysis.

[53] ibid.

[54] JB Weiner, 'Better Regulation in Europe' (2006) 59 *Current Legal Problems* 483–84.

[55] ibid.

[56] OECD (n 21) 18; Sinden, 'Unquantified Benefits' (2018) 28–33.

[57] Wool (n 4) 635.

[58] OECD (n 21) 12–13.

any resulting instrument.[59] Lastly, it is important to review the actual achievement of EB on an ex-post basis, that is, after the implementation process has occurred.

For those undertaking the EA, it is important to be aware of potential challenges which may be faced at each of these stages regarding: the availability of data, the ability to undertake accurate empirical modelling, the ability to prove the existence of any causal relationships, and the need to make numerous assumptions, particularly on an *ex-ante* basis.[60]

From a practical perspective, a number of OECD countries have already adopted the recommended approach of a two-stage EA process.[61] This involves undertaking a preliminary assessment of policy proposals in the first stage of the process, prior to conducting a full assessment in the second stage.[62] This is particularly useful when only limited data is available at the inception of the regulatory proposal. In this way, the second stage acts as a review of the first stage evaluation, inclusive of more complete information.

The data shows that most OECD countries include information on both costs and benefits in their assessments, but only 10 countries currently require regulators to demonstrate that the benefits outweigh the identified costs.[63] One reason why *net* benefits are not systematically calculated is because costs and benefits are often qualitatively as opposed to quantitatively assessed.[64] As such, from a structural, systematic perspective, a regulatory management system can ensure that EA includes evidence-based *ex-ante* and ex-post evaluations as a matter of course.[65] Benefits should be clearly communicated and regulations reviewed periodically to eliminate or replace those which are inefficient.[66]

While it is common for there to be challenges regarding the quality and timeliness of EA, it should be viewed as a fundamental element of improving regulatory reform. Likewise, ex-post EA should be integrated into the policy process, and support must be provided to the agencies, departments and staff members responsible for the EA, in order to improve the evidence basis for regulation and ongoing reform.[67] While more data will be available post implementation, assumptions and confidence levels will necessarily be included in the initial analysis.

The ex-post EA must be systematically undertaken and compared with *ex-ante* stated objectives and the principles of better regulation.[68] Ex-post EA must be built into the system through automatic regulatory review procedures, such as the inclusion of sun-setting clauses.[69] There should additionally be centralised and independent expert

[59] ibid.

[60] Wool (n 4) 637–38. The magnitude of such challenges will be dependent upon whether the particular form of EA employed proceeds from a priori or a posteriori reasoning.

[61] OECD (n 21) 18.

[62] ibid.

[63] Malyshev, 'Regulatory Impact Assessment' (2017).

[64] ibid.

[65] OECD (n 6) Annex, 6.

[66] OECD (n 6) Annex, 6; OECD, 'Guiding Principles' (n 6) 3.

[67] ibid; Johns and Saltane (n 2).

[68] OECD, 'Guiding Principles' (n 6) 4.

[69] ibid.

oversight of the EA process. In this manner, assessments will be reviewed by an objective party with technical expertise, and results will more likely carry greater weight in influencing national governments and reducing political risk.

Likewise, expert EA oversight should be strengthened. While an independent government body is responsible for EA oversight in 26 OECD countries, the oversight body is only empowered to send back inadequate EAs in 19 countries.[70] Additionally, most oversight bodies are currently not external from government, which needs to change in order to increase the effectiveness of the process.[71] Independent central expert oversight should be implemented across countries, with the expert oversight body possessing the power to send back inadequate EAs. In this manner, EAs can be reviewed on the merits of the quantitative assessment and assumptions, which will mitigate political influence.

Currently, it is uncommon to observe requirements to publish full EA documents.[72] This, combined with a lack of central oversight, undermines the effectiveness of the process. As stated above, it is important for EA documents to be made publicly available so that the quantitative analysis and data assumptions are both replicable and challengeable. A further requirement is for the data sources to be publicly accessible, which will facilitate the review function.

The independent expert oversight function should include: quality control and review of the EA; the return of inadequate EAs for recalculation; the facilitation of systematic and effective regulatory solutions; actively managing ex-post evaluation for policy revision and continuous improvement of ex-ante methods; and the provision of EA education and training.[73] Lastly, the performance of the expert oversight body, including the quality control and review functions, should be periodically assessed by independent analysts.[74] Further, continuous process improvement should be sought, as discussed in the following section.

D. The Ex-post Evaluation should Involve a Clear Feedback Loop

The final proposed guideline is that the ex-post evaluation should not merely be window dressing but must involve a clear feedback loop (see Figure 5.2) which can inform future EAs. The use of a feedback loop should result in the timely provision of information which can drive policy revisions. Further, EA process data and results should be utilised to reduce political risk wherever possible.

Countries with the most widespread experience in conducting EAs concede that there are only a small percentage of EAs which successfully calculate benefits and costs, and create a robust net present value.[75] The availability of measurable data on the

[70] Malyshev (n 10).
[71] ibid.
[72] ibid; Johns and Saltane (n 2).
[73] OECD (n 6) 9.
[74] ibid 9, 13.
[75] OECD (n 21) 35.

degree to which EA ultimately succeed in evaluating benefits and costs is limited.[76] One example of this is the US EPA, which revealed in reported data that approximately 39 per cent of EA prepared by this agency between 1996 and 1999 resulted in a net benefit figure.[77] It should be noted that this signified a sizable improvement on figures provided in earlier periods.[78] Another analysis undertaken in Australia in 2001 identified that 29 per cent of EAs fully computed costs.[79] A separate analysis undertaken in the state of Victoria, Australia more recently revealed an improvement in the volume of EAs measuring costs from 17 per cent to 50 per cent within a 12-month period.[80]

Nonetheless, the ability to truly measure the costs and benefits will likely continue to be impaired by the limits of available data within required timeframes, a lack of resources, and the education of analysts undertaking EA, among other factors.[81] There is certainly a trade-off in terms of accuracy and timeliness of analysis *ex ante*. Those conducting the EA must balance interests, meet time requirements for policy decisions, and balance availability of data with advanced modelling techniques.[82] While appropriate advanced methodologies, increased computing power and software packages, and data parameters are all of benefit to accuracy, these trade-offs must be understood by decision-makers.[83]

Further, economists acknowledge that modern regulatory policy is far too complex for a simple set of guidelines to achieve optimal EA.[84] Lawyers must work with economists to understand possible linkages and indirect effects of regulation; trade-offs and substitution impacts *ex ante*; and the effects of resource constraints.[85] Advanced modelling techniques then allow economists to explore EA results, understand which key parameters and/or data drive results, and how changes in these key assumptions change the overall EA.[86]

If an independent agency is responsible for carrying out the EA, it must be ensured that sufficient capability exists and quality is maintained.[87] If this occurs, benefits are likely to arise regarding the independence of the assessment. This is in contrast to situations in which government agencies may be responsible for both drafting and assessing regulations. Here, the challenge will be to maintain independence during the EA process. In the case of international agencies, regulatory cooperation is paramount, given the complexity and proliferation of transnational regulation.[88]

By necessity the EA process is well suited to the evaluation of current regulation as well as to the examination of new regulatory proposals *ex ante*.[89] There is little doubt

[76] ibid.
[77] ibid.
[78] ibid.
[79] R Deighton-Smith, 'Regulatory Impact Assessment in Australia: A Survey of 20 Years of RIA Implementation' in Kirkpatrick and Parker (n 10); OECD (n 21) 35.
[80] ibid.
[81] OECD (n 21), 35; Johns and Saltane (n 2).
[82] Roland-Holst and Evans, 'An Introduction to General Equilibrium Policy Modeling' (2015).
[83] ibid.
[84] ibid.
[85] ibid; HM Treasury (n 10).
[86] ibid.
[87] This has been difficult to achieve in financial regulation. cf R Bubb, 'The OIRA Model for Institutionalizing CBA of Financial Regulation' (2015) 78 *Law and Contemporary Problems* 47; Revesz (n 22) 545.
[88] OECD (n 18).
[89] ibid 47.

that EA outcomes are more likely to be accurate when applied to current regulation, given that the implementation procedure leads to the generation of a sizable amount of new data for use in the assessment, which was not available prior to enactment (Figure 5.2).[90]

Figure 5.2 Ex-post feedback loop

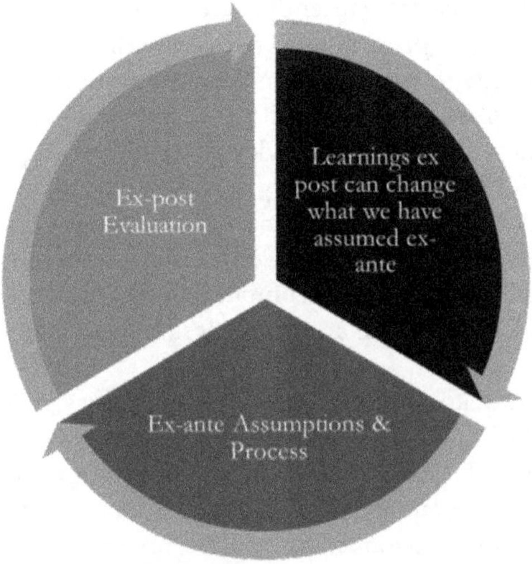

The quality of *ex-ante* EA may be improved by introducing a requirement for ex-post review of the regulatory effects. If regulators are made aware that the EA will be reviewed shortly after it has been completed, this may serve as a deterrent against any self-interested manipulation of the analysis to support the implementation of the regulation.[91]

Furthermore, ex-post review will assist in uncovering systematic errors in EA procedures and thus lead to advances in methodology over time. Achieving this, however, requires the results of ex-post reviews to be methodically evaluated, and any conclusions incorporated into subsequent EA process improvement.[92] As stated, this may be achieved through the use of systematic review periods and sunset clauses. For example, in the case of ISO, a maximum period is set before systematic review must occur: in the case of an international standard this is five years, and for a technical specification the maximum period is three years.[93]

According to the OECD, as of 2006 a sizable percentage of EAs still failed to measure significant benefits and costs in quantifiable terms, which was attributable to data

[90] ibid.
[91] OECD (n 18) 53.
[92] ibid.
[93] OECD and ISO, 'The Case of the International Organization for Standardization (ISO)' (2016) 54. Here, the systematic review can result in one of the following outcomes regarding the standard: its confirmation, revision, withdrawal or conversion to another form of deliverable.

and analytical shortfalls. As a result, a variety of other methods also continue to be used on a regular basis in undertaking EA, suggesting that the practical application of the theoretical guidance was restricted due to empirical limitations.[94]

Regulatory studies and reform are largely focused on economic efficiency and rates of return; yet, at is core, the regulatory process is largely political.[95] Regulation is influenced by political forces, and does not simply involve the straightforward pursuit of social welfare aims, even if this is seldom acknowledged.[96] Indeed, as Haines has argued, the principal issue faced when regulatory reform is pursued is not of a technical or actuarial nature, but rather involves the reduction of political risk in order to achieve regulatory aims.[97] While it is often perceived that regulation is based on an identified problem to be remedied or to reduce costs, Haines submits that this is equally a political issue; and this must be understood in the context of regulatory reform efforts.[98] At the international level, regulatory reform can most effectively be analysed as a political process, even though the politics are often disguised by technical or economic reasoning.[99]

From an economic standpoint, standardisation has been associated with the occurrence of distributional conflicts.[100] Given that international standardisation involves the harmonisation of areas of law which were previously very different in practice, this means that at least some jurisdictions will incur adjustment costs.[101] Resultantly, conflicts of interest may arise over the equitable distribution of such adjustment costs, and this is posited to be the case even when new international standards are expected to lead to far greater benefits as compared with the anticipated adjustment costs which will be borne by nations.[102]

Importantly, the use of advanced EA techniques both *ex ante* and ex post will provide insight regarding who will benefit from proposed regulation and who will incur costs. This information can be used to enlist 'winners' to support the regulatory efforts and to identify 'losers' and determine how they can be compensated.[103] As such, much must be invested in the transition and implementation process, inclusive of educational initiatives and institutional involvement. The EA results must then be communicated in such a way as to mitigate political risk. That is, results and recommendations should be explained *without* the use of jargon and technical detail; and in a manner which addresses the various concerns of policy-makers.[104]

[94] OECD (n 18) 73.

[95] J Jordana and D Levi-Faur, *The Politics of Regulation: Institutions And Regulatory Reforms for the Age of Governance* (Cheltenham, Edward Elgar, 2005); T Büthe and W Mattli, *The New Global Rulers: The Privatization of Regulation in the World Economy* (Princeton NJ, Princeton University Press, 2011) 12.

[96] ibid.

[97] F Haines. *The Paradox of Regulation: What Regulation Can Achieve and What It Cannot* (Cheltenham, Edward Elgar 2011) 232.

[98] ibid; Büthe and Mattli, *The New Global Rulers* (2011) 12.

[99] ibid 12.

[100] ibid 42. The authors note that from an economic standpoint International standardisation resembles what game theorists refer to as a coordination game with distributional conflict.

[101] ibid.

[102] ibid. Given that distributional conflicts necessarily imply that international regulation generates winners and losers, Barcia further explains that 'New [international] standards can be the source of enormous wealth or the death of corporate empires. With so much at stake, standards arouse violent passions'.

[103] Roland-Holst and Evans (n 28).

[104] ibid.

In light of the above, successful EA is dependent on the level of political commitment expressed, as well as properly incentivising public officials involved in the process. Further to the latter point, another important strategy is to increase the political costs of non-compliance with EA results and ICLR instruments.[105] Additionally, transparency through public consultation and the involvement of relevant stakeholder groups is recommended.[106]

As previously stated, regulatory policy-makers require evidence about identified costs and benefits. Therefore, economic models make a lasting contribution to EA processes when the following key conditions are met (Figure 5.3 below):

(1) the EA must incorporate advanced data and methods;
(2) data should be publicly available, or made so post publication of the EA;
(3) results must be transparent; and
(4) the EA itself should be replicable.

Figure 5.3 Key conditions for the use of economic models in EA

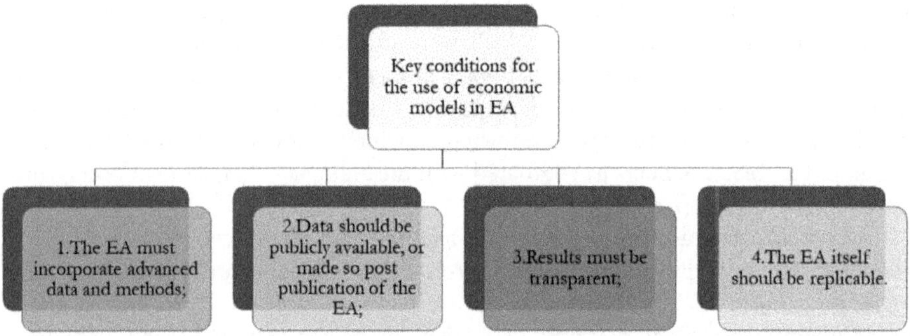

II. Conclusion

This chapter has proposed a set of best practice guidelines in five areas which are critical to conducting EA of ICLR in particular, inclusive of practical guidelines and components which are key to implementation at the international level. Taking from a disparate body of literature at both international and national levels, it attempts to distil key principles which are in line with current economic research and will support the aims of law reform and harmonisation efforts in a data-driven manner. It is hoped that the application of such principles will assist in streamlining the EA process across

[105] In this regard, signalling theory adds to the understanding of compliance incentives under international law: cf DH Moore, 'A Signaling Theory of Human Rights Compliance' (2003) 97 *Northwestern University Law Review* 879; JR Hollyer and BP Rosendorff, 'Why Do Authoritarian Regimes Sign the Convention Against Torture? Signaling, Domestic Politics and Non-Compliance' (2011) 6 *Quarterly Journal of Political Science* 275.

[106] Johns and Saltane (n 2); Malyshev (n 10).

international organisations, while being of comparative use to governmental and non-governmental bodies, policy-makers, and third-party stakeholders. Public availability, transparency and replicability are key components of any such assessment. This will ensure that EA results will be comparable, and consultation will be both constructive and backed by data. Systematic quantification and transparency will allow for the curtailment of political influence of decision-making processes, as much as this is possible. In this way, EA processes will be streamlined, which will allow for better law-making at the international level, implementation at the country level, and evidence-based moves towards harmonisation.

PART III

The Challenge of the Digital Economy

6

Cyberspace Institutions, Community and Legitimate Authority

CHRIS REED

To its users, cyberspace appears to be almost completely harmonised. Online services such as Facebook, Google and eBay have a near identical appearance no matter where in the world the user is located, and seem to work identically too. Geography and nationality are apparently irrelevant.

Under the surface, though, there is a mass of diverging law and regulation which these services need to cope with in order to achieve their apparent universality. Some of these legal and regulatory differences reflect fundamental societal choices which cannot easily be harmonised, if at all.[1] But many of the differences are just contingent accidents of history. Ideally, they would be harmonised if that were possible.

Harmonisation[2] usually requires positive collective action to achieve. Admittedly the arrival of cyberspace has sometimes led to convergence of national law and regulation without such collective action. Probably the best-known example is the law on electronic signatures which, following an initial burst of legislative activity, rapidly coalesced around a two-tier model of electronic signatures which has become almost universal. But this convergence was only possible because electronic signatures were a previously unknown phenomenon, and thus no legal system already had an entrenched view about what should be the proper law and system of regulation. This allowed law-makers to abandon false starts and copy better solutions from elsewhere once these became known. But even here, the coordination work undertaken by UNCITRAL in producing model laws was highly influential, and the convergence might not have happened without it.

Further useful harmonisation of laws affecting cyberspace will usually require the adaptation of existing systems of law and regulation, rather than devising completely new laws. Most of the easy wins have now been achieved. So, if further harmonisation

[1] Perhaps the clearest example is the wide divergence of national attitudes to freedom of speech, illustrated in the series of cases involving Yahoo! and France's anti-Nazi laws – see *Yahoo! Inc v LICRA* TGI de Paris, 22 May 2000, 20 November 2000; *Yahoo! Inc v La Ligue Contre Le Racisme Et L'Antisemitisme*, 169 F Supp 2d 1181 (ND Cal, 2001), 379 F 3d 1120 (9th Cir 2004).

[2] Used here to cover both harmonisation and approximation of laws.

is to take place, positive collective action will be necessary. The question this chapter examines is a simple one: are the world's existing transnational institutions capable of undertaking this work and, if not, what kinds of institution will we need for the purpose?

I. The Authority of Current Institutions

A. Sources of Authority

Authority is a claim that some person should obey a rule, or at least conform his or her behaviour to the precepts of the person making the claim. The main difficulty facing our existing transnational institutions when trying to achieve harmonisation is that their authority claims are generally very weak.

Authority is traditionally conceptualised in terms of the nation state. The state has constitutional authority to make obedience claims because its constitution derives from the consent, or at least acquiescence, of its citizens. Additionally, the state has effective authority[3] because it has enforcement powers against those resident in its territory. Each state claims unlimited authority to regulate those activities which fall within the scope of its constitutional authority.[4]

Few transnational institutions have authority of this kind.[5] The EU might be seen as one, but its constitutional authority is limited to a geographical region, rather than claiming global law-making authority.[6] A global example might be the World Trade Organisation (WTO) which derives constitutional authority from the WTO Treaty, and also has some enforcement powers through the WTO tribunal.[7] The World Intellectual Property Organisation (WIPO) might also be seen as having constitutional authority, through the WIPO Treaty, though it has no direct enforcement powers against a state which refuses to modify its intellectual property laws in accordance with the Treaty. In both cases, the authority only requires compliance by states, and not by individuals.

It is, perhaps, worthy of note that although WIPO has achieved formal harmonisation of copyright law as it applies to cyberspace, by introducing a right of communication to the public,[8] this harmonisation has not been successful in persuading the majority of cyberspace users to comply with the law. One might suspect that the combined constitutional authority of WIPO and the states whose law follows the Treaty is inadequate for this purpose, and I will return later to the reasons why this might be so.

[3] J Raz, *The Authority of Law*, 2nd edn (Oxford, Oxford University Press, 2009) 5.

[4] ibid 119, and see text to n 27.

[5] Note, though, Linarelli's argument that the collective body of transnational law for each area of commercial activity has sufficient authority to amount to an independent legal system. See J Linarelli, 'Analytical Jurisprudence and the Concept of Commercial Law' (2009) 114 *Penn State Law Review* 119.

[6] In the field of data protection the EU asserts global authority over personal data processing involving EU citizens or residents – see eg Article 29 Working Party, Guidelines on the implementation of the Court of Justice of the EU judgment on 'Google Spain and inc v Agencia Española de Protección de Datos (AEPD) and Mario Costeja González' C-131/12 (14/EN WP 225, 26 November 2014) – but it does not claim authority to regulate processing where there is no connection to its constitutionally established geographical region.

[7] JP Trachtman, 'The Domain of WTO Dispute Resolution' (1999) 40 *Harvard International Law Journal* 333, 338–39.

[8] WIPO Copyright Treaty, Art 8.

Other international institutions, such as UNCITRAL, OECD or ICC, do not even have constitutions which impose compliance obligations on those to whom their authority claims are addressed. These institutions have a different kind of authority, known as charismatic authority. Charismatic authority derives from the acceptance of a person or group as leader, which thus legitimates the authority claim to obedience through the affectual or emotional effects which arise from such acceptance.[9] Unless this authority is institutionalised[10] through law-making and enforcement mechanisms, by means of a constitution of some kind, such institutions can therefore only attempt to persuade others, in our instance most commonly states, to adopt the harmonisation models they propose. How persuasive they are depends on both the respect in which those who crafted the proposal are held, and also on the quality and workability of the proposal as a mechanism for achieving harmonisation.

B. Success or Failure?

Where transnational institutions have used their charismatic authority to persuade states to remove barriers to online activity, they have in general been successful. The best-known example is probably the work of UNCITRAL. The majority of states worldwide has taken inspiration from the Model Law on Electronic Commerce, and has modified (when necessary) its contract law to enable online transactions to take place. The Model Law on Electronic Signatures sets out the fundamental principles which should be applied to decide whether a particular form of online authentication should be treated as a valid electronic signature, and these are reflected in instruments such as the US E-Sign Act 2000[11] and the EU eIDAS Regulation.[12]

However, these institutions have not been well-equipped to deal with those areas of online activity which have allowed cyberspace users to engage in socially undesirable behaviours. Charismatic authority seems to be sufficient to persuade states to harmonise by removing legal barriers to desirable activities. But because constraining undesirable activities requires enforcement action against those who do not comply voluntarily, transnational institutions have largely left harmonisation efforts as matters for the state level. And state attempts to regulate (for example) the unauthorised online dissemination of copyright works, or infringements of digital privacy, or online defamation, have almost uniformly been unsuccessful in achieving their aims.[13]

An important reason for these failures is that there is a deficit in the legitimacy of authority. There is no global transnational institution which focuses primarily on

[9] M Weber, *Economy and Society: An Outline of Interpretive Sociology* (Berkley, University of California Press, 1968) 1139ff.

[10] See ME Spencer, 'Weber on Legitimate Norms and Authority' (1970) 21 *British Journal of Sociology* 123, 124–25.

[11] 15 USC §96.

[12] Regulation 910/2014 on electronic identification and trust services for electronic transactions in the internal market and repealing Directive 1999/93/EC, OJ L 257 28 August 2014, 73–114.

[13] See eg MI Franklin, 'Digital Dilemmas: Transnational Politics in the Twenty-First Century' (2010) 16 *Brown Journal of World Affairs* 67, 69; T Hartley, '"Libel Tourism" and Conflict of Laws' (2010) 59 *International & Comparative Law Quarterly* 25. Copyright is explored further below.

online defamation or data privacy[14] and might therefore claim charismatic authority to shape regulation in either field. Even if there were such an institution its authority claims would normally be addressed to states, not individuals.[15] States have a legitimate authority claim to regulate the activity of those who are physically present in their territory, but because cyberspace transcends national territories then in practice those claims are also addressed to cyberspace users who are located elsewhere. To these users the legitimate authority of state claims is at best doubtful.[16]

The difficulties which copyright law has faced in regulating cyberspace activities illustrate clearly why there is a legitimacy deficit. Copyright laws are shaped through the WIPO Treaty, and WIPO has constitutional authority by virtue of that Treaty. WIPO's authority claims are addressed to states, who implement treaty changes in their national law, and these states have constitutional authority and also effective authority because of their enforcement powers. How can a deficit of legitimate authority have arisen?

The fact that there is such a deficit is without doubt, simply because of the widespread unauthorised use of copyright works which occurs throughout cyberspace.[17] It is now an established norm among cyberspace users that sharing content, at least if the sharing is not for profit, is generally acceptable. Cotterrell suggests that:

> It might be tempting, then, to think of authority as something primarily *claimed* in support of power by its holders, and legitimacy as something primarily *conferred* on power by those subject to it or who observe it; that is to say, legitimacy indicates an acceptance of the claim of authority as successfully made.[18]

Clearly, the vast mass of cyberspace users does not accept the legitimacy of the WIPO copyright treaty, or its implementations in national law.

If a law has a legitimate claim to authority, it is likely to be obeyed because of the social norm that we should all act lawfully.[19] But the empirical work of Tyler has shown that copyright law lies outside this social norm: 'one crucial problem is the lack of a public feeling that breaking intellectual property laws is wrong. In the absence of such a conception, there is little reason for people to follow intellectual property laws'.[20] Partly this is because some aspects of copyright in the digital world are perceived

[14] It is, though, arguable that the EU's Article 29 Working Party has achieved a high degree of charismatic authority in the field of data protection, such that its recommendations often (though not always) set the shape of law and regulation in other countries. I am grateful to my colleague Professor Christopher Millard for this insight.

[15] And further, because regulation would be seeking compliance from individuals, the institution's lack of enforcement powers would weaken the effective authority of such claims.

[16] For detailed analysis of why this might be so see C Reed and A Murray, *Rethinking the Jurisprudence of Cyberspace* (Cheltenham, Edward Elgar, 2018).

[17] See C Reed, *Making Laws for Cyberspace* (Oxford, Oxford University Press, 2012) ch 1.

[18] R Cotterrell, 'Legal Authority in a Transnational World/ Autotytet prawa w świecie transnarodym', The Leon Petrazycki Lecture, University of Warsaw, 22 May 2014 (Warsaw, University of Warsaw Faculty of Law and Administration, 2014) 43.

[19] HLA Hart in *The Concept of Law*, 2nd edn (Oxford, Oxford University Press, 1994) accepts as foundational that obedience to the law is dependent on general acceptance of the social norm that it should be obeyed (112–18), although his primary distinction is between norms which are obeyed only because of social pressure, and law, whose norms obeyed because they emanate from official lawmaking sources.

[20] TR Tyler, 'Compliance with Intellectual Property Laws: A Psychological Perspective' (1997) 29 *New York University Journal of International Law and Politics* 219, 226.

as unfair; for example, there is a strong belief that content should have to be paid for only once.[21] Mainly, though, even ordinary citizens (and cyberspace users even more so) do not accept that intellectual property laws have legitimate authority to direct their lives.

Jensen has demonstrated[22] that the law of copyright was developed mainly in order to regulate relations between those involved in the exploitation of creative works, to a lesser extent to regulate relationships with creators, and hardly at all in relation to the use of works by the general public. Because the law was not developed for 'ordinary' people, they do not perceive it as imposing meaningful obligations on them:

> Voluntary compliance with intellectual property laws in general and copyright laws in particular suffer from a perceived lack of procedural fairness and public mistrust. The process of drafting copyright legislation often amounts to little more than negotiations among narrow interest groups; without a seat at the bargaining table, the public has no meaningful opportunity to participate in the legislative process. This process fosters the (often accurate) perception that copyright law is designed by and for the benefit of a small circle of vested interests. This widespread sense of unfairness – that copyright protections exist for the benefit of Microsoft and Disney – undermines voluntary compliance with copyright law.[23]

If copyright is not addressed to the ordinary citizen, it is hardly surprising that the citizen does not consider that it makes any legitimate claims on him or her.[24]

If we are looking for further harmonisation in cyberspace, it seems clear that it is unlikely to come from our existing transnational institutions. New institutions will be needed, and they will need to possess a high level of legitimate authority, such that their laws and regulations are likely to be obeyed voluntarily by cyberspace users. Reliance on state law enforcement mechanisms is largely ineffective, as the case of copyright law shows. All cyberspace users are foreign residents, except for their home state, and their only connection with the national territory of any other state which claims authority over them is merely a consequence of the user's activities in cyberspace. They will be reluctant to accept the authority claims of a foreign state, because there is no relationship of state and citizen or resident, and the foreign state is likely to have limited enforcement powers over the user and thus little effective authority. Even worse, when multiple states claim authority over the same activity, cyberspace users will inevitably ask which, if any, of those laws ought to be obeyed; or, to put it in jurisprudential terms, whether those law-makers have any authority at all to claim obedience to their laws.

[21] ibid 228.

[22] C Jensen, 'The More Things Change, the More They Stay the Same: copyright, digital technology, and social norms' (2003) 56 *Stanford Law Review* 531.

[23] ibid 540. The story of the negotiation of the US Digital Millennium Copyright Act 1998, 17 USC §512(g), illustrates clearly how little part the interests of content users played in its enactment – see J Litman, *Digital Copyright* (Amherst NY, Prometheus Books, 2001).

[24] See Jensen, 'The More Things Change' (2003) 543: 'groups such as authors and publishers formed relatively small communities of repeat players. As such, they knew the rules of the game and knew that, as repeat players, following the rules in one transaction would affect their success in future interactions with other players. In this context, constructing a widely embraced normative justification for copyright law was unnecessary to ensure that the commercially significant players obeyed the law. Under any circumstances, the game went on outside the view of the ordinary consumer of copyrighted works, who remained unsocialized in any "copyright culture" that developed among those involved in the business of making and selling copyrighted works.'

We therefore need to understand where legitimate authority comes from in cyberspace, so that we can understand how a transnational institution could achieve voluntary compliance, and this may tell us what kinds of institutions we need to develop.

II. Legitimate Authority in Cyberspace

A. The Distinction between Legitimacy and Authority

It is important to begin by recognising that although legitimacy and authority are closely connected, they are nonetheless conceptually separate. Cotterrell recognises this separation when, as we saw earlier, he proposes that authority is a claim by power, whilst legitimacy is the acceptance of that claim.[25] This might be an accurate description of the relationship in the physical world,[26] but I would suggest that in cyberspace things work differently. This is because authority and legitimacy in the physical world can be, and usually are, assessed at the systemic level. The question is whether this particular institution's or legal system's overall claim to authority should be accepted, on the basis that membership of the system requires either that all the rules of the system should be obeyed, or that none need to be. Raz describes this as 'comprehensive' authority and argues that legal systems: 'claim authority to regulate any type of behaviour … They do not acknowledge any limitation of the spheres of behaviour which they claim authority to regulate'.[27] In Raz's terms authority is an all-or-nothing proposition – either *all* the system's laws have authority, or *none* of them do.

But this can only hold true for members of the rule system.[28] No state claims comprehensive authority over the residents of other states. So far as outsiders are concerned, authority claims are only made in respect of specific rules, and only when the outsider's activity brings him or her within the ambit of the rule, for example when the activity has effects within the territory of a nation state. The majority of cyberspace users are outsiders[29] to any particular rule system, and this tells us that we need to consider the question of authority at the level of each individual authority claim, rather than assessing the authority of the rule system as a whole. It also means that we have to determine the answer afresh for each cyberspace user, because an authority claim is only made if the user's activities fall within the ambit of the rule and also because merely falling within that ambit does not itself legitimate the authority claim.

[25] See text to n 18.

[26] Though I have doubts whether legitimacy is demonstrated simply by the fact of acceptance of authority. Hart's gunman (see Hart, *The Concept of Law* (1994) 19–23) is obeyed, but only through fear and not because there is any normative obligation to do so. His claim to obedience is surely illegitimate, and if the fear is removed by the gunman being disarmed there is no reason why anyone should even considering following his orders.

[27] Raz, *The Authority of Law* (2009) 116–17.

[28] I adopt this term to avoid needing to discuss how far 'law' is limited to rules issued by a nation state, and where the boundaries lie between law and regulation, and between 'hard' and 'soft' law.

[29] Or at the least, are likely to consider themselves to be outsiders. As we are focusing on voluntary compliance, recognising that rule enforcement in cyberspace is inevitably problematic, it is the internal understanding of actors which is the most important factor, rather than whether the rules of public and private international law hold them to be subject to the rule system.

An assessment of legitimate authority is thus a three-stage process. First, we must examine the authority claim to see if it is made against the particular cyberspace user. This requires us to evaluate the meaning of the rule and, also, if the claim is made by a national legal system, to decide if that system's rules of public and private international law make the rule applicable to that user.

Second, we must decide if the claim is legitimate.[30] Addressees of an authority claim are, of course, entitled to ignore an illegitimate claim. But if the claim is legitimate, this does not itself determine whether the claim has authority. Cyberspace users are faced with a multitude of legitimate authority claims, and because they cannot comply with them all they are forced to choose between them. Authority claims which are routinely ignored cannot, with any accuracy, be said to have any actual authority. Thus legitimacy determines whether the user is under a normative obligation to consider the authority claim; it is what gets the claim a hearing.

Finally, we need to decide if the claim is accepted by a sufficiently large number[31] of those cyberspace users to whom it applies. To have authority a law-maker needs a legitimating community,[32] and that community confirms the legitimacy of the claim by accepting it, and thus granting the law-maker authority.

B. Achieving Institutional Legitimacy

An institution might assert, with reference to its constitution, that its authority claims are legitimate. But this does not tell us whether legitimacy has in fact been achieved.[33] Instead, we must recognise that legitimate authority is a political rather than a legal construct, and a matter of fact which can only be determined by observing the behaviour of those to whom its claims are addressed: 'An institution is legitimate in the sociological sense when it is widely believed to have the right to rule.'[34] This tells us that it is necessary to identify the group to which those claims are directed, which will thus constitute the institution's legitimating community.

It is difficult to envisage a transnational institution which could realistically claim that the entire group of cyberspace users constituted its legitimating community.

[30] In cyberspace, the legitimacy of a law's authority claim cannot be assessed purely by reference to the constitution of the state making that claim, but additionally needs to achieve legitimacy in the eyes of those to whom it is addressed through the fairness, justice and appropriateness of the claims it makes –Reed and Murray, *Jurisprudence of Cyberspace* (2018) ch 7.

[31] It is worth noting that in some fields of cyberspace activity there may be a small number of cyberspace actors who effectively set the standards for the other players in that arena, or perhaps even only one, and acceptance by that group or single entity might be sufficient to establish authority and legitimacy. Amazon, Facebook and Google are obvious candidates. Again, my thanks are due to Professor Christopher Millard. This issue is explored further in A Murray, 'Nodes and Gravity in Virtual Space' (2011) 5 *Legisprudence* 195.

[32] See CA Thomas, 'The Uses and Abuses of Legitimacy in International Law' (2014) 34 *Oxford Journal of Legal Studies* 729, 747–49.

[33] See N Luhmann, *Law as a Social System* (trans KA Ziegart) (Oxford, Oxford University Press, 2008) 407ff, discussing the paradox that the legality of a constitution can only be determined by the institutions established by that constitution, which therefore have to presuppose the constitution's legality in order to give themselves power to decide the question.

[34] A Buchanan and RO Keohane, 'The Legitimacy of Global Governance Institutions' (2006) 20 *Ethics & International Affairs* 405.

But we can easily find cyberspace institutions whose communities consist of identifiable subsets of the actors in cyberspace. Three examples of such institutions are examined in section III.

A cyberspace institution is likely to have at least some degree of constitutional authority to make rules and regulations for its community. However, that authority is likely to be weaker than in the case of physical world institutions, because of the more remote and impersonal nature of relationships in cyberspace. This suggests that cyberspace institutions will need to achieve a high level of charismatic authority, in addition to their constitutional authority. Charismatic authority would also assist intermediary service providers who wish to persuade their own user communities to comply with an institution's rules.

Both constitutional and charismatic authority, but especially the latter, can be enhanced by focusing on non-constitutional normative sources of legitimacy. These are what Paiement describes as the input, throughput and output aspects of law-making.[35] Input legitimacy concentrates on the participatory nature and inclusiveness of the norm-creation process, while throughput legitimacy examines the rule-making processes for procedural fairness and impartiality. Both of these are likely to be visible only to involved members of the institution's legitimating community, and so will mainly work to enhance constitutional legitimacy.

Output legitimacy is based on the quality of the rules themselves, particularly in terms of achieving their desired outcomes. This is something which is visible to all those who become aware of an institution's rules, not merely to involved members of its community, and is therefore a very strong component of that institution's charismatic authority.

One important element of output legitimacy is the status of the institution as a credible rule-maker. This is something which the institution itself, or the community which establishes it, can control through the development of its constitution and the selection of its members. But, so far as individual cyberspace users are concerned, this is perhaps the least visible element of output legitimacy.

Far more important is the manner in which the institution makes its authority claim, and also the normative content of the claim. Unlike the physical world where a resident must either accept all the claims of a state's law system or deny them all,[36] in cyberspace the addressee can choose to accept only some of those claims and reject others.

What, then, will influence a cyberspace user's decision to accept the legitimacy of a law's authority claim? Three factors seem particularly important:

- the extent to which the law is perceived as being addressed to the cyberspace user, rather than to some other person;

[35] P Paiement, 'Paradox and Legitimacy in Transnational Legal Pluralism' (2013) 4 *Transnational Legal Theory* 197, 213–15.

[36] See J Finnis, *Natural Law and Natural Rights* (Oxford, Clarendon Press, 1980) 317: 'each obligation-stipulating law is a member of a system of laws which cannot be weighed or played off one against the other but which constitute a set coherently applicable to all situations and which exclude all unregulated or private picking and choosing amongst the members of the set. … either you obey the *particular* law, or you reveal yourself as lacking or defective in allegiance to the *whole* [system], as well as to the particular.'

- how far the law's provisions are congruent with the rest of the environment in which the cyberspace user acts; and
- the perceived fairness and justice of the law's claims to obedience.

There is insufficient space in this chapter to examine these in detail,[37] but a single example of a spectacular failure of output legitimacy might serve to illustrate the pitfalls of ignoring these factors.

In 2003 the UK Financial Services Authority (FSA), the then financial regulator, attempted to impose the requirements of the e-Money Directive 2000[38] on mobile telephony companies.[39] Under the Directive issuers of e-money were prohibited from engaging in non-financial service activities, which of course includes providing telephony services.[40] At that time mobile telephony companies were starting to allow pre-pay customers to make payments using the unspent float on their accounts. The FSA interpreted this as issuing e-money and sent letters to those companies requiring them to obtain authorisation as e-money issuers.

These letters highlighted the first problem of legitimacy. The mobile telephony companies did not dispute that the EU could legitimately regulate e-money, or that the FSA had constitutional legitimacy to seek compliance with financial regulation. But the e-Money Directive appeared to be addressed to new market entrants, who intended their main business to be the provision of a new kind of payment mechanism, and not to established businesses in other fields who were offering a payment service as a sideline to their main activities. Because it was not apparently directed to telephony companies, they perceived the claim that it should regulate their activities as unwarranted.

The second problem of legitimacy arose because the prohibition on non-financial services activities placed the companies in an impossible dilemma. If they complied with the FSA demand and registered as e-money issuers they would be prohibited from continuing to offer telephony services and would thus be in breach of their telecommunications licence terms as well as being forced out of business. If they continued to offer telephony services, they could not seek authorisation as e-money issuers. They thus denied that the FSA had any legitimate claim to apply the Directive to them, because it required behaviour which was practically impossible for them.

There followed a period of negotiation between the FSA, in which the companies proposed various solutions which would have enabled them to comply with the Directive while still carrying on business in telephony, but the FSA refused to consider any solution other than registration as e-money issuers or ceasing to offer payment services. The companies considered this application of the law to be illegitimate because they saw it as producing unfair and unjust results, the third legitimacy deficit. So they responded in a commercially realistic way by defying the FSA and refusing to register, thus denying the legitimate authority of the Directive and the FSA's interpretation of

[37] See further Reed and Murray (n 16) ch 7.

[38] Directive 2000/46/EC of the European Parliament and of the Council on the taking up, pursuit of and prudential supervision of the business of electronic money institutions, OJ L 275/39, 27 October 2000 ('e-Money Directive 2000').

[39] UK FSA, Electronic Money: perimeter guidance (February 2003).

[40] e-Money Directive 2000, Art 1(5).

it. Rather than force the issue, the FSA backed down and left the matter to be resolved as part of a then forthcoming review of payment services regulation at EU level, which eventually abandoned the prohibition on undertaking non-financial activities.[41]

The story is instructive because it shows that mere constitutional legitimacy, which was never in doubt, is not necessarily sufficient to achieve voluntary compliance with rules, even within a nation state's legal and regulatory system. It should be clear from this narrative how much less effective mere constitutional legitimacy will be in cyberspace, where institutions are likely to lack enforcement powers or experience real practical difficulties in exercising them.

III. New Kinds of Institutions?

Most of our current institutions derive their legitimacy from nation states; in other words, their legitimating community is made up of states rather than individuals. This makes them ill-suited to regulate many cyberspace activities because, so far as achieving compliance by individual cyberspace users are concerned, they have to rely on national law implementation of their rules. Unless all (or at least most) states agree to implement those rules the cyberspace user is faced with a multiplicity of differing rules about the matter, all of which have an equal claim to constitutional legitimacy and none of which can convincingly assert that they should be obeyed in preference to their rivals.[42] And the areas of law where harmonisation would be desirable are generally those where states disagree substantially about what the rules should be.

This suggests that further harmonisation in cyberspace will need to be achieved through new kinds of institution which can regulate individual cyberspace users directly, bypassing the authority of nation states. What, ideally, might such an institution look like?

First, it will need to have a legitimating community which consists of that subset of cyberspace users to which the institution's rules are directed. The development of an institution which attempts to deal with all the harmonisation issues in cyberspace is unlikely because its legitimating community would consist of almost every person in

[41] Directive 2009/110/EC of the European Parliament and of the Council of 16 September 2009 on the taking up, pursuit and prudential supervision of the business of electronic money institutions amending Directives 2005/60/EC and 2006/48/EC and repealing Directive 2000/46/EC, OJ L267/7 10 October 2009 Art 6(1)(b). In theory this Directive, together with the Payment Services Directive (Directive 2007/64/EC of the European Parliament and of the Council on payment services in the internal market amending Directives 97/7/EC, 2002/65/EC, 2005/60/EC and 2006/48/EC and repealing Directive 97/5/EC, OJ L 319/1, 5 December 2007), creates a coordinated system of regulation for non-credit institution payment services. However, the dividing line between e-money issuers and other payment service providers is by no means clear, and this opens the way to further contradiction.

[42] DR Johnson and DG Post 'Law And Borders – The Rise of Law in Cyberspace' (1996) 48 *Stanford Law Review* 1367, 1376 (emphasis added): 'Because events on the Net occur everywhere but nowhere in particular, are engaged in by online personae who are both "real" (possessing reputations, able to perform services, and deploy intellectual assets) and "intangible" (not necessarily or traceably tied to any particular person in the physical sense), and concern "things" (messages, databases, standing relationships) that are not necessarily separated from one another by any physical boundaries, *no physical jurisdiction has a more compelling claim than any other to subject these events exclusively to its laws.*'

the world. It is possible, though, to imagine an institution which attempts to regulate a single field of activity, and thus has a legitimating community which is limited to those cyberspace users who take part in that activity.[43]

Second, the institution itself will need a high degree of constitutional legitimacy. This can be achieved if the constitution is developed in partnership with members of the legitimating community and updated as the activities and needs of the community develop. This constitutional legitimacy can be enhanced by focusing on input and throughput legitimacy in the rule-making process. Community members, or their representatives, need to be involved in identifying the need for rules and devising their form.

Third, the rules produced by the institution should exhibit a high degree of output legitimacy. Achieving voluntary compliance has to be the aim, and this requires community members to be convinced about the appropriateness and fairness of the rules. Finally, there should be some mechanism for enforcing the rules against that minority of community members who refuse to comply voluntarily.

At first sight, this looks like a highly idealistic wish list. Nation states, even those with a long history of effective law-making and citizen acceptance, cannot meet all its requirements. And yet, there is already a small number of cyberspace institutions which largely does so.

A. ICANN

The Internet Corporation for Assigned Names and Numbers (ICANN) is a US not-for-profit corporation which controls the internet's addressing systems, without which the internet would simply not work. It is clearly one of the most important regulators in cyberspace.

ICANN's authority as regulator derives from the charismatic authority of John Postel, who effectively ran both the IP number addressing system and the top-level (transnational) domain name system[44] from the early 1970s until the mid-1990s. ICANN took on these functions when it was formed in 1998 and has controlled them ever since.[45]

From the moment of its formation ICANN's constitutional legitimacy was challenged.[46] Initially it was governed by a board of directors who consisted mainly of

[43] This voluntary participation in the activity is what gives normative force to the institution's rules. See Linarelli, 'Analytical Jurisprudence' (2009) 196: 'In a normative community that is not determined by state boundaries, the internal reflective attitude exists in both norm givers and norm users, towards both secondary and primary rules. … Role or identity seems to be key in understanding the practical authority of rules in normative communities not formed by political borders. For example, if a person accepts a role or identity of a merchant, then the law merchant rules relevant to that merchant grouping apply to her.'

[44] This maps human-readable names, such as bloomsburyprofessional.com, to numerical IP addresses.

[45] For a history of this period, including the attempt by the US Government to assert control over the system, see SP Sonbuchner, 'Master of Your Domain: Should the US Government Maintain Control Over the Internet's Root?' (2008) 17 *Minnesota Journal of International Law* 183, 187–97.

[46] See JP Kesan and AA Gallo, 'Pondering the Politics of Private Procedures: the case of ICANN' (2008) 4 *I/S: A Journal of Law and Policy for the Information Society* 345; SM Ryan, RA Plzak and J Curran, 'Legal and Policy Aspects of Internet Number Resources' (2008) 24 *Santa Clara Computer & High Tech Law Journal* 335.

well-known figures from the internet technical community, but successors were merely appointed by the board and there was no effective representation of the user community. Eventually ICANN recognised the need to legitimate its authority, and adopted a new constitution which represents each of its legitimating communities, primarily registries and registrars, the internet technical community and national governments. All these have representation on the board and involvement in standards-setting and rule-making.[47] In 2016 the US agreed to relinquish its residual elements of control in ICANN's governance, which is to be revised to increase ICANN's constitutional legitimacy.[48] Once this process is complete, there should be few doubts as to ICANN's legitimacy, in input and throughput terms as well as constitutionally.

But even before this work on legitimacy began, ICANN developed a rule system for dealing with disputes over the ownership of domain names. These disputes tend to arise because, although the system in theory operates on a first-come-first-served basis, in practice many of those who claim strong rights to the usage of a name (eg through registered or unregistered trademarks) find that someone else has beaten them to registration and wish to seek a remedy.

The rule system is embodied in ICANN's Uniform Domain Name Dispute Resolution Policy (UDRP).[49] These rules apply only to the top-level domains (most importantly .com, .org and .net) over which ICANN asserts its authority, but the country-level domain systems have adopted very similar principles in their own regulations. The rules of the UDRP define when a domain name should be transferred to a claimant, and disputes are decided by online arbitration, which is outsourced to a number of providers, most importantly WIPO.[50]

The UDRP is the constitution for this rule system, and registrars sign up to the ICANN rules when seeking authorisation, while registrants of domain names enter into contracts with registrars which oblige them to submit to the dispute resolution system. Similarly, complainants who wish to contest a domain name registration sign up to the rules when submitting their complaint. This creates a web of contractual obligations which demonstrates the acceptance of the constitution by all those who have agreed to take part.

The UDRP has remained unamended since it was devised in 1999, so there is no space for community participation in rule-setting. The fairness and justice of arbitration panel decisions is inevitably a matter of debate, with suggestions that decisions tend to favour trademark-holders over ordinary cyberspace users,[51] but choices made by complainants[52] suggest that these decisions have strong legitimacy, in their eyes at least.

[47] Details of the constitution and working processes can be found in the *ICANN Accountability & Transparency Frameworks and Principles* (ICANN, January 2008), available at www.icann.org/en/system/files/files/acct-trans-frameworks-principles-10jan08-en.pdf.

[48] www.icann.org/stewardship-accountability.

[49] www.icann.org/udrp/udrp-policy-24oct99.htm.

[50] WIPO decisions can be found at www.wipo.int/amc/en/domains/decisionsx/index.html.

[51] See M Geist, 'Fair.Com: An Examination of the Allegations of Systemic Unfairness in the ICANN UDRP' (2002) 27 *Brook Journal of International Law* 903; D Klerman, 'Forum Selling and Domain-Name Disputes' (2016) 48 *Loyola University Chicago Law Journal* 561.

[52] Participant choice, where such a choice is possible, has been proposed as a strong measure of the quality of a rule system – see A Schmidt, 'Radbruch in Cyberspace: about law-system quality and ICT innovation' (2009) 3 *Masaryk University Journal of Law and Technology* 195.

The system runs in parallel to national trademark law, so complainants can choose between litigation and the UDRP, but the volume of complaints submitted to the WIPO element of the system alone (over 3,000 per annum in the last three years to the end of 2018[53]) suggests that the UDRP is seen as more legitimate by a very substantial margin.

Additionally, UDRP decisions are directly enforceable. Where a decision is in favour of a complainant, the registrar of the domain name is instructed to transfer it to the complainant. Registrars comply with these instructions because they are obliged to do so by the terms of their authorisation from ICANN. In theory a recalcitrant registrar could be forced to comply or have its authorisation removed, but there are no reports of this ever happening.

It can be seen that the ICANN UDRP rule system largely meets all four elements of the legitimacy wish list. This is fortunate, because ICANN comes very close to regulating the whole community of cyberspace users within its limited sphere of activity. It is, though, a very complex institution which has taken nearly 20 years to achieve this state, and might not therefore be an ideal model for institutions which aim to regulate smaller communities.

B. eBay

The regulatory problem facing eBay was simply that national law is inadequate to resolve disputes between its buyers and sellers. Most disputes are for small sums, usually far less than the fees chargeable even in national law small claims proceedings. Where seller and buyer are in different countries, national law is even less effective. This led eBay to develop its own rule system for consumer protection, which has been copied with some additional elements by other online trading platforms such as Alibaba. Schultz suggests that this system is so much superior to national law in practice that it could be seen as a community legal system, operating outside national law.[54]

The earliest eBay users developed a set of trading norms which achieved a high level of voluntary compliance because the eBay community was so small that participants felt they knew each other. As the community of traders and buyers grew this feeling could not be sustained, and so a feedback system was introduced to give each participant a public reputation, based on the experiences and comments of their trading partners.[55] Ultimately, continued growth produced the need for a formal way of resolving disputes, and so the community's trading norms were entrenched in the eBay user terms, to which buyers and seller must sign up to become members.[56]

[53] www.wipo.int/amc/en/domains/statistics/cases.jsp.

[54] T Schultz, 'Private Legal Systems: What Cyberspace Might Teach Legal Theorists' (2007) 10 *Yale Journal of Law & Technology* 151.

[55] A useful short history of the development of norms in eBay is in J Goldsmith and T Wu, *Who Controls the Internet? Illusions of a borderless world* (New York, Oxford University Press, 2006) 130–45.

[56] For ebay.com, http://pages.ebay.com/help/policies/user-agreement.html, and for ebay.co.uk http://pages.ebay.co.uk/help/policies/user-agreement.html. All the eBay User Agreements, so far as is possible under the national laws which apply, impose the same trading obligations on sellers and buyers.

The resulting rule system is known (in English) as the 'eBay Money Back Guarantee', and is included in substantially identical wording, allowing for language differences, in the terms of the eBay sites for the US, UK, France, Germany, Ireland and Australia. It appears probable that it is drafted to achieve the same effect in all of eBay's other sites. eBay claims that its sites attract buyers from 208 countries,[57] so there is no doubt that this system is a global one.

Sellers agree to comply with the procedures which underpin the Money Back Guarantee, and buyers are promised that eBay will operate those procedures to give redress in the specified circumstances so long as the buyer purchased using one of the specified payment methods.[58]

The eBay seller's obligations under the scheme are simple:

(a) sellers must deliver the products they sell; and
(b) the products must be substantially as described by the seller.

If sellers fail to meet these obligations, eBay runs an online mechanism for mediating and determining disputes. It begins by requiring buyer and seller to communicate in an attempt to reach a mutually acceptable settlement. If a settlement cannot be agreed, eBay staff review the claims of each side and decide whether the seller was in breach. If the buyer is successful eBay arranges for a refund; if PayPal was used, the seller's account with Paypal will be debited,[59] or if the eBay site offers alternative payment mechanisms, then eBay deducts the amount from monies it owes to the seller or otherwise reclaims the funds from the seller.[60] Most disputes are resolved within 14 days without any fee being charged.[61]

The eBay rule system garners some minimal constitutional legitimacy from the contractual agreement by sellers and complaining buyers to participate in it, though the rules themselves are controlled autocratically by eBay so there is no element of input legitimacy here. There appear to be few complaints that the dispute resolution process itself is flawed, though there are plenty of complaints by sellers that the results unfairly favour buyers (and, unsurprisingly therefore, few complaints about fairness from buyers). Perhaps the most telling measure of the system's legitimacy is how extensively it is used in preference to national law, even though national law in theory provides buyers with far more extensive rights than the eBay rules in many countries.[62] In 2010, the last year for which statistics appear to have been released, eBay handled in excess

[57] https://web.archive.org/web/20160425033304/http://sellercentre.ebay.co.uk/where-to-sell-internationally (April 2016).

[58] PayPal is always one of the specified methods, and still the most popular one, but eBay also operates the Money Back Guarantee if payment is made by credit card, debit card via eBay as an intermediary, or (in Australia) via the Paymate system.

[59] Under the PayPal User Agreement (clauses 5.3, 10.1 and 13 for UK customers, see www.paypal.com/uk/webapps/mpp/ua/useragreement-full?locale.x=en_GB#4, June 2019).

[60] See Australian eBay User Agreement Clause 10, available at http://pages.ebay.com.au/help/policies/user-agreement.html.

[61] Though this, of course, means that the cost of the system is covered from the seller fees collectively and thus, ultimately, shared between all buyers.

[62] For example, the EU Consumer Rights Directive 2011/83/EU gives EU consumers the rights, inter alia, to prior information about the seller and charges, a right to withdraw from the contract, and rights to receive goods of appropriate quality. None of these are provided for in the eBay rules.

of 60 million disputes worldwide, averaging US$70–100 in value.[63] To put this number in context, in 2011 the *total* number of small claims handled by the UK courts (under £5,000 at that time) was in the region of 30,000, and the vast majority of these did not relate to complaints by buyers of products.[64] If any eBay buyer is dissatisfied with a decision there is nothing in the rules to prevent bringing a national law claim against the seller, but there appear to have been few if any such cases.

eBay's decisions under this rule system are enforceable entirely by eBay itself, without the need to refer to external legal systems. eBay has sole decision-making power once a buyer has referred a dispute to the process and, because the only remedy available is a refund, can enforce that remedy autonomously through its relationships with payment providers. In practice the eBay rule-system operates like an autonomous transnational law system and is the primary source of regulation for the trading activities of its participants.

C. Google Search and the Right to be Forgotten

In 2014 the CJEU decided in *Google Spain SL, Google Inc v Agencia Española de Protección de Datos (AEPD) and Mario Costeja González (Google Spain)*[65] that individual data subjects would sometimes have the right to request under the Data Protection Directive[66] that particular elements of their personal data available on third-party websites should no longer be disclosed by internet search engines. The court's reasoning, in simplified terms, was that in the case before it the information in question was so outdated that its continued processing by Google for the purposes of search had ceased to be fair, as required by Article 6 of the Directive.[67] This is usually referred to as the 'right to be forgotten', though it would be more accurate to described it as a right to be delisted.

Importantly, though almost in passing, the court made it clear that the decision whether any such demand was justified should initially be made by the data controller, ie the internet search provider: 'Requests … may be addressed by the data subject directly to the controller who must then duly examine their merits and, as the case may be, end processing of the data in question.'[68] However, the court gave no guidance as to

[63] LF Del Duca, C Rule and B Cressman, 'Lessons and Best Practices for Designers of Fast Track, Low Value, High Volume Global E-Commerce ODR Systems' (2015) 4 *Penn State Journal of Law & International Affairs* 243, 248, citing eBay Corporate Factsheet Q4 2010.

[64] UK Ministry of Justice, *Court Statistics Quarterly October to December 2012* 12, figure 1.3.

[65] C-131/12, 13 May 2014.

[66] Directive 95/46/EC on the protection of individuals with regard to the processing of personal data and on the free movement of such data, OJ L281/31, 23 November 1995. The rights in question were to request erasure and blocking of data (Art 12(b)) and to object to further processing (Art 14(1)). The Directive has since been replaced by Regulation (EU) 2016/679 of the European Parliament and of the Council of 27 April 2016 on the protection of natural persons with regard to the processing of personal data and on the free movement of such data, and repealing Directive 95/46/EC (General Data Protection Regulation), OJ L119/1, 4 May 2016 (GDPR), but data subjects continue to have all these rights under the Regulation.

[67] *Google Spain* (n 65), para 72.

[68] ibid, para 77.

how internet search providers should make these decisions, other than that they should follow the provisions of the law.

Following the initial spike of requests, the number of requests to Google fell slowly from an average of around 4,000 per week in November 2014 to around 2,000 per week in September 2017 and appears to have settled at that figure.[69] The volume of these requests has made it necessary for Google to set up an internal system for deciding whether to de-list; in effect, a non-state transnational judicial system.

Notionally, the rules to be applied by Google are those set out in the CJEU judgment. But, as commentators have pointed out,[70] that judgment does not explain in sufficient detail which rules are to be applied and how they interact, and in particular how the right to be forgotten should be balanced against other fundamental rights such as that to free speech. It is to be hoped that at some point Google will find a way of publishing key decisions whilst maintaining data subject privacy, but at present the body of decisions is rightly described as 'a jurisprudence built in the dark'.[71]

What is interesting for the purposes of this chapter is the ways in which Google has (and has not) sought to achieve legitimacy for its decision-making system. The constitutional legitimacy of the system is established by the CJEU judgment, which holds that the law requires Google to make these decisions, but as we have seen, constitutional legitimacy alone is rarely sufficient to achieve user acceptance.

To date, Google's main focus has been on the input legitimacy of the system. Because the CJEU did not fully explain the rules which Google should apply, Google has adopted two external documents for this purpose. The first is the opinion of the EU's Article 29 Working Party, which was published in November 2014 and attempts to consolidate the views of the EU's national data protection supervisors about the rules and the process which should properly be applied.[72] Google has committed largely to follow these guidelines in making its decisions: 'We have carefully developed criteria in alignment with the Article 29 Working Party's guidelines.'[73] The second is a report by the Advisory Council which Google set up following the CJEU judgment. The Advisory Council held hearings in seven European capitals in the autumn of 2014, video of which is available online,[74] and took written evidence following a public call. The Council's report was published in February 2015,[75] and Google states that its findings will 'inform' the development of Google's de-listing policies.[76]

[69] Data from graph in https://transparencyreport.google.com/eu-privacy/overview.

[70] See eg P Gryffroy, 'Delisting as a part of the decay of information in the digital age: a critical evaluation of Google Spain (C-131/12) and the right to delist it has created' (2016) *Computer and Telecommunications Law Review* 149, 158–59.

[71] 'Open Letter to Google from 80 Internet Scholars: Release RTBF Compliance Data' (13 May 2015), available at https://medium.com/@ellgood/open-letter-to-google-from-80-internet-scholars-release-rtbf-compliance-datacbfc6d59f1bd.

[72] Article 29 Working Party, 'Guidelines on the Implementation of the Court of Justice of the EU judgment on "Google Spain and Inc v Agencia Española de Protección de Datos (AEPD) and Mario Costeja GonzáLez" C-131/12' (WP225, 26 November 2014).

[73] https://transparencyreport.google.com/eu-privacy/overview.

[74] https://archive.google.com/advisorycouncil.

[75] https://static.googleusercontent.com/media/archive.google.com/en//advisorycouncil/advisement/advisory-report.pdf.

[76] https://archive.google.com/advisorycouncil.

How far this legitimates the rules and process design is still a matter for debate. It is clear that in one respect, at least, Google is not following the recommendations of the Article 29 Working Party because it informs webmasters when their web pages are de-listed for a particular name search and also informs search users that some results are omitted under data protection law. Both these run counter to the Working Party's recommendations.[77] The work of Google's Advisory Council has been analysed at length by Chenou and Radu,[78] who point out that Google selected the topics for discussion in the public meetings, that the membership of the Council was largely chosen to be sympathetic to Google's interests, and that the public interest, particularly the view of data protection supervisors, was not adequately represented in the discussions. They conclude that: 'Rather than a broad dialogue, the work of the Advisory Council on "the right to be forgotten" can be better described as a framed and controlled process aiming to legitimize Google's practices.'[79] It seems likely that over time Google will need to do more to enhance the input legitimacy of its system.

So far, little attention has been paid to throughput and output legitimacy. The decisions made within Google remain obscure, and were not even available to the Advisory Council as part of its work.[80] Google has made some attempt to bolster output legitimacy by publishing brief summaries of decisions which it believes raise important points of principle, as part of its Transparency Report,[81] but as at May 2019 only 108 summaries were disclosed from over 800,000 de-listing requests, although aggregated data analysis of the reasons for refusals to de-list is also published.[82] Although this information is interesting, it is hardly an adequate basis on which to assess whether the decisions Google makes are fair and just.

It is too early to predict how things will develop, but it seems clear that at some point Google will need to address the independence of this decision-making system because there is a conflict between Google's judicial role and its commercial interest in disseminating as much information as possible as widely as possible.[83] Other search providers such as Bing and Yahoo! are necessarily developing their own systems, and it would seem obvious for them to pool their experiences and develop a consolidated set of guidelines for making de-listing decisions. These might in turn evolve into a quasi-independent decision-making system, funded by search providers but not directly controlled by them, which would help legitimate the system further by demonstrating a degree of independence.

[77] WP225 (n 72) 9–10.

[78] J-M Chenou and R Radu, 'The "Right to Be Forgotten": Negotiating Public and Private Ordering in the European Union' (2017) *Business & Society* 1, 12–23.

[79] ibid 16.

[80] ibid 16.

[81] https://transparencyreport.google.com/eu-privacy/overview.

[82] https://storage.googleapis.com/transparencyreport/faqs/eu-privacy/Google_EU_privacy_data_nov2015.pdf.

[83] See Chenou and Radou, 'The "Right to Be Forgotten"' (2017) 20: 'The power delegation from the public to the private sector transforms the latter not only by adding new responsibilities (from indexing information to assessing the content of the links) but also by entrusting the corporation to adopt a public interest approach that would be typical of an independent agency. In principle, the public interest logic would encourage the deindexing of content, yet the corporate strategy would advise in favor of minimizing risks.'

IV. Conclusions

Can we, then, predict when and where these new kinds of transnational cyberspace institution are likely to develop? I suggest that there are three factors which, when they occur together, are likely to lead to a new institution.

First, there must be a single transnational problem in cyberspace, or a set of related problems, which nation states seem powerless to resolve. Powerless here means powerless in practice – it might be that states could in theory coordinate to solve the problem, but the time it will take to do so is longer than cyberspace users can tolerate. All the institutions discussed in section III were formed in reaction to an immediate need.

Second, the problem will need to affect a subset of cyberspace actors whose membership is sufficiently clear, usually from their participation in the regulated activity, that they can constitute the transnational legitimating community for an institution. Additionally, those members (or some of them) will need to be in a position to set up an institution and sufficiently motivated, often by their commercial interests, to do so.

Third, there will usually need to be tools of enforcement which do not require the involvement of national legal systems, and which the institution can control. These are likely to be technical/commercial tools, operating via the technological architecture of cyberspace.

To be successful, such an institution will need to legitimate its activities, primarily through the output legitimacy achieved by issuing decisions which are perceived by the legitimating community as being fair and just. If the institution achieves this, it arguably has greater legitimacy to regulate the problem than does any nation state or any transnational institution based on nation states.[84]

It might be objected that such institutions oust the authority of nation states, but as the examples in section III show, this is not so. Those institutions all defer to judgments of national courts, if judgments are issued. But such judgments are rare (I would argue because community members perceive the institution to be a more appropriate decision-maker), and in their absence the institutions instead operate, simply, as if the concept of the nation state did not exist. It should be clear that for all the examples, in the unlikely event that all the world's nation states simply disappeared, then the institutions could continue their operations without interruption and without changing their rules. On a day-to-day basis, nation states are simply irrelevant to them.

Lawyers are often unhappy when it appears that private 'law' is taking over a domain previously reserved to national or international law, most likely because their training

[84] As between states, comparative legitimacy is embodied in the principle of comity which requires that a state should not claim to regulate persons within another state unless it is reasonable to do so, which normally means that regulation should be undertaken by the state which has the greater interest in so doing – see eg Restatement (Third) of Foreign Relations Law of the United States §403(1) (1987). In the case of a dispute between an eBay buyer and seller who are located in different states, it is hard to argue that either state has a closer connection with the dispute than eBay.

and experience is based on traditional understandings of law. But it must be remembered that this phenomenon is neither new nor exceptional. As Graz points out:[85]

> On a long-term historical basis, the influence of non-state actors is not necessarily new. The state as we know it now, related to a given territory, controlling a closely defined population whose sovereignty is allegedly embodied in it, centralising monetary emission in conjunction with private agents – all this is a creation of the last third of the nineteenth century in the western world.[86] As Halliday points out, 'non-state' is in fact a continuation of something that prevailed until the modern state was formed'.[87]

[85] J-C Graz, 'Hybrids and regulation in the global political economy' (2006) 10 *Competition & Change* 230, 235.

[86] E Helleiner and A Pickel (eds), *Economic Nationalism in a Globalizing World* (Ithaca, Cornell University Press, 2005).

[87] F Halliday, 'The romance of non-state actors' in D Josselin and W Wallace (eds), *Non-state Actors in World Politics* (London, Palgrave, 2001) 27.

7

Data-driven Mergers under EU Competition Law

ANCA D CHIRITA*

This chapter aims to review data-driven mergers including, but not limited to, major conglomerates involving large-scale individual user data, known as 'big data', by Facebook (WhatsApp), Microsoft (Yahoo!, Skype and LinkedIn), Google (DoubleClick), TomTom (Tele Atlas), Publicis/Omnicon, Telefonica/Vodafone UK, and so on. These mergers have been unconditionally cleared based on the traditional law and economic analysis of mergers, known as a 'significant impediment to effective competition' legal test. The test disregards public policy concerns, including the economics of privacy, as in concerns relating to data analytics, data-sharing with third parties, such as publishers or retailers, and data-selling. The chapter draws on previous research on the rise of big data and the loss of privacy, which sheds light inter alia on the ineffectiveness of the data, consumer and competition rules and on the intrusive privacy policies of the various digital platforms.

This chapter argues that the current assessment of mergers has to activate the public policy clause under Article 21(4) of the EU Merger Control Regulation 139/2004, which allows Member States to 'take appropriate measures to protect legitimate interests other than those taken into consideration by this Regulation' and to consider the economic implications of privacy following a merger. No merger should be unconditionally cleared if it involves a large amount of users' data.

The chapter arrives at the conclusion that the new data protection framework is insufficiently robust. The contract theory of informed consent associated with the

* Earlier drafts were presented at the Annual Seminar of the Society of Legal Scholars on 'The Future of Commercial Law' in 2017 held in Durham, the 13th Annual Conference of the Academic Society for Competition Law on 'The Effects of Digitalization, Globalization and Nationalism on Competition Law' held at the New York University School of Law and the Annual Competition Policy Conference on 'The relationship between antitrust, innovation and investment' of the Royal Institute of International Affairs (Chatham House) in 2018 and benefitted from helpful suggestions, comments or questions from academics and practitioners including Massimiliano Kadar, Maurice Stucke, Thomas Vinje, Konrad Ost, Han Li Toh, John Linarelli, Sir Roy Goode QC, Louise Gullifer QC (Hon), Chris Reed, Orkun Akseli, Michal Gal and Simonetta Vezzoso.

potential of sharing anonymised and aggregated data means that digital platforms are able to exploit data protection loopholes and abuse users' trust in digital platforms. In addition, the chapter looks at the treatment of innovative digital platforms from the perspective of Schumpeterian economics and therefore identifies the fallacy of too great a reliance on ephemeral market shares. It discusses more critically the expectation of a robust and coherent theory of harm to consumers in the context of digital markets.

I. Institutional Cooperation: A Pragmatic Solution in the Age of Big-Data Mergers?

In the digital age, the technological advance has contributed to a myriad of mega-mergers. In the last decade, the European Commission reviewed a number of large-scale acquisitions ranging from $3.1 billion paid by Google to acquire DoubleClick in 2008; €2.9 billion paid by TomTom to acquire Tele Atlas in 2008; $45 billion paid by Microsoft for Yahoo! Search in 2010, $8.5 billion for Skype in 2011 and $26 billion for LinkedIn in 2017; $19 billion paid by Facebook to acquire WhatsApp in 2014; and $35 billion for the collapsed merger between Publicis and Omnicom.[1] What all these mergers had in common was a vast amount of users' data available on digital platforms, known as 'big data'.

Such acquisitions might well have been driven by the desire to invest existing profits and encourage even more innovation. Retrospectively, it is questionable whether any of the much smaller entities acquired by these giants have become more successful innovative entities.

However, the acquisition of less successful businesses cannot remain unchallenged by the hidden value of big data. Indeed, we have witnessed the emergence of highly innovative technologies based on intelligent business solutions where platform users pay nothing in return for the use of a service. Nonetheless, such users pay with their own data. Should ownership of an online platform change, then the new owner will take over large amounts of data. This process shifts the focus from an interest in pure innovation to an interest in data, as the latter possesses an intrinsic monetary value. Even if it is not sold at an internet-based auction, such data is valuable for sharing.

How, then, was it possible that these large transactions went ahead without attracting any attention? The first Data Protection Act was a directive in 1995 and, following suggestions from the European Data Protection Supervisor (EDPS), it was not until 2012 that, at the European Commission's initiative, this area of law became the subject of a major reform spanning over five years.[2] The EDPS's Opinion in 2016 further

[1] See, eg, COMP M 4731, *Google/DoubleClick*, 11 March 2008; COMP M 5727, *Microsoft/Yahoo! Search*, 18 February 2010; COMP M 6281, *Microsoft/Skype*, 7 October 2011; COMP M 8124, *Microsoft/LinkedIn*, 20 January 2017; COMP/M 7217, *Facebook/WhatsApp*, 3 October 2014.

[2] See, eg, Directive 95/46/EC, the European Data Protection Directive on the protection of individuals with regard to the processing of personal data and on the free movement of such data; European Data Protection Supervisor's Opinion on European Commission's Communication 'A Comprehensive Approach to Personal Data Protection in the EU', 22 June 2011; the European Commission's proposal to strengthen online privacy rights and the digital economy, 25 January 2012; European Data Protection Supervisor's Opinion on EC

informed the wider debate by reference to a triangle among data, consumer protection and anti-trust enforcement, with a specific focus on mergers.[3] By recognising that cyber space is a threat to privacy, personal data and the very basic principle of non-discrimination, the EDPS united these three areas of law through the legal requirement of fairness, that of fair processing of data versus fair competition to consumers (B2C) and protection against unfair competition (B2B).

In digital markets, it is often the case that anti-competitive practices will infringe two or more applicable legal frameworks. It is therefore expected that consumer, data and competition authorities should work together towards establishing forms of mutual and practical cooperation during investigations. But this problem is not resolved so simply. As is often the case, cooperation can cause delays. Furthermore, too large a chain of responsible actors might also lead to an ineffective solution. Instead, a more pragmatic approach to big data is for the European Commission to activate its public policy clause whenever this is really needed. The answer to this last question will be offered in the final section.

II. Data-driven Mergers – A Few Preliminary Observations

Recent years have witnessed a number of high-profile merger cases in high-technology markets, as shown in Table 7.1 below.

The effects of the above data-driven mergers have come to be felt and understood by not only competition scholars, but also practitioners.[4] In her recent speech, the

data protection reform package, 7 March 2012; The Article 29 Working Party's Opinion on data protection reform proposal, 23 March 2012; WP 29 update on data protection reform, 5 October 2012; the EU Parliament adopted the General Data Protection Regulation on 12 March 2014 with overwhelming support in its favour; European Data Protection Supervisor's recommendations on the final text of the GDPR, 27 July 2015; the European Parliament, European Commission and Council reach an agreement on the GDPR on 15 December 2015; Article 29 Working Party's action plan for the implementation of the GDPR, 2 February 2016; and finally, on 27 April 2016 Regulation (EU) 2016/679 on the protection of natural persons with regard to the processing of personal data and on the free movement of such data is adopted, which entered into force on 25 May 2018, as well as Directive (EU) 2016/680 on the protection of natural persons with regard to the processing of personal data by competent authorities for the purposes of the prevention, investigation, detection or prosecution of criminal offences or the execution of criminal penalties, and on the free movement of such data; on 10 January 2017, the European Commission proposed two new regulations on privacy and electronic communications (ePrivacy) and on the data protection rules applicable to EU institutions (Regulation 45/2001) that align the existing rules to the GDPR; Data Protection Directive for the police and justice sectors into national legislation on 6 May 2018; Proposal for a Regulation on the protection of personal data in EU institutions on 22 May 2018.

[3] See the European Data Protection Supervisor's Executive Summary of the Opinion of the European Data Protection Supervisor on effective enforcement in a digital society economy, OJ C 463/09 [2016], highlighting how cyber space represents a threat to privacy, personal data and the principle of non-discrimination as 'antitrust has its roots in political decisions to disrupt abusive monopoly power for the benefit of society at large. Consumer rights emerged as a bulwark against abusive traders. Big Data opportunities for boosting productivity and connectivity should be accompanied by Big Data Protection safeguards'.

[4] Nonetheless, there is scant literature on the subject, which is largely attributed to notoriously lengthy merger decisions. For further references by practitioners, see P Werner, S Clerckk and H de la Barre, 'Commission Expansionism in EU Merger Control – Fact and Fiction' (2018) 9 *Journal of European Competition Law & Practice* 139; G Lougher and S Kalmanowicz, 'EU Competition Law in the Sharing Economy' (2016) 7 *Journal of European Competition Law & Practice* 92, 99–101. For a case-by-case brief review,

Commissioner for Competition, Margrethe Vestager, explained: 'People understand that handing over data has a cost. Because each time we share our data, we give up something very valuable. Something that could be used against us'.[5] Hopefully, the vast array of data from the above mergers will not come back to haunt us, the users of online platforms and other digital services. Five years ago, Vestager's predecessor mentioned that 'traditionally, the storage and treatment of personal data has been the province of laws and regulations designed to protect the privacy of citizens'; indeed, Joaquín Almunia was right that 'this will remain of paramount importance in the foreseeable future', as has recently been proven by the study of big data analytics.[6] As shown in Table 7.1 below, the European Commission reviewed a number of merger decisions where a large scale of accumulation of data was a potential motive behind the merger.

Table 7.1 Mergers and acquisitions

Platform/service	Acquisition/merger with
Microsoft	Skype, a provider of internet-based communications services and software
Microsoft, inter alia a provider of software solutions for customer relationship management	LinkedIn, a provider of sales intelligence solutions
Facebook	WhatsApp, a provider of text, photo, voice and video message apps for smartphones
TomTom, the largest supplier of portable navigation services in Europe	Tele Atlas, a producer of navigable digital map databases
Omnicom, a US-based global advertising, marketing and corporate communications company	Publicis, a French international communications and advertising group
Telefonica UK, Vodafone UK and Everything Everywhere	mCommerce, a joint venture offering various mobile commerce services to businesses in the UK as a 'Wallet' platform
Google	Joint venture involving Sanofi, a global pharmaceutical group, offering services for the management and treatment of diabetes
IMS	Cegedim, active in the IT sector, offering solutions to measure and improve the performance of companies active in the healthcare sector

see M Kadar and M Bogdan, 'Big Data and EU Merger Control – A Case Review' (2017) 8 *Journal of European Competition Law & Practice* 1; B Holles de Peyer, 'EU Merger Control and Big Data' (2017) 13 *Journal of Competition Law & Economics* 767, with a focus on so-called 'theories of harm' but arguing against the review of privacy considerations in mergers.

[5] See EU Commission, Commissioner for Competition, 'When Technology Serves People', speech, Budapest, 1 June 2018, 2.

[6] See, eg, EU Commission, Commissioner for Competition, J Almunia, 'Competition and personal data protection', speech, Brussels, 26 November 2012. Although the Commission did not define a market for

A. Free Product or Service in Return for Data

First, it is helpful to illustrate the relevance of data in the context of free products or services. In the area of mergers, the decision in *Publicis/Omnicom* offers an excellent definition of 'big data' analytics. Its primary goal is to help 'companies make better business decisions by enabling data scientists and other users to analyse large volumes of transaction data as well as other data sources that may not be assessed by conventional business intelligence programmes'.[7] Data and its analytics are the 'raw' material and a 'tool' used by advertising agencies to create advertising messages and deliver them to consumers.[8] In essence, one can simply say that the study of data analytics is effectively examining the means to implement and achieve marketing strategies and targeted advertising, which is normally captured by consumer law.

Subsequently, this decision also makes an extremely important distinction among three different kinds of services offering marketing information, market research and media measurement.[9] The first consists in the provision of data to individual consumers for direct marketing purposes, which is tantamount to targeted advertising. The second consists of measuring actual purchasing patterns through retail tracking or data obtained from consumer panels. The last one refers to measuring the audience of specific media, such as television and the Internet.

One of the most important instances of gradual recognition in data-driven mergers is the free offering of a product or service which can be monetised through other means. For example, in *Facebook/WhatsApp, Microsoft/LinkedIn* and *Microsoft/Yahoo*, consumer communications apps, social and professional networking services, and internet search services are all recognised as being provided 'free of charge' or free from 'monetary charges' but they could, nonetheless, be 'monetised' through other means, including advertising or charges for premium services.[10] In *Microsoft/Skype*, it was mentioned that it is difficult to monetise consumer communications, as competitors offer them free of charge, and an estimated 75 per cent of Skype users would even give up Skype rather than pay for its use.[11] The General Court stated on appeal that

> the fact that the services are offered free of charge is a relevant factor in assessing the market power of the new entity. […] any attempt to make users pay would run the risk of reducing the attractiveness of those services and of encouraging switching.[12]

In *Facebook/WhatsApp*, it was noted that 'users of consumer communications apps tend to be very price-sensitive and expect communications apps to be provided for free'.[13]

personal data, the Commissioner considered that this was not something that should be ruled out altogether. The *Google/DoubleClick* merger, however, involved a combination of personal data about search and web browsing behaviour, but was, unfortunately, not considered as such.

[7] COMP M 7023, *Publicis/Omnicom*, 9 January 2014, para 617.

[8] ibid para 622.

[9] ibid para 618.

[10] See, eg, COMP/M 7217, *Facebook/WhatsApp*, 3 October 2014, paras 31 and 47; COMP/M 8124, *Microsoft/LinkedIn*, 20 January 2017, para 87; COMP/M 5727, *Microsoft/Yahoo! Search*, 18 February 2010, para 33.

[11] COMP/M 6281, *Microsoft/Skype*, 7 October 2011, paras 86 and 76.

[12] *Cisco Systems Inc and Messagenet SpA v Commission*, Case T-79/12, ECLI:EU:T:2013:635, para 73.

[13] COMP/M 7217, *Facebook/WhatsApp*, 3 October 2014, para 90.

A contrasting example of monetisation is *Hutchinson 3G UK/Telefonica UK*, which acknowledges that the mobile market in the UK is 'more and more data centric, customer demand for data is increasing and all operators seek to monetise this trend' and that data has become 'an important competitive criterion'.[14] Very close to a similar recognition of data analytics services is *Publicis/Omnicom* where the merging parties have marketing data analytics capabilities which were used in-house for targeted advertising.[15] In other words, the parties claim that their analysis of consumer data is 'an intrinsic part' of their own service.

In *Telefonica/Vodafone/Everything Everywhere/JV*, the most significant inquiry is into the relevant market for data analytics services in order to collect and analyse mobile usage data from the merging parties and advertising services and to provide customers with 'valuable insights into consumer behaviour'.[16] Business analytics of this kind include prospective analytics with a view to increasing the customer base, cross-selling and loyalty analytics.[17] The Commission recalled that, in *WPP/TMS*, it had previously identified a separate market for research services and media measurement services aimed at measuring and understanding consumer attitudes and purchasing behaviour and the market for marketing information services in *VNU/ACNielsen*.[18] The latter referred to the supply of personal and/or sensitive data, such as address, age, social group, activities, habits of consumption etc, which could be used for direct marketing purposes. Due to the rather ambiguous responses received, the Commission left it open whether there should be a separate market for online and mobile data analytics.[19]

However, from the area of abuse of a dominant position, the recent decision in the *Google Comparison Shopping* case highlighted that the fact that a product or service is offered free of charge does not prevent such an offering from being considered an economic activity.[20] This is an evolutionary recognition of data as the new currency in digital markets.

It is difficult but not impossible to examine a degradation of quality. As advanced elsewhere, the focus can be shifted from the price variation to small but significant and non-transitory changes in quality (SSNIQ).[21] Another excellent point raised by Gal

[14] COMP/M7612, *Hutchinson 3G UK/Telefonica UK*, 11 May 2016, paras 435 and 517 respectively. At para 794, there is a further reference to another mobile operator, O2's plans to make data sharing between mobile devices and people 'easier than ever before'. Later, at para 1076, Virgin Media and TalkTalk are mentioned as 'ideally placed to offload a proportion of their mobile customers' data traffic onto their fixed networks in a cost efficient manner'. These examples show how internet companies are also capable of harvesting big data.

[15] COMP/M 7023, *Publicis/Omnicom*, 9 January 2014, paras 11 and 619.

[16] COMP/M 6314, *Telefonica UK/Vodafone UK/Everything Everywhere/JV*, 4 September 2012, para 191.

[17] ibid paras 192 and 193.

[18] ibid para 197; COMP/M 5232, *WPP/TMS*, 23 September 2004, para 13; COMP/M 2291, *VNU/ACNielsen*, 12 February 2001, paras 10–12.

[19] COMP/M 6314, *Telefonica UK/Vodafone UK/Everything Everywhere/JV*, 4 September 2012, paras 202 and 203.

[20] See EU Commission, COMP Case AT 39740, *Google Search (Shopping)* decision, 27 June 2017, published on 18 December 2017, para 152; citing the General Court rulings in *Microsoft* and *Cisco & Messagenet*, see GC, Case T-201/04, *Microsoft*, ECLI:EU:T:2007:289, paras 966–970, and GC, Case T-79/12, *Cisco Systems and Messagenet v Commission*, ECLI:EU:T:2013:635, paras 65–74.

[21] See, eg, M Gal and D Rubinfeld, 'The Hidden Costs of Free Goods: Implications for Antitrust Enforcement'. (2016) 80 *Antitrust Law Journal* 540.

and Rubinfeld is that 'we should not automatically exempt free goods from antitrust scrutiny'.[22] Ultimately, there is no 'free' product. As one commentator observed:

> We do not pay money for Google's services. But someone pays for its thousands of engineers, and that someone is advertisers. [...] We also pay in our ignorance of how the company operates [...], and how it uses the data it collects.[23]

B. Dual-sided Platforms

The second important recognition in the above merger decisions is that such services are offered through the medium of 'two-' or 'multi-sided' platforms.[24] As in traditional transactions, such dual-sided platforms might offer one service for free, but extract revenues from the other side of the same platform.[25] The economic designation of these online platforms is circular, as the transaction itself is still a bilateral contract rather than the unilateral stipulation of a free gift.

Therefore, despite the convoluted terminology, online platforms continue to operate legally under the same assumption of a traditional contract of sale. In this scenario, in return for a free service, users then offer their own experience data. Third parties, such as advertisers or retailers, may even secretly offer monetary considerations to have access to such data.

The cause of multi-sidedness is, of course, data which accounts for monetary consideration. This is not surprising, as digital payments have nowadays resulted in the lapse of money in favour of more innovative technologies where use of cards has overtaken the use of money in exchange for goods. So why not have *data* in return for service offerings? Whilst the driver of such platforms is inevitably an exploration of new avenues for attracting users to the mousetrap of a free service, the transactional exchange of data has de facto become the new currency operating in digital markets. In the area of abuse of a dominant position, it has more recently been recognised in the *Google Comparison Shopping* case that 'offering a service free of charge can be an advantageous commercial strategy, in particular for two-sided platforms'.[26]

[22] See, eg, ibid at 542; this is because 'a free good does not imply a lack of adverse welfare effects'. The authors suggested the use of a presumption of legality for free goods, with the burden of proof on those arguing otherwise. In practice, this would imply that competition authorities would need to produce evidence of consumer harm inflicted by free goods.

[23] See, eg, F Pasquale, *The Black Box Society: The Secret Algorithms That Control Money and Information* (Cambridge, MA, Harvard University Press, 2016) 66.

[24] *Microsoft/Yahoo! Search*, 18 February 2010, para 47; COMP/M 8124, *Microsoft/LinkedIn*, 20 January 2017, para 87: LinkedIn offers a multi-sided platform, which enables users 'to connect, share, discover and communicate with each other across multiple devices and means'; COMP/M 4731, *Google/DoubleClick*, 11 March 2008, para 290; COMP/M 4523, *Travelport/Worldspan*, 21 August 2007, where the Commission defined the two-sided market for Global Distribution Systems which operates as a wider platform between upstream travel providers, such as airports, hotels and car rentals, and downstream intermediary agents.

[25] On the benefits of dual-sided online platforms, see AD Chirita, 'Google's Anti-Competitive and Unfair Practices in Digital Leisure Markets' (2015) 11 *Competition Law Review* 113 and the general literature referred to in fn 33.

[26] EU Commission, COMP Case AT 39740, *Google Search (Shopping)* decision, 27 June 2017, published on 18 December 2017, para 159.

'Even though users do not pay a monetary consideration for the use of general search services, they contribute to the monetisation of the service by providing data with each query.'[27] This paragraph effectively recognises competition that is not based on price, as there are other parameters of competition.[28] In the same spirit, the Director-General for Competition, Johannes Laitenberger, declared: 'Now in many digital markets, price – as we used to understand it – plays no decisive role since the services are not monetised on the consumer side, or at least there is no price expressed in monetary terms.'[29] Data protection has therefore been recognised as 'an important parameter of competition' on the basis of quality.[30]

To sum up, cyber space is driven by online platforms which know how to monetise, monopolise and control their users' online experiences and behaviour.[31]

C. To Define, or not to Define the Relevant Markets: That is the Question, but what are the Practical Implications?

In the overwhelming majority of the merger decisions under review, the Commission has been rather Kaplowian,[32] as it has repeatedly ruled that 'the exact market definition' can be 'left open'.[33] A sensible explanation provided in Kaplow's scholarship is that the process of defining markets 'entails unnecessary work' and the outcomes are 'inferior to those arising when it is eschewed entirely'.[34]

The Commission, however, spent considerable energy in analysing each potentially narrower relevant market. In *Facebook/WhatsApp* and *Microsoft/LinkedIn*, for example, it questioned whether social networking services and consumer communications apps could be further divided accorded to their intended use.[35] On the basis

[27] ibid para 158.

[28] ibid para 160: 'even though general search services do not compete on price, there are other parameters of competition between general search services', which include the relevance of results, the speed with which results are provided, the attractiveness of the user interface and the depth of indexing the web.

[29] EU Commission, Director-General for Competition, Johannes Laitenberger, ' EU Competition Law in Innovation and Digital markets: Fairness and the Consumer Welfare Perspective', speech, Brussels, 10 October 2017, 6.

[30] ibid 9 ('we see data protection as an element of the quality of the product'), 10.

[31] In the same vein, see, eg, CJ Hoofnagle, *Federal Trade Commission Privacy Law and Policy* (Cambridge, Cambridge University Press, 2016) ch 6, 46.

[32] See, eg, L Kaplow, 'Why (Ever) Define Markets?' (2010) 124 *Harvard Law Review* 438, 515, suggesting that 'it is difficult to render coherent the process of inferring market power from market shares in redefined markets'.

[33] See, eg, COMP/M 7217, *Facebook/WhatsApp*, 3 October 2014, para 33; COMP/M 5727, *Microsoft/Yahoo! Search*, 18 February 2010, para 81; COMP/M 6281, *Microsoft/Skype*, 7 October 2011, para 43; COMP/M 8124, *Microsoft/LinkedIn*, 20 January 2017, para 87.

[34] See, eg, L Kaplow, 'Market Definition' in RD Blair and DD Sokol (eds) *The Oxford Handbook of International Antitrust Economics* (Oxford, Oxford University Press, 2015) vol 1, 350. In support of Kaplow's assertion, see, eg, MA Lemley and MP McKenna, 'Is Pepsi Really a Substitute for Coke? Market Definition in Antitrust and IP' in Blair and Sokol (ibid) 195. On the pitfalls of too narrow or too wide market definitions, see, Anca D Chirita, 'Editorial: Competition and Regulatory Trends in Digital Markets' (2017) 12 *Competition Law Review* 122.

[35] See, eg, COMP/M 7217, *Facebook/WhatsApp*, 3 October 2014, para 60, where Facebook offers a richer experience compared to WhatsApp, which offers a 'more personal and targeted' one; COMP/M 8124, *Microsoft/LinkedIn*, 20 January 2017, paras 95 and 97; there is an increasingly overlapping pattern where

of functionality and the availability on operating systems and on different platforms, consumer communications apps can indeed be divided further. WhatsApp was offered only on smartphones, but not on tablets and PCs.[36] In *Microsoft/Yahoo Search!*, the Commission questioned an eventual distinction between search and non-search advertising and whether, beyond advertising, intermediation via software vendors, internet search providers and distribution agreements, with hardware manufacturers on entry points to search engines, are relevant markets.[37] Similarly, in *Microsoft/Skype*, the Commission questioned a further division of the market for consumer communications on the basis of its functionalities (IM, voice or video calls); operating systems (Windows, Mac, Linux, Android, etc); and platforms (PCs, smartphones and tablets).[38] It recognised that there was a market for enterprise communications.[39] Narrowly defined markets for the provision of online advertising space, intermediation in online advertising and the provision of ad serving for display ads was yet another useful recognition in *Google/DoubleClick*.[40] For the latter market, the Commission contemplated a further subdivision between the provision of such services to advertisers and publishers.[41] It considered, however, that there was no need to identify even narrower markets for the provision of search and non-search advertising space or further subdivisions of intermediation.[42]

However, in *Facebook/WhatsApp*, the Commission was not yet prepared to recognise separate markets for the 'provision of data or data analytics services'.[43] Similarly, in *Publicis/Omnicom*, the Commission considered that there was no need to further narrow down the sales side of the 'media buying services' market into large- and small-scale advertisers or on the basis of the type of media, sector or size of account.[44] As previously, the Commission considered that the 'exact scope of the relevant product market can be left open'; this is because the merger did not raise serious doubts regarding any possible market definition.[45]

In *TomTom/Tele Atlas*, the Commission examined the relevant upstream market for the provision of digital map databases and the intermediation software market.[46]

similar services initially targeting individuals have expanded to reach out to professionals; see para 89; COMP/M 8124, *Microsoft/LinkedIn*, 20 January 2017, para 87; COMP/M 5727, *Microsoft/Yahoo! Search*, 18 February 2010, para 33.

[36] COMP/M 7217, *Facebook/WhatsApp*, 3 October 2014, para 18.

[37] *Microsoft/Yahoo! Search*, 18 February 2010, paras 75 and 87.

[38] COMP/M 6281, *Microsoft/Skype*, 7 October 2011, paras 29, 42 and 55. It did so also for the market for enterprise communications services, questioning whether this particular market needs to be further narrowed on the basis of operating systems.

[39] ibid para 187.

[40] COMP/M 4731, *Google/DoubleClick*, 11 March 2008, paras 56, 68 and 81 respectively.

[41] ibid para 81.

[42] ibid paras 56 and 73 respectively.

[43] See, eg, COMP/M 7217, *Facebook/WhatsApp*, 3 October 2014, para 72.

[44] COMP/M 7023, *Publicis/Omnicom*, 9 January 2014, paras 27, 70, 75, 79 and 80.

[45] ibid para 92. This was because the combined market share of the merging parties was below 15%; see para 142.

[46] See, eg, COMP/M 4854, *TomTom/Tele Atlas*, 14 May 2008, paras 38 and 45. A digital map will normally include relevant data, such as street names, addresses, driving directions, turn restrictions and speed limits; see para 17. Digital maps are sold to manufacturers of navigation devices for address location, route planning and navigation; see para 19. There are on-board, off-board and hybrid navigation software systems;

The latter uses an algorithm to calculate routes, including offering voice guidance.[47] TomTom is active in two downstream markets for the provision of navigation software and as a manufacturer of portable navigation devices.[48] Companies active in these markets use the same input. Although the Commission contemplated, again, narrowing down the relevant market for navigable digital map databases according to the type of navigation device, eg, Personal Digital Assistant, GPS-enabled mobile telephone and 'in-dash' navigation device, it ultimately chose not to do so.[49] It left open the exact delineation of the relevant product markets, as this did not affect the proposed merger.[50]

In *Hutchinson 3G UK/Telefonica UK*, the Commission defined a single market for retail mobile telecommunications services to end customers, but did not divide it further by type of service (eg voice, data or SMS), type of network technology (eg 2G, 3G and 4G), or end-user.[51] It considered it inappropriate to narrow down separate markets for voice services, SMS/MMS services and data services,[52] which could have considered the implications of data usage and traffic. Similarly, in *Telefonica/Vodafone*, the Commission examined a fast-growing sector of mobile Commerce, 'mCommerce', including mobile payments, advertising and, most importantly, data analytics.[53] It identified the relevant market for the wholesale supply of mobile wallet platforms, but 'left open' whether a market for secure storage also includes secure storage on devices attached to the handset or cloud-based solutions, or whether the market for online advertising should be narrowed down further to search and non-search services.[54]

The narrowest relevant market could be the market for mobile contactless or offline payments.[55] Leaving these aside, JV would be acting as an intermediary for the one-stop-shop sale of digital advertising, including 'push' and 'intelligent bulk' SMSs, 'pull offers', display advertising, coupons and vouchers.[56] With regard to 'non-intelligent' bulk SMSs, the respondents submitted to the Commission that these are part of generic

see para 46. The Commission considered that it was inappropriate to identify separate markets depending on the type of navigation device in which the software is used; see para 51.

[47] More specifically on algorithmic consumers, as systems likely to collect, record and aggregate immense volumes of personal data; see, eg, M Gal and N Elkin-Koren, 'Algorithmic Consumers' (2017) 30 *Harvard Journal of Law and Technology* 324.

[48] COMP/M 4854, *TomTom/Tele Atlas*, 14 May 2008, para 14. This vertical merger is a case of upstream market integration where a producer acquires its main provider of an important input.

[49] ibid paras 28 and 29. There was, however, a limited substitutability of navigable digital map databases (see para 32), as the 'greater the geographic coverage of map data and content, the higher the licence fee' that had to be paid (see para 31).

[50] ibid, 14 May 2008, para 38, ie, whether or not individual country or regional licences constitute separate product markets.

[51] See, eg, COMP/M7612, *Hutchinson 3G UK/Telefonica UK*, 11 May 2016, paras 251, 255 and 259. This was because all providers offer all these kinds of services to end-customers. At para 265, it was noted, however, that in the UK, competition in the mobile market is increasingly 'data-centric', ie, based on sale of data packages. The latter cover Internet data usage and traffic as part of a monthly data allowance.

[52] ibid para 262.

[53] ibid paras 26 and 88.

[54] ibid paras 102, 110 and 151 respectively.

[55] ibid para 123.

[56] ibid paras 140–142. However, JV would not be acting for the supply of intermediation services for search advertising.

advertising and therefore not interchangeable with targeted advertising.[57] In contrast, the merging parties submitted that targeted advertising should be treated similarly to display advertising in order to reach out to their desired consumer audience.[58]

Due to the technical and commercial features of mobile advertising, eg, the size of ads and the possibility of advertising outlets near the location of a smartphone-holder, the Commission considered the existence of a sub-market for mobile search advertising; thus, this was also 'left open'.[59] However, the majority of the respondents to the Commission's survey submitted that, within mobile advertising, targeted marketing messaging should be considered as a separate market from search and non-search advertising.[60] The two markets were not substitutable due to existing differences in marketing scope and reach, campaign objectives, advertising functions, pricing models, targeting possibilities, consumer data collection and consumer behaviour.[61]

In 2012, the recognition of such a market would have been significant, as the tracking technology would have clearly been able to exploit the personal location data of mobile subscribers. As described in this merger decision, the conduct would have involved targeted advertising only, rather than the sharing of location data with retailers, more specifically, for achieving online price discrimination. However, one could also argue that targeted advertising on the basis of location tracking is only a first necessary step towards the implementation of behavioural price discrimination.[62]

In *Microsoft/LinkedIn*, the software solution offered by Microsoft helps companies to manage customer interactions from sales, marketing or customer databases. It is involved in the collection of data sets so as to boost sales or improve data quality.[63] LinkedIn offers sales intelligence solutions to professionals interested in personal data, financial information or contacts metrics in order to reach out to potential customers.[64] To its premium members, LinkedIn offers a Sales Navigator solution, which uses its users' database to identify sales opportunities. Here, the Commission identified another relevant market for the provision of intelligence sales solutions.[65] However, it did not narrow down the market for social networking platforms based on their intended use, ie, personal and professional-centric social networks, due to an overlap of functionalities.[66]

[57] ibid paras 189 and 190. Therefore, retail bulk SMS services constituted a separate market from active marketing messaging.

[58] ibid para 146.

[59] ibid paras 152 and 159.

[60] ibid para 160. This is because the two services were seen as complementary, not substitutable.

[61] ibid para 161. For the characteristics of 'mobile push advertising', see para 168, namely, being highly targeted to users, able to elicit an immediate customer response, to allow the advertisers to accurately measure the campaign success and consumer engagement and very attractive to users as offers are clipped to the wallet and can be redeemed simultaneously with the payment.

[62] For earlier arguments on these issues and, more specifically, on targeted advertising and online price discrimination, see Anca D Chirita, 'The Rise of Big Data and the Loss of Privacy' in M Bakhoum, B Gallego Conde, MO Mackenordt and G Surblyte (eds), *Personal Data in Competition, Consumer Protection and IP Law – Towards a Holistic Approach?* (Berlin, Heidelberg, Springer, 2018) 11; specifically, on behavioural price discrimination, see A Ezrachi and M Stucke, *Virtual Competition: The Promise and Perils of the Algorithm-Driven Economy* (Cambridge, MA, Harvard University Press, 2016) 112.

[63] COMP/M 8124, *Microsoft/LinkedIn*, 20 January 2017, para 31.

[64] ibid para 57.

[65] ibid para 68.

[66] ibid paras 97 and 98. Respondents to the Commission's survey suggested that the creation and updating of a detailed resume or CV is an essential functionality of this platform, see para 101.

In *Sanofi/Google/DMI JV*, the newly created joint venture offered several services using an integrated digital e-medicine platform developed by Google for the system delivery and monitoring of insulin and glucose for the management and treatment of diabetes as well as data analytics services.[67] The exact scope of the market definition was initially left open, but later focused on data collection, display, storage, analysis and transmission related to the management and treatment of diabetes.[68] The Commission referred to its previous examinations of data analytics, outside the healthcare sector, where it was appropriate to differentiate between marketing information, market research and media measurement services.[69] Some of the respondents submitted to the Commission that the algorithms and tools used to analyse healthcare data are comparable to those used for the analysis of other types of data.[70] However, the joint venture did not raise competition concerns, regardless of whether there is a separate product market for algorithms for analysing healthcare data.[71]

In *IMS Health/Cegedim Business*, the Commission examined healthcare professional databases; sales tracking data; data for the provision of real world evidence, ie, observational studies, data collected on actual patient experiences and use of a product in clinical trials; and the primary market research services.[72] Business intelligent solutions included tracking technologies and data analytics, including aggregation, matching, consolidation and verification.[73] Again, the exact delineation of the markets for the provision of healthcare professional databases and for sales tracking data was left open.[74] The Commission did not narrow down the market for the provision of business intelligence solutions,[75] though the latter could have looked at the functionality of the software for reporting and analysis or for advanced analytics, including data mining and statistics.[76]

Thus, one could reach a preliminary conclusion. The implications of offering 'open' rather than closed market definitions is adding to a nebulous understanding of online platforms, as these are actively involved in a variety of tiny markets; some of the latter are engaged in the study of big data analytics.

D. Is a Quick Look at the Market Shares Self-revealing or Self-defeating?

In the market for consumer communications, there were only two close competitors: WhatsApp, with a 20–30 per cent share of this market, and Facebook Messenger,

[67] COMP/M 7813, *Sanofi/Google/DMI JV*, 23 February 2016, paras 6 and 17.
[68] ibid paras 37, 38 and 42.
[69] ibid para 17.
[70] ibid para 46.
[71] ibid para 48. In fact, the parties considered it inappropriate to narrow down the market for data analytics and argued instead that health data is subject to special regulation, see para 45.
[72] COMP/M 7337, *IMS Health/Cegedim Business*, 19 December 2014, paras 9–24, 26, 49.
[73] ibid paras 40–41.
[74] ibid paras 73 and 80.
[75] ibid para 105.
[76] ibid para 99.

with 10–20 per cent, alongside Skype, with 5–10 per cent and Twitter, with 5–10 per cent.[77] Following the *Facebook/WhatsApp* merger, Facebook could have strengthened its position in the market for social networking services by adding users and/or functionalities.[78] This aspect was, however, mitigated by the fact that around 70–90 per cent of WhatsApp's users were already active on Facebook, too.[79]

In the worldwide market for the provision of navigable digital map databases within the European Economic Area, Tele Atlas was the largest duopoly player.[80] Similarly, in *Publicis/Omnicom*, the merger was likely to lead to a duopoly in certain national 'media buying marketing' markets.[81]

DoubleClick and 24/7 Real Media/OpenAdStream on the one hand, and DoubleClick and Quantitative Atlas on the other, enjoyed 40–50 per cent and 35 per cent shares of the market respectively, while Microsoft enjoyed a just below 5 per cent market share of the marketing segment.[82] In the UK, the retail market for mobile telecommunications services was found to be 'very concentrated' in *Hutchinson 3G UK/Telefonica UK*, being dominated by four players with over 90 per cent of all subscriptions and revenues.[83]

Looking at the revenues from advertising, in 2006, Google possessed an approximately 20–40 per cent share of online advertising worldwide, whilst Microsoft's Dynamic 365 solution was fourth after Oracle's Adaptive Intelligent Apps by Data Cloud.[84] In terms of usage, Facebook Messenger attracted around 100–200 million users in the European Economic Area compared to 50–150 million users of WhatsApp.

Google was clearly dominant in the area of universal search with 90–100 per cent compared to Microsoft with 20–30 per cent and Yahoo Search with 10–20 per cent in the EU, including shares below 5–10 per cent in 2009. LinkedIn's Sales Navigator relies on a database of around 430 million users and could, therefore, become an 'important input'.[85] Microsoft's Windows Live Messenger had an approximately 90–100 per cent market share, with Skype having 70–80 per cent on PCs in 2011, Microsoft's WLM having around 30–40 per cent, and Skype's video calls having 40–50 per cent. This showed that both Microsoft and Skype were close competitors. Having attracted 600 million users, WhatsApp was definitely more popular than Facebook Messenger in 2014 compared to the latter with 250–350 million.[86]

[77] COMP/M 7217, *Facebook/WhatsApp*, 3 October 2014, paras 84 and 94.

[78] ibid para 159. Another example where the merging parties were close competitors is COMP/M 7612, *Hutchinson 3G UK/Telefonica UK*, 11 May 2016, para 417.

[79] COMP/M 7217, *Facebook/WhatsApp*, 3 October 2014, paras 159 and 162.

[80] COMP/M 4854, *TomTom/Tele Atlas*, 14 May 2008, para 80.

[81] COMP/M 7023, *Publicis/Omnicom*, 9 January 2014, para 631. This will enable the merging parties to impose conditions on media vendors and to attract more advertisers, to the competitive disadvantage of smaller rivals.

[82] COMP/M 8124, *Microsoft/LinkedIn*, 20 January 2017, para 268. Given that this is a highly innovative business model, what should matter most is the potential to exploit the relevant data rather than the market share coverage.

[83] COMP/M 7612, *Hutchinson 3G UK/Telefonica UK*, 11 May 2016, para 411.

[84] COMP/M 8124, *Microsoft/LinkedIn*, 20 January 2017, paras 198 and 200. Oracle's app offered access to over five billion global consumer profiles and 400 million business-to-business profiles. Adobe's analytics is also active in marketing, being second most competitive in terms of price.

[85] ibid paras 203 and 246 respectively.

[86] COMP/M 7217, *Facebook/WhatsApp*, 3 October 2014, para 128.

The philosophy underpinning the Commission's interpretation of market shares is that in the fast-growing high-technology sector 'high market shares are not particularly indicative of competitive strength'.[87] These figures are not self-defeating but must, nonetheless, be seen in the context of dynamic competition based on innovation. Therefore, in *Microsoft/Skype* and *Facebook/WhatsApp*, the Commission repeatedly stated the same underlying assumption, namely, that 'the consumer communications sector is a recent and fast-growing sector which is characterised by short innovation cycles in which large market shares may turn out to be ephemeral'.[88] Furthermore, following the appeal in *Cisco & Messagenet*, the same contextual consideration of dynamic competition prevails in *Facebook/WhatsApp*, in that 'the very high market shares and very high degree of concentration on the narrow market, to which the Commission referred merely as a basis for its analysis, are not necessarily indicative of market power'.[89] The only difference is a subsequent reference to the above context as enabling 'the new entity to significantly impede effective competition' in *Cisco & Messagenet* and to 'lasting damage to competition' in *Facebook/WhatsApp* respectively.

Finally, one could say that looking at market shares is a bit delusional given the particular context of high-technology markets, but the temporal dimension is more helpful in correcting such misperceptions.

E. Were Alternatives Available?

This is a straightforward question in the merger decisions under consideration, but it is dependent on how narrow the relevant markets had previously been defined. In four of these mergers, namely, *Facebook/WhatsApp*, *Microsoft/LinkedIn*, *Microsoft/Yahoo!Search* and *Google/DoubleClick*, a good number of available alternatives to both merging parties were found as follows: to Facebook, eg, Google+, LinkedIn, MySpace, Pinterest, InterNations;[90] and WhatsApp, eg, iMessage (Apple), BBM (Blackberry), ChatON (Samsung), Hangouts (Google), Android, and Skype (Microsoft);[91] to LinkedIn, there are a number of alternatives available that are specialised in 'social networking services', eg, Xing, Viadeo, GoldenLine, Academia, Behance, Doximity;[92] and Microsoft, eg, LinkedIn's Sales Navigator (Avention), Data.com, Dun & Bradstreet, InsideView, and Twitter;[93] to Yahoo, eg, Google, Microsoft, Yahoo, Ask, Yandex, AOL, Baidu and, obviously, to Microsoft; to DoubleClick, eg, Google's AdSense, Yahoo! Publisher

[87] COMP/M 6281, *Microsoft/Skype*, 7 October 2011; on appeal, *see Cisco Systems Inc and Messagenet SpA v Commission*, Case T-79/12, ECLI:EU:T:2013:635, para 51.

[88] *Cisco Systems Inc and Messagenet SpA v Commission*, Case T-79/12, ECLI:EU:T:2013:635, para 65; COMP/M 7217, *Facebook/WhatsApp*, 3 October 2014, para 99.

[89] *Cisco Systems Inc and Messagenet SpA v Commission*, Case T-79/12, ECLI:EU:T:2013:635, para 74.

[90] COMP/M 7217, *Facebook/WhatsApp*, 3 October 2014, para 49.

[91] ibid para 85.

[92] COMP/M 8124, *Microsoft/LinkedIn*, 20 January 2017, para 90. As enterprise social networks facilitating communication among employees, see 'Facebook's Workplace', para 93. On available alternatives, see paras 108 and 109. Respondents indicated that it would be difficult to transform a personal social platform into a professional one, para 110.

[93] ibid para 225.

Network, Drive PM, Trade Double, Zanox, AdLink, Interactive Media, and AOL etc; and to Google, eg, Yahoo! and Microsoft for search advertising.[94] Alternative competitors to *Publicis/Omnicom*'s data analytics space included measurement and analytics providers, such as Omiture (Adobe), Google Analytics, Coremetrics (IBM), webtrends, comScore, Nielsen, Flurry, Marketshare, Neuralitic, Agent, Localytics and Tracksimple (Bluekai); Independent providers such as Turn, Invite Media (Google), Efficient Frontier (Adobe), The Trade Desk, MediaMath, DataXu and Accordant Media; and other ad agencies, such as WPP, IPG, Havas, Dentsu-Aegis, MDC Partners and iCrossing.[95]

It was solely in *Microsoft/Skype* that the merging parties were indeed close competitors; this was despite there being a number of alternatives, for example, Microsoft's Windows Live Messenger, Skype, Google, Apple, Facebook, Yahoo! and AOL and Microsoft enterprise comms, Cisco, Citrix, IMB and Skype.[96] By contrast, Facebook Messenger and WhatsApp were found not to be close competitors on the basis of several indicia including, inter alia, the identifiers used to access the services, ie, phone number for WhatsApp; the source of the contacts, ie, users' address book for WhatsApp; user experience, which was richer for Facebook; the privacy policy on data collection for advertising and sharing; and the usage frequency.[97]

F. Barriers to Entry and Switching Costs

As has rightfully been argued elsewhere,[98] the most important barriers to data collection, sharing and transferring are, of course, data protection and privacy laws.

In *Facebook/WhatsApp* and *Microsoft/Skype*, there were very low and low barriers to entry respectively.[99] Although there were no legal barriers to entry, such as patents, know-how and IPRs, in *Facebook/WhatsApp*, there were additional issues such as portability and interoperability.[100] Switching was therefore problematic, as users, then, could lose all of their data and interaction history; thus, the messaging history remained accessible on smartphones.[101] There was, however, evidence of consumer switching in Germany.[102] Data portability was 'unlikely to result in a lock-in of users who typically

[94] COMP/M 7217, *Facebook/WhatsApp*, 3 October 2014; COMP/M 8124, *Microsoft/LinkedIn*, 20 January 2017; COMP/M 5727, *Microsoft/Yahoo! Search*, 18 February 2010; COMP/M 4731, *Google/DoubleClick*, 11 March 2008.

[95] COMP/M 7023, *Publicis/Omnicom*, 9 January 2014, para 622.

[96] COMP/M 6281, *Microsoft/Skype*, 7 October 2011.

[97] COMP/M 7217, *Facebook/WhatsApp*, 3 October 2014, paras 93, 102 and 107.

[98] For the view that data protection and privacy laws create legal barriers to the collection of data that can be circumvented through anonymisation, see D Rubinfeld and M Gal, 'Access Barriers to Big Data' (2017) 59 *Arizona Law Review* 339, 360. The authors note that, although paternalistic, privacy-based limitations of data collection protect the public interest. ibid 361.

[99] COMP/M 7217, *Facebook/WhatsApp*, 3 October 2014, para 94; COMP/M 6281, *Microsoft/Skype*, 7 October 2011, para 77.

[100] COMP/M 7217, *Facebook/WhatsApp*, 3 October 2014, paras 120 and 122 respectively.

[101] ibid para 113.

[102] ibid para 174.

retain access to message history on their handset even if they start using another consumer communications app'.[103]

In *TomTom/Tele Atlas*, customers had to reconfigure the new database when switching suppliers of navigable digital map databases. The Commission identified that barriers to switching were relatively limited to the reconfiguration cost, including that of modifying production tools to handle different data formats.[104] Elsewhere, however, it was recognised that, in the event of switching, a producer of digital map databases would have to spend substantial resources to collect any additional data necessary for navigation.[105]

In *Microsoft/Skype*, switching costs were higher if the users were charged for the service after a long time, but there were no technical or economic constraints.[106] In contrast, in *Microsoft/Yahoo Search!*, barriers to entry were very high; for example, $1 billion needed to be invested in hardware and human resources respectively.[107] It was also found that advertisers would no longer switch from adCenter to Panama.[108] Switching between ad serving suppliers also entailed additional costs in *Google/DoubleClick*, eg, staff training and deployment. Although some of such costs could be significant, they are still 'manageable'.[109]

Ultimately, in *Publicis/Omnicom*, it was 'very easy' or 'somewhat easy' for advertisers to switch with no significant costs other than the cost of re-tendering.[110] As the market for marketing communications services is a 'highly fragmented and creativity-driven' market, barriers to entry are low, and termination of contracts is easy without incurring significant costs.[111] In addition, large advertising networks, including WPP, IPG, Dentsu-Aegis and Havas, will probably exert a significant competitive constraint on the merged entity.[112]

Finally, in *Facebook/WhatsApp*, the existence of network effects was 'unlikely to shield the merged entity from competition from new and existing consumer communications apps'.[113]

[103] ibid para 137. In addition, it was noted that users of consumer communications apps cannot be locked in to any particular physical network or hardware solution. Neither Facebook Messenger nor WhatsApp are pre-installed on a large base of datasets and there is no 'status quo bias' potentially affecting consumer choice.

[104] COMP/M 4854, *TomTom/TeleAtlas*, 14 May 2008, paras 106 and 99 respectively. However, the costs of handling different database formats are not significant; see para 102.

[105] ibid para 25. This is more so since compiling and processing the necessary data is 'a very time-consuming process' (see para 26) because vast volumes of data have to be collected from various sources, and field survey teams have to drive down every road in the EEA and record all features on the way; see para 132.

[106] COMP/M 6281, *Microsoft/Skype*, 7 October 2011, para 77; on appeal, *see Cisco Systems Inc and Messagenet SpA v Commission*, Case T-79/12, ECLI:EU:T:2013:635, para 80.

[107] COMP/M 5727, *Microsoft/Yahoo! Search*, 18 February 2010, para 111.

[108] ibid para 181.

[109] COMP/M 4731, *Google/DoubleClick*, 11 March 2008, paras 137, 297 and 329.

[110] COMP/M 7023, *Publicis/Omnicom*, 9 January 2014, paras 227, 233 and 614.

[111] ibid para 598. See also para 603, where respondents identified creativity as a key factor on the basis of which marketing communications service agencies are selected by customers alongside expertise, quality, delivery, price scale and absence of conflicts of interest.

[112] ibid para 602.

[113] COMP/M 7217, *Facebook/WhatsApp*, 3 October 2014, para 135.

III. Post-merger Innovation Incentives: Dead or Alive?

In the digital markets under scrutiny, one sensitive issue has been whether the merged entity will continue to invest in innovation. In *Facebook/WhatsApp*, the underlying assumption was that customers could easily switch to competing services if the merged entity were to reduce the amount of innovation.[114] Being recognised as 'recent and fast-growing', the consumer communications sector was portrayed as characterised by 'frequent market entry and short innovation cycles in which large market shares turn out to be ephemeral'.[115] However, as recent events have shown, digital giants like Facebook could lose their market share due to reputational damage following data breaches rather than to their innovation cycles. The latter are also referred to in *Microsoft/Skype* under the same assumption that, in these markets, innovation cycles are short-lived.[116] As both software and platforms are constantly redeveloped, innovators lead the market solely for a short while.[117]

In both *Microsoft/LinkedIn* and *Microsoft/Yahoo Search!*, there is recognition that the former entity, Microsoft, could make it more difficult for alternative intelligent solutions 'to compete and bring innovation in the market', whilst the latter, Yahoo, would require heavy investments in upgrading data, storage for a web search index and advanced algorithms.[118] There is a potential contradiction as, although Yahoo was recognised as a 'weak innovative force' that 'may lose the ability to provide important innovations', Yahoo's incentives to innovate would not be reduced, as Google would have similar incentives.[119] The same conclusion was valid for Microsoft, in that it would be unlikely to reduce its incentives to innovate.[120] It was assumed that the new platform (*Microsoft/Yahoo Search!*) could compete more effectively with Google.[121]

Prospectively, these predictions have proved to be inaccurate. The post-merger reality is often a different one in which not all conglomerates become successful innovators. Retrospectively, one could question whether Yahoo/Search or LinkedIn are better services than before, in particular whether significant achievements based on innovation could also be highlighted.

[114] ibid para 94.

[115] ibid para 99. A Schumpeterian understanding of innovation cautions against the risks for competition authorities when assessing innovation incentives ex ante, which is also pervasive in the area of merger control. Anca D Chirita, 'Editorial: Competition and Regulatory Trends in Digital Markets' (2017) 12 *Competition Law Review* 126.

[116] COMP/M 6281, *Microsoft/Skype*, 7 October 2011, para 83.

[117] ibid para 83.

[118] COMP/M 8124, *Microsoft/LinkedIn*, 20 January 2017, para 246; COMP/M 5727, *Microsoft/Yahoo! Search*, 18 February 2010, para 140.

[119] COMP/M 5727, *Microsoft/Yahoo! Search*, 18 February 2010, paras 141, 203, 206 and 219.

[120] COMP/M 8124, *Microsoft/LinkedIn*, 20 January 2017, para 275.

[121] COMP/M 5727, *Microsoft/Yahoo! Search*, 18 February 2010, para 192.

IV. From Fictional Assumptions Disregarding Data to the Growing Relevance of Data

Prospectively, one could challenge such assumptions, which are known in mergers as 'counterfactual' scenarios. In *Google/DoubleClick*, there were a number of competitive advantages for Google following the integration of DoubleClick's ad serving technology with ad intermediation services, DoubleClick's customer base among publishers and advertisers, and data about consumer behaviour collected through ad serving.[122] This was a first indicator of the role of data. Furthermore, DoubleClick represented a 'key input into distribution channels that compete with Google's AdSense'; however, the combination of users' databases was thought unlikely to provide 'a considerable additional competitive advantage'.[123] A portability issue became apparent as advertisers had to transfer 'past' data from one system to another.[124] It was, however, estimated that less than one per cent of former customers would require the migration of historical delivery data upon switching.

Another aspect that was neglected in *Google/DoubleClick* was the data collected by DoubleClick, which contained information about a rich subset of the web-browsing behaviour of DoubleClick users across all publishers' websites engaged in targeted advertising.[125] The latter had the potential to inflict consumer harm given that publishers are normally either paid or at least sponsored by businesses, including retailers. For example, tracking technologies could facilitate online price discrimination on the basis of such targeted advertising.[126] DoubleClick's justification was that, although it had indeed collected behavioural data from its users, such data was used for a legitimate purpose only, namely, improving DoubleClick's service experience offered to advertisers.[127] Furthermore, the record of ads containing the 'prices paid by different ad networks' was in the form of *aggregated* data.[128] This could have partially met the data protection requirements.

Nonetheless, the variation in pricing could have been investigated further, in particular regarding whether tracking technologies were used to monitor users and whether the latter had meaningfully consented to this procedure. Rather, increasing the confusion, there is another specific reference to the fact that DoubleClick could not possibly have made the data in question available to 'others', presumably third parties, publishers or advertisers, subject to a contractual express prohibition that was unlikely to be changed

[122] COMP/M 4731, *Google/DoubleClick*, 11 March 2008, para 225.

[123] ibid paras 286 and 298. In contrast, the US FTC concluded that 'neither the data available to Google, nor the data available to DoubleClick, constitute an essential input to a successful online advertising product'. See Pamela Jones Harbour, Dissenting Statement in the Matter of Google/DoubleClick FTC, file no 071-0170 (2007) p. 12.

[124] COMP/M 4731, *Google/DoubleClick*, 11 March 2008, para 140.

[125] ibid para 182.

[126] For a suggestion that the ability to price discriminate on the basis of consumer preferences may be 'substantial', see Rubinfeld and Gal, 'Access Barriers' (2017) 378. The final conclusion, however, goes to the opposite direction by suggesting that the 'collection and analysis of big data has *undoubtedly* increased social welfare'; ibid 381.

[127] COMP/M 4731, *Google/DoubleClick*, 11 March 2008, paras 183 and 184.

[128] ibid para 187.

in the future.[129] This seemingly indicated that there was an inner circle of publishers and advertisers with which DoubleClick must have had a contractual relationship in return for an adequate consideration of their business interests. The argument based on confidentiality grounds is particularly weak. In this respect, DoubleClick argued that the relevant data would have been of limited use anyway. This was because of the confidentiality clauses included in the contractual arrangements with both advertisers and publishers.[130]

The *Google/DoubleClick* merger decision includes nevertheless a significant disclaimer at paragraph 360:

> it is not excluded that [...] the merged entity would be able to combine DoubleClick's and Google's data collections, eg, users' IP addresses, cookies IDs, connection times to correctly match records from both databases. Such combination could result in individual users' search histories being linked to the same users' past surfing behaviour on the internet [...] the merged entity may know that the same user has searched for terms A, B and C and visited pages X, Y and Z in the past week. Such information could potentially be used to better target ads to users.[131]

There is no better evidence elsewhere that the merged entity could only consolidate its previous accumulation of data, which would make the tracking of users' locations easier.

All in all, in 2008, it was simply too early for data experts to be articulate about the monetisation of data, which justifies the above positive assumption about the lack of a competitive advantage based on data. It will be argued that the exclusionary focus based on access to data, or an ability to accumulate it, is a fallacy. What matters most is how data, once accumulated, is used to exploit online consumers.

However, many years later, in *Facebook/WhatsApp*, a closer examination of the data collected by the merging parties revealed that, on the one hand, Facebook collects data for the purpose of serving its users more targeted advertisements; Facebook also claimed that it does not sell or provide data analytics to advertisers or third parties.[132] On the other hand, WhatsApp claimed that neither does it sell advertising, or store or collect users' data for advertising purposes, and nor does WhatsApp collect its users' personal data such as verified name, sensitive data such as age and gender, and any other personally identifiable data including social groups, activities, consumer habits or other characteristics that are valuable for advertising purposes.[133] Based on WhatsApp's disclosure, it would appear that this platform offered its users enhanced privacy protection. This was, however, not so, as in 2012, WhatsApp was investigated by the Office of the Privacy Commissioner of Canada and the Dutch Data Protection Authority for having forced its users to give access to their entire address book without consent.[134] Apart from this, WhatsApp's privacy policy of 2012 is self-explanatory, as

[129] ibid paras 188, 257 and 265.
[130] ibid para 277.
[131] ibid para 360.
[132] COMP/M 7217, *Facebook/WhatsApp*, 3 October 2014, para 70.
[133] ibid paras 71 and 166.
[134] See L Clark, 'WhatsApp Breached Data Privacy Laws by Storing Non-User Contact Details', *Wired*, 29 January 2013, available at www.wired.co.uk/article/whatsapp-privacy. For the findings of the international

WhatsApp claimed that it did not collect its users' mobile address book, but actually, the company collected its users' mobile phone numbers. It also claimed not to collect location data or to target its users with advertisements.[135] Indeed, the policy clearly mentioned that WhatsApp does not 'sell or share your Personally Identifiable Information (such as mobile phone number) with other third-party companies for their commercial or marketing use without your consent or except as part of a specific programme or feature' for which users had the ability to opt in or out.

Ultimately, the objective justifications for data collection and sharing by WhatsApp are in line with those of similar platforms including, for example, the performance, improvement and maintenance of WhatsApp's own service or as part of a legal requirement, such as a court order, subpoena, search warrant or other equivalent. Another similar procedural safeguard put in place referred to the event of a merger, where

> in the event that WhatsApp is acquired by or merged with a third party entity, we reserve the right to transfer or assign the information we have collected from our users as part of such merger, acquisition, sale, or other change of control.[136]

The above disclaimer is technically a procedural waiver for WhatsApp's previous data collection, which was intended to facilitate the transfer of data. However, such a procedural notice is given too early for its users to express any meaningful and informed consent, and personal data could simply be purchased from elsewhere, such as through other third parties.[137] Furthermore, such users had no realistic choice of blocking the merger anyway. The material scope of application of the data protection regime is confined to data breaches, not to merger reviews.

Facebook's submission was, however, in sharp contrast to Facebook's own privacy policy, which mentioned that it collects behavioural data, including its users' location, which Facebook shares not only with companies that are part of Facebook, but also with integrated third-party apps, websites or other services, including third-party advertisers.[138] Facebook sought consent only for sharing personally identifiable users' data with 'third party advertisers and analytics partners', but not for *aggregated* data sent to vendors, service providers and partners. Given Facebook's business model of offering a social networking platform free of charge, the revenues were extracted from advertising so that targeted advertising represented Facebook's default terms and conditions of trade. Indeed, Facebook did not consider asking its users for consent to use targeted advertising. Obviously, this model did not comply with the data protection regime, as whilst general advertising is annoying, targeted advertising must have exploited

investigation by the Canadian and Dutch data protection authorities, see Office of the Privacy Commissioner of Canada, Final Report of the Findings: Investigation into the personal information handling practices of WhatsApp Inc, 15 January 2013, available at https://autoriteitpersoonsgegevens.nl/sites/default/files/downloads/rapporten/rap_2013-whatsapp-opc-final-report-of-findings.pdf.

[135] See, eg, WhatsApp's archived privacy policy of July 2012, available at www.whatsapp.com/legal?doc=privacy-policy&version=20120707, subject to several notable safeguards concerning the security of the data and the opt-in and opt-out available procedures.

[136] See also WhatsApp's archived privacy policy of July 2012.

[137] For the view that the 'notice-and-choice' frameworks are deeply undermined by the 'third-party problem', see Hoofnagle, *Federal Trade Commission* (2016) 146.

[138] See Chirita, 'The Rise of Big Data and the Loss of Privacy' (2018) 17.

Facebook users' behavioural data. Also, the reference to advertisers as business partners is used interchangeably with vendors, which could include retailers or any other interested business parties.

Most notably, Facebook also claimed that it would be 'unable to automatically and reliably associate a Facebook ID with a valid phone number used by a user on WhatsApp' and that technical integration of the two services was unlikely.[139] Nonetheless, in August 2016, WhatsApp updated its privacy policy to allow for linking WhatsApp users' phone numbers with Facebook users' identity in a move which was intended to 'improve customer experience'. The previous statement was proven to have been misleading and the Commission sent its statement of objections.[140] Due to such misleading statements, the Commission did not investigate the market for the provision of data or data analytics services.[141]

In *Publicis/Omnicom*, the merging parties made an astonishing revelation: first, that they did not control the primary source of data and, second, that they needed clients' databases and needed 'to purchase such data from various first-party data sources'.[142] The revelation should be persuasive for commentators who still question whether there is a dark rather than an open market for the sale of data. The Commission concluded that navigable digital map databases are 'important inputs' for device manufacturers and providers of navigation software.[143]

In *Microsoft/LinkedIn*, providers of competing software solutions claimed that LinkedIn's Sales Navigator could represent an 'important input'; furthermore, Microsoft could make it more difficult for alternative intelligent solutions 'to compete and bring innovation' into the market following this merger.[144] The LinkedIn Sales Navigator could potentially share users' datasets with third parties.[145] Again, this consideration was ignored because the sharing of personal data would undermine LinkedIn's own business model.

For example, in *Telefonica/Vodafone/Everything Everywhere/JV*, JV would send targeted marketing messages solely to mobile subscribers who had opted in to receive them.[146] This would then be fully compliant with the data protection framework. Yet, had such subscribers not understood the hidden pitfalls of the terms and conditions of privacy, their consent might not have been meaningful. In addition, JV would aggregate behavioural data in the market for retail bulk SMSs, with the assistance of computer software for originating messages, including routing SMS to any destination.[147]

[139] COMP/M 7217, *Facebook/WhatsApp*, 3 October 2014, paras 138 and 139.

[140] See European Commission, COMP/M 8228, *Facebook/WhatsApp*, press release of 20 December 2016, 'Mergers: Commission alleges Facebook provided misleading information about WhatsApp takeover'. As a result, a €110 million fine was imposed on Facebook for providing misleading information about the WhatsApp merger.

[141] COMP/M 7217, *Facebook/WhatsApp*, 3 October 2014, para 72.

[142] COMP/M 7023, *Publicis/Omnicom*, 9 January 2014, para 624.

[143] COMP/M 4854, *TomTom/Tele Atlas*, 14 May 2008, para 165. Thus, most providers considered navigable digital map databases as a 'key input' for navigation software, see para 164.

[144] COMP/M 8124, *Microsoft/LinkedIn*, 20 January 2017, para 246.

[145] ibid paras 247 and 248.

[146] COMP/M 6314, *Telefonica UK/Vodafone UK/Everything Everywhere/JV*, 4 September 2012, paras 26 and 88.

[147] ibid paras 493 and 494.

This would, however, require a significant investment in software and systems and the analysis of vast amounts of data.[148] The Commission considered it unlikely that the merging parties would discriminate between the bulk of SMSs sent by JV and those sent by competitors.[149]

It was put forward that JV's data analytics would involve the analysis of data on customers and their behaviour. JV would collect data from its mobile wallet platform and its advertising intermediation services so as to provide customers with valuable insight into consumer behaviour.[150] However, JV would not offer standalone data analytics. The personal and/or sensitive data including inter alia age, residential status, profession and location would be anonymised, which will then meet the data protection requirements.[151] Some respondents were concerned that JV would develop a database that would become an essential input for targeted mobile advertising.[152] The merging parties mentioned competition from a range of data analytics providers, such as Google Analytics, Apple, Facebook, Visa, MasterCard, Experian, Acxiom, Amazon or eBay.[153] All of them possess sophisticated databases used for targeted advertising. Another concern was whether JV could foreclose competing providers of data analytics or advertising services by combining personal, location, response, social behaviour and browsing data. In other words, could JV create a unique database that would become an essential input for targeted mobile advertising that no other provider would be able to duplicate?[154] This was not the case, as the above data sets were already available to Google, Apple, Facebook, card issuers, reference agencies or retailers.[155] For example, Microsoft submitted that it can provide the 'same level of granularity' with regard to geo-location data.[156]

In conclusion, JV would be able to collect a vast array of consumer data for its mobile data analytics and advertising services.[157] As there are 'strong and established' competing players, JV could not possibly foreclose competition in the respective markets for mobile data analytics, market research and marketing information services.[158]

On a positive note, in *IMS Health/Cegedim Business*, IMS provides pharmaceutical companies with sales data on the basis of a predefined geographical segmentation without any identification of sales to individual pharmacies or customers, as is required by data protection law.[159]

[148] ibid para 511.
[149] ibid para 514.
[150] ibid para 531.
[151] ibid para 532.
[152] ibid para 534.
[153] ibid para 535. In the UK, the market for data analytics and market research is worth £2.8 billion per year. See para 536.
[154] ibid para 539.
[155] ibid para 543.
[156] ibid para 545. In addition, social behavioural data could be collected from Facebook or LinkedIn, see para 547; browsing data from Google, cookies or Apple iPhone.
[157] ibid para 557.
[158] ibid para 558. The same conclusion is subsequently found in the market for advertising services, see para 579.
[159] COMP/M 7337, *IMS Health/Cegedim Business*, 19 December 2014, para 20.

V. The Corporatist Model of Data Control – Where Terms and Conditions of Privacy are Imposed on Consumers: Is Huge Accumulation of Data a 'Road to Serfdom'?[160]

In recent years, privacy has been the focus of the United Nations' Special Rapporteur on the right to privacy, who noted that: 'There are strong indicators that Privacy has become an important commercial consideration with some major vendors adopting it as a selling point. If there is a market for privacy, market forces will provide for that market.'[161]

Corporations do not need to accumulate a vast amount of data to make online platforms work. Although everyone accepts it, the objective necessity justification for the accumulation of data is implausible. It can be argued, for example, that the Google Maps app cannot work if location tracking is disabled; however, many other services do not need to use tracking technologies other than for their own commercial interests. In the vast majority of cases, corporations allow the disclosure of data in order for them to respond to legal proceedings. But there is no objective justification for exploiting behavioural data for the targeted advertising of users in exchange for a monetary consideration from advertisers or publishers.

Who, then, dictates the corporatist model of data control?[162] Users have no other realistic choice but to agree to exploitative terms and conditions of privacy where data is the new currency. Beyond corporations, whose sole interest is boosting corporate profits from advertising, the state, too, has an interest in having such corporations disclose relevant data for legitimate legal proceedings. Thus, creating a disclosure mechanism of data puts a strain on the balance of legitimacy between proper functioning or service maintenance and judicial or administrative expectations.

The state ultimately empowers corporations by enacting insufficiently robust legislation without proper coordination with other areas that might be affected by the accumulation of data. So, the initial question in the heading of this section might not have an easy answer. It is clear that there is a tyranny of the corporatist model based on data; however, the role of the state in nurturing the supremacy of data accumulation over the fundamental value of privacy is dubious at its best. By contrast, competition authorities have proceeded cautiously. In the assessment of privacy, care has been taken not to upset the balance of power and to overstep the traditional role of the competition

[160] Generally, on the paradigmatic shift from capitalism to socialism and totalitarianism, see FA von Hayek, *The Road to Serfdom* (London, Routledge, 2001), originally published in 1944.

[161] Report of the Special Rapporteur on the Right to Privacy, Joseph A Cannataci, United Nations' Human Rights Council, Doc No A/HRC/31/64 of 8 March 2016.

[162] A first answer is that states can and do engage in massive surveillance, see M Bohlander, 'The Global Panopticon: Mass Surveillance and Data Privacy Intrusion as a Crime against Humanity' in M Böse, M Bohlander, A Klip and O Lagodny (eds), *Justice Without Borders: Essays in Honour of Wolfgang Schomburg* (Leiden, Boston, Brill Nijhoff, 2018). A second answer is that individuals can also influence the model by rejecting a lower privacy standard, which is, after all, a subjective preference. For the view that both quality and privacy are subjective preferences, see K Waehrer, 'Online Services and the Analysis of Competitive Merger Effects in Privacy Protections and Other Quality Dimensions' (8 July 2016), available at https://ssrn.com/abstract=2701927.

authorities. The latter had not dealt with privacy before. At a first glance, privacy is an exotic fruit grown in the field of mergers. In reality, the terms and conditions of privacy are a mere sub-division of a standard form agreement offered by online platforms to their users.

To get back to basics, transactional contract theory is applicable in the sense that privacy terms and conditions might be unfairly imposed on users. Under the myriad of contract theories based on will, reliance, fairness, efficiency and good value, the consent theory of contract has replaced the traditional ones.[163] Although the requirement of consent also implies transactional costs, the consent theory was better able to capture what the doctrine of consideration was unable to due to the lack of monetary consideration. A showing of consent is, therefore, prima facie sufficient to make an online platform's user agreement legally enforceable. Furthermore, the consent theory recognises the need to enforce gratuitous commitments and, in this respect, the consent theory has sorted out the issue of the lack of monetary consideration of the many online services offered free of charge. The perils of the consent theory, as it is applicable to the context of online platforms, is that it protects a promisee's reliance (ie, online platform) on a promisor's consent (ie, online users), even in those instances where, for example, online users did not subjectively intend to be bound, eg, for the lack of any reading or comprehension of privacy terms and conditions.[164]

All in all, it has been shown above that the modern transactional theory of contract based on consent, although pragmatically helpful in many respects, as with many other theories applied in practice, is still a theory that is unable to resolve all problems. Put briefly, it is a theory that fails lamentably in practice.

In *Facebook/WhatsApp*, there is also a welcome recognition of a number of important areas of improvement, in particular, 'privacy and security, the importance of which varies from user to user but which are becoming increasingly valued, as shown by the introduction of consumer communications apps specifically addressing privacy and security issues'.[165] Privacy concerns have largely been dismissed based on the division of competence between competition and data protection law. For example, in *Facebook/WhatsApp*, it was stated that:

> Any privacy-related concerns flowing from the increased concentration of data within the control of Facebook as a result of the Transaction do not fall within the scope of the EU competition law rules but within the scope of the EU data protection rules.[166]

[163] For an excellent narrative of the above contract theories, see RE Barnett, 'A Consent Theory of Contract' (1986) 86 *Colombia Law Review* 269, including: (i) will theory dependent on the will of the parties, with moral implications and subjective intent; (ii) reliance on promises based on the intuition that we ought to be contractually liable; (iii) efficiency theory based on the maximisation of wealth; (iv) fairness theories based on substantive or procedural fairness; (v) bargain theory; and, finally, (vi) consent theory.

[164] For the consent theory, see ibid.

[165] COMP/M 7217, *Facebook/WhatsApp*, 3 October 2014, para 87.

[166] COMP/M 7217, *Facebook/WhatsApp*, 3 October 2014, para 164. For the criticism that both the EU Commission and the US Federal Trade Commission have underestimated the 'true' value of data, see A Ezrachi, *EU Competition Law: An Analytical Guide to the Leading Cases*, 5th edn (Oxford, Hart Publishing, 2016) 454.

A nearly identical statement was made in *Sanofi/Google/DMI JV*, specifically, that:

> For the purposes of this decision, the Commission notes that any privacy-related concerns flowing from the use of data within the control of the Parties do not fall within the scope of the EU competition law rules but within the scope of the EU data protection rules.[167]

Although sensible, at least one of the above statements was at odds with the fact that Facebook's privacy policy had expressly stated that in the case of a change in ownership or control, users are subject to data transfer.[168] However, in *Sanofi/Google/DMI JV*, the parties lacked the ability to lock in patients by limiting or preventing the portability of their data.[169]

A similar approach was, more recently, used in *Microsoft/LinkedIn*, specifically, that 'the merger does not raise competition concerns resulting from the possible post-merger combination of the data', including more specifically, personal and behavioural data, and that 'any such data combination […] could only be implemented by the merged entity to the extent it is allowed by applicable data protection law'.[170] The merging parties had made it clear that they did not make data available to third parties for the purpose of advertising subject to 'very limited exceptions'.[171]

In the early years of consideration of data-driven mergers in *Google/DoubleClick*, the decision simply paid attention to the legal framework, mentioning that it is 'without prejudice' to Directive 95/46/EC and Directive 2002/58/EC.[172] This conveyed an impression that there was no appetite for any review of data and privacy implications. It, nonetheless, highlighted the need for greater coordination between competition and data protection.

In *Microsoft/LinkedIn*, privacy considerations were effectively ignored with the justification that the merger

> does not raise competition concerns resulting from the possible post-merger combination of data (essentially consisting of personal information, such as information about an individual's job, career history and professional connections, and/or her or his email or other contacts, search behaviour etc. about the users of their services) held by each of the Parties in relation to online advertising.[173]

The problem associated with this approach overlooking privacy is that the Commission too readily accepted that such a data combination is already compliant with data protection law. Instead, it examined horizontal effects since actual or potential competitors will need to collect 'even more data to compete effectively with the new entity'.[174]

[167] COMP/M 7813, *Sanofi/Google/DMI JV*, 23 February 2016, para 70.

[168] For Facebook's privacy policy, see https://www.facebook.com/about/privacy?ref=new_policy. Currently, unlike Google, Facebook does not display its archived privacy policies. Similar provisions in the event of a merger were adopted by Whisper: Chirita (62) 19.

[169] COMP/M 7813, *Sanofi/Google/DMI JV*, 23 February 2016, para 69. This is due to the new data protection regime.

[170] COMP/M 8124, *Microsoft/LinkedIn*, 20 January 2017, paras 176 and 177.

[171] COMP/M 8124, *Microsoft/LinkedIn*, 20 January 2017, para 180.

[172] COMP/M 4731, *Google/DoubleClick*, 11 March 2008, para 368.

[173] COMP/M 8124, *Microsoft/LinkedIn*, 20 January 2017, para 176.

[174] ibid para 179.

Both merging parties were believed not to compete against each other in advertising on the basis of data and not to make data available to third parties for advertising but for 'very limited exceptions'.[175]

Nonetheless, too much faith was placed in the General Data Protection Regulation (2016/679),[176] one year ahead of its entry into force. Indeed, the new regime might not be as effective in addressing the existing loopholes regarding data. In particular, the decision noted that the new regulation could limit Microsoft's ability to have access to LinkedIn's full data and process personal data, 'thereby strengthening the existing rights and empowering individuals with more control over personal data'.[177] This remains rather wishful thinking since Microsoft's strategic move was simply the acquisition of 'more data'.

As has previously been noted with regard to the *Facebook/WhatsApp* merger, the data protection regulation is not empowered to block mergers and acquisitions. Competition authorities are therefore best placed to consider the implications of a large accumulation of data and to review unfair terms and conditions of privacy. Furthermore, the dismissal of privacy considerations on grounds based largely on the classical divide between competition and data protection is unhelpful in instrumenting the case against behavioural price discrimination, which is something that privacy cannot deal with. As one commentator explained, first-degree price discrimination is one manifestation of the significant privacy and autonomy risks, 'But privacy may not be the right tool to address the problem'.[178]

Finally, regarding the new data protection regime and the question of whether it is, indeed, offering better protection against data breaches, the answer is that one can only hope so. Again, it is rather wishful thinking that we expect data protection authorities to take action against the exploitation of aggregated and anonymised behavioural data that could negatively affect the economic interests of consumers. Recital 75 of the new Data Protection Regulation 679/2016 refers to discrimination and to any other significant economic disadvantage, to personal economic situation, personal preferences or interests, behaviour, location or movements, all of which depict the landscape of data analytics analysed above in the context of mergers. Article 3(1) of the Directive 680/2016 recognises name, identification number, location, online identifier and economic identity as personal data. In other words, the legal framework recognises individual rights to an online personal identity; thus, in the wake of the market studies and research involving aggregated personal identities, the enforcement of individual rights to an online personal identity relies on the legal tests foreseen by the data protection law. It will, however, be argued that the enforcement of individual rights to online

[175] ibid para 180. Microsoft submitted that it did not hold 'a significant percentage of valuable data for advertising purposes'.

[176] See Regulation (EU) 2016/679 of the EU Parliament and of the Council of 27 April 2016 on the protection of natural persons with regard to the processing of personal data and on the free movement of such data, OJ L 119/2016.

[177] COMP/M 8124, *Microsoft/LinkedIn*, 20 January 2017, paras 178 and 368 respectively.

[178] Hoofnagle (n 31) 147. Hoofnagle also refers to another paradox, namely, the inconsistency between consumer desires for more privacy and their actual behaviour of exposing an excessive wealth of personal information on social platforms.

economic identity, envisioning the economic rights referred to above, could solely be enforced by competition authorities. We cannot, and should not, accept that data and privacy experts deal with cases of online price discrimination.

VI. Towards a Workable Theory of Harm?

Several attempts have already been made to address the nefarious effects of the accumulation of data by advancing theories of harm to consumers. None of these so-called 'theories' was ultimately a workable theory that could be applicable to all data-driven mergers in recent practice. This section will map the most relevant theories of harm and, based on their criticism, offer a workable theory of harm.

A. Consumer Harm Due to Degradation of Quality and Targeted Advertising

Both *Facebook/WhatsApp* and *Microsoft/Yahoo! Search* offer a different kind of theory of harm, which is discussed as a 'theoretical' possibility, leading to a bifurcated analysis of 'targeted advertising' and 'degradation', ie diminution, of quality.[179] The catalyst for this bifurcated theory is the consumer-protection function inherent in competition law,[180] as the primary focus of consumer law is on advertising and quality. In recent years, most notably after the enactment of the Guidance Paper on the prioritisation of cases under Article 102 TFEU, there has been an extension of the consumer-protection function with a further welcome focus on consumer choice and implications for innovation. As the areas of abuse of dominance and mergers are intertwined, this extension of enforcement is helpful and pragmatic. More specifically, the legal test applicable to mergers is focused on the 'creation or strengthening' of a dominant position following the merger. Disregarding such consumer considerations could therefore lead to an enforcement gap;[181] consumer law is not equipped to deal either with monopolistic power or with mergers.

In the first scenario in *Facebook/WhatsApp*, the Commission examined the theoretical possibility of introducing targeted advertising following a change in

[179] COMP/M 7217, *Facebook/WhatsApp*, 3 October 2014; COMP/M 5727, *Microsoft/Yahoo! Search*, 18 February 2010.

[180] See R Whish and D Bailey, *Competition Law*, 8th edn (Oxford, Oxford University Press, 2015) 20, favouring a consumer-protection function applicable, more generally, to competition law; in the area of mergers, see the reference to the reduction of quality in the Guidelines on the assessment of horizontal mergers under the Council Regulation on the control of mergers between undertakings, OJ [2004] C 31/5, para 36 on decreasing quality; para 65 on deteriorating quality; and specifically for the prohibition of abuse of a dominant position, see, eg, Anca D Chirita, 'Undistorted, (Un)fair Competition, Consumer Welfare and the Interpretation of Article 102 TFEU' (2010) 3 *World Competition Law and Economics Review* 417. In the context of free goods, as more emphasis has to be placed on quality, rather than on price, this could therefore enforce a consumer-protection function of competition law. See Gal and Rubinfeld, 'The Hidden Costs of Free Goods' (2016) 542.

[181] In the same vein, see Gal and Rubinfeld (n 21) 546, fn 143 on Facebook's privacy cases, highlighting that, due to the absence of monetary consideration, some courts decided that consumer law does not apply.

WhatsApp's privacy policy and data collection for the same purpose of targeted advertising.[182] These scenarios were dismissed due to the possibility of switching from Facebook and WhatsApp to other services and the existence of alternative providers of data for the purpose of advertising, eg, Apple, Amazon, eBay, Microsoft, AOL, Twitter, Yahoo!, IAC, LinkedIn, Adobe and Yelp.[183]

In the second scenario, in *Microsoft/Yahoo! Search*, the Commission examined the theoretical possibility of degradation of the organic search due to the trade off from paid results. This possibility was easily dismissed because 'when a platform tries to attract more users through greater relevance on the organic search it runs the risk of losing revenues on the advertising side'.[184] As adCenter and Bing will process more traffic, more data will then be available for experimentation which, in turn, will also 'tend to increase' the quality of the new product through better ad matching and higher conversion rates of sale. It was firmly believed that the new platform would eventually become an effective competitor of Google.[185] In *Google/DoubleClick*, there was also consideration of the same possibility of the degradation of DoubleClick tool's quality, including bundling DoubleClick with Google's intermediation services.[186]

In *Publicis/Omnicom*, the Commission also examined whether big data may facilitate online targeted advertising and become crucial to conducting a business and to attracting new advertisers.[187] By contrast, in *TomTom/TeleAtlas*, the Commission found that the merged entity was most likely to have the ability to increase prices, degrade quality or delay access for some manufacturers and navigation software providers of digital maps.[188] However, confidentiality concerns were considered similar to product degradation in that the perceived value of the navigable digital map for manufacturers would be lower if the latter feared that confidential information would be shared with TomTom.[189] These concerns were later dismissed due to the limited amount of information of competitive value exchanged between Tele Atlas and its customers.[190]

Given the dismissal of the above counterfactual scenarios, one could extract as a preliminary conclusion that the consumer harm caused in these cases by an accumulation of data was not taken too seriously. The most plausible explanation is that both the degradation of quality and targeted advertising are primarily the mission of consumer laws. In contrast, the mission of competition law in the area of mergers is to balance the existence of conglomerate effects. Both *Microsoft/Yahoo Search* and *Microsoft/Skype* evaluated these effects but, nonetheless, dismissed them.[191]

[182] See COMP/M 7217, *Facebook/WhatsApp*, 3 October 2014, paras 173 and 185 and para 180 respectively.
[183] ibid para 188.
[184] COMP/M 5727, *Microsoft/Yahoo! Search*, 18 February 2010, para 204.
[185] ibid para 192.
[186] COMP/M 4731, *Google/DoubleClick*, 11 March 2008, para 289.
[187] COMP/M 7023, *Publicis/Omnicom*, 9 January 2014, para 625.
[188] COMP/M 4854, *TomTom/TeleAtlas*, 14 May 2008, para 210.
[189] ibid para 274.
[190] ibid para 276.
[191] COMP/M 5727, *Microsoft/Yahoo! Search*, 18 February 2010, paras 244; COMP/M 6281, *Microsoft/Skype*, 7 October 2011, paras 158 and 214.

B. Consumer Harm due to Horizontal Effects

In *Microsoft/Skype*, consideration was given to the horizontal effects on consumer communications including instant messaging, voice and video calls on PCs having Microsoft's Windows operating system, and on enterprise communications.[192] None of these effects were considered to be significant. In *Facebook/WhatsApp*, the horizontal effects were dismissed since only Facebook is active in the provision of online advertising services.[193] In *Telefonica/Vodafone/Everything Everywhere/JV*, the Commission examined whether the merger could give rise to horizontal effects, but concluded that JV could face competition from a number of market participants, including Google and Apple.[194] Given the low market shares and the presence of several strong competitors, no horizontal effects were identifiable in *IMS Health/Cegedim Business* with regard to intelligent business solutions; nonetheless, such effects were identified with regard to the provision of syndicated primary market research.[195]

C. Consumer Harm Due to Conglomerate Effects through Tying or Bundling

In *Microsoft/Yahoo Search*, it was found that the existence of conglomerate effects may increase Microsoft's ability to leverage its market power in areas other than online advertising including notably its PC operating systems and personal productivity apps.[196] In particular, Microsoft could negotiate distribution agreements with manufacturers for the default making of its search technology. The consumer harm inflicted through such bundling was rather surprisingly considered 'unlikely to be significant'.[197] In *Microsoft/Skype*, similar conglomerate effects were identified due to Microsoft's dominant position in the market for Windows operating systems, the Internet Explorer browser and Office apps software.[198] In particular, Microsoft could degrade the interoperability of Skype with competing operating systems and platforms and instead interoperate solely with Microsoft's Lync app.[199] Furthermore, Microsoft could technologically integrate Skype and Windows as a 'must-have' product or engage in commercial bundling of Skype with Microsoft's Windows operating system or Office app.[200] On appeal, the Commission was criticised for not having considered such conglomerate effects, in particular 'the ability of and the incentives for the new entity to use its position on the consumer

[192] COMP/M 6281, *Microsoft/Skype*, 7 October 2011; on appeal, *see Cisco Systems Inc and Messagenet SpA v Commission*, Case T-79/12, ECLI:EU:T:2013:635.
[193] COMP/M 7217, *Facebook/WhatsApp*, 3 October 2014, para 165.
[194] COMP/M 6314, *Telefonica UK/Vodafone UK/Everything Everywhere/JV*, 4 September 2012, paras 523–528.
[195] COMP/M 7337, *IMS Health/Cegedim Business*, 19 December 2014, paras 166 and 189 respectively.
[196] COMP/M 5727, *Microsoft/Yahoo! Search*, 18 February 2010, paras 243.
[197] ibid paras 244.
[198] COMP/M 6281, *Microsoft/Skype*, 7 October 2011, para 133.
[199] ibid paras 135 and 213.
[200] ibid paras 137 and 138.

communications market as leverage to distort competition on the enterprise communications market'.[201] However, the General Court found that the theory of harm based on conglomerate effects was 'complex and abstract' based on a generic assumption that 'concentrations giving rise to conglomerates do not usually generate competition concerns'.[202] Conglomerate effects were also dismissed in *Publicis/Omnicom* because the parties would not have the ability or incentive to leverage a position on one market to another by means of tying or bundling or other exclusionary practices.[203] In *Telefonica/Vodafone/Everything Everywhere/JV*, the Commission considered any conglomerate effects stemming from the combination of products in related markets which may facilitate the ability and incentive of the merging parties to leverage a strong market position from one market to another through tying or bundling; thus, no concerns were identified.[204]

In *Sanofi/Google/DMI JV*, the Commission also looked at the potential for conglomerate effects.[205] It examined the ability to foreclose rivals through tying, bundling or limiting the interoperability with competing providers.[206] The Commission found that neither JV, nor the parties had a market position which could be leveraged to exclude third-party device manufacturers, insulin providers or providers of digital services for the management and treatment of diabetes. The parties also lack such an incentive; otherwise, by preventing third-parties' insulins and devices from working, JV would drive patients away.[207] No conglomerate effects were found in *IMS Health/Cegedim Business*.[208]

D. Consumer Harm due to Exclusionary Effects of Data Combination

In *Facebook/WhatsApp* and *Google/DoubleClick*, the overarching theory of consumer harm is based on the exclusionary effects of data combination. Again, the existing concerns were too easily dismissed, often with not too plausible explanations. For example, in *Facebook/WhatsApp*, it was simply mentioned that 'there will continue to be a large amount of Internet user data that are valuable for advertising purposes and that are not within Facebook's exclusive control' and that 'there are currently a significant number of market participants that collect user data alongside Facebook'.[209] Although this was an

[201] *Cisco Systems Inc and Messagenet SpA v Commission*, Case T-79/12, ECLI:EU:T:2013:635, para 107.

[202] ibid para 112; subsequently, the Court rejected the theory of harm based on conglomerate effects as purely speculative, at para 121.

[203] COMP/M 7023, *Publicis/Omnicom*, 9 January 2014, para 673. However, one competitor submitted to the market investigation that the merged entity will be able to leverage its market power in price negotiations with media vendors, which will lead to higher barriers to market entry, see para 679; this was counterbalanced by the broad choice of alternative agencies and the buyer power of media vendors.

[204] COMP/M 6314, *Telefonica UK/Vodafone UK/Everything Everywhere/JV*, 4 September 2012, paras 518–22.

[205] COMP/M 7813, *Sanofi/Google/DMI JV*, 23 February 2016, para 85; thus, this was not the case.

[206] ibid para 84.

[207] ibid para 84.

[208] COMP/M 7337, *IMS Health/Cegedim Business*, 19 December 2014, para 275.

[209] See COMP/M 7217, *Facebook/WhatsApp*, 3 October 2014, paras 189 and 188 respectively.

easy way of dismissing any exclusionary effects on competing rivals, this statement did not helpfully consider how the data combination could subsequently exploit consumers. A similar approach to foreclosure effects was applied to *Google/DoubleClick*. It highlighted that the data collected by DoubleClick was 'relatively narrow in scope' and that 'other companies active in online advertising have the ability to collect large amounts of more or less similar information that is potentially useful for' targeted advertising, eg, Yahoo!'s Blue Lithium collection of behavioural data.[210] All in all, neither the merged entity, nor DoubleClick alone could access 'unique, non-replicable data'.[211] Indeed, the merged entity would need to renegotiate contractual terms.[212] This was the theory of harm underpinning the combination of data. Although targeted advertising was a cause for concern, the available technology to implement it was still at an early stage: 'the type of behavioural targeting that lies at the core of these network effects is an emerging technology which neither Double Click nor Google have developed vis-à-vis Yahoo!, Blue Lithium or AOL's Tacoda'.[213]

Publicis/Omnicom underwent a similar assessment where it was noted that the large majority of competing rivals are 'at least similarly placed to the merged entity to get access to big data analytics'.[214] Again, the focus was exclusionary, which examined whether competing advertising agencies would continue to have access following the merger. Competitors offered mixed responses: some were still relying on the offline world, whilst others noted the increasing importance of big data.[215] They confirmed, however, that there would be access to a large number of third-party providers of big data analytics and that some of them had already developed their own data analytics tools.[216] But none of the rival media owners believed *Publicis/Omnicom* to be 'better placed than its competitors post-merger to get access to big data analytics'.[217] Even if the merged entity were to block access to Publicis/Omnicom's own data analytics platform, the impact would still be rather limited, as 'many other providers are developing big data platforms, or will be able to access similar data and not be disadvantaged'.[218] Based on this survey, the Commission concluded that there are no serious doubts with regard to big data since a sufficient number of alternative providers of big data analytics will still be available.[219] However, a number of manufacturers of portable navigable devices

[210] COMP/M 4731, *Google/DoubleClick*, 11 March 2008, paras 269 and 270.

[211] One could add here the explanation that data is 'non-rivalrous' in the sense that its collection cannot prevent others from collecting identical data. See Rubinfeld and Gal (n 98) 369.

[212] COMP/M 4731, *Google/DoubleClick*, 11 March 2008, para 303.

[213] ibid para 303.

[214] COMP/M 7023, *Publicis/Omnicom*, 9 January 2014, para 628.

[215] ibid para 626.

[216] ibid para 627. See also para 628, where one competitor emphasised that third-party providers of data such as Twitter, Facebook, Google and blogs offer aggregated data free of charge or for a fee.

[217] ibid para 628.

[218] ibid para 629; a small minority of respondents noted, however, that the impact on them will be negative.

[219] ibid para 630. See para 660, where the Commission arrives at the conclusion that it is 'unlikely that the merged entity will have the ability and the incentive to restrict the access to the advertising space to competitors of the merged entity's media buying agencies or to discriminate against these competitors'. Furthermore, the sale of advertising space in cinema is not an important product for the downstream market (see para 665); hence, any input foreclosure will not be profitable (see paras 664 and 669).

were concerned that the merged entity would increase map database prices, offer lower quality or delay the availability of new features and updates.[220]

By contrast, in *TomTom/Tele Atlas*, the Commission arrived at the conclusion that, although the merged entity had the ability to foreclose, it would simply lack any incentive to do so.[221] Any price increase in the downstream market would not be profitable for the merged entity. More important, however, was that the merged entity would gain access to commercially sensitive information regarding the downstream activity of rivals.[222] This would allow it to compete less aggressively or make entry and expansion less attractive for competitors. Due to vertical integration, confidential information could be shared with TomTom.[223] In this respect, the Commission considered it unlikely that such confidentiality issues could lead to a significant impediment to effective competition in the market for navigable digital map databases and that the merged entity would still have the incentive to protect its customers' confidential information.[224]

In *Telefonica/Vodafone/Everything Everywhere/JV*, the Commission considered the likelihood of a strategy to technically or commercially foreclose access to essential inputs for the provision of mobile wallet products offered to final consumers.[225] This was found not to be the case, as there are a considerable number of alternative banks.[226] In reaching its view, the Commission subsequently noted that the market concerned is a 'nascent and evolving' one and that there will be additional competition coming from future new technologies based on software, cloud-based SEs, micro-SD, NFC stickers and sleeves.[227] It questioned whether the merging parties would indeed have the technical ability to substantially foreclose access to SIM-based SEs to competing mobile wallet providers, including the ability to degrade competing mobile wallets functioning with an alternative SE.[228] Due to the availability of dual architecture smartphones, competitors could offer their products using embedded SEs, including stickers for maximising consumer reach.[229] Relying on Ofcom's technical expertise, the Commission examined whether the merging parties had a technical ability to foreclose competing mobile wallet providers, including preventing the downloading of a competing mobile wallet app without blocking access to the entire app store.[230] Following an in-depth technical analysis, it was felt that the blocking of the entire traffic from a given IP address

[220] COMP/M 4854, *TomTom/Tele Atlas*, 14 May 2008, para 190. Elsewhere, see para 198, the merging parties argued that quality degradation or delayed release of updates would be impossible because Tele Atlas offers only one core digital navigable map database for any given geographical area. Furthermore, quality degradation would be technically difficult; see para 199.

[221] ibid para 230. Earlier, see para 210; it was, however, acknowledged that the merged entity is likely to have the ability to increase prices or degrade quality or delay access for some manufacturers and navigation software providers competing with TomTom; thus, quality degradation would be unprofitable; see para 220.

[222] ibid para 252, with further reference to para 78 of the Guidelines on the assessment of non-horizontal mergers under the Council Regulation on the control of concentrations between undertakings, OJ C 265/07 [2008].

[223] COMP/M 4854, *TomTom/Tele Atlas*, 14 May 2008, para 253.

[224] ibid paras 254 and 255 respectively.

[225] COMP/M 6314, *Telefonica UK/Vodafone UK/Everything Everywhere/JV*, 4 September 2012, para 248.

[226] ibid para 249.

[227] ibid para 259.

[228] ibid para 263.

[229] ibid para 268.

[230] ibid paras 294, 295 to 306.

'would not make economic sense' for the merging parties and would be detected by consumers.[231] It was therefore concluded that the parties would have no ability either to technically block or to degrade a competing mobile wallet app from being downloaded, installed or updated on a handset operating on the network of the parties, including the automatic setting of preferences to SIM-based SE or further delisting of mobile datasets capable of supporting rival mobile wallets.[232]

In *Sanofi/Google/DMI JV*, with regard to data analytics services in the field of healthcare, the Commission did not identify any risk of market foreclosure; there were alternative providers, including one competitor offering data analytics tools in-house.[233] In *IMS Health/Cegedim Business*, the Commission found that IMS does not have the ability or the incentive to successfully foreclose access to experience and clinical trials data.[234] A majority of competitors submitted to the Commission that it was difficult to collect such data from multiple sources, which also involves a considerable cost.[235] Thus, the transaction did not raise vertical effects.[236] There are alternative suppliers of healthcare professional databases, including aPureBase and Veeva.[237] The Commission identified vertical foreclosure effects with regard to healthcare professional databases and sales tracking data. It reached the conclusion that IMS will effectively have the ability to foreclose access to its brick structure to competing providers of such databases or make access more onerous for customers.[238] IMS will be the owner of a stronger offer in the customer interaction software.

In *Microsoft/LinkedIn*, the Commission tipped the balance in favour of pro-competitive benefits following two counter-factual merger scenarios, specifically, assuming that LinkedIn had no incentive to monetise its data on a standalone basis and that Microsoft would have access to LinkedIn's data and use it to improve its software solutions. Then, the merger may have pro-competitive effects, such as in new products or improvements to existing ones to the benefit of consumers 'based on a dataset to which otherwise no one would have access'.[239] The Commission's optimism was fuelled by uncertainty over whether LinkedIn's Sales Navigator could become an important input.[240] Therefore, no foreclosure of competing providers of alternative software solutions was foreseeable.[241] As Intel explained, although LinkedIn's data is 'very useful', it is not the only source of data. There are many other sources available of 'unstructured

[231] ibid paras 307 and 308. For adverse consumer reactions, see para 435.

[232] ibid paras 307, 313 and 347 respectively. The same is valid even after the installation of an embedded SE, see para 322 and subsequently paras 450 and 491.

[233] COMP/M 7813, *Sanofi/Google/DMI JV*, 23 February 2016, paras 72 and 76.

[234] COMP/M 7337, *IMS Health/Cegedim Business*, 19 Dec2014, paras 211 and 213.

[235] ibid para 214.

[236] ibid para 217.

[237] ibid para 229.

[238] ibid paras 242, 244, 254 and 257.

[239] COMP M. 8124, *Microsoft/LinkedIn*, 20 January 2017, para 249. In the absence of the present merger scenario, LinkedIn did not plan licensing its data to any third-parties, *see* para 376.

[240] ibid para 250. LinkedIn Sales Navigator's competitors and half of its customers submitted that LinkedIn's solution is, or will become, an important input; see para 257. In contrast, the Commission suggested that all major vendors have already started offering advance functionalities, including SalesForce, Zoho and E-Deal.

[241] ibid paras 253 and 267. Due to LinkedIn's insignificant market share, the merged entity would not have the ability to foreclose competing providers of software solutions; see para 373.

information about commercial markets and cognitive solutions'.[242] The majority of competing intelligent solutions providers submitted that the impact on effective competition of the proposed merger would be negative.[243] In contrast, the Commission considered it unlikely that the overall impact would be negative and unlikely to lead to consumer harm.[244] Even if Microsoft were to use LinkedIn's data, this is unlikely to affect a significant number of Microsoft's competitors through a significant price increase or a reduction in the incentives to innovate.[245] The underpinning philosophy of this final assessment is recognition that, although 'data is a relevant input', it is not an 'essential' one.[246]

Referring to the *Microsoft/LinkedIn* merger where the quest was 'whether bringing the companies' data together would make it too hard for others to compete', the Commissioner for Competition suggested that 'controlling a large amount of data shouldn't become a way to shut rivals out of the market'.[247] However, 'this wasn't an issue [...] as other companies still had access to plenty of data'.

On the basis of all the above merger decisions, a preliminary conclusion would suggest that the exclusionary focus based on the question of whether rivals have access to even more data is unhelpful if it does not address the harm caused to consumers through the exploitative use of data. It is furthermore submitted that an exclusive reliance on the market foreclosure test is not in the spirit of consumer and data protection laws.

VII. Merger Control in the Public Interest: Are Privacy Considerations Taken Seriously in Data-driven Mergers?

One could come to regret after having accepted the terms and conditions of privacy imposed by various online platforms, including software companies, not because one could not be bothered to read them, but because one did not have the time. However, many people, who might have taken the time to read them, may have not properly understood all the privacy implications.

After having read and reviewed the most relevant data-driven mergers, one could say that significant resources have been spent on understanding and explaining the intricacies of data analytics and the potential harm to consumers through the prism of the traditional economic analysis of horizontal, vertical and conglomerate effects. In 2008, it was not very clear whether competition authorities were well-equipped to deal with

[242] ibid para 263.
[243] ibid para 273.
[244] ibid paras 274 and 275 respectively as well as para 380. The majority of the respondents expected the effects of this merger to be neutral; see para 378.
[245] ibid para 275.
[246] ibid para 276.
[247] See EU Commission, Commissioner for Competition, M Vestager, 'Clearing the Path for Innovation', speech, Lisbon, 7 November 2017, 4.

data; after 2016, it became clear that the learning curve has made it possible to examine data analytics in more depth than before. One could, nonetheless, argue that privacy considerations of an economic nature could be taken into account even more seriously than before. The assessment of mergers has been based more on economic considerations rather than on any legal interpretation. It could, otherwise, be argued that the analysis of the expected merger-specific efficiencies brought about by the proposed merger could be endangered by unwanted political attention and hidden considerations. However, economics can no longer ignore a wider social context that requires a careful balancing of privacy considerations which bear economic weight.

One commentator has already rejected the consideration of privacy as being in breach of the EU Merger Regulation.[248] Based on a literal interpretation of the Regulation, privacy consideration might not be a good fit. However, there are wider public policy considerations than a narrower focus on privacy. The legal instrument is Article 21(4) of the EU Merger Control Regulation 139/2004, which allows Member States to 'take appropriate measures to protect legitimate interests other than those taken into consideration by this Regulation and compatible with the general principles and other provisions of Community law'.

Under the Merger Control Regulation, the protection of privacy could be seen to fall under the remit of other 'legitimate interests', being a concrete matter of public interest. One potential obstacle against this projection is the wording of the second sentence of Article 21(4), which, under the concept of a 'recognised public interest', includes more specifically 'public security, plurality of the media and prudential rules'. This shortcoming could easily be overcome by reliance on the last paragraph of Article 21(4), which mandates that 'any other public interest' be communicated to the Commission for an evaluation on a case-by-case basis,[249] and so it could successfully include privacy considerations as a sub-type of terms and conditions of use for online platforms. Although 'other legitimate public interest' grounds have, only very rarely, been invoked,[250] high-tech could be recognised as a strategic sector, as certain corporations have become influential tools of the unprecedented mass surveillance of individuals. On balance, there is a greater public interest in cushioning individuals against the pervasive powers of self-interested multinational corporations.

The blocking of a merger on grounds of public interest remains a solution of last resort; it would attract unwanted criticism for being based on politics, rather than on economic considerations.[251] It is, however, obvious that the motives for the market study of data analysis are for profit-seeking. As has already been recognised elsewhere, merger

[248] See BH de Peyer, 'EU Merger Control and Big Data' (2017) 13 *Journal of Competition Law & Economics* 767 and ff.

[249] On the distinction between recognised and non-recognised interests, see C Bengtsson, JM Carpi Badia and M Kadar, 'Mergers' in J Faull and A Nikpay (eds) *The EU Law of Competition*, 3rd edn (Oxford, Oxford University Press, 2014) 607, paras 5.283 and 5.284.

[250] For this view, see Vivien Rose and David Bailey (eds), Bellamy and Child, *European Union Law of Competition*, 7th edn (Oxford, Oxford University Press, 2013) 568, 569, para 8.104.

[251] For a number of politically controversial merger decisions, see O Koch, 'Fundamentals of European Merger Control' in G Hirsch, F Montag and FJ Säcker (eds) *Competition Law: European Community Practice and Procedure* (London, Sweet & Maxwell, 2008) 1918–19, paras 5-1-073–5-1-077, and fns 210–13.

decisions are often economic and/or political decisions.[252] In the merger enforcement of the last decade, one could see this from the alternative perspective: merger decisions are in essence economic decisions, and only exceptionally based on legal interpretation. Ultimately, the politics of privacy will triumph, hopefully for those people who take the time to read privacy policies but have no choice but to leave an online platform.

VIII. Conclusion

From the *Google/DoubleClick* merger in 2008 up to *Microsoft/LinkedIn* in 2016, the assessment of data and privacy considerations in mergers slightly improved and hopefully will continue to do so. Overall, the acquisition of large data sets has represented an intelligent and strategic move towards harvesting even more useful data. The focus has been on the exclusionary likelihood of competition on the basis of data rather than on the exploitative likelihood and actual harm caused to consumers following the use of data.

One enforcement weakness has been the unconditional approval of several data-driven mergers. Another enforcement weakness has been the belief that data and consumer protection laws are capable of calibrating the imbalance caused by aggressive competition on the basis of data. Nowadays, data has been recognised as a competitive indicator of performance. In transactional theory, the performance indicator has traditionally been the price or the monetary consideration. In online platforms, exchanges have therefore substituted the price with data. However, users of online platforms possess weaker bargaining power; they have no choice but to consent to default terms and conditions and give in to notices of privacy changes. These developments are nefarious and should have been approached differently by the competition authorities.

First, reliance on consumer law is a fallacy, as, although the latter deals with misleading and comparative advertising, competition law could also activate its consumer-protection function to address targeted advertising and the degradation of quality in the context of online platforms.

Second, reliance on data protection is another fallacy, as the former cannot block mergers or acquisitions. Furthermore, a data protection compliance checklist may confirm that online platforms indeed attempt to be fully compliant with data protection, eg, (i) platform users have freely given their consent, even if they had decided not to read lengthy privacy conditions or a platform's terms of use; and (ii) their aggregated data was anonymised and then shared or transferred. Third, reliance on the market-foreclosure test as a panacea for competition based on data with a comprehensive but conservative evaluation of access to data and barriers to market entry, often serves mostly competing rivals who need access to the data in question. Without an extension of the test of foreclosure to the analysis of consumer harm from exploitation, there is a risk of under-enforcement.

The vast majority of data-driven mergers have given rise to horizontal effects, eg, *Google/DoubleClick*, *Facebook/WhatsApp*, *Microsoft/Yahoo! Search*, *Microsoft/Skype*,

[252] F Rittner and M Kulka, *Wettbewerbs – und Kartellrecht* (Heidelberg, CF Müller, 2008) 381.

Publicis/Omnicom, *Cisco & Messagenet*, rather than vertical effects, eg, *TomTom/Tele Atlas*. Based on the horizontal and vertical dichotomy, only a tiny minority, eg, *Microsoft/Skype* and *Cisco & Messagenet*, have given rise to conglomerate effects. Nurturing conglomerates in the long run is therefore no longer remotely possible. Too much faith in ephemeral high market shares and a reduction in innovation is also dangerous. In the end, conglomerates become largely bureaucratic, ie, inefficient, which can only inhibit entrepreneurship and innovation.

How could these concerns be addressed? There is a clear need for better coordination of the enforcement efforts with regard to digital platforms. Institutional cooperation may also help better inform about the wider scope of competition, consumer and data protection laws. It could address enforcement gaps and empower one authority for areas that cannot be dealt with by the others, especially when dealing with monopolies or mergers. Ultimately, existing tests have to be adapted to the requirements and particularities of digital markets.

No doubt, some of the competition concerns have already been addressed through specific remedies. Some remedies have inter alia ensured that manufacturers or distributors of PCs do not pre-install LinkedIn on the Windows operating system, that LinkedIn can be removed if pre-installed, and that the interoperability of competing service providers with Windows' office apps is duly maintained.

PART IV

Tensions for Sale of Goods Law

8

Circular Economy, Title and Harmonisation of Commercial Law

SEAN THOMAS

In the middle of the nineteenth century, Leone Levi produced a compendium of the commercial laws of a vast array of jurisdictions, prefaced with a salutary reminder of the importance of cross-jurisdictional observation and analysis:

> In an epoch when commercial relations embrace the greatest public and private interest, when nationalities are all but blended into each other, when work, improvement, and welfare, are the all-prevailing ideas; and, when the rapidity of communication demands in a corresponding degree security and protection; the revision of the laws, statutes, usages, and customs of all countries becomes imperative. As nations are approaching each other, each is enabled to profit by the common experience; and it is of the utmost importance to watch carefully all innovations, and mark the reason and the starting point of all essential and permanent progress.[1]

Here, the aim is somewhat different, but the basic rationale remains the same: examine commercial law and practice in an era of changes to law, of technological change, and of developments in jurisprudential relationships. This chapter considers the effect of circular economy on law, and vice versa. Section I outlines circular economic thought, and identifies the need to focus on aspects of ownership and control regarding goods. Section II will set out a specific problematic issue of English law in light of a need to shift from ownership to use in circular economies. This issue concerns the interrelationship between contract and property as control mechanisms for downstream parties in a chain of transactions. Section III then examines the harmonisation of commercial law. The problems faced by circular economies in terms of obtaining necessary levels of legal harmonisation will be identified. Two possible directions for harmonisation will be considered: (1) application of property control mechanisms; and (2) application of contractual control mechanisms. The likely success of the latter direction will not result

[1] L Levi, *Commercial Law, Its Principles and Administration; or, the Mercantile Law of Great Britain* (William Benning & Co, London, 1850) vol 1, vii. See further GR Rubin, 'Levi, Leone (1821–1888)' in *Oxford Dictionary of National Biography* (Oxford, Oxford University Press, 2004), available at www.oxforddnb.com/view/article/16551.

in the direct harmonisation of a circular economy law or laws, but this will not preclude a profusion of contractual control mechanisms to enable effective implementation of circular economic practices. Section IV concludes.

I. Circular Economy

The notion of a circular economy is a relatively recent development, though it has academic antecedents across a broad range of disciplines.[2] It has come to fruition in recent years by means of NGO and think-tank analyses,[3] before being taken up by domestic, regional and international governmental and institutional organs. These efforts have also found considerable support from corporate interests, both directly,[4] and via interest and lobby groups,[5] as well as via charitable organisations.[6] Additionally, there is governmental support (in the UK) in the form of recent funding calls offering

[2] See, eg, WR Stahel, 'The Product-Life Factor' (1982), available at www.product-life.org/en/major-publications/the-product-life-factor; WR Stahel and G Reday-Mulvey, *Jobs for Tomorrow: The Potential for Substituting Manpower for Energy* (New York, Vantage Press, 1981) (examining the notions of closing loops in systems); R Frosch and N Gallopoulos, 'Strategies for Manufacturing' (1989) 261 *Scientific American* 94–102 (analogy between industrial and biological ecosystems); M Fischer-Kowalski and W Hüttler, 'Society's metabolism: The intellectual history of materials flow analysis, part II: 1970–1998' (1998) 2 *Journal of Industrial Ecology* 107 (the impact of socio-economics); M Braungart and W McDonough, *Cradle to Cradle: Remaking the Way We Make Things* ([2002] London, Vintage, 2009) (arguing that the 3Rs approach (reduce, reuse, recycle) is too wasteful, and a more intensive cycling of products is necessary). As to the importance of public (mis)perception, whilst 59% of respondents in a client survey thought recycling helps the transition to a circular economy the most, the role of recycling is much more limited in a circular economy: G Hieminga, *Rethinking Finance in a Circular Economy: Financial Implications of Circular Business Models* (May 2015), available at www.ing.com/About-us/Ourstories/Features/Circular-economy-challenges-financial-business-models.htm 12. At the 'Creativity within the Circular Economy' symposium, The Westminster Law and Theory Lab, University of Westminster, 24 March 2016, Jules Hayward of the Ellen MacArthur Foundation noted that the current approach to circular economic thought is a synthesis of existing work concerning the performance economy (Stahel), cradle to cradle (McDonough), natural capitalism (P Hawkin, A Lovins and LH Lovins, *Natural Capitalism: Creating the Next Industrial Revolution* (New York, Little, Brown and Co, 1999)), industrial ecology and symbiosis (MR Chertow, 'Industrial Symbiosis: Literature and Taxonomy' (2000) 25 *Annual Review of Energy and the Environment* 313) and biomimicry (https://biomimicry.org). See generally www.ellenmacarthurfoundation.org/circular-economy/concept/schools-of-thought.

[3] F Preston, 'A Global Redesign? Shaping the Circular Economy' (Chatham House Briefing Paper, 1 March 2012), available at www.chathamhouse.org/publications/papers/view/182376; Ellen MacArthur Foundation, 'Towards the Circular Economy: Economic and Business Rationale for an Accelerated Transition' (2013), available at www.ellenmacarthurfoundation.org/assets/downloads/publications/Ellen-MacArthur-Foundation-Towards-the-Circular-Economy-vol.1.pdf. See also www.product-life.org (the Product-Life Institute was founded by Stahel, amongst others); P Lacy and J Rutqvist, *Waste to Wealth: The Circular Economy Advantage* (Basingstoke, Palgrave MacMillan, 2015).

[4] See, eg, www.veolia.co.uk/circulareconomy (a waste management business); Hieminga, *Rethinking Finance in a Circular Economy* (2015) (bank).

[5] For example, the management consultants McKinsey provide substantial research for the Ellen MacArthur Foundation's work on circular economy, and the Ellen MacArthur Foundation is heavily supported by corporate interests: www.ellenmacarthurfoundation.org/about/partners. See also Chartered Institute of Wastes Management, 'The Circular Economy: What does it Mean for the Waste and Resource Management Sector?' (October 2014), available at www.ciwm-journal.co.uk/downloads/CIWM_Circular_Economy_Report-FULL_FINAL_Oct_2014.pdf.

[6] www.wrap.org.uk/content/about-us; www.theguardian.com/environment/bike-blog/2016/oct/21/islabikes-radical-new-plan-means-you-may-never-need-to-buy-your-child-a-bike-again.

to support the study of the circular economy,[7] as well as more direct governmental agencies engaging in the issue.[8] Most recently, the new waste strategy announced by the Department of Environment, Food and Rural Affairs (DEFRA) in December 2018 explicitly ties future UK policy to adopting circular economic approaches,[9] and there have been EU efforts to deal with the environmental problems of plastics within a circular economic framework.[10] These efforts often complement and refer to each other.[11] Academic interest has also accelerated,[12] with a growing legal literature.[13] What, therefore, is the circular economy?

A circular economy is often presented quite simply, as a form of interconnected (hence circular) sectors of economic practices, which enable minimisation of waste products leaking out by various means at the different stages of the creation-consumption

[7] www.epsrc.ac.uk/funding/calls/circulareconomy; https://epsrc.ukri.org/funding/calls/uk-research-and-innovation-call-creative-circular-economy-approaches-to-eliminate-plastics-waste/ (nb the author was part of an unsuccessful application to this funding call). The EPSRC also provides a position statement which provides a useful overview of the circular economy concept: www.epsrc.ac.uk/files/funding/calls/2015/circulareconomypositionstatement.

[8] See, eg Collaboration for a Circular Economy, Innovate UK at https://connect.innovateuk.org/web/collaborations-circular-economy/overview; Department for Environment, Food and Rural Affairs, 'UK response to European Commission consultation of member states on the circular economy' (11 November 2015), available at www.gov.uk/government/publications/circular-economy-and-waste-markets-uk-government-response-to-european-commission-consultations.

[9] Department of Environment, Food and Rural Affairs, 'Our waste, Our Resources: A Strategy for England' (18 December 2018), available at www.gov.uk/government/publications/resources-and-waste-strategy-for-england. September 2019 saw the publication of plans for a Circular Economy Bill before the Scottish Parliament: www.gov.scot/publications/protecting-scotlands-future-governments-programme-scotland-2019-20/pages/4.

[10] European Commission, 'A European Strategy for Plastics in a Circular Economy', COM(2018) 28 final (at eur-lex.europa.eu/legal-content/EN/TXT/?qid=1516265440535&uri=COM:2018:28:FIN; European Commission, 'Proposal for a Directive of the European Parliament and of the Council on the reduction of the impact of certain plastic products on the environment', COM(2018) 340 final, available at ec.europa.eu/environment/circular-economy/pdf/single-use_plastics_proposal.pdf).

[11] See, eg, DEFRA, 'Circular economy' (2015) 8 (referring to the Ellen MacArthur Foundation and Hieminga (n 2)).

[12] See, eg, www.lead-journal.org/content/call_for_papers.pdf; www.greatrecovery.org.uk/resources/what-is-the-great-recovery ('The Great Recovery is a project run by the RSA and supported by Innovate UK. It looks at the challenges of waste and the opportunities of a circular economy through the lens of design.'); https://sites.google.com/view/pace2019 (SLS One-Day Conference on Rethinking Property Approaches in Resources for the Circular Economy).

[13] F Bonciu, 'The European Economy: From a Linear to a Circular Economy' (2014) 14 *Romanian Journal of European Affairs* 78; C Dalhammar, 'The Application of "Life Cycle Thinking" in European Environmental Law: Theory and Practice' (2015) 12 *Journal of European Environmental & Planning Law* 97; TJ de Römph, 'Terminological Challenges to the Incorporation of Landfill Mining in EU Waste Law in View of the Circular Economy' (2016) 25 *European Energy and Environmental Law Review* 106; K Steenmans, J Marriott and R Malcolm, 'Commodification of Waste: Legal and Theoretical Approaches to Industrial Symbiosis as part of a Circular Economy' (9 June 2017) working paper presented at the SMART conference 'Life-cycle Based Management and Reporting for Sustainable Business' (29–30 November 2016), available at ssrn.com/abstract=2983631; C Backes, *Law for a Circular Economy* ((The Hague, Eleven International Publishing, 2017), available at www.uu.nl/sites/default/files/rgl-ucowsl-backes-law_for_a_circular_economy.pdf; S Thomas, 'Law, Smart Technology, and Circular Economy: All Watched Over By Machines of Loving Grace?' (2018) 10 *Law, Innovation & Technology* 230; JT Mähönen, 'Financing Sustainable Market Actors in Circular Economy' (26 October 2018) University of Oslo Faculty of Law Research Paper No 2018–28, available at ssrn.com/abstract=3273263; S Thomas, 'Law and the Circular Economy' [2019] *Journal of Business Law* 62; M Burger, 'Materials Consumption and Solid Waste' in MB Gerrard and J Dernbach (eds), *Legal Pathways to Deep Decarbonization in the United States* (Washington DC, ELI Books, 2019); E Maitre-Ekern and C Dalhammar, 'Towards a hierarchy of consumption behaviour in the circular economy' (2019) 26 *Maastricht Journal of European and Comparative Law* 394.

process. However, the simplicity of this approach contrasts with the many different definitions that can be found in the literature:[14] what appears common is the basic notion of maximising value and minimising waste by means of better design at the outset and reuse/recycling at the end. The charitable organisation WRAP puts it this way:

> A circular economy is an alternative to a traditional linear economy (make, use, dispose) in which we keep resources in use for as long as possible, extract the maximum value from them whilst in use, then recover and regenerate products and materials at the end of each service life.[15]

It is important, though, to recognise that waste is just one aspect of circular economy.[16] At the Creativity within the Circular Economy symposium,[17] Hayward suggested there were three principles at the heart of circular economic thought: (1) preservation and enhancement of natural capital; (2) optimisation of resource yields; and (3) fostering system effectiveness by revealing and designing out negative externalities. Put another way: circular economy is concerned not just with waste, but with designing and utilising mechanisms and systems for the long-term *use* of material objects.[18] Circular economy thus requires analysis of the transference mechanisms by which goods transition to different sectors of the circular economy.

Despite the necessarily holistic nature of circular economies, the centrality of waste and waste management, connected to claims as to environmental benefits, has resulted in regulatory regimes being structured around waste.[19] One of the earliest instances of the regulatory turn can be found in the Circular Economy Promotion Law of the People's Republic of China, which was promulgated in August 2008 and came into force in January 2009.[20] It defined a 'circular economy' as 'a generic term for the reducing, reusing and recycling activities conducted in the process of production, circulation and consumption'.[21] This will 'be propelled by the government, led by the market, effected by enterprises and participated in by the public'.[22] In this sense,

[14] J Kirchherr, D Reike and M Hekkert, 'Conceptualizing the Circular Economy: An Analysis of 114 Definitions' (2017) 127 *Resources, Conservation & Recycling* 221; C Babbitt, G Gaustad, A Fisher, G Liu and W Chen (eds), 'Sustainable Resource Management and the Circular Economy' (2018) 135 *Resources, Conservation and Recycling* 1.

[15] cf www.wrap.org.uk/content/wrap-and-circular-economy.

[16] See, eg, www.ellenmacarthurfoundation.org/circular-economy/concept.

[17] Above n 2.

[18] This explanation should clearly demonstrate why this chapter's focus is on material objects: intangible things, such as digital products, are not subject to the same sort of deterioration resulting from usage and can potentially exist forever (not least because, under the current technological framework, digital products are invariably duplicated when transmitted, and at worst are duplicable without any significant cost). See generally Ellen MacArthur Foundation, 'Intelligent Assets: Unlocking the circular economy potential' (8 February 2016), available at www.ellenmacarthurfoundation.org/publications; and in particular, Thomas, 'Law, Smart Technology, and Circular Economy' (2018).

[19] The centrality of waste to circular economic thought is likely to be part of a rhetorical tactic in order to enhance the ethical standing of circular economic analysis and related work: N Gregson, M Crang, S Fuller and H Holmes, 'Interrogating the circular economy: the moral economy of resources recovery in the EU' (2015) 44 *Economy and Society* 218.

[20] For a translation, see eg, www.lawinfochina.com/display.aspx?id=7025&lib=law. See also G Chen and B F C Hsu, 'Law and Policy in the Sustainability of Affordable Housing: The Case of China' (2012–13) 30 *UCLA Pacific Basin Law Journal* 259, 284–86.

[21] Circular Economy Promotion Law, Art 2.

[22] ibid Art 3.

the Chinese first-step has been copied broadly by later adopters, for whom the role of government is key. This is illustrated in the preference for circular business practices in public procurement,[23] which would be mirrored by the UK Government some six years later (noted below). The PRC also set out provisions that impose obligations to recycle certain named products onto producers, who are covered even if the material is 'deserted' (abandoned).[24] The heavy focus on waste (the nature, role and processing of waste) in the PRC's law would come to be replicated within the EU's own later circular economy strategy.[25] The EU's aim is to 'close the loop', and reduce waste sent to landfill.[26] Although it may be argued that the EU's strategy is more waste-focused,[27] it is not without reference to the need to engage producers to design and manufacture in circle-appropriate ways:[28] this may well just reflect the rather tortured history of this strategy which involved a failed attempt to produce a waste directive before moving into the broader circular economy field.[29]

The UK Government's response to the EU Commission's consultations was initially,[30] unsurprisingly, in favour of the circular economic concept in general, with preferences for a light-touch regulatory approach which would amongst other things reduce the obligations to reuse/recycle waste for SMEs and other such groups,[31] as well as increasing data capture, usage and sharing across the single market (for design and waste aspects) to more effectively create and maintain circular business.[32]

[23] ibid Art 47.

[24] ibid Art 15. cf R Linzer and S Salhofer, 'Municipal Solid Waste Recycling and the Significance of Informal Sector in Urban China' (2014) 32 *Waste Management and Research* 896 (substantial proportion of recyclables are collected and processed by informal waste collectors); E Ryan, 'The Elaborate Paper Tiger: Environmental Enforcement and the Rule of Law in China' (2014) 24 *Duke Environmental Law and Policy Forum* 183, 189–90: 'The Circular Economy Law … is largely exhortatory and contains few enforceable provisions.' B Gillin, 'Keeping Up with Chinese Consumerism: Offsetting China's Individually Generated Garbage with Regulatory and Social Mechanisms' (2011–12) 13 *Vermont Journal of Environmental Law* 69 (regulatory changes will not work without corresponding effective social changes).

[25] http://ec.europa.eu/environment/circular-economy/index_en.htm, and above n 10. The relationship between the PRC and the EU on circular economy is illustrated by The Memorandum of Understanding on Circular Economy between the European Commission and the National Development and Reform Commission of the People's Republic of China (16 July 2018), available at http://ec.europa.eu/environment/circular-economy/pdf/circular_economy_MoU_EN.pdf). See also www.ellenmacarthurfoundation.org/news/china-eu-agreement-paves-way-for-global-adoption-of-circular-economy.

[26] EC, 'Closing the loop – An EU Action Plan for the Circular Economy' (COM(2015) 614). See, eg, YM Gordeeva, 'Recent Developments in EU Environmental Policy and Legislation' (2016) 13 *Journal of European Environmental & Planning Law* 120, 120–21.

[27] cf Gregson et al, 'Interrogating the circular economy' (2015) 228–30: the UK's system of municipal materials recovery facilities is focused on weight as a costing system, thus the overall quality of recovered waste is generally irrelevant, which creates problems for the circular economy. This is arguably the consequence of focusing on waste-diversion, rather than resource-recovery, as 'the driving metric'.

[28] EC, 'Closing the Loop' Annex 1 (2015) 614 (listing the various ways in which the EU plans to achieve its aims).

[29] See, eg, D Moore, 'Commission Pledges Tough Circular Economy Package Enforcement' (6 April 2016), available at www.ciwm-journal.co.uk/commission-pledges-tough-enforcement-circular-economy-package/.

[30] www.gov.uk/government/publications/circular-economy-and-waste-markets-uk-government-response-to-european-commission-consultations.

[31] DEFRA, 'UK response' (2015) 3: 'Exemptions for some SMEs from registering as waste carriers if they only transport small amounts of their own non-hazardous waste for example a small shop owner; Removing the need for applying for permit exemptions for activities that pose little risk, such as small-scale composting by schools.'

[32] See generally DEFRA (n 8).

The volume of consumption in the form of public procurement, and the way that can contribute to a circular economy, was also recognised.[33] Whilst there are some other brief acknowledgements of the potential impact of moving towards circular economies on our understanding of property and commerce (in the sense of ownership),[34] the DEFRA report appeared content to refer to the work undertaken by the ING banking group,[35] which is examined in the next section. In December 2018, as noted above, DEFRA published a new waste strategy. This marked a signal change, as circular economics was integrated throughout that report. As well as providing sector-specific policies, reflecting contemporary concerns over plastics for instance, the report recognises the centrality to circular economy of avoiding waste.[36] One means to achieve this is the development of 'regulatory or economic instruments if necessary and appropriate'.[37] However, the specific implications for legal doctrine are unclear, with a general assumption that transactions other than the disposition of ownership are what are needed for circular economics.[38]

There is thus an identifiable duality at the heart of circular economic thought: on one hand it is presented as an opportunity for dealing with production and waste in a more efficient manner in terms of environmental costs; on the other hand it can be understood as a commercially focused ideology resting on new methods of diffusing ownership and use-rights in transaction chains. This latter understanding will now be explored.

II. The Shift from Controlling Ownership to Controlling Use in the Circular Economy

The literature on circular economy has so far failed to identify and examine legal issues in any depth, and such brief examples that exist simply raise more questions than anything else. Property and ownership issues are at best acknowledged, then swiftly overflown.[39] One rare (but still limited) example comes from Hieminga of ING:

> [T]he legal and financial systems that support the current business environment may not be very conducive to the new setting that the circular economy requires. For example, the

[33] ibid 2–3.

[34] ibid 16: facilitation of reuse through eg 'Examining other opportunities to promote greater reusability and reparability in product design and support trade in second hand products while continuing to ensure effective regulation, including product standards for reuse and repair.'

[35] DEFRA, 'UK Response' (n 8) 8.

[36] DEFRA, 'Our waste, Our Resources' (2018) 26: 'The "lifecycle" approach complements the circular economy model. It requires us to focus not just on managing waste responsibly, but on preventing its creation in the first place. It means taking into account how decisions taken during the design stage – at the start of the lifecycle – affect how a product is used and then disposed of by the consumer. At every stage of a product's lifecycle there is scope for people to do all they can to maximise resource value and minimise waste.'

[37] ibid 17.

[38] ibid 30, 37, 55.

[39] See, eg, M Howard and K Webster, 'Circular business advantage: what organisations need to know' (24 October 2018), available at https://medium.com/circulatenews/circular-business-advantage-what-organisations-need-to-know-c7ae1954cc46 (noting, inter alia, how 'Product ownership will become a thing

> circular economy is based on the principle that waste does not exist and is a valuable resource in (perhaps another company's) production. But the circular economy faces a lot of legal barriers that limit the use of waste as an input.[40]

There are undoubtedly ownership difficulties surrounding reuse, recycling and waste,[41] and this could generate control problems: 'Even in a case where producers would – in the legal sense – keep ownership over sold products, the actual control over the products would be difficult to ensure.'[42] One way around this might be through adopting a so-called 'ownership-heavy' approach. Hieminga suggests that such an approach can be effective in circular economic practice. He uses the example of how Van Scherpenzeel, a Dutch recycling company, owns the materials throughout their supply chain in the recycling sector. They own the waste from its collection, through its recycling, until it is reused.[43]

This ownership-heavy approach has a flip-side: contracting becomes key in controlling the use of goods. This is in turn connected to another change, though this is more conceptual and policy-orientated: a shift from ownership to access and use as being central to consumption.[44] This requires acknowledging a key effect of taking an ownership-heavy approach. Such an approach will concentrate and centralise ownership in the initiator in a circular economic transaction. They will want to control as many aspects of the goods' use as possible. These brief points alert us to potential problems regarding property, ownership and control in commercial context in circular economies. Three interconnected issues arise here when examined through a circular economy lens. First, what will be the effect of the shift from ownership to use? Second, what will be the role of property (title/ownership) in governing transactions (and the consequence of transactions) in circular economies? Interrelated to this examination is the role of contracts in this field: where property rules fail to fully and/or accurately replicate participants' wishes, contracts will step in. Third, given the role of property in sales, and the importance of contracting in circular economic transactions, are circular economic transactions capable of being sales?

of the past'). The problems can be seen in reports underlying the 2016 New Plastics Economy Initiative (newplasticseconomy.org/about/the-initiative) led by the Ellen MacArthur Foundation: World Economic Forum, Ellen MacArthur Foundation and McKinsey & Company, 'The New Plastics Economy – Rethinking the Future of Plastics' (2016), available at newplasticseconomy.org/about/publications/report-2016; and World Economic Forum, Ellen MacArthur Foundation and McKinsey & Company, 'The New Plastics Economy – Catalysing action' (2017), available at newplasticseconomy.org/about/publications/report-2017. 'Catalysing action' very briefly mentions (at 40) laws concerning plastic packaging, but makes no mention of other legal issues. 'Rethinking the Future of Plastics' has a section on legal responses (at 37), though these are merely identified regulatory actions almost all in the form of prohibitions, as well as a brief reference (60–61) to potential implications for public procurement.

[40] See, eg, Hieminga (n 2) 35.

[41] C Dalhammar, 'The Application of "Life Cycle Thinking" in European Environmental Law: Theory and Practice' (2015) 12 *Journal of European Environmental & Planning Law* 97, 106–07.

[42] ibid 107, fn 31.

[43] Hieminga (n 2) 32.

[44] ibid 6. This shift is clearly evident in circular economy literature, such as the 'Intelligent Assets' report (2016), for which see generally Thomas (n 13).

A. Shift from 'Ownership' to 'Use'

Fundamental to circular economy is the need to shift focus away from an 'ownership' perspective to a 'use' perspective as to our relationship with goods.[45] What needs to be understood is that this shift from ownership to use is one of permanent consequence for the lifespan of the goods. Ownership acts as a potential blockage to circular economies; focusing on the use of the goods enables a more fine-grained level of control and thus opening up the contractual agreements for use to greater modification than ordinarily would be case. This may require contemplation of alternative commercial transactions which would more accurately represent a use-exchange model.

Hieminga provides eight conclusions about what may be necessary for financing practice in circular economies; it is suggested they also have broader commercial and legal implications, impacting on specific areas such as sale. The eight conclusions are:[46]

(1) multiple forms of capital will be needed for financing circular business models;
(2) pay per use models require emphasising cash flow timings;
(3) '[c]ontracts are pivotal in financing circular economic models';[47]
(4) pay per use increases the importance of creditworthiness;
(5) value will be sought and found in second-hand markets;
(6) end of use value needs to be accounted for;
(7) '[s]upply chain finance can facilitate the circularity of supply chains and is expected to evolve towards earlier states of the supply chain';[48]
(8) there are different and unpredictable implications.

These points reveal various different potential methods for concentrating ownership and extending control through multiple parties. It is worth expanding on some of Hieminga's analysis.

Contracts will be 'pivotal'. This is both a cause and consequence of concentrating ownership. In the context of developments in pay per use, 'pay per use models value is first and of all created in the continuation of the contract instead of a one time sales value in the linear business model'.[49] The potential for long-term contracting, throughout the supply chain, further emphasises the importance of contractual continuity.[50] This is matched by the importance of the terms of such contracts. As Hieminga suggests,

> If producers retain ownership of products during their life cycle it provides them with strong incentives to look after these products, maintain them well and make them valuable at the end

[45] See, eg, Braungart and McDonough, *Cradle to Cradle* (2009) 111: 'Instead of assuming that all products are to be bought, owned and disposed of by "consumers", products containing valuable technical nutrients – cars, televisions, carpeting, computers, and refrigerators, for example, would be reconceived as services people want to enjoy … When they finish with the product, or are simply ready to upgrade to a newer version, the manufacturer replaces it, taking the old model back.' Lacy and Rutqvist, *Waste to Wealth* (2015) 61: 'Companies need to find ways to control the return flow.'

[46] ibid 37–46.

[47] ibid 39.

[48] ibid 44.

[49] ibid 38.

[50] ibid 45.

of life. From a circular point of view this has strong advantages but it comes with increased financial obligations.[51]

It is not difficult to see, in light of the proprietary nature of English asset financing law generally, that the shift from ownership to contracted use could be problematic for asset financing in a circular economy.[52] The structures of property rights, and ownership interests, could impinge on material flows within a circular economy. Manipulating proprietary interests in assets, by utilising legal and equitable divisions, may be less flexible than delineating between personal use rights.[53] What follows illustrates how shifts towards use may create conceptual problems between English law and circular economy, whilst also indicating possible ways in which English law would fit well in circular economies.

Proponents of circular economy seem to suggest quite radical transaction forms, and some see potential structural danger with the shift from ownership to use. For Gregson et al, it involves 'nothing short of a wholesale transformation of the basis of contemporary capitalism and consumption'.[54] Hieminga suggests a possible shift from business to business (B2B) or business to consumer (B2C) transactions using money as an exchange medium, to one where:

> New market segments arise in which consumers interact with other consumers (C2C) and in which economic agents act both as manufacturer as well as consumer (C2B). Money is the main, but not necessarily the sole, medium of exchange as goods or services are for example exchanged against energy, time or waste.[55]

This change may well have implications in the conceptualisation of circular economy transactions, but it is worth remembering that English law occasionally displays considerable ambivalence towards attaching overriding importance to ownership. It is quite content with consequences of dividing types of transaction according to whether they transfer ownership. The obvious historical example is the development of hire purchase in the late nineteenth century, which resulted in a doctrinal distinction between sales and hire purchase.[56] Most recently the Supreme Court set the framework for *sui generis* retention of title clauses outside the sales law framework; this will be examined further below.[57]

Consumption for use rather than ownership seems to have rapidly become the prime form of consumption in the car market. Recent trends towards transactions that enable financiers to maintain control down the chain of transactions has led to

[51] ibid 46.

[52] ibid 39.

[53] ibid 51: 'traditional leasing models are structured for manufacturers or vendors of "hard assets" such as cars, trucks, trailers, copiers or medical equipment. These assets can be repossessed and remarketed in case of default or bankruptcy which makes it "true asset backed finance". The circular economy however is not limited to these "hard assets" with well-developed second hand markets. Developing leasing models for "softer assets" first requires acceptance by financers of contractual comfort instead of legal ownership over assets.'

[54] Gregson et al (n 19) 224, citing B Su, A Heshmati, Y Geng, and X Yu, 'A Review of the Circular Economy in China: Moving from Rhetoric to Implementation' (2013) 42 *Journal of Cleaner Production* 215, 217.

[55] Hieminga (n 2) 6.

[56] *Helby v Matthews* [1895] AC 471.

[57] Text following n 93.

concerns about the volumes of debt accrued through such transactions.[58] Prior to that there were concerns about the development of sub-prime asset financing through so-called log-book loans. There were numerous calls for reform, which appear to be succeeding with the introduction of a Goods Mortgages Bill in the June 2017 Queen's Speech following a Law Commission Report into this area.[59] However, that reform failed, with the withdrawal of the Bill in May 2018 following lobbying from the lending industry.[60] Yet the point here is that this is just another illustration of consumers being willing to trade ownership (or at least a risk to ownership) whilst being able to retain use rights, and the likely form of the legislation will be that such trade-offs will continue to be allowed.[61] Such analysis can be applied to potential circular economies more broadly. And as will be seen, whilst there may be changes wrought on commercial practices, moves to contract-focused transactions at the expense of ownership would be hardly novel in terms of modern English legal history.

On the other hand, problems might arise in the context of accession of goods. Hieminga gives the example of a situation where Philips, the electronics giant, might want to install a pay per use lighting system, 'and take responsibility for end of life disposal of the armatures and lamps', but in doing so they run the risk that such goods accede to the realty and become subject to third-party claims.[62] Hieminga goes on to suggest that ownership and accession issues will be resolved through contract:

> There are practical workarounds available. Although legal ownership could be lost through accession parties can remain the economic owner of the goods through binding agreements. Parties can sign a contract that not only specifies the payment structure to use the service, but they can also agree upon what should be done in case things go wrong. And legally agreements must always be kept! In legal terminology: pacta sunt servanda. This might give both the supplier and financer enough comfort to close a deal.[63]

This approach is legally dubious. English law has regrettably, and arguably incorrectly, taken the approach that where goods become fixtures any prior owner or supplier loses priority regardless of any contractual agreement with the receiver.[64] One ray of hope here is in the final sentence in the quote above: if the supplier agrees with third parties that they have some form of priority then than can be protected, though only contractually.[65]

[58] P Inman, 'MPs and Charities Urge Car Leasers to Publish Sub-Prime Loan Figures', *The Observer* (2 July 2017), available at www.theguardian.com/money/2017/jul/02/car-leasers-publish-sub-prime-lending-figures-mps-charities.

[59] Details of the bill are available at: www.gov.uk/government/publications/queens-speech-2017-background-briefing-notes. See also Law Commission, 'Bills of Sale' (Law Com No 396, 12 September 2016); 'Replacing bills of sale: a new Goods Mortgages Bill. Consultation on draft clauses' (July 2017).

[60] www.lawcom.gov.uk/government-shelves-goods-mortgages-bill.

[61] It is suggested that a similar process will likely occur with the car-finance market, ie such transactions will be regulated (lightly) but not prohibited.

[62] Hieminga (n 2) 39.

[63] ibid 39.

[64] S Thomas, 'Mortgages, Fixtures, Fittings and Security over Personal Property' (2015) 66 *Northern Ireland Legal Quarterly* 343 (noting the convoluted judicial attempts to reconcile old doctrine with new commercial practices which involved novel utilisations of goods).

[65] ibid 39: 'As such the circular business must yield a high enough return to compensate for the additional risk.'

Another approach is to reverse our focus, and examine the extent to which proactive control in the absence of ownership rights can function to maintain circular economies. In the context of the Philips lighting example above, Philips runs the risk of a liquidator terminating the contract. However,

> Philips can build in a technical feature that allows them to turn off the service (lighting) remotely. With such a 'red button option' the liquidator has a strong incentive to continue the contract because otherwise the suppliers turns off the service and the property is worth less. However, such technical solutions are not always available or could raise legal issues.[66]

Contemporary and future shifts from ownership to use will likely be brought about by, and accelerated by, changes in technology as much as any other factor. Technological development, encapsulated in memetic phrases such as 'the internet of things',[67] 'autonomous vehicles', 'wearable tech', and so on, points strongly towards trends of automation, miniaturisation, connectivity and ultimately control.[68] Smart objects enable digital control and manipulation, both *of* the environment and more crucially *by* the environment.[69] Interactivity is generally a multidirectional process, enabling connections to be drawn and maintained at very limited cost over long time periods.[70] Such control capacity has been a boon to those operating in the field of smart goods and technology, as intellectual property law regimes provide effective mechanisms for down-chain legal and practical control of the use of objects.[71]

Three brief, and notorious, examples will illustrate: Amazon's deletion of text-files purchased by Amazon Kindle e-reader owners where the files breached copyright (ironically of *1984* and *Animal Farm*);[72] the printer manufacturer HP using a firmware

[66] ibid 40.

[67] See, eg, http://ec.europa.eu/digital-agenda/en/internet-things; http://www.internet-of-things-research.eu; Thomas (n 13); K Manwaring, 'A Legal Analysis of Socio-Technological Change Arising out of eObjects' (5 January 2016) UNSW Law Research Paper No 2016–15, available at http://ssrn.com/abstract=2690024; WK Hon, C Millard and J Singh, 'Twenty Legal Considerations for Clouds of Things' (4 January 2016) Queen Mary School of Law Legal Studies Research Paper No 216/2016, available at http://ssrn.com/abstract=2716966.

[68] Privacy concerns burn brightly here: AG Ferguson, 'The Internet of Things and the Fourth Amendment of Effects' (2016) 104 *California Law Review* 807; MW Bailey, 'Seduction by Technology: Why Consumers Opt Out of Privacy by Buying into the Internet of Things' (2016) 84 *Texas Law Review* 1023.

[69] See, eg, M Hildebrandt, *Smart Technologies and the End(s) of Law* (Cheltenham, Edward Elgar, 2015) 11: 'Pre-emptive smart environments begin to transform our dealings with artefacts.'

[70] cf Hieminga (n 2) 46: 'Tracking sold products and services in order to perform maintenance over the life span or take them back at the end of the lifecycle requires knowledge about the whereabouts and conditions of the so called 'installed base'. Innovations like the "internet of things" make easy tracking possible but require investments.'

[71] See generally Thomas (n 13); S Thomas, 'Sale of Goods and Intellectual Property: Problems with Ownership' (2014) *Intellectual Property Forum* 25; S Thomas, 'Goods with Embedded Software: Obligations under Section 12 of the Sale of Goods Act 1979' (2012) 26 *International Review of Law, Computers & Technology* 165. See also MA Lemley, 'IP in a World Without Scarcity' (2015) 90 *New York University Law Review* 460 (the reduced relevance of scarcity brought about by technological change may lead to reactions by IPR holders, such as attempts to control goods).

[72] B Stone, 'Amazon erases Orwell books from Kindle devices' *New York Times* (17 July 2009), available at http://www.nytimes.com/2009/07/18/technology/companies/18amazon.html; 'Amazon sued for Kindle deletion of Orwell' CBS News (31 July 2009), available at http://www.cbsnews.com/stories/2009/07/31/tech/main5201198.shtml;.

update to prevent printers using non-proprietary ink;[73] and the agricultural plant manufacturer John Deere attempting to prevent users from modifying software and hardware elements of goods.[74] Each example points to different behaviour by both user and manufacturer, and there was no consistency in the end result,[75] but at the core for each was an illustration of the downstream control that could be maintained in the practical sense. The technological capacity to unilaterally delete an infringing file, or to alter the nature of the goods, is clear in the first two examples. But for both examples, and more pertinently the third, what is also on show is the legal strength backing up such contractually based actions against digital assets (software) and its capacity to extend into controlling the use of tangible things.[76] This may help to protect the assets in the face of rather unclear and possibly flimsy provisions for the transfer of property rights in digital assets.[77]

These examples show the importance of two aspects underlying any shift in the relationship between ownership and use: the role of contracting (especially that of licencing) and the (related) capacity to manipulate the location and effect of the title of goods.[78] Manipulating title and retaining ownership may seem like a powerful response, but as will be seen, it is only really a catalyst for drawing attention to any underlying contractual agreement as between relevant parties. In this context, we must be wary of the potential impact of licences, which grows in the context of digital technologies.[79] Moreover, we must acknowledge the different timescales that technological and legal developments operate on. The shift from ownership to use is a policy goal of circular economies. Such shifts can be accommodated in English law. However, policy goals for circular economies will more likely be first met by technological developments, and law will invariably be playing catch-up. This should make us aware of the possibility of English law utilising pre-existing forms and structures in order to cope with novel commercial practices; how this utilisation can occur thus needs analysis.

[73] www.dailymail.co.uk/news/article-3797408/Licence-print-money-HP-faces-backlash-blocking-customers-using-cheaper-ink-cartridges-printers.html; www.theguardian.com/technology/2016/sep/20/hp-inkjet-printers-unofficial-cartridges-software-update.

[74] K Wiens, 'We Can't Let John Deere Destroy the Very Idea of Ownership' Wired Business (21 April 2015), available at www.wired.com/2015/04/dmca-ownership-john-deere. John Deere (and Apple) has also lobbied against rights to repair: O Sohn, 'A Right to Repair: Why Nebraska Farmers Are Taking on John Deere and Apple' *The Guardian* (6 March 2017), available at www.theguardian.com/environment/2017/mar/06/nebraska-farmers-right-to-repair-john-deereapple.

[75] Amazon refused to back down. HP did back down: www.bbc.co.uk/news/technology-37503139. The John Deere case is continuing.

[76] See also L Feiler, 'Separation of Ownership and the Authorization to use Personal Computers: Unintended effects of EU and US Law on IT security' (2011) 27 *Santa Clara Computer & High Technology Law Journal* 131, 132–33 (noting different instances of IPR holders affecting ownership and/or usage of goods).

[77] See, eg, S Thomas, 'Security Interests in Intellectual Property: Proposals for Reform' (2017) 37 *Legal Studies* 214; MBM Loos and C Mak, 'Remedies for Buyers in Case of Contracts for the Supply of Digital Content', ad hoc briefing paper for the European Parliament's Committee on Legal Affairs, May 2012, (Amsterdam Law School Legal Studies Research Paper No 2012–71, 2012), available at http://ssrn.com/abstract=2087626 (recommending greater clarity on the transfer of ownership rights over digital content).

[78] This is not to deny any other element's role in this process. Here the focus is limited for clarity and economy.

[79] Above n 71. See also AJ Casey and A Niblett, 'Self-Driving Contracts' (1 March 2017), available at https://ssrn.com/abstract=2927459.

B. Role of 'Property' and 'Title' in Sales

The meaning and treatment of ownership, in a practical sense and in terms of the structure and content of legal regimes, is clearly commercially important. Whereas sales are functional commercial activities, in the sense of being easily affected and manipulated by connected aspects of practical commerce such as financing choices and requirements, business structuring decisions, and decisions over control and use of assets, they still are governed by a body of formal rules combining in a property regime.[80] The Sale of Goods Act 1979 provides a body of rules pertaining to the transfer of property in sales, which is somewhat necessary by virtue of the definition of sale as being the transfer of property in the goods.[81] The rules on property concern various different aspects of transactions, providing structures which help ascertain who has standing, as well as determining liability for aspects such as loss or damage to goods.[82] Section 12 of the 1979 Act sets out an obligation to pass good title, and failure to do so voids the sale.[83] Property in the goods is deemed not to pass in unascertained goods,[84] but party intention is key to determining whether property has passed.[85] In the event of a failure to ascertain an appropriate intention, the Sale of Goods Act 1979, section 18 provides a variety of different rules to enable that intention to be determined. Passing title is essential, and you cannot pass a title that you do not have: *nemo dat quod non habet.*[86] In such cases an unsuspecting purchaser may be able to avail themselves of a number of exceptions to the *nemo dat* rule,[87] though it is often a complicated and treacherous path to success.[88] There have been relatively recent important changes concerning the

[80] cf J Devenney and M Kenny, 'The Omission of Personal Property Law from the Proposed Common European Sales Law: The Hamlet Syndrome … Without the Prince?' [2015] *Journal of Business Law* 607, 618: 'Given that the sale of goods is, *fundamentally*, about the passing of property, any exclusion of property is significant because it threatens the overall coherence as well as the future prospects of the proposed CESL.'

[81] Sale of Goods Act 1979, s 2(1).

[82] *Re Waite* [1927] 1 Ch 606; *Re Goldcorp Exchange* [1995] 1 AC 74. Determining property is important for insurance purposes as well, because in English law, under the Sale of Goods Act 1979, s 20(1), unless otherwise agreed, risk of loss passes with property. Tort law is also relevant here. In the event of a conversion or negligence claim, the claimant must be at least entitled to a right to possess the goods: *The Aliakmon* [1986] AC 785 (negligence); *Kuwait Airways v Iraqi Airways* [2002] 2 AC 883 (conversion). However, this chapter will focus on the sales regime.

[83] *Rowland v Divall* [1923] 2 KB 500.

[84] Sale of Goods Act 1979, s 16.

[85] Sale of Goods Act 1979, s 17.

[86] Sale of Goods Act 1979, s 21.

[87] The core exceptions are found in Sale of Goods Act 1979, ss 21 (estoppel), 23 (voidable title), 24 (seller in possession), and 25 (buyer in possession). The other core provisions are mercantile agency in the Factors Act 1889, s 2, and the hire-purchase exception for motor vehicles under the Hire-Purchase Act 1964, Part II (re-enacted by the Consumer Credit Act 1974, s 192, Sch 4, para 22; amended by the Sale of Goods Act 1979, s 63 and Sch 2, para 4).

[88] See, eg, S Thomas, 'The Role of Authorization in Title Conflicts Involving Retention of Title Clauses: Some American Lessons' (2014) 43 *Common Law World Review* 29 (concerning the complicated relationship between the very similar provisions on seller and buyer in possession under the Factors Act 1889, ss 8 and 9 and those in the Sale of Goods Act 1979); S Thomas, 'Transfers of Documents of Title under English Law and the Uniform Commercial Code' [2012] *Lloyd's Maritime and Commercial Law Quarterly* 573–605 (problems with voidable title).

property rights in bulks,[89] and most recently there has been a removal and replication of provisions concerning consumers.[90]

The importance of property, title and ownership concepts, how they are used (and can be abused, or may not work well), is clear for English law.[91] Despite some confusion and debate of the meaning of 'property' and 'title',[92] this chapter will side-step that issue by focusing on some other implications. Here three points can be drawn out. The first concerns the problems in English law concerning recent case law on retention of title clauses. The second and third points broaden the examination and illustrate how on one hand a wide variety of jurisdictions employ rules concerning obligations to pass good title, and then on the other hand how the UN Convention on the International Sale of Goods operates its notoriously property-free regime. This will show how contracts can often take precedence as the determining factor in ascertaining the location and transference of property, but that this may have problematic results. Furthermore, the prevalence of rules protecting purchasers by obliging owners to pass good title creates a tension between a body of doctrine allowing commercial control of goods down a chain of transactions through contractual manipulation of property and another body of doctrine protecting those downstream from suffering such infringements.

i. Retention of Title

English commercial law's avoidance of an overly strict regulation of commerce along with a tendency to assume that parties can, and are best left to, sort things out for themselves, means, as Gullifer puts it, 'the [statutory] provisions as to the passing of property … exemplify freedom of contract'.[93] English law provides that a seller can

[89] Sale of Goods Act 1979, ss 20A and 20B.

[90] The Consumer Rights Act 2015 has the functional effect of removing all consumer law from the Sale of Goods Act 1979, which can now be considered a type of commercial code. The Consumer Rights Act 2015 makes some changes (such as those concerning digital products) and removed and retained some recent changes to the old statutory regime (such as rules providing that risk does not pass to consumers until delivery in Consumer Rights Act 2015, s 29), but a number of property rules remain the same (such as those concerning transfer of property in Consumer Rights Act 2015, s 4, the obligation to pass good title in Consumer Rights Act 2015, s 17, and title conflicts, which the explanatory notes para 33 directs back to the Sale of Goods Act 1979 provisions). Economy unfortunately prevents analysis of these issues here. See further eg S Whittaker, 'Distinctive Features of the New Consumer Contract Law' (2017) 133 *Law Quarterly Review* 47 (property noted once in passing); P Giliker, 'The Consumer Rights Act 2015 – A Bastion of European Consumer Rights?' (2017) 37 *Legal Studies* 78 (no mention of property).

[91] G Battersby and AD Preston, 'The Concepts of "Property," "Title" and "Owner" Used in the Sale of Goods Act 1893' (1972) 35 *Modern Law Review* 268; LC Ho, 'Some Reflection on "Property" and "Title" in the Sale of Goods Act' [1997] 56 *Cambridge Law Journal* 571; G Battersby, 'A Reconsideration of "Property" and "Title" in the Sale of Goods Act' [2001] *Journal of Business Law* 1. See generally C Debattista, 'Transferring Property in International Sales: Conflicts and Substantive Rules under English law' (1995) 26 *Journal of Maritime Law and Commerce* 29; T O'Sullivan, 'The Sale of Goods Act 1908: Rules for Passing of Property in Specific Goods. One Hundred Years On – Have the Rules Stood the Test of Time?' (2008) 14 *New Zealand Business Law Quarterly* 190.

[92] cf KN Llewellyn, *Cases and Materials in the Law of Sales* (Chicago, Callaghan and Co, 1933) xiv; KN Llewellyn, 'Through Title to Contract and a Bit Beyond' (1938) 15 *NYU Law Quarterly Review* 159.

[93] L Gullifer, '"Sales" on Retention of Title Terms: Is the English Law Analysis Broken?' (2017) 133 *Law Quarterly Review* 244, 245.

retain title. The Sale of Goods Act 1979, section 19 states that sellers can impose obligations, making the passing of property contingent on other events (eg full payment). In addition, there has been a 40-year juridical meander from this legislative starting point, resulting in a complex and unclear body of law.[94] It is not clear the extent to which parties holding a retention of title clause can reach into and beyond assets, products and mixtures, though we can agree with Gullifer that retention of title clauses give sellers 'a powerful method of proprietary protection'. For the purposes of her analysis, she noted this was protection against 'counterparty credit risk', looking to the retention of title's usual role as securing the seller.[95] Acknowledging the primary function of retention of title clauses is to secure the seller in lending to the purchaser,[96] such clauses also demonstrate the role of contract in ascertaining proprietary rights. This can creates problems, whether due to deliberate skilled negotiating and drafting, or whether due to error or incompetence.[97] In addition, there is the impact (or lack thereof) of the Sale of Goods Act 1979, section 49(1): the seller's right to sue on the price depends on the passage of property. As the sale under retention of title terms will not lead to passage of property until the terms are met, then the seller could not sue on the price until that point.

Matters have been recently complicated by the Court of Appeal in the *Caterpillar* case,[98] and the Supreme Court's decision in the *Bunkers* case.[99] In *Caterpillar* the Court of Appeal held that the effect of the Sale of Goods Act, section 49(1) – the seller's right to sue on the price depends on the passage of property – meant that the seller could not actually sue on the price due to the presence of a retention of title clause. Only when title passed would the right arise. Whilst Longmore LJ notoriously left this argument by declaiming this just showed there were costs as well as benefits to the retention of title clause,[100] Gullifer criticised this on the policy grounds that it ignores the fact that in cases of solvent buyers sellers want the price, not repossessed goods,[101] and welcomed the Supreme Court's overruling on this point.[102] In the *Bunkers* case the Supreme Court held, in essence, that the contract concerned was not a contract of sale, a conclusion Gullifer rightly describes as having 'far reaching consequences'.[103]

[94] *Aluminium Industrie Vaassen BV v Romalpa Aluminium* [1976] 1 WLR 676 (CA); *Re Bond Worth Ltd* [1980] Ch 228; *Borden (UK) Ltd v Scottish Timber Products Ltd* [1981] Ch 25; *Clough Mill Ltd v Martin* [1984] 3 All ER 982; *Hendy Lennox (Industrial Engines Ltd v Grahame Puttick Ltd* [1984] 1 WLR 485; *E Pfeiffer Weinkellerei-Weineinkauf GmbH v Arbuthnot Factors Ltd* [1988] 1 WLR 150; *Compaq Computer Ltd v Abercorn Group Ltd* [1991] BCC 484; *Armour v Thyssen Edelstahlwerke AG* [1991] 2 AC 339. See generally L Gullifer, 'Retention of Title Clauses: A Question of Balance' in A Burrows and E Peel (eds), *Contract Terms* (Oxford, Oxford University Press, 2007) 285.

[95] Gullifer, '"Sales" on Retention of Title Terms' (2017) 246.

[96] There is a long and complex debate about whether retention of title clauses are, or if not whether they could be recharacterised, as a security interest. Here it is simply assumed that such clauses function as security interests.

[97] Gullifer (n 92) 249–50.

[98] *Caterpillar (NI) Ltd (formerly FG Wilson (Engineering) Ltd) v John Holt & Co (Liverpool) Ltd* [2013] EWCA Civ 1232, [2014] 1 WLR 2365.

[99] *PST Energy 7 Shipping LLC v OW Bunker Malta Ltd* [2016] UKSC 23, [2016] AC 1034. See also A Tettenborn, 'Of Bunkers and Retention of Title: When is a Sale Not a Sale?' [2016] *Lloyds Maritime & Commercial Law Quarterly* 24.

[100] *Caterpillar* [2014] 1 WLR 2365 [56].

[101] Louise Gullifer, 'The Interpretation of Retention of Title Clauses: Some Difficulties' [2014] *Lloyds Maritime & Commercial Law Quarterly* 564.

[102] ibid 253.

[103] ibid 254.

Gullifer has provided an excellent overview of the state of law following these decisions,[104] noting how the retention of title doctrine and the Sale of Goods Act 1979 are no longer compatible due to the Act's age and conceptual shortcomings.[105] Her criticism of the agency explanation given by the Court of Appeal in *Caterpillar* as opening up a raft of commercial difficulties in financing context is on point.[106] For the purposes of this chapter, it is worth noting that the effect of these decisions, in the context of the agency rationale, is to reinforce the contractual dominance of sales transactions which in itself will actually fit well within the context of the circular economy. This point is developed further in section III C below.

It is also worth teasing out a specific boon for circular economic practice arising from the Supreme Court's approach in *Bunkers*. By demonstrating the potential of a contractual transaction for the using up of tangibles that *does not* meet the requirements of a contract of sale of goods, the Court has provided (almost certainly inadvertently) a mechanism for commercial initiators in circular economies to restrict the nature of the transaction in a way that will be to their benefit.[107] By making sure that the transaction is not one of sale, complications arising from obligations to pass good title might be avoided, as might obligations against interference with quiet possession. Gullifer suggested that the obligations to pass good title are one particular thorny problem with the result of *Bunkers*, and she argued inter alia that a *sui generis* legislative response would need to implement a version of section 12 in order to resolve those problems.[108] Here it is suggested that circular economic practitioners, especially initiators of circular economic transactions, would resist such moves.

A particular implication not explicitly considered, but which arises by implication of Gullifer's examination of the effects of this case law on the using up or perishing of goods,[109] is that on *Re Highways Food* situations.[110] When A sells to B on retention of title terms, and B sells to C on the same terms, which prevent title passing until the price is paid, it is possible now to say such transactions are not sales. In *Benjamin on Sale*, it states that

> where an owner is bound by a *sui generis* supply contract [of the sort in *Bunkers*] concluded by a mercantile agent, it should follow, though the position is not free from doubt, that the recipient of goods remains at liberty to use or consume them, even if the property has not yet passed, accounting to the agent supplying the goods for the price.[111]

Whether the same logic applies in the *Re Highway Foods* situation is doubtful (*Benjamin on Sale* appears to reject the possibility). The extent of this effect of *Bunkers* must be

[104] ibid.

[105] ibid 250.

[106] ibid.

[107] At this point, 'initiators' is used instead of 'sellers'. Such actors will initiate the commercial transaction (whether circular or linear) by being the first to dispose of the goods, but, and this will become clearer later in this chapter, they will not be disposing of the property in the goods and thus cannot be technically be called "sellers". See further Thomas (n 13) 63.

[108] Gullifer (n 92) 262–63.

[109] ibid 259–60.

[110] *Re Highway Foods International Ltd, Mills v Harris (Wholesale Meat Ltd)* [1995] 1 BCLC 209, [1995] BCC 271. See generally S Thomas, 'The Role of Authorization in Title Conflicts Involving Retention of Title Clauses: Some American Lessons' (2014) 43 *Common Law World Review* 29.

[111] MG Bridge (ed), *Benjamin on Sale*, 9th edn (London, Sweet & Maxwell, 2014) [7-048].

left to another time, but the suggested consequence has the effect of further indicating the increased importance that is attached to the contractual arrangement between the parties.

ii. Obligations to Pass Good Title

The obligation to pass good title, under the Sale of Goods Act 1979, section 12 (for consumers, the Consumer Rights Act 2015, section 17) is not a particularly ancient implied term, arising only in the mid-nineteenth century.[112] Nevertheless, its importance was shown during a House of Commons Public Bill Committee Debate on the Consumer Rights Bill: 'Being able to use something freely and fairly is a fundamental part of buying it.'[113] The obligations under section 12 consist of a condition that the seller has the right to sell the goods, and two warranties of quiet possession and freedom from encumbrances. The right to sell has been interpreted as being distinct from the power to pass to title, ie to sell.[114] Failure to meet this obligation can have significant and potentially questionable results, such as a windfall for purchasers who effectively face no set-off for their use of the goods between acquisition and termination for breach of section 12.[115] Yet it should not be thought that the warranties are of limited import here. Though their status means no right to terminate arises from their breach, consideration of the implications of their potential reach reveals some potential problems. In *Microbeads AG v Vinhurst Road Markings Ltd*,[116] an English company bought a line-marking machine from a Swiss company. Some years later a different English company sued for patent infringement, seeking an injunction to prevent the use of the machines. Lord Denning MR held that although the infringement of the warranty of quiet possession arose after the initial sale, the obligation to prevent this infringement continued regardless of the seller's innocence. The seller had to bear the loss.[117] More recently the unauthorised imposition of a time lock on a computer system was held to be a breach of the warranty of quite possession.[118] Combined, these cases begin to provide the basis for a valuable form of protection against actions based on downstream facing attempts to exert control over the use of goods. What is particularly valuable is the application of the section 12 protections here in the context of claims by intellectual property rights holders; patents in the case above, and trademarks in the earlier case *Niblett Ltd v Confectioners' Materials Co Ltd*.[119]

[112] *Morely v Attenborough* (1849) 3 Ex Ch 500 (denied the existence of an implied warranty of title); *Eichholz v Bannister* (1864) 17 CB NS 708 (the very act of selling goods meant the seller held out that he was the owner of the goods unless the circumstances implied otherwise).

[113] Consumer Rights Bill Deb 25 February 2014, col 165 (The Parliamentary Under-Secretary of State for Business, Innovation and Skills (Jenny Willott MP)).

[114] *Niblett Ltd v Confectioners' Materials Co Ltd* [1921] 3 KB 387; *Great Elephant Corp v Trafigura Beheer BV (The Crudesky)* [2012] EWHC 1745 (Comm), [2013] 1 All ER (Comm) 415, [2012] 2 Lloyd's Rep 503 (reversed on appeal: [2013] EWCA Civ 905: this was on different grounds, and the conclusions from the QBD on the SGA s 12 points were expressly approved: paras 20–21.

[115] *Rowland v Divall* [1923] 2 KB 500.

[116] [1975] 1 WLR 218.

[117] ibid 222–23.

[118] *Rubicon Computer Systems Ltd v United Paints Ltd (CA)* (2000) 2 TCLR 453.

[119] [1921] 3 KB 387.

This power of intangible rights holders to control the use of tangibles,[120] begins to disturb notions of ownership as much as any claims by retention of title clause-holders. In the event of successful actions, the goods-holders are liable to the rights holder, and their source of recourse is their vendor.[121] In the event of vendor insolvency or disappearance the loss thus falls on the purchaser. A similar logic of course applies to the section 12 condition as it does to the warranties; the liability to the rights-holder causes the liability, but the financial loss caused falls on the purchaser if they have no chance of claiming damages even if they can terminate the contract. The overwhelming volumes of intellectual property rights encased in smart objects raises two potential problems. The first is whether or not the section 12 jurisprudence will easily apply to the quite different conditions of contemporary objects of commerce compared to the 1970s (*Microbeads*) or the 1920s (*Niblett*). The second, and more dangerous, is potential utilisation of the inequality of bargaining power by parties wishing to authorise the use of their intellectual property by means of contracted-for licences. This would be in line with the shifting from ownership to control. Rather than using the sword or spear of retention of title clauses, there may be a preference for the entanglement possibility of contractual licences, limiting ownership *and* enhancing control over not only that specific intellectual property which the licence covers but by the consequences of technological integration the goods the intellectual property inheres in.[122] By taking situations outside section 12, following *Bunkers*, control without corresponding obligations is a strong possibility.

iii. CISG

A useful, brute, comparator to the English sales regime is the CISG. There, the lack of specific rules on property law is well known.[123] Article 4 states that the CISG only governs 'the formation of the contract of the sale'; the 'effect which the contract may

[120] See, eg, S Thomas, 'Security Interests in Intellectual Property: Proposals for Reform' (2017) 37 *Legal Studies* 214, 240–42.

[121] For a very recent demonstration, see, eg, *R v M and others* [2017] UKSC 58 (no differentiation between goods produced without authorisation from a trademark holder, and goods sold without authorisation (so called 'grey goods') vis-à-vis criminalisation under the Trade Marks Act 1994, s 92(1)).

[122] See generally Thomas (n 13).

[123] See generally TQ Thang, 'Passing of Property Under Contracts for the International Sale of Goods: Should the CISG Regulate the Transfer of Property?' (2004), available at www.cisg.law.pace.edu/cisg/biblio/thang.html; M Wesiack, 'Is the CISG Too Much Influenced by Civil Law Principles of Contract Law Rather than Common Law Principles of Contract Law? Should the CISG Contain a Rule on the Passing of Property?' (2004) available at www.cisg.law.pace.edu/cisg/biblio/wesiack.html; M Torsello, 'Transfer of Ownership and the 1980 Vienna Sales Convention: A Regretful Lack of Uniform Regulation?' (2000) *International Business Law Journal* 939; E Visser, 'Favor Emptoris: Does the CISG Favor the Buyer?' (1998) 67 *UMKC Law Review* 77; W Khoo, 'Article 4' in C Bianca and M Bonell (eds), *Commentary on the International Sales Law: The 1980 Vienna Sales Convention (1987)* 44, available at www.cisg.law.pace.edu/cisg/biblio/khoo-bb4.html; RM Goode, 'Reflections on the Harmonisation of Commercial Law' (1991) 1 *Uniform Law Review* 54; A Romein, 'The Passing of Risk: A Comparison Between the Passing of Risk under the CISG and German Law' (Heidelberg, June 1999), available at www.cisg.law.pace.edu/cisg/biblio/romein.html.

have on the property in the goods sold' is not a concern of the CISG 'except as otherwise expressly provided'.[124] According to the CISG Secretariat Commentary, this

> makes it clear that the Convention does not govern the passing of property in the goods sold. In some legal systems property passes at the time of the conclusion of the contract. In other legal systems property passes at some later time such as the time at which the goods are delivered to the buyer. It was not regarded possible to unify the rule on this point nor was it regarded necessary to do so since rules are provided by this Convention for several questions linked, at least in certain legal systems, to the passing of property; the obligation of the seller to transfer the goods free from any right or claim of a third person [see CISG articles 41 and 42]; the obligation of the buyer to pay the price [see CISG Article 53]; the passing of the risk of loss or damage to the goods [see CISG Articles 66–70]; the obligation to preserve the goods [see CISG Articles 85–88].[125]

There are other areas of the CISG where property is to be found, as a referent or a subject of a provision. CISG Article 30 states that 'The seller must deliver the goods, hand over any documents relating to them and transfer the property in the goods, as required by the contract and this Convention', indicating that the CISG, whilst rejecting any attempt to provide rules on property, still requires the transference of property, and the governance of this transference of property is to be undertaken by the contract itself (and not the CISG). Thus on the issue of property in sales of goods, the CISG is content with the consensual approaches reached in individual transactions by the relevant parties to that transaction.

One of the major problems here concerns situations involving the insolvency or disappearance of parties to sales. Security interests and retention of title clauses, by being property matters, are subject to domestic determination.[126] By forcing parties to rely on domestic law the CISG's claim to uniformity is undermined, and there may be practical problems for such parties if the international transaction suddenly gets grounded in one or another domestic jurisdiction.[127] However, the CISG does provide guidance regarding obligations to pass good title, in Articles 41 and 42. Article 41 obliges sellers

[124] CISG Art 4.

[125] The Secretariat Commentary to the CISG, available at http://www.cisg.law.pace.edu/cisg/text/secomm/secomm-04.html#1.

[126] *Roder Zelt-und Hallenkonstruktionen GmbH v Rosedown Park Pty Ltd and Reginald R Eustace* [1995] 57 FCR 216 (Federal Court of Australia) (http://cisgw3.law.pace.edu/cases/950428a2.html); *Usinor Industeel v Leeco Steel Products* (2002 US DC (Ill)) 209 F Supp 2d 880; 47 UCC Rep Serv2d 887 (http://cisgw3.law.pace.edu/cases/020328u1.html); *St Paul Guardian Insurance Co v Neuromed Medical System & Support* (2002 US DC (NY)) 2002 WL 465312 (http://cisgw3.law.pace.edu/cases/020326u1.html); *Stolen Automobile Case* (21 March 2007, Appellate Court Dresden, Germany) (http://cisgw3.law.pace.edu/cases/070321g1.html) (see also *Automobile Case* (22 August 2002, District Court Freiburg, Germany; http://cisgw3.law.pace.edu/cases/020822g1.html – essentially identical); *Milk Packaging Equipment Case* (15 July 2008, Foreign Trade Court of Arbitration attached to the Serbian Chamber of Commerce) (http://cisgw3.law.pace.edu/cases/080715sb.html).

[127] As such there have been proposals to introduce property rules to the CISG: Proposal by Switzerland on possible future work by UNCITRAL in the area of international contract law, 8 May 2012 (UN Doc A/CN.9/758). See also L Galler, 'An Historical and Policy Analysis of the Title Passage Rule in International Sales of Personal Property' (1991) 52 *University of Pittsburgh Law Review* 521; SS Grewal, 'Risk of Loss in Goods Sold During Transit: A Comparative Study of the UN Convention on Contracts for the International Sale of Goods, the UCC, and the British Sale of Goods Act' (1991) 14 *Loyola LA International & Comparative Law Journal* 93.

to deliver goods 'free from any right or claim of a third party'. Article 42 provides for such freedom 'from any right or claim of a third party based on industrial property or other intellectual property, of which at the time of the conclusion of the contract the seller knew or could not have been aware'.[128] There has not been much in the way of extensive analysis of this provision, rendering its scope and meaning quite unclear.[129] However, the most reasonable interpretation has to be that it would have the same broad effect as the English doctrine. Article 42 essentially formalises something similar to the approach taken by the English courts considering section 12.

This raises a question: if there is similarity between a 'property-heavy' regime and a 'property-light' regime as to the importance of protecting purchasers by means of holding sellers liable for breaches of third-party rights is that pointing to the importance of the role of property, or is it pointing more towards identifying the role of contract?

C. How and Why Contracting may Eradicate Sales in the Circular Economy

It is generally considered that there are a far greater proportion of formal contracts in international commercial transactions compared to domestic transactions. This is partially due to a lack of trust between such parties,[130] but there may be a wide range of reasons why the parties in international transactions might want a greater level of formality. This difference in use of contracts is a key factor when contextualising the multi-party, cross-border nature of circular economic problems. The potential for control of goods by initial parties in the chain of transactions in a circular economy, in order to implement shifts from ownership to use as the governing conceptual basis for the transactional value of the thing, raises issue of negotiation of the contract, and of contractual licences.

The extent of the use of standard form contracts is related to the nature of the subject of sale. Commodity transactions are very often undertaken using standard form contracts, often issued by relevant trade bodies. On the other hand, sales of bespoke

[128] Article 42(1). Article 42(2) imposes the same notice/knowledge test on the buyer.

[129] The extent of the literature on this Article is: S Kröll, 'Article 42' in S Kröll, L Mitselis and P Perales Viscasillas (eds), *UN Convention on Contracts for the International Sale of Goods (CISG)* (Munich and Oxford, C H Beck & Hart Publishing, 2011) 647; B Zeller, 'Intellectual Property Rights & the CISG Article 42' (2011–12) 15 *Vindobona Journal of International Commercial Law and Arbitration* 289; I Schwenzer, *Schlechtriem & Schwenzer: Commentary on the UN Convention on the International sale of Goods (CISG)*, 3rd edn (Oxford, Oxford University Press, 2010) 648; RM Janal, 'The Seller's Responsibility for Third Party Intellectual Property Rights under the Vienna Sales Convention' in CB Andersen and UG Schroeter (eds), *Sharing International Commercial Law Across National Boundaries: Fechtschrift for Albert H Kritzer on the Occasion of his Eightieth Birthday* (Wildy, Simonds & Hill Publishing, 2008) 203; JA Van Duzer, 'A Seller's Responsibility for Third Party Intellectual Property Claims: Are the UN Sales Convention Rules Better?' (2001) 4 *Canadian International Lawyer* 187; C Rauda and G Etier, 'Warranty for Intellectual Property Rights in the International Sale of Goods' (2000) 4 *Vindobona Journal of International Commercial Law and Arbitration* 30; AM Shinn, 'Liabilities under Article 42 of the UN Convention on the International Sale of Goods' (1993) 2 *Minnesota Journal of Global Trade* 115.

[130] V Gessner, RP Appelbaum and WLF Felstiner, 'Introduction: The Legal Culture of Global Business Transactions' in RP Appelbaum, WL Felstiner and V Gessner (eds), *Rules and Networks: The Legal Culture of Global Business Transactions* (Oxford, Hart, 2001) 1, 23.

or non-fungible goods may well take place under the aegis of a unique, negotiated contract. In the context of circular economy though, transactions may, oddly enough, involve both types of contracts, in the sense that there may be bespoke contractual arrangements with regard to the whole asset combined with standard form agreements for specific aspects or contents of that asset. This is most likely to be the case with smart objects: goods which are able to interact with other objects and persons, consisting of hardware and software integrated so coherently that it is not possible to alter either element with affecting the functions of the smart object.

The authority to use IPRs is invariably by licence. Licences pervade the digital world. The capacity to access software is conditional on agreement to licence terms. These licences set out the extent of your powers as a user. The power to alienate, or modify, may be (almost certainly will be) restricted. They may include obligations regarding data capture and use. Moreover, the capacity to negotiate such terms is limited, not least by the fact that at least in a consumer context, they are often not even read.[131] Licences may also contain break clauses, having the effect of removing authorisation for use. Combined with the technical capacity to prevent use of goods for infringements of licences to use software integral to the goods, the power of licences for some commercial parties becomes evident.[132] The breadth of possibility afforded by licences should no doubt attract initiators in circular economies, for whom the task is as much about controlling the use of goods down long chains of transactions as it is about locating ownership in a particular owner.[133]

Another point worth briefly mentioning concerns the fact that long-term contractual relationships will need to be catered for, and the capacity of English law to provide for such a commercial model has been the subject of much debate.[134] There is a possible avenue for further research in terms of mapping on conceptualisations of relational contracts to circular economic practices. There will no doubt be room for examining in particular notions of potentially infinite relationships requiring continuing in-contract negotiation and planning for a future other than that of contract termination. These are likely to be key normative battlegrounds in the debate as to law and circular economy, especially as to how it relates to B2C transactions. This would be from a pragmatic stance, ie locking consumers in, to more political and theoretical questions concerning

[131] See, eg, Y Bakos, F Marotta-Wurgler and DR Trossen, 'Does Anyone Read the Fine Print? Consumer Attention to Standard-Form Contracts' (2014) 43 *The Journal of Legal Studies* 1 For an amusing example, see A Hern, 'Thousands Sign up to Clean Sewage Because They Didn't Read the Small Print' *The Guardian* (17 July 2017), available at www.theguardian.com/technology/2017/jul/14/wifi-terms-and-conditions-thousands-sign-up-clean-sewage-did-not-read-small-print.

[132] A further complication arises when the possibility of self-driving contract, contracts which automatically determine enforceable terms in order to reach a defined end result for both parties, is considered. Licences may well be manipulated beforehand, or during, automatically without human interferences. See Casey and Niblett, 'Self-Driving Contracts' (2017).

[133] See, eg, Thomas (n 13) 255–63.

[134] See, eg, H Collins, *Regulating Contracts* (Oxford, Oxford University Press, 1999). The nature of relational contracts has a rich literature, often starting with Stewart Macaulay, 'Non-Contractual Relations in Business: A Preliminary Study' (1968) 28 *American Sociology Review* 55. The work of Ian Macneil is often at the heart of the debate; for a useful overview and development of his work, see R Austen-Baker, 'Comprehensive Contract Theory: a Four-Norm Model of Contract Relations' (2009) 25 *Journal of Contract Law* 216.

whether such transactions/agreements are suitable in liberal democracies,[135] or whether they will perpetuate debt.[136]

It can thus be asked whether circular economic transactions will ever be sales. As has been seen, English law has recently shifted, towards treating retention of title transactions as quite distinct from sales. This may have a dual effect: retention of title will not limit the possibility to claim for damages in the event of a failure to pay the 'price', which in turn increases the likelihood of individualised contracts designed to escape the potential dangers of the Sale of Goods Act 1979. The other effect is to potentially collapse together understanding of dispositions of digital information such as software under copyright licence and dispositions of goods under a retention of title clause, into the same type of transactions where title is retained *and* use is authorised by means of a contractual licence, with whatever additional constraints that that form of authorisation can hold. This in turn allows for distribution of the licence, through sub-licences to all further users, which would help avoid the potential title conflicts that could arise where retention of title clauses were utilised in an attempt to achieve the same end. The shift to control over goods, to enable their most appropriate journey around a circular economy, will be achieved with greater ease.

III. Harmonisation

The circular economy will inevitably be cross-jurisdictional, immediately raising questions of harmonisation. Will circular economies require pre-existing legal harmonisation? Or will circular economic practices of themselves result in the harmonisation of legal doctrine? These questions will be tentatively explored here, before considering whether something other than harmonisation may prevail. It is necessary to caveat this discussion: the claims that follow about harmonisation are big, and what will be suggested is only a possible direction for developments. It is hoped though that this part will provoke debate about the relationship between circular economy and harmonisation, especially in the face of multilateral technological–managerial developments that will come with moves towards circular economy.[137]

Harmonisation is a tricky, multifaceted concept.[138] We could see harmonisation as unification. However, unification may lead to formal doctrinal rules and a

[135] cf MJ Radin, *Boilerplate: The Fine Print, Vanishing Rights, and the Rule of Law* (Princeton, Princeton University Press, 2013).

[136] cf D Graeber, *Debt: The First 5,000 Years* (London, Melville House Publishing, 2014) arguing exchange is definitely terminable, because it is between equals, but unequal transactions will continue, creating debt, for ever.

[137] On the importance of taking account of technological management in law, see generally R Brownsword, 'In the Year 2061: From Law to Technological Management' (2015) 7 *Law, Innovation and Technology* 1; R Brownsword, 'Technological Management and the Rule of Law' (2016) 8 *Law, Innovation and Technology* 100; R Brownsword, 'From Erewhon to AlphaGo: For the Sake of Human Dignity, Should we Destroy the Machines' (2017) 9 *Law, Innovation and Technology* 117.

[138] D Nelken, 'Comparative Law and Comparative Legal Studies' in E Örücü and D Nelken (eds), *Comparative Law: A Handbook* (Oxford, Hart Publishing, 2007) 3, 31 (making this point in the context of EU harmonisation projects). See also N Foster, 'Transmigration and Transferability of Commercial Law in a Globalized

prescriptive legal regime, limiting participant capacity to avoid or manipulate such rules. There may also be difficulties with the creation and maintenance of such rules, with tensions between different commercial cultures restricting effective implementation of harmonised regimes.[139] The history of the property rules in the CISG is a good example of this. Issues more internal to different regimes, such as incoherence and unpredictability, both in terms of internal assessments of legal regimes and in terms of correlating different jurisdictions, will impact on any moves towards harmonisation (or unification).[140] Other difficulties may be more in the political sphere; recent events such as Brexit, and the Trump Administration's withdrawal from the Trans-Pacific Partnership and the Paris climate accord, illustrate how political debates about sovereignty (however ill-informed) can impact on commerce and trade.[141] There are thus issues concerning identifying the subjects of harmonisation, the process of harmonisation, and the mechanism for maintaining harmonised positions (in the event of potential future ruptures).[142]

These are tough issues, and it may be that there is value in non-harmonisation, in difference. Even if we could accept that harmonisation might be a good thing, on balance,[143] we might still never properly resolve the underlying socio-cultural difference that gave rise to the differences that entailed the question of harmonisation in the first place.[144] Furthermore, as Nelken perceptively observes, 'The development of the international economy often uses, emphasises or exacerbates differences in the places which produce goods and services even as it spreads homogenous appetites for such goods.'[145] What this means to the broader question of whether circular economy

World' in A Harding and E Örücü (eds), *Comparative Law in the 21st Century* (London, Kluwer, 2002) 55; M Andenas and CB Andersen (eds), *Theory and Practice of Harmonisation* (Cheltenham, Edward Elgar, 2011); R Goode, 'Reflections on the Harmonization of Commercial Law' in R Cranston and R Goode (eds), *Commercial and Consumer Law: National and International Dimensions* (Oxford, Clarendon Press, 1993) 3; LF Del Duca, 'Developing Transnational Harmonization Procedures for the Twenty-First Century' in ibid, 28–40; I Fletcher, L Mistelis and M Cremona (eds), *Foundations And Perspectives of International Trade Law* (London, Sweet & Maxwell, 2001); ES Lasaballett, 'Conceptualizing harmonization: the case for contract law' (2019) 24 *Uniform Law Review* 73.

[139] NHD Foster, 'Comparative Commercial Law: Rules or Context?' in Örücü and Nelken (ibid) 263–86.

[140] See eg JM Smits, 'Convergence of Private Law in Europe: Towards a New Ius Commune?' in Örücü and Nelken), *Comparative Law* (2007) 219–40.

[141] This article makes no specific claims one way or another about Brexit, or Trump. Rather, it merely notes that claims as to sovereignty were made by the proponents of such actions. For a valuable analysis of potential implications of Brexit on IP, see eg, GB Dinwoodie and RC Dreyfuss, 'Brexit and IP: The Great Unraveling?' (2017) 39 *Cardozo Law Review* 967.

[142] cf M Siems, *Comparative Law* (Cambridge, Cambridge University Press, 2014) 233, differentiating 'convergence' and 'harmonisation' on the basis that the latter is 'based on a deliberate programme for legal unification'.

[143] For some general criticisms on harmonisation, see, eg, L Mistelis, 'Is Harmonisation a Necessary Evil? The Future of Harmonisation and New Sources of International Trade Law' in I Fletcher, L Mistelis and M Cremona), *Foundations And Perspectives* (2001) 1; L Mistelis, 'Regulatory Aspects: Globalization, Harmonization, Legal transplants and Law reform – Some Fundamental Observations', (2000) 34 *International Law* 1055.

[144] cf P Legrand, 'How to Compare Now' (1996) 26 *Legal Studies* 232; P Legrand, 'The Impossibility of Legal Transplants' (1997) 4 *Maastricht Journal of European and Comparative Law* 111; L Nottage, 'Convergence, Divergence, and the Middle Way in Unifying or Harmonising Private Law' (2004) 1 *Annual of German and European Law* 166; R Cotterrell, 'Is it so Bad to be Different: Comparative Law and the Appreciation of Diversity' in Örücü and Nelken (n 138) 133–54.

[145] D Nelken, 'Comparative Law' (2007) 3, 31.

needs legal harmonisation though is unclear, but for the sake of clarity it is assumed that there may be something close to legal harmonisation in developments towards circular economy.[146] Two reasons support this claim.

On one hand, we could see harmonisation as less about formal unification,[147] and more about reaching some form of commonality between different legal systems, resembling something like the post-war European *acquis* or *ius commune*.[148] This sort of harmonisation results from a combination of political and socio-economic trends.[149] Another form of harmonisation may result from the globalised nature of circular economy: some form of harmony between different legal systems may be practically necessary in order for circular economy to work in anything other than jurisdictional autarky.[150] The following subsections expand on the harmonisation process in commercial context, and will suggest possible directions for harmonisation and circular economy.

A. What Sort of Harmonisation would be Best for the Circular Economy?

Foster has usefully suggested three main (though not exhaustive or exclusive) categories of harmonisation processes: 'institutionally organised; customary, market-based; and pressure to conform/inter-jurisdictional competition'.[151] The first concerns those efforts such as the CISG, the UNCITRAL Model Law on International Commercial Arbitration, the Principles of International Commercial Contracts, the Model Guide on Secured Transactions. The second 'arises out of international transactions. They are not consciously planned, and *a fortiori* are not conceived within any institution.'[152] The third concerns, broadly, legal transplants (of various forms and styles).

For circular economies, movement towards harmonised *aspects* of commercial law may be required not least because doctrinal similarity will be necessary to prevent offshoots and breakages in circular economic processes as they flit through jurisdictions

[146] cf Siems, *Comparative Law* (2014) ch 9 generally, and 255–58 in particular, for an overview of the pros and cons of what he calls convergence (though for our purposes the arguments apply to harmonisation, if distinguished from convergence), with a tendency towards seeing convergence in a positive light.

[147] cf Mistelis, 'Is harmonisation a necessary evil?' (2001) 4: 'harmonisation is a process which may result in unification of law subject to a number of (often utopian) conditions being fulfilled, such as, for example, wide or universal geographical acceptance of harmonisation instruments, and with wide scope of harmonising instruments which effectively substitute all pre-existing law'.

[148] This would include development of the Draft Common Frame of Reference and the Principles of European Law, amongst other things.

[149] See, eg, M Gelter, 'EU Company Law Harmonization Between Convergence and Varieties of Capitalism' (30 May 2017) in H Wells (ed), *Research Handbook on the History of Corporation and Company Law* (forthcoming), Fordham Law Legal Studies Research Paper No 2977500, European Corporate Governance Institute (ECGI) – Law Working Paper No 355/2017, available at https://ssrn.com/abstract=2977500 (suggesting a shift in economic perspectives with the entry of the UK to the then EC in 1972 affected EU corporate law).

[150] Foster, 'Comparative Commercial Law' (2007) 56: 'Commerce is by its nature international, and there is therefore no field in which there is more harmonization than commercial law, with numerous transplants … Globalization is itself largely a commercial phenomenon.'

[151] ibid 57. Mistelis, 'Is harmonisation a necessary evil?' (n 143), elucidates may various categorisations of harmonisation. Foster's is taken here purely for clarity.

[152] ibid 58.

and across boundaries. This can be conceptualised as a tension between focusing on global and local perspectives. Cotterrell explains it thus:

> I take globalization simply to mean tendencies (however interpreted) towards transactional uniformity in economic or social arrangement, institutions and values. Localization is taken here to refer to counter-tendencies (of whatever kind) towards protection, assertion or facilitation of diversity, difference, independence, separation or autonomy of groups, nations or territories, most often in matters of government or common values or traditions. … Globalization seems pre-eminently to be about seeking similarity by unifying social, economic and often legal arrangements. Localization seems to be about appreciating difference by creating, preserving or rediscovering conditions in which difference (for example, political or cultural) can flourish and be respected.[153]

Circular economies are cross-jurisdictional, in multiple locations connected through various tangible and intangible means across multiple nodes. In order to operate such economies, there needs to be mechanisms for long-term and long-distance control, which must necessarily cross over any of the potential boundaries to which circular economies are potentially susceptible. This is obviously going to be a difficult task, for each of the counter-tendencies towards localism Cotterrell identified could themselves operate powerful and potentially fatal attacks to the unifying effects of harmonisation. However, it is not difficult to discern this happening in the field of commercial activity, the stronghold of harmonisation activity.

Commercial harmonisation efforts have had various degrees of success. This is still no such thing as an International Code of Commerce or a worldwide commercial court. Moreover, those harmonisation efforts often portrayed as successful are either specific in focus (Cape Town Convention), or have well-known exceptions and limitations in scope of coverage and substantive content (CISG). Yet as much as there is difficulty extending towards full harmonisation, this does not mean lessons cannot be learnt from harmonisation efforts about how to deal with the contest between global and local approaches.

B. What is Likely to Happen?

Cotterrell sets out the urgency in harmonisation efforts: 'The question is not "whether or when?", but "how and on what model?"' Comparative law may help in such efforts by identifying 'sources of friction' and bypassing or eradicating them, 'by inventively smoothing out legal differences, creatively interpreting legal change to those who must accept it, or preserving familiar forms, concepts and styles of legal practice and thought while adjusting to meet transnational requirements'.[154] The implication here is that the effect of harmonisation efforts can be tied, loosely or tightly, to the tasks deemed necessary to get around problems in such processes. It is worth recognising the implication that harmonisation may be the result of efforts in *preservation* of legal doctrine and action.

[153] R Cotterrell, 'Seeking Similarity, Appreciating Difference: Comparative Law and Communities' in Harding and Örücü, *Comparative Law* (2002) 35, 43.
[154] ibid 45.

The role of industry is also recognised as being an essential element in the success of commercial law harmonisation in many other contexts (and conversely, absence of an effective industrial voice in the process can have a fatal effect on harmonisation efforts).[155] Cotterrell sets out that

> the opening of trade and commerce on an ever wider transnational basis, the development of international banking and financial systems, the world-wide control and exploitation of intellectual property, the development of the internet, and the control of transnational crime of many kinds. All of these projects are seen to require, for their efficient pursuit, significant harmonization of nation states, or the creation of new transnational regulatory regimes.[156]

A useful example here is the Cape Town Convention, and the protocol thereto on aircraft financing.[157] One of the core factors in the success of this Convention is often thought to be the role of industry, in particular the aviation industry, as a major driving force.[158] A strong level of harmonisation amongst elites who operate and maintain a particular regime may eradicate underlying cultural differences.[159] These elites need not be political elites; commercial harmonisation has been driven by self-interested commercial parties and organisations. Such commercial bodies have communality of purpose, and act in accordance with a broad body of rules and principles (whether formal or otherwise). Without getting into the debate about the presence or otherwise of a contemporary (or even historical) *lex mercatoria*, it is simply suggested that commercial actors can be discerned to be acting in sufficient concert as to constitute an international commercial culture (or at least, related cultures). In this sense, the elites have not so much eradicated underlying cultural differences as much as their cultural communality has become the dominant factor.[160] This can be seen in not just the Cape Town Conventions, but in other agreements, whether in the form of treaties such as the CISG, or in uniform or model guides such as UNCITRAL's UPCC, or the Model Guides on Secured Transactions. At the end of the scale classic soft law such as the ICC's UCP on documentary credit also demonstrates a strong cultural communality as between the financiers (who basically insist on the UCP) and the users of such action (who readily accept it in the event of a letter of credit transaction).

On the other hand, Smits has suggested that the success of private law harmonisation efforts is due partly to the communality in the globalised commercial world as to contracting law; this is demonstrated by contra-distinction with the status of property law harmonisation.[161] For Smits, 'The great difference between contract law and property law thus seems to be that the former is much more tied to a non-national

[155] For example, the lack of enthusiasm from commercial and consumer interests scuttled the proposed Common European Sales Law.

[156] Cotterrell, 'Seeking Similarity' (2002) 44, citing J Weiner, *Globalization and the Harmonization of Law* (London, Pinter, 1999).

[157] www.unidroit.org/instruments/security-interests/cape-town-convention. There is a valuable bibliography at www.unidroit.org/biblio-2001capetown.

[158] MJ Sundahl, 'The Cape Town Approach: A New Method of Making International Law' (2006) 44 *Columbia Journal of Transnational Law* 339, 349–54.

[159] Foster (n 139).

[160] cf Foster (n 139) 68–69.

[161] J Smits, 'On Successful Legal Transplants in a Future *Ius Commune Euorpaeum*' in Harding and Örücü (n 138) 137, 147.

environment than the latter one', though with the caveat that there may need to be division between different 'segments' of contract (say, between commercial and consumer contracts).[162] It should be noted that Smits was concerned with real property. However, we have seen above the effect of the differences over personal property rules, and as such we must recognise that element of truth implied by Smits' analysis: the contractual field provides great flexibility for parties to manipulate and control their relationships across a wide range, but property law(s) may militate against such a tendency due to a more static social position.[163]

We can therefore compare the possible trajectory of harmonisation for circular economy with that of two other harmonisation projects which are generally deemed successful: CISG, and the Cape Town Convention on Mobile Equipment. CISG involved a variety of jurisdictions with different social, economic, cultural and other differences. Compromises were necessary and the absence of property rules is one of the more obvious examples of the exclusionary effects of compromise. For circular economy that is not an insurmountable problem. As seen, the shift away from ownership to use will arguably come partially as a result of contracting licences as the primary method of disposition, with the exacerbating factor of recharacterising retention of title transactions as something other than sales, might combined have the effect of showing that circular economy will not be concerned with sales transactions as we commonly understand them. This could lead to two positions. First, the CISG will not be a suitable umbrella for such transactions, as they are both divorced from sale and likely to be too diverse for CISG to be an appropriate framework. Second, the potentially limited role for sales might actually mean that those transactions that actually are sales (and which may still be necessary in a circular economy) may be more appropriately dealt with under the pre-existing harmonisation scheme offered by CISG. Nevertheless, without progress on the status of property in the CISG this suggestion must be made with considerable caution.

For the Cape Town Convention the story is slightly different, and the end result quite different. The Cape Town Convention involved a variety of powerful industry interests, alongside a stellar academic background, and proceeded to produce a viable and elegant system involving an international register of transactions. Despite its success, its applicability as a harmonisation project to circular economy is severely limited. The Cape Town Convention involved a rather specific type of goods (aircraft),[164] whereas circular economies will involve vast ranges of goods, notwithstanding the necessary extension to the production and disposition sides (covering material inputs and waste products). Registration of interests is economically feasible in the context of mobile equipment as per Cape Town, but such an approach would be unfeasible for circular economy transactions. This is not to say though that no registration is possible. Aspects of the circular economy would no doubt be subject to registration, as is already the case with vast swathes of the economy. These registers will begin to converge as a result of technological development, rendering the process of registration and the storage and use costs of

[162] ibid 148.
[163] ibid 150–51.
[164] Other types of goods such as rail stock, were also covered, but it is the aircraft sector which was and remains the dominant power here.

the data more marginal as time progresses. A 'central' register for all circular economic transactions though is most unlikely. Furthermore, licences will not be cost-neutral; there will invariably be negotiations and modifications by both parties. The danger is that cost-inducing actions such as negotiating at the outset or bargaining for authorisation to modify, will be born by the unequal partner in the arrangement, suggesting a likely down-chain transfer of costs.

Comparing CISG and Cape Town reveals a conceptual issue that any harmonisation process will need to engage with. CISG concerned sales. Cape Town concerned secured transactions. At the heart of both concepts is the idea of property (even if CISG has taken an idiosyncratic approach to property), and in particular at a commercial level, it is about transfers of property interests for commercial gain. However, circular economy transactions will reflect a move from ownership to use, expressed in a move from proprietorian to personal control. This may create problems for the conceptual bases of CISG and Cape Town, with the development of new transactional forms that may merge or mutate previous forms. Thus a further note of caution must be noted. If there is to be harmonisation in order to achieve circular economic goals, it is essential to first ascertain the new sorts of transactional relationships that will arise (with attendant issues concerning the commercial/consumer relationship). As suggested, the focus will be on the contract aspect of such relationships rather than property. Thus the direction harmonisation would likely take, at least at the outset, is in harmonisation of contract control mechanisms. However, this claim must be caveated by the likely pre-emption of any directed harmonisation processes by means of profusion amongst circular economy participants of contract relationships that reflect the urge to have cross-jurisdictional control of goods in order to reflect the shift from ownership to use.

C. Is Something other than Harmonisation more Appropriate?

Hugh Collins has effectively critiqued the potential dangers of transnational private law, focusing on its dislocated nature separate from any underlying fixed social grounding.[165] Whilst private law, whether national or transnational, operates from a rather narrow starting point, certain types of transnational private law operate from even more narrow foundations. This can be compared with domestic private law regimes which take into account broader concepts of social justice (including, Collins argues with some success, principles of cosmopolitanism). Collins recognised that private law has to deal with some thick concepts of social ordering: 'the rules governing ownership of property, the protection of material and personal interests, and the system for governing transactions can be viewed [as] the cement that holds the different parts of society together'.[166] The effect of this is that transnational legal systems might be able to 'provide a scheme of justice that could be embedded in global or regional markets', and thus might be able to promise 'secure normative foundations for markets that are no longer

[165] H Collins, 'Cosmopolitanism and Transnational Private Law' (2012) 3 *European Review of Contract Law* 312.

[166] ibid 312.

effectively governed by a nation state',[167] but they fail to do so because they either suffer sectoral limitations (in the case of the *lex mercatoria* systems), or because they fail to respond in a sufficiently broad, encompassing and flexible way to encompass the social justice embedded within currently domestic private law regimes (this is the case of EU private law).[168]

Similar to Collins is Cotterrell's argument that even if we think of law as being a conglomeration of different cultures, meaning 'Different kinds or areas of law relate to different *types of community*', then there is a danger with overvaluing one particular community over another. He raises the issue of an '*instrumental* community as the kind of social relationships that are based on common or convergent purposes – especially, but not necessarily, economic purposes', and notes that while harmonisation efforts are often driven by perceptions of that community's status, 'if law serves it exclusively at the expense of protecting and promoting the well-being of other kinds of social bonds, other types of community, it fails to meet some important demands'.[169] Although such communities can be provided with highly tailored harmonisation efforts, they serve 'social groups (especially commercial enterprises, trade networks and economic interest groups) that mutate rapidly as national and international markets alter'.[170]

Circular economy may suffer similar difficulties. On one hand, there may be sectoral limitations if circular economic practice is unable to extend beyond sub-specific examples; it will need to be able to provide 'whole-regime' responses to issues concerning all types of private law concepts. Potentially more fatal to circular economic practice might be the difficulties arising from the almost paradigmatic shifts that will occur in terms of how transactions occur and what the effect of such transactions will be, in order to support long-term down-chain control, necessary for effective implementation of circular economic practices. This will probably lead to some form of political contestation, and this can be seen in the context of the EU-centric nature of some circular economic thought.[171]

We must be wary of the fact that:

> Legal cultures are thus overlapping and inter-related and may come together in unexpected ways. The method of law-making by Directive of the Commission of the European Union is closer to civil than it is to common law tradition, but much of the substance of such laws has to with common law influenced ideas of liberalism and the free market.[172]

Regardless of the complexities arising from Brexit, the point to be taken from Nelken's analysis is that normative and formative issues concerning law and society may combine in interesting ways. The circular economy necessarily raises such issues of combination, and thus engagement with the possible ways of encompassing circular economy

[167] ibid 324.
[168] ibid 324–25. cf Nelken (n 138) 31: 'Convergence can also be pursued as part of a deliberate political project such as harmonisation of law in the European Union. Because this is something in which comparative lawyers play an important part it has led to heated debate about whether harmonisation leads to the sacrifice of diversity and whether this is something to be resisted.'
[169] Cotterrell (n 153) 47.
[170] ibid
[171] Gregson et al (n 19) 225.
[172] Nelken (n 138) 29.

as cross-border society raises the need for a new form of governance that can respond to an era of technologically enforced hyper-globalisation and confusing and often reactionary behaviour by states and corporations.

Mere harmonisation or unification of doctrine will not suffice. The very act of harmonisation/unification has been subject to so much critique from a theoretical perspective, and can be demonstrated as giving rise to far too many problems at all stages (proposal, application, maintenance), that it arguably is not worth attempting in any situations more complex than those that focus on a very narrow sector operated by and for particular elite participants (such as that found with the Cape Town Convention). The circular economy necessarily encompasses too broad a range of stuff, and will involve multiple different participants causing a potentially complex debate over the content of any harmonising instrument.

Where there may be successful harmonisation (or harmonisation-like activity) may be at the very soft end of the spectrum. This is likely to occur in the context of enhanced attention being paid to the content and structure of contracts for the use of goods at different points along the circular economy. There are a number of benefits of such an approach, particularly for commercial organisations. First, the retreat to contract is a retreat to a point of accepted safety: party autonomy is such a strong principle within the intellectual framework of international commercial law (and, importantly, amongst international commercial *lawyers*) that challenges are usually unsuccessful. By going to contract, and claiming the principle of party autonomy, commercial entities will essentially have a rhetorical trump card which may have a blinding effect on practitioners, legislators, regulators and academics.[173] Second, the shift from ownership to use, within the ideology and foundational normative work on the circular economy, can be analogised with the recent developments in English law with regard to the effect of retention of title clauses. In such cases, there is no contract of sale. The proprietary element of the transaction is that which takes it out of the SGA framework, which in turn necessarily increases the importance of the contractual framework of the specific agreement(s). Moreover, the shift away from ownership, which is a shift away from sale, means that there is unlikely to be harmonisation with CISG in the context of a response to circular economy. Third, the move to contractual control will provide bargaining power to those with the strongest negotiating position; this is likely to be commercial organisations. This raises obviously tough questions in terms of the status of consumers in circular economies, but it would be wrong to ignore the point that commercial inequality can be just as great. Furthermore, the advantage of being an initiator in circular economic transactions is that one has the power to control later transactions. Since there will invariably be a number of down-chain transactions, notwithstanding any interactions with other circular economies (due to the complexity of modern globalised commercial practices), the reification of contractual control will provide those parties capable of negotiating and modify their contracts with especially valuable power. The benefits suggest that non-formal harmonisation, with contracts (and contracting practices) functioning as operative harmonising instruments in a soft law context, will be acceptable for certain commercial parties.

[173] This is certainly the consequence of reasoning such as in *R v M and others* [2017] UKSC 58 (n 121).

IV. Conclusion

Circular economic ideas are relatively novel; commercial practices instigating such ideas are even newer. Despite increasing attention being paid to the legal issues of circular economies, there remains much work to be done. Here it is been suggested that one of the core underlying shifts engendered by circular economy is a move away from 'ownership' to 'use' as governing practices for commercial engagement with goods. One of the results of this will be a reconceptualisation of the notion of sale: transaction chains will transmogrify into circles, with 'initiators' (rather than 'sellers') beginning the process and controlling the objects' journey around the circular economy and capturing and recalling back any waste products that do break out of the circle. This in turn presents a number of challenges for commercial law, in particular the purpose and nature of property and title ideas that have stood the test of time as central foundations of the English commercial law. Recent case law on retention of title clauses indicates a break between such clauses and the sales regime; such agreements can be considered *sui generis* providing the parties retaining title with a wider array of potential remedies against recalcitrant purchasers. The full implications of the *Bunkers* case are yet to be seen, but that case arguably enhances the role of the contract and the use of the goods, rather than the ownership and the property in/of the goods. By accepting that it is not a zero-sum game and that one can both retain title and not have a sales transaction, the door is open for licences to use goods to burst through. Initiators can retain title, which can then be used as an additional protection, whilst maintaining that the contract with the first acquirer is a non-sale contract. This would help to avoid some of the potential traps arising from the section 12 obligations. Furthermore, by taking advantage of the role licences could play, especially as they can control more sub-acquirers in more subtle and more complex ways, initiators can increase the chances of their control of far greater proportions of the circular transactions. Contracts with the power of property – contracts which extend their reach through multiple participants – will not only happen due to the nature of free market bargaining (within obvious limitations), but because of the necessity of accepting loss of control for participation (other than as an initiator) within a circular economy.

Law and circular economy are already in an unknowing, unwitting relationship. Regulatory frameworks exist, even if they are lacking in detail and substance. More importantly, commercial practices on circular economic lines are already evident and occurring; small suggestions as to potentially large fissures in the law have already been made. Most importantly, circular economic thought is attracting interest from various commercial and corporate lobby and interest groups. Drawing on the environmental benefits (however speculative) will no doubt help the commercial side gel with the NGO participants in this debate; it is certainly helping to attract governmental attention. It is therefore possible that law and circular economy will come together, but this will require us to rethink our understanding of the practices of commercial transactions.

9

Service Contracts and the CISG

PROF DR INGEBORG SCHWENZER, JULIAN RANETUNGE AND FERNANDO TAFUR

The story of the UN Convention on Contracts for the International Sale of Goods ('CISG' or 'the Convention') is one of worldwide success. It has been ratified by 85 states, potentially covering more than 80 per cent of world trade. Its profound effect on the law governing the international sale of goods is well documented. Despite its name, however, the CISG has the potential to be much more than just a sales convention. It can also govern the international supply of services. Indeed, according to Article 3(2) CISG, mixed contracts[1] are subject to the CISG if the preponderant part of the obligations of the party who furnishes the goods does not consist in the supply of labour or other services. In other words, the CISG already governs service obligations, albeit those contained within a contract characterised as one for the sale of goods.

Traditionally, when compared with goods, services were viewed by economists as non-storable, intangible and non-tradable.[2] Modern economic analysis takes a different view. Today, many economists point out that 'the boundaries between manufacturing goods and services are blurring', and regard the debate on the demarcation of services from goods as 'inconclusive'.[3] The ambiguity of the divide between goods and services becomes all the more pronounced when considered in light of major modern industries engaged in international trade – entertainment and mass media, telecommunications; computer, information and financial services – and of the increasing amalgamation of goods and services in 'smart' goods or the 'internet of things'. This recent scepticism towards maintaining a strict distinction between sales and services in the field of economics has corresponded with a prominent rise in the prevalence of service contracts in international trade.[4] The question now arises whether the distinction between sales and services can and should be maintained in law.

[1] Contracts containing both sale of goods and supply of services obligations.

[2] B Damien, 'Services, Trade in Services and Trade of Services Industries' (2014) 48 *Journal of World Trade* 31.

[3] ibid 33.

[4] 'The 2011 World Development Indicators show that the services sector accounted for almost 71% of global GDP in 2010 [...]. Moreover, trade in services is growing at a pace faster than trade in goods since the 1980s and in 2011, commercial services exports grew 11% to US$ 4.1 trillion' United Nations Conference on Trade and Development (UNCTAD), available at http://unctad.org/en/conferences/publicsymposium/2014/Pages/importance-of-services.aspx.

Thus far, there has been little discussion of this issue in the context of the CISG. Previous literature has focused either solely on arguments about the suitability of the CISG to govern service contracts[5] or on the process of amending the CISG to include provisions which explicitly govern service contracts.[6] This paper takes a different approach by considering the reasons why the CISG excludes service contracts from its scope, by undertaking comparative analysis of domestic legal systems in their attempt to grapple with the distinction between sales and services, and by providing an account of how the most contentious provisions of the CISG can be applied to service contracts.

Section I argues that the most plausible reason why the CISG excludes service contracts from its scope is because domestic jurisdictions do the same, but that there is no valid reason why domestic jurisdictions do so. In fact, domestic jurisdictions continue to struggle with differential treatment between sales and service transactions because they have failed to provide a clear and consistent basis upon which to distinguish the two and impose starkly different consequences of classifying contracts as sales or services (section II). Section III argues that there are good theoretical and practical reasons for applying the CISG to service contracts, in their guise both as pure service contracts and as mixed contracts which are predominantly for the supply of services. With reference to cases which apply – without difficulty – the CISG to service obligations, it argues that the CISG in its current form can govern service contracts by considering the most contentious provisions of the CISG in this context.

I. Why does the CISG Exclude Service Contracts from its Scope?

Looking back at the historical development of the CISG, as far back as Ernst Rabel's seminal 1936 work *Recht des Warenkaufs*, there is a noticeable absence of discussion on why the CISG – a convention to promote international trade[7] – should be confined to contracts for the sale of goods. It was only at the Vienna Conference in 1980 that the issue received (brief) mention for the first time. The Czechoslovakian representative on the First Committee opened discussions by proposing that the CISG should govern both sales and service contracts.[8] He saw 'no reason' why service contracts should be excluded from the scope of the Convention. Although the Committee rejected this proposal, its exact reasons for doing so are unclear. Those who rejected the proposal either did not provide reasons for their position or merely stated that it would be '[un]desirable'.[9]

[5] E Karner and H Koziol, *Zur Anwendbarkeit des UN-Kaufrechts bei Werk-und Dienstleistungen* (Vienna, Jan Sramek Verlag, 2015).

[6] L Tripodi, *Towards a New CISG* (Leiden, Brill Nijhoff, 2015).

[7] Preamble to the CISG, paras 2, 3.

[8] United Nations Conference on Contracts for the International Sale of Goods, Official Records (UN 1991) A/CONF.97/19, 241.

[9] ibid.

In many ways, the Czech proposal had no chance of gaining traction at the Vienna Conference. As Honnold reports, at the Conference,

> the time for review of the [Draft Convention of 1978] was limited. Thus proponents of amendments had a heavy burden: they needed to show not only that a change was needed but also that a proposed amendment was clearly drafted and would not lead to untoward consequences in relation to other provisions of the law.[10]

The proposal came too late: the delegates arrived in Vienna under the impression they were going to refine a draft convention on the international sale of goods, not one on the supply of services. More precisely, the proposal was 16 years too late. The 1964 Hague Conventions,[11] the predecessors of the CISG, contained similar (but not identical) provisions to Article 3(1) CISG. For example, Article 6 ULIS (concerning the supply of materials by the buyer) pursues the same purpose: to exclude from the convention's scope any contracts in which the parties' obligations were substantially anything other than the delivery of goods for a price.

This does not mean, however, that the historical development of the CISG does not leave behind clues about the reasons for the exclusion of service contracts. In 1969, UNCITRAL made a pivotal decision to abandon the promotion of the Hague Conventions just five years after their conclusion because of a failure to command widespread adoption among states. This failure 'stemmed from inadequate participation by representatives of different legal backgrounds in the preparation of the 1964 Conventions', which were seen as 'essentially the product of the legal scholarship of Western Europe'.[12] Thus, the decision to abandon the Hague Conventions was borne out of a desire to create a new instrument that would command acceptance across *all* states in order to enjoy universal adoption. But this desire for universal adoption came at a price. UNCITRAL had not only instructed the Working Group to produce legislation that would be acceptable 'by countries of different legal, social, and economic systems',[13] it had also insisted that decisions be made by consensus. An increase in diversity of opinion usually shrinks the areas upon which consensus can be reached. Thus, despite having nine years to draft the new convention, the 14 Member States of the Working Group had limited room for academic debate about the inclusion of service contracts within the scope of a convention on the sale of goods. They invariably avoided 'contestable terms that [were] inconsistent with domestic law and thus potentially objectionable to some participants'.[14]

These observations about the historical development of the CISG lend significant credence to Perales Viscasillas's suggestion that the CISG only excludes service contracts from its scope because Member States do the same: they exclude service

[10] J Honnold, *Uniform Law for International Sales under the 1980 United Nations Convention*, 3rd edn (The Hague, Kluwer Law International, 1999) 10.

[11] Uniform Law for the International Sale of Goods (ULIS) and Uniform Law on the Formation of Contracts for the International Sale of Goods (ULF).

[12] Honnold, *Uniform Law for International Sales* (1999) 8.

[13] ibid 8.

[14] C Gillette and S Walt, *The UN Convention on Contracts for the International Sale of Goods: Theory and Practice* (Cambridge, Cambridge University Press, 2016) 8.

contracts from the scope of their domestic laws on the sale of goods.[15] It is highly probable that the CISG's drafters, when faced with the particularly contentious issue over the scope of the Convention, chose to simply reflect domestic legal tradition. This solution avoided the need to confront yet another divisive issue that may have compromised the overriding desire for universal adoption. As such, in order to understand why the *CISG* differentiates between sales and service contracts, it is necessary to consider why *domestic jurisdictions* differentiate between sales and service contracts. Why do domestic systems organise their laws such that sales transactions are governed by largely coherent, sale-specific laws or codes, while service transactions are not so governed? The answer to this question could hold the key to understanding why the CISG excludes service contracts from its scope, and whether there is any good reason for doing so.

Unfortunately, domestic jurisdictions do not provide explicit reasons for differential treatment of sales and services either. Common sense suggests two possible reasons. Firstly, since trade in goods was much more commonplace in early civilisation than trade in services, perhaps laws governing sales were developed long before those governing services, and the two were never unified. Differential treatment is a result of historical accident. However, while it may be true that trade in goods was more prevalent in the past, it is not true to suggest that laws governing the supply of services are new. Roman law developed its own body of law governing the supply of services, and Roman legal scholars themselves were vexed by the question of where to draw the line between sales (*emptio venditio*) and services (*locatio conductio*).[16] It is not plausible to argue that this failure to treat services and sales laws alike is really a failure to address a historical quirk that has prevailed for nearly two millennia. It seems more likely that their separation is intentional.

Secondly, it could be argued that sales and services are treated differently in law because of the different standards of liability they entail. Sales transactions entail strict liability, derived from contract law. Service transactions entail negligent or fault-based liability, traditionally derived from tort or delict law. Tort and contract pursue different aims. While contract governs voluntary transfers and protects expectations created after an exchange of promises, tort governs involuntary transfers and protects the status quo against wrongful harm. Indeed, it was on this basis that Roman law divided duties into those in contract and those in delict.[17] Similarly, it could forcefully be argued that it is unfair to impose a 'duty of result' on a service provider, for example, a strict duty on a doctor to cure a patient. The problem with this reasoning is twofold. Firstly, unlike other relationships in which negligent liability arises, the supply of services does not arise in a tortious context. Even though liability in service transactions is frequently fault-based, every other characteristic of a service transaction is contractual: the parties negotiate, form a contract and seek to have their expectations upheld. And while it may be inappropriate to impose duties of result on certain types of

[15] CISG Advisory Council Opinion No 4, 'Contracts for the Sale of Goods to Be Manufactured or Produced and Mixed Contracts (Article 3 CISG)' (24 October 2004), available at www.cisgac.com/cisgac-opinion-no4.

[16] R Zimmerman, *The Law of Obligations* (Oxford, Oxford University Press, 1990) 234, 235.

[17] ibid 10, 11.

service provider (eg doctors), it may well be appropriate to impose such duties on other types of service provider (eg construction contractors). A similar distinction between two kinds of service transaction was recognised in Roman law: while contracts for work and services (*locatio conductio operis*) entailed strict duties of result, contracts of personal services (*locatio conductio operum*) entailed fault-based liability.[18] Secondly, this argument does not account for civil law systems, in which sales do not necessarily entail strict liability. One approach in civil law is to impose strict liability on the seller only for hidden defects; the buyer accepts liability for obvious defects. Another civil law approach only imposes strict liability if the seller has either specifically guaranteed the presence of certain features or the goods are so defective as to substantially diminish their intended use.[19] As such, the argument that differential treatment is justified because of different standard of liability is unconvincing. In sum, there does not appear to be any good reason why domestic jurisdictions organise their laws such that sales are treated differently from services.

II. Domestic Distinctions between Sales and Service Contracts

Thus far, it has been argued that there is no sound basis on which the CISG excludes service contracts from its scope. The Convention only excludes service contracts because domestic jurisdictions do the same, but the latter offer no sound basis on which service contracts are excluded from their sales laws. The following section explores this claim by considering: (a) the basis on which domestic jurisdictions distinguish between sales and services contracts; and (b) the consequences of classifying a contract as sales or services.

A. On what Basis do Domestic Jurisdictions Distinguish between Sales and Service Contracts?

The basic definition of a contract of sale is the reciprocal exchange of goods for a price.[20] While exact definitions vary from jurisdiction to jurisdiction – the common law, for instance, focuses on the notion of tangibility while civil law does not at the outset restrict the definition on this basis – the basic definition is the same across all jurisdictions and seems relatively clear. By contrast, the basic definition of a contract for the supply of services is far less precise. Most civil law systems are content to define a service contract as a 'contract for the supply of services' without further defining what

[18] ibid 32, 397.
[19] I Schwenzer, P Hachem and C Kee, *Global Sales and Contract Law* (Oxford, Oxford University Press 2012) para 31.26ff.
[20] ibid para 7.01.

a 'service' is.[21] The position in common law countries is more or less the same. Service contracts are defined widely as, for instance, 'contract[s] under which a person … agrees to carry out a service'.[22] These wide definitions are usually circumscribed by the removal of discrete kinds of services from the definition of a 'services' contract,[23] but this does little to clarify the definition.

Given the vague definition of a service contract, it is unsurprising that courts have struggled to distinguish between sales and service contracts when classifying mixed contracts. There appear to be two ways of conducting classification – two types of tests that are used. The first type classifies the whole contract according to its 'essence' or 'substance'. If 'work' is the essence of the contract, the entire contract is classified as a services contract; if the 'delivery of goods for a price' is the essence of the contract, the entire contract is one for the sale of goods. This test is followed by most common law jurisdictions and a few civil law jurisdictions such as Spain and France.[24] The second type of test, referred to as the 'gravamen of the action' test, involves splitting the contract into more than one part. The court then applies whichever law – sales law or services law – is relevant to the alleged problem. For example, in a contract for the removal of old cabinets and the supply and installation of new cabinets, the court would apply services law to defects in the removal and installation of the cabinets, and sales law to defects with the cabinets themselves.[25] This approach is followed by Germanic legal systems and some French and US courts.[26]

Both tests suffer from flaws. The 'substance' of the contract test is ineffective to deal with those contracts in which neither sales nor services dominates. In many ways, it does not make sense to assert that the 'substance' of, for example, a delivery and installation contract is the delivery (sales) or the installation (services); one is just as important as the other. Indeed, in common law jurisdictions, the case law shows that some common law judges have exploited the difficulties with this test to prioritise fair

[21] A Bénabent, *Droit des contrats spéciaux civils et commerciaux*, 11th edn (Paris, LGDJ, 2015) para 472 (France); P Malaurie, L Aynès and P Gautier, *Droit des contrats spéciaux*, 8th edn (Paris, LGDJ, 2016) para 72ff (France); see also Art 1165 Code Civil: '*contrats de prestation de services*' without any further definition (France); § 611 BGB (Germany).

[22] Australian Consumer Law, s 2(1)(a) (Competition and Consumer Act 2010, Sch 2) (Australia); Supply of Goods and Services Act 1982, s 12 (England); Consumer Protection Act 1986, s 2(o) (India).

[23] eg contracts of tenancy, the services rendered by an arbitrator, the services rendered by a director to a company: Australian Consumer Law, s 2(1)(b) (Australia); M Bridge, *The Sale of Goods*, 3rd edn (Oxford, Oxford University Press, 2014) paras 7.150, 7.151 (England).

[24] C Turner, *Australian Commercial Law* (Sydney, LBC Information Services, 1997) 263 (Australia); M Bridge (ed), *Benjamin's Sale of Goods*, 9th edn (London,Sweet & Maxwell, 2016) para 1-041 (England); Malaurie, Aynès and Gautier, *Droit des contrats spéciaux* (2016) paras 11–16 (France); N Bhadbhade, *Contract Law in India* (The Hague, Kluwer Law International, 2010) 264 (India); C Lasarte, *Contratos* (Madrid, Marcial Pons, 2008) 108 ('characteristic obligation') (Spain); L Lawrence, *Anderson on the Uniform Commercial Code*, 3rd edn (Toronto, Thomson Reuters 2016) § 2-105:88 ('predominant factor' test) (US).

[25] *JO Hooker & Sons Inc v Roberts Cabinet Co Inc* 683 So 2d 396 (Miss 1996).

[26] Malaurie, Aynès and Gautier (n 21) paras 12–21 (France); G Brudermüller, J Ellenberger, I Götz, C Grüneberg, S Herrler, H Sprau, K Thorn, W Weidenkaff, D Weidlich and H Wicke (eds), *Palandt – Bürgerliches Gesetzbuch*, 75th edn (München, CH Beck, 2016) Palandt/Grüneberg, Überbl v § 311, paras 242–26 (Germany); BGE 139 III 49, E 3.3 (Switzerland); H Honsell, N Vogt and W Wiegand (eds), *Basler Kommentar OR I*, 6th edn (Basel, Helbing Lichtenhahn, 2015) M Amstutz/A Morin, Einleitung vor Art 184 ff, para 23 (Switzerland); T Quinn, *Quinn's Uniform Commercial Code Commentary and Law Digest*, 2nd rev edn (Toronto, Thomson Reuters, 2016) vol 1 § 2-102[A][1][a] (US).

outcomes for claimants over consistent classification 'according to the book'. While there were no form requirements on service contracts, the English Statute of Frauds 1677 imposed form requirements on contracts of sale. This affected judicial approaches to classification. Courts did not want contract-breakers to avoid the consequences of breach by claiming that their contracts never existed for want of form. As such, courts would classify contracts involving the sale of goods as contracts for the supply of services so that the lack of conformity with form requirements did not invalidate the contract. Thus, courts classified contracts not on the basis of their content or terms but on the basis of reaching fair outcomes.[27] This purposive classification led to the development of artificial, often conflicting, case law on determining whether a contract was for sales or services. Unfortunately, courts continue to use this old case law as the starting point in deciding how a contract should be classified.[28] As such, in common law, the classification of contracts as sales or services 'often rather fluid'.[29] While England has abolished these form requirements, some common law jurisdictions maintain such requirements (most notably the UCC in the USA)[30] and so likely continue to espouse a fluid approach to contract classification. The shorter limitation period which in the US applies only to sales contracts may be a further factor affecting judicial approaches to classification.[31] Turning to the second test, the insurmountable difficulty with the gravamen of the action test is that parties will find it very difficult to plan for the legal effects of their transactions if more than one legal regime could operate to govern the transaction.[32]

In conclusion, neither civil nor common law has found a way to clearly and consistently distinguish between sales and services contracts. This suggests that there are more similarities than differences between the two, a view supported by the analogous application of sale of goods provisions to service contracts in the common law.[33] In practice, courts have relied on an assortment of factors to make a distinction, with little attempt to follow any particular rationale.[34]

Despite the absence of a clear distinguishing basis, it appears that a degree of consensus among legal systems is emerging about the kinds of contracts that should be considered 'services contracts'. Agency contracts,[35] and consultancy and professional

[27] S Whittaker, 'Contracts for Services in English Law and in the DCFR' in R Zimmermann (ed), *Service Contracts* (Tübingen, Mohr Siebeck, 2010) 120; Bridge, *Benjamin's Sale of Goods* (2016) para 1-041.

[28] See, eg, the conflicting cases of *Lee v Griffin* (1861) 30 LJ QB 252 and *Robinson v Graves* [1935] 1 KB 579.

[29] Whittaker, 'Contracts for Services' (2010) 121.

[30] §2-201 UCC; Sale of Goods Act 1896, s 9 (Tasmania, Australia); Sale of Goods Act 1895, s 4 (Western Australia, Australia).

[31] *Frommert v Bobson Const Co* 219 Mich App 735 (1996).

[32] W Hawkland, F Miller, L Rusch, C Bjerre, J Byrne, S Harris, W Henning, S Hughes, L Lawrence, R Nimmer and H Patchel (eds), *Hawkland's Uniform Commercial Code Series* (Toronto, Thomson Reuters, 2016) vol 1 § 2-102:2.

[33] *Clark v Macourt* [2013] HCA 56 (Australia); Bridge (n 24) paras 1-031, 1-041 (England).

[34] CISG AC Opinion No 4 (n 15) para 1.4.

[35] P Gillies, *Business Law*, 12th edn (New South Wales, The Federation Press, 2004) 470 (Australia); P Watts (ed), *Bowstead & Reynolds on Agency*, 20th edn (London, Sweet & Maxwell, 2016) para 6-012 (England); M Arzt, K Berger, H-J Bieber, M Henssler, W Krüger, J Harke, M Häublein, C Hergenröder, D Hesse, R Müller-Glöge, M Schmid, G Wagner and K Zehelein (eds), *Münchener Kommentar zum Bürgerlichen Gesetzbuch*, 6th edn (München, CH Beck, 2016) Band 4, MünchKoBGB/Müller-Glöge § 611

services contracts (rendered by eg auditors and accountants),[36] are considered by most legal systems to be service contracts. It is very likely that franchising,[37] licensing,[38] distribution and legal service contracts[39] are also so considered. Turnkey contracts,[40] construction contracts and contracts with architects, engineers and the like[41] are treated as service contracts by the common law, whereas civil law countries typically characterise such contracts as contracts for work and labour, for which there are special provisions in their respective civil codes.[42] Doctor–patient contracts are considered service contracts by the common law whereas the civil law position is unclear.[43]

paras 1–2 (Germany); Bhadbhade, *India* (2010) 264 (India); A Koller, 'Dienstleistungsverträge – Begriff, Arten, rechtliche Grundlagen' (2014) 12 *AJP/PJA* 1627, 1629 (Switzerland); Laurence, *Anderson* (2016) § 2-105:81 (US).

[36] *Astley v Austrust Ltd* (1999) 197 CLR 1, *Honeychurch Management Pty Ltd v Deloitte Touche Tohmatsu* [2005] TASSC 13, *Stone James & Co v Investment Holdings Ltd* [1987] WAR 363 (Australia); H Beale (ed), *Chitty on Contracts*, 32nd edn (London, Sweet & Maxwell, 2015) para 14-037 (England); Malaurie, Aynès and Gautier (n 21) 287 (France); *Corporate Counsel's Guide to Warranties* (2015) <Westlaw> accessed 1 December 2016 §1.14 (US).

[37] Under Swiss Law, franchising contracts are considered mixed contracts with inter alia components of labour, rent and mandate contracts (Honsell, N Vogt and W Wiegand, *Basler Kommentar* OR I, Amstutz/Morin (2015) Einl vor Art 184ff, para 133). In German law, while the nature of franchising contracts is disputed, they are considered by some as mixed contracts with components of lease, sale, rent and contracts for management of affairs (Palandt/Weidenkaff (n 26) Einf v § 581, para 22); Laurence (n 24) § 2-105:81 (US).

[38] Civil law countries tend to consider licence contracts as mixed contracts with components of sale, lease, rent and corporate law: H Bitain, *Droit des créations immatérielles* (Paris, Wolters Kluwer France, 2010) para 278ff (France); Palandt/Weidenkaff (n 26) Einf v § 581, para 7 (Germany); *Basler Kommentar* OR I, Amstutz/Morin (n 26) Einl vor Art 184ff, para (Switzerland). Common law: Laurence (n 24) § 2-105:81; H Hunter, *Modern Law of Contracts* (Toronto, Thomson Reuters, 2016) § 9:12 (US).

[39] Though some legal systems may specifically exclude some types of legal services from regulation by the general law on supply of services eg in England, the services of an advocate in court, and in carrying out preliminary work directly affecting the conduct of the hearing, are excluded from the supply of services regime (Supply of Services (Exclusion of Implied Terms) Order 1982 (SI 1982/1771) (England); *Giannarelli v Wraith* (1988) HCA 52 (Australia). Under Swiss law, legal service contracts are in principle governed by provisions on mandate contracts (*Basler Kommentar* OR I, Amstutz/Morin (n 26) Einl vor Art 184ff, para 272).

[40] *Chocolate Factory Apartments v Westpoint Finance* [2005] NSWSC 784 (Australia); J Huse, *Understanding and Negotiating Turnkey Contracts* (London, Sweet & Maxwell, 1997) para 2–4 (England); *Semler v Knowling* 325 NW 2d 395 (Iowa 1982); *Speight v Walters Dev Co Ltd* 744 NW 2d 108, 110 (Iowa 2008); *Guaranteed Const Co v Gold Bond Products* 153 Mich App 385, 395 (1986); *Reilly Const Co Inc v Bachelder Inc* 863 NW 2d 302 (Iowa App 2015) (US).

[41] Gillies, *Business Law* (2004) 404 (Australia); V Ramsay and S Furst (eds), *Keating on Construction Contracts*, 10th edn (London, Sweet & Maxwell, 2016) para 3-053; R Barrister and N Dennys (ed), *Hudson's Building and Engineering Contracts*, 13th edn (London, Sweet & Maxwell, 2015) para 2-011 (England); Bhadbhade (n 24) 266 (India); J White, R Summers and R Hillman (eds), *White & Summers' Uniform Commercial Code*, 6th edn (München, Thomson Reuters, 2010) 450; *Corporate Counsel's Guide to Warranties* (2015) §§11.2–4, 11.11 (US).

[42] Construction contracts: Arts 1787–1799(1) Civil Code (France); §§ 631–651 BGB (Germany); Arts 1544, 1586–1600 Civil Code (Spain); Arts 363–379 Code of Obligations (Switzerland). Turnkey contracts: Méga Code Civil, Art 1787, para 113 (Dalloz, 2012) (France); H Prütting, G Wege and G Weinreich (eds), *BGB Kommentar*, 11th edn (Tübingen, Luchterhand Verlag, 2015) § 631, para 19 (Germany); Lasarte, *Contratos* (2018) 283 (Spain); BGE 114 II 53; *Basler Kommentar* OR I, Zindel/Pulver (n 26) Art 353, para 13 (Switzerland).

[43] *Eyre v Measday* (1986) 1 All ER 488 (CA) (England); *State Of Punjab v Shiv Ram & Ors* [2005] INSC 447 (India); H Flechtner, 'Service Contracts in the United States (and from an Economic Perspective)' in R Zimmermann (ed), *Service Contracts* (Paris, Mohr Siebeck, 2010) 158, though some kinds of medical contracts found to be sales contracts: White, Summers and Hillman, *White & Summers* (2010) 448 (US).

It is disputed by common law countries whether contracts for the development of software are sales or service contracts.[44] In civil law countries, such contracts are in principle considered contracts for work and services.[45] While employment can be considered a service, most legal systems place employment contracts outside the scope of the 'services' regime because of the need for a more bespoke regime to protect employees.[46]

B. Consequences of Classification as Sales or Service Contracts

The difficulty courts have with discerning between sales and services contracts suggests that there are more similarities than differences between the two. Despite this similarity, the classification of contracts as sales or services has wide-ranging implications on parties' relationships. Four main consequences of classification are as follows.

Firstly, classification determines *how* the contract is regulated by the law: by, on the one hand, statute or code, and on the other, judicial discretion. Most common and civil law jurisdictions have extensive and well-settled codes on the sale of goods, such as the Sale of Goods Act in England, the UCC in the US, the French, Spanish and German Civil Codes and the Swiss Code of Obligations.[47] By contrast, the laws regulating the supply of services are far less organised or coherent. In common law, the rules governing the supply of services remain largely uncodified. Such rules are found almost exclusively in case law or in general contract law principles.[48] It is true that, in civil law jurisdictions, there is greater codification of rules governing services. Codes usually contain specific chapters governing a handful of particular types of service contract, such as mandate (agency) contracts.[49] However, there is no overarching, comprehensive and coherent set of rules that govern all types of service contracts.[50] This means that, when faced with an *uncodified* service contract, a civil law judge looks to other parts of the code to find provisions that are most suitable to apply to the services contract. The 'law' that is ultimately applied to the uncodified service contract is in fact a mishmash of provisions

[44] Turner, *Australian Commercial Law* (1997) 263 (Australia); *St Albans City and DC v International Computers Ltd* [1996] 4 All ER 481, 492–93, (heavily criticised) (England); White, Summers and Hillman (n 41) § 2.1, contrast with *Micro Data Base Systems Inc v Dharma Systems Inc* 148 F3d 649 (7th Cir 1998) (US).

[45] However, if mass-produced software is delivered with a lifetime licence, then they are classified as sales contracts: H Bitain, *Droit des contrats informatiques et pratique expertale* (Toronto, Wolters Kluwer France, 2007) para 124 (France); Palandt/Weidenkaff (n 26) § 433, para 9 (Germany); *Basler Kommentar* OR I, M Amstutz/A Morin (n 26) Einl vor Art 184 ff, para 267 (Switzerland).

[46] Australian Consumer Law, s 2(1) (Australia); Supply of Goods and Services Act 1982, s 12(2) (England); Code du Travail (France); §§ 611–630 BGB (Germany); Bhadbhade (n 24) 263 (India); Art 1 *Ley de Estatuto de Trabajadores* (Spain); Arts 319–362 OR (Switzerland).

[47] Goods Act 1958 (Victoria, Australia); Sale of Goods Act 1979 (England); Arts 1582–85 Code Civil (France); §§ 433–479 BGB (Germany); Sale of Goods Act 1930 (India); Arts 1445–537 Codigo Civil (Spain); Arts 184–236 OR (Switzerland); Art 2 Uniform Commercial Code (2002) (US).

[48] Whittaker (n 27) 116 (England); Bhadbhade (n 24) 263 (India); R Lord (ed), *Williston on Contracts*, 4th edn (München, Thomson Reuters, 2016) vol 20 § 26:20 (US).

[49] Arts 1984–2010 Code Civil (France); §§ 662–75b BGB (Germany); Arts 1709–39 Civil Code (Spain); Arts 394–406 OR (Switzerland).

[50] J Barendrecht, C Jansen and M Loos, *Principles of European Law on Service Contracts* (Paris, Sellier European Law Publishers, 2007) 135, 136.

drawn from whichever chapters of the code the judge deems most suitable to apply – an approach that generates uncertainty for parties about the content of the law that will be applied to their dispute. For example, while a Swiss court might apply provisions from rent, corporate and labour law chapters to govern franchise contracts,[51] a German court might apply provisions from rent, lease, sale and management of affairs chapters.[52] Overall, this absence of codified rules in both civil and common law means that the law governing the supply of services is difficult to ascertain, unclear and inconsistently applied. Its development is left almost entirely to judicial discretion. Secondly, classification may have consequences relating to procedural rules, such as those mentioned above regarding different form requirements and limitation periods.[53]

Thirdly, classification usually defines the obligations of the parties. If a contract is classified as a sales contract (and, in civil law jurisdictions, as a contract for work and labour), the seller owes an *obligation de résultat* (obligation of result); if a contract is classified as a service contract, the service provider generally owes an *obligation de moyens* (obligation of means). Under the former, there is a breach of contract if the result has not been achieved, regardless of whether reasonable skill and judgment is exercised (ie strict liability). Under an *obligation de moyens*, the contract is not breached as long as the obligor has used reasonable skill and judgment, in other words, was not at fault (ie negligence liability).[54] There are instances, however, where classification does not define the standard of liability; where, instead, service contracts attract *obligations de résultat*.[55] In common law jurisdictions, examples of the kinds of service contracts in which strict liability obligations have been implied include construction[56] and turnkey contracts[57] and contracts for the development of software.[58] Some civil law jurisdictions have also applied strict liability obligations to software contracts[59] and doctor–patient contracts.[60] Strict liability in these aforementioned types of service contracts is usually only implied if it is found that the service-recipient reasonably relied on the service provider's expertise.[61]

The fourth main consequence of classification relates to the availability of certain remedies. For instance, in most civil law jurisdictions, the remedy of price reduction in cases of non-conformity is only available with sales contracts.[62] The French Civil

[51] *Basler Kommentar* OR I, Amstutz/Morin (n 26) Einl vor Art 184 ff, para 133.

[52] Palandt/Weidenkaff (n 26) Einf v § 581, para 22.

[53] See section II A above from the text associated with nn 30–32.

[54] P Malaurie, L Aynès and P Stoffel Munck, *Droit des obligations*, 8th edn (Paris, LGDJ, 2016) para 942 (France): the obligor owes 'une diligence suffisante'.

[55] Beale, *Chitty on Contracts* (2015) para 14-037.

[56] *Greaves & Co (Contractors) Ltd v Baynham Meikle & Partners* [1975] 1 WLR 1095 (CA) (England); Bhadbhade (n 24) 266 (India).

[57] Huse, *Turnkey Contracts* (1997 para 2–4; *Basildon DC v JE Lesser (Properties) Ltd* [1985] QB 839; see also *Vancouver Water District v North American Pipe & Steel Ltd and Moody International Ltd* [2012] BCCA 337; *MT Hojgaard A/S v E.ON Climate and Renewables UK Robin Rigg East Ltd* [2015] EWCA Civ 407 (England); *Semler v Knowling*, 325 NW 2d 395 (Iowa 1982).

[58] *St Albans v IDC* (n 44) (England).

[59] eg in France: Cour de cassation, Chambre Commercial, 25 Novembre 1997; Cour d'appel de Bastia, 19 November 2002, 2002/00772; Cour de cassation, Chambre Commercial, 1 Mars 2005, 01-15.007.

[60] D Mainguy, *Contrats spéciaux*, 10th edn (Paris, Dalloz, 2016) para 576.

[61] *Corporate Counsel's Guide to Warranties* (n 36) § 11.16 (US).

[62] § 441 BGB (Germany); Art 1486 Codigo Civil (Spain); Art 205 OR (Switzerland).

Code is the exception: the recent amendments which came into force on 1 October 2016 extend the availability of this remedy to all contracts.[63] In common law, the defence of contributory negligence is only available in service contracts.[64] This defence reduces the liability of the breaching party to take account of the aggrieved party's contribution to the breach. For example, the liability of an architect who had negligently designed a fire suppression system was reduced by two-thirds because the claimants had provided inaccurate information to the architect about the appropriate type of fire-suppressing material that should have been used.[65]

In sum, despite the many factual similarities between sales and service transactions, the outcome of the classification exercise undertaken by domestic courts has wide-ranging legal consequences on the relationship between the parties. Parties to mixed contracts may face uncertainty about the extent of judicial discretion in the determination of their dispute, the validity of their contract in light of form requirements, applicable limitation periods, the standard of liability (*résultat* or *moyen*) and the availability of certain remedies or defences. This differential treatment runs contrary to the legal axiom that like cases should be treated alike unless there is a valid reason to treat them differently. It impugns the internal consistency of the law, undermines parties' legitimate expectations, and increases the costs of resolving disputes.

III. Is the CISG Suitable to Govern Service Contracts?

Thus far, it has been shown that there is no sound basis on which the CISG excludes service contracts from its scope or, indeed, on which domestic jurisdictions exclude service contracts from the scope of their sales laws. Despite the wide-ranging consequences attached to the classification of mixed contracts, there are many similarities between sales and service transactions and it is often difficult to discern between the two. In light of this, it is doubtful that sales and service contracts merit differential treatment to the extent that they currently do in domestic legal systems.

A. Should the CISG Govern Service Contracts?

There are convincing reasons why the CISG should govern service contracts. Firstly, there are good doctrinal reasons. Not only would it align the CISG with modern economic thought,[66] it would also fulfil the wider purpose of the CISG to 'promote development of international trade' and 'contribute to the removal of legal barriers

[63] Art 1223 Code Civil (France).

[64] N Seddon, R Bigwood and M Ellinghaus, *Cheshire and Fifoot: Law of Contract*, 10th Australian edn (Chatswood, NSW, LexisNexis Australia, 2012) 1108 (Australia); *Forsikringsaktieselskapet Vesta v Butcher* [1989] AC 852 (CA) (England); A Singh, *Law of Contract and Specific Relief*, 9th edn (Lucknow, Eastern Book Co, 2005) 451 (India); Laurence (n 24) § 2-314:560 (US). This defence is not available where the supplier's obligation is one of strict liability.

[65] *Sahib Foods Ltd (In Liquidation) v Paskin Kyriakides Sands (A Firm)* [2003] EWCA Civ 1832 (England).

[66] See Introduction.

in international trade'.[67] Secondly, there are compelling practical and commercial reasons why the CISG should govern service contracts. Parties engaged in international commerce usually want the whole of their relationship to be governed by the same system of law.[68] However, a prevalent legal problem faced by such parties is the application by the court of multiple laws to the same transaction, against the parties' wishes and against commercial sense. Parties to contracts governed by the CISG are not immune from these problems. For example, in a contract for the delivery, installation and initial maintenance of a factory, arbitral tribunals have been known to apply the CISG to the sales part of the contract (delivery) but apply domestic law to the services part (installation and maintenance).[69] Alternatively, the tribunal might find that the value of installation and maintenance exceeds – even by a fractional amount – the value of delivery, and consequently decline to apply the CISG altogether. This creates numerous problems for the parties: greater difficulty in pricing risk into contracts and greater uncertainty of outcome in the event of a dispute. In addition, the benefits that parties enjoy from the application of the CISG to their disputes – its international character, balance between different legal cultures and neutrality between the domestic laws of each party – are lost. The application of the CISG to service contracts would solve these problems. It would mean that a single set of rules would apply to a transaction in which goods and services are closely related.

This paper, however, goes further than calling for the application of the CISG to mixed contracts. It also argues that the CISG should govern 'pure' service contracts – contracts for the supply of services which do not contain any sale of goods obligations. The primary argument in favour of this position is based on taking existing provisions in the CISG to their logical conclusion. If, as is widely acknowledged,[70] the CISG already applies to supply of service obligations (albeit those found within contracts classified as sales contracts) there is no reason why the CISG should not also govern pure service contracts. Similar problems call for similar solutions.[71] Exactly *how* the CISG would govern pure service contracts will be illustrated later in this part with reference to cases already decided under the CISG which apply the CISG to service obligations. The question then arises: to what kind of pure service contracts is the CISG most apt to govern? The answer to this question, this paper suggests, should draw inspiration from those kinds of service contracts which domestic legal systems, by consensus, deem as service contracts. These are listed above in the final paragraph of section II A. This would mean that, for instance, cases such as *RT v WT*[72] (regarding a turnkey contract) and the *Market Study* case[73] would be decided differently and brought within the scope of the CISG.

[67] CISG, preamble para 3; Official Records of Vienna Conference (n 8) 195, para 2.

[68] An assumption made by many legal systems (failing indication to the contrary). See, eg, Giuliano-Lagarde Report on the Rome Convention [1980] OJ C282/1, 17 para 4; *Sulamérica Cia Nacional de Seguros SA and others v Enesa Engenharia SA and others* [2012] EWCA Civ 638 (CA) [11] (England).

[69] A problem anticipated three decades ago by Schlechtriem: P Schlechtriem, *Uniform Sales Law – The UN Convention on Contracts for the International Sale of Goods* (Vienna, Manz Vienna, 1986) 31.

[70] See, eg, Honnold (n 10) 58.

[71] ibid 60.

[72] HG Zürich, 9 July 2002, CISG-online 726 (contract to plan, deliver, assemble, and initially operate a plant for the breaking down and separation of cardboard packaging).

[73] OLG Köln, 26 August 1994, CISG-online 132 (contract to conduct scientific study of specific segment of German express-services market).

For the avoidance of doubt, parties may wish to specify in their pure service contracts that the CISG does indeed apply.[74]

B. Can the CISG Govern Service Contracts?

Previous literature has given no more than cursory consideration to the issue of how the CISG's provisions might apply to non-sales contracts.[75] What follows is a more extensive consideration of this issue, together with examples of case law which applies the CISG to service obligations.

i. Requirements to Establish Liability

The following issues surrounding liability for breach of a services contract will be considered: determining conformity (Article 35 CISG), third-party rights or claims to the services rendered (Articles 41 and 42 CISG), obligations to examine the service and give notice of defects (Articles 38, 39 and 43 CISG) and causation by the aggrieved party (Article 80 CISG).

Article 35(1)–(2) CISG sets out the two ways in which conformity of goods can be established. According to Article 35(1) CISG, goods must comply with the contractually stipulated quantity, quality, description and packaging. In the absence of contractual stipulation, Article 35(2) contains fallback provisions designed to objectively establish whether performance is in conformity with the contract. It asks what rights and duties reasonable persons in the shoes of the parties would have agreed to if they had put their minds to such a question. Goods must be fit for their ordinary or particular purpose, conform to any sample and be adequately packaged.

The primary objection to including pure service contracts within the ambit of the CISG is that the provisions of the CISG are not suitable for service contracts. In particular, Karner and Koziol argue that the CISG is not suitable to govern conformity in service contracts because of the absence of provisions on reasonable care and skill. The first point to note about these arguments is that they only concern one kind of breach of contract – non-conformity – and do not concern other types of breach, such as delayed performance and complete non-performance.[76] This is because the specific provisions with which Karner and Koziol take issue – Articles 35, 46(3) and 50 CISG – are only applicable if the goods do not conform to the contract. The significance of this is that their objections do not hold currency in cases of non-performance and delayed performance. It cannot be argued that non-performance and delayed performance

[74] A course of action endorsed by many authorities such as Schlechtriem, *Uniform Sales Law* (1986) 30 and the 'UNCITRAL Legal Guide on Drawing Up International Contracts for the Construction of Industrial Works' (UNCITRAL, 1988) 304.

[75] See, eg, F Enderlein and D Maskow, *International Sales Law* (New York, Oceana, 1992) 37. For slightly more detailed consideration: P Schlechtriem, 'Interpretation, gap-filling and further development of the UN Sales Convention' (tr M Koehler, 2004), available at http://cisgw3.law.pace.edu/cisg/biblio/schlechtriem6.html#*.

[76] Karner and Koziol, *Zur Anwendbarkeit des UN-Kaufrechts bei Werk-und Dienstleistungen* (2015) para 79.

merit different treatment as between sales and service contracts.[77] This is evidenced by civil law codes which apply rules on non-performance and delayed performance to all kinds of contracts, sales and services alike.[78]

It is still, of course, important to address Karner and Koziol's arguments as made in the context of non-conformity. It is submitted that the definition of liability in Article 35(1) CISG is appropriate for any kind of contract, including services contracts, because it is primarily the stipulations of the parties which determine their obligations. Conformity with stipulated quality will be the main issue in service contracts, but an issue with conforming quantity may also arise, for instance, if a service is contracted to be rendered twice a week but is instead rendered once a week. In rare cases packaging may also play a role in service contracts.[79] As the criterion of description was specifically included to address problems arising in the sales laws of civil jurisdictions,[80] it is unlikely to apply to service contracts.

The provisions in Article 35(2) CISG can also be applied to service contracts. It was noted above that service contracts can attract two kinds of implied terms: those of *résultat* and those of *moyens*. Firstly, in contracts in which it is reasonable to expect a service to produce a result, the Article 35(2) CISG provision on fitness for purpose can be used as a benchmark to determine conformity in the same way it is used in sale of goods cases. This raises the question: in what kinds of contracts would it be reasonable to expect a service to produce a result? Guidance can be found both in existing laws[81] and in harmonisation projects. The Principles of European Law on Service Contracts extend *obligations de résultat* to construction, processing, storage and design contracts on the basis that, in these contexts, a reasonable service-recipient in the same circumstances as the service-recipient concerned would have no reason to believe there was a substantial risk that the result envisaged would not be achieved by the service.[82] This is useful guidance for a court which finds itself considering the kinds of service contracts which might attract strict liability standards found in Article 35(2) CISG. Article 35(2) CISG has already been applied to determine the conformity of service obligations where strict liability was imposed, for example, on obligations to develop software[83] or to dismantle a factory.[84]

Secondly, Article 35(2) CISG can also be used to determine conformity where the service provider owes an *obligation du moyen* or duty of reasonable care and skill. As mentioned above, Article 35(2) CISG provides an objective standard to evaluate conformity. In cases of *obligations de moyens*, one would simply ask: 'what degree of

[77] Karner & Koziol (n 5), paras 73, 78 (referring to employment contracts).

[78] See in the respective civil codes the general provisions for contracts. Arts 1–142 OR (Switzerland); §§241-347 BGB (Germany); Arts 1101–369-11 Civil Code (France); Arts 1088–213 Civil Code (Spain).

[79] For example, a service contract to repair a machine might require proper packaging before the machine's return.

[80] Schwenzer, Hachem and Kee, *Global Sales* (2012) para 31.15ff (the distinction between *aliud* and *peius*).

[81] Some types of service contracts attract implied terms of strict liability in common law – see section 2 B above from the text associated with nn 56–58.

[82] Barendrecht, Jansen and Loos, *Principles of European Law* (2007) 134.

[83] Cour d'appel de Lyon, 18 December 2003, CISG-online 871.

[84] Cour d'appel de Grenoble, 26 April 1995, CISG-online 154 (English translation available at http://cisgw3.law.pace.edu/cases/950426f2.html).

reasonable care and skill would be expected in these circumstances from an objectively reasonable perspective?'. In each circumstance, this could encompass any particular purpose, sample or packaging. As such, courts applying Article 35(2) CISG to service contracts would essentially be replacing the word 'goods' in the Article with the word 'services'. This exercise of reading words into the CISG can be justified through one of two routes within the CISG. Firstly, according to Article 6 CISG, parties may vary the effect of any of the Convention's provisions. As such, parties could agree to vary Article 35(2) CISG to replace the word 'goods' with 'services'.[85] Secondly, the tribunal could undertake common-sense gap-filling to arrive at such a reading of Article 35(2) CISG.[86] The argument for such an interpretation of Article 35(2) CISG would apply a fortiori if parties to service contracts expressly opt into the CISG.

Articles 41 and 42 CISG require the seller to deliver goods which are free from, firstly, *general* third-party property rights or claims and, secondly, third-party *intellectual property* rights or claims. In the services context, while issues of general third-party rights will not usually pose a problem, third-party intellectual property rights or claims are an especially important issue, one which the CISG is more adept than domestic systems at resolving. Take, for example, a scenario where a third-party developer has an intellectual property right to software that was developed in India and used in Germany. Domestic systems require the seller to guarantee that the goods are free from third-party intellectual property rights worldwide.[87] This would impose on the Indian developer the onerous task of investigating all potentially conflicting intellectual property rights worldwide. By contrast, Article 42 CISG requires the seller to guarantee only that the goods are free from third-party intellectual property rights *under the laws of narrow categories of countries*: the place where the goods would be resold or the place of the buyer's business. This resolves the issue faced by service providers who would otherwise be expected to have knowledge of all potentially conflicting rights worldwide. Thus, Articles 41 and 42 CISG are not only equally applicable to service contracts, they are also more suitable than domestic provisions which would otherwise govern this aspect of the contract.

The CISG obliges the buyer to examine the goods (Article 38 CISG) and give notice to the seller of any non-conformity (Article 39 CISG) or third-party rights or claims (Article 43 CISG). If the buyer fails to do so, it loses the right to rely on potential non-conformity of the goods or on Articles 41 and 42 CISG. Because of the absence of comprehensive, codified rules on service contracts in domestic jurisdictions, it might, at first glance, have seemed unlikely that legal systems would have considered the issue of notice requirements in service contracts. However, it appears that notice requirements do apply to service contracts in some contexts. For instance, under the Directive on Package Holidays,[88] the consumer must communicate any failure in the performance of a contract to the supplier of the service. If such a duty is appropriate to impose on consumers, it is a fortiori appropriate to impose on commercial service users. This is

[85] Schlechtriem, *Uniform Sales Law* (1986) 30.

[86] Schlechtriem, 'Gap-filling' (2004) part II, 4.

[87] Official Records of Vienna Conference (n 8) 37, Art 40, paras 3–5.

[88] Council Directive (EEC) 90/314 on package travel, package holidays and package tours (EC Package Holidays Directive) [1990] OJ L158, Art 5(4).

nothing more than an expression of the principle of good faith and fair dealing in international commerce. Thus it does not come as a surprise that the Principles of European Law on Service Contracts oblige the service-recipient to notify the service provider if it discovers that the service will fail or has failed to achieve the result it envisaged,[89] and that the consequences of the service-recipient's failure to notify range from losing the right to rely on non-conformity to compensating the service provider.[90] It is also unsurprising that courts have already applied the rights and duties under Article 39 CISG to service obligations, notably in a contract for the development of software[91] and in a contract for design, installation and waste management.[92]

According to Article 80 CISG, a party may not rely on a failure of the other party to perform to the extent that such failure was caused by the first party's act or omission. Underlying Article 80 is the general principle that each party must account for its own sphere of risk.[93] This principle is not restricted to sales contracts; it is generally applicable to any kind of contract,[94] including service contracts.

In conclusion, the CISG's provisions on conformity, third-party rights and claims, examination and notice of defects and causation are equally suitable to establish whether contracts for the supply of services have been breached.

ii. Remedies

The remedies provisions of the CISG are also suitable to govern service contracts. Both sale of goods and supply of service provisions are specialised rules of general contract law, and so it follows that the rules governing breach of a services contract are virtually the same as those governing breach of a sales contract.[95] There is no question that the seller's remedies against the buyer (set out in Article 61 CISG) are very well suited for the service provider too. Thus, the service provider may claim for the price (Article 62 CISG), fix additional time for the service-recipient's performance (Article 63 CISG), declare the contract avoided upon fundamental breach (Article 64 CISG) and specify certain features of the service itself in default of the service-recipient doing so as required under the contract (Article 65 CISG). It is suitability of the buyer's remedies against the seller for the service-recipient that is more controversial. Thus, the following remedies will be considered in the context of service contracts: specific performance (Articles 28, 46(2) and 46(3) CISG), avoidance (Articles 49(1)(a), 51 and 25 CISG), damages (Article 74 CISG), exemption (Article 79 CISG) and price reduction (Article 50 CISG).

[89] Art 1.113 Principles of European Law on Service Contracts.

[90] Barendrecht, Jansen and Loos (n 50) 283–85.

[91] Cour d'appel de Lyon, 18 December 2000, CISG-online 871.

[92] LG Mainz, 26 November 1998, CISG-online 563. See also CISG Advisory Council Opinion No 4 (n 15) n 31 referring to a Belgian decision (Rechtbank van Koophandel Hasselt, 4 February 2004, CISG-online 863) which stated that the rules on notice in the CISG applied to the services part of the relevant contract.

[93] I Schwenzer (ed), *Schlechtriem & Schwenzer: Commentary on the UN Convention on the International Sale of Goods*, 4th edn (Oxford, Oxford University Press, 2016) Art 80, para 1. See also Art 42(2)(b) CISG.

[94] UNIDROIT Principles, Art 7.1.2.

[95] Law Commission of England & Wales, Law Com No 156, 'Law of Contract: Implied Terms in Contracts for the Supply of Services' (1986) Cmnd 9773.

Under the CISG, while specific performance is generally available, a court is not bound to enter a judgment for specific performance unless it would do so under its own law in respect of similar contracts (Article 28 CISG). The lack of case law on Article 28 CISG suggests that, in practice, commercial parties do not rely on this expansive remedy.[96] In cases of non-conformity, specific performance assumes the guise of replacement and repair, addressed in Articles 46(2) and 46(3) CISG. It has been argued that specific performance cannot be available in service contracts because defective performance cannot be cured without contemporaneous cooperation from the aggrieved party.[97] This objection is misplaced. It is in the very nature of an order for specific performance, in a sales context or any other, that the aggrieved party's cooperation will be required, not least in its patience while the defective performance is cured. There does not appear to be any good reason why the CISG's remedy of specific performance cannot also be suitably applied to service contracts.[98] Indeed, Article 46(3) CISG has already been used to determine whether a seller had cured its defective dismantling of a factory by replacing the parts which were damaged during the dismantling.[99]

Avoidance is the most onerous remedy for breach of contract. Thus, in line with the common law approach, both the CISG and the UNIDROIT principles grant avoidance only in cases of fundamental breach.[100] That many domestic legal systems follow this approach, applying it to all kinds of contracts including service contracts,[101] suggests it is equally appropriate for the CISG to approach the avoidance of service contracts on the same basis. Indeed, Articles 25 and 49 CISG have already been used to determine whether breach of an obligation to dismantle a factory can amount to fundamental breach and thereby justify avoidance.[102] As Schlechtriem rightly explains, if the non-performance itself constitutes fundamental breach, such as when installation is not completed by a stipulated date, the services portion of the contract can be avoided, enabling the buyer to purchase services elsewhere and claim the additional expenses as damages under Article 75 CISG.[103] Likewise the so-called *Nachfrist* principle,[104] according to which an original non-fundamental breach arising from non-performance may constitute a fundamental breach if the party does not adhere to the additional period fixed for performance, is suitable to apply to service contracts.[105]

[96] Schwenzer, *Schlechtriem & Schwenzer* (2016) Art 28, para 4 (Müller-Chen).

[97] Karner and Koziol (n 5) fn 138 for references.

[98] Karner and Koziol reach the same conclusion (n 5) para 75.

[99] Cour d'appel de Grenoble, 26 April 1995, CISG-online 154.

[100] Arts 49(1)(a), 51, 25 CISG; UNIDROIT Principles Arts 7.3.1(1), (2).

[101] Civil law countries contain this remedy within the general part of their codes of obligations, thus it is applicable to all contracts: Arts 1224–30 Civil Code (France); § 323 BGB (Germany); Art 1124 Codigo Civil (Spain); Arts 97, 107–09 OR (Switzerland). Common law countries do not appear to differentiate between the operation of this remedy in the sales and services context, as seen in leading case law such as *Hong Kong Fir*, which concerned an owner's (services) obligation to maintain the ship in 'seaworthy' condition – *Hong Kong Fir Shipping Co Ltd v Kawasaki Kisen Kaisa Ltd* [1962] 2 QB 26 (England); *Koompahtoo Local Aboriginal Land Council v Sanpine Pty Ltd* [2007] HCA 61 (Australia); R Padia (ed), *Mulla Indian Contract and Specific Relief Acts*, 13th edn (India, Lexis Nexis, 2006) 1488 (India); *Printing Center of Texas, Inc v Supermind Pub Co Inc*, 669 SW 2d 779 (Tex 1984) (USA).

[102] Cour d'Appel de Grenoble, 26 April 1995, CISG-online 154.

[103] Schlechtriem (n 75) part II, 4(a)(cc).

[104] Article 49(1)(b) CISG; UNIDROIT Principles Arts 7.3.1(3), 7.1.5.

[105] Schlechtriem (n 75) part II, 4(a)(cc).

Modern provisions on damages, such as those in Article 74 CISG or Articles 7.4.2 and 7.4.4 UNIDROIT Principles, provide for full compensation of reasonably foreseeable losses flowing from the breach. This rule can be traced to the seminal common law case *Hadley v Baxendale* which, incidentally, concerned the breach of a service obligation in a contract for the transport of a crankshaft.[106] Courts have not in the past had problems applying Article 74 CISG to service obligations in mixed contracts, for instance, in a contract for construction, transport, assembly and initial operation of a processing centre.[107] There should be little dispute that the CISG damages provisions can be applied to service contracts.[108]

Article 79 CISG exempts a party from liability in damages if breach is due to an unforeseeable impediment beyond its control.[109] It represents a middle ground between the narrow common law doctrine of frustration and the wider fault principle found in most civil law jurisdictions. In most cases, the decisive element is whether the impediment was 'beyond [the party's] control'. As with its application in sale of goods cases, Article 79 CISG is equally capable of exempting a party to a services contract that is under an *obligation de résultat*. The question remains how Article 79 CISG would regulate an alleged breach of *obligations de moyens*. If a party complies with its duty to take reasonable care and skill, there is no breach under Article 35 CISG and so exemption under Article 79 CISG would not be in issue. If, however, a party does not comply with its *obligation de moyens* and so is in breach under Article 35 CISG, Article 79 CISG might be pleaded as a way of exempting the promisor from paying damages. This could happen in a situation where it is not only the service provider that is responsible for the breach. For instance, in a contract for the delivery, erection and installation of wall partitions, the court applied Article 79 CISG to exempt the supplier from liability for the defective installation (unintended gaps between the top of the partitions and the ceiling) because the defective installation was carried out by a third party.[110] Thus, the service provider is exempted because the failure to perform is due to an impediment beyond its control. One of the deciding factors should, as with sale of goods cases, be the sphere of risk service provider. Only external objective circumstances outside of the sphere of risk of the service provider should be taken into account. When defining the sphere of risk, the court should consider the contractual allocation of risk (alternatively, practices and usages of the parties), the reasonableness of the service provider's failure to take the impediment into account at the time of contract formation, and the difficulty for the service provider to overcome the impediment or its consequences.[111] Increased costs of performing the service should not suffice for exemption. As such, Article 79 CISG may govern service contracts.

In cases of non-conformity, the CISG gives the buyer a right to reduce the purchase price.[112] While this remedy is indispensable in civil law because of the exceptional

[106] [1854] EWHC J70 (England).

[107] Tribunal de commerce de Namur, 15 January 2002, CISG-online 759; see also OGer Aargau, 3 March 2009, CISG-online 2013; OGer Zug, 19 December 2006, CISG-online 1427 (also cited as CISG-online 1565).

[108] Schlechtriem (n 75) part II, 4(a)(bb).

[109] See also UNIDROIT Principles Art 7.1.7; Art 1218 Civil Code (France) now follows this approach.

[110] Tribunale d'appello Ticino, 29 October 2003, CISG-online 912.

[111] Schwenzer (n 93) Art 79 paras 12–15 (Schwenzer).

[112] Art 50 CISG.

nature of a damages award, it is not known to the common law. For this reason, it is disputed whether the price reduction remedy can be applied to service contracts. Some authors opine that price reduction is not suitable in a services context because there is no market price for services.[113] This argument is not convincing. Price reduction is nothing more than a partial avoidance of the contract. The French Civil Code now provides for price reduction in its general part of obligations thus applying it to all kinds of contracts, including service contracts.[114] Following this reasoning, the CISG price reduction remedy should also be applied to service contracts.[115]

A further argument made against the inclusion of services in the ambit of the CISG is that services are typically rendered under long-term contracts.[116] In these contexts, an important issue is the effect on long-term obligations of a short-term breach of contract – an issue, it is argued, the CISG is not suitable to govern. However, the CISG itself contains a provision dealing with instalment contracts that is suitable for any long-term contract. According to Article 73(1) CISG, in a case of fundamental breach of contract, a partial non-conformity primarily allows the obligee to avoid the contract with respect to the part concerned. If there are good grounds to conclude that a fundamental breach will occur with respect to future performances, the promisee may avoid the contract for the future (Article 73(2) CISG). In addition, a buyer who declares the contract avoided in respect of any single performance may at the same time declare the contract void in respect of past or future performances of the same obligation if the respective obligations are interdependent (Article 73(3) CISG). Evidently, these provisions are capable of governing services rendered under long-term contracts.

Finally, it is further argued that service contracts typically require both parties to work closely together, and that the sales provisions of the CISG are incapable of dealing with this kind of relationship.[117] However, practice shows that such close cooperation is also a common feature of complex sales contracts. Any questions of apportioning liability between the parties can be addressed using Article 80 CISG, which allows for an attribution of liability to the extent that the failure has been caused by the respective party.[118]

In sum, both the liabilities and remedies provisions of the CISG are suitable to govern service contracts. To overcome the obstacles posed by Article 3(2) CISG and for the avoidance of doubt, parties to contracts containing service obligations may wish to 'opt in' to the application of the CISG to their contracts.[119]

IV. Conclusion

Both the CISG and its earlier iterations envisaged a convention that would govern the international sale of goods. Despite allowing the Convention to govern service

[113] K Tillmanns, *Strukturfragen des Dienstvertrages: Leistungsstörungen im freien Dienstvertrag und im Arbeitsvertrag* (Tübingen, Mohr Siebeck, 2007) 402ff; cf Karner and Koziol (n 5) para 81.
[114] Art 1223 Civil Code (France).
[115] Karner and Koziol (n 5) Schlechtriem (n 75) part II, 4(a)(dd).
[116] Karner and Koziol (n 5) para 68, fn 138.
[117] Karner and Koziol (n 5) paras 67, 86.
[118] Schwenzer (n 93) Art 80, para 7ff.
[119] Schwenzer (n 93) Art 6, para 31.

obligations, its drafters thus limited its application to those contracts that are, in the main, for the sale of goods. While the decision to exclude service contracts (in their guise either as pure service contracts or as mixed contracts which are predominantly for the supply of services) may have been a reasonable one, it was nonetheless a decision without valid justification. The exclusion aimed to secure the overriding aim of consensus by reflecting domestic legal tradition on the issue of the scope of the Convention. Yet it failed to recognise the difficulties associated with such differential treatment that domestic jurisdictions themselves face: the absence of a clear and consistent basis upon which to distinguish sales and service contracts, and the failure to treat like cases alike by imposing starkly different consequences of classification.

Amidst the confusing and outdated distinctions drawn by domestic jurisdictions, the CISG holds great potential to lead the way in the application of a single legal instrument to contexts in which sales and services are closely intertwined and in contexts of pure service contracts. This approach makes theoretical and practical sense. Above all, it would greatly enhance predictability in international trade by avoiding conflict-of-laws disputes about the law applicable to the services part of the contract. The Convention was expressly designed to apply to service obligations, albeit those contained within sales contracts, and it has indeed been so applied without difficulty. This supports the proposition that the Convention in its current form is suitable to govern service contracts.

PART V

Law for Access to Finance

10

The Financing of Micro-businesses in the United Kingdom: The Current Position and the Way Forward

LOUISE GULLIFER*

Micro-businesses, the very smallest business enterprises in the world, are the most numerous and are of great importance to any economy, developed or developing. Globally, there is considerable evidence of a large financing gap in relation to these businesses. The author has previously mapped the reasons for this gap, identified problems caused by the unique characteristics of micro-businesses, and suggested some legal and institutional responses.[1] This chapter takes that analytical framework and applies it to the financing of micro-businesses in the UK. Drawing on the most recent government and other data, it describes the current access to finance in these jurisdictions, considers what solutions, if any, exist to the potential problems previously identified and discusses possible ways forward.

Many definitions of a micro-business exist in national and international legislation, and institutions such as the World Bank use specific definitions for the purposes of their statistics.[2] The UK Government surveys referred to in this chapter use the definition of businesses with 0–9 employees, while the UK Companies Act 2006 defines a 'micro-entity' as one which fulfils at least two of the following conditions: turnover not more than £632,000; balance sheet total not more than £316,000; and number of employees not more than 10.[3] Much of the discussion in this chapter does not need a 'hard' definition of a micro-business, but is focused on the very smallest businesses, which have most or all of the characteristics described in the next section.

* Many thanks are due to Professor Ignacio Tirado for his helpful and insightful comments on this chapter.

[1] L Gullifer and I Tirado, 'A global tug of war: a topography of micro-business financing' (2017) 81 *Law and Contemporary Problems* 109.

[2] In 'A global tug of war' (ibid) we used the World Bank definition of an enterprise of not more than four employees.

[3] At present, this is for the purposes of determining what accounts must be filed by such companies (charities and financial companies are excluded from this regime) but a similar definition was included in ss 33 and 34 of the Small Business, Enterprise and Employment Act 2015 in relation to corporate and non-corporate entities with a view to this being used in legislation to relieve other regulatory burdens from these types of entities.

I. Problems Likely to Occur in the Financing of Micro-businesses

Wherever they are based in the world, micro-businesses have some or all of the following characteristics. They usually are either individual entrepreneurs or family businesses, which means that there is a close interrelationship between the business and the household. To the extent that they require external finance, they seek to borrow small amounts of money. However, they also often have few, or even no, assets to give as collateral to secure the financing. Moreover, those running the business are relatively unsophisticated, with low levels of financial literacy, which means, amongst other things, that the financial information available to lenders is limited or of poor quality.

As a result of these characteristics, micro-businesses are likely to encounter some or all of the following problems in the course of attempting to obtain, or obtaining, finance.[4] First, some issues arise in relation to the initial decision to lend. Potential creditors are not able to obtain satisfactory financial information on which to make a decision to lend, and frequently the costs of assessing risk outweigh the benefit to the lender of making the loan. Moreover, although in many cases micro-businesses do not have assets which can be offered as satisfactory collateral, if they do, there is a danger that the lender will rely too heavily on collateral and will not make a proper risk assessment. A second set of issues relate to potential oppression of micro-business borrowers because of inequality in bargaining power between them and the creditors. Thus, lenders typically demand guarantees from those connected with the micro-business which, although sometimes beneficial, can be oppressive to the guarantors and cause social problems when enforced. Further, the inequality of bargaining power can lead to abusive or onerous terms in the loan or security agreements. A third set of issues relate to the behaviour of creditors during the life cycle of the credit. One is moral hazard: often creditors do not do sufficient monitoring since the amounts involved are too small and, if the credit is secured, the creditor is likely to be over-collateralised, which also reduces the incentive to monitor and to take early action on default. This can lead to, in relation to the borrower, insolvency and, in relation to the lender, non-performing loans. Moreover, creditors can be either are too passive or too aggressive in relation to enforcement: both of which can lead to value destruction and lack of rescue of viable businesses.[5]

The extent to which these problems arise, and the legal response to them, is considered in the rest of this chapter in relation to the financing of micro-businesses in the UK.

[4] For more discussion, see Gullifer and Tirado, 'A global tug of war' (2017) 114–34.

[5] Two other potential problems were identified in 'A global tug of war' (n 1), which are not considered in this chapter because of consideration of space. One relates to the difficulties of enforcement against micro-businesses, especially in relation to secured lending, and the other to the effect of prudential regulation of banks on incentives to lend to such businesses.

II. Financing of Micro-businesses in the United Kingdom

This section considers the techniques used by micro-businesses in the UK to obtain external finance, made more concrete by the use of a simple example. Statistical details of the incidence of these types of financing obtained from the latest Government Small Business Survey are provided in the footnotes.[6]

Sixty-seven per cent of UK micro-businesses and 48 per cent of businesses with no employees had external financing in 2017,[7] which means that a significant proportion do not use external financing at all, and rely on initial equity, retained profits, supplies on credit and income to run their businesses. Obtaining finance seems to be a major problem for a significant minority of micro-businesses in the UK: 18 per cent of employer micro-businesses and 13 per cent of businesses with no employees thought that obtaining financing was a major obstacle to the success of their business in general.[8] Moreover, nine per cent of employer micro-businesses and eight per cent of businesses with no employees who required finance were discouraged from applying for finance at all,[9] a point which is discussed later in this chapter.

The example chosen here is that of a micro-business which manufactures goods on a small scale, despite the fact that that is not necessarily typical.[10] It is chosen because it potentially can obtain finance from many different sources, thus illustrating the options theoretically available to micro-businesses, although not all options will be available to all businesses.[11] It takes the form of a limited liability company,[12] since this is a form chosen by many micro-businesses, partly for tax reasons as the rate of corporation tax is lower than that of income tax,[13] and partly to limit liability, although

[6] Department for Business, Energy and Industrial Strategy (BEIS), 'Longitudinal Small Business Survey 2017, available at www.gov.uk/government/statistics/small-business-survey-2017-businesses-with-employees, including data tables (survey 1); and BEIS, 'Longitudinal Small Business Survey 2017: Businesses with no employees: cross-sectional report', available at www.gov.uk/government/statistics/small-business-survey-2017-businesses-with-no-employees, including data tables (survey 2).

[7] Survey 1 para 64 and survey 2 para 43. 'External finance' is not defined in the survey but the examples asked about in particular are credit card finance, bank overdrafts, loans from financial institutions, business associates or family and friends, leasing, receivables financing, peer-to-peer lending, commercial mortgages, government grants or schemes, equity finance from external sources. Most of these are discussed in this section of the chapter.

[8] Survey 1 table 76 and survey 2 table 75. Of those who applied for finance, 8% of employer micro-businesses (survey 1 table 105) and 5% of businesses with no employees (survey 2 table 89) had had an application for finance rejected in the last 10 years, but only 17% of employer micro-businesses who applied for finance in 2017 obtained all of it (survey 1 table 101) (no equivalent figures for businesses with no employees).

[9] Survey 1 table 107 and survey 2 table 90.

[10] It should be noted that manufacturing businesses are a small proportion of (a) all businesses (5.2% of all businesses registered for tax purposes in the UK in 2016, see Office of National Statistics, 'UK business; activity, size and location: 2016' 5, (b) 5% of UK micro-businesses employing 1–9 employees (these will be referred to as 'employer micro-businesses', see survey 1 table 9, and (c) 4% of UK businesses with no employees, see survey 2 table 9.

[11] For example, a micro-business providing services will not need to obtain raw materials on credit.

[12] 63% of employer micro-businesses are private companies limited by shares (survey 1 data tables) table 10.

[13] The rate of corporate tax is 19%, while income tax, leaving aside the personal allowance, is 20%, with a higher rate of 40% applying for incomes over £46,351.

this may be qualified by the fact that the directors frequently give a personal guarantee to lenders and other creditors. As is typical, the one director (A) is also the sole shareholder. The equity capital is nominal: two shares of £1 each. A invested £2,000 of his personal savings in the company, but this is in the form of subordinated loan as this is more tax efficient.[14] It has five employees.

Finance is required for the business at different stages of its life cycle. Broadly, this can be split into investment capital[15] and working capital (or cash flow). When it was starting up, investment capital was required to acquire machinery, to pay the deposit on its lease of business premises, and for other start-up costs. Later on, as the business progresses, it will have to meet regular expenses, including the acquisition of raw materials, rent for the premises, payments for utilities and services, wages for employees and marketing costs, as well as the ongoing cost of the initial financing.

The business has a number of options for meeting its investment capital financing needs. As well as an injection of a relatively small amount of capital into the business by A, if the business is attractive enough, he may try to raise some equity capital from crowdfunding, although, given the size of the business, this is likely to be donation or advance purchase crowdfunding[16] rather than equity crowdfunding, since the costs of administrating the latter will outweigh the benefits.[17]

This paragraph considers the options for the micro-business in terms of debt finance. There is a thriving market for asset finance in the UK, and the business is likely to be able to obtain machinery or vehicles on either hire purchase terms or under a leasing agreement from a specialist finance company to whom the initial vendor has sold the vehicle or machinery.[18] Small items would have to be bought outright using cash. It is at this stage that financing of investment capital shades into financing of working capital. While a term bank loan is possible, and appropriate for the provision of investment capital, the most common types of finance used by micro-businesses in the UK for working capital are credit card and bank overdraft finance.[19] These revolving credit facilities can provide finance at a relatively low level: their availability will depend on the finance provider's willingness to extend credit, which is examined in the next paragraph. Trade credit is another possible source of finance. Depending on the relevant market, the business will be able to obtain raw materials on credit:[20] ideally the credit

[14] Interest payments can be deducted for tax purposes. 15% of micro-businesses currently had loans from business partners, directors or owners, see survey 1 (table 80), with 5% having loans from family or friends. The figures are 8% and 6% respectively of all businesses with no employees, see survey 2 (table 79).

[15] This refers to expenditure which has to be met before the business started producing any income.

[16] See J Armour and L Enriques, 'The Promise and Perils of Crowdfunding: Between Corporate Finance and Consumer Contracts' (2018) 81 *Modern Law Review* 51.

[17] Only 1% of micro-businesses currently use equity financing, see survey 1 data tables (table 80).

[18] 20% of micro-businesses currently use leading/hire purchase finance, see survey 1 (table 80) and 9% of all businesses with no employees, see survey 2 (table 79).

[19] Credit card finance is used by 31% and bank overdraft finance by 31% of UK micro-businesses, see survey 1 (table 80); 25% of UK businesses with no employees used credit card finance and 22% of such businesses use bank overdraft finance, see survey 2 (table 79). 16% of micro-businesses currently have a bank loan, see survey 1 (table 80), and 8% of businesses with no employees, see survey 2 (table 80).

[20] 92% of manufacturing SMEs obtained credit in the UK in 2017, see survey 1 (table 148) (no figures just for micro-businesses in this sector) and 74% of manufacturing businesses with no employees (see survey 2 table 125). In the UK goods supplied on trade credit are extremely likely to be supplied on retention of title terms, but this will only be effective as regards goods which have not yet lost their identity in the manufacturing process.

period being longer than it takes the business to manufacture and sell the product and obtain payment. As the business sells its products to the wholesale market, this is likely also to be on credit terms,[21] however, so the business will need finance to smooth out the mismatch between the date payment is due to the supplier and the date it receives income from sales. Possible ways of doing this are also explored below.

The availability of most of the debt finance options discussed in the previous paragraph will depend on whether the micro-business can offer collateral to the finance provider. Credit card finance is usually unsecured, but is very expensive and short-term. Revolving facilities or term loans provided by banks, however, are likely to be on a secured basis, if collateral is available. Although land is highly valued as collateral, in the present example, as is typical, the business leases its premises, so it has no land to offer as collateral. Any tangible assets acquired on asset finance terms will not be available to be given as collateral, although a lender can take a security interest over the benefit of the leasing contracts and its lease of its premises. Raw materials in the possession of the micro-business are likely to be supplied on retention of title terms and cannot, therefore, be used as collateral, but products could be:[22] their usefulness in this regard will depend on the length of time they remain unsold. Once they are sold, it is the receivable generated which are available as collateral (plus the benefit of the contract if they are sold on ROT terms). In addition, the micro-business can offer security over its bank account, its intellectual property (if any), the benefit of other contracts it has, such as insurance contracts, and its 'goodwill' (the difference in the value of the business as a going concern and the break-up value). In the UK, it is likely that a lender providing a term loan or a revolving facility (such as an overdraft) will take security (a fixed and floating charge debenture) over all the assets of the company mentioned, with a view to enforcing by selling the business as a going concern if necessary.[23] In this financing model, it is important that English law[24] permits the taking of security over all types of assets (including intangibles such as intellectual property and goodwill), and also future assets, so that at any one time the lender has security over all the assets of the business.[25]

However, a lender is not permitted to take a floating charge over the assets of an unincorporated business,[26] thus such a business is likely to borrow unsecured,

[21] 84% of manufacturing SMEs gave credit in the UK in 2017, see survey 1 (table 147) (no figures just for micro-businesses in this sector) and 60% of manufacturing businesses with no employees (see survey 2, table 124).

[22] Any attempt by the seller to extend its retention of title clause to products is very likely to be recharacterised as a charge, and is therefore almost certainly to be void for non-registration, see *Re Bond Worth Ltd* [1980] Ch. 228; *Borden (UK) Ltd v Scottish Timber Products Ltd* [1981] Ch. 25; *Clough Mill Ltd v Martin* [1985] 1 WLR 111.

[23] See L Gullifer and J Payne, *Corporate Finance Law: Principles and Policy*, 2nd edn (Oxford, Hart Publishing, 2015) 7.3.3.1.

[24] There are some differences in Scottish law, see Scottish Law Commission, Report on Moveable Transactions Volume 2: Security over Moveable Property (No 249, 2017) Vol 2 ch 17.

[25] This is so that the lender has the power to appoint an administrator out of court under Insolvency Act 1986, Sch B1, para 14.

[26] This is because ss 5 and s 9 of, and the Schedule to, the Bills of Sale Act (1878) Amendment Act 1882 (which applies to the taking of security over goods owned by non-corporate debtors) require goods over which security is taken to be specifically listed in a schedule to the bill of sale and provide that the bill is void in relation to any goods specified which are not owned by the debtor at the time of the bill. See also *Thomas v Kelly* (1888) 13 App Cas 506. The Law Commission has included a discussion of extending the floating charge

except perhaps for asset finance[27] or receivables finance.[28] The lender will also want other forms of protection in addition to security interests. It will take a guarantee from A, the director, partly in order to have access to any non-business assets A has (over which it will take security), and also in order to align A's incentives with those of the lender, in that A will lose his own assets if the business cannot repay the lender. It may also require guarantees from others, such as members of A's family.

Mention should be made of other possible sources of finance for A's business. If a SME business is turned down by a bank for funding, the Small and Medium Sized Business (Finance Platforms) Regulations 2015 require the bank to pass on information about the applicant to financing platforms designated by the Government, if the applicant agrees.[29] Some financing may be obtainable from government or local authority schemes.[30] Another possibility is peer-to-peer lending,[31] although this still represents a tiny percentage of loan finance to micro-businesses in the UK.[32]

A more established option is receivables financing. As mentioned, since A's business sells on credit, the revolving asset which is likely to be available for the longest period of time as collateral is receivables (since raw materials are not available at all, and products are, hopefully, sold quickly). In the UK, the type of receivables financing most appropriate for micro-businesses is 'factoring' ie notification financing where the account debtor pays direct to the financier.[33] This is because non-notification financing (invoice discounting) requires a robust collection and retention of payments structure which many micro-businesses do not have.[34] Financiers will usually not factor receivables containing an anti-assignment clause, which has resulted in more limited availability of this type of finance.[35] This problem will be overcome soon in the UK with the advent of regulations overriding such clauses in trade receivables owed to small and medium-sized businesses, which would include A's micro-business[36]

to non-corporate businesses in its consultation paper on Bills of Sale (cp 225) App D, but concluded that it required a separate project, largely because of the need for consequential law reform in other areas. A floating charge can be given by an unincorporated agricultural business under the Agricultural Credits Act 1928.

[27] See above text to n 18.

[28] See below text to nn 33–36.

[29] The designated platforms are Alternative Business Finance (www.alternativebusinessfunding.co.uk), Funding Options (www.fundingoptions.com) and Funding Xchange (www.fxe.co.uk) and have access to many bank and non-bank funding sources.

[30] 7% of micro-businesses used such finance in 2017 (survey 1 table 80) but only 1% of businesses with no employees (survey 2 table 79).

[31] This is lending available via a platform which brings together potential lenders, often private individuals, with potential borrowers in a manner similar to equity crowdfunding. Many peer-to-peer platforms now provide diversification services to lenders, resulting in loans being made by a large number of lenders, see FCA, 'Loan-based ("peer-to-peer") and investment-based crowdfunding platforms: Feedback on our post-implementation review and proposed changes to the regulatory framework' (CP18-20) ch 3.

[32] 1% of micro-businesses (see survey 1 table 80) and 1% of businesses with no employees (0% of such manufacturing businesses) (see survey 2 table 79).

[33] According to the surveys, relatively few micro-businesses are financed by receivables financing (5% of micro-businesses (survey 1 table 80) and 1% of businesses with no employees (see survey 2 table 79)). UK Finance figures for Q4 2017 receivables financing, show that 12,952 businesses with a turnover of less than £500,000 were clients of UK Finance members at the end of Q4 2017, with advances totalling £ 833m. While not directly comparable, the UK Finance figures for bank financing (including some asset finance) for end of Q4 2017 show gross lending of £409m to 3.7m small businesses (with a turnover of less than £1m–2m).

[34] L Gullifer, H Beale and S Paterson, 'A Case for Interfering with Freedom of Contract? An Empirically-Informed Study of Bans on Assignment' [2016] 3 *Journal of Business Law* 203, 214, 218.

[35] ibid 220.

[36] The Business Contract Terms (Assignment of Receivables) Regulations 2018 (SI 2018/1254)

III. Legal Framework

This section will examine the problems identified in section II in the light of the legal framework in the UK, to see whether these problems exist, and, if not, why not.

A. Issues Relating to the Original Decision whether to Extend Credit

i. Financial Information

The first potential problem is the difficulty creditors may have in obtaining satisfactory financial information on which to make a decision to lend. In general, this arises where the micro-business is not a registered entity or is not under an obligation to draw up audited accounts for other purposes. It is unlikely to be a significant problem in the UK for the reasons set out below. First, companies will be considered, and then unincorporated businesses.

In 2017 in the UK, 63 per cent of employer micro-businesses[37] and 34 per cent of micro-businesses with no employees are companies limited by shares.[38] Companies in the UK are required to file accounts at Companies House.[39] A reduced regime, based on Article 36 of the Directive on annual financial statements[40] including exceptions for micro-undertakings,[41] has been included in the Companies Act 2006.[42] The overall obligation that the accounts must give a true and fair view of financial position of the company[43] still applies, though the information required is reduced) and the micro-entity minimum accounting items included in the company's accounts for the year are presumed to give the required true and fair view.[44] Thus, where a micro-business is incorporated, there will be financial information publicly available to a potential lender. The accounts may not be audited, since most micro-businesses will fall within the small business audited accounts exception.[45] The publicly available information is limited, however, as the filed accounts are, by their nature, historic and private companies are only obliged to file within nine months from the end of the accounting period.[46] Moreover, micro-businesses fall under the small companies regime, which only requires filing of a balance sheet, though further information can be filed if desired.[47] Moreover, since a profit and loss account is still required to be drawn up,[48] a potential lender can

[37] Survey 1 para 185.

[38] Survey 2 para 111.

[39] See Companies Act 2006, Pt 15.

[40] Directive 2013/34/EU.

[41] See text to n 3 above.

[42] Small Companies (Micro-Entities' Accounts) Regulations 2013 (2013/3008) and Companies Act 2006, ss 393–397, 444 and 444A.

[43] Companies Act 2006, s 393(1).

[44] Companies Act 2006, s 444(5) and see also ss 393(1A), 396(2A)(6), 415(1)(a) and 444(5) (see also s 495(3A) where the accounts are audited).

[45] Companies Act 2006, s 477. Auditing is required if any member or members holding more than 10% of the share capital require it (s 476).

[46] Companies Act 2006, s 442.

[47] Companies Act, s 444. A micro-entity does not need to draw up a directors report, s 415(1A).

[48] Companies Act 2006, s 396.

demand to see these even if they are not publicly filed, and could also require accounts to be audited. Incorporated micro-businesses also have to produce accounts for tax purposes.

Even if a micro-business is not a company, it may be required to file accounts for other reasons. For example, six per cent of employer micro-businesses were charities, most of whom who have to file accounts. Charities with a turnover of £25,000 to £250,000 a year can file simple, though audited, accounts,[49] and those with a turnover of less than £25,000 can file unaudited accounts.[50] Moreover, any business with a turnover of more than £85,000 a year, whatever its legal status, must register for VAT (and businesses with a lower turnover may do so). Such businesses have to keep records, and make an annual return to Her Majesty's Revenue and Customs (HMRC).[51] Most micro-businesses which are not companies are sole proprietorships:[52] even these are likely to have accounts (often audited) because the individual proprietor will be liable for income tax and will have to produce accounts as part of his or her tax return. Most micro-businesses in the UK will have a business current bank account,[53] and bank statements can also provide valuable information to lenders about cash flow. There are also private companies which collect available information and produce credit rankings for businesses,[54] largely for the benefit of potential lenders.

Lenders to micro-businesses tend to rely on a combination of these sources of information, and will insist on the production of accounts, bank statements and VAT returns.[55]

ii. Costs of Assessing Risk

Another potential problem is that the costs of assessing risk outweigh the benefit to the creditor of extending the credit. Where loans are very small, there are certain basic risk assessment procedures which have to be gone through in order for a loan to be made without incurring undue risk to the lender. These vary slightly according to the amount of the loan, but there is a minimum level below which a lender cannot, and should not, go. Certain steps can be taken to reduce costs, particularly using standardisation and online forms, but the danger of this is that proper risk assessment is not carried out, and the borrower may well be unable to repay, which is a bad outcome for both the lender and the borrower.

Complicated and lengthy application processes are a disincentive to a borrower to apply for a small loan, as well as to a lender to make a small loan. One way of overcoming this is for lenders to have online portals where potential borrowers can quickly check their eligibility for a loan, thus making sure that they are not wasting their time

[49] www.gov.uk/prepare-charitys-annual-accounts/y/no/over-25-000-to-250-000.

[50] www.gov.uk/prepare-charitys-annual-accounts/y/no/up-to-25-000.

[51] HMRC is the UK tax authority.

[52] 16% of employer micro-businesses (survey 1 table 1) and 51% of micro-businesses with no employees (survey 2 table 1).

[53] 96% of employer micro-businesses (Survey 1 table 79) and 72% of micro-businesses with no employees (survey 2 table 78) had a business current account. All others used a personal current account.

[54] For example, Experian, see www.experian.co.uk/about-us/index.html.

[55] See, for example, www.iwoca.co.uk/faq; www.business.hsbc.uk/en-gb/finance-and-borrowing/credit-and-lending/small-business-loan.

when they do apply.[56] Further, the availability of accounts, as discussed above, may help reduce the costs of assessment, as can reliable information about the business's bank accounts: while this can come from bank statements, the borrower's own bank is in a better position than others to acquire this information, and some banks make it a condition of making a loan that the business already has a current account with them.[57] The Government initiative of Open Banking is designed to make bank information more available to other potential lenders, where the borrower agrees.[58]

iii. *Availability of Finance*

In the UK there does not appear to be a real difficulty in obtaining small amounts of finance if that is what is required. This section will consider the position in two ways. First, the evidence from the BEIS Longitudinal Small Business Survey 2017 about size and availability of financing will be examined. Secondly, a Government initiative which spreads the costs away from initial decision-making into monitoring will be examined.

The survey showed that the amounts of financing applied for by micro-businesses are predominantly small. Sixty per cent of employer micro-businesses[59] and 89 per cent of micro-businesses without employees[60] who applied for finance in the previous 12 months applied for less than £50,000. Of these, 18 per cent of employer micro-businesses and 40 per cent of micro-businesses without employees applied for less than £10,000. Only 73 per cent of employer micro-businesses[61] and 52 per cent of micro-businesses without employees[62] who applied for finance were successful, but of those who obtained finance, 65 per cent of employer micro-businesses[63] and 74 per cent of micro-businesses with no employers[64] obtained less than £50,000. 23 per cent of employer micro-businesses obtained less than £10,000 and 34 per cent of micro-businesses with no employers. While only 12 per cent of employer micro-businesses[65] and five per cent of micro-businesses with no employees[66] surveyed applied for finance in 2017, only nine per cent of employer micro-businesses[67] and eight per cent of micro-businesses with no employees[68] said they had a need for finance in the past 12 months. Three major reasons for not applying among those who had a need for finance but did not apply appeared to be concern that it would be too expensive,[69] fear of rejection[70]

[56] See, for example, https://creditindication.business.hsbc.co.uk; www.fundingcircle.com/businesses/apply.
[57] See, for example, www.santander.co.uk/uk/business/borrowing-finance/business-loans.
[58] See text to n 144 below.
[59] Survey 1 table 99.
[60] Survey 2 table 87.
[61] Survey 1 para 88. Another 14% only obtained part of the finance applied for.
[62] Survey 2 para 59.
[63] Survey 1 table 100.
[64] Survey 2 table 88.
[65] Survey 1 table 82.
[66] Survey 2 table 80.
[67] Survey 1 table 107.
[68] Survey 2 table 90.
[69] 50% of employer micro-businesses cited this (survey 1 table 108) and 32% of micro-businesses with no employees (survey 2 table 91).
[70] 31% of employer micro-businesses and 39% of micro-businesses with no employees.

and concern that it would take too long or be too onerous,[71] although the predominant reason was a disinclination to take on any more risk.[72]

The British Business Bank Plc is wholly owned by the UK Government, and has various schemes in the UK for financing small businesses. Its programme for start-up loans, funded by government money, involves the submission of very little hard data on application for a loan, but requires a business plan, cash flow forecast and 'personal survival budget'.[73] Credit risk is managed by 12 months of free mentoring: the assessment if based on future prospects rather than past data.

iv. Collateral

A third issue concerns the availability of satisfactory collateral that can be offered by micro-businesses, who rarely own land or valuable fixed assets over which security can be taken.[74] The reasonably liberal rules in the UK as to what can be the subject of a security interest help to overcome this problem, at least in relation to corporate micro-businesses. The assets a micro-business is most likely to be able to offer as collateral are circulating assets such as inventory or receivables, together perhaps with some low-value equipment and, in some cases, intellectual property. There is no legal problem in the UK to prevent corporate micro-businesses granting security over all their assets, including circulating assets, by using a combination of fixed and floating charges, and this is very likely to be the case where such businesses are granted overdrafts or term loans.[75] Individuals and unincorporated businesses cannot give this type of security over goods,[76] although it can be done over receivables.[77] Micro-businesses can also obtain trade credit, which is extensively used,[78] and asset finance to obtain equipment, which is less used.[79]

The provision of collateral can, in theory, mean that sometimes a lender does not make a proper risk assessment or monitor properly. As discussed below, lending to businesses is, unlike lending to consumers, generally not a regulated activity[80] in the UK, and so the Financial Conduct Authority (FCA) does not directly supervise the risk assessments made by most lenders. One exception is where the borrower is an unincorporated business and is borrowing less then £25,000. This type of credit agreement[81] is

[71] 35% of employer micro-businesses and 32% of micro-businesses with no employees.

[72] 59% of employer micro-businesses and 55% of micro-businesses with no employees.

[73] See www.startuploans.co.uk/how-to-apply.

[74] See L Gullifer and I Tirado, 'Financing Micro-businesses and the UNCITRAL Model Law on Secured Transactions' (2017) 4 *Uniform Law Review* 642.

[75] See n 19. The statistics do not show whether the overdrafts or loans are secured or not, but it is very likely that they will be.

[76] See n 26.

[77] *Tailby v the Official Receiver* (1888) 13 App Cas 523.

[78] 64% of micro-businesses (survey 1 table 148) and 41% of businesses with no employees (survey 2 table 125). The figures were much higher (around 75%) for businesses in the manufacturing and retail sectors, and it is likely that these reflect the supply of goods on retention of title terms.

[79] See n 18 above.

[80] That is, it does not fall within the FSMA (Regulated Activities) Order 2001.

[81] Loans and asset finance are included.

regulated within the consumer credit regime, and the FCA handbook provides that a lender must make a 'reasonable assessment of credit-worthiness'.[82]

In relation to other lending to micro-businesses, there is an industry code. The Standards of Lending Practice[83] apply to members of the Lending Standards Board[84] (about 30 major banking groups and other lenders) and govern lending to business customers with a turnover of less than £6.5m. These standards provide, amongst other relevant standards, that before granting credit 'firms should assess, from the information available at the time, whether the customer will be able to repay it in a sustainable manner without incurring financial difficulty'. While these standards are not enforceable per se by the FCA, senior employees in regulated firms[85] must comply with individual standards,[86] including observing proper standards of market conduct.[87] The FCA have recently stated that compliance with an industry code will normally amount to observing such standards[88] and intend to publicly recognise certain codes, although none have been recognised so far. While doubt has been expressed as to the effectiveness of industry codes,[89] the FCA see this move as a soft way of extending the regulatory net, and, at present, do not intend to extend the obligation to observe proper market standards in relation to unregulated activities to firms themselves,[90] nor to make lending to businesses a regulated activity.[91]

While the regime is not comprehensive, and there is always a risk of non-compliance, some controls are at least in place in the UK to ensure that a proper assessment is made of the ability of the borrower to repay, rather than focusing on enforcement against collateral.

B. Issues Arising in Relation to Inequality of Bargaining Power

i. Guarantees

As well as collateral, lenders often require guarantees from those connected with the micro-business. This can be beneficial, in that it makes it more likely that credit will be extended, and, from the point of view of the lender, aligns the incentives of the guarantor with that of the business. However, it can also be oppressive to the guarantors, particularly those who are not commercially part of the business but are, for example, part of the entrepreneur's family.

[82] Consumer Credit Sourcebook (CONC) Rule 5.2A. Credit-worthiness means the ability of the borrower to make repayments, and must be assessed without taking account of the existence of a guarantee or security (rules 5.2A.12 and 5.2A.14).

[83] www.lendingstandardsboard.org.uk/the-standards-for-business-customers.

[84] www.lendingstandardsboard.org.uk/registered-firms.

[85] At present this is limited to banks, building societies, credit unions and dual regulated investment firms, but will extend to other regulated firms in December 2019.

[86] Code of Conduct (COCON) 1.1.

[87] Code of Conduct (COCON) 2.1 rule 5.

[88] FCA Policy Statement PS18/18, 8–9.

[89] See House of Commons Treasury Committee report on SME Finance ('Treasury Committee report') HC 805 para 80 (26 October 2018).

[90] FCA Policy Statement PS18/18, 23–24.

[91] See below section III C.

In theory, English common law contains a number of protections for a guarantor, who is seen to be in a vulnerable position as he or she is not a party to the debt contract, and (at least in theory) receives no direct benefit from the guarantee,[92] although this justification is much less strong where the guarantor is a director of a corporate business. Thus, there is a limited duty of disclosure of unusual features of the credit arrangement,[93] and a guarantor's liability is discharged[94] if the liability of the principal debtor is void, unenforceable, discharged, released or varied without the guarantor's consent.[95] Moreover, given that the bargaining power usually favours the creditor, a contract of guarantee is traditionally construed strictly against the creditor[96] and, although this approach has been somewhat softened recently, clear words are still necessary to derogate from the normal incidents and protections of a guarantee contract, such as a right of set-off against the creditor.[97] A body of law has been developed, in addition, whereby a contract of guarantee entered into as a result of fraud, misrepresentation, duress or undue influence can be set aside, whether the vitiating factor was as a result of the conduct of the creditor or another person (if the creditor had constructive notice of this).[98] If the guarantor is an individual who is acting wholly or mainly outside their business (for example, a relation of the entrepreneur, though not the entrepreneur themselves), the controls on unfair terms in the Consumer Rights Act 2015 will apply.[99] Thus the fairness of any term can be assessed by the court, except to the extent that it specifies the main subject matter of the contract or the appropriateness of the price,[100] and, to the extent it is unfair, it will be unenforceable against the consumer.[101]

As well as this protection under the general law, there is some specific protection under the Standards of Lending Practice addressing some of the more egregious potential problems with guarantees.[102] First, the lender must make a potential guarantor aware of their obligations and give them the option to seek legal advice,[103] which mirrors the common law on undue influence, since the provision of independent legal advice to

[92] *Blest v Brown* (1862) 4 De GF & J 367.

[93] *Royal Bank of Scotland v Etridge (No 2)* [2001] UKHL 44 [188].

[94] See G Andrews and R Millett, *Law of Guarantees*, 7th edn (London, Sweet & Maxwell, 2015) 6-018–6-029.

[95] *Holme v Brunskill* (1878) 3 QBD 495.

[96] *Trafalgar House Construction (Regions) Ltd v General Surety & Guarantee Co Ltd* [1996] AC 199, 208.

[97] *Liberty Mutual Insurance Co (UK) Ltd v HSBC Bank plc* [2002] EWCA Civ 691 [56]–[59]. Exclusion of a right of set-off would also fall within s 3 of the Unfair Contract Terms Act 1977 if on the creditor's standard terms, and would be unenforceable unless it was reasonable; *Governor and Co of the Bank of Scotland v Singh* (unreported, 17 June 2005) QB Mercantile Ct, Manchester. Other exclusions of rights would be unlikely to fall within that Act, however, see H Beale (ed), *Chitty on Contracts*, 33rd edn (London, Sweet & Maxwell, 2018) 45.152–45.154.

[98] *Royal Bank of Scotland v Etridge (No 2)* [2001] UKHL 44. Constructive notice will only arise in relation to a non-commercial guarantor, ibid [87]–[88].

[99] Consumer Rights Act 2015, Pt 2 (see below section III B ii). While there was previously uncertainty whether these controls applied to contracts of guarantee, this has been made clear by the CJEU case of *Tarcău v Banca Comercială Intesa Sanpaolo România SA* C-74/15, EU, interpreting the 1993 Directive on which this part of the Consumer Rights Act is based. The definition of 'consumer' in s 2(3) of the Act to include those acting *mainly* outside their business also makes it more likely that family member guarantees will be within the controls.

[100] Consumer Rights Act 2015, s 64 (1).

[101] Consumer Rights Act 2015, s 62.

[102] See section III a iv above in relation to the regulatory status of this code.

[103] Product sale, standard 13.

the guarantor will usually rebut any presumption of undue influence or constructive notice.[104] Second, lenders should not accept unlimited guarantees[105] and, third, should provide information to guarantors on their current level of liability on request providing the borrower gives permission.

While the protection of guarantors is not comprehensive under English law, it does seek to reach a reasonable balance between increasing access to finance by enabling family creditworthiness and assets to be used to support business borrowing, and protecting the more vulnerable family members[106] and, to some extent, individual entrepreneurs.

ii. Loan or Security Agreements

Given the, often extreme, difference in bargaining power between the micro-business and the lender, there is a further danger that abusive or onerous terms will be included in the loan or security agreements.[107]

In terms of the overall fairness of the bargain between the parties, there are not controls in relation to lending to corporate micro-businesses, except the requirements of disclosure in the Standards of Lending Practice. In relation to lending to unincorporated businesses, the Consumer Credit Act provisions enabling an 'unfair relationship' to be set aside by the court[108] apply to business lending to such businesses without any limit on the amount of lending.[109] Although there have been a number of cases establishing that an 'unfair relationship' is very unlikely to be found in a commercial context where the parties are of equal or near equal bargaining power,[110] it is much more strongly arguable that this jurisdiction could apply in the context of lending to micro-businesses. However, even in a consumer lending situation, one-sidedness alone is not enough to make a relationship unfair.[111] The terms of the agreement have to be unfair in all the circumstances, which includes the characteristics and sophistication of the borrower and the market choices available.[112] The courts' seeming reluctance to find relationships unfair in the consumer context,[113] which may be affected by the draconian remedy of setting aside the entire agreement, does not indicate that this jurisdiction is a very robust protection for micro-businesses in anything but the most egregious situations.

[104] *Royal Bank of Scotland v Etridge (No 2)* [2001] UKHL 44, [50]–[63].

[105] Product sale standard 14.

[106] *Barclays Bank Plc v O'Brien* [1994] 1 AC 180, 188 and *Royal Bank of Scotland v Etridge (No 2)* [2001] UKHL 44, [37].

[107] See House of Commons debate on 'RBS Global Restructuring Group and SMEs': Hansard, HC Vol 634 col 1086 (18 January 2018).

[108] Consumer Credit Act 1974, s 140A.

[109] This is because business lending over £25,000 is an 'exempt agreement' under the Financial Services and Markets Act 2000 (Regulated Activities) Order 2001, reg 60C, but exempt agreements are included within s 140A.

[110] *Rahman v HBSC* [2012] EWHC 11 (Ch) [285]; *Deutsche Bank (Suisse) SA v Khan* [2013] EWHC 482 (Comm); *Commercial First Business Ltd v Pickup* [2017] CTLC 1 [75].

[111] *Plevin v Paragon Personal Finance Ltd* [2014] UKSC 61, [9].

[112] *Plevin v Paragon Personal Finance Ltd* [2014] UKSC 61, [17].

[113] Eg *Consolidated Finance Ltd v Hunter* [2010] BPIR 1322; *Carey v HSBC* [2009] EWHC 3417 (QB); *Julie McMullon v Secure the Bridge Limited* [2015] EWCA Civ 884; cf *Link Financial Ltd v Wilson* [2014] EWHC 252 (Ch), which was a fraud case.

While there is control of unfair terms in contracts in the UK, particularly in the consumer field,[114] this is limited in relation to businesses. The Unfair Contract Terms Act 1977 applies a requirement of reasonableness to terms which are included in the written standard terms of business of a contracting party,[115] which requirements includes consideration of the relative bargaining power of the parties.[116] However, it only applies to clauses excluding or limiting liability for breach of contract, relied upon by the party on whose standard terms the contract is made. The abusive or onerous terms in a loan agreement are not likely to be this type of term. 'Penalty clauses' are also unenforceable under the common law. While this jurisdiction is more likely to cover, for example, an extra charge if there is a brief default in payment, it is limited in that it only applies to stipulated amounts payable on breach,[117] and also only applies where the amount payable is in excess of a 'genuine pre-estimate of loss' but also where it is not fixed to protect a 'legitimate interest' of the party not in breach.[118] While this latter qualification is more likely to apply where the parties are of equal bargaining power, the test has been applied in a consumer case to validate a parking 'fine' which was greatly in excess of any loss.[119]

The regulation of unfair terms in consumer contracts in the Consumer Rights Act[120] is much wider in scope, and there have been proposals to extend this to micro-businesses, although these have not been implemented.[121] This control is much more measured than that under the Consumer Credit Act, since only the unfair term is unenforceable, and would be more appropriate. The vulnerability of those running very small businesses, and the very thin line between a sole entrepreneur and a consumer,[122] was recently noted by the House of Commons Treasury Committee.[123] Since there is now a definition of 'micro-business' in sections 33 and 34 of the Small Business, Enterprise and Employment Act 2015, thus overcoming one of the objections to the previous proposals,[124] extending the Consumer Rights Act protection to such businesses could be an effective way of dealing with the inequality of bargaining power identified here.

C. Behaviour of Creditors during the Life Cycle of the Loan

Another issue identified[125] in relation to micro-business finance in general is that, due to the small size of the loans made to micro-businesses, and also to the fact that lenders

[114] See Consumer Right Act 2015, Pt 2.
[115] Unfair Contract Terms Act 1977, s 3.
[116] Unfair Contract Terms Act 1977, Sch 2, para (a).
[117] *Cavendish Square Holding BV v Talal El Makdessi* [2015] UKSC 67, [41]–[43].
[118] ibid.
[119] *Parking Eye Limited v Beavis* [2015] UKSC 67.
[120] See above III B i.
[121] Law Commission, Unfair Terms in Contracts Report LC292 (2005).
[122] The Financial Services Consumer Panel, in their evidence to the Treasury Committee, said that 'the small business consumer is often simply an individual consumer wearing a business hat and needs the same protection as an individual'.
[123] Treasury Committee report (n 89) paras 72–76.
[124] Namely, that it was difficult to define 'micro-business' in a satisfactory way, see Law Commission, 'Unfair Terms in Contracts' LC 292 (2005) 2.37–2.40, 5.35.
[125] See section I above.

may be over-collateralised, there is little incentive on them to monitor the loan or financial situation of the business. Moreover, lenders may also be either too passive or too aggressive in relation to enforcement of loans, leading to value destruction and failure to rescue a viable business.

In relation to the UK, there has been recent concern about the behaviour of lenders. The House of Commons Treasury Committee considered certain examples of lender misconduct over the past few years in relation to SMEs in its very recent report. The report was not specifically focused on micro-businesses, although the arguments contained in it seem to apply particularly to micro-businesses.[126] These related both to the origination of loans[127] and the treatment of borrowers during the currency of the loan.[128] The examples were taken from a debate in the House of Commons in January 2018 when many examples of such misconduct were given, most of which related to aggressive enforcement of loans, often in a situation where there was a dispute over whether there had been a default, as a result of a revaluation of assets or some other recalibration of an existing deal.[129]

As a result, a number of solutions have been proposed by MPs, by the Treasury Committee and the FCA. The first, which has already been discussed, is the recognition of codes of conduct by the FCA, and the acknowledgement that senior managers can comply with their regulatory requirements by abiding by such codes. While this is helpful, it is only necessary because commercial lending is not a 'regulated activity' under the Financial Services and Markets Act 2000 ('FSMA'). This means that an institution can lend to businesses without having to be authorised or regulated by the FCA,[130] and that the conduct of business standards, which apply to regulated entities, do not apply in relation to commercial lending.

One set of arguments about why business lending is not a regulated activity, as opposed to, for example, dealing in investments, is that loans are governed entirely by contract law, and, in many situations, both lenders and borrowers can protect themselves adequately by the use of contract. However, this assumes that the borrowers are in a position to do so, and this may not be the case for micro-businesses. Consumer lending, on the other hand, was within the regulatory net long before FSMA.[131] When the ambit of the regulation brought about by FSMA was being considered, it was decided not to include any commercial lending within its scope, on the grounds that all businesses could 'fend for themselves',[132] and that regulation would drive up the cost of lending and reduce access to credit. This conclusion is now being rethought, on the grounds, which chime with the thesis set out in this paper, that owners of SMEs are no more sophisticated or financially experienced than consumers, and, in many cases, are individuals whose only experience of finance is as a consumer. The Treasury

[126] The only exception to this is the discussion of SME access to the Financial Ombudsman Service (FOS), since micro-businesses with a turnover of up to €2 million can already access the FOS.

[127] Treasury Committee report (n 89) paras 53–54.

[128] Treasury Committee report (n 89) para 76.

[129] House of Commons debate on 'RBS Global Restructuring Group and SMEs' (n 107). Many banks, and their advisers, were implicated in the debate.

[130] Lending by consumers on a peer-to-peer platform is regulated, see n 144 below.

[131] The Consumer Credit Act was introduced in 1974, but many of the provisions originated many years before in, for example, moneylending legislation (see Beale, *Chitty* (2018) 39–298.

[132] Treasury Committee report (n 89) paras 70–71

Committee have concluded that the regulatory net should be extended so as to provide 'adequate protection' to SMEs, which, in order to be proportionate and not to adversely affect the availability and cost of credit, should be 'targeted at those SMEs that show the greatest need for additional protection'.[133] Arguably, this should include, at least, micro-businesses.

Another additional solution proposed in the debate in the House of Commons was to provide a readier avenue for redress for SMEs, since many of the businesses who complained of the conduct of lenders also complained of the expensive and slow resolution of disputes by the courts.[134] The FCA is increasing access to the Financial Services Ombudsman, but since micro-businesses already have such access, this is beyond the scope of this chapter. A proposal for a Financial Services Tribunal has proved more controversial and was not recommended by the review carried out by Walker in 2018.[135] Despite this, it is recommended by the Treasury Committee.

One of the results of the misconduct referred to above is that there appears to have been a reduction of trust in the banking system by SMEs, including micro-businesses. This emerged in the evidence given to the Treasury Committee as a reason for discouragement in relation to seeking finance from banks.[136] The issue of discouragement will be considered in the next section, but one possible response in the context of the issues discussed in this section is a market one. If banks are seen as failing to monitor or to respond properly to real or perceived difficulties experienced by borrowers, alternative finance providers could offer 'relationship banking' including closer monitoring as an attractive selling point.[137]

IV. Access to Finance

As mentioned above,[138] a significant proportion of micro-businesses felt that lack of finance was a major problem, and many were discouraged from even applying. It is clear from the Longitudinal Small Business Survey 2017 and from the work done on its data by the Enterprise Research Centre that discouragement is a particular problem among micro-businesses.[139] While the most cited reason for discouragement was concern over taking on additional risk,[140] other significant reasons were fear of rejection[141] and lack of speed.[142]

[133] Treasury Committee report (n 89) paras 86–88. The FCA is more cautious, and would like to wait to discover whether the plan of recognising codes of conduct can meet the regulatory aim without more.

[134] House of Commons debate on 'RBS Global Restructuring Group and SMEs' (n 107).

[135] S Walker, 'Review into the complaints and alternative dispute resolution (ADR) landscape for the UK's SME market' (UK Finance, 23 October 2018).

[136] Treasury Committee report (n 89), para 12.

[137] See, for example, the package offered at https://fleximize.com/services.

[138] Section III a iii.

[139] Enterprise Research Centre, 'An empirical Examination of discouraged borrowers in the UK' (ERC Research Paper 69, 2018) 41.

[140] Survey 1 table 109 (27%), survey 2 table 92 (29%)

[141] Survey 1 table 109 (12%), survey 2 table 92 (16%). This reason was also highlighted by the Treasury Committee (n 89), para 14–15.

[142] Survey 1 table 109 (12%), survey 2 table 92 (13%).

Both of these issues could be targeted by more competition, as could the lack of trust in banks discussed in the previous section. For example, one of the selling points of peer-to-peer lending platforms is that they can make credit decisions far more quickly than a bank can,[143] although, in order to protect the borrower from the dangers discussed in section IV B above, it would be necessary for the alternative finance providers to be under the same regulatory regime as the banks.[144] Increased competition is also a possible answer to the problem of inequality of bargaining power, at least in relation to interest rates and other obvious comparators. It is perhaps too much to expect detailed comparison of other terms by unsophisticated borrowers, although comparison websites can assist.[145]

Competition to bank lending is growing in the UK, and, although some types are not yet used extensively by micro-businesses,[146] this could change with more information and encouragement. As mentioned earlier, banks are now required to pass on information to alternative finance providers if they refuse to extend finance.[147] The lack of reliable credit information that sometimes holds back alternative finance providers is being addressed by Open Banking, an initiative set up by the Competition and Markets Authority, which enables micro-businesses to make their bank information available securely to regulated providers, including comparison websites.[148]

V. Conclusion

This chapter has considered the financing of micro-businesses in the UK using the analytical framework developed in relation to the financing of micro-businesses globally. In some areas, the UK scores quite well: while a significant proportion of micro-businesses find access to finance a problem, this is well below the global finance gap, which is estimated at 50 per cent.[149] Moreover, some of the potential problems with micro-business finance are mitigated by a legal response, which in some areas (such as the law of security, and the provision of reliable information) is quite robust. However, there are still gaps in the legal response. Two examples, namely the restrictions on the giving of security over tangible assets by unincorporated businesses and the limited control of unfair contract terms in contracts not governed by the Consumer Rights Act, have been the subject of recommendations for reform by the Law Commission which have not yet been implemented.

Having said this, there are still considerable problems, both relating to bank conduct and more generally to discouragement of applications for finance. There are two possible areas of response to this. One is increased regulation, both self-regulation by

[143] Treasury Committee report (n 89), para 40.

[144] Most peer-to-peer platforms are regulated by the FCA if consumers are involved either as lenders or borrowers, see FSMA (Regulated Activities) Order 2001, Art 36H.

[145] See, for example, in relation to peer-to-peer lending www.p2pmoney.co.uk.

[146] See n 30 above. Even receivables financing is not yet extensively used, see n 31.

[147] See text to n 29 above.

[148] See www.openbanking.org.uk.

[149] Gullifer and Tirado (n 1) 649.

industry and regulation imposed by the FCA, and there is movement in this direction from the FCA and the Government. However, the response needs to be proportionate, since heavy regulation may increase costs, stifling access to finance and increasing its cost.[150] The other response is increased competition. This is occurring within the UK at a fast pace, ranging from well-established receivables financing to innovative finance initiatives such as peer-to-peer lending. These come with their own dangers, and, again, the balance will need to be struck between protection and cost, but, for now, increased competition seems to be a way to improve both access to finance for micro-businesses and the quality of the experience for financed micro-businesses.

[150] Gullifer and Tirado (n 1) 124.

11

Equity Crowdfunding to Facilitate Access to Finance for Small Business: The Regulatory Response and the Indirect Impact on Company Law*

TERESA RODRÍGUEZ DE LAS HERAS BALLELL

I. 'Access to Finance' Challenges and the Search for Alternative Sources

Credit availability and access to finance with reasonable conditions are declared to be the most pressing factors in the launching and the development of business projects.[1] Particularly, entrepreneurs and small-and-medium sized enterprises (SMEs) in their start-up stage face financing problems.[2] The financial crisis visibly aggravated the situation, bringing with it a serious funds shortage, higher credit costs (direct costs such as interest rates as well as indirect costs such greater demands for additional suretyships and security interests), and a general reluctance to support innovative, creative or emerging projects with higher levels of risk.

Financing strategies can be shaped by internal funding sources or external ones and are essentially based on equity or debt. Start-ups and entrepreneurs tend to rely

* This chapter has been prepared during a visit as a Chair of Excellence at the University of Oxford (Commercial Law Center, Harris Manchester College), reciprocal with Professor Louise Gullifer (University of Oxford) at the Universidad Carlos III de Madrid in the framework of *UC3M-Santander Chair of Excellence program*. The author would like to acknowledge Universidad Carlos III of Madrid and Santander bank for the granting of the Chair of Excellence, and the Harris Manchester College for the warm reception.

[1] According to the European Commission '2015 Survey on the Access to Finance of Enterprises (SAFE): Analytical Report' (December), available at http://ec.europa.eu/DocsRoom/documents/14321/attachments/1/translations/en/renditions/native, only 41% of EU SMEs declare not to encounter difficulties in accessing credit. The Ipsos Mori '2013 SMEs' Access to Finance Survey: Analytical Report' (European Commission, 14 December), available at http://ec.europa.eu/DocsRoom/documents/7864/attachments/1/translations/en/renditions/native also came to a similar conclusion.

[2] Relevant data and wide analysis of the finance gap for micro-businesses, in particular, L Gullifer and I Tirado, 'Financing Micro-Businesses and UNCITRAL's Model Law on Secured Transactions' (2017) 22 *Uniform Law Review* 642.

on external financing.[3] Limited retained earnings in the start-up period and a lack of personal financial availability usually force them to look for external funds sources in multiple forms: bank loans, credit lines, public grants, borrowing funds from family and friends, or investments from business angels or venture capitalists.[4] All these types of external financing present benefits and risks, advantages and drawbacks. Likewise, not every external funding model is suitable for all business projects. The economic sector in which a business operates, the growth potential, and the development phase are determinant factors in assessing the most suitable (or simply the available) external funding method for each business project.[5]

Another recent trend is a progressive shift of venture capital and bank finance towards subsequent phases of the business finance curve ('funding escalator').[6] Venture capitalist and banks are continuously displacing their targets to projects of bigger size, higher financial needs and, as a consequence, lower risk. Below such quantitative thresholds, the finance gap is becoming broader and broader accordingly. The resultant effect of that tendency is an appreciable abandonment of start-up initiatives, innovative projects and emerging business.

The perverse combination of the contraction of traditional financing sources and the increasing finance gap proves to be devastating for the market of start-up business finance. Hence, entrepreneurs and start-ups are pressed to explore and find alternative financing sources beyond the traditional framework of equity- and debt-based funding options. Diversification of financing sources, along with the needed recovery of the credit market, has become a crucial strategy in economic stimulus policies.[7] In such a context, crowdfunding has burst into our economies and stands to fill the gap.[8]

Certainly, crowdfunding is not a new phenomenon. The possibility of funding a project by raising small (albeit, continuously increasing) contributions from many sources (investors, lenders, donors, users), instead of relying on a few investors to put in the whole amount, has launched many projects and made them feasible throughout history. However, the extraordinary vigour, exponential growth and increasing popularity of crowdfunding at the present time mark a clear inflexion point. More than a simple emulation in digital form of public funds collection, crowdfunding has today gained a unique profile[9] and has become a genuine alternative model for the financing market.

[3] Ipsos Mori '2013 SMEs' Access to Finance Survey' (n 1) at 6.

[4] 'European Commission Staff Working Document, Capital Markets Union: First Status Report' (25 April 2016) 23–33, SWD(2016) 147 final, available at https://ec.europa.eu/info/system/files/cmu-first-status-report_en.pdf.

[5] ibid 23.

[6] BIS, 'SME Access to External Finance' (BIS Economics Paper No 16, 2012) 19ff, available at www.gov.uk/government/uploads/system/uploads/attachment_data/file/32263/12-539-sme-access-external-finance.pdf.

[7] 'Crowdfunding in the EU Capital Markets Union' (3 May 2016) SWD(2016) 154 final, available at http://ec.europa.eu/finance/general-policy/docs/crowdfunding/160428-crowdfunding-study_en.pdf.

[8] L Collins and Y Pierrakis, 'The Venture Crowd: Crowdfunding Equity – Investment into Business', *Nesta*, July 2012, 4, available at www.nesta.org.uk/sites/default/files/the_venture_crowd.pdf.

[9] T Rodríguez de las Heras Ballell, 'A Comparative Analysis of Crowdfunding Rules in the EU and U.S', Stanford TTLF Working Paper Series, Working Paper no 28, available at https://law.stanford.edu/publications/no-28-a-comparative-analysis-of-crowdfunding-rules-in-the-eu-and-u-s; see also T Rodríguez de las Heras Ballell, 'Las plataformas de financiación participativa (crowdfunding) en el Proyecto de Ley de Fomento de la Financiación Empresarial: Concepto y funciones' (2014) 15 *Revista de Derecho del Mercado de Valores* 8.

Recent studies provide data endorsing the revolutionary potential of crowdfunding for the future of the business finance market.[10]

Three concurrent factors explain its emergence and increasing popularity.[11] Although the above-described retraction in traditional financing sources and the narrowing of available credit are the trigger for the need to search for alternative funding sources, a social factor and a technological enabler have been decisive in forming the current shape of crowdfunding.

On the one hand, a social movement towards the empowering of communities has encouraged the design of bottom-up processes and decentralised structures. Crowdfunding takes advantage of crowd-based decision-making, collective creation and innovation, and virality of digital activities, and applies them to the funding of projects or businesses.[12] As a matter of fact, crowdfunding seems to be inspired by and, at the same time, share to a great extent, the philosophy of the growing 'sharing economy'. This describes an economic model that is fuelled by trust,[13] is built of communities and evolves through interaction,[14] collaboration and co-participation relationships.[15]

On the other hand, the advent of electronic platforms has created the ideal structural conditions for realising an authentic crowd-based financing alternative. Digital technology has been a powerful enabler for the creation of multilateral environments based on centralised management, peer-to-peer interaction schemes and contract-based operations.[16]

II. Crowdfunding: Concept and Variations

According to the description formulated by the World Bank, 'crowdfunding is an Internet-enabled way for businesses or other organizations to raise money in the form of either donations or investments from multiple individuals'.[17] Certainly, in its infancy,

[10] InfoDev/World Bank, 'Crowdfunding's Potential for the Developing World' (2013), available at www.infodev.org/infodev-files/infodev_crowdfunding_study_0.pdf, estimated the total market potential for crowdfunding by 2025 would be up to US$90–96 billion per year, ie 1.8 times today's global venture capital industry.

[11] As previously explained in T Rodríguez de las Heras Ballell, 'El Crowdfunding como mecanismo alternativo de financiación de proyectos' (2014) 1 *Revista de Derecho Empresarial* 121, available at www.redemcr.org/contenido/el-crowdfunding-como-mecanismo-alternativo-de-financiacion-de-proyectos.

[12] InfoDev/World Bank, Crowdfunding's Potential (2013) 8.

[13] N Luhman, 'Familiarity, confidence, trust: problems and alternatives' in DG Gambetta (ed), *Trust* (New York, Basil Blackwell, 1988) 94–107; F Fukuyuma, *Trust: The Social Virtues and the Creation of Prosperity* (New York, The Free Press, 1995); JD Lewis and A Weigert, 'Trust as a Social Reality' (1985) 63 *Social Forces* 967.

[14] Y Benkler, *The Wealth of Networks: How Social Production Transforms Market and Freedom* (New Haven, Yale University Press, 2006).

[15] The community-building approach is further elaborated on in Teresa Rodríguez de las Heras Ballell, 'Refusal to Deal, Abuse of Rights and Competition Law in Electronic Markets and Digital Communities' (2014) 22 *European Review of Private Law* 685.

[16] A comprehensive analysis of platform-based models and proposals for devising a legal framework in T Rodríguez de las Heras Ballell, *Régimen Jurídico de los Mercados Electrónicos Cerrados (e-Marketplaces)* (Madrid, Marcial Pons, 2006). A new updated overview of platforms as a prior assessment for a prospective EU regulatory action, T Rodríguez de las Heras Ballell, 'The Legal Anatomy of Electronic Platforms: A Prior Study to Assess the Need of a Law of Platforms in the EU' (2017) 3 *The Italian Law Journal* 149.

[17] InfoDev/World Bank (n 10) 8.

crowdfunding appeared on the market simply as a 'crowd-based funding' method. Nonetheless, it promptly evolved into a more comprehensive model assisting entrepreneurs and SMEs, especially in developing their business strategy. Today, crowdfunding provides more than just funding.[18] Crowdfunding permeates the whole business model and helps project promoters to launch marketing campaigns, test markets, interact with clients, validate products and process feedback.[19] At present, crowdfunding is a more complex phenomenon with varied implications.

It is commonplace to classify crowdfunding models into several variations according to the nature of the relationship entered into between contributors and promoters and the main driving motivations of funders.[20] Beyond mere classification purposes, the interest in identifying the diverse categories and their differences is multi-fold. First, through the spectrum of crowdfunding variations one can trace and discover the evolutionary line of crowdfunding. Second, it is easier to visualise and more clearly understand the scope and application of the regulatory rules that have been enacted or are in the process of being adopted. Here, a cross comparison of different crowdfunding models reveals how a variety of interest-protection mechanisms is available, but that they are different in each case. Thirdly, as the market moves towards financial crowdfunding models, namely equity-based and debt-based crowdfunding, the impact on corporate governance requirements and on business strategy needs appreciably intensifies.

Within the context outlined above, the following variations are already quite familiar in European jurisdictions. In donation-based crowdfunding, donors contribute to projects without expecting any monetary or financial compensation. Reward-based crowdfunding has several variations. In pure reward models, funders receive a token gift of appreciation in return for the contribution. Under pre-sale models, however, the amount contributed by funders represents advance payment of the price for the provision of future services or delivery of goods. Unlike pure rewards, where the value of the gift is symbolic, in pre-sale crowdfunding the contribution may equal the price.

Invoice trading is a form of asset-based financing whereby promoters sell unpaid invoices or receivables, individually or in a bundle, to a pool of investors through the crowdfunding platform. Should the crowdfunding model be based on debt, funders contribute an amount of money that will be deemed a loan. Accordingly, they will receive in return a debt instrument entitling them to interest and return of principal on the stipulated date. In social lending models, however, no interest is expected. More sophisticated models are equity-based ones. Two variations may operate here.[21] The

[18] 'In addition to providing an alternative source of financing directly, crowdfunding can offer other benefits to firms: it can give proof of concept and idea validation to the project seeker; help attract other sources of funding, such as venture capital and business angels; give access to a large number of people providing the entrepreneur with insights and information; and be a marketing tool if a campaign is successful.' 'Crowdfunding in the EU Capital Markets Union' (2016) 3.

[19] JH Armour and L Enriques, 'The Promise and Perils of Crowdfunding: Between Corporate Finance and Consumer Contracts' (2018) 81 *Modern Law Review* 51.

[20] K Buysere, O Gajda, R Kleverlaan and D Marom, 'A Framework for European Crowdfunding' (2012) 10ff, available at http://eurocrowd.winball2.de/wp-content/blogs.dir/sites/85/2013/06/FRAMEWORK_EU_CROWDFUNDING.pdf.

[21] Association for UK Interactive Entertainment, 'UKIE Crowd Funding Report: A Proposal to Facilitate Crowd Funding in the UK' (February 2012) 2, available at http://ukie.org.uk.

securities model implies that investors receive equity instruments in return for their investment and become partners/shareholders of the funded company. Contrarily, the collective investment scheme (CIS) model does not deem funders' contributions to be equity. Funders can only participate in profits under profit-sharing arrangements without exercising ownership or partners' rights. Therefore, the second category may be more accurately defined as investment-based crowdfunding. Independently of the adopted classification, these variants may be grouped under a financial-crowdfunding sub-category insofar as the central benefit is the expected financial return.[22]

All the above-mentioned crowdfunding variations co-exist in the market, but with different levels of popularity, intensity of presence and potential for growth depending on the sector.[23] Nonetheless, an invisible line of evolution can be traced – not from non-commercial financial models (donation and reward) but from more conventional, commercial financial models, namely, lending and equity, in recent times.[24] The trend towards financial models has contributed to crowdfunding emerging as a real alternative to traditional financing techniques.

Furthermore, that progressive shift has immediately attracted regulators' attention and increasingly aroused legal concerns. Considering existing regulations, regulatory and supervisory focus has undoubtedly been placed on financial models, namely, equity-based crowdfunding and lending crowdfunding repayable with interest. Funders in donation-based and reward-based crowdfunding models would arguably be protected by general contract rules and consumer protection legislation, but lending and equity-based variations invade the realm of the financial regulations, interweaving multiple public and private interests. Although specific risks have been identified and denounced in non-financial crowdfunding, greater concern arises from financial models of crowdfunding. The legislative milestones reached up until now and the path of regulation reveal the focus of the approach.

Concurrently, the progressive intensification of institutional involvement in crowdfunding is reported.[25] Venture capital, angel investors and even bank entities

[22] Nonetheless, very interestingly, adding potential nonfinancial benefits (entertainment value, political expression, patron of the arts, altruism, community and creativity) to the expectation or chance of financial return could make securities crowdfunding (overall, financial variants) more attractive, even than donation-based or reward-based: AA Schwartz, 'The Nonfinancial Returns of Crowdfunding' (2015) 34 *Review of Banking and Financial Law* 565.

[23] A large percentage of platforms were involved in reward-based crowdfunding (30%), followed by platforms involved in equity crowdfunding (23%) and loan-based crowdfunding (21%). 'Crowdfunding in the EU Capital Markets Union' (n 7).

[24] According to the '2nd European Alternative Finance Industry Report' prepared by the Cambridge Center for Alternative Finance (September 2016) (available at www.jbs.cam.ac.uk/fileadmin/user_upload/research/centres/alternative-finance/downloads/2016-european-alternative-finance-report-sustaining-momentum.pdf): 'Peer-to-peer consumer lending is the largest market segment of alternative finance, with €366m recorded for 2015 in Europe. Peer-to-peer business lending is the second largest segment with €212m, with equity-based crowdfunding in third with €159m and reward-based crowdfunding, fourth, with €139m in 2015. However, invoice trading is the fastest-growing alternative finance model in Europe registering €81m in 2015, up significantly from the low base of just €7m in 2014' (p 20). Even if in global terms, donation- and reward-based crowdfunding is still ranking second in amount ($5.5b) as per Massolution 'Crowdfunding Industry 2015 Report' (available at http://crowdexpert.com/crowdfunding-industry-statistics).

[25] Revealingly, in 2015 the European Investment Bank approved a pilot project to provide financing to small and medium-sized enterprises (SMEs) in the UK through a crowdlending platform, for an amount

increasingly co-invest, along with or in parallel to 'crowd investors' through crowdfunding platforms. This trend would confirm the thesis that crowdfunding is permeating the financial markets beyond the limits of the 'finance-gap' area and is shaping an entire financing model. The growing involvement of both institutional and professional investors, and the consequent increase in the average amount of contributions, is also enabling a continuous expansion of sectors and industries. Thus, crowdfunding activity is increasing in renewable energy and real estate.

From the perspective of corporate governance and business strategy, crowdfunding affects various layers. Donation-based crowdfunding and, above all, reward crowdfunding in the pre-sale model exert a visible influence on product design and the deployment of business strategy.[26] It illustrates the contrast with traditional financing contexts where entrepreneurs first seek funds in order to subsequently run the project and attract clients. In contrast, crowdfunding encourages entrepreneurs to restructure the stages of the business strategy process. Hence, promoters first publish their project, test the market, attract clients/users and, subsequently, with a critical mass of clients and a tested idea, address prospective investors for fund-raising. Donation and reward crowdfunding infuse business models with the opportunity to exploit different priorities and competitive advantages.

Lending and, primarily, equity-based crowdfunding are the types that more directly influence promoters' corporate governance requirements and corporate structure. Certainly, as further discussed below, the crowd of investors/lenders calls for a corporate structure that is suitable for managing scattered and numerous financial partners. Likewise, the funding campaign requires more sophisticated and complex disclosures similar to standards that underpin the transparency paradigm in financial markets. However, crowdfunded projects lack a genuine trading market providing liquidity. As a consequence, promoters have to deal with entry and exit requests from existing and prospective investors using available company law tools. This inside effect has nevertheless been mostly disregarded in recent regulations on crowdfunding. Specific solutions provided by funding platforms, creative responses formulated by promoters or the general rules of company laws are the main boundary markers for exploring issues and proposing possible solutions.

As a consequence of the high illiquidity of crowdfunding securities, market price does not adjust depending on demand.[27] Yet, equity-crowdfunding investors are much more exposed than those investing in regulated markets where market price incorporates publicly available information and therefore represents the best estimate of securities' value.

of approximately £100m (European Investment Bank, 2015). Likewise, as per the market survey conducted within the EU, 45% of platforms in the UK reported institutional involvement. Cambridge Centre for Alternative Finance and Nesta, 'Pushing Boundaries: The 2015 UK Alternative Finance Industry Report' (February 2016), available at www.nesta.org.uk/sites/default/files/pushing_boundaries_0.pdf.

[26] P Crosetto and T Regner, 'Crowdfunding: Determinants of Success and Funding Dynamics', Jena Economic Research Papers, 2014-035.

[27] Armour and Enriques, 'The Promise and Perils of Crowdfunding' (2018) 59.

III. Regulatory Model for Funding Platforms: 'Outside Effect'

The number of crowdfunding platforms and funded projects has skyrocketed in recent years[28] and the average amount of funds raised has significantly increased.[29] Interestingly, an expansion of crowdfunding beyond micro-credits and micro-investments is more and more visible. Some expansion trends clearly reveal the ambitious enlargement of the scope of crowdfunding. First, as indicated above, the participation of accredited investors or the running of funding platforms where solely accredited investors are eligible entails an increase in investments, funds raised and projects.[30] Second, business angels and venture capitalists are acknowledging more and more the great added value that funding platforms contribute to the financing process (reduction of transaction costs, transparency, centralisation of resources, economies of scale, rating services, provision of searchers, comparators or aggregators). Accordingly, these professional and institutional investors are willing to participate as users (prospective investors) in crowdfunding platforms.[31] Wisely, funding platforms are not only filling the gap left by the shift of banks and investors towards later stages of the finance curve, but they are also serving as enablers and intermediaries at the very core of professional investment. Thirdly, as an example of how project budget is increasing and how the focus on start-up projects is being displaced to other economic sectors further from genuinely innovative fields, real estate crowdfunding platforms are making their debut.[32]

Whereas some crowdfunding models, such as donation-based or reward-based ones, have peacefully settled in sectors (such as music, arts, scientific research) that

[28] According to the data provided by the Massolution 'Crowdfunding Industry 2015 Report' (n 24), fundraising volume in 2015 for the global industry is estimated in $34b, representing P2P lending $25b; reward and donation crowdfunding: $5.5b; and equity crowdfunding $2.5b. See previous data and statistics in 'Crowdfunding Industry Report. Market Trends, Composition and Crowdfunding platforms', Massolution (May 2012), www.crowdsourcing.org. Growth by region prediction for 2015 was estimated of 82% for North America and 98.6% for Europe. In predicted funding volume, however, North American region leads the industry with $17.2b whereas Europe ranks at a third position with $6.48b and the Asian region is second with $10.54b.

[29] 'Mapping EU Markets and Events Study' (European Commission Crowdfunding, 30 September 2015), available at http://ec.europa.eu/finance/general-policy/docs/crowdfunding/20150930-crowdfunding-study_en.pdf.

[30] 'Online platforms for accredited investors are fuelling the continued growth in angel investing', according to the Angel Capital Association, '2015 PENSCO Crowdfunding Report' (20 March 2015), available at http://info.pensco.com/2015-crowdfunding-report.

[31] JK Haar, RE Lee and JK Haar Jr in 'The Institutional Crowd' in '2015 PENSCO Crowdfunding Report' (ibid) 38–40 do vehemently endorse this tendency: 'The continuing evolution of the industry can be expected to result in a number of related trends, including a growing interest among traditionally institutional sponsors, […], to use crowdfunding platforms for larger, higher profile investments. […] We also believe that the type of opportunities sponsors allocate to crowdfunding platforms will broaden – from basic debt and equity offerings to preferred and mezzanine capital. Finally, larger funds, private REITs and other national operators will be attracted to the lower cost of raising capital and streamlined investor relations that web portals provide, as well as the expanded access to private accredited investors and family offices.' See also WealthInsight Report at www.wealthinsight.com/IndexReports, estimating the growth prediction of high-net-worth individuals.

[32] As per '2015CF-RE. Crowdfunding for Real Estate', Report prepared by Crowdsourcing, available at http://reports.crowdsourcing.org/?route=product/product&product_id=52, real estate crowdfunding has emerged as one of the most attractive crowdfunding categories with significant growth rates and appreciable higher average amounts per campaign. According to these data, real estate crowdfunding grew 156% in 2014, breaking the $1 billion mark, with campaigns ranging in size from less than $100,000 to over $25 million. In global terms, real estate crowdfunding is expected to increase by 150%, equalling $2.57 billion in 2015, making it one of the fastest-growing industry segments of crowd capitalism.

eagerly claimed the diversification of financing sources, the purely financial version, namely, equity crowdfunding and debt crowdfunding, soon aroused legal concerns and attracted regulators' attention, insofar as it invades the natural field of regulated markets. Notwithstanding the complexity added by the cross-border, or delocalised, factor in crowdfunding financing transactions, general contract rules and consumer laws apply to donation-based and reward-based crowdfunding. Therefore, general protection mechanisms for consumer transactions would be activated in the pre-sales, reward-based or, to a certain extent, donation-based model. Nonetheless, such crowdfunding schemes are not totally free of legal concerns. It might be well worth noting, for instance, that the mere conceptualisation of crowdfunding financing transactions as being consumer transactions in all cases is indeed questioned. In pre-sales models where the promoter carries out the activity on a regular basis, the application of consumer rules is more easily justified. However, in many peer-to-peer (P2P) transactions (activities that are undertaken sporadically, such as micro-credit for personal/family purposes, donations for non-professional projects, social lending, non-habitual activities) the imbalance between parties is less and this undermines claims for weak-party protection.

In contrast, lending and equity-based crowdfunding encroach upon highly regulated sectors. Attempts to subsume these transactions within the general legal framework for lending contracts and corporate finance might not be enough. Supervision and schemes to regulate intermediaries, market conditions and client protection rules require more complex consideration than just devising legal machinery for financial crowdfunding.[33]

The regulatory challenges posed by crowdfunding have been addressed at different pace in the EU and the US. As a consequence, both the adopted approach and the resulting regulatory outcomes differ appreciably.

US Rules on Crowdfunding are essentially comprised of the legal provisions of Title III 'Capital Raising Online While Deterring Fraud and Unethical Non-Disclosure Act of 2012' of *Jumpstart Our Business Startups Act*,[34] *JOBS Act* (hereinafter, US Crowdfund Act), which is implemented by the final rules adopted by the Securities Exchange Commission (SEC) under the Securities Act of 1933 and the Securities Exchange Act of 1934 (hereinafter, SEC Rules or SEC Regulation or Crowdfunding Regulation).[35] The final rules and forms went into effect May 16, 2016, except that instruction 3 adding part 227 and instruction 14 amending Form ID went into effect 29 January 2016.

The EU Rules on Crowdfunding are multiple and combine domestic bespoke regimes and EU-harmonised rules. The legal regime for crowdfunding within the EU is the (incomplete) outcome of a process of integrating EU-wide general rules on financial

[33] Nonetheless the foregoing assumption, regulatory approaches in different jurisdictions may differ and depart from the presumed conclusion that equity crowdfunding would be more stringently regulated than reward crowdfunding. A comparison between US and UK approaches better illustrate the possible diverging policies. Whereas, under the framework of EU law, UK has essentially encouraged securities crowdfunding with a disclosure-obligation-exempting solution, the US opts for requiring appreciable disclosure obligations. Contrariwise, reward crowdfunding is subject to broad consumer protection laws in the UK, deriving from EU laws, whereas in the US they are no equivalent solution. As clearly explained by Armour and Enriques (n 19) 64.

[34] HR 3606, of 5 of April of 2012.

[35] 17 CFR Parts 200, 227, 232, 239, 240, 249, 269 and 274 [Release Nos. 33–9974; 34–76324; File No S7-09-13] RIN 3235-AL37.

markets, domestic general rules, and nationwide crowdfunding-specific regimes. Therefore, the legal framework is multi-layered. In general terms, there are two regulatory approaches. First, there is the approach led by the attempt to subsume debt- and equity-crowdfunding in existing legal categories. In that regard, some EU Directives[36] tackle crowdfunding-related issues, although the directives were not originally envisioned to regulate crowdfunding. This approach achieves stability and provides a common playing field for all market players, both traditional and newcomers. Besides, since these rules are adopted at a European level, albeit under the form of Directive, harmonisation across the EU is potentially higher. But this approach may to fail address the particularities of crowdfunding and, as a consequence, block the emergence of the new sector with unsuitable requirements. Second, some national jurisdictions have enacted, or are planning to adopt, specific legislation for crowdfunding – in most of the cases, for lending and equity crowdfunding.

The EU is also working on a harmonisation solution for crowdfunding. To that end, an expert group called the European Crowdfunding Stakeholders Forum (ECSF) was set up in June 2014 to assist the European Commission in exploring the potential and the risks of this growing form of finance, as well as the national legal frameworks applicable to it, in order to identify whether there should be a European-level policy action in this field. Compared to the non-specific approach, this one is more likely to produce a consistent solution covering all legal issues related to crowdfunding. Nonetheless, there is a risk of treating market players providing competing financial services differently (traditional financial intermediaries and funding platforms) – which must be carefully managed and attenuated. It is argued that given the predominantly local nature of crowdfunding and the limited cross-border activity – as revealed by available data[37] – there is no strong case for EU-level policy intervention at present. National frameworks that have been developed so far are considered by the Commission to be broadly consistent in terms of the objectives and outcomes, even if they are tailored to local markets and domestic regulatory approaches. Therefore, EU monitoring of the

[36] Directive 2003/71/EC of 4 November 2003, on the prospectus to be published when securities are offered to the public or admitted to trading, as amended by Directive 2010/73/EU of 24 November 2010 [2010] OJ L327/1 (Prospectus Directive), subsequently repealed by Regulation (EU) 2017/1129 of the European Parliament and of the Council of 14 June 2017 on the prospectus to be published when securities are offered to the public or admitted to trading on a regulated market, and repealing Directive 2003/71/EC Text with EEA relevance regulates fund-raising by companies. Directive 2009/65/EC of 13 July 2009 on the coordination of laws, regulations and administrative provisions relating to undertakings for collective investment in transferable securities [2009] OJ L302/32 deals with fundraising by investment companies. Directive 2006/48/EC of 14 June 2006 relating to the taking up and pursuit of the business of credit institutions [2006] OJ L177/1 (Capital Requirements Directive) and Directive 2009/110/EC of 16 September 2009 on the taking up, pursuit and prudential supervision of the business of electronic money institutions [2009] OJ L267/7 (E-Money Directive) governs crowdfunding platforms, and Directive 2011/61/EU of 8 June 2011 on Alternative Investment Fund Managers [2011] OJ L174/1 (Alternative Investment Fund Manager Directive) regulates their dealings with investment companies. Directive 2004/39/EC of 21 April 2004 on markets in financial instruments [2004] OJ L145/1 (Market in Financial Instrument Directive, MiFID), repealed by Directive 2014/65/EU of the European Parliament and of the Council of 15 May 2014 on markets in financial instruments and amending Directive 2002/92/EC and Directive 2011/61/EU – and Regulation (EU) No 600/2014 of the European Parliament and of the Council of 15 May 2014 on markets in financial instruments and amending Regulation (EU) No 648/2012 can also impact on the regulation of crowdfunding platforms.

[37] According to the '2nd European Alternative Finance Industry Report' (2016) prepared by the Cambridge Center for Alternative Finance (n 24), data reveal that market activity in the crowdfunding sector remains mostly domestic. Their findings show that foreign inflows (none in 46% of the operating platforms) and foreign outflows (none in 76% of the platforms) represent very limited percentages in the whole activity.

sector can be expected to test the adequacy of national approaches and their progressive degree of convergence, to facilitate the consideration of a more intense response at EU level. Finally, it has been published in the last quarter of 2017 an inception impact assessment in relation to a *legislative proposal for an EU framework on crowd and peer-to-peer finance*, to inform stakeholders and allow them to provide feedback on this initiative.[38]

In accordance with the latest overview of the crowdfunding regulatory frameworks (updated January 2017) provided by the Expert Group of the European Securities Committee, the following EU Member States have adopted bespoken regimes for investment-based crowdfunding: Austria (1 September 2015),[39] Belgium ('crowdfunding exception' in prospectus regime, 17 May 2014), Spain (29 April 2015),[40] France (1 October 2014),[41] United Kingdom (1 April 2014),[42] Italy (17 December 2012, Law, and 26 June 2013, Regulation),[43] Germany (10 July 2015),[44] Portugal (24 August 2015 pending regulatory ruling to enter into force),[45] Finland (1 September 2016)[46] and Lithuania (1 December 2016).[47] With regard to lending-based crowdfunding, only a few countries have adopted specific rules: Spain (within the scope of the Crowdfunding legislation, 29 April 2015), France (within the scope of the Crowdfunding regulations, 1 October 2014), UK (within the scope, 1 April 2014), and Portugal (expected).

[38] https://ec.europa.eu/info/law/better-regulation/initiatives/ares-2017-5288649_en.

[39] Federal Act on alternative means of financing (Alternative Financing Act – *Alternativfinanzierungsgesetz, AltFG*) – Obligations for issuing bodies as well as operators of internet platforms ('crowdfunding') regarding the financing of terrorism (s 4, para 5 and s 5 para 1 (2)), Federal Law Gazette Vol I No 114/2015).

[40] Business Finance Promotion Act, number 5 of 2015 (hereinafter, LFFE 2015), of 27 of April (*Ley 5/2015, de 27 de abril, de Fomento de la Financiación Empresarial*), as published in the Official Bulletin (BOE) num 101, of 28 of April of 2015. Title V is entirely devoted to crowdfunding platforms legally named 'Plataformas de Financiación Participativa'.

[41] *Décret n° 2014-1053 du 16 septembre 2014 relatif au financement participatif/Ordonnance n° 2014-559 du 30 mai 2014. Ordonnance n° 2014-559 du 30 mai 2014 relative au financement participatif*, JORF n°0125 du 31 mai 2014 page 9075, texte n° 14, available at www.legifrance.gouv.fr/eli/ordonnance/2014/5/30/FCPX1406454R/jo/texte (*Ordonnance*).

[42] Policy statement 14/4, 'The FCA's regulatory approach to crowdfunding over the internet, and the promotion of non-readily realisable securities by other media', March 2014, available at www.fca.org.uk/static/documents/policy-statements/ps14-04.pdf (PS 14/4). FCA's February 2015 'Review of the regulatory regime for crowdfunding and the promotion of non-readily realizable securities by other media', available at www.fca.org.uk/static/documents/crowdfunding-review.pdf (the *Review*). Financial Services and Markets Act 2000 (FSMA). A call for input to the post-implementation review of FCA's crowdfunding rules was conducted and concluded in 8 September 2016: www.fca.org.uk/publications/calls-input/post-implementation-review-fca-crowdfunding-rules.

[43] *Legge 221/2012*, of 17 December 2012, *di conversione in legge, con modificazioni, del decreto-legge 18 ottobre 2012, n. 179, recante ulteriori misure urgenti per la crescita del Paese.*(12G0244), in force since 13th of January of 2014. Subsequently, CONSOB (*Commissione Nazionale per le Società e la Borsa*) adopted *Regolamento sulla raccolta di capitali di rischio da parte di start-up innovative tramite portali on-line. Delibera* num. 18592 and the attached Regulation of 26 of June of 2013 were published in *Gazzetta Ufficiale* num. 162 dated on 12 of July of 2013.

[44] Small Investor Protection Act, *Kleinanlegerschutzgesetz, Budesgesetzbakatt Teil I*, 2015, Nr 28 vom 09.07.2015.

[45] Lei n° 102/2015 de 24 de agosto, *Regime jurídico do financiamento colaborativo, Diário da República*, First série (in Portuguese) – N° 164 – 24 August 2015.

[46] Press release on Finnish Crowdfunding Act at http://vm.fi/artikkeli/-/asset_publisher/joukkorahoituslaki-tuo-toimialalle-kevytta-saantelya?_101_INSTANCE_C91M3tdJeutx_languageId=en_US.

[47] A brief note on the enactment of the legislation and an outline of the main points of the Lithuanian Crowdfunding Act is available at www.crowdfundinsider.com/2016/11/92020-lithuania-approves-bespoke-crowdfunding-regulations-platforms-may-raise-e5-million.

All the regulatory initiatives stem from observing that funding platforms have entered the capital market scene and joined the ecosystem of financial intermediaries. A number of regulatory and supervisory issues immediately derive from that development. This is the most visible effect of crowdfunding – the *outside effect* – which regulators have perceived and skilfully tackled. Tellingly, many of the rules adopted so far deal with issues such as risk management goals, protecting investors' interests, preventing systemic effects, ensuring smooth functioning of the market and enhancing transparency.[48]

Schematically, regulations adopted at all levels provide for rules relating to three actors engaged in crowdfunding financing, namely funding platforms, project promoters and investors/lenders ('the crowd'). These three pillars of regulation are discussed below.

A. Crowdfunding Platforms

With regard to crowdfunding platforms, although legal models differ in their specific requirements, the regulatory schemes are essentially underpinned by several or all the following elements: registration, licence/approval and prudential requirements (minimum capital, insurance, organisational form). Under such a regulatory policy, two main approaches seem to be feasible.

On the one hand, countries may opt to subject crowdfunding platform operators to the general rules of financial intermediaries provided that the operators effectively provide regulated services (for example, under the US Crowdfund Act). A funding platform must hold a broker licence and comply with broker-dealer regulations. On the other hand, legislators may decide to devise a new (bespoke) legal framework for crowdfunding platforms. Newly adopted regulatory requirements may arguably result in a trade-off between (1) the need to protect involved interests and prevent unfair competition with incumbent players; and (2) the inadvisability of imposing an excessive regulatory burden on crowdfunding platforms, which is likely to asphyxiate the emerging sector. So, in France, platform operators must obtain a newly created licence as an 'investment-crowdfunding adviser' (*conseillers en investessements participatifs*) (Ordonnance No 2014-559, Art 1).[49] As well, in Spain, under the Business Finance Promotion Act 2015 (LFFE 2015),[50] platforms have to be registered, obtain a licence and be named, on an exclusive basis, as a 'participative financing platform' (*Plataforma de Financiación Participativa* (PFP)). Italy provides an alternative hybrid model, as platforms must be attached to a financial institution.

[48] JF Baritot, 'Increasing Protection for Crowdfunding Investors Under the Jobs Act' (2012) 13 *UC Davis Business Law Journal* 259; E Burkett, 'A Crowdfunding Exemption? Online Investment Crowdfunding and U.S. Securities Regulation' (2011) 13 *Transactions: Tennessee Journal of Business Law* 63; AC Fink, 'Protecting the Crowd and Raising Capital through the Crowdfund Act' (2012) 90 *University of Detroit Mercy Law Review* 1; R Weinstein, 'Crowdfunding in the U.S. and Abroad: What to Expect When You're Expecting' (2013) 46 *Cornell International Law Journal* 428.

[49] n 41.

[50] n 40.

Under the EU approach, four broad models of authorisation for crowdfunding platforms adopted by EU Members in accordance with national legislation can be identified. First, authorisation under EC Directive 2004/39/EC[51] and related Directives grants a passport to carry out regulated services and activities throughout the EU (Austria, Germany and France, for transferable securities). This Directive (also known as MiFID, short for Markets in Financial Instruments Directive) enables crowdfunding platforms to provide specified investment services listed in the Directives in relation to listed financial instruments, in particular transferable securities (such as shares and bonds) or units of collective investment undertakings.

Second, there is the national authorisation model developed under the exemption provided in MiFID.[52] In this approach, employed in Italy, authorised platforms can carry on crowdfunding-related services and activities at national level also in relation to MiFID financial instruments, but they are not allowed to passport their activities across the EU without getting a full MiFID authorisation. In the third national model, authorisation for crowdfunding platforms enables them to carry out non-MiFID activities and/or activities not related to instruments covered by MiFID (such as stakes in private companies insofar as they are not deemed negotiable instruments). Spain and Portugal have adopted this model. The fourth national authorisation model is outside the MiFID framework and is tailored for crowdfunding platforms.

In sum, all the regulatory requirements create barriers to entry, limit the number of players in the market and impose costs on the platforms accordingly. On the other hand, regulatory requirements are expected to prevent fraud, enhance market stability, enable supervision and minimise risks. Compliance entails costs and, insofar as domestic regulations differ, forum shopping risk increases.

B. Investor Protection

Along with the commonplace protection measures, based on disclosure duties and due diligence requirements, a specific additional technique has been commonly implemented in crowdfunding regulations for investor protection purposes: fixing limits on the maximum investable amounts in crowdfunding. This legislative policy decision instils a visible degree of caution and containment in the crowdfunding sector. In practice, setting caps on investable amount restricts the magnitude of competition among finance sources and restrains the effective size of the crowdfunding market. Therefore, it represents a legal solution specifically tailored for crowdfunding transactions.

Although setting investment limits is then a commonplace measure for protecting investors in crowdfunding regulations (with exceptions of France, and, to a certain extent, Italy and UK), nevertheless, investment limits for protection purposes and the very formulation of such limits and their conditions have been debated, questioned

[51] European Council Directive 2004/39/EC (MiFID).

[52] Under MiFID, Art 3, Member States may choose not to apply the Directive to any person for whom they are the home Member State who: are not allowed to hold clients' funds or securities; are not allowed to provide any investment service except the reception and transmission of orders and the provision of investment advice; in the course of providing that service, are allowed to transmit orders only to authorized entities; provided that the activities of those persons are regulated at national level.

and reconsidered. On the one hand, they appear to be objective mechanisms and operate as effective loss-containing techniques, provided that the formulation is clear and easy to apply. But, on the other hand, they constrain the financial capacity of investors and, in practice, are based on setting thresholds with estimated figures and percentages that can always be challenged.

Not surprisingly, comments received by the SEC on the Proposing Release[53] to implement Title III of JOBS Act referred to investment limits and reflected opposing views regarding the establishment of any type of limits, the proposed amount, and the application of limits in practice. Member States' domestic legislation, if they have contemplated investment limits, differ in amount and scope. Local particularities and specific market conditions explain the diversity of formulations. These limitations take different forms and range from fixed maximum ceilings to variable shares of personal income, wealth or financial assets. Whereas under certain regulations these ceilings are calculated per offering, other specific regimes estimate based on the total investment in a given timeframe (typically, one year). In general, the investment limits depend on the categories of investors, which are classified as retail, sophisticated and professional investors; accredited and non-accredited investors; and natural and legal persons. In essence, such disparities prove the variability that the measure permits and the inconsistency of the underlying legal policy.

Regardless of these questions, investment limits are present in most crowdfunding regulations. Certainly, they prove to be effective loss-containing mechanism. Should the statutory language aim to clarify ambiguities and ensure easy calculations of maximum permitted amounts, investment limits may operate with objectivity and automatism. Likewise, the quantitative limitation of investment provides a resultant effective control of risks that facilitate insurability on both sides. Considering those advantages, the limit-based regulatory option has been preferred by regulators.

From a macro perspective, the option of investment limits also impacts the crowdfunding sector as a whole. Due to these limits on the investable amount in crowdfunding projects, it could be that crowdfunding remains a secondary investment option that completes investment decisions in other traditional areas in the investor's portfolio. At the same time, investment limits tend to preserve the crowd distribution structure of crowdfunding campaigns and preserve the micro character of the contribution, especially if the caps apply to all types of investors. The latter effect seems to reinforce the roots of crowdfunding as an alternative finance method for microfinance.

In general terms, quantitative caps are effective, easy to apply and free of interpretation difficulties. Nevertheless, protection purposes can be achieved or enhanced by the implementation of more sophisticated mechanisms. The provision of a set of obligations to inform helps potential investors to make an informed decision, assess risks and protect themselves. These mechanisms operate on a qualitative basis and alleviate the rigidities arising from the application of simple quantitative thresholds. Legislation does indeed combine both approaches.[54]

[53] Rel No. 33–9470 (23 October 2013) [78 FR 66427 (5 November 2013)] (the 'Proposing Release'), available at www.sec.gov/rules/proposed/2013/33-9470.pdf.

[54] Spanish legislation (LFFE 2015), for example, relies on a combination of limits on investment. First, investors are divided into two categories – accredited and not accredited – according to a set of criteria

Quantitative thresholds are intended to lessen the financial risk taken on by non-accredited investors. Certainly, setting a cap on investment per specific project reduces risk exposure in case of failure and forces diversification. Under Austrian[55] and Portuguese[56] laws, limits on investable amounts per year (and per individual and/or per project) established by statute are not applicable to legal persons and professional investors. German[57] rules fix different limits on investable amount according to a double test of available assets and monthly income.

It might be worth pointing out here some of the trust-generating formulas implemented in national legislation aiming to provide retail investors with additional factors to assess the risks and potential benefits of each project. The participation of professional investors or own funding platforms in crowdfunding campaigns is supposed to infuse credibility indicia into decision-making and valuation. In that regard, Italian regulation (Regolamento),[58] for example, requires that five per cent of the subscription of shares (equity crowdfunding) is to be made by professional investors. Professional investors are here playing the role of trusted third parties. A critical point to further investigate would be potential liability arising from wrong valuation by professional investors.

Theoretically, crowdfunding platforms could perform the role of trusted third parties as well. However, more legal concerns are aroused by the participation of funding platforms, because a trade-off between the prescription effect (trust generation) and the risk of conflict of interest should be carefully managed. On the one hand, when funding platforms are required to invest in every project they agree to publish, a serious valuation and precautionary risk analysis of the project can be expected to be undertaken by other investors. On the other hand, conflicts of interests are more likely to arise, insofar as the funding platform is no longer a neutral venue and is more inclined to favour projects in which it holds an interest or otherwise participates.

Spanish rules on crowdfunding illustrate how a compromise can be managed. First, funding platforms must formulate and publish a policy to prevent conflicts of interest and internal rules guiding the participation of the platform in projects. Secondly, funding platforms are entitled (but not obliged) to participate in any project that they publish within a limit. The platform's participation can neither be higher than ten per cent of the financing goal nor entitle it to control the company (LFFE 2015, Art 63). Moreover, in such cases, investors have to be readily informed about the participation (LFFE 2015, Arts 63.1.b and 63.2.b). Specific rules on the management of conflicts of interest, the obligation to adopt reasonable steps to avoid and prevent conflicts, and disclosure duties

(incomes, revenues, patrimony) (LFFE 2015, Art 81). Second, funding platforms are required to monitor non-accredited investors' investment decisions and prevent them from investing either more than €3,000 in the same project as published in one platform or a higher total amount of 10,000 in all projects published in the same platform within a period of 12 months (LFFE 2015, Art 82.1).

[55] Austria, Alternative Financing Act (Federal Act on alternative means of financing, Federal Law Gazette Vol I No 114/2015, *Alternativfinanzierungsgesetz*, AltFG), Obligations for issuing bodies as well as operators of Internet platforms ('crowdfunding') regarding the financing of terrorism (s 4 para 5 and s 5 para 1(2).

[56] Portugal (n 45).

[57] Germany (n 44).

[58] Italy (n 43).

are similarly provided for under Italian (Title III Regolamento),[59] Portuguese[60] and UK[61] regulations.

Nevertheless, it has long been discussed whether the simple fixing of investment limits, as well as accreditation requirements, are wise decisions, particularly given that non-accredited investors cannot request to be deemed accredited investors unless they can prove that they meet the accreditation criteria. As a matter of fact, some successful funding platforms operating before the enactment of the currently in-force legislation in Spain were intended to offer a platform for business angels (www.thecrowdangel.com). Average investing funds were far from micro-investments, for instance, with a minimum of €3,000 per contribution. Clearly under the newly enacted rules only accredited investors are eligible investors (LFFE 2015, Art 81). The rationale behind that crowdfunding business model is to exploit crowd-based benefits at a later stage of the business finance cycle. Searching, monitoring and transaction costs also impact on the investment process of business angels, venture capitalists and other private equity investors. Funding platforms provide them with a centralised venue to access available projects, compare variables, make selections in accordance with predetermined factors, exchange information, request further data and then decide about investing.

Additionally, SMEs are entitled to be deemed accredited investors on request, provided that the funding platform evaluates the requestor's experience and knowledge and ensures the investor can take informed investing decisions and understand the risks involved (LFFE 2015, Art 81.2.d). The reasonableness of limits is only to be assessed in relation to non-accredited investors. These points of reference can be compared to other jurisdictions.

US regulators elected to limit the amount and frequency of investments. Individuals can annually invest up to a threshold. If the investor's net worth plus income is less than US$40,000, he or she can only invest up to US$2,000. If his or her net worth and income combined are less than US$100,000, investment is limited to five per cent of his or her income. When income or net worth is greater than US$100,000, the investment limit is raised to 10 per cent of his or her income (US Crowdfund Act 2012, s 302).

C. Regulating Projects and Crowdfunding Campaigns

Rules applicable to project promoters and their crowdfunding campaigns are commonly classified in three areas: disclosure and information duties; liability for misstatements; and limits on the capital raised or a duty to prepare and issue a prospectus, depending on the size of the offer.

Along with other specific requirements (reporting, filing, advertising), in some jurisdictions, most regulations impose on promoters (issuers) disclosure duties,

[59] Italy, mainly Titolo III, *Regole di Condotta, Regolamento sulla raccolta di capitali di rischio da parte di start-up innovative tramite portali on-line* (n 43).

[60] Portugal, Lei 2015 (n 45), in particular Arts 11 and 21.

[61] Policy statement 14/4 (March 2014) (UK, FCA); see also Financial Conduct Authority, 'Review of the Regulatory Regime for Crowdfunding and the Promotion of Non-Readily Realisable Securities by Other Media' (April 2015).

and obligations to disclose risk warnings and information to platform operators and prospective investors. Except for some jurisdictions that make these obligations conditional upon certain thresholds (such as in Austria or Lithuania when the offer must be at least up to €100,000), disclosure is required in all equity-crowdfunding campaigns (the rest of EU Member States that have adopted specific regimes), and in crowd-lending campaigns where regulated (Spain, France, UK, Portugal). The rationale behind disclosure and risk warnings is to remedy underlying information asymmetries and enable well-informed and educated investment decisions by future investors. Given that, however, legislation differs on the policy decisions regarding the allocation of risks and obligations. Incentives-allocation outcomes are therefore diverse. Where some jurisdictions impose disclosure obligations on project promoters, others opt for placing these obligations on platform operators on an isolated basis (ie in Spain, except for the liability of the promoter on the information provided to investors) or concurrently with promoters (ie France, US SEC Final Rules p 68). These rules should be driven by the desire to allocate duties to the least cost avoider – the party who will incur the lowest cost of care to prevent or avoid risks or damages – and the desire to effectively implement measures to protect interests involved. From this perspective, promoters can better provide information about the project and the offer, whereas platform operators are prepared to supply information about the platform, general risks warnings about investing in the projects published on the platforms, and other key information relevant for investors in crowdfunding campaigns (Lithuania, Spain, Portugal or Finland). Under the US Crowdfunding Regulation, these disclosures and risk warnings are included in the educational material to be provided by the operators.[62]

Disclosure obligations are crucial in alleviating asymmetries, and should be carefully devised. The decision to impose obligations on platform operators defines the role of operators in different ways. At the same time, clear rules allocating obligations and risks enable operators to better devise their business models.

The other rule commonly included in existing crowdfunding regulations is the establishment of maximum amount of funds that can be raised through crowdfunding. Normally, setting this threshold is intimately associated with prospectus requirements in financial regulations. As a result, crowdfunding tends to fill the finance gap and is relieved of the formalities and complexities that offerings of certain magnitude are otherwise subject to. Within the EU, quantitative thresholds and time limits differ. A common threshold is €5 million over a 12-month period (Finland, Lithuania, UK or Italy). Spain lowers the threshold to €2 million per project and per platform and maintain the €5 million limit for offers limited to accredited investors. This latter condition is also embraced by Portugal, which also fixes a general limit of €1 million in all other cases.

Since the Commission published its report on 'Crowdfunding in the EU Capital Markets Union' in May 2016, several developments in the regulatory framework for crowdfunding activities have taken place, both at EU and the domestic level. On 8 December 2016, the European Parliament, the Council, and the Commission decided to revamp prospectus regulations in order to improve access to finance for companies

[62] Rule 302(b)(1) of Regulation Crowdfunding would require intermediaries to deliver to investors, at account opening, educational materials including a list of specific items.

and simplify information for investors. Under the reformed regulation, the smallest capital raisings and crowdfunding projects up to €1 million will not need to issue a prospectus at all. Thus, the costs and complexities for these projects are alleviated and the burden of the prospected lifted. On the other hand, some domestic legislative amendments aligned to the EU policy to enable access to finance have been undertaken. For example, a 2016 reform in France raised the size of offers from €1 million to €2.5 million per year per project.

Under the US regulatory framework, the exemption from registration provided by section 4(a)(6) is available to a US issuer provided that 'the aggregate amount sold to all investors by the issuer, including any amount sold in reliance on the exemption provided under [section 4(a)(6)] during the 12-month period preceding the date of such transaction, is not more than $1,000,000.' Consistent with the statute, Rule 100(a) of US Crowdfunding Regulation limits the aggregate amount sold to all investors by the issuer in reliance on the new exemption to $1 million during a 12-month period. Capital raised through other exempt transactions would not be counted in determining the aggregate amount sold in reliance on section 4(a)(6).

IV. Crowdfunded Businesses and Corporate Governance: The *Inside Effect*

Notwithstanding the regulation of crowdfunding discussed above, a second effect has been largely unperceived: the *inside effect*. This is about the effect crowdfunding has on the inside of the company raising capital from the crowd. In effect, a crowdfunding-based financing strategy challenges traditional company law rules. Rules governing non-public companies are, overall, neither well designed nor effectively operational for managing multiple dispersed partners, atomised capital and go-public-like demands. Since recent rules on crowdfunding are mainly inspired by capital-market regulatory concerns, the dysfunctions are amplified.

Non-public companies embarking on crowdfunding campaigns must suddenly struggle through an unfamiliar field of challenges. These include corporate governance requirements, disclosure duties, complex decision-making, exit strategies when facing illiquidity, finding pure investing partners, public exposure and reputational strategies. Is company law flexible enough to internalise all these required adaptations? Can solutions be implemented in bylaws? Or is legal reform needed? Moving forward, these are important questions for law and public policy. The challenges thrown up by crowdfunding are several. They include the issue of separation of ownership and control, liquidity problems for investors, and disclosure duties for crowdfunded businesses.

A. Separation of Ownership and Control

First, there is an issue concerning crowdfunded companies prioritising investors' interests over management's motivations and shareholding patterns in closely held corporations.[63] Under the traditional distinction between public and private (or more precisely, closely held) companies, the latter are commonly characterised by the singular involvement of shareholders[64] in company matters. Since the personal features of shareholders in closed corporations matter, they are not usually deemed to be simple investors but are supposed to be interested in decision-making, management and business development generally. With crowdfunding, a closely held corporation can become more and more open, in which case the presence of investors or purely financial shareholders is more and more likely.

In sum, starting from the hypothesis that many, albeit not all, companies launching crowdfunding campaigns are in the start-up stages of the evolutionary line, they will have to deal with different types of shareholders. Along with the founders and subsequent shareholders willing to engage in company issues, most other participants will be simply motivated by financial aims. Even more, a number of micro/small investors will co-exist with founding shareholders. Such a scattered, fragmented and extensive ownership base has to be managed.

Decision-making criteria, director appointment process and voting majorities should be devised accordingly. When a scattered and fragmented base of investing shareholders strengthens, on the one hand, control is concentred in a reduced number of shareholders. But on the other hand, if control is very extensive or broad-based, it may also dilute the decision-making process due to absenteeism, passivity and investors being motivated solely by financial interests in the form of higher dividends.

B. Liquidity for Investments: Some Possibilities

Secondly, equity investment in non-public companies is highly illiquid due to the absence of a secondary market. Therefore, exit options have to be carefully considered in bylaws. Illiquidity certainly is the weakest operational feature of crowdfunding as an alternative finance model compared to exchange markets or other functionally equivalent competing schemes. Crowdfunding emulates exchange markets' operation in the fundraising stage insofar as it facilitates the entry and escalates the benefits of collecting funds from the public. Yet today it is still unable to provide liquidity at the exit phase.

Along with business risks, crowd-investors have to face and manage exit risks. Crowdfunding investments lack the uniformity and standardisation that can enable negotiability in a liquid market. Investors are exposed to the risk of becoming prisoners of projects. Illiquidity is not a problem created or aggravated by crowdfunding.

[63] The general statement may certainly require precision and its accuracy depends on the crowdfunding model, kind of project, sector and other circumstances. In fact, the survey 'Crowdfunding from an Investor Perspective' (Financial Services Users Group, 2015) revealed that investors in P2P lending cared more about returns, while interest and excitement are more important drivers of investment in equity crowdfunding. Poor returns or losses are the most important risk factors. The survey is cited by the European Commission Staff Working Document, 'Crowdfunding in the EU Capital Markets Union' (n 7) 15.

[64] The term 'shareholders' is used, for convenience and simplification purposes, to refer to those 'members' of the company holding shares or parts or units of the company. In some jurisdictions, members of private companies, with separate legal personality and limited liability for members, would not be shareholders because capital stock is not divided into shares. The contributors of their capital are usually described as members in general.

Certainly, investors and business angels also face such exit difficulties when investing in start-ups and emerging businesses. Nevertheless, illiquidity does hamper the ability of crowdfunding to effectively compete with traditional financial markets. It would be reasonable to foresee that in response to illiquidity investors would tend to maintain their contributions at limited amounts. Accordingly, it would be very difficult for crowdfunding to take off.

It is therefore vital that crowdfunding platforms evolve and develop secondary market functionalities. Within the same crowdfunding platform, as an added-value service, or through another platform entirely specialising in enabling negotiability/liquidity, a secondary market to trade interests (shares, stakes, units) in crowdfunding projects can operate. Thus, funding platforms can be fuelled by higher liquidity. Although this service is not provided systematically, there are already some examples of different models and forms providing such secondary marketplaces.[65]

One model entails the direct involvement of the crowdfunding platform, enabling the connecting and interaction among investors who intend to sell and potential acquirers of such investments. In practice, such liquidity-providing platforms acting as emerging exchanges will likely compete with traditional markets. It might be predicted that the regulatory response would be similar to the approach initially followed in dealing with Alternative Trading Systems, or Multilateral Trading Facilities, as labelled under EU MiFID).[66] In another model, crowdfunding platforms may opt to collaborate with existing trading platforms for unlisted companies and thus enable investors to buy and sell securities that have been offered through crowdfunding platforms.

In enabling liquidity, any restriction on the transfer of shares, securities or other interests held by investors in crowdfunded companies as laid down in regulations (such as a minimum holding period or transfer solely under limited circumstances) should be taken into consideration to assess the scope and the feasibility of proposed secondary-market facilities. Likewise, provisions in shareholders'/partners' agreements will be relevant to assess the marketability of shares, securities or other interests.

C. Disclosure Duties for Crowdfunded Companies

Third, whereas publicly traded companies are familiar with multifarious disclosure duties, these duties can represent a huge burden for unlisted companies, particularly for small private enterprises.[67] Regulations on crowdfunding have essentially opted for

[65] European Commission Staff Working Document, 'Capital Markets Union: First Status Report' (n 4).

[66] J De Bel, 'Automated Trading Systems and the Concept of an "Exchange" in an International Context. Proprietary Systems: A Regulatory Headache!' (1993) 14 *University of Pennsylvania Journal of International Business Law* 169; R Lee, *What is an Exchange? The Automation, Management, and Regulation of Financial Markets* (Oxford, Oxford University Press 1998) 117–39; TH Maynard, 'What is an "Exchange"? Proprietary Electronic Securities Trading Systems and the Statutory Definition of an Exchange' (1992) 49 *Washington and Lee Law Review* 833; P Nyquist 'Failure to Engage: The Regulation of Proprietary Trading Systems' (1995) 13 *Yale Law and Policy Review* 281.

[67] Some commentators stress the enormous potential benefits of crowdfunding as being a genuine revolution for corporate finance. See, eg, T Privé, 'Top 10 Benefits of Crowdfunding', *Forbes*, 10 December 2012. But there have also been criticisms about the complexity of investments, difficulties in standardising the investment process and the high cost of regulation compliance (D Isenberg, 'The Road to Crowdfunding Hell', *Harvard Business Review*, 23 April 2012, available at https://hbr.org/2012/04/the-road-to-crowdfunding-hell).

disclosure duties as the most effective instrument to enhance transparency, market efficiency and investor protection. As in stock markets, project promoters have to disclose relevant information and provide the platform, prospective investors and investors with increasingly varied data.[68]

The ultimate aim is to prevent insider trading and ensure informed investing decisions. Benefits of large access to finance would arguably compensate publicly traded companies for the high cost of complying with disclosure duties. For start-ups and SMEs, however, the increasing information requirements might exhaust the expected benefits of collecting funds. Along with other legal concerns related to confidentiality issues and idea protection, disclosure and reporting duties in crowdfunding should ideally find an equilibrium between, on the one hand, the need to protect investors and promote market efficiency and, on the other, the costs for project promoters and the reasonableness of such duties, taking into consideration the size, early evolutionary stage and organisational base of enterprises.

In France and Portugal, the required information has to be provided in a certain document or format.[69] In the United Kingdom, there is a general obligation to provide sufficient information in a clear, fair and not misleading manner.[70] More interestingly, domestic laws differ in the solution adopted about the allocation of such disclosure of information duties and liability. Whereas under some legislation all obligations regarding information are imposed on the promoter, other legal models also entrust platform operators with some duties regarding the provision of sufficient information. Although responsibility for the information should be ultimately taken on by the promoter, the latter model would be expected to encourage platforms to implement procedures and rules to ensure that the required information is provided in a timely manner and is sufficient for investor decision-making.[71]

Certainly, if the specific aim of regulation reform is to provide regulatory relief to emerging growth companies to encourage initial public offerings, that should entail exemptions or phasing-in of certain requirements. But, if duties and requirements are not properly gauged, the process may become expensive and time-consuming.

V. Corporate Governance Structures for Crowdfunded Companies

It is important that crowdfunded (non-public) companies adopt appropriate structures for their governance. Certainly, crowdfunding provides an extraordinary

[68] See, eg, Spain (LFFE 2015, Arts 70, 72, 73, 75, 76, or 78); Portugal (Lei No 102/2015, Arts 14, 17 or 19).

[69] Under French regulations, key information has to be provided in a predefined template (Annex 1 to the Autorité des Marches Financiers (AMF) instruction DOC-2014-12). The format in which to provide the required information, as well as the key data to include, are considered in the public consultation launched by the Portuguese Securities Market Commission (CMVM) (Portuguese Financial Markets Authority 2015).

[70] United Kingdom (Financial Conduct Authority Review (UK) 2015); Spain (LFFE 2015, Art 70.1).

[71] Spanish legislation provides an illustrative example in that regard. LFFE 2015, Art 71 sets out that the platform shall ensure that the information supplied by the promoter is complete and provided in accordance with the legal provisions, and shall publish any information pertaining to the project and/or the promoter in its possession; LFFE 2015, Art 73 states that the promoters will be accountable to investors for all the information provided to the platform for publication.

opportunity for start-ups and SMEs, along with individuals and unincorporated businesses, to access finance. In return, project promoters opting for crowdfunding must accept market scrutiny. Likewise, should funding campaigns result in a wide and fragmented investing mass/crowd, promoters would suddenly face the complications, needs and challenges that openness entails and which a small/closely held corporation is not usually familiar with. The concluding section discusses some options for the governance of crowdfunded companies and the use of digital technologies in the effort.

A. Shareholder Participation and Digital Technologies

First, the crowdfunded company should protect and facilitate the exercise of shareholders' rights. Given the potentially high number of investors, the supposedly reduced participation in the company, the possible cross-border element, and the investing/financial profile of investors, crowdfunded companies will have to design and adopt corporate schemes to facilitate the decision-making process. In that regard, Spanish legislation requires that bylaws should include the right to participate and attend shareholders' meetings through electronic means and the right to use a proxy to be represented at meetings by any person (LFFE 2015, Art 80.1.a). Provisions regulating both rights necessarily have to be included in promoters' bylaws, and any provision in the bylaws that is likely to infringe the said legal provisions shall be null and void (LFFE 2015, Art 80.2). The use of digital technology in company operations can hugely minimise the corporate governance challenges for crowdfunded companies. The availability of digital functionalities for corporate purposes can remove obstacles to the free and widespread exercise of shareholders' rights.

Effective use of digital technology and implementation of interactive applications can facilitate the management of a company, irrespective of the size and the number of members, with due protection of different rights and interests. Nonetheless, an effective electronic exercise of rights has to be based on state-of-the-art electronic procedures and interactive environments. Cost and accessibility to technology are other important factors. Crowdfunding platforms can find here an appealing business opportunity. These platforms can decide to offer, as an added value to their users (promoters and investors), technological infrastructure to enable digital meetings, live interaction and other functionalities to assist promoters in the management of crowdfunded companies.

B. Dealing with Large Shareholder Bases

From a different perspective, the problem of a massive number of shareholders (especially minority shareholders) in start-ups or small-sized companies can be managed by the implementation of structural solutions aimed at 'isolating' crowdfunded corporations from their 'crowds'. According to applicable legislation, available options may differ.

i. Minimum Shareholding Requirements for Voting

The rationale of effective shareholder participation would be behind the need to consider fixing by bylaws the minimum number of shares to be held for attending and/or voting at company meetings. Otherwise, it might happen that shareholders' meetings become massive, that a quorum is in practice difficult to attain, or that the exercise of the right to be informed about company issues overloads company managers with information requests.

ii. Use of Non-Equity Models

Investment can be in convertible bonds that will be subsequently converted or be susceptible of conversion into equity within a specific period or at a specific date at a predetermined conversion rate – transitioning from debt-based crowdfunding to equity-based crowdfunding. Alternatively, investment can be articulated as a profit-sharing/revenue-sharing model. In such models, investors do not hold ownership interests in the company. Their contribution to and the participation in the project operate through contractual instruments (for example, silent partnerships, *cuentas en participación*), aimed at regulating distribution of revenues and, if agreed, losses.

iii. Use of Nominee Accounts

When possible under applicable legislation, investors may invest in the equity of a crowdfunded company through a nominee account, whereby a third party holds the legal title to the equity on behalf of the investors who would be beneficial owners of the securities. Crowdfunding platforms can also offer, require or simply permit the use of organisational vehicles to gather investors, unify and channel investors' decisions and participate as a sole shareholder in the crowdfunded company. In this structure, crowd-funded companies would benefit from having a more limited number of shareholders to deal with. There would be less complexity in managing a highly atomised ownership base, and the structure could also contribute to controlling transaction costs in enabling the effective exercise of shareholder rights, and streamlining company decision-making processes and structures.

iv. Intermediary Vehicles

In the intermediary organisational model, investors do not invest directly in crowd-funded companies; instead they join and participate in an organisational vehicle acting as an intermediary. The role of that vehicle is merely and solely instrumental, as it aims to merge dispersed and varied shareholders into a single layer and direct their participation on a unified basis towards the target company. At a second layer, the intermediary vehicle becomes a shareholder of the crowdfunded company. Investors only participate indirectly in the target company.

The intermediary vehicle, as a separate and distinct legal entity, may in principle adopt any legal form available under applicable legislation (partnership, closed corporation, limited liability company, stock corporation, collective investment scheme). It would be advisable to choose a legal form that is not too costly to create and sufficiently simple and flexible to manage. Should the intermediary vehicle be likely to generate costs, a decision to distribute and allocate such costs should be discussed.

If the prospective investors are expected to be minority partners, given the envisaged amount of their contributions, the allocation of costs associated with the intermediary-based structure to backers would seem inadequate and will very likely be a clear disincentive for small investors. Alternatively, either the platform or the promoter may consider taking responsibility for the structure. So, on the one hand, it might be offered as an added-value service provided by the platform, or, on the other hand, it might be assumed to be an inherent cost of the fund-raising process by the promoter. Besides, it should be remembered that any actions likely to delay the immediacy presumed in online transactions, to hinder the advantages of a non-intermediated financial environment or to complicate or prolong investment decisions may exert destructive effects on the competitiveness of crowdfunding models compared to other funding options. Consequently, the option for implementing any of the described structural schemes as a business strategy should be carefully considered.

Another critical issue is to ensure that the distribution of power according to investors' contributions in the vehicle is not distorted in the second stage and a reasonable level of representativeness is achieved. As the intermediary vehicle is the only genuine shareholder in the crowdfunded company, decision-making processes and management rules within the intermediary vehicle have to be carefully devised. Decisions are first adopted within the intermediary vehicle and, subsequently, its designated representative or agent will participate in deliberations and vote to adopt decisions in the target company's meetings. If the intermediary company internally applies measures aimed at limiting voting rights by fixing caps or imposing the holding of a minimum number of units/shares in order to attend meetings and/or to vote, the participation expectations of investors in the target company could be frustrated.

In fact, having voting majorities (minimum number of votes representing capital and/or number of members to validly adopt decisions) and quorum rules (minimum number of members holding or duly representing capital attending the meeting to deem it constituted) are also decisive issues. As an example, should the threshold for adopting decisions (voting majority) be too low, minority members in the intermediary vehicle will see their (indirect) representation significantly diluted in the target company.

The complexity of the implementation of an intermediate organisational level could dissuade from creating an intermediary legal entity. Hence, other solutions should be considered. An associative or simply consensual formula might provide effective solutions without the costs and drawbacks of an intermediary legal entity. To the extent that the applicable legislation permits, the following solutions can be considered.

v. Co-ownership Agreements

Investors can hold as co-owners the stakes (whole or part) of the target company offered in crowdfunding. Each investor would hold a portion or quota of the total. An agreement signed among the co-investors would provide the rules on the distribution of dividends and profits, representation scheme and decision-making. Structurally and operationally, the 'crowd' forms a community that acts in unity through its designated representative in the running of the target company. As a result, the crowdfunded company is not headed towards the complex situation of managing a high number of small and dispersed shareholders.

vi. Syndicates and Voting Agreements

Voting agreements, syndication or functionally equivalent formulae may provide a solution to the management of decision-making processes involving numerous shareholders. Under a voting agreement, the legal title would remain with individual shareholders. Therefore, the solution is partial. It only ensures united action in the exercise of the right to vote by the delegation of the right, on a revocable basis, to a representative under the voting agreement. But the company still has to manage multiplicity and dispersion in the compliance of its information duties, distribution of dividends and in other situations. Even more, in many cases, the voting agreement would not involve the designation of a representative. Parties to voting agreements can agree to vote separately and individually, although in the same agreed direction. In some jurisdictions, voting trusts are available as an alternative device.

Any agreement (voting syndication, shareholders' agreement) affecting voting rights in a company to any extent may impact upon the merchantability of the company's shares/stakes due to any conditions or limitations that are imposed. These should be disclosed and immediately communicated to all members of the company. Such a rule is provided for in Spanish legislation, which extends a typically financial-market-oriented mechanism to unlisted companies (LFFE 2015, Art 80.1.c). The same rule is stated in Italian regulations (Regolamento, Art 24.1.b).

Efforts to consider and carefully manage the new corporate governance challenges for crowdfunded companies will make the inside effect of crowdfunding more perceptible. A first step would be to assess the degree of adaptability of company law schemes to emerging needs. As access to financial markets has shaped the legal regime for publicly held companies, crowdfunding-based finance options also impact on company issues. The success of a crowdfunding campaign, especially the continuity of the financed project, depends upon the adequacy of the organisational model and the suitability of the corporate decisions made in the strategic configuration of the organisation running the project.

Crowdfunding rules adopted in several domestic jurisdictions do not tackle organisational issues, or they do so only tangentially. The outside effect requires more prompt and effective attention due to the potential systemic risks and interests at stake. The inside effect should now be considered to contribute to the development of crowdfunding as an alternative finance option and the consolidation of crowdfunded projects. The organisational and governance dimensions of crowdfunded projects are critical enablers that should be strategically designed and effectively implemented in the market given the specific features and particular implications of crowdfunding campaigns.

PART VI

Secured Transactions: Global and National Movements

12

Global Secured Transactions Law-making and National Law Reforms: Quo Vadis Secured Transactions Law?

N ORKUN AKSELI*

I. Introduction

Over recent decades there has been a debate about the desirability of harmonising and modernising secured transactions laws. International organisations and international financial institutions have taken active part in producing legislative standards and instruments. The general aim of these instruments has been to improve the law of secured credit with the assumption that harmonised modernisation of secured transactions law lowers the cost of credit. Harmonisation efforts on secured transactions have been generally justified on the grounds of commercial necessity, usefulness as a law reform toolkit, necessity for cross-border transactional certainty and modernisation of law to respond to the needs of businesses. Domestic law reform activities have also been taking place during the same period.[1] These international harmonisation and domestic law reform efforts have been both criticised and favoured.

* Associate Professor of Commercial Law, Durham University Law School.

[1] Eg UCC Art 9 was revised in the late 1990s. For example, in England there have been significant but unsuccessful attempts on the reform of secured credit laws. Crowther Committee Report on Consumer Credit (Cmnd 4596, 1971); Report of the Review Committee on Insolvency Law and Practice (Cmnd 8558, 1982); A Review of Security Interests in Property (Diamond Report, HMSO, 1989); Law Commission, 'Registration of Security Interests: Company Charges and Property other than Land' (Law Com Consultation Paper No 164, 2002); Law Commission, 'Company Security Interests, a Consultative Report' (Law Com Consultation Paper No 176, 2004); Law Commission Report on Company Security Interests (Law Com No 296, 2005). New Zealand Personal Property Security Act was enacted 1999. Secured transactions law reform was introduced in the former Soviet Republics and Eastern European countries in the 1990s. In civil law jurisdictions France has reformed its secured transactions laws. See eg ME Ancel, 'Recent Reform in France: The Renaissance of a civilian collateral regime?' in F Dahan and J Simpson (eds), Secured Transactions Reform and Access to Credit (Cheltenham, Edward Elgar, 2008) 259ff. For recent reforms and a general overview See L Gullifer and O Akseli, *Secured Transactions Law Reform: Principles. Policies and Practice* (Oxford, Hart, 2016); SV Bazinas and O Akseli, *International and Comparative Secured Transactions Law* (Oxford, Hart, 2017).

However, generally speaking, it is not possible to say that there has been a meaningful law reform in the field of secured transactions law that accompanies the globalisation of financial markets and the market interdependency. Secured transactions law is at the crossroads of the law of contracts, commercial law (in particular, insolvency law), consumer law and the law of property which are deeply rooted in the traditional domestic legal culture and history of a country.[2] The traditional roots of secured transactions law and the resistance (or reluctance) of stakeholders to law reform are considered to be tension points in the modernisation of secured transactions.[3] This debate is not confined to international efforts but also domestic ones. Particularly, modernising law via transnational texts has been regarded as a conduit of legal imperialism whereby secured transactions concepts of economically developed nations, which are embedded in the transnational texts, are transplanted into reforming legal systems. Businesses have legitimate expectations from the law and the state has a responsibility to establish a financial and legal framework which understands the barriers to access to finance, and either addresses those barriers efficiently or enables businesses to negotiate them. Law reform in the light of uniform law texts prepared by mandated international organs may positively improve our current understanding and efficiency of secured transactions law. These norms may also provide useful comparators as to how the law reform should take place. Particularly, the UNCITRAL Legislative Guide on Secured Transactions and the Model Law on Secured Transactions have the educative value as to how the reform can take shape. The regulatory competition as to whose law is better should be left aside in favour of the quest as to how the law can best respond to the needs of businesses.

The general aim of these international instruments can be explained as follows: first, they are useful as educational texts and act as law reform toolkits in national law reform activities which may assist legislators to better respond to the ever changing needs of businesses. Secondly, less complex and accessible norms written in codified language in secured transactions law are desirable for cross-border transactional certainty and, controversially, improving the rankings in the World Bank *Doing Business* tables.[4] Thirdly, transnational texts are drafted with a view to increase the effectiveness and efficiency of secured transactions laws. Finally, these texts also broaden the view of national approaches to law reform with the assumption that modernisation of secured transactions law may lead to the reduction of cost of credit by promoting simplicity in the law.[5]

[2] See also F Dahan, 'Secured Transactions Law in Western Advanced Economies: Exposing Myths' (2000) *Law in Transition* 37, 39; R Cuming, 'The Internationalization of Secured Financing Law: The Spreading Influence of the Concepts UCC, Article 9 and its Progeny' in R Cranston (ed), *Making Commercial Law Essays in Honour of Roy Goode* (Oxford, Clarendon, 1997) 499, arguing that the law of secured transactions 'is perceived as embodying cultural attitudes and public policy choices that vary greatly among states'.

[3] Typically arguments revolve around concerns as to how financiers and clients' interests will be protected, thus why mend something if it's not broken.

[4] For an economic efficiency perspective and criticism see eg M Renaudin, 'The role of the economic efficiency paradigm in commercial law reforms: a French Perspective' (2015) 6 *Journal of Business Law* 472.

[5] Here, simplicity is understood as clarity, certainty, accessibility and expedition with economic results. See R Calnan, 'What makes a good law of security?' in F Dahan (ed), *Research Handbook on Secured Financing in Commercial Transactions* (Cheltenham, Edward Elgar, 2015) 451, 455. For lowering the cost of credit argument, see eg S Bazinas, 'Lowering the Cost of Credit: the Promise in the Future UNCITRAL Convention on Assignment of Receivables in International Trade' (2001) 9 *Tulane Journal of International and Comparative Law* 259. However, whether modernisation or harmonisation, in fact, lowers the cost of credit requires statistical certainty which can, only, be achieved, perhaps, by an empirical study.

Meanwhile, national law reform activities both in common and civil law jurisdictions have gained impetus since the 1990s. These activities have taken two distinct approaches. On one hand, jurisdictions such as New Zealand[6] and Australia,[7] Belgium,[8] Canada,[9] Malawi,[10] Colombia[11] and Honduras[12] have thoroughly overhauled and fundamentally changed the way their national laws regard security rights over moveables. This category of jurisdictions implemented non-possessory security interests, eliminated multiple security devices and established a general registration system – as point of public notice and priority – for third-party effectiveness in their legal frameworks. This is the approach taken under the Uniform Commercial Code Article 9 which was revised in 1999 and amended several times, and the international texts most notably the UNCITRAL Legislative Guide on Secured Transactions, OAS Inter-American Model Law on Secured Transactions, and the UNCITRAL Model Law on Secured Transactions.

On the other hand, a number of other jurisdictions have preferred to implement law reform in a piecemeal fashion. These jurisdictions enact limited reform legislation incrementally that improves the existing law while preserving the fundamental structures of secured credit law. The rationale for the incrementalist approach to law reform is threefold:[13] firstly, while the law may be fragmented or have shortcomings, it may work well in domestic practice whereby lenders may take still security over a broad range of assets. This could be explained with the innovative nature of the domestic law. Therefore, there may be resistance from domestic stakeholders with strong lobby power to a change that may affect their current priority status. Second, a broad reform that removes floating charge and carve-out rules introduced by the Enterprise Act 2002 may affect the well-established practices. Third, international standards and other domestic laws that may influence reform may not be fully compatible the reforming jurisdiction. The incompatibility may be related to a number of factors and concerns including differing business practices, the style of regulation and, more importantly, whether a movement towards a functional system in security interests could replace formalism and conceptualism. These concerns have affected a broad spectrum law reform in a number of jurisdictions.

[6] New Zealand Personal Property Security Act 1999. See M Gedye, 'The Development of New Zealand's secured transactions jurisprudence' (2011) 34 *University of New South Wales Law Journal* 704.

[7] Australian Personal Property Securities Act 2009. A statutory review was conducted in relation to the Australian PPSA 2009 in 2015; see www.ag.gov.au/consultations/pages/StatutoryreviewofthePersonalPropertySecuritiesAct2009.aspx.

[8] See eg E Dirix, 'The Reform of Security Law in Belgium' in A Apers, S Bouly, E DeWitte and D Gruyaert (eds), *Property Law Perspectives III* (Cambridge, Intersentia, 2015) 135.

[9] See eg RCC Cuming, C Walsh and RJ Wood, *Personal Property Security Law*, 2nd edn (Toronto, Irwin Law, 2012).

[10] M Dubovec and C Kambili, *A Guide to the Personal Property Security Act The Case of Malawi* (Pretoria, PULP, 2015).

[11] www.garantiasmobiliarias.com.co/Default.aspx.

[12] M Dubovec, 'A Guide to a successful adoption and implementation of the Organisation of American States Model Law on Secured Transactions and Registry Regulations in Honduras – The National Law Experience' 43 *Uniform Commercial Code Law Journal* 825 (2011).

[13] For similar views see also N McGrath, 'International standards and the reform of English Personal Property Securities Law' in. Akseli (ed), *Availability of Credit and Secured Transactions in a Time of Crisis* (Cambridge, Cambridge University Press, 2013).

This chapter's overarching theme is that modernising the law of secured transactions by taking examples from uniform law prepared by the mandated international organs and weaving them into argument with the current domestic law would improve our understanding of how secured transactions law should be and how credit can be facilitated. This is because taking multiple perspectives is enriching and may improve legislative quality. In this connection, this chapter connects comparative law and the law of secured transactions at the crossroads of modernisation and global secured transactions law-making.

II. Significance of Secured Credit

The ability to take security and to raise finance through security is important. From an economic perspective, companies and incorporated businesses should have the ability to utilise both moveables and intangibles as collateral. Access to low-cost credit by businesses through utilising all of their economically valuable assets is expected to drive economic growth, according to studies conducted by the World Bank.[14] Modernisation of secured transactions laws, by improving the national legal framework, may provide better access to low-cost credit for borrowers, while increasing the confidence of lenders as to transactional certainty maintained by harmonised rules.[15] Confidence of lenders may be maintained by transactional certainty provided by clear rules that they will be repaid in case of debtor default.[16] The existence of collateral reduces the risk of non-payment and this has a positive impact on credit terms (lower interest rates, longer repayment periods and larger amounts of credit). Transactional certainty provides predictable and transparent rules where both parties to a transaction are aware of the legal outcome of their transactions. Harmonised rules on security rights may sustain cross-border lending, and open up local markets that do not have mature and balanced rules on securities. Therefore, facilitation of credit at the national level may be achieved by modern rules and at the international level by harmonised rules, which makes harmonisation the foremost key policy issue for the availability of credit across national borders.

The many differences among national laws in secured transactions laws are felt acutely in small companies' access to credit. These differences are mainly experienced

[14] R Levine, 'Finance and Growth: Theory and Evidence' (2004) National Bureau of Economic Research Working Paper 10766, 85, available at www.nber.org/papers/w10766.pdf; PM Machoka, 'Towards financial sector development – the role of the draft UNCITRAL Legislative Guide on Secured Transactions' (2006) 21 *Journal of International Banking Law and Regulation* 529.

[15] For a similar view See B Kozolchyk, 'Modernisation of Commercial Law: International Uniformity and Economic Development' (2009) 34 *Brooklyn Journal of International Law* 709, 718–19 arguing financial institutions 'had ample lending capital at their disposal, yet very few were willing to lend to small businesses unless their owners were very well known to the banks and could supply their "personal" signatures and "good" real estate mortgages as collateral.'

[16] Certainty has been part of the development of English commercial law. See eg *Vallejo v Wheeler* (1774) 1 Cowper 143, 153, 98 ER 1012, 1017: 'In all mercantile transactions the great object should be certainty: and therefore, it is of more consequence that a rule should be certain, than whether the rule is established one way or the other.'

in the key areas of secured credit transactions, including the creation, perfection, priority and enforcement of a security interest. The law of secured transactions has been influenced by cultural, historical, economic and social factors, and has close links to the law of property, contracts and insolvency. These historical, social, cultural and economic factors have prevented the law of secured transactions from being modernised in the light of uniform or harmonised law texts prepared by international legislative institutions.[17] The last decade has witnessed increasing efforts at the harmonisation and modernisation of the law of secured transactions by international legislative bodies and financial organisations. These efforts have been based on the idea that law reform is necessary to enable businesses to access credit at affordable levels and use all their economically valuable assets as collateral. Access to credit and the ability to use all types of economically valuable assets is a significant problem for small businesses. Small businesses access credit mainly on a secured as opposed to an unsecured basis, because of the risk of default carried by small businesses.[18] The risk of default is mainly due to fact that small businesses do not have the necessary creditworthiness or assets that they can use as collateral, and the financiers require security as a condition to extend credit. There is a correlation between the borrower's financial strength and the attraction to secured credit. Ronald Mann points out that 'borrowers exhibit an increasing tendency toward unsecured debt as their financial strength increases'.[19] Philip Wood observes similarly that public companies usually borrow on an unsecured basis and rather use negative pledge clauses in their contracts because of their credit strength and need to spread their sources of finance.[20] The Law Commission in England has also pointed out this tendency and reported that 'well-established public companies are able to borrow readily on an unsecured basis, but for many smaller enterprises credit can be obtained on significantly better terms … if the borrower is able to offer security to the lender'.[21]

Most small businesses do not have assets apart from their receivables and it is important for them to be able to utilise their receivables as collateral in order to be able access to further credit. Between 2001 and 2005, the World Bank in its Enterprise Surveys, conducted in 60 low- and middle-income countries, established that 22 per cent of company assets are land and buildings, 34 per cent accounts receivables, and 44 per cent machinery; nevertheless, as collateral only nine per cent accounts receivables, 18 per cent machinery, and 73 per cent lands and buildings are accepted.[22] While it is clear that in unreformed legal systems there is a tendency to accept tangible moveable and immoveable property as collateral, within the framework of an effective and efficient secured transactions regime this may be regarded as an inadequate system that fails

[17] C Walsh, 'The "Law" in Law and Development' (2000) *Law in Transition* 7, 12–13.

[18] J Armour, 'The Law and Economics Debate About Secured Lending: Lessons For European Lawmaking?' in H Eidenmüller and EM Kieninger (eds), *The Future of Secured Credit in Europe* (European Company and Financial Law Review, 2008) 3, 9.

[19] RJ Mann, 'Explaining the Pattern of Secured Credit' (1997) 110 *Harvard Law Review*, 625, 674 and 683 concluding that secured credit '[enhances] the borrower's ability to give a credible commitment to refrain from excessive future borrowing and by limiting the borrower's ability to engage in conduct that lessens the likelihood of payment'.

[20] P Wood, *Law and Practice of International Finance* (London, Sweet and Maxwell, 2008) 253.

[21] Law Commission Report No 296 (2005), para 1.2.

[22] M Safavian, H Fleisig and J Steinbuks, 'Unlocking Dead Capital' *Viewpoint*, Note Number 307 (March 2006) 2 and Figure 3.

to promote secured credit.[23] Empirical studies conducted by economists 'demonstrate a strong positive link between the functioning of the financial system and long-run economic growth'.[24]

Legal systems with secured transactions laws that do not respond to businesses' needs pose risks for lenders. Businesses expect certain standards from secured credit law aimed at allowing to assess and to price the risk in a transaction. These can be summarised as the ability to take security over any type of assets – future or existing – to secure any type of obligations, transparent and predictable information system that informs interested parties of the possible encumbrances over the debtor's assets, predictable priority system to regulate competing claims of the debtor's possible creditors, effective enforcement systems, fair and balanced insolvency rules that protect the interests of all parties, the application of perfection and priority rules equally to other devices that perform security functions but are not apparent to third parties, and clear, transparent and easily accessible rules.[25] Furthermore, a security interest created in one jurisdiction may not provide the same protection that would otherwise provide in the home jurisdiction of the lender. So, modern rules in one state may not be enough for the provision of credit across national borders and this means that there is a need for harmonised rules on matters such as the creation, perfection, priority and enforcement of a security interest. Lack of these predictable rules may have negative impact on the lending decisions to emerging economies.[26]

III. Rationale for Taking Security

There are certain reasons why lenders take security. Firstly, security reduces the risk of non-payment and where there are competing claims, reducing the risk means ensuring priority.[27] The lender bargains for the priority position and takes security in order to increase its repayment chances in the event of a debtor's insolvency or default in

[23] See A/CN.9/631, Recommendation 1 for elements of an effective secured transactions law regime.

[24] Levine, 'Finance and Growth' (2004) 85.

[25] 'Secured Transactions Law Reform: The Case for Reform', available at http://securedtransactionsproject.wordpress.com/case-for-reform.

[26] PL Freedman and RW Click, 'Banks That Don't Lend? Unlocking Credit to Spur Growth in Developing Countries' (2006) 24 *Development Policy Review* 279, 291, stating that 'Substantial deficiencies in the legal and regulatory environment in developing countries constitute the primary reason for the low degree of credit extended to the private sector'.

[27] For a debate as to whether unqualified security is good and whether there should be carve-outs for unsecured creditors under the UCC Art 9 see eg E Warren, 'Making Policy with Imperfect Information: The Article 9 Full Priority Debates' (1997) 82 *Cornell Law Review* 1373; KN Klee, 'Barbarians at the Trough: Riposte in Defense of the Warren Carve-out Proposal' (1997) 82 *Cornell Law Review* 1467; LM LoPucki, 'Should the Secured Credit Carve-Out Apply Only in Bankruptcy? A Systems/Strategic Analysis' (1997) 82 *Cornell Law Review*, 1483; SL Harris and CW Mooney, 'Measuring the Social Costs and Benefits and Identifying the Victims of Subordinating Security Interests in Bankruptcy' (1997) 82 *Cornell Law Review* 1349; LA Bebchuk and JM Fried, 'The Uneasy case for the Priority of Secured Claims in Bankruptcy: Further Thoughts and a Reply to Critics' (1997) 82 *Cornell Law Review* 1279; R Scott, 'The Truth about Secured Financing' (1997) 82 *Cornell Law Review* 1436, 1437–38; A Schwartz, 'Priority Contracts and Priority in Bankruptcy' (1997) 82 *Cornell Law Review*, 1396.

payment.[28] Security enables a lender to be repaid before other creditors in the event of insolvency of the debtor. The priority function of security is a safety element for the lender. The lender decides to lend if satisfactory collateral is provided and given a priority position in the event of debtor's insolvency. Secondly, security affords control whereby the lender monitors the business decisions of the debtor during the period of the security interest to prevent the debtor from reducing the value of the collateral. This is a natural outcome of security interests in the sense that the lender has bargained for the secured creditor position and provided credit at a lower interest rate. Therefore, it has the ability to monitor the business decisions of the debtor in order to maintain the value of the collateral which is left with the debtor. Monitoring over the collateral is particularly important in terms of equipment financing. The security interest created in one jurisdiction may not afford the same protection as a security interest created in the lender's jurisdiction. It has been noted that

> the primary purpose of a security interest may be to give a secured creditor a priority over a firm's other creditors in the event that the firm encounters financial distress and cannot meet its fixed obligations. In the case of the equipment financier, however, the security interest may serve a different purpose. A lender may lend because it is confident that the procedures available to it in the event of default will allow it to realise much of the amount of the loan in the event of default. Thus, the lender may take a security interest in large part because its rights upon default against the debtor are greater that they would be if it did not take security.[29]

Precisely, this is also one of the fundamental reasons why uniform or harmonised law texts that aim to improve secured transactions law should be supported. Thirdly, security assists the expansion of business and enables borrower to access credit with better terms. The ability to offer collateral increases chances of obtaining credit[30] and this will have a positive impact in accessing low-cost credit whereby interest rates may be reduced (as the risk premium is not included in the rate) and lending may occur with longer maturities. Fourthly, ability to take security in legal systems that respond to business needs enables the secured creditor to be able to enjoy self-help remedies. Efficient enforcement mechanisms are likely to have a beneficial impact on the availability and the cost of credit. Fifthly, taking security is deemed as 'a fair exchange for credit'.[31] Thus the ability to take security should be facilitated. This can be achieved by a transparent and predictable secured credit law which endorses the creation of security over moveable

[28] There is a classical debate, largely confined to the US, on the efficiency of secured lending as to whether security in fact lowers the cost of credit and whether allowing full priority to secured creditors is a good thing. This debate is partly based on the political idea that lenders have too much power and are over-dominant in insolvencies. On these matters see eg T Jackson and A Kronman, 'Secured Financing and Priorities Among Creditors' (1979) 88 *Yale Law Journal* 1143; W Woodward, 'The Realist and Secured Credit: Grant Gilmore, Common Law Courts and the Article 9 Reform Process' (1997) 82 *Cornell Law Review* 1511; M LoPucki 'The Unsecured Creditor's Bargain' (1994) 80 *Virginia Law Review* 1887, 1947.

[29] D Baird, 'Security Interests Reconsidered' 80 *Virginia Law Review* 2249, 2252 (1994).

[30] U Drobnig, 'Secured Credit in International Insolvency Proceedings' (1998) 33 *Texas International Law Review* 53, 54. This is also reflected in documents such as Basel Accord 1988 and the EU Capital Adequacy Directive 2006/49 according to which for capital adequacy purposes security has significance and critical for risk-weighting of capital.

[31] Wood, *International Finance* (2008) 250.

assets and protects the interests of the lender and is recognised even if the moveable asset crosses borders. This is equally applicable to intangibles, especially receivables, and the choice of law in the contract should not prejudice the encumbrance with security right. Finally, the ability to take security may lead to economic growth. Lenders may extend credit in reliance on the protection provided by security. If the cost of credit is low, small businesses may obtain credit at better and affordable conditions and this may lead to economic growth.[32] Economically less developed nations' laws do not support security or make it difficult for creditors to obtain security. Furthermore, intangibles are not considered as acceptable collateral and this, in turn, risks increasing the cost of credit.[33] The origin of law which is based on culture, political conditions, history and social factors may have significant effect on financial development.[34] Economically less developed nations generally have an antagonistic approach to intangibles and security based on intangible property. A link between common law and economic growth was found to exist whereby common law has a better response characteristic than other legal traditions.[35] According to this link legal systems mainly based on common law tradition are more receptive to rules and institutions that may assist the growth of financial markets and business transactions. Unlike their civil law counterparts, they do not accept rules that would impede 'economic freedom and market efficiency'.[36] Similar arguments are equally applicable as to availability of credit and the ability of firms' access to credit.[37]

[32] See eg 'Number Crunching the Credit Crunch' Federation of Small Businesses, available at www.fsb.org.uk/frontpage/assets/credit%20crunch%20figures.pdf, which suggests that in the UK there are 4.7million SMEs with 13.5million employees and their contribution to UK economy is more than half of turnover. Similarly in International Finance Corporation's (IFC) figures, 90% of businesses globally are small and medium sized and account for 50% of employment worldwide. IFC Issue Brief, 'Small Businesses' (September 2012). See also B Kozolchyk, 'Secured Lending and Its Poverty Reduction Effect' (2007) 42 *Texas International Law Journal* 727.

[33] For an empirical study on the use of immoveables and moveables as opposed to intangibles as collateral see M Safavian, 'Firm level evidence on collateral and access to finance' in Dahan and Simpson (eds), Secured Transactions Reform (2003) 110.

[34] See generally R La Porta, F Lopez de Silanes and A Schleifer, 'The Economic Consequences of Legal origins' 46 (2008) *Journal of Economic Literature* 285; T Beck, A Demirguc-Kunt and R Levine, 'Law and Finance: Why Does Legal Origin Matter? (2003) 31 *Journal of Comparative Economics* 653, 672–73. Beck et al suggest that legal systems based on German or British legal traditions have better developed financial norms than the French influenced legal systems and note that 'legal origin matters because legal traditions differ in their ability to adjust efficiently to evolving socioeconomic conditions. Legal systems that adapt efficiently to minimize the gap between the financial needs of the economy and the capabilities of the legal system will foster financial development more effectively than will more rigid legal systems'.

[35] R Epstein, 'The Static Conception of the Common Law' 9 (1980) *Journal of Legal Studies* 253. For a similar argument supported by empirical findings See R La Porta, F Lopez de Silanes, A Shleifer and R Vishny, 'Legal Determinants of External Finance' (1997) 52 *Journal of Finance* 1131; R La Porta, F Lopez de Silanes, A Shleifer and R Vishny, 'Law and Finance' (1998) 106 *Journal of Political Economy* 1113.

[36] See N Garoupa and T Ginsburg, 'Economic Analysis and Comparative Law' in M Bussani and U Mattei (eds), *The Cambridge Companion to Comparative Law* (Cambridge, Cambridge University Press, 2012) 57, 67. P Mahoney, 'The Common Law and Economic Growth: Hayek Might be Right' (2001) 30 *Journal of Legal Studies* 503.

[37] T Beck, A Demirguc-Kunt and R Levine, 'Law and Firms' Access to Finance' (2005) 7 *American Law and Economics Review* 211.

IV. Harmonisation in the Context of Secured Transactions Law

A. Rationale for Harmonised Modernisation

The functional meaning of harmonisation in the context of secured transactions should be understood as approximating similar concepts or principles in certain key areas (such as the creation, perfection, priority and enforcement of security interests) for the purposes of improving the law, reducing the cost and facilitating the flow of credit which will establish transactional certainty both in domestic and international secured credit transactions and assist legislators in law reform. Thus, harmonisation should not be regarded as means to export laws of powerful states to weaker states, but rather a positive practical and conceptual development which involves input from different legal traditions. Modern standards introduced by international texts therefore provide harmonised or similar rules in reforming jurisdictions.

There is certainly desirability, not an absolute necessity, of harmonisation of secured transactions laws. Divergence in national secured transactions laws complicates cross-border trade and obstructs businesses to have access to low-cost credit. This is because choice of law rules are unpredictable, costs for searching and learning the applicable may be high and the applicable law may have inefficient rules that do not endorse security.[38] In that context, it is critical to harmonise secured transactions laws at the international level by including all legal cultures and achieve a modern, harmonised and predictable set of rules for secured credit transactions which may serve as a model for domestic law reform initiatives. Whether or not this may occur in practice has not been tested, but it is clear that harmonised secured transactions legislative texts provide benefits to both economically developed and developing nations in their perceptions of secured transactions law, and may act as useful sources in law reform activities.[39] International organisations and international financial institutions have been active since the early 1970s in the field of secured transactions law. The general aim of these harmonisation activities is based on the understanding that the harmonised application of modern set of rules on the law of secured credit may assist transactional and legal certainty in lending decisions and lower the cost of credit. Harmonised legislative texts may assist developed nations to improve and reform their laws on secured transactions and provide better sets of norms that may serve business better.[40] By the same token, for emerging economies harmonised texts may help to facilitate credit for their small businesses to achieve economic growth.

[38] N Cohen, 'Internationalizing the Law of Secured Credit: Perspectives from the U.S. Experience' (1999) 20 *University of Pennsylvania Journal of International Economic Law* 423, 432.

[39] Harmonisation may be achieved by eliminating divergent aspects of secured transactions law. G Hermann, 'The Role of UNCITRAL' in I Fletcher, M Cremona and L Mistelis (eds), *Foundations And Perspectives of International Trade Law* (London, Sweet and Maxwell, 2001) 28, 32 suggesting 'preventive unification' to unify an area of law that none of the nations has ever done.

[40] For example, the UNCITRAL Guide has clear set of rules in terms of creation, perfection, priority and enforcement of security interests where many national laws fail to provide predictable and transparent rules. As an example under English law there are at least 10 distinct priority rules. While registration is a feature under English law Companies Act 2006, Pt 25, this requirement is somewhat burdensome (as this

The rationale for harmonisation may be summarised as the commercial necessity to minimise the effects of divergent laws on the cost of credit and to facilitate cross-border flow of credit, minimisation of legal conflicts and costs in international transactions,[41] its effect as a means for legal reform and economic growth, and the need to ensure the use of intangible property in cross-border transactions.[42] Harmonisation and modernisation of secured credit are important to the international finance community for the following four reasons. Firstly, modernisation and harmonisation support economic growth. The causal link between the legal reforms and economic growth has been established in the UNCITRAL studies.[43] One method to achieve economic growth through appropriate law reforms is to eliminate certain barriers (such as trade, language and legal) and facilitate the flow of credit across borders. The World Bank in its 'Principles for Effective Insolvency and Creditor Rights Systems' study aimed to establish an efficient and reliable system of creditors' rights and insolvency. The Principles have been formulated 'to assist countries in their efforts to evaluate and improve core aspects of their commercial law systems that are fundamental to a sound investment climate and to promote commerce and economic growth'.[44] Secondly, modern secured transactions systems improve financial stability, thus robustness in the face of financial crises may be enabled. Thirdly, convergence of diverse legal systems enables the facilitation of globalisation in various fields but particularly in commerce by facilitating the flow of credit. Finally, with the advancement of technology it is possible to avoid transaction and litigation costs through harmonised rules.[45] The globalisation of markets, increasing cross-border transaction costs and the diversity of rules on secured credit have justified the efforts of international harmonisation of secured transactions law.

Three arguments have been made against harmonisation. These are loss of sovereignty, loss of legal competition and loss of legal culture.[46] But these are unconvincing. A number of brief observations are in order. By adopting English common law

is a transactions filing rather than notice filing) and the entire security document needs to be filed (unlike under the Guide where the notice filing is required). CA 2006, Pt 25 has been revised on a very limited scale and the changes to this part will apply as of April 2013. For further information see eg BIS, 'Revised Scheme for Registration of Charges Created by Companies and Limited Liability Partnerships, Proposed revision of Part 25, Companies Act 2006', (August 2011).

[41] See eg GP Miller, 'The Legal-Economic Analysis of Comparative Civil Procedure' (1997) 45 *American Journal of Comparative Law* 905, 917 noting that harmonisation reduces transaction costs, 'since the parties to international legal transactions might have a somewhat better sense of the risks and costs of litigation they face in a harmonized system than they do in a diverse one'. For the advantages of harmonisation in the reduction of high transaction costs see J Wool, 'Rethinking the Notion of Uniformity in the Drafting of International Commercial Law: A Preliminary Proposal for the Development of a Policy Based Unification Model' (1997) 2 *Uniform Law Review* 46, 47ff; J Wool, 'The Case for a Commercial Orientation to the Proposed Unidroit Convention as applied to aircraft equipment' (1999) 4 *Uniform Law Review* 289, 291–92.

[42] See eg HL Buxbaum, 'Unification of the Law Governing Secured Transactions: Progress and Prospects for Reform' (2003) 8 *Uniform Law Review* 322, 324.

[43] A/CN.9/512, para 4.

[44] The World Bank Principles for Effective Insolvency and Creditor Rights Systems, 2005, at 2.

[45] For these four reasons see V Tata, 'The Role of Multilaterals in the Promotion of Modern Securities Law' Comments at the Congress to Celebrate the 40th Annual Session of UNCITRAL, available at www.uncitral.org/pdf/english/congress/Tata-revised.pdf.

[46] For a summary of these objections to harmonisation see eg G McCormack, *Secured Credit, UNCITRAL and the Harmonisation of Law* (Cheltenham, Edward Elgar, 2011) 33–41.

Commonwealth nations have not lost their sovereignty, their competition of laws or their legal culture. Even if one assumes that they have lost, as a result of British imperial rule, it is not possible to compare this with a uniform law text that is not binding. Similarly, continental European states have not lost their sovereignty or their legal culture by adopting the harmonised Roman law. Finally, using the UCC Article 2 and the CISG as metaphor, the former is preferred more by American lawyers despite the fact that the USA adopted the CISG in 1988. The reason is that lawyers either do not know the CISG, do not wish to learn new law or feel comfortable with their domestic law. Obviously behind these reasons there may be a point where lawyers do not wish to risk their clients' or stakeholders' interest by learning new law or supporting new law.[47] Thus the underpinning point of this argument is that adopting an international legislative text does not always necessarily lead to the application of that international text by lawyers, as they may prefer a more familiar text. Linking this argument to the UNCITRAL Guide, it can be argued that the Guide intends to supplement and improve domestic law. Therefore, loss of sovereignty or loss of legal competition may not occur in the end. Every nation may decide to adopt and adapt the recommendations of the Guide or the UNCITRAL Model Law on Secured Transactions according to their business needs.

Harmonisation has been the basic tenor of international legislative activities on various aspects of private law. In the context of international activities on secured transactions, the intention is certainly to harmonise the law and provide a different perspective to nations that would like to improve their laws and their understanding of secured transactions law that can respond to the needs of business in the ever changing system of financial markets.[48] The law evolves through business practices. This phenomenon may also be labelled as the 'bottom-up evolution of law' according to which commercial law norms, in particular, are based on pre-existing business practices and social norms of a country.[49] One method to prevent difficulties in access to credit is to have standards that support access to credit at affordable rates. This can be achieved by either domestic law reforms in the light of harmonised international legislative texts or by transplantation of laws of other countries as part of the law reform agenda. Harmonisation can be regarded as a fair method of modernising the law over legal transplantation. This is because while harmonisation reduces the possibilities of choice of law and subjecting the transaction to unpredictable laws, it enables, at the

[47] For an interesting discussion on this point see eg HA Hamoudi, 'The American Commercial Religion' (2012) 10 *DePaul International Law Journal* 107, 152 noting that 'while the CISG may be formally ratified, all too often it ends up in judicial application being more mirage than expression of transnational harmony'. See also L Spagnolo, 'Through the Kaleidoscope: Choices of Law and the CISG (Kaleidoscope Part I)' (2009) 13 *Vindobona Journal of International Commercial Law and Arbitration* 135, 135–36 noting that CISG is generally opted out.

[48] The term 'harmonisation' has been defined on the UNCITRAL's website as follows: '"Harmonisation" may conceptually be thought of as the process through which domestic laws may be modified to enhance predictability in cross-border commercial transactions.' www.uncitral.org/uncitral/en/about/origin_faq.html.

[49] R Cooter, 'Normative Failure Theory of Law' (1997) 82 *Cornell Law Review* 947, 948. In terms of UCC Art 9 see eg R Scott, 'The Politics of Article 9' (1994) 80 *Virginia Law Review* 1783, 1850, noting that 'Article 9 regulates asset-based financers, a paradigmatic example of well-organized and cohesive interests, the process is susceptible to disproportionate influence by a single active interest group representing particular financial interests … [and suggests that] the law revision process [tends] to propose rules that are both transactionally efficient and distributionally favourable to the dominating interests.'

same time, different legal systems and cultures to express their views and have an input. Critics of convergence of laws argue that jurisdictional competition promotes rules that offer better solutions.[50] Creditors in states with laws that do not support security have legitimate concerns to lose their trust, hence the need to modernise the law of secured credit. Scholars further argue that if 'particular States adopt the Guide, then this creates an environment that is comfortable and familiar for US business interests'.[51] The Guide and Model Law are soft law texts which are offered to states for adoption. Whether and, if so, how they will be adopted are the sovereign decision of the states. In addition, while the Guide and Model Law have been influenced by the UCC Article 9, they have been also influenced by the Canadian PPSA, New Zealand PPSA and number of uniform law texts, such as the EBRD and the OAS Model Laws on Secured Transactions, and the Cape Town Convention on International Interests in Mobile Equipment. It should also be added that, in any case, the measure of success of any law depends, not on its qualifier as US or UK law, but rather on the extent to which the law responds to the needs of businesses, promotes economic growth and thus commands influence abroad.[52]

B. Obstacles to Modernisation

Conceptualising modernisation in the context of the law of secured transactions will assist our understanding as to why it is necessary and how it can assist in achieving economic growth. Economic growth occurs through individuals who are entrepreneurs who represent the business community at large.[53] Entrepreneurs need to be supported by dynamic rules that allow the use of economically valuable assets as collateral and recognise and enable financing techniques that facilitate the flow of credit. The causal link between modern law of secured transactions and economic growth has been established by the UNCITRAL and the World Bank.[54] Rules that can facilitate transactional certainty have the ability to adjust to external shocks and to attract external finance. Secured transactions laws that respond to business needs and establish *ex ante* transactional predictability may enable states to utilise the benefits of modern financial and international credit markets.[55]

[50] See generally eg U Mattei, 'Efficiency in Legal Transplants: An Essay in Comparative Law and Economics' (1994) 14 *International Review of Law and Economics* 3.

[51] G McCormack, 'American private law writ large? The UNCITRAL secured transactions guide' (2011) 60 *International & Comparative Law Quarterly* 597, 604 (citing Commercial Finance Association senior counsel's statement).

[52] See generally R Goode, 'Insularity or Leadership? The Role of the United Kingdom in the Harmonisation of Commercial Law' (2001) 50 *International & Comparative Law Quarterly* 751.

[53] See generally J Schumpeter, *Capitalism, Socialism and Democracy* (Oxford, Routledge, 2003). See also W Rostow, 'Five Stages of Economic Growth' (1959) 12 *The Economic History Review* 1.

[54] A/CN.9/512, para 4; The World Bank Principles for Effective Insolvency and Creditor Rights Systems, 2005, at 2. The Principles have been formulated 'to assist countries in their efforts to evaluate and improve core aspects of their commercial law systems that are fundamental to a sound investment climate and to promote commerce and economic growth'.

[55] For a similar view see H Burman, 'The Commercial Challenge in Modernizing Secured Transactions Law' (2003) 8 *Uniform Law Review* 347, 349.

There are several obstacles to the modernisation of national secured transactions laws. The main impediment is that this area of law has been deeply influenced by the social, cultural and historical factors that reflect the business practices of each jurisdiction. The same impediment may be cited as the reason why the law of secured transactions has remained within the boundaries of domestic law with close links to the law of property, contracts and insolvency.[56] In these areas of law there are cultural attitudes and public policy preferences that vary from state to state. In the international harmonisation activities the economic or political expectations, the competition among legal systems, the tensions inherent in international law-making[57] play a significant role. All of these factors are influential in the decisions of countries as to whether to adopt or reject the legislative texts prepared by international organisations. There is certainly a role for the scepticism of legal practitioners and academics towards new rules and adapting to them in order to protect their clients and certain ideologies.[58] While divergence of laws does not mean that the laws are inefficient per se,[59] diversity of secured transactions laws causes 'uncertainty and transaction costs that lower the expected value of a transaction to the creditor'.[60]

The term *modernisation* has often been misunderstood as the 'development' and 'introduction' of rules imposed by states or international organisations on other economically less advanced states. However, it can be argued that modernisation is an element of development (social/societal, economic, legal, political). The change can be achieved through law which is 'a vehicle for social change'.[61] Its responsiveness to social and business needs is necessary. Nonet and Selznick note that '[a responsive law] perceives social pressures as sources of knowledge and opportunities for self-correction'.[62] Therefore, modernisation achieved through law may be defined as '"progressional", even evolutionary, notion of social, economic, and political change'.[63] In the context of the law of secured transactions, modernisation can be defined as a

[56] See generally S van Erp, 'Civil and Common Property law: Caveat Comparator – The Value of Legal Historical-Comparative Analysis' (2003) 11 *European Review of Private Law* 394. Divergence of laws stem from the proprietary aspects of law. See R Goode, 'Security in Cross Border Transactions' (1998) 33 *Texas International Law Review* 47, 48.

[57] See R Goode, 'Rule, Practice, and Pragmatism in Transnational Commercial Law' (2005) 54 *International & Comparative Law Quarterly* 539.

[58] See generally A Ogus, 'The Economic Base of Legal Culture: Networks and Monopolization' (2002) *Oxford Journal of Legal Studies* 419; A Ogus, 'Competition between National Legal Systems: A Contribution of Economic Analysis of Comparative Law' (1999) 48 *International & Comparative Law Quarterly* 405. See Garoupa and Ginsburg, 'Economic Analysis' (2012) 69, where it is noted that 'there are obstacles to convergence that result from local rent-seeking (essentially by the legal professions), legal culture, and other forms of transaction costs'.

[59] See generally Garoupa and Ginsburg (n 36) 69.

[60] N Cohen, 'Harmonizing the Law Governing Secured Credit: The Next Frontier' (1998) 33 *Texas International Law Review* 173, 176.

[61] R Wacks, *Philosophy of Law: A Very Short Introduction* (Oxford, Oxford University Press, 2006) xii.

[62] P Nonet and P Selznick, *Law and Society in Transition Toward Responsive Law* (New York, Harper Torchbooks, 1954) 77.

[63] JA Gardner, *Legal Imperialism, American Lawyers and Foreign Aid in Latin America* (Madison, University of Wisconsin Press, 1981) 261. For modernisation of societies through law see eg J Linarelli, 'Law, Rights and Development' in J Linarelli (ed), *Research Handbook on Global Justice and International Economic Law* (Cheltenham, Edward Elgar, 2013).

process whereby a society goes through a period of transition in relation to rules that recognise and enable financing techniques which respond to the changing nature of business and global finance and that create transactional certainty.

As part of this scepticism, one argument forwarded against the way the harmonised texts were prepared was that certain powerful states in international organisations use harmonisation or convergence process and the legitimacy of international organisations to transplant their laws through uniform law texts into economically less powerful states. Arguments suggest that harmonisation process is used to further imperialistic ambitions and attempt to link two absolutely distinct concepts at the crossroads of imperialism: harmonisation and legal transplants.[64] Imperialism argument has been based on Ugo Mattei's theory that 'imperial law is produced, in the interest of international capital'.[65] However, these two distinct concepts do not converge in their goals and certainly harmonisation has nothing to do with imperialism. Imperial law, in its literal meaning, is really what one can find of English common law in the common law of Australia or New Zealand, and in the context of secured transactions law even those two jurisdictions have rejected the original imperial common law. Critics of harmonisation or modernisation and international legislative texts contend that, the UNCITRAL Guide and Model Law in particular have been heavily influenced by the UCC Article 9 and thus, it is, in a sense, there to impose an imperialistic law.[66] The argument is that the UNCITRAL Guide, with its concepts similar to the UCC Article 9, impose an 'American tone' on law reform activities globally.[67] There are also empirically obtained evidence based arguments.[68] Socio-legal scholars examine the arguments that the UN legislative texts impose economically powerful nations' laws, from the perspective of who is represented in the working group and commission meetings, who actually attends and who contributes to the deliberations.[69] The conclusion by Halliday et al suggest that the legitimacy of the UNCITRAL's legislative texts is not measured by the inclusiveness of the working methods of the UNCITRAL, but by who actually contributes and whose domestic legal norms are enshrined in the fundamental principles of those texts.[70] It can be submitted that the persuasiveness of each text depends on how effectively it addresses the needs and concerns of all states and on the balance of the legislative process.

[64] See eg McCormack, 'UNCITRAL' (2011); McCormack, 'American private law' (2011).

[65] U Mattei, 'A theory of Imperial Law: A Study on US Hegemony and the Latin Resistance' (2002) 10 *Indiana Journal of Global Legal Studies* 383, 383.

[66] See eg McCormack (n 46).

[67] See generally McCormack (n 51).

[68] See eg TC Halliday, J Pacewicz and S Block-Lieb, 'Who Governs? Delegations and Delegates in global trade lawmaking' (2013) 7 *Regulation & Governance* 279; S Block-Lieb and TC Halliday, 'Incrementalisms in Global Lawmaking' (2007) 32 *Brooklyn Journal of International Law* 851; S Block-Lieb and TC Halliday 'Legitimation and Global Lawmaking' Fordham Law Legal Studies Research Paper No 952492 (2006), available at http://ssrn.com/abstract=952492; S Block-Lieb and TC Halliday, 'Harmonisation and Modernisation in UNCITRAL's Legislative Guide on Insolvency Law' (2007) 42 *Texas International Law Journal* 481.

[69] See generally Halliday, Pacewicz and Block-Lieb (ibid).

[70] See ibid.

C. Legal Transplantation is not Synonymous with Harmonisation or Modernisation

Firstly, legal transplantation[71] mostly works.[72] Legal transplantation is a method of law reform where a foreign law (donor state) is imported to another state (host state).[73] Uniform or harmonised law is non-binding and not imposed by international legislative organs that prepare uniform or harmonised law. Some scholars base their arguments on 'superiority' of the donor state's law.[74] Other scholars base their arguments on the 'prestige' that it offers.[75] However, the success of transplantation process requires simultaneous importation and digestion of precedents, case law, doctrinal commentaries and education material which then need to be followed up by continuous reform in the light of the donor state's reform of that particular law.[76] The donor state develops its legal order internally (so the law evolves from bottom up) and builds the legal order on its business practices and ethics with which its population is generally familiar. The host state that transplants the legal order needs to structure its business understanding and practices according to the adopted legal order so that the transplant works.[77] However, this is not always necessary. The host state may adopt the law together with its jurisprudence, case law and legal doctrines and over the years with internal reforms adjust

[71] For harmonisation and transplantation see eg M Ancel, 'From the Unification of Law to its Harmonisation' 51 *Tulsa Law Review* (1976) 108, 114–17; A Watson, 'Legal Transplants and Law Reform' (1976) 92 *Law Quarterly Review* 79; A Watson, *Legal Transplants An Approach to Comparative Law* (Edinburgh, Scottish Academic Press 1974) 30ff explaining various types of reception, eg imposed reception, solicited reception, infiltration, penetration, etc. RA Macdonald, 'Three Metaphors of Norm Migration in International Context' (2009) 34 *Brooklyn Journal of International Law* 603 suggesting that there are three metaphors namely harmonisation, transplantation and viral propagation.

[72] Successful examples are Swiss law adopted by Turkey, German–Roman law adopted by Japan and Common law in Africa. H Kronke, 'Why Transplants Rarely work-why convergence is insufficient in Commercial Law – methodical changes in paradigm in the harmonisation of commercial law', available at www.law.qmul.ac.uk/events/docs/London_February_2008_Kronke.ppt#1. Professor Kronke correctly states two types of successful transplantation: (1) through imperialism; and (2) through invitation or shared values/ideology. Doubtful transplantation examples are those attempted by invited or solicited scholars.

[73] For more information see eg Watson, *Legal Transplants* (1974).

[74] Eg McCormack (n 51) 601. E Örücü, 'Critical Comparative Law: Considering Paradoxes for Legal Systems in Transition' (2000) 4.1 *EJCL*, available at www.ejcl.org/41/art41-1.html, noting that the reception of laws by Turkey was a radically reformist approach to tear up the foundations of the old legal system and to build a new one on the basis of the relationship of people and not on the religious values or customs and thus the reform was a significant example of 'social engineering through law'. See also A Watson, *The Nature of Law* (Edinburgh, Edinburgh University Press, 1977) 111 noting that 'A particular type of massive transplant is the voluntary adoption of a Western-style civil code by an economically under-developed nation with the deliberate intention of helping or forcing that country into the 'modern world'.

[75] For 'prestige' see Mattei, 'Efficiency in Legal Transplants' (1994) 4 (citing and rightly criticising Rudolfo Sacco's view that legal transplants occur because they offer prestige: R Sacco, 'Legal Formats, A Dynamic Approach to Comparative Law (1991) 39 *American Journal of Comparative Law* 1).

[76] For example, since the adoption of the Swiss law, law reform and amendments to Turkish Civil and Obligations Codes have been made closely and comparatively following the reforms to the Swiss Civil and Obligations Codes while taking Turkey's legal needs into account. That practice is in line with Professor Watson's suggestion that 'A successful legal transplant … will grow in its new body, and become part of that body just as the rule or institution would have continued to develop in its parent system. Subsequent development in the host system should not be confused with rejection.' Watson (n 71) 27.

[77] See D Berkowitz, K Pistor and J-F Richard, 'Economic Development, Legality and the Transplant Effect' (2003) 47 *European Economic Review* 165.

the adopted law according to its internal needs. Thus the adopted law, while keeping the philosophy and spirit of the donor law, will become part of the host state's culture, legal tradition and ideological perspective.[78] But, of course, the main issue is that prior to adoption or transplantation appropriate choice needs to be made. Knowledge of legal and economic systems of the host and adapting the donor state's rules accordingly carry significant value in the success of transplantation.[79]

In particular, in secured transactions similar economic development, social and administrative infrastructure levels are necessary for a considerable success. In other words, using the well-known 'exportability of the UCC Article 9' example, unless a country has similar business practices, well-developed social and market infrastructure and financial level as the United States has, transplantation or exportation of the UCC Article 9 theory cannot create workable results. Berkowitz et al argue that the law-making mechanism rather than the contents of legal rules determine the effectiveness and success of transplantation, and that the law and its institutions develop better when the evolution happens internally rather than external imposition.[80] This argument supports 'bottom-up' evolution of legal norms. However, Berkowitz et al also suggest that for the success of transplants the law needs to be 'compatible with the pre-existing social norms' and that 'the population is already familiar with the basic principles of these laws'.[81] This argument seems to suggest that there should be historical ties, cultural relations or even colonialism relationship between the host and donor states. It is arguable that this viewpoint is valid for law reform activities where a foreign law is introduced or imposed from above without any concerns as to their compatibility with the recipient or host jurisdiction. However, the argument seems to over-generalise and include where the adoption is made consciously, and the law is revised throughout the years to reflect the business practices, social fabric or culture of the population.

Secondly, propagation of global norms happens in a number of ways. Some scholars address this as 'isomorphism' or 'convergence'.[82] According to DiMaggio and Powell isomorphic change (convergence) occurs either through political influence (*coercive isomorphism*) or by responses to uncertainty (*mimetic isomorphism*) or stems from professionalisation (*normative isomorphism*).[83] Coercive isomorphism occurs when political pressures require a reform.[84] This type of reform may be unproductive in the

[78] Turkish civil and obligations codes which were adopted from Swiss law can be given as an example.

[79] For more discussion on this see Walsh, 'The "Law"' (2000) 12.

[80] D Berkowitz, K Pistor and J-F Richard, 'The Transplant Effect' 51 *American Journal of Comparative Law* (2003) 163, 189–90. Berkowitz et al also suggest that secured transactions legislative texts are marketed by the Western states to the Eastern states with promises of financial aid or membership to the EU; see at 164. See also G Ajani, 'By Chance and Prestige: Legal Transplants in Russia and Eastern Europe' (1995) 43 *American Journal of Comparative Law* 93. One cannot agree with this presumptive observation within the context of the UNCITRAL Legislative Guide on Secured Transactions.

[81] See Berkowitz, Pistor and Richard, 'The Transplant Effect' (2003) 190. For similar lines of arguments K Pistor, Y Kienan, J Kleinheisterkamp and M West, 'Innovation in Corporate Law' (2003) 31 *Journal of Comparative Economics* 676.

[82] See eg PJ DiMaggio and WW Powell, 'The Iron Cage Revisited: Institutional Isomorphism and Collective Rationality in Organizational Fields' (1983) 48 *American Sociological Review* 147; T Halliday and B Carruthers, *Bankrupt: Global Lawmaking and Systematic Financial Crisis* (Stanford, Stanford University Press, 2009) xxiii.

[83] DiMaggio and Powell (ibid) 150ff.

[84] Halliday and Carruthers exemplified this with the reform of laws as a condition of credit by the IMF. See ibid, xxiii and 173–74.

long term due to the fact that the host state has no prior exposure or evaluation because outside factors determine whether or not the chosen law is worth adopting.[85] Mimetic isomorphism is similar to legal transplantation and occurs when a system is modelled upon another in order to overcome uncertainty.[86] Finally, the normative isomorphism is where professionals define and determine the rules or laws as appropriate.[87]

It is clear that the term 'transplant' connotes negative meaning and is used to explain ideological agendas when it is compared with 'harmonisation', which is an apolitical term. In order to make secured credit affordable the law needs to respond to the needs of businesses by ensuring transactional certainty. One way to achieve this is to modernise the law in the light of the texts prepared by the international legislative organs. The other way is to import foreign law and adapt its legal rules together with academic opinions, precedents and jurisprudence.

Guide and model law are soft-law texts. They contain commentary, guide to enactment, sections and recommendations. Guide is no law and by definition it cannot be prescriptive. It contains general rules and 'the greater the generality of the rule (the wider the range of situations that the rule applies to), the greater will be the need to tune its application to the particular circumstances of the case'.[88]

The risk in law reform which is based on legal transplants is that the rules of the donor country may not necessarily fit perfectly to the economic and social conditions of the host country. This is due to the fact that the legal rules evolve from bottom to top[89] and they are based on social, cultural and economic conditions, and business practices of a country.[90] More serious risk can be experienced when legal advisors who are not sensitive to the legal culture or social conditions in the host nation attempt to write new laws for countries that need modernisation.[91] Legal transplants may seem to be unworkable as the law and institutions of another state may not be suitable to be used in law-making.[92] It is argued that this line of argument applies squarely to legal transplants but does not extend to harmonisation or modernisation as these include different legal cultures and states with varied level of economic development.

[85] F Schauer, 'The Politics and Incentives of Legal Transplantation' (2000) Center for International Development at Harvard Working Paper No 44, 24, available at www.cid.harvard.edu/cidwp/044.htm. See also J Armour, S Deakin, P Lele and M Siems, 'How do legal rules evolve? Evidence from a Cross-Country Comparison of Shareholder, Creditor and Worker Protection' (2009) 57 *American Journal of Comparative Law* 579. Armour et al suggest that legal culture may be open to change but this needs to be based on concepts that the legal culture is familiar with.

[86] It can be argued that the adoption of the Swiss Civil and Obligations Codes, doctrines, scholarly writings and judicial precedents by Turkey in 1926 seems to explain this concept.

[87] Halliday and Carruthers, *Bankrupt* (2009) xxiii; DiMaggio and Powell, 'The Iron Cage Revisited' (1983) 152ff.

[88] M Chen-Wishart, 'Legal Transplant and Undue Influence: lost in translation or a working misunderstanding?' (2013) 62 *International & Comparative Law Quarterly* 1, 25.

[89] See generally Cooter, 'Normative Failure' (1999).

[90] See eg H Collins 'European Private Law and Cultural Identity of States' (1995) *European Review of Private Law* 353. Some scholars reject the idea of legal transplants on the grounds of culture see eg P Legrand 'The Impossibility of Legal Transplants' (1997) 4 *Maastricht Journal of European and Comparative Law* 111.

[91] For more information on legal reforms and problems during that process see L Mistelis, 'Regulatory Aspects: Globalization, Harmonisation, Legal Transplants and Law reform-Some Fundamental Observations' (2000) 34 *International Law* 1055, 1064–65.

[92] O. Kahn-Freund, 'On Uses and Misuses of Comparative Law' (1974) 37 *Modern Law Review* 1, 12ff.

D. What Harmonisation is and is not

It is axiomatic that one of the fundamental reasons why there are divergent views on the efficiency of harmonised modernisation of secured transactions laws is that the meaning of harmonisation has not been understood properly. For that reason, harmonisation or harmonised modernisation of laws has been regarded as one of the methods of disguised imposition of economically developed nations' laws onto the developing or transitional nations. This has been based on the fact that, particularly, within the scope of the work of UNCITRAL, certain economically developed nations have been very active in terms of attendance as delegations, the same delegates' frequency of attendance and the relationship of non-governmental organisations with those economically developed nations.[93]

Private and global law-making bring together concerns regarding legitimacy. Legitimacy, in that sense, attributes effectiveness and powerfulness to the international organisation and the legal instrument prepared by that organisation.[94] Incorporation of divergent views and inclusiveness are antidotes to arguments of lack of legitimacy and of persuasiveness.[95] It can be submitted in the secured transactions field, and the presence of non-governmental organisations (NGOs), lobbying groups and states in the same process is a positive thing. It is the members of these organisations and lawyers who are represented by the NGOs who will be end users. Further, NGOs and market players bring their expertise.[96] Their input enriches the end product, though in UNCITRAL NGOs do not take part in the decision-making process and have no votes. This does not mean that the product has to be accepted or will be a perfect piece of legislation. It means that the product, the legislative text, takes into account business practices and the interest of lenders (by providing 'transactional certainty') and borrowers (by being 'distributionally favorable').[97]

V. Conclusions

Modernisation of secured transactions laws is an essential process for businesses in both emerging and developed economies. The UNCITRAL Guide and the Model Law introduce modern principles that apply in both domestic and cross-border

[93] See generally Halliday, Pacewicz and Block-Lieb, 'Who Governs?' (2013).

[94] Black and Rouch suggest four criteria: Democratic, Constitutional, Functional or performance-based legitimacy, and Values and objectives-based criteria. See J Black and D Rouch, 'The Development of the Global Markets as Rule-makers: Engagement and Legitimacy' (2008) 2 *Law and Financial Markets Review* 218, 225. For discussion of legitimacy related to UNCITRAL, see CR Kelly (2009) 'The Politics of International Economic Law: Legitimacy and the UNCITRAL Working Methods', Brooklyn Law School Legal Studies Research Papers Working Paper Series No 140.

[95] Block-Lieb and Halliday 'Legitimation and Global Lawmaking' (2006).

[96] For example, Cape Town Convention provides a very good example of how global law-making should be. During the deliberations of the Convention market players, airline representatives, manufacturers, etc took active part and the Convention with its ratification numbers can be regarded as a July 2019.

[97] For a discussion of lawmaking and revision of the UCC Art 9 see R Scott, 'The Politics of Article 9' (1994) 80 *Virginia Law Review* 1784, 1850.

financing transactions. The fact that the Guide and the Model Law have certain aspects of the UCC Article 9 does not mean that they propagate imperialistic law. Law is 'a vehicle for social change'[98] and it needs to be responsive to financial, social and cultural changes.[99] That social change, as a result of global financial crisis, occurs both in the developed and developing economies. Comparative law is there to assist even the most developed legal systems. Every jurisdiction has a lot to learn from other jurisdictions and international legislative texts that introduce modern principles.

[98] R Wacks, *Philosophy of Law: A Very Short Introduction* (Oxford, Oxford University Press, 2006) xii.

[99] See generally P Nonet and P Selznick, *Law and Society in Transition Toward Responsive Law* (New York, Harper & Row, 1978).

13

The Role of Innovation in Cross-Border Lending

RICHARD M KOHN

Recent years have witnessed the rapid globalisation of US middle-market companies. Today's middle-market company has customers in other countries, imports inventory from foreign suppliers, sets up foreign distribution and manufacturing operations and acquires foreign companies. Middle-market companies form the backbone of our globalised economy. According to the US Department of Commerce, in 2016, 98 per cent of all US exporters and 97 per cent of all US importers were small and medium-sized businesses (SMEs), defined for that purpose as companies having fewer than 500 employees.[1]

These cross-border activities require significant working capital and acquisition financing, a circumstance that has posed a serious challenge for lenders to middle-market companies. Until fairly recently, most US lenders were extremely reluctant to engage in cross-border lending. Instead, they confined their middle-market lending to purely domestic transactions in which the borrower, the guarantors and the collateral all were located in the US. As a result, many US companies were unable to obtain the financing they needed to fund their escalating cross-border activities.

However, recent years have witnessed a sea-change in the attitudes of many US lenders. Motivated by a desire to accommodate the rapidly increasing cross-border financing needs of their existing and prospective borrowers, US lenders have risen to the challenge, pushing themselves to find ways to lend to borrowers, and against assets, located in other countries. This transformation is not confined to large money-centre banks; smaller banks, and non-banks as well, have increasingly been making cross-border loans.

This sea-change in attitude has been accompanied by a rich profusion of innovative ideas. The innovation has taken three principal forms: (i) innovation in the ways that US lenders have been willing to step out of the comfort zone of their domestic laws to make loans in other countries having legal regimes that are not conducive to US-style lending; (ii) innovation in the way that lenders and their lawyers have developed creative legal concepts and loan structures to bridge the gap between the laws of these other

[1] www.trade.gov/mas/ian/build/groups/public/@tg_ian/documents/webcontent/tg_ian_005538.pdf.

countries and the needs of modern financing transactions; and (iii) innovation in the way that international organisations such as UNCITRAL, UNIDROIT and the World Bank are helping countries modernise their secured transactions laws to promote low-cost secured credit that stimulates the creation of jobs, higher standards of living and general economic growth. This chapter discusses all of these forms of innovation.

I. The Increasing Willingness of US Lenders to Make Cross-border Loans

Unable to find more than a few countries that have adopted secured transactions laws even remotely similar to US laws, many US lenders have searched instead for countries in which the laws offer the functional equivalent of the legal protections they enjoy under US law.

As a result, the list of countries in which US lenders are willing to make loans has grown steadily in recent years. Even 15 years ago, loans by US lenders to companies located in the UK, the Netherlands and Germany were considered to be pioneering. Now they are routine. Moreover, the list of 'lender-friendly' jurisdictions has grown over the past 15 years to include Australia, Belgium, Canada, Germany, Hong Kong, Ireland, the Netherlands, New Zealand, Singapore, Switzerland and the UK, among others, and the list continues to grow.

The expansion of the list of lender-friendly countries has been driven primarily by market forces, as middle-market companies have requested lenders to consider lending in the countries in which these companies are conducting business. Mexico provides a real-time laboratory that reveals how this process occurs. Until recently, many US lenders would not consider lending in Mexico, primarily out of a concern as to the quality of the Mexican courts. However, in recent years US lending in Mexico has increased, in part because automotive manufacturers in Mexico recently began to insist that their suppliers in the US and other countries set up manufacturing or assembly plants in Mexico. This, in turn, created a need on the part of such suppliers to finance their newly established Mexican operations, which translated into more requests by such suppliers to US lenders to make loans secured by Mexican collateral. In response, some US lenders have re-evaluated their previous reluctance to make loans in Mexico in an effort to accommodate these suppliers. At the same time, Mexico has been taking steps to improve the quality of its laws and judicial system, and otherwise to rebrand itself as a commercially vibrant and welcoming jurisdiction. For example, according to the US Department of Commerce, as of April 2019 Mexico had entered into free-trade agreements with more countries than any other country.[2] As a result of these factors, it is highly probable that Mexico will increasingly be viewed as a lender-friendly country, and that US lenders will increasingly make loans there. The extent to which the current protectionist attitude of the US Government will affect trade between the US and Mexico and dampen the willingness of US lenders to lend in Mexico remains to be seen. However, it

[2] www.export.gov/article?id=Mexico-Trade-Agreements.

is quite possible that a reduction in US–Mexico trade would merely create a vacuum in Mexico that lenders in other countries would fill.

Even if US lenders are willing to make a loan in given country, they often are confronted with secured transactions laws that pose legal risks not present under US law. Examples of such risks abound, and the manner in which lenders have addressed them in specific financing transactions provides graphic illustrations of innovation in action. Unlike the innovation discussed in section II below, which results in the birth of new legal concepts and loan structures, these instances of innovation express themselves as a metamorphosis of traditional US domestic lending practices to address, or ultimately accept, the perceived legal risks of lending under unfamiliar legal regimes. The following list examines some of those risks, and the ways in which US lenders have addressed them.

(1) *Priority claims.* A lender may discover that the laws of another country provide for preferential claims that take priority over the lender's security interest. This may take the form of a statute providing that tax or wage claims are granted priority over the lender's pre-existing security interest in the borrower's assets. It may also take the form of a 'carve-out' for unsecured creditors, which mandates that a share of the proceeds of certain types of collateral be set aside for the benefit of unsecured creditors. In the UK, for example, the law provides that approximately 20 per cent of the proceeds of a 'floating charge', up to a specified cap, be set aside for the benefit of unsecured creditors. Another example is provided by Finnish law, which imposes a carve-out for unsecured creditors of 50 per cent of the proceeds of an enterprise mortgage.

The manner in which US lenders respond to the existence of these claims typically will depend upon the type of financing in which the lenders are engaged. For those lenders that provide 'asset-based lending' – a form of financing prevalent in the US in which revolving loans are made against a 'borrowing base' comprised of the borrower's eligible receivables or inventory (or both) – the response to the existence of priority claims often will be to reserve (ie hold back) a portion of the loan proceeds sufficient to cover the projected amount of the priority claims. However, lenders have also developed other ways to address priority claims. For example, in the case of the UK carve-out discussed above, current UK jurisprudence enables lenders to avoid the carve-out when financing receivables by converting the 'floating charge' (which is subject to the carve-out) to a 'fixed charge' (which is not subject to the carve-out). To accomplish this, the borrower is required to notify its account debtors to make payments directly to a bank account under the control of the lender. These proceeds are transferred by the depository bank to the lender on a daily basis to reduce the outstanding balance of the loan, free of the carve-out.

Countries are increasingly recognising the adverse impact that priority claims can have on the availability of credit. For example, in recent years, both Sweden and Belgium have repealed their carve-outs for unsecured lenders in an effort to promote lending.

(2) *Retention-of-title claims.* In many jurisdictions, it is common for suppliers of goods to retain title to the goods until the purchase price for the goods is paid in full. As a result, the borrower may not own the inventory that it uses in the operation of its business, a circumstance that presents a challenge for US lenders, given that

retention-of title claims are not recognised under US law.[3] Moreover, in most jurisdictions that recognise retention-of-title claims, the supplier is not required to register a public notice of the claim. As a result, the lender may not even be aware of the existence of these claims of suppliers. Also, in some jurisdictions, such as Germany, it is possible for the supplier to obtain an 'extended' retention-of-title claim that reaches beyond the goods themselves into the receivables generated when the goods are sold. Nevertheless, when lending in a jurisdiction that recognises retention-of-title claims, US lenders have been willing to address the possible existence of these claims through a combination of due diligence (by examining the purchase orders and other documents evidencing the borrower's purchases of goods from its suppliers), reliance on the borrower's representations concerning the absence of such claims and adjustments to the borrowing base.

(3) *Anti-assignment clauses.* In many countries, it is quite common for the documents evidencing a receivable to include a restriction on the ability of the owner of the receivable to assign or encumber it. This is particularly the case where the debtor on the receivable has a superior bargaining position. Anti-assignment clauses pose an unfamiliar risk for US lenders, given that US law renders such clauses unenforceable in the case of most trade receivables.[4] Nevertheless, US lenders have shown a willingness to conduct the extra due diligence required to determine whether anti-assignment clauses exist in the receivables they are being asked to finance and to treat the affected receivables as ineligible for borrowing.

(4) *Additional formalities.* One of the hallmarks of the Uniform Commercial Code (UCC) is the efficiency with which it enables security interests to be created and enforced. In stark contrast, the laws of many countries adopt a highly formalistic approach that is significantly less efficient. For example, they may require that a separate security document be used for each category of collateral, rather than permitting a 'blanket' security agreement that efficiently covers all forms of personal property, or they may require that the lender and borrower appear (either in person or pursuant to a prescribed form of power of attorney) before a professional notary in connection with the execution of certain types of security document. In addition, the unavailability of non-judicial remedies in many jurisdictions adds time and complexity to the enforcement of security interests, a situation that is unfamiliar to US lenders, who are accustomed to the availability of efficient non-judicial remedies under the UCC. However, US lenders have been willing to educate themselves concerning these requirements in order to the accommodate the needs of their borrowers.

(5) *The unavailability of a non-possessory security interest.* In some jurisdictions, it is not possible to obtain a non-possessory security interest in tangible moveable property such as inventory, a circumstance that precludes lenders from financing inventory where the borrower needs to retain possession of the inventory for purposes of manufacture or

[3] Under US law, contractual retention-of-title provisions are treated as unperfected security interests. UCC, §§ 1-201(b)(35) and 2-401(1).

[4] UCC, §9-406(d).

assembly. US lenders have demonstrated a willingness to search for creative solutions to this problem, such as by identifying situations in which a customer of the borrower, a warehouse or other bailee may be willing to serve as the lender's agent for purposes of establishing possession. As discussed below, in at least one instance, lawyers in the country itself were able to offer an innovative solution by developing a creative new security device.[5]

(6) *The unavailability of a security interest in future receivables and inventory.* Another important characteristic of the UCC is the ease with which it permits security interests to be created in future receivables as they arise, and future inventory as it is acquired, in the ordinary course of the borrower's business. In many other countries, obtaining a security interest in future receivables and inventory requires the execution of additional documents or registrations, which can add complexity and cost to a financing transaction. Here, US lenders have shown a willingness to understand and adjust to the procedures prescribed by foreign law by incorporating them in their loan documents.

(7) *The absence of an efficient secured transactions registry.* The cornerstone of a modern secured transactions regime is a registry that enables secured creditors to register their security interests and search for potentially competing security interests, and the absence of such a registry in a given country can pose a major impediment to lending in that country. In some countries, registrations can only be made with the intervention of a professional notary. In other countries, the registry is not searchable, but exists only to serve the evidentiary function of enabling a secured creditor to prove that its security interest was created at a particular time. In still other countries, there is no registry at all, forcing lenders to rely primarily upon representations from their borrower as to the absence of competing security rights – a circumstance that poses a significant challenge for US lenders accustomed to relying on the highly efficient and transparent UCC registries.

In some countries that do have a fully searchable registry, the law inserts a complication in the form of a grace period for registration: A security interest registered within a specified number of days after the execution of the security agreement is deemed to have been registered as of the date of execution of the security agreement for purposes of determining the priority of the security interest vis-à-vis competing security interests. Although these grace periods are intended to provide an accommodation for secured parties, they also create the risk that a search of the registry might not reveal a competing security interest that could still achieve priority.[6] In spite of these differences with

[5] See discussion of the Belgian tolling arrangement in section II D.

[6] This risk can be illustrated by the following example: The law of a particular country provides for a 21-day grace period for registration of security interests. Lender 1 signs a security agreement with Borrower on Day 1 but does not register a notice of its security interest immediately. On Day 10, Lender 2 conducts a search of the registry that reveals no competing security interests. Lender 2 signs a security agreement with Borrower on Day 11, which it registers on Day 12. Lender 1 then registers its security interest on Day 15, within its 21-day grace period. Under these facts, Lender 2's security interest would have priority.

US registries, US lenders have increasingly been willing to venture out of their comfort zones to accommodate the needs of their borrowers.

Impediments to secured lending are not only found in a country's secured transactions laws; they may also be found in other bodies of law. An 'upstream' guarantee (that is, a guarantee by a subsidiary company of a loan made to its parent company) is a case in point. Imagine a US parent company with a foreign subsidiary that wishes to obtain credit from a US bank based upon the value of inventory owned by the subsidiary and located in the subsidiary's jurisdiction of organisation. It is quite common to structure such financing as a loan to the US parent company supported by a guarantee given by the subsidiary, which guarantee would be secured by a security interest in the subsidiary's inventory. However, the lender may find that the laws of the subsidiary's jurisdiction impose severe limits upon the ability of the subsidiary to guarantee a loan made to its parent company. For example, such restrictions may limit the amount of the guarantee to (i) the amount of cash proceeds that the subsidiary actually receives from the financing, or (ii) a specified percentage of the subsidiary's net worth determined at the time the guarantee is given. In some cases, the law may provide that the subsidiary may not make a payment in respect of the guarantee to the extent that doing so would render it insolvent, determined at the time of enforcement. Such a restriction precludes the lender from relying upon the guarantee when it structures the financing transaction, because the lender cannot know, at the time it receives the guarantee, what the financial condition of the guarantor will be at the time of enforcement. Faced with this circumstance, the lender is compelled to examine alternative loan structures, such as making a loan directly to the subsidiary, or reducing the amount of credit it extends.

'Financial assistance' laws provide an additional example. Laws in many EU Member States and elsewhere make it illegal for a company domiciled in the state to grant a guarantee or a security interest in its assets to secure a loan made to finance the acquisition of the company's shares (a transaction often referred to as a 'leveraged buyout'). Recognising that these laws can present a serious obstacle to financing transactions, in recent years the UK, the Netherlands and Singapore have repealed their financial assistance laws for private companies in an effort to promote the availability of credit.

Other frequently encountered impediments are a corrupt or unfair judicial system, under which the rights of a non-domestic lender may not be recognized in a fair and efficient manner, and an insolvency law that fails to recognise properly documented and otherwise enforceable security interests. In evaluating a judicial system or an insolvency law, lenders typically do not apply a standard that is biased in favour of creditors, but rather one that can assure merely a reasonable degree of certainty that their rights will be respected. However, in those countries in which this standard cannot be met, lenders may innovate by exploring security devices that operate independently of the courts and insolvency laws. An example is the Mexican *fideicomiso de garantía*, a legislatively created security device in which the assets serving as collateral are transferred to a security trust that is 'bankruptcy remote' (that is, the assets of the grantor will not form a part of the grantor's insolvency estate) and with respect to which the parties are free to agree upon non-judicial enforcement proceedings in the event of the borrower's default.

II. The Willingness of Lenders and their Lawyers to Develop Innovative Legal Concepts and Loan Structures

Recent years have witnessed some striking examples of ways in which lenders and their lawyers have developed innovative legal concepts and loan structures to bridge the gap between the realities of outmoded secured transactions regimes and the needs of modern financing transactions. This section of the chapter discusses four of those examples: 'centralisation' of receivables; the collateral allocation mechanism; parallel debt; and Belgian tolling arrangements.

A. 'Centralisation' of Receivables

Some multi-national companies have corporate structures in which one or more of the entities comprising the structure are domiciled in countries with laws that are not conducive to obtaining financing. Often, these corporate structures are designed to achieve a beneficial tax structure for the group, but in some cases insufficient consideration is given to the impact that the structure may have upon the group's ability to obtain needed financing.

Assume that a corporate group that wishes to obtain receivables financing is comprised of a US parent holding company and subsidiaries in a number of jurisdictions with laws inhospitable to receivables financing. Here, a principle called 'centralisation' has been developed by lenders and their lawyers. Under this principle, receivables are transferred to another member of the borrower's corporate group domiciled in a country where laws are more favourable, such as the UK, the Netherlands or Ireland (the 'finance affiliate'). This can occur using one of two methods. Under the first method, receivables generated by a foreign member of the corporate group are assigned to the finance affiliate pursuant to a 'true sale' (ie an arm's-length transaction that will withstand attack from the creditors, or an insolvency representative, of the transferring company). Under the second method, the receivables are generated in the first place by the finance affiliate. Under either method, the result is that the receivables are owned by an entity that is located in a lender-friendly country. The implementation of either method can be costly, as well as operationally disruptive; however, the cost and disruption can be more than outweighed by the increased access to financing that can be achieved using centralisation.

B. The Collateral Allocation Mechanism

Sometimes the impediment to making a cross-border loan is internal to the lender: the inability to make loans to a foreign borrower. This issue arises often in syndicated loans to corporate groups having borrowers in the US and also in foreign countries, where some lenders in the syndicate are not able or willing to make loans to a non-US borrower.

To address this issue, lenders and their lawyers have developed a concept known as the collateral allocation mechanism (CAM), under which loans to the US borrowers in the corporate group are made by those lenders that are able to make loans to US entities, and loans to the non-US borrowers in the corporate group are made by those lenders that are able to make loans to non-US entities. The loan documents provide that, upon the occurrence a significant triggering event, such as material default by the borrowers resulting in acceleration of the loans, each of the lenders is required to 'true up' its position in the loan facility by purchasing interests in the loan position of each of the other lenders, with the result that each lender bears a proportionate share of both the US loans and the foreign loans. Using the CAM, the loan syndicate is able to accommodate lenders that are able to make foreign loans and those that are not, thereby increasing the range of lenders that are available to participate in the borrowers' credit facility and enhancing the borrowers' access to credit.

C. Parallel Debt

In some civil law jurisdictions, each time the composition of the parties to certain types of security device is changed, the documents evidencing the security device must be amended. This presents a serious problem in syndicated loan facilities, where the composition of the syndicate of lenders may change often as lenders assign all or portions of their interest in the loans to other lenders.

In many countries, this issue is addressed by using an administrative agent (a concept based upon agency law) or a security trustee (a concept based upon trust law), but in some civil law jurisdictions these mechanisms are not available. To address this circumstance, lenders and their lawyers have developed a concept known as 'parallel debt'.

The idea is this: in addition to the debt owing to the lenders under the credit agreement (the 'corresponding debt'), a second debt (the 'parallel debt') is created. The parallel debt functions in tandem with the corresponding debt: Payments on the corresponding debt also reduce the parallel debt; payments on the parallel debt also reduce the corresponding debt; and the total of the parallel debt and the corresponding debt can never exceed the corresponding debt. The security interests secure only the parallel debt and not the corresponding debt; thus, lenders may move freely in and out of the syndicate (under which only the corresponding debt is owing) without triggering the requirement of an amendment to the security documents.

Although there is little legal authority supporting the concept of parallel debt,[7] billions of dollar-, euro- and sterling-denominated credit facilities have employed a parallel debt structure predicated on the presumed effectiveness of this highly innovative concept.

[7] The principal case usually cited as authority for the enforceability of parallel debt is the decision of the French Cour de Cassation in the *Belvédère* case, Arrêt n° 840 du 13 Septembre 2011 (10-25.633; 10-25.731; 10-25.908), Cour de Cassation, France. However, the case is less than ideal as authority, given that the French Supreme Court merely enforced a parallel debt provision in a credit agreement governed by New York law on the ground that the provision did not violate French public policy. A second judicial decision often cited in support of parallel debt is the decision of the Supreme Court of Poland of 9 October 2009 (file no IV CSK 145/09), which implied that it was possible to use a parallel debt mechanism under Polish law. However, the case has little value as precedent because the parallel debt feature of the credit facility involved in that case was not challenged.

D. Belgian Tolling Arrangements

One of the most innovative techniques developed by lenders and lawyers to facilitate modern financing transactions is the Belgian 'tolling arrangement'. Prior to the effectiveness of Belgium's new secured transactions regime on 1 January 2018, Belgian law did not recognise the concept of a non-possessory security interest in tangible moveable property such as inventory (except in the limited case of an enterprise mortgage, which was available only to qualified lenders, and only covered 50 per cent of the grantor's inventory). Thus, in order for a lender to obtain an enforceable security interest in inventory owned by its borrower and located in Belgium, the lender had to maintain possession of the inventory, either directly or indirectly through an agent. As noted above,[8] this situation made it highly impractical for lenders to finance a borrower's inventory, since it is normally essential for the borrower to maintain possession of its inventory for use in the operation of its business, unless the inventory is of a type that can practically be stored in a public warehouse under the lender's control.

However, in an effort to address this situation, Belgian lawyers devised an ingenious solution known as a 'tolling structure'. The concept underlying the tolling structure is to detach the possession of the inventory from its legal ownership. Thus, title to the inventory would be held by one member of the corporate group, while another member of the corporate group – the member that conducted the manufacturing or assembly operations – maintained actual possession of the inventory and was thereby able to use the inventory in the operation of its business. The latter entity would then agree to hold the inventory as the agent of the lender, thereby enabling the lender to satisfy the requirement of possession. An example of the structure is depicted in Figure 13.1.

Figure 13.1 Tolling structure diagram

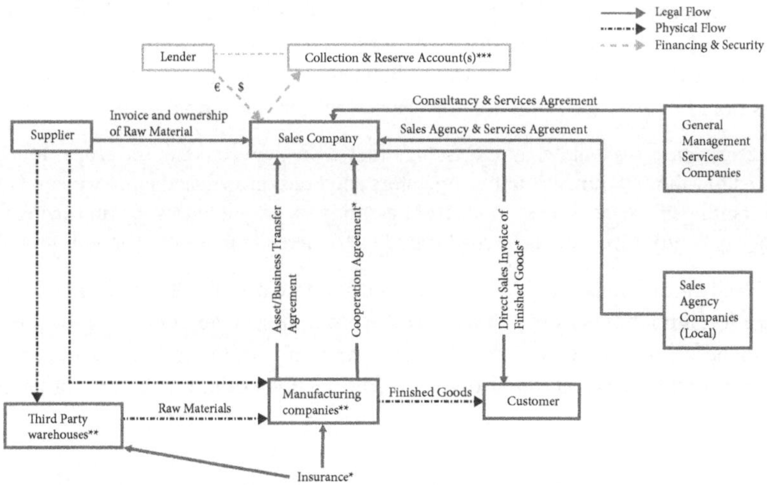

* Pledge or similar security over Receivables resulting out of Key Contract and Trade Contracts
** Pledge or similar security over Inventory, including Raw Material, Work in Progress and Finished Products
*** Pledge or similar security over Collection and Reserve Account(s)

Source: This chart is reprinted with the kind permission of the Belgian law firm Lydian.

[8] See list item (5) in section I.

The Belgian tolling structure only works for corporate groups in which it is practical for one entity in the group to hold title and another to hold possession. Fortunately for Belgian borrowers, the need for tolling structures was significantly reduced when Belgium's new secured transactions law, which recognises non-possessory security interests in inventory, became effective on 1 January 2018, although the Belgian finance market still views the tolling structure as beneficial for borrowers and lenders in various respects. However, the tolling structure, like the other innovative concepts discussed in this section, demonstrates the great extent to which lenders and their lawyers are willing to innovate in order to meet the needs of modern financing transactions.

III. Innovation Through Secured Transactions Reform

So far, this chapter has focused on innovations in cross-border lending contributed by the world of corporate finance. However, the world of secured transactions reform has provided another, equally powerful, source of innovation.

It has always seemed to me that the genius of UNCITRAL resides in its recognition of the power of commerce as a force for promoting peace, by helping businesses to grow, creating jobs, raising standards of living and stimulating overall economic growth. Equally significant is UNCITRAL's recognition that one of the most effective ways of stimulating commerce is the promotion of low-cost secured credit. These recognitions are also integral to the philosophies and achievements of the World Bank, UNIDROIT and the other international organisations that devote themselves to secured transactions reform.

The recognition that secured credit can be a powerful economic driver has found increasing acceptance. For example, the new Belgian secured transactions law referred to above, which was inspired, in part, by the UNCITRAL Legislative Guide on Secured Transactions (2007), was rooted in the recognition that the availability of secured credit for Belgian SMEs was an effective way to help Belgium lift itself from the Great Recession. As noted in a report to the Belgian Parliament in December 2012:

> The economic crisis that Belgium is facing recalled the importance of the proper functioning of credit facilities to fund economic operators and boost growth and employment. However, the granting of credits is inseparable from granting security interests. By improving the efficiency of security, we reduce the cost of credit and therefore promote economic growth.[9]

The secured credit envisioned by this report can come not only from domestic lenders, but from foreign lenders as well. Like credit from domestic lenders, cross-border credit helps businesses grow, creates jobs, improves standards of living and stimulates overall economic growth. However, cross-border credit has the additional benefit of promoting

[9] See, 'Exposé introductif de Mme AnnemieTurtelboom, ministre de la justice, sur les projets de loi DOC 53 463/001 et DOC 53 2464/001' in *Rapport fait au nom de la commission de la justice par Mme Carina Van Cauter*, 21 December 2012: '*La crise économique à laquelle la Belgique est confrontée a rappelé l'importance d'un bon fonctionnement des mécanismes de crédit pour financer les opérateurs économiques et stimuler la croissance et l'emploi. Or, l'octroi de crédits est indissociable de la constitution de droits de sûreté. En améliorant l'efficacité de ces derniers, l'on réduit le coût du crédit et l'on favorise donc la croissance économique.*'

economic interdependence of countries, as well as welcome communication and relationships among business people in those countries.

The world of cross-border corporate finance and the world of secured transactions reform are quite different, yet they intersect in ways that enhance the impact of their respective innovations. The very same laws championed by international organisations to enable an SME in a developing economy to obtain credit can also encourage a major money-centre bank to fund a large multi-national corporate credit facility to a borrower with a subsidiary in that country. In this way, secured transactions reform facilitates corporate finance. On the other hand, the increased willingness of lenders in developed economies to make cross-border loans encourages other countries to modernise their secured transactions laws in order to attract capital, demonstrating that the world of corporate finance can also influence secured transactions reform.

We owe a debt of gratitude to both worlds: to the world of secured transactions reform for the innovation it displays as it encourages countries to modernise their laws to promote low-cost credit, and to the world of corporate finance for the innovation it displays in searching for ways to serve an increasingly globalised middle market. Each world helps to weave the tapestry of commerce that blankets the earth, improving the quality of life for diverse peoples and enhancing trust and economic bonds across national boundaries.

14

Reform of Moveable Transactions Law in Scotland

ANDREW STEVEN

'Law reform takes time', Sir Roy Goode has written.[1] I agree without reservation.[2] Moveable transactions law reform in Scotland is very much a case in point. This area of law equates broadly with what is known as 'personal property security law' in common law jurisdictions. Since at least 1897 there have been serious calls for reform,[3] but apart from the controversial introduction of the floating charge in 1961 very little has happened.

The subject, however, is presently much to the fore because the Scottish Law Commission (SLC) has recently completed a long-term project on the area. This has culminated in the publication of a report and draft legislation. It is now a matter for the Scottish Government to decide whether to take forward the SLC's recommendations.

This chapter attempts to provide an overview of the subject set against the general background of the issue of harmonisation of commercial law. It will be structured as follows. Section I will consider the current law. Section II will look at previous attempts to reform the law. Section III describes the SLC project. Section IV discusses the question of harmonisation, in particular with the law of England and Wales. Section V considers the recommendations that the SLC has made.

I. Current Law

A. General

'Moveable transactions law' is a term which will be searched for in vain in books on Scottish law. It was coined only to describe the SLC's project. As the name suggests, it

[1] R Goode, 'Reforming the Law of Secured Transactions in Jersey' in L Gullifer and O Akseli (eds), *Secured Transactions Law Reform: Principles, Policies and Practice* (Oxford, Hart, 2016) 207.

[2] cf, however, Lord Thomas of Cwmgiedd, 'Law Reform Now in 21st Century Britain: Brexit and Beyond', Scarman Lecture 27 June 2017 available at www.judiciary.gov.uk/announcements/speech-by-the-lord-chief-justice-law-reform-now-in-21st-century-britain-brexit-and-beyond.

[3] WM Gloag and JM Irvine, *Law of Rights in Security, Heritable and Moveable including Cautionary Obligations* (Edinburgh, W Green, 1897, reprinted 1987) 187–88.

is about moveable rather than immoveable property. Beyond that it divides into two broad areas: (a) transfer of moveable property; and (b) security over moveable property. Moveable property can be divided into two types: (1) corporeal moveable property; and (2) incorporeal moveable property.[4] The former equates broadly with what English law calls 'chattels' or 'choses in possession' and the latter with 'intangibles' or 'choses in action'. Thus, moveable transactions law can be divided into four subcategories: (a) transfer of corporeal moveable property; (b) transfer of incorporeal moveable property; (c) security over corporeal moveable property; and (d) security over incorporeal moveable property.

The usual reason for transfer of property is sale. In relation to subcategory (a), sale is regulated by the Sale of Goods Act 1979. As is well known, this legislation applies throughout the UK. Its predecessor, the Sale of Goods Act 1893, controversially replaced the Scottish common law with a codification primarily based on English law.[5] Under the previous law, delivery was required to transfer ownership and this remains the case for donation and barter. Given the UK-wide legislation on sale, subcategory (a) was outwith the scope of the SLC project and will not be discussed further here.

B. Transfer of Incorporeal Moveable Property

The most common form of incorporeal moveable property is a 'personal right', that is to say a right against another person to the performance of an obligation. Another way of expressing this concept is by using the word 'claim'.[6] The typical example of a claim is the right to be paid money. While a claim is the ordinary type of incorporeal moveable property, there are also special types such as financial instruments and intellectual property. The transfer of these, like the sale of goods, is usually a matter regulated by UK-wide legislation[7] and was also therefore beyond the scope of the SLC project.

Transfer of claims in Scotland is primarily governed by the common law, ie non-statute law. The only significant statutory inroad has been the Transmission of Moveable Property (Scotland) Act 1862, passed in the year that Queen Victoria celebrated her Silver Jubilee. A claim is transferred by means of an 'assignation'.[8] The word of course is very similar to 'assignment', the technical term for the equivalent transaction in English law. But there the similarity stops. In England assignments are equitable or legal. Scottish property law, being firmly grounded in Roman law, recognises no such distinction.[9]

[4] See further GL Gretton and AJM Steven, *Property, Trusts and Succession*, 3rd edn (Haywards Heath, Bloomsbury, 2017) paras 1.20–1.23.

[5] See, eg, DL Carey Miller, 'Scots and South African Property: Problem Transplants' in E Cooke (ed), *Modern Studies in Property Law Vol 1: Property 2000* (Oxford, Hart, 2001) 293–308.

[6] See, eg, Baron D Hume, *Lectures 1786–1822* (Edinburgh, Stair Society, 1952) vol 15, III,1; RG Anderson and J Biemans, 'Reform of Assignation in Security: Lessons from the Netherlands' (2012) 16 *Edinburgh Law Review* 24, 26.

[7] See, eg, the Stock Transfer Act 1963, the Copyright, Designs and Patents Act 1988 and the Trade Marks Act 1994.

[8] The leading modern text is RG Anderson, *Assignation* (Edinburgh, Edinburgh Legal Education Trust, 2008).

[9] On equity in Scots law see DJ Carr, *Ideas of Equity* (Edinburgh, Edinburgh Legal Education Trust, 2017).

A Scottish assignation alone, in contrast to an English equitable assignment, does not transfer the claim. For that to happen in Scotland the additional step of intimation is required. In other words, the account debtor must be notified or there can be no transfer. As Bankton, the eighteenth-century institutional writer,[10] puts it: 'The assignation is not completed by executing and delivering it to the assignee, but it must likewise be intimated to the debtor, till which is done, the [assignor] is not understood in our law to be denuded.'[11]

At common law intimation required a public act involving no less than five individuals. The 1862 Act reformed this to allow intimation by post (requiring a copy of the assignation to be sent) or by a notary. This formally remains the law today, but the courts have recently taken a more relaxed approach,[12] although the efficacy of a non-1862 Act intimation has yet to be fully considered in a case where the assignor has become insolvent. Business requires certainty on this issue.

It should be stressed that an unintimated assignation cannot be regarded as having transferred the claim as between assignor and assignee.[13] Scottish law following Roman law holds to the principle that ownership cannot be with one party for some purposes and another party for other purposes. Until intimation the claim continues to be held by the assignor for all purposes.

The requirement of intimation for transfer inhibits commerce and Scotland must be one of the few countries in the world still to have this rule.[14] The rule is cumbersome because a single assignation, for example in an invoice discounting transaction, might assign numerous claims against numerous debtors and will need to be intimated numerous times. If the 1862 Act is followed a copy of the assignation must be delivered with the intimation. Such documents may be lengthy and contain confidential information. Electronic intimation is not authorised because, unsurprisingly, the 1862 Act has nothing to say on this. Another major difficulty concerns future claims. A business cannot validly assign its future invoices because, until the claim which leads to the invoice arises, the identity of the debtor will typically be unknown, so that assignation is impossible.

These difficulties have led to Scottish lawyers being forced to use workarounds such as trust law or writing contracts under English law so that the need to intimate is removed. But such workarounds are not without risk or difficulty.[15] They also increase transaction costs.

[10] The institutional writers wrote texts in the 17th to 19th centuries based on the Roman model, which remain influential today in certain areas, notably property law. They include Stair, Bankton, Erskine and Bell.

[11] Bankton, *An Institute of the Laws of Scotland in Civil Rights: With Observations upon the Agreement or Diversity between them and the Laws of England* (1751–53, reprinted Edinburgh, Stair Society 1993–95), vols 41–43, 1.1.6.

[12] See *Christie Owen and Davies plc v Campbell* [2009] CSIH 26 and *Promontoria (Ram) Ltd v Moore* [2017] CSOH 88.

[13] See KGC Reid, 'Unintimated Assignations' 1989 *Scots Law Times (News)* 267, 269.

[14] See AF Salomons, 'Deformalisation of Assignment Law and the Position of the Debtor in European Property Law' (2007) 5 *European Review of Private Law* 639 and now French Civil Code, Art 1323 (in force 1 October 2016).

[15] See *Joint Administrators of Rangers Football Club Plc, Noters* [2012] CSOH 55, on which see GL Gretton, 'The Laws of the Game' (2012) 16 *Edinburgh Law Review* 414; Lord Reed, 'Triremes and Steamships: Scholars, Judges and the Use of the Past', The Scrymgeour Lecture, University of Dundee, 30 October 2015, 9–10, available at www.supremecourt.uk/docs/speech-151030.pdf.

C. Security Over Corporeal Moveable Property

This is another area where the common law principally governs matters and with one exception would be recognisable to a lawyer of the seventeenth century.[16] That exception is the floating charge which, as mentioned at the outset of this chapter, was introduced in 1961.[17] This reform was effected because of the restrictive nature of the common law, where effectively the only security right that can be granted is pledge.[18] As is familiar in many jurisdictions, pledge requires delivery of the property to the creditor. This is typically impractical because a business cannot operate without core assets such as computers and vehicles. Moreover, banks do not want to have to keep these. Only where goods are already being stored on premises owned by a third party, such as whisky in a warehouse, is pledge a practical option. But even here Scots law puts up a legal barrier because there is case authority that pledge can only be carried out by means of actual delivery.[19] If this is correct,[20] then pledge by intimation to a custodier[21] or by handing over a bill of lading is not competent.

The floating charge was borrowed from English law and operates at a practical level in the same way in Scotland. Only companies and a limited number of other corporations can grant floating charges.[22] They are typically granted over all assets including land. But they only require to be registered at Companies House and not in any other register such as the Land Register. The corporation is free to deal with its property despite it being subject to the charge. But on the charge being enforced, whether on insolvency or otherwise, it 'attaches'[23] to the corporation's property which can then be realised to recover the secured debt. Although floating charges were introduced in 1961, receivership did not follow until 1972.[24] As in England and Wales, floating charges are subject to the Insolvency Act 1986. They have a lower ranking in insolvency than fixed securities. Expenses of an administration,[25] preferential creditors[26] and the 'prescribed part'[27] carve-out for unsecured creditors must be paid first. Since the Enterprise Act 2002 the ability to appoint a receiver has been curbed and floating charges are normally now enforced by an administrator.[28]

Undoubtedly, the floating charge is popular amongst financial institutions in Scotland. But as a legal transplant it has been highly controversial. The reason for this is

[16] See AJM Steven, 'Scottish Property Law 2017' 2017 *Juridical Review* 21, 27.

[17] Companies (Floating Charges) (Scotland) Act 1961.

[18] See Eighth Report of the Law Reform Committee for Scotland (Cmnd 1017, 1960) para 2.

[19] *Hamilton v Western Bank* (1856) 19 R 152.

[20] For criticism, See, eg, AF Rodger, 'Pledge of Bills of Lading' 1971 *Juridical Review* 193.

[21] Note that attornment, whereby the custodian must confirm to the creditor that the goods are being held for that party, is not part of Scots law. Mere intimation suffices. See C Anderson, 'Delivery of Goods in the Custody of a Third Party: Operation and Basis' (2015) 19 *Edinburgh Law Review* 165.

[22] Companies Act 1985, s 462.

[23] For a comprehensive analysis, see AJD MacPherson, *The Attachment of the Floating Charge*, PhD Thesis, University of Edinburgh, 2017.

[24] Companies (Floating Charges and Receivers) (Scotland) Act 1972.

[25] Insolvency Act 1986, Sch B1, para 99(3).

[26] Insolvency Act 1986, s 59.

[27] Insolvency Act 1986, s 176A.

[28] Enterprise Act 2002, s 250, which amended the Insolvency Act 1986.

set out well by Lord Drummond Young in the important five-judge case of *MacMillan v T Leith Developments Ltd (in receivership and liquidation)*[29] where he states:

> The introduction of the floating charge into Scots law, and subsequently the concept of receivership, have created significant practical problems. A large part of the difficulty has, I think, been an attempt to reproduce concepts of English equity in a legal system that has no similar institution. The conceptual structure of English equity is distinctive, being based, in its original form, on a series of general principles that can be adapted to produce justice in individual cases. It is difficult to translate the institutions of English equity into another legal system, especially one based on the more rigorous conceptual structure of Roman law, as is the case with Scots law and most other European legal systems other than English law.[30]

This lack of coherence had been pointed out even more strongly by Lord President Cooper decades before when he said: 'It is clear in principle and amply supported by authority that a floating charge is utterly repugnant to the principles of Scots law.'[31] In *Sharp v Thomson*[32] the efforts of the House of Lords to integrate the statutory scheme for this security with the rules on transfer of ownership of land threatened the systematic foundations of Scottish property law.[33] The matter was referred to the SLC which produced a report recommending reforms,[34] but in the meantime the decision in *Burnett's Trustee v Grainger*[35] significantly reduced the impact of *Sharp*. The law on floating charges became the subject of a wider review by the SLC, which is discussed in the next section.

Scots law also recognises aircraft mortgages and ship mortgages, where the law is more or less the same as in England and Wales.[36] Clearly, however, these have a limited scope for use.

The restrictive nature of formal ('true') security rights over corporeal moveable property has meant that functional securities are commonly used.[37] Typically, ownership of the asset will be held by the creditor until the secured obligation is performed. For example, in commercial sales contracts there is a general practice of retaining ownership until all sums due by the purchaser have been paid and such clauses have been upheld by the courts.[38] Hire-purchase is another functional security which works in a similar way.

[29] [2017] CSIH 23. See AJD MacPherson, 'The Circle Squared? Floating Charges and Diligence after *MacMillan v T Leith Developments Ltd*' 2019 *Juridical Review* 230.

[30] [2017] CSIH 23 at [121].

[31] *Carse v Coppen* 1951 SC 233 at 239.

[32] 1997 SC (HL) 66.

[33] See, eg, GL Gretton, 'Scots Law in Shock: Real Rights and Equitable Interests' (1999) 6 *European Review of Private Law* 403.

[34] Scottish Law Commission, Report on *Sharp v Thomson* (Scot Law Com No 298, 2007).

[35] 2004 SC (HL) 19.

[36] Thus, security over aircraft can also be achieved now under the Cape Town Convention. See The International Interests in Aircraft Equipment (Cape Town Convention) Regulations 2015 (SI 2015/912).

[37] *See* AJM Steven and H Patrick, 'Reforming secured transactions law in Scotland' in Gullifer and Akseli (eds), *Secured Transactions Law Reform* (2016) 253 at 259–60.

[38] *Armour v Thyssen Edelstahlwerke AG* 1990 SLT 891. For the background to that decision see AJM Steven, 'George Gretton and the Scots Law of Rights in Security' in AJM Steven, RG Anderson and J MacLeod (eds), *'Nothing so Practical as a Good Theory': Festschrift for George L Gretton* (Edinburgh, Avizandum, 2017) 235, 243–46.

Both these cases involve property being acquired by the debtor. Where that party already owns the asset, a lender might seek to take security over it by means of a transfer of ownership, but without possession changing. Thus, the debtor will sell the goods to the financing party but retain possession on the basis of another contract such as a finance or operating lease. The legal difficulty with such arrangements is that section 62(4) of the Sale of Goods Act 1979 disapplies that Act as regards 'a contract of sale which is intended to operate as by way of mortgage, pledge, charge or other security'. The effect is that the common law applies and therefore delivery is required. Whether section 62(4) applies will depend on the precise facts and circumstances.[39] A sale at fair value followed by a lease on standard commercial terms is unlikely to engage it. Since the effect of section 62(4) is not to invalidate transactions but only to make them subject to the common law, what is sometimes done in practice is that the goods are delivered to the creditor and immediately redelivered.[40] It is unclear whether this is effective because the delivery can be argued to be too transient.

D. Security Over Incorporeal Moveable Property

Apart from the floating charge, security over incorporeal property can only be achieved by means of transferring it to the creditor. This is normally done by an assignation in security. For example, if a company has intellectual property and wants to use this to obtain finance, it will have to transfer the intellectual property to the creditor. For example, in 2015 Rangers Football Club was reported to have granted security over its trademarks by means of assignation.[41] Another example is shares in a company. A transfer to the creditor is required and the creditor will need to be registered by the company as the shareholder.[42] There is no counterpart in Scotland to the English fixed charge over shares,[43] or indeed over other intangibles such as intellectual property.

The effect of an assignation of course is that the creditor acquires the asset and the debtor is left with a right to a reconveyance on the loan being repaid. The nature of a transfer is that this is only possible once. If a company assigns its trademarks in security to a bank it cannot grant an effective assignation of these to another bank. Multiple securities are impossible. All the company can offer as security to another creditor is its contingent right to a re-assignation but taking a security in respect of that is complex.

There are other disadvantages of transfer too, the underlying issue being that it gives the creditor more than it actually requires. Complex contractual arrangements have to

[39] See GL Gretton, 'The Concept of Security' in DJ Cusine (ed), *A Scots Conveyancing Miscellany: Essays in Honour of Professor J M Halliday* (Edinburgh, W Green 1987) 126.

[40] See Scottish Executive Central Research Unit, 'Business Finance and Security over Moveable Property' (2002) 66: 'One interviewee explained that in one transaction involving a bus company that wished to raise finance though a sale and leaseback of the buses it owned, the financier had to let (hire) a warehouse for one night so that the buses could be driven in and out of the warehouse in order that delivery to the financier be effective.'

[41] See www.bbc.co.uk/sport/0/football/32280000.

[42] Except in the case of bearer shares. But there is now a prohibition on the issue of such shares and the conversion or cancellation of existing ones. See the Small Business, Enterprise and Employment Act 2015, s 84 and Sch 4.

[43] See *Farstad Supply A/S v Envirico Ltd* [2011] UKSC 16 at [4] per Lord Collins of Mapesbury.

be entered into in the case of intellectual property to allow its now former holder to be able to continue to deal with it, such as granting licences.[44] For shares there requires to be provision made to enable voting rights to be exercisable by the transferor, as well as to maintain its entitlement to dividends. Since the property is now held by the creditor there is a risk to the provider if that party becomes insolvent. Given that the provider merely holds a right to a reconveyance this may not be effective against an insolvency official, although it might be argued that the law would imply a trust in favour of the provider.[45]

E. Summary

This brief account has demonstrated how inadequate current moveable transactions law is in Scotland. Assignation is hampered by the need for intimation. For security to be taken over corporeal moveable property, unless a floating charge (with its relatively low ranking) can be used, only pledge is available. For security in respect of incorporeal moveable property the only method aside from the floating charge is transfer. In the words of Bruce Wood, a leading asset finance practitioner, 'it is an area desperately in need of reform'.[46] Some might ask, however, if the need is so desperate why there has not been reform already. The answer is that there have been previous attempts, but they have proved unsuccessful.

II. Previous Attempts at Reform

A. Chronology

As mentioned at the outset of this chapter, the only significant reform of moveable transactions law to take place in the last 120 years has been the introduction of the floating charge in 1961. Ten years later came the Crowther Report[47] in relation to consumer credit. Some recommendations in that report were implemented by the Consumer Credit Act 1974. But its more radical proposals[48] to introduce a functional approach to security rights based on Uniform Commercial Code Article 9 of the USA (UCC-9) were not. The Report recommended that this approach should be taken in Scotland as well as south of the border, but that the differences between the respective legal systems merited separate legislation.[49] The Government of the day was not persuaded.[50]

[44] See, eg, A Orr and T Guthrie, 'Fixed Security Rights over Intellectual Property in Scotland' [1996] 18 *European Intellectual Property Review* 596.

[45] *Compare Purnell v Shannon* (1894) 22 R 74.

[46] *The Scotsman* 28 August 2011, available at www.scotsman.com/news/it-s-an-area-of-scots-law-desperately-in-need-of-reform-1-1816927.

[47] Report of the Committee on Consumer Credit (Cmnd 5427, 1973).

[48] Crowther Report Part 5.

[49] Crowther Report para 5.2.21.

[50] White Paper on Reform of the Law of Secured Credit (Cmnd 5427, 1973).

But a working party was subsequently established by the SLC under the chairmanship of Professor Jack Halliday to examine how such an approach might be introduced in Scotland, in particular to 'consider the legal and technical problems which would arise or to be likely to arise'.[51] It reported in 1986 and in fact somewhat went beyond its remit of technical issues by actively recommending the introduction of a scheme based on UCC-9 but with some deviations.[52] Floating charges were apparently to remain.[53] Nothing ever came of this report.

The Diamond Report of 1989,[54] which once again recommended an approach based on UCC-9 for Scotland as well as for England and Wales, was also not taken forward. Like Crowther it advised that there should be separate legislation for the two legal systems.[55]

The Murray Report of 1994[56] concerned only Scots law. It rejected the UCC-9 approach, stating that it 'would have involved a radical departure from the current law, and would have required, when fully specified, a very complex set of new rules'.[57] Its main recommendations were that (a) the floating charge should be made available to non-corporate debtors but only for moveable property and not for consumer goods; and (b) a new fixed security right should be introduced which would be created by registration in a new Register of Security Interests. This would be kept at Companies House.[58]

While the Murray Report was not taken forward, some of its proposed reforms in relation to floating charges are echoed by Part 2 of the Bankruptcy and Diligence etc (Scotland) Act 2007. The genesis of Part 2 lies in the SLC Report on Registration of Rights in Security by Companies, which was published in 2004.[59] The SLC had been asked to consider the law in relation to floating charges because of the difficulties mentioned above in relation to how these interacted with the underlying law. The Report recommended a new legislative scheme which involved the establishment of a new Scottish Register of Floating Charges (RFC). This would be run by Registers of Scotland. Floating charges over Scottish assets would have to be registered in the new register instead of at Companies House. The scheme formed the basis of Part 2 of the 2007 Act and thus reached the statute book.

But those who hoped that reform had been achieved were to be disappointed. After the legislation was passed the Committee of Scottish Clearing Bankers wrote a letter to the Scottish Government which argued against Part 2 being brought into force.

[51] The Report is available on the SLC website. See also CK Davidson, 'The Scottish Law Commission 1965–1995' (1995) 1 *Scottish Law and Practice Quarterly* 18, 21–22.

[52] In particular that certain types of property would be excluded, notably consumer goods, equipment used to secure low-value loans, intellectual property and company shares.

[53] See Scottish Law Commission, Discussion Paper on Moveable Transactions (Scot Law Com DP No 151, 2011) para 10.17.

[54] AL Diamond, *A Review of Security Interests in Property* (Department of Trade and Industry, 1989).

[55] Diamond Report para 8.4.4.

[56] 'Security over Moveable Property in Scotland: A Consultation Paper' (Department of Trade and Industry 1994), known as the Murray Report after its chair, Professor John Murray QC.

[57] Murray Report, para 2.5.

[58] For discussion of the Murray Report recommendations see H Patrick, 'Reform of Security over Moveable Property: Some General Comments' 1995 *Scots Law Times (News)* 42; AJM Steven, 'Reform of Security over Moveable Property: Some Further Thoughts' 1995 *Scots Law Times (News)* 120.

[59] Scot Law Com No 197, 2004.

The new law, it was said, would lead to increased costs for business.[60] The main basis of this argument was that a UK company with assets both in Scotland and England would have to make two registrations (in the RFC and at Companies House) rather the one registration at Companies House. The Scottish Government set up a technical working group to consider the issue, which was coordinated by Registers of Scotland. The group's report proposed three options:[61] (1) implement Part 2 without amendment; (2) implement with amendment; and (3) do not implement. The Scottish Government subsequently carried out a consultation on these in 2012. It has made no statement on the fate of Part 2 since, but it can be safely assumed that it will not now be brought into force.

B. Commentary

In its Report on Moveable Transactions the SLC seeks to analyse why the previous attempts at reform have been unsuccessful.[62] It sets out some possible explanations.

As has been seen, the Crowther, Halliday and Diamond Reports all recommended an approach based on UCC-9. Several reasons can be adduced as to why this approach was not adopted. First, it would seem that it was simply too radical.[63] Secondly, unreformed Scottish law is not in as unsatisfactory a state as secured transactions law was in the US prior to the introduction of UCC-9. For example, that law had no equivalent to the floating charge.[64] Jurisdictions which have introduced a Personal Property Security Act (PPSA), which takes the same functional approach to security interests as UCC-9, have often done so to replace a multiplicity of local and asset-specific registers with the one nationwide (or, in the case of Canada, province-wide) register. At least in respect of security rights granted by companies in the UK there is a national register in the form of Companies House. Thirdly, some are reluctant to move away from the familiarity of the current law. As Professor Hugh Beale has commented on unreformed English law: 'I agree that the current system works – just as steam trains still work'.[65] Fourthly, there are aspects of the UCC-9/PPSA approach which may not be attractive to businesses when compared with the current law, for example the need to register functional securities such as retention of title and hire-purchase in order for these to have priority over third parties and thus to have to pay a registration fee. No such registration is required at present. Finally, the UCC-9/PPSA approach is less easy to reconcile with Scottish

[60] The letter is reproduced as Appendix 3 to 'Register of Floating Charges Technical Working Group: Report to Scottish Government' (2011) available at www.gov.scot/Resource/Doc/254430/0121799.pdf.

[61] ibid.

[62] See Scottish Law Commission, Report on Moveable Transactions (Scot Law Com No 249, 2017) paras 18.32–18.43, available at www.scotlawcom.gov.uk.

[63] Professor Michael Bridge has drawn the same conclusion in relation to the proposals made the Law Commission for England and Wales in the earlier 2000s to reform English law along the lines of the UCC-9 model, which attracted strong opposition and were not taken forward. See MG Bridge, 'The Scope and Limits of Security Interests' in H Eidenmüller and E-M Kieninger (eds), *The Future of Secured Credit in Europe* (Berlin, De Gruyter, 2008) 180, 184.

[64] *Benedict v Ratner* 268 US 353 (1925).

[65] H Beale, 'The Exportability of North American Chattel Security Regimes: The Fate of the English Law Commission's Proposals' (2006) 43 *Canadian Business Law Journal* 178, 198.

property law compared with property law in common law jurisdictions. This is a matter which will be discussed again later.[66]

In contrast, the approach of the Murray Report was a more modest one and it is not so obvious why it was not taken forward. Part of the reason may be that it was sponsored by the then Department of Trade and Industry in London prior to devolution. Scotland-only commercial law reforms at Westminster were then rare because they had to compete with other priorities for legislation. Five years after the Report and, following devolution in 1999, the Scottish Justice Minister commissioned research into 'the perception that businesses in Scotland are being inhibited in raising capital because, under Scots law, they cannot create a security over moveable property without giving up possession.'[67] As a result of this, in 2002 the Central Research Unit's Report, 'Business Finance and Security over Moveable Property', was published. It concluded that there was

> little empirical evidence to support the suggestion that business finance is more difficult to obtain in Scotland because SMEs are unable to grant a non-possessory security over moveable assets, or that it is more difficult for unincorporated Scottish SMEs to obtain finance because they cannot grant a floating charge.[68]

This finding probably sealed any lingering chance that the Murray Report would yet be implemented. And yet, as discussed below, it was only a matter of a few years more, before the SLC was urged to return to the subject.[69]

Part 2 of the Bankruptcy and Diligence etc (Scotland) Act 2007 can be dealt with relatively briefly. It was opposed by the banks, who are important stakeholders in relation to reform of moveable transactions law. They did not want a scheme for floating charges and in particular a registration scheme that was different for Scotland from England and Wales. In other words, they opposed the harmonised regime already existing north and south of the border being broken up. Once again, this issue will be returned to later.[70]

III. The SLC Project

The SLC is the independent public body responsible for promoting law reform in Scotland.[71] It periodically agrees programmes of work with the Scottish Government. The moveable transactions project had its origins in the consultation preceding the Seventh Programme of Law Reform (2005–2009). The Law Society of Scotland and other legal bodies lobbied for a project on assignation of, and security over, incorporeal moveable property.[72] The SLC accepted the need for this considering the importance of this area to business and the fact that the existing common law rules were now unfit

[66] See section IV.
[67] Parliamentary Written Answer S1W-1719 (29 September 1999).
[68] Scottish Executive Central Research Unit, *Business Finance and Security over Moveable Property* (2002).
[69] See section III.
[70] See section IV below.
[71] It was established by the Law Commissions Act 1965.
[72] Scottish Law Commission, Seventh Programme of Law Reform (Scot Law Com No 198, 2005) para 2.32.

for purpose. Progress, however, during the period of the Seventh Programme was slow because the relevant team at the SLC was committed to other work.[73] By the time it came to announce the Eighth Programme of Law Reform (2010–2014), the SLC had decided to widen the project to include security over corporeal moveable property.[74] Once again this was because of lobbying by stakeholders. The result was the three-part moveable transactions project covering: (a) assignation (transfer) of incorporeal moveable property; (b) security over incorporeal moveable property; and (c) security over corporeal moveable property.

In common with its usual practice the SLC scoped the project and appointed an advisory group comprising academics and practitioners. The project was led by Professor George Gretton.[75] The SLC published a Discussion Paper in the summer of 2011.[76] This proposed significant statutory reform of the area. The most significant proposals were the abolition of intimation as a requirement for an assignation and the creation of a new security right over corporeal and incorporeal moveable property, which could be granted by any person and not just by companies, etc as is the case with the floating charge. There should, however, be certain restrictions to protect consumers.[77]

At this stage leadership of the project changed because Professor Gretton's term at the SLC came to an end. I succeeded him. Meanwhile the Discussion Paper was undergoing its three-month consultation period. Responses were received from key stakeholders including CBI Scotland, the Committee of Scottish Clearing Bankers, the Federation of Small Businesses and the Law Society of Scotland. There was also a seminar held in October 2011 at the University of Edinburgh to discuss the security aspects of the project.[78]

The proposals made in the Discussion Paper were broadly supported by stakeholders and enabled the SLC to proceed to the complex and lengthy task of producing a Report and draft Bill. From the beginning of the project significant regard was had to legislation in other countries,[79] notably UCC-9 and the PPSAs.[80] International instruments such as the Draft Common Frame of Reference (2009)[81] and the UNCITRAL Model Law on Secured Transactions (2016)[82] were also considered.

[73] In particular a large project on land registration, which led to the Land Registration etc (Scotland) Act 2012. For the background, see KGC Reid and GL Gretton, *Land Registration* (Edinburgh, Avizandum 2017) ch 1.

[74] Scottish Law Commission, Eighth Programme of Law Reform (Scot Law Com No 220, 2005) para 2.5.

[75] Professor Gretton served as a Scottish Law Commissioner from 2006 to 2011. He recounts his experience in G L Gretton, 'Of Law Commissioning' (2013) 17 *Edinburgh Law Review* 119.

[76] Scottish Law Commission, Discussion Paper on Moveable Transactions (n 53).

[77] Such as preventing them granting security over future assets.

[78] The papers, by Professor Gretton, Dr Hamish Patrick, Dr Ross Anderson and Professor Hugh Beale were subsequently published at (2012) 16 *Edinburgh Law Review* 261.

[79] See Sir G Palmer, 'The Law Reform Enterprise: Evaluating the Past and Charting the Future' (2015) 131 *Law Quarterly Review* 402, 415.

[80] Including the Security Interests (Jersey) Law 2012.

[81] C von Bar and E Clive, *Principles, Definitions and Model Rules of Private Law: Draft Common Frame of Reference* (6 vols) (Oxford, Oxford University Press, 2009). Book IX (Proprietary security rights in movable assets) is particularly relevant. For the official commentary on this, see U Drobnig and O Böger, *Proprietary Security in Movable Assets* (Oxford, Oxford University Press, 2014). But Book III (Obligations and corresponding rights) in relation to assignment is also of great interest.

[82] Available at www.uncitral.org/uncitral/en/uncitral_texts/security/2016Model_secured.html.

Closer to home, a watchful eye was kept on the work of both the Financial Law Committee of the City of London Law Society, which has prepared a draft Secured Transactions Code for England and Wales[83] and the Secured Transactions Law Reform Project.[84] In considering the law and proposals for reform elsewhere, the question of harmonisation arose. To what extent should Scotland have a moveable transactions law which is similar to other jurisdictions and most especially the law of its nearest neighbours? This is the subject of the next section.

IV. Harmonisation

In 2014, Lord Hodge, one of the Scottish Justices at the UK Supreme Court, delivered the Annual Lecture of the Edinburgh Centre for Commercial Law. Its title was 'Does Scotland need its own commercial law?'[85] He began: 'The answer to the question posed in the title of this lecture is yes and no.' He went on to say:

> The basic structure of our commercial law, with a clear distinction between the law of property and the law of obligations, is radically different from Common Law systems with their dichotomy between law and equity. For that reason, if for no other, we need our own commercial law.[86]

But he counselled against particularism: 'Law reformers, academics, and judges must be open to good things from elsewhere and must build bridges to make our commercial law accessible to those outside our borders with whom we do business.'[87]

These comments are germane to reform of Scottish moveable transactions law and the question of harmonisation with the law of England and Wales. Of course, in many areas of commercial law, notably company law, corporate insolvency law, intellectual property, partnership law and sale of goods, there is already harmonisation; indeed, there has been since the nineteenth century.[88] But while moveable transactions law is *functionally* an area of commercial law, it is *formally* an area of property law. Its subject matter is therefore covered in the synonymous LLB courses for both areas as well as

[83] Available at www.citysolicitors.org.uk/index.php?option=com_content&view=category&id=129; see also R Calnan, 'A Secured Transactions Code' (2015) 30 *Butterworths Journal of International Banking and Financial* Law 473.

[84] See https://securedtransactionslawreformproject.org; see also WJ Chan, 'Secured Transactions Law Reform: The Long and Winding Road' (2017) 32 *Butterworths Journal of International Banking and Financial Law* 215.

[85] The lecture was subsequently published at (2015) 19 *Edinburgh Law Review* 299. And see also J Hardman, 'Some Legal Determinants of External Finance in Scotland: A Response to Lord Hodge' (2017) 21 *Edinburgh Law Review* 30.

[86] (2015) 19 *Edinburgh Law Review* 299, 301.

[87] (2015) 19 *Edinburgh Law Review* 299, 310.

[88] See, eg, AF Rodger, 'The Codification of Commercial Law in Victorian Britain' (1992) 108 *Law Quarterly Review* 570. And there have been periodic calls for greater harmonisation. See, eg, J Dove Wilson, 'A Scottish Judge Ordinar' (1907–08) 17 *Yale Law Journal* 171, 234: 'it is absurd that a small country like Scotland, so intimately connected with a large country like England should still keep its law, and uniformity should extend, not only over the UK, but over the British Empire.'

in standard textbooks for both areas.[89] As Lord Hodge noted in his lecture, Scottish property law is fundamentally different from that in England and Wales. This has meant that attempts to harmonise areas of commercial law which involve property law have been problematic. The Sale of Goods Act 1893 (the predecessor of the Sale of Goods Act 1979) has been the subject of sharp criticism for its imposition of the English law of sale in Scotland.[90] Earlier in this essay,[91] the difficulties with the floating charge, summarised by Lord Drummond Young, were considered.

Over 30 years ago, George Gretton, in a review of the second edition of Goode's *Legal Problems of Credit and Security*,[92] said:

> Professor Goode's book, among its many other merits, shows to a Scottish reader, just how fathomless a gulf separates Scots and English security law. Or, to change the image, they are like two railway systems with different gauges, the Anglo-Americans on broad gauge and the Scots and most of Europe on standard gauge. If the two systems are to be united, it must either be on broad gauge, or standard gauge, or a new gauge. The second possibility will not be adopted. And the first and third would involve tearing up the tracks.[93]

The gauges are the underlying systems of property law. In the intervening decades, it is the UCC-9/PPSA approach which has established itself as the dominant one internationally.[94] It has strongly influenced important international instruments such as the DCFR and the UNCITRAL Model Law. Such an approach sits more easily within common law systems of property law than systems based on Roman law, as can be seen from the jurisdictions that have adopted it. Thus, for example, in Canada it is the common law provinces that have a PPSA. The Quebec Civil Code takes a different approach.[95]

The attachment/perfection distinction, which is at the core of the UCC-9/PPSA approach, poses particular challenges for Germanic property law systems where a property right is either effective against the world or against nobody.[96] In contrast, the concept of attachment is that a security interest is good between the parties but requires perfection to be good against all third parties. But Scots property law generally does not

[89] For example, chapters on rights in security can be found in Gretton and Steven, *Property, Trusts and Succession* (n 4), C Anderson, *Property: A Guide to Scots Law* (Edinburgh, W Green, 2016), IG MacNeill (ed), *Scots Commercial Law* (Edinburgh, Avizandum, 2014) and F Davidson, DJ Garrity, LJ Macgregor and L Richardson, *Commercial Law in Scotland*, 5th edn (Edinburgh, W Green, 2018). See also AJM Steven, 'Real Security Rights: Time for Cinderella to Go to the Ball?' in S Scott and J van Wyk (eds), *Property Law Under Scrutiny* (Claremont, Juta, 2015) 61, 62–64.

[90] See generally TB Smith, *Property Problems in Sale* (London, Sweet & Maxwell, 1978); see also Miller, 'Scots and South African Property' (2001) 293.

[91] Above at section I.

[92] RM Goode, *Legal Problems of Credit and Security*, 2nd edn (London, Sweet & Maxwell, 1988).

[93] GL Gretton, 'Book Review' (1989) 57 *Scottish Law Gazette* 28.

[94] As Duncan Sheehan has noted, the World Bank in the Credit section of its 'Doing Business' ratings effectively ranks countries on the basis of how closely they follow UCC-9. See D Sheehan, *The Principles of Personal Property Law*, 2nd edn (Oxford, Hart, 2017) 386.

[95] Although there has been some UCC-9/PPSA influence. See C Walsh, 'Transplanting Article 9: The Canadian PPSA Experience' in Gullifer and Akseli (n 1) 49, 50.

[96] See Scottish Law Commission, Discussion Paper on Moveable Transactions (n 53) paras 13.20–13.29; See also GL Gretton, 'Security over Moveables in Scots Law' in J De Lacy (ed), *Reform of UK Personal Property Security Law* (London, Routledge, 2010) 270, 278. But cf H Kuhn, 'The UNCITRAL Model Law on Secured Transactions – A Swiss Perspective' in B Foëx (ed), *The Draft UNCITRAL Model Law on Secured Transactions: Why and How?* (Geneva, Schulthess, 2016) 61, 83.

accept such an idea.[97] Yet for common law systems, where the concept of a proprietary interest being created by consent is a familiar one, there is less difficulty. Even, however, in UCC-9/PPSA systems there remain questions about how the scheme integrates with the general law of moveable property. It has been said that UCC-9 'lies over the top of the underlying property law, like a tea towel laid over a pile of unwashed dishes'.[98] This is not without difficulties.[99]

It can therefore cogently be argued that harmonising the Scottish and English law of moveable transactions on a UCC-9/PPSA approach may be too challenging an option because of the difficulties of integration, particularly with Scottish property law.[100] Although reform along the lines of this approach nevertheless has at least one notable supporter in Scotland,[101] it was not in any event a realistic option for the SLC in its moveable transactions project. The principal reason for this, perhaps oddly in the light of what has just been said, is harmonisation. As has already been noted, the UCC-9/PPSA approach would be a radical departure from both current Scottish and English law. It is apparent that attempting law reform in Scotland which required notice filing of functional security interests such as retention of title, hire-purchase and trusts in Scotland for priority purposes, when no such filing was required south of the Scottish border, would attract strong opposition. While Scottish and English moveable transactions laws are indeed different as we have seen, there is no appetite to make them more different. The experience of Part 2 of the 2007 Act[102] is but one piece of evidence for this.[103] As the SLC noted in its Discussion Paper: 'The UK has a high degree of economic unity, and that fact gives rise to pressure for legal approximation or even unification – not in all areas, but in many. That this is a fact cannot be ignored.'[104]

[97] It is possible to find exceptions. One is the company charges registration scheme provided for by the Companies Act 2006, Pt 25. This scheme and its predecessors have been part of Scots law since the floating charge was introduced. For criticism, see GL Gretton, 'Registration of Company Charges' (2002) 6 *Edinburgh Law Review* 146.

[98] Scottish Law Commission, Discussion Paper on Moveable Transactions (n 53) para 13.10.

[99] See, eg, the interaction of the NZ PPSA with the law of estoppel, as discussed in M Gedye, RC Cuming and RJ Wood, *Personal Property Securities in New Zealand* (Wellington, Thomson Brookers, 2002) 539–40.

[100] On the need to make reforms consistent with the underlying law, see also AJM Steven, 'Reform of Security over Moveables: Still a Longstanding Reform Agenda in Scots Law' in D Bain, RRM Paisley, ARC Simpson and NJM Tait (eds), *Northern Lights: Essays in Private Law in Memory of Professor David Carey Miller* (Aberdeen, Aberdeen University Press, 2018) 217, 231–32.

[101] Lord Drummond Young, the former Chairman of the SLC, who played an important part in the decision to widen the assignation and security over incorporeal moveable property project to include security over corporeal moveable property. In *MacMillan v T Leith Developments Ltd (in receivership and liquidation)* (n 29) at para 122 he stated: 'It is noticeable that in the English-speaking world, in systems which are for the most part based on English law (and equity), the modern tendency has been towards the systematic codification of property and security rights. This produces greater certainty and has generally superseded the traditional form of floating charge. Such a tendency towards systemization can be seen in the provisions of Article 9 of the Uniform Commercial Code in the US and the Personal Property Security Acts, based on the UCC, found in the Canadian provinces, New Zealand and most recently Australia. These statutes provide a clear and coherent structure for property rights and for systematic registration so that property rights are at all times a matter of public record.' But the functional approach of UCC-9 and the PPSAs has its critics in Scotland. See J MacLeod, 'Thirty Years After: The Concept of Security Revisited' in Steven, Anderson and MacLeod (eds), *'Nothing so Practical as a Good Theory'* (2017) 177, 190–92.

[102] See section II.

[103] For another see Hardman, 'Some Legal Determinants of External Finance in Scotland' (n 85).

[104] Scottish Law Commission, Discussion Paper on Moveable Transactions (n 53) para 1.22.

V. The SLC Recommendations

With this in mind, the approach of the SLC was less radical. It sought to reform Scottish moveable transactions law in the places where it is most needed: (a) to remove intimation as a mandatory requirement in assignation of claims; (b) to provide a non-possessory security over corporeal moveable property; and (c) to provide a security over incorporeal moveable property that does not require title to the property to be transferred to the secured creditor. Its recommendations were published in December 2017 in a three-volume Report.[105] These follow broadly what was proposed in its Discussion Paper.[106] The Report is accompanied by a draft Bill of 124 sections[107] and an impact assessment.

The SLC sought to produce a Bill which is within the legislative competence of the Scottish Parliament in terms of the Scotland Act 1998.[108] This meant working within the terms of existing legislation which is reserved to the UK Parliament. In particular, corporate insolvency law is reserved.[109] Therefore the fixed/floating distinction in relation to security rights had to be accepted, despite the fact that there is widespread support for its reform.[110] Another example is the law of business associations[111] and therefore the rules on registration of company charges (securities) will remain.[112] Other reserved areas are also relevant.[113]

In relation to assignation of claims the SLC recommends that registration in a new Register of Assignations should be an alternative to intimation.[114] This would facilitate assignation of multiple claims and in particular of multiple future claims, where intimation is cumbersome or indeed impossible (until the future claim arises and there is an identifiable debtor). Registration would take place online under an automated electronic system. While the assignation document would be registrable it could describe the claims by reference to a class (for example, 'our April 2020 invoices'). There would be no need for individual specification.

[105] Scottish Law Commission, Report on Moveable Transactions (n 62). For overviews, see AJD MacPherson, 'The Future of Moveable Security in Scots Law'? Comments on the Scottish Law Commission's Report on Moveable Transactions' 2018 *Juridical Review* 98 and H Patrick and A Steven, 'Moveable transactions law reform coming in Scotland?' (2018) 33 *Butterworths Journal of International Banking and Financial Law* 71.

[106] See section III.

[107] The Draft Bill was the subject of a consultation in July 2017.

[108] For a negative reaction to this, see J Hardman, 'Three Steps Forward, Two Steps Back: A View from Corporate Security Practice of the Moveable Transactions (Scotland) Bill' (2018) 22 *Edinburgh Law Review* 266, 272–73.

[109] Scotland Act 1998, Sch 5, Part II head C2.

[110] The Financial Law Committee of the City of London Law Society in its Discussion Paper on Secured Transactions Reform (n 83) para 4.24 describes it as 'a running sore in our legal system'.

[111] Scotland Act 1998, Sch 5, part II head C1.

[112] The interaction of the scheme recommended in the Report with the rules on registration of company charges was one which the SLC found particularly difficult. See Report on Moveable Transactions (n 62) ch 36. A requirement for double registration is patently unattractive but for the reasons set out in the Report the SLC with some reluctance concluded that it was the most realistic approach at least initially. Jonathan Hardman (in 'Three Steps Forward, Two Steps' (2018) argues that there is a 'simple' solution for corporate granters of the new security: registration solely in the Companies Register. But if that solution were so simple the SLC would doubtless have adopted it.

[113] These include intellectual property and the subject matter of the Consumer Credit Act 1974.

[114] Scottish Law Commission, Report on Moveable Transactions (n 62) ch 5.

It is anticipated that the registration option would be used widely in the invoice financing sector. In other areas the parties may wish to continue to proceed by means of intimation and the SLC therefore recommends that the rules here are put onto a modern statutory footing and that the Transmission of Moveable Property (Scotland) Act 1862 is repealed. In particular it recommends that electronic intimation should be competent.

The approach recommended for registration of assignations differs from that of UCC-9 and the PPSAs, and indeed that being contemplated for reform of English law, in three principal ways.

The first is that registration would be necessary to transfer the claim, rather than merely for it to have effect against third parties. This approach fits with underlying Scottish property law and reflects the fact that the SLC's consultees rejected the attachment/perfection distinction.

The second is that assignations in security would not be recharacterised as security rights/interests because this was also rejected by the SLC's consultees.

The third is that intimation would remain as an alternative to registration. This would allow flexibility. The counter-argument, however, is that a third party cannot solely rely on the register. They require to make enquiries with the account debtor too to see if there has been an intimation. This 'defeat[s] the purpose of the register'.[115] But, as suggested above, the SLC expects that assignations of receivables in favour of financing institutions would always be registered because this would be much simpler and cheaper than intimations to multiple debtors. In addition, intimation would not be possible for future claims. A prospective assignee is effectively only at risk from a fraudulent or negligent assignor who does not disclose that the claim has already been assigned by intimation. The SLC's advisory group noted that financial institutions factor in such risks.

The proposals for reform of English law deal with receivables, in essence invoices under contracts for goods, services or incorporeal assets.[116] Other claims are excluded. In contrast, the SLC's recommendations relate to claims in general. The SLC concluded that there would be merit in giving the Scottish Ministers the power to specify types of claim for which registration would be compulsory to transfer the claim.[117] Intimation would not be available as an alternative. Hence if registration for assignments of receivables effectively became compulsory in England and Wales, albeit there only to achieve priority against third parties, there might be support for this also in Scotland for assignations of receivables.

In relation to security, the SLC recommends the introduction of a new 'statutory pledge'.[118] Whereas the current common law pledge requires delivery to the secured creditor for it to be created, its new younger sibling would need registration in a new Register of Statutory Pledges. Thus, for corporeal moveable property the provider of

[115] Secured Transactions Law Reform Project, Discussion Paper Series: Sale of Receivables (2017) para 3.D.iii.

[116] See Secured Transactions Law Reform Project, Discussion Paper Series: Sale of Receivables (n 115) and City of London Law Society Financial Law Committee draft Secured Transactions Code (n 83) ss 35 and 38.

[117] Scottish Law Commission, Report on Moveable Transactions (n 62) paras 5.19–5.22.

[118] Scottish Law Commission, Report on Moveable Transactions (n 62) vol 2.

a statutory pledge would not require to give up possession of the asset. Unlike the floating charge the statutory pledge could be granted by any person and not just by companies, etc.

The SLC's proposal in its Discussion Paper was that the new security right should have both a 'fixed' and 'floating' version for the purposes of corporate insolvency law.[119] The floating version was provisionally termed the 'floating lien'. But consultees criticised this approach on the basis that there would be an overlap with floating charges and therefore the SLC recommends in its Report that the statutory pledge should be a fixed security only.[120]

For incorporeal moveable property, the SLC recommends that at least initially the statutory pledge can be granted over financial instruments and intellectual property only.[121] The reasons for this are pragmatic. First, these are the incorporeals in respect of which the current law of security in Scotland causes the most significant problems.[122] Secondly, there are very difficult issues as regards taking fixed security over claims and proceeds. English law struggles with these against the background of the Insolvency Act 1986.[123] This legislation applies in Scotland too and is reserved to the UK Parliament. An attempt to place the rules of English equity on control of sums into Scottish legislation is unpalatable given, as mentioned above, that there is pressure in England and Wales to reform the fixed/floating distinction. Thirdly, security over claims in Scotland meantime can be taken by assignation, with less difficulty than transferring financial instruments or intellectual property in security. Finally, restricting the scope of the statutory pledge would reduce the impact on insolvency law as not all assets could be encumbered. The SLC was conscious of the inter-relationship between secured transactions laws and insolvency law.[124] Indeed some of its consultees wanted the project to be extended to include reform of insolvency law. This, however, given the already considerable scale of the project and the limited resources at the SLC was not feasible. Furthermore, as has already been mentioned, corporate insolvency law (including the 1986 Act) is reserved to the UK Parliament.

The SLC recommends the same broad battery of remedies for enforcing possessory pledge and statutory pledge, including sale and appropriation.[125] The rationale is that there is no compelling reason for different remedies simply because the two types of pledge are constituted in a different way. But the enforcement regime would not apply to pawns by consumers in respect of which there is already a legislative scheme provided for by the Consumer Credit Act 1974.[126]

[119] Scottish Law Commission, Discussion Paper on Moveable Transactions (n 53) ch 22.

[120] Scottish Law Commission, Report on Moveable Transactions (n 62) ch 20.

[121] Scottish Law Commission, Report on Moveable Transactions (n 62) ch 22.

[122] For example, in relation to taking security over intellectual property, one leading Scottish law firm has described Scottish law as 'stuck in the 19th century'. See www.brodies.com/node/3607.

[123] The leading case is *National Westminster Bank plc v Spectrum Plus Ltd* [2005] UKHL 41, [2005] 2 AC 680, on which see J Getzler and J Payne (eds), *Company Charges: Spectrum and Beyond* (Oxford, Oxford University Press, 2006).

[124] See, eg, G McCormack and R Bork (eds), *Security Rights and the European Insolvency Regulation* (Cambridge, Intersentia, 2017).

[125] Scottish Law Commission, Report on Moveable Transactions (n 62) chs 27 and 28.

[126] Consumer Credit Act 1974, ss 114–122. This legislation is reserved to the UK Parliament.

The Register of Statutory Pledges would work on the same broad basis as the Register of Assignations.[127] Once again registration would take place online using an automated system. But because a statutory pledge is a *right*, in contrast to an assignation, which is a *transfer*, there would be differences. Thus, it would be possible for the entry in the register for a statutory pledge to be amended to add more secured property. And ultimately when the statutory pledge is extinguished, such as when the secured obligation is performed in full, the secured creditor could have the entry deleted. UCC-9/PPSA legislation typically provides for a registration to lapse after a set number of years (although it can be renewed).[128] The SLC's consultees were strongly opposed to such a rule. Another difference between the scheme that the SLC recommends and the UCC-9/PPSA approach, is that a distinction is made between juristic acts affecting a statutory pledge (such as an amendment adding property) and inaccuracies. The former would enter the register by *registration* and the latter would be dealt with by means of a *correction.* In contrast the UCC-9/PPSA approach is for both to enter the register in the same way by means of a supplementary notice, sometimes called a 'financing change statement'.[129] The approach taken by the SLC is more faithful to the underlying law.

The SLC, however, in working towards its recommendations drew on several aspects of the UCC-9/PPSA model. Thus, as already mentioned, the new registers would be electronic and registration would be automated. Whether a registration is effective or not would depend on the data registered not being 'seriously misleading'.[130] There would be a change demand system for statutory pledges allowing the registered creditor to be called upon to correct the register.[131] There would also be duties imposed on the secured creditor to provide certain information to a limited category of persons.[132] It might be questioned why there is a need for such duties when the assignation or statutory pledge document would be registered, in contrast to mere notice filing. But the information on the register may not be comprehensive. For example, the assignation may be of claims or the statutory pledge may be of assets only identified specifically in off-register documents. And the register may not be up to date in respect of a statutory pledge, for example where property has been released from the security off-register.

It is true that the SLC scheme is one which recommends piecemeal reform. This approach to reform has been criticised.[133] But the SLC concluded that wholesale reform at this time was simply not feasible.[134] Indeed, it was opposed by its consultees.

[127] Scottish Law Commission, Report on Moveable Transactions (n 62) chs 29–35.

[128] For example, in New Zealand the period is five years. In Australia, however, the party making the registration has to specify its duration, with higher fees for longer durations. See B Allan, *The Law of Secured Credit* (Wellington, Thomson Reuters, 2016) 486–87.

[129] See, eg, NZ PPSA 1999, s 135.

[130] See, eg, UCC § 9-506; NZ PPSA 1999, s 149; Australian PPSA 2009, s 164.

[131] See, eg, Ontario PPSA 1990, s 56; NZ PPSA 1999, ss 162–69.

[132] See, eg, UCC § 9-210; NZ PPSA 1999, ss 177–183; DCFR IX. 3:319–3:324.

[133] See L Gullifer, 'Piecemeal reform: Is it the Answer?' in F Dahan (ed), *Research Handbook on Secured Financing in Commercial Transactions* (Cheltenham, Edward Elgar, 2016) 421.

[134] Scottish Law Commission, Report on Moveable Transactions (n 62) paras 18.52–18.54.

VI. Conclusion

Scottish moveable transactions law is clearly in an unsatisfactory state. Consisting primarily of common law rules which have little changed in centuries, it does not meet the needs of modern commerce. Nevertheless, it has proven an area where it has been difficult to achieve statutory reform. The SLC's recommendations now provide a basis on which to do this. In the words of a practising commercial lawyer, Scots law now hopefully 'will be on its way to a long-awaited reform in this area'.[135]

[135] E Arcari, 'Corporate Briefing' (2017) 62 *Journal of the Law Society of Scotland* (September) 29, 30.

PART VII

Public–Private Partnerships: An Area for Future Reform?

15

Public–Private Partnerships and Harmonisation: The Public Private Partnership Act

RICHARD CRAVEN

For better or for worse,[1] across the globe it is now commonplace to find the private sector playing a pivotal role in the delivery of 'public' services, back office and public-facing, via contract. These arrangements often attract the label 'public–private partnerships' (PPP). PPP is an ill-defined concept. Typically (and superficially), the phrase is used to refer to a sophisticated contractual agreement between a public body and a private partner (a consortium of private actors), entailing provision of finance for capital infrastructure or for establishing services by the private sector provider, which then recoups its costs (and profits) by charging, eg for facilities management, over an extended period of time, typically 20 to 30 years. As with any form of privatisation, PPPs are controversial and, unsurprisingly, they have been the focus of much academic[2] and policy scrutiny. This is not so, however, when it comes to the legal regulation of PPPs.

[1] David Hall's reports for the European Federation of Public Service Unions (EPSU) on the Public–Private Partnership (PPP) model stands out for its critical stance: see D Hall, 'Public–Private Partnerships (PPPs): Summary paper' (EPSU, October 2008); D Hall, 'Alternatives to PPPs: positive action for in-house services' (EPSU, October 2008); D Hall, 'Protecting workers in PPPs' (October 2008); D Hall, 'Critique of PPPs' (EPSU, October 2008), available at www.epsu.org/article/public-private-partnerships-summary-paper-and-reports-ppps#critique.

[2] There are numerous examples. See J Delmon, *Public–Private Partnership projects in infrastructure; an essential guide for policy makers*, 2nd edn (Cambridge, Cambridge University Press, 2017); A Akintoye, M Beck and M Kumaraswamy (eds), *Public Private Partnerships: A Global Review* (London, Routledge, 2016); E Engel, R Fischer and A Galetovic, *The Economics of Public Private Partnerships* (Cambridge, Cambridge University Press, 2014); P de Vries and E Yehoue (eds), *The Routledge Companion to Public-Private Partnerships* (Abingdon, Routledge, 2013); C Greve and G Hodge (eds), *Rethinking Public-Private Partnerships: Strategies for Turbulent Times* (London, Routledge, 2013); G Hodge, C Greve and A Boardman (eds), *International handbook on Public–Private Partnerships* (Cheltenham, Edward Elgar, 2012); D Grimsey and M Lewis (eds), *Public Private Partnerships: The Worldwide Revolution in Infrastructure Provision and Project Finance* (Cheltenham, Edward Elgar, 2004); S Osborne, *Public Private Partnerships: Theory and Practice in International Perspective* (London, Taylor & Francis, 2002).

Despite the importance of the topic – for example, in terms of transparency and accountability – legal academic research here is only recently emerging.[3]

The 'Public Private Partnership Act' – the subtitle of this chapter – refers to PPP-specific legislation that has become increasingly prevalent over the course of the last decade, in particular following the 2007/08 financial crisis, across the developing world. The World Bank's Public-Private Partnership in Infrastructure Resource Center provides a convenient reference point for many of these PPP laws.[4] The growth of this law emphasises the continuing flourishing (and promotion) of PPP, something the 2007/08 financial crisis might potentially have disrupted.[5] In fact, for some, PPPs are the answer to the 2007/08 financial crisis:

> The financial crisis of 2008 onwards brought about renewed interest in PPP in both developed and developing countries. Facing constraints on public resources and fiscal space, while recognizing the importance of investment in infrastructure to help their economies grow, governments are increasingly turning to the private sector as an alternative additional source of funding to meet the funding gap.[6]

The PPP-specific laws, arguably, serve mainly to signal to private investors – debt funders – a state's preparedness for the implementation and operation of these sophisticated projects, and in particular seeking to assuage any doubts there may be over the safety of an investment: the PPP-specific laws give the impression of 'a clear and stable legal environment for PPP projects in order to reduce the perception of risk, attract more competition for projects, attract more competition for finance, and therefore reduce project costs'.[7]

It is therefore unsurprising that multilateral trade organisations, like UNCITRAL, are moving to explore the potential for a model law on PPPs in the same vein as the model law for public procurement.[8] This would supplement UNCITRAL's legislative guide on Privately Financed Infrastructure (PFI), produced in 2000, and model legislative provisions on PFI projects.[9] This chapter is primarily concerned to discuss the potential contents of a model law on PPPs. In essence, PPP-specific legislative harmonisation, whilst it may serve a valid objective, especially in countries with a civil law tradition, obscures many difficult, technical decisions. This is the particular focus of this chapter. The chapter will, however, begin with discussion on the growth of PPP, the globalisation of PPP regulation and the need for harmonisation. The chapter then

[3] Y Marique, *Public–Private Partnerships and the Law: Regulation, Institutions and Community* (Cheltenham, Edward Elgar, 2014).

[4] See http://ppp.worldbank.org/public-private-partnership/legislation-regulation/laws/ppp-and-concession-laws. Unfortunately, the website is now dated and many of the hyperlinks are broken.

[5] According to the European Investment Bank's most recent review of the European PPP market for 2016, 69 PPP transactions reached financial close, representing an aggregate value of €12 billion. It is reported that the most active market was the UK (by value and number of projects). www.eib.org/infocentre/publications/all/epec-market-update-2016.htm.

[6] World Bank Group, Government objectives: benefits and risks of PPPs: http://ppp.worldbank.org/public-private-partnership/overview/ppp-objectives.

[7] Delmon, *Public–Private Partnership projects in infrastructure* (2017) 29.

[8] UNCITRAL Model Law on Public Procurement (1 July 2011).

[9] UNCITRAL Legislative Guide on Privately Financed Infrastructure Projects (29 June 2000); UNCITRAL Model Legislative Provisions on Privately Financed Infrastructure Projects (7 July 2003).

moves on to discuss some of the key issues that UNCITRAL will need to confront in the development of a model law on PPP. These include questions relating to how PPP might be defined, and, as such, the scope of the law, the support provided by particular government institutions, for example in developing policy on PPP or developing standardised documents, whether or not any limitations may be necessary in relation to the availability of the PPP model, for example when PPP can be used and what public bodies may make use of the PPP model, whether PPP demands a special procurement process, such as the EU's competitive dialogue, and issues to do with the PPP contract.

The chapter concludes with a note of caution. The difficulty for legal harmonisation in this area relates to a perceived commercial need for flexibility, for example, so as not to constrain the advancement of PPP contracting. Importantly, as accepted by the multilateral development banks, including the World Bank, 'There is no single, model PPP framework. A government's PPP framework typically evolves over time, often in response to specific challenges facing its PPP program'.[10] The extent to which a model law would therefore be beneficial remains to be seen. A further concern would be that legal rules might, to an extent, distract from capacity building, in particular the important need for high-level skills, and experience in government to organise and deliver these projects.

I. The Globalisation of PPP Regulation

This section will concentrate on the reasons for the spread of strikingly similar PPP-specific legislation in recent years, especially noticeable in developing countries. This legislation resembles and appears to be modelled on the experience in certain jurisdictions with mature PPP markets, like the UK, and thus aspects of the UK PPP experience will be the focus of the discussion after this.

The idea behind PPP is not new. Indeed, Wettenhall suggests that the concept – cooperation between the public sector and private sector – has been around since the early civilisations.[11] However, these arrangements gained prominence late-on in the twentieth century, as governments embraced the New Public Management – which, for the purposes of chapter, refers to the refashioning of the state as a private actor, involving the appropriation of modern management techniques from the private sector and influenced by public choice theory.[12] For the UK in particular, the New Public Management radically transformed the public sector, involving, amongst other developments, privatisation of public owned-assets, compulsory competitive tendering, which made it mandatory for local authorities to put a range of services, traditionally delivered

[10] PPP Knowledge Lab, 'Public Private Partnerships reference guide: version 3', available at https://pppknowledgelab.org/guide/sections/83-what-is-the-ppp-reference-guide.

[11] R Wettenhall, 'Mixes and Partnerships Through Time' in G Hodge, C Greve and A Boardman (eds), *International Handbook on Public-Private Partnerships* (Cheltenham, Edward Elgar, 2010) 17.

[12] See P Dunleavy and C Hood, 'From Old Public Administration to New Public Management' (1994) 14 *Public Money & Management* 9; C Hood and R Dixon, 'Not What it Said on the Tin? Reflections on Three Decades of UK Public Management Reform' (2016) 32 *Financial Accountability and Management* 409; C Hood, *The Art of the State: Culture, Rhetoric, and Public Management* (Oxford, Oxford University Press, 2000); C Hood, 'A Public Management for All Seasons' (1991) 69 *Public Administration* 3.

in-house, out to competitive tender (due to resulting criticism and animosity generated by compulsory competitive tendering it was replaced with a 'Best Value' system in 1997), and the promotion of PPPs, notably under the UK's infamous Private Finance Initiative (PFI).[13]

The UK's PFI – launched in 1992 as a means of increasing 'the scope for private financing of capital project',[14] and now operating under the guise of Private Finance 2 (PF2)[15] – is a notorious PPP investment scheme. The National Audit Office reports that, as of 18 January 2018, there are 761 PFI and PF2 projects either under construction or in operation in the UK, with a total capital value of £59.4 billion.[16] In view of this experience, the UK is often recognised to be at the vanguard of the development of PPP, and the UK experience is an important reference point for states, including developing countries, as they look to roll out PPP programmes.

The UK – mainly but not exclusively in the common law tradition – has not relied upon legislation for the implementation and operation of PFI/PF2. Instead, legal regulation is provided by general public and private law, though legal rules deriving from the EU are in place to regulate the procurement process. This regulation is supplemented by a considerable amount of non-legislative advice and guidance (soft law). For UK central government, the non-legislative Green Book, provides authoritative regulation for PPP,[17] and there are also a number of standardised documents, including a standardised contract.[18]

The PPP-specific legislation, which is increasingly prominent across the developing world, bears striking resemblance to the systems developed in advanced economies, like under the UK's PFI. However, it is not entirely evident why a template so heavily indebted to regulatory systems of advanced economies is being adopted.

In their ground-breaking study on the globalisation of business regulation (as distinct from the globalisation of businesses or markets), the socio-legal scholars, Braithwaite and Drahos, explain there to be a variety of social, economic or political processes that cause regulation to travel across borders:[19] 'regulatory globalisation is a process in which different types of actors use various mechanisms to push for or against principles'.[20] For instance, the mechanisms involved could, depending on the context, be military coercion, economic coercion and systems of reward – for example, the 'conditionality' associated with multilateral development banks, like the World Bank – modelling, reciprocal adjustment and non-reciprocal coordination, and capacity building.[21]

[13] There exists a significant amount of negative press coverage, political opposition and public scepticism surrounding PFI, especially in recent days following the insolvency of Carillion Plc, a key player in the global PPP market. See,eg, 'Fears Fallout from Carillion Collapse will Spread to Other Companies' *Guardian* (5 January 2018), available at www.theguardian.com/business/2018/jan/15/jobs-carillion-liquidation-construction-hs2.

[14] Norman Lamont MP (Chancellor of the Exchequer), Hansard (HC) vol 213, col 998 (12 November 1992).

[15] HM Treasury, 'A New Approach to Public Private Partnerships' (December 2012). It was announced in the 2018 budget that PFI and PF2 would be abolished for future building projects: see www.gov.uk/government/publications/budget-2018-documents/budget-2018.

[16] National Audit Office, 'PFI and PF2' (17 January 2018) 23.

[17] HM Treasury, 'The Green Book: Appraisal and Evaluation in Central Government' (2003, updated July 2011); HM Treasury, 'Value for Money Assessment Guidance' (Aug 2004, updated November 2006).

[18] HM Treasury, 'Standardisation of PF2 contracts: draft' (December 2012).

[19] J Braithwaite and P Drahos, *Global Business Regulation* (Cambridge, Cambridge University Press, 2004).

[20] ibid 9.

[21] ibid 17.

There are potentially a number of the above mechanisms at work here, in particular economic coercion and also capacity building. The PPP-specific laws are clearly in place to provide, or at least to symbolise to investors, the presence of a robust system, in which private investment is secure and worthwhile:

> Given the significant and long-term commitments involved, it is difficult to pursue a PPP programme without strong and stable political commitment. This is essential if both the public and private sector partners are to be expected to spend significant time and money preparing, investing in and implementing projects.[22]

So, multilateral development banks, which have emerged as strong backers of PPP,[23] can exert pressure for a particular model of PPP. The European Bank of Reconstruction and Development's Legal Transition Programme has had a particular focus on assisting governments committed to bringing PPP laws in line with 'better standards and promoting sound practices'.[24] In addition, the PPP framework, including PPP institutions and specific legislation, can form part of 'good governance' initiatives, and so be a focus in capacity building. For instance, 'PPP institution building' is a strategic priority for the Public–Private Infrastructure Advisory Facility (PPIAF), established in 1999, 'a multi-donor technical assistance facility that is financed by 11 multilateral and bilateral donors'.[25]

Braithwaite and Drahos found 'modelling' (mentioned above),[26] which may in some ways be equated with 'regulatory export',[27] to be especially significant in the globalisation of regulation. The model here is the PFI. It has been on display in the UK since it was rolled out in 1992 and has been symbolically interpreted and copied by other international actors, including other states and multilateral development banks.

The chapter will now proceed to discuss the possible contents of an UNCITRAL model law on PPPs, and, based on the UK PPP experience, it will identify potential complications, and choices that may need to be made in agreeing a text.

II. Defining PPP

This section of the chapter concerns the need to define the phrase/acronym PPP in a model law. In defining PPP, we are concerned with the scope of application of PPP-specific legislation.

[22] European PPP Expertise Centre, 'PPP Motivations and Challenges for the Public sector' (October 2015) 12.

[23] C Tan and L Cotula, 'Regulating Development Partnerships: PPPs, Blended Finance and Responsible Investment Provisions' (23 March 2018), available at investmentpolicyhub.unctad.org/blog.

[24] See www.ebrd.com/what-we-do/sectors/legal-reform/ppp-concessions.html; European Bank of Reconstruction and Development, 'Update on Best International Practices in Public Private Partnership with Regards to Regional Policy Issues' (November 2005).

[25] See https://ppiaf.org/about-us.

[26] J Braithwaite, 'A Sociology of Modelling and the Politics of Empowerment' (1994) 45 *The British Journal of Sociology* 445.

[27] K Raustiala, 'The Architecture of International Cooperation: Transgovernmental Networks and the Future of International Law (2002) 43 *Virginia Journal of International Law* 1, 7.

There is no universally accepted definition of PPP. The meaning of the phrase varies depending on context, in particular between countries. In the UK, for instance, there is no legal definition of PPP. Nevertheless, government publications use the term as an overarching phrase to refer to a variety of arrangements that sit on a spectrum between traditional procurement and in-house provision of public services, and full-blown privatisation.[28] These include the contracting out of services that conventionally delivered by the public sector to private providers, privately financed infrastructure (described above), and institutional PPPs involving a public body and private partner setting up a joint venture to provide infrastructure and/or deliver services. Unhelpfully, the phrase PPP can also be used in a narrower sense, for example as projects procured under the UK's PFI were renamed PPP when New Labour was in government. PFI has since evolved under subsequent governments and is now referred to as PF2.[29]

From a commercial perspective, the UK is seen to have benefited from not restricting the development of PPP by rigidly defining it and, over time, PPP has entailed a variety of private investment opportunities.[30] In any particular setting, the PPP model is bound to evolve, for example, with changes in politics and financial conditions. For example, the recent introduction of PF2 represents the recent Conservative–Liberal Democrat coalition Government response, in the wake of financial crisis, to perceived over-reliance on private finance under the previous Government (New Labour). So, amongst other things, PF2 places greater emphasis on appropriate risk allocation and seeks to ensure less reliance on bank debt.[31] Similarly, there has been much interest in the Non-Profit Distributing (NPD) model, pioneered by the Scottish Government in recent years, which supposedly provides many of the benefits of traditional PPP, but places a cap on private sector profits.[32]

There are also numerous definitions for PPP in circulation at the international level, and these tend to try to accommodate the different shapes PPP may take, often highlighting risk-sharing – a central feature and perceived benefit of PPP arrangements. This can be seen in the definition adopted by the World Bank's 'PPP Knowledge Lab': A PPP is 'A long-term contract between a private party and a government entity, for providing a public asset or service, in which the private party bears significant risk and management responsibility and remuneration is linked to performance'.[33] This is a wide definition that covers many of the different PPP, and, from an infrastructure perspective, various shapes an agreement may take, such as Design-Build-Finance-Operate (DBFO), Build-Operate-Transfer (BOT), and Build-Own-Operate (BOO).

[28] HM Treasury, 'Public Private Partnerships: The Government's Approach' (2000) 10.

[29] HM Treasury, 'A New Approach' (2012).

[30] KPMG, 'Public Private Partnerships: Emerging Global Trends and the Implications for Future Infrastructure Development in Australia' (June 2015) 18.

[31] HM Treasury (n 15).

[32] See Scottish Futures Trust, 'NPD Model Explanatory Note' (December 2011), available at www.scottishfuturestrust.org.uk/files/publications/Explanatory_Note_on_the_NPD_Model_(Updated_December_2011).pdf.

[33] http://ppp.worldbank.org/public-private-partnership/overview/what-are-public-private-partnerships.

EU law fails to provide a legal definition for PPP. The variety of approaches to PPPs found, for example, even across the relatively close-knit Member States of the EU,[34] suggests that any rigid or narrow definition for PPP would not be a viable option.

Although EU law does not regulate PPPs specifically, EU public procurement law – internal market legislation – has struggled to deal with the idiosyncrasies of certain Member States in this regard. The EU regulates the procurement of goods, works and services by 'contracting authorities' in Member States in order to open markets to EU-wide competition. EU law prohibits barriers to trade, such as national bias in the award of contracts, and, since the 1970s, detailed regulation, in the form of directives, seeks to require specified procurement deemed to be of cross-border interest to adhere to contract award procedures based on principles of transparency, equal treatment and non-discrimination. There are presently separate directives governing public contracts,[35] concessions,[36] utilities[37] and defence,[38] and these are supported by a system of enforcement and remedies.[39] The separate directives mean that there are different sets of rules for PPPs that are public contracts and PPPs that are concessions (explained below), and the need for such separate sets of rules lacks any convincing economic justification. The distinction in treatment is down to historical and cultural reasons: it is just that certain Member States, notably France, have a history of regarding concessions as different.[40]

The construction of a motorway can be used to provide a basic illustration of the difference between a public contract PPP and a concession PPP. The authority procures the finance and construction of the motorway; along with operation and maintenance services for a 20-year period. Under a concession arrangement, the private partner will recoup its costs and make a profit by levying a toll on individual members of the public who travel on the motorway. In a public contract payment for the operational and

[34] Indeed, experiences with different PPP programmes across Member States, for example, UK's PFI, Germany's *vorfinanzierungsmodell*, Belgium's *contrats de promotion*, France's *marchés d'entreprises de travaux publics*, and Italy's *TAV formula* – have differed.

[35] Directive 2014/24/EU of the European Parliament and of the Council of 26 February 2014 on public procurement and repealing Directive 2004/18/EC (OJ L 94, 28.3.2014, p 1–64).

[36] Directive 2014/23/EU of the European Parliament and of the Council of 26 February 2014 on the award of concession contracts (OJ L 94, 28.3.2014, p 65–242).

[37] Directive 2014/25/EU of the European Parliament and of the Council of 26 February 2014 on procurement by entities operating in the water, energy, transport and postal services sectors and repealing Directive 2004/17/EC (OJ L 94, 28.3.2014, p 243–374).

[38] Directive 2009/81/EC of the European Parliament and of the Council of 13 July 2009 on the coordination of procedures for the award of certain works contracts, supply contracts and service contracts by contracting authorities or entities in the fields of defence and security and amending Directives 2004/17/EC and 2004/18/EC (OJ L 216, 20.8.2009, p 76–136).

[39] Council Directive of 21 December 1989 on the coordination of the laws, regulations and administrative provisions relating to the application of review procedures to the award of public supply and public works contracts (89/665/EEC) (OJ L 395 30.12.1989, p 33); Council Directive 92/13/EEC of 25 February 1992 coordinating the laws, regulations and administrative provisions relating to the application of Community rules on the procurement procedures of entities operating in the water, energy, transport and telecommunications sectors (OJ L 395 30.12.1989, p 33); Directive 2007/66/EC of the European Parliament and of the Council of 11 December 2007 amending Council Directives 89/665/EEC and 92/13/EEC with regard to improving the effectiveness of review procedures concerning the award of public contracts (OJ L 335, 20.12.2007, p 31–46).

[40] See Allen and Overy, *Global Guide to Public–Private Partnerships* (March 2010) ch 4.

maintenance services would be provided by the public sector. The procurement rules applicable therefore vary according to the classification of the contract (a much lighter regime applies to concessions), and, because of the arguably unnecessary distinction, the clarity and intelligibility of the regulatory system is undermined. This has been a controversial area in EU public procurement, especially prior to the introduction of the 2014 Concessions Directive – when there existed different rules for public contracts, works concessions and services concessions. The 2014 Concessions Directive now confirms that a concession 'consists either solely in the right to exploit the works/services that are the subject of the contract or in that right together with payment',[41] and the award of the concession 'shall involve the transfer to the concessionaire of an operating risk in exploiting those works or services encompassing demand or supply risk or both',[42] but important legal grey areas remain.[43]

In addition to the distinction above between PPPs that are public contracts and PPPs that are concession arrangements, the European Commission has distinguished between (1) purely contractual PPPs, where the relationship between a public body and the private partner is based solely on contract; and (2) what it terms institutional PPPs (IPPP), which involve cooperation between the public body and private partner in a distinct mixed-capital entity that performs public contracts/concessions.[44] A joint venture company established by the public body and private partner could therefore be classified as an IPPP, as could an arrangement where a proportion of shares in an existing public sector entity are transferred to the private sector. The distinction is made mainly due to uncertainty surrounding the application of EU public procurement law. For example, to establish a joint venture a public body will need to select the private partner based on a tendering exercise; however, as EU procurement law does not apply to purely inhouse provision (the so-called *Teckal* exemption),[45] must the joint venture then compete for further public contracts procured by the public body, or does it escape the procurement rules? These uncertainties have produced a line of case law from the Court of Justice of the EU.

EU public procurement law has also struggled to grapple with, so-called, 'development agreements', which may also be classified as PPP. The procurement rules generally apply to procurement, ie acquisition, activities. To what extent should the law apply to 'gifts' made by public bodies in cases where procurement by such bodies would otherwise be regulated under the directive? An authority may wish to do make a gift of land based on the proviso that the private contractor will develop the land. As above, in relation to the *Teckal* exemption, the Court of Justice of the EU has repeatedly been called upon to delineate these boundaries within and around EU public procurement law.

[41] Article 5(1)(a) and (b).

[42] Article 5(1).

[43] R Craven, 'EU's 2014 Concessions Directive' (2014) 4 *Public Procurement Law Review* 188.

[44] Commission interpretative communication on the application of Community law on Public Procurement and Concessions to institutionalised PPP (OJ C 91, 12.4.2008, p 4–9).

[45] *Teckal Srl v Comune de Viano and Azienda Gas-Acqua Consorziale (AGAC) di Reggio Emilia* (C-107/98) [1999] ECR I-8121.

III. PPP Institutions

PPP-specific legislation invariably contains provisions on institutional arrangements, for example, designating oversight responsibilities to departments and/or non-departmental public bodies, or, more realistically, in view of the need for flexibility, providing a power to set up such institutional arrangements. This section will outline the history of the UK's PFI, which, as it will be seen, entails constant restructuring of the institutional arrangements for PFI, changes brought about by changes in and within governments, and varying due to the challenges faced, such as the 2007–08 financial crisis.[46] Due to the complexity of the institutional framework, the chapter will focus on the main institutions set up to administer PFI in England. The description cannot be completely comprehensive. In particular, the overview does not concern itself with PPP institutions specific to Scotland, Wales and Northern Ireland.

The PFI was officially launched in 1992 under a Conservative government. Prior to 1992, between 1981 and 1989, the Ryrie Rules had governed the availability of private finance in the provision of public infrastructure and services, and the PFI was intended to increase scope for such projects. Following a slow start under PFI, the Private Finance Panel was established in 1993, its personnel drawn from both the private and public sectors in order to promote and help expand PFI. In 1994, the 'universal test' was introduced: HM Treasury would only allow capital projects if private finance options had been explored.

The PFI-era truly dawned when the New Labour Government came to power in 1997. Swiftly, a review of PFI was carried out, resulting in the 1997 Bates Report, which made 29 recommendations. In 1997, the universal test was dropped. The Treasury Taskforce, replacing the Private Finance Panel, was created within HM Treasury. It would have two arms: a policy arm, staffed by public sector employees, and a projects arm, staffed by individuals representing the private sector. As a consequence of a second Bates Report in 1999, the projects arm of the Treasury Taskforce was replaced by Partnerships UK, itself a PPP, which would have an arm's-length relationship with HM Treasury, operational independence, and 51 per cent of its equity would be owned by the private sector.

In April 2000, the Office of Government Commerce (OGC), an independent office of HM Treasury, was established in place of the policy arm of the Treasury Taskforce. The OGC was an independent office of HM Treasury, established to help government deliver best value from its spending. In addition, the OGC had the lead role in developing procurement skills across the public sector and coordinated responses in EU infraction cases against the UK.

In addition, two significant PFI investment schemes instituted under the Labour Government in England – Building Schools for the Future (BSF), which aimed to rebuild or renew every secondary school in England (over 700 schools received investment), and National Health Service Local Improvement Finance Trusts (LIFT), relating to investment in primary care and community-based facilities and services – would be

[46] European PPP Expertise Centre, 'United Kingdom – England: PPP Units and Related Institutional Framework' (June 2012); OECD, OECD, 'Review of Public Governance of Public–Private Partnerships in the United Kingdom' (GOV/PGC/SBO(2015)8) (December 2015).

promoted and administered through new institutions: Partnerships for Schools (BSF) and Community Health Partnerships (LIFT). In these schemes, investment was delivered via a joint venture, a Local Education Partnership (BSF) or LIFT Company (LIFT), involving local authorities, the private sector and either Partnerships for Schools or Community Health Partnerships (depending on the scheme). The joint venture would enter into long-term strategic partnership agreements with the procuring authority to deliver an area's BSF or LIFT programme, which may consist of PFI and conventionally financed design and build infrastructure.[47]

The financial crisis, and the lack of available finance that resulted, led to the establishment of the HM Treasury Infrastructure Finance Unit (now part of Infrastructure UK; see below) in March 2009.[48] Essentially, its objective was to step in to provide lending for PFI deals on the same terms as commercial lenders to ensure that infrastructure projects make it to financial close. In April 2009, it was necessary for the Treasury Infrastructure Finance Unit to rescue the Greater Manchester's waste disposal PFI with a £120 million loan.

The Conservative–Liberal Democrat coalition Government came to power in 2010, confirming its commitment to PPP, despite mounting hostility: 'The Government has confirmed it remains committed to Public Private Partnerships (PPP), including those delivered via [PFI], and that such arrangements will continue to play an important role in delivering Britain's future infrastructure'.[49]

In June 2010 it was announced that responsibility for the OGC (as well as the public sector procurement agency, Buying Solutions) would move from HM Treasury to Cabinet Office where it would form part of a new Efficiency and Reform Group (closed in October 2014).[50] In 2011, it was announced that Partnerships UK would be dissolved, and Infrastructure UK, part of HM Treasury, would take over much of its role. In 2016, Infrastructure UK was merged with the Major Projects Authority, becoming the Infrastructure and Projects Authority.[51]

Specific institutions were also deemed necessary for the local level. In 1996 the Public Private Partnerships Programme (4Ps) was set up in England and Wales to encourage the growth of PPPs, particularly PFI. In 2009, this was absorbed into a new joint venture between the Local Government Organisation and Partnerships UK: Local Partnerships.[52]

The above sketch of the institutional landscape emphasises the versatile approach to PPP policy and practice in the UK, something that would have been at risk of being inhibited by an approach reliant on legal rules resulting from legal harmonisation. Arguably, the 'chop and change' approach to the institutions involved in administering PFI provides little stability. However, because of the political importance of PPP and public spending more generally, it is questionable whether a legal framework would, in reality, provide a greater degree of certainty.

[47] Deloitte, 'Building Flexibility: New Delivery Models for Public Infrastructure Projects' (2006).
[48] HM Treasury, 'Treasury lending to PFI projects and the Treasury's Infrastructure Finance Unit', letter (4 May 2009).
[49] HM Treasury, 'Public-private partnerships – technical update number 2010' (2010).
[50] www.gov.uk/government/organisations/efficiency-and-reform-group.
[51] www.gov.uk/government/organisations/infrastructure-and-projects-authority.
[52] http://localpartnerships.org.uk.

IV. The Decision to Use PPP

This section will consider reasons for limiting the use of PPP, in particular the rationales for restricting the use of PPP so that it is only used for appropriate reasons and limiting the types of public bodies that may use PPP, and how these restrictions might be carried out.

There are a number of attractions to PPP. At the present time, with many nations under pressure to keep sovereign debt and deficit levels in check, the prospect of upfront private finance[53] can be seductive: PPP may be looked upon as a means of delivering capital infrastructure and/or services that would otherwise not be affordable, for example, because tax rises would not be palatable politically, though this depends on the accounting treatment of PPP, and whether the project will count as capital spending for the year in which the investment occurs.

In a traditional public procurement involving public finance, typically, the public sector records spending as it is incurred, eg during the construction. This is not necessarily the case in PPP procurement. It may be possible to structure a PPP so that it is 'off-balance sheet'. This, clearly, from a political perspective can make PPP a very attractive option: a government can meet demands for improved infrastructure and/or public services, and, at the same time, can claim to be fiscally prudent. However, in the long term, from a standard economic point of view, relying on private finance to deliver infrastructure and/or services only because sufficient public funds are not available (ie there are no supplementary cost savings or value-for-money arguments) would be unwise. The main reason for this is that in spreading the cost of payment the Government will inevitably pay more than it would otherwise do, and governments can raise finance on the bond markets at a much lower rate than the private sector can, which, naturally, will inflate the cost borne by a future government.

For some, a more legitimate argument for PPP is that it can lead to efficiency savings and enhanced value for public money, as in 'the optimum combination of whole life cost and quality (or fitness for purpose) to meet the user's requirement'.[54] Efficiency savings can be associated with socially detrimental practices, such as job losses, but, in this regard, risk-sharing is commonly highlighted as the major selling point of PPP. Unlike a traditional procurement, in a PPP risks may be transferred to the party best placed to manage them. A public body may be relieved of bearing the risk of cost overruns during the construction phase, construction delays and long-term maintenance of an asset.[55]

In the UK, the Government's position has long been that PPP/PFI should only be used in place of public finance where it is the value-for-money option. Accurately making this determination has, however, been problematic, and there has been criticism that projects have been delivered under PPP/PFI when value for money was debatable. The decision whether or not to use PPP would be made by reference to a public sector

[53] The financial crisis has meant that the prominence of other means of financing PPP has risen. See, eg, European PPP Expertise Centre, 'Financing PPPs with Project Bonds' (October 2012).

[54] HM Treasury, 'PFI: Strengthening Long-Term Partnerships' (2006) 29.

[55] See, eg, P Hovy, 'Risk Allocation in Public-Private Partnerships: Maximizing Value for Money' (International Institute for Sustainable Development, August 2015).

comparator: a cost and risk estimate of a public financed project delivering the same outputs as those of the intended PPP project. The financial projections involved in this comparison exercise are complex and will depend on future unknowns and assumptions. The figures are open to manipulation, and, if there is, in reality, no non-PFI alternative (for example, because of funding constraints) when the comparison is made, there can be strong incentives to be optimistic about PFI.

The accounting treatment for PFI – when should the capital expenditure feature on public sector accounts and when should it feature on private sector accounts – has been a particular cause for concern, because off-balance sheet accounting may incentivise PFI even where value for money is not present. This is an incredibly complex matter, and regrettably there is not scope in this chapter to do justice to that complexity.[56] However, in looking at accounting practices, a crucial concern in PPP procurement and therefore any legal harmonisation efforts, much harmonisation has already taken place. In basic terms, the situation has developed over time showing two accounting approaches in competition: 'risk and rewards' and 'control'.[57] In the early days of PFI, much PFI spending would have been regarded as off the public sector balance sheet,[58] and sometimes off the private sector balance sheet as well.[59] The treatment would depend on certain complex determinations in accordance with Generally Accepted Accounting Practice (GAAP), but, for the public sector, in the main, the debt would be off-balance sheet where the majority of the risk had been transferred to the private partner. The UK eventually switched to International Financial Reporting Standards (IFRS), introduced across the public sector in 2009–10, which emphasises the criterion of control, rather than risk and reward (the criterion under GAAP). The switch has brought most PFI/PPP on to the public sector balance sheet, according to the government, but there are doubts as to the accuracy of this.

There are differences between the above accounting and the national accounts. The position under the European System of Accounts,[60] which all Member States of the EU must prepare national accounts in accordance with, favours the risk and rewards approach, and thus the public sector net debt excludes most PFI liabilities. This comparatively lax system has been tightened up in recent years;[61] however, this has tended to mean that the system works against new forms of PPP that have developed in response to criticisms, such as the NPD PPP model in Scotland (see above). As with conventional public sector procurement, such new methods are more likely to adversely affect

[56] David Heald, George Georgiou and others have, however, written some detailed and accessible publications on the subject. See D Heald and G Georgiou, 'The Substance of Accounting for Public-Private Partnerships' (2011) 27 *Financial Accounting and Management* 217; D Heald and G Georgiou, 'Accounting for PPPs in a Converging World' in G Hodge, AC Greve and AE Boardman (eds), *International Handbook on Public Private Partnerships* (Cheltenham, Edward Elgar, 2010) 237; D Heald, 'Value for Money Tests and Accounting Treatment in PFI Schemes' (2003) 16 *Accounting, Auditing and Accountability Journal* 342; D Heald and N Geaughan, 'The Private Financing of Public Infrastructure' in G Stoker (ed), *The New Management of Local Governance: Audit of an Era of Change in Britain* (London, Macmillan, 1999) 222.

[57] Heald and Georgiou, 'The Substance of Accounting' (2011).

[58] ibid 224–25.

[59] ibid 227.

[60] Eurostat, European System of Accounts, ESA 2010.

[61] See Eurostat, 'A Guide to the Statistical Treatment of PPPs' (September 2016).

government balance sheets in comparison to traditional PPP models.[62] Nevertheless, in spite of the more relaxed system, UK government has adopted measures to enhance transparency about the cost of PPPs: the Whole of Government Accounts, 'a consolidated set of financial statements for the UK public sector', first published in 2009–10, reports on the position in accordance with IFRS, thus including most PPP debt.

At the local level, the UK was, at an early stage, keen to free up and support local authorities to enable local government to utilise the PFI model. In particular, local authorities could apply for PFI credits, which, if granted, would cover the capital element of the charges owed to the private provider.[63] In view of criticisms about the overreliance and abuse of PFI in local government, this system was abolished in 2010[64] in order to engender 'a level playing field for all forms of public procurement, thus seeking to ensure that procuring authorities consider all reasonable options for meeting their requirements'.[65] However, in examining this topic, the House of Commons Treasury Select Committee, has noted that PFI credits remain in operation, but in a rebadged form under the Government's National Infrastructure plan 2011,[66] and evidence heard by the Committee suggests that the end of PFI credits had not, in any significant way, reduced the incentives for local authorities to use PPP/PFI. It was argued that the incentives remained due to constraints on local authority capital budgets, such that without PPP projects would be unaffordable.[67]

A model law could make an important contribution if it encouraged PPP use to be limited to only projects in which it can be demonstrated, on a case-by-case basis, that there is a particularly strong economic justification for using the PPP route over conventional public financing. However, international agreements on this aspect of a model PPP law would be difficult, and the approach to such a limitation would be far from straightforward.

V. The PPP Procurement Process

The procurement process is important for PPP. It is through this that the contractual terms – or deviations from standard term contracts – will be nailed down. The UNCITRAL Model Law on Public Procurement arguably provides suitable procurement procedures for PPP. However, to what extent does PPP-specific legislation need to specify the use of a particular procedure for the procurement of PPP? In relation to

[62] S McCann, 'Is Non-Profit Distributing PPP Dead? Long live PF2?' (Blake Morgan, October 2016), available at www.blakemorgan.co.uk/training-knowledge/features-and-articles/non-profit-distributing-ppp-dead.

[63] See J Sharland, *A Practical Approach to Local Government Law*, 2nd edn (Oxford, Oxford University Press, 2006) for further detail on these PFI inducements.

[64] HM Treasury, 'Public Private Partnerships – Technical Update 2010,' available at https://assets.publishing.service.gov.uk/government/uploads/system/uploads/attachment_data/file/215079/ppp_technical_update.pdf.

[65] HM Treasury (n 15) 71.

[66] House of Commons Treasury Select Committee, 'Private Finance 2' (House of Commons, 12 March 2014) para 18.

[67] ibid.

this decision, we potentially encounter tensions between the desire for transparency (for example, to deter corruption), the need to maintain competitive tension, and the need for a streamlined, low-cost process, in which wide-ranging negotiations between the public body and bidders – arguably vital for maximising value for money – are possible. The EU, in regulating PPP procurement, has grappled with a similar tension in recent years, and so this experience is the focus of this section.[68]

In 2004, a new procedure, competitive dialogue, was introduced into the EU procurement rules to strike an appropriate balance between transparency and flexibility with regard to PPP procurement.[69] For the UK, this new procedure suggested major changes would be needed to PPP procurement practice. Prior to competitive dialogue, in the UK, in line with government guidance, procuring authorities had relied upon the negotiated procedure for PFI procurement.[70] The negotiated procedure is a flexible procedure, with few stipulations in addition to a requirement to advertise the procurement EU-wide in the *Official Journal of the European Union*. This flexibility allowed authorities to run quite streamlined procurements, often characterised by a swift reduction of bidder numbers and early identification of a preferred bidder with which to negotiate the detail of the deal. This practice reduced bid costs for all involved, but raised question marks over the transparency of, and competitive tension maintained throughout, the negotiations.

The use of the negotiated procedure was problematic, especially for the European Commission, which considered that the procedure was being used inappropriately in the UK and, thus, in relation to the PFI procurement for a school in London, issued a reasoned opinion against the UK under Article 258 TFEU.

In 2004, a new procedure was introduced, specifically designed with PPP procurement in mind: competitive dialogue. This new procedure enabled negotiations between public bodies and bidders by incorporating a dialogue stage, in which all aspects of the contract could be discussed, but also sought to remove the scope for preferred bidder negotiations (that is, negotiations, when just one bidder was left in the process, of the kind seen in the UK): following the formal close of the dialogue stage, when the public body could identify the solution/s capable of meeting its needs, it was required to invite final tenders, and uncertain legal rules restricted the scope for any further work on proposals or tenders.

On paper, the new legal rules appear to strike a sensible balance. However, in practice, there were teething problems, and the law was ultimately reformed in 2014.[71] In particular, problems arose due to the way in which the rules required competitive bidding to be maintained until much later on in the process: the resources this entailed for both public bodies and bidders made the procedure unattractive, especially when bidders might be required to invest heavily in pulling a bid together with little certainty

[68] S Arrowsmith and S Treumer (eds), *Competitive Dialogue in EU Procurement* (Cambridge, Cambridge University Press 2012).

[69] Article 29, Directive 2004/18/EC of the European Parliament and of the Council of 31 March 2004 on the coordination of procedures for the award of public works contracts, public supply contracts and public service contracts (L 134/114).

[70] S Arrowsmith and R Craven, 'Competitive Dialogue in the United Kingdom' in Arrowsmith and Treumer, *Competitive Dialogue* (2012) 181.

[71] Directive 2014/24/EU (Public Procurement Directive), Art 30 (n 35).

of success. Such problems were magnified following the 2007–08 financial crisis. In addition, because of the way in which the financial crisis impacted on debt financers – like banks – the regulatory framework – specifically the restrictions on post-dialogue negotiations – came under severe strain, for example, as banks demanded changes to agreements after the close of the dialogue stage, immediately prior to contract close. This exceptional period would prompt the regulatory reforms.[72]

The 2014 reforms introduce greater flexibility, placing more trust in the hands of national policy-makers and procurement professionals. Importantly, the wording around the post-dialogue work that can be undertaken with bidders was relaxed, with it now emphasising the need to avoid changes that might distort competition or cause discrimination. A new procedure – the competitive procedure with negotiation – was also introduced, replacing the old negotiated procedure, as a flexible alternative to sit alongside the competitive dialogue.[73]

From the viewpoint of regulatory globalisation, it is noteworthy to see the EU terminology – competitive dialogue – travel. A competitive dialogue procurement procedure can now be found in the World Banks's procurement framework.[74] The procedural rules also resemble those of the EU's competitive dialogue (pre-reform), essentially the EU's PPP procurement procedure. However, although competitive dialogue is available for PPP procurement, there is no sign in the rules that it is the preferred method for PPP.[75]

VI. The Contract

This final section focuses on the PPP contract. The PPP contract is obviously of critical importance, dealing with central issues such as risk transfer, ownership, service delivery, payment, dispute resolution, etc. In the UK, all such issues are dealt with through standard form contracts.[76] In recent times, in the UK, due to PFI failures (eg due to expense or poor service delivery), the debate has emphasised the operation of penalty clauses, termination and termination costs. In addition, this chapter has already touched upon new PPP models, like PF2 and Scotland's NPD – which attempt to constrain risk transfer and profiteering. This section, however, shifts the focus away from the UK experience, concerning itself with a more neglected topic, but one of particular relevance to PPP arising through the involvement of development banks: the way in which the PPP contract may serve to percolate 'public law values into private law and into corporate self-regulation',[77] so-called 'publicization of the private'.[78] From a global perspective, Tan and Cotula note that 'the private turn [in development policy] brings into sharp

[72] See Aspey and Craven, 'Regulating Complex Contracting: A Socio-Legal Study of Decision-Making under EU and UK law' (2018) 81 *Modern Law Review* 191.

[73] Directive 2014/24/EU (Public Procurement Directive), Art 29 (n 35).

[74] World Bank, 'Procurement Regulations for IPF Borrowers' (July 2016), Annex XIII; P Trepte, 'All Change at the World Bank? The New Procurement Framework' (2016) 4 *Public Procurement Law Review* 121.

[75] See Trepte (ibid) fn 52.

[76] HM Treasury, 'Standardisation of PF2 contracts, draft' (December 2012).

[77] J Braithwaite, 'Strategic Socialism, Strategic Privatisation and Crises' (2013) 28 *Australian Journal of Corporate Law* 35.

[78] J Freeman, 'Extending Public Law Norms through Privatization' (2003) 116 *Harvard Law Review* 1285.

focus the relationship between the "public goods" mandate of donors and international financial institutions …, and the commercial interests of the private investors they seek to incentivise'.[79] However, in UK PPP policy, these issues receive little attention, despite the apparent political attractions.

PPPs are traditionally seen as a threat to public law values, such as fairness, equality, participation, transparency and accountability, as well as a threat to democracy. There are clearly deep and legitimate concerns in this regard. However, Jody Freeman turns the debate on its head, viewing privatisation in a more optimistic light. For Freeman, privatisation presents an opportunity to use public contracts (like PPP) to enhance public law values, 'by extending them to realms where they typically do not play a role'.[80] Freeman contends that 'publicization' can align with pragmatic arguments behind PPP, having to do with maximising value for money, She, however, accepts that 'public law norms might be costly for private providers, and those costs might undermine the potential for efficiency gains',[81] for example, because private companies are deterred from bidding for work. Publicisation may not be appropriate for all PPP contracts, therefore, but in many situations, it may be unwise for public actors to approach PPP contracts with a purely commercial attitude.

In this regard, scholars note how the rise in use of PPP for development might be used to promote international instruments on, for example, labour conditions, the environment, corruption and human rights (such as the United Nations Guiding Principles on Business and Human Rights).[82] If an organisation like UNCITRAL is to involve itself in further legal harmonisation in this area, particularly with the take-up of the PPP model in the developing world where governments may be overly reliant on standardised documentation, proposals relating to 'publicization' are worthy of consideration.

VII. Conclusion

In view of UNCITRAL undertaking additional work on legal harmonisation on PPP, this chapter has sought to flesh out many of the difficult areas that will need to be addressed by PPP-specific laws, using the UK experience as a case study. The chapter has thus worked through different parts of the 'PPP Act' – PPP-specific legislation emerging throughout the developing world – including the definition of PPP, PPP institutions, the decision to use PPP, the PPP procurement process, and the contract. In relation to the UK, behind each heading lies a highly complex set of arrangements that continue to evolve in line with the economic, social and political climate, which necessarily makes agreement over a model law contentious, particularly one that addressed the main issues in a meaningful way, and liable to date relatively quickly. That said, the pick-and-choose approach of the model law on public procurement, supplemented by a detailed guide, is a valuable tool, and such an approach here may be similarly worthwhile.

[79] Tan and Cotula, 'Regulating Development' (2018).
[80] Freeman, 'Extending Public Law Norms' (2003) 1314.
[81] ibid 1339.
[82] Tan and Cotula (n 23).

The chapter highlights two aspects of PPP in which continued work at international level would be helpful, especially for countries inexperienced in PPP procurement, so that they may learn from mistakes made in places like the UK. The first relates to the decision to use PPP. In the UK, much criticism derives from a perception of PPP overuse due to a bias in favour of PPP over conventional public procurement because of its off-balance sheet accounting treatment. The UK has taken steps to address this, however, with IFRS across government and also introducing the Whole of Government Accounts. The other aspect concerns the PPP contract. In the UK, commentators have criticised PPP contracts for being unreasonably advantageous to the private sector, for example, due to inappropriate risk transfer. New modes of delivering PPP are emerging that seek to counter these criticisms – such as Scotland's NPD (above), and there is scope to encourage a more balanced approach to PPP, as in pursuing 'publicization' in PPP contracts, which would seem appropriate in view of the role of the multilateral development banks post the 2007/09 financial crisis in the global spread of PPP procurement.

16

Regulation of Public–Private Partnership in China: The Search for Coherence, Consistency and Certainty

PING WANG

Public–private partnerships (PPPs) have developed rapidly in the past three decades due to financial shortages in the public sector and PPP's ability to harness additional financial resources, innovation and operating efficiencies inherent to the private sector.[1]

China is at the forefront of this development in terms of market size. PPPs emerged in China in the 1980s in the form of Build-Operate-Transfer (BOT) projects. Since then, PPPs have evolved through six phases, with the term 'concession' introduced in 2004 and the term 'PPP', as a distinctive legal concept, introduced in 2014 through various ministerial decrees and local legislation. Statistics from the World Bank's Private Participation in Infrastructure (PPI) database indicates 1,337 PPP projects have reached financial closure in China since 1990 with a total investment $130,985 million as of September 2018.[2] Brazil, China, India, Mexico and Turkey are regarded as top five countries in terms of total investment commitments in infrastructure PPPs from 1991 to 2015 with 54 per cent share of total investment in 2015.[3] As of June 2018, 7749 PPP projects are included in the PPP Project Library established by the Ministry of Finance (MoF) with total investment of CNY 11.9 trillion. Amongst these projects, 3,668 (47.3 per cent) reached financial close with investment of CNY 6 trillion, execution/construction

[1] For an overview of PPP development see G Hodge, C Greve and M Biygautane, 'Do PPPs Work? What and How Have we Been Learning so far? (2018) 20 *Public Management Review* 1105; T Bovaird 'A Brief Intellectual History of the Public–private Partnership Movement.' in G Hodge, C Greve and A Boardman (eds), *International Handbook on Public–private Partnerships* (Cheltenham, Edward Elgar, 2010) 43; European Commission, 'Guidelines for Successful Public–private Partnerships' (March 2003) 14.

[2] See https://pppknowledgelab.org/countries/china. Asian Development Bank (ADB)'s 2017 PPP country monitor presents slightly different but comparable figures: 1990–2016, 1052 PPP projects reaching financial close with $139 billion total investment. See Asian Development Bank, Public–Private Partnership Monitor (2017) ch 6, available at www.adb.org/sites/default/files/publication/381681/ppp-monitor.pdf#page=328.

[3] World Bank, 'Benchmarking Public–private Partnerships Procurement 2017: Assessing Government Capability to Prepare, Procure, and Manage PPPs' (2016) 12.

started with regard to 1,684 projects (45.9 per cent).[4] With so many projects in the pipeline for a considerable value, China is regarded as 'the largest PPP market in the region'.[5] Furthermore, it is predicted by the global ratings agency Fitch that PPPs will be the main financing model used by Chinese local governments for infrastructure investments up to 2020.[6]

It is widely recognised that a sound and enabling regulatory environment plays a critical role to a sustainable PPP. Referred to as the 'PPP framework' by the World Bank, it 'consists of the policies, procedures, institutions, and rules that together define how PPPs will be identified, assessed, selected, prioritised, budgeted for, procured, monitored, and accounted for and who will be responsible for these tasks'.[7] In particular, an enabling regulatory environment for PPPs has to minimise the regulatory risk and must be sufficiently clear, reliable and predictable as to encourage private participation and investment. If the legal and judicial environment is not clearly defined, investors and project participants will see the project as 'unpredictable and highly risky'.[8]

However, current incoherent, inconsistent and ambiguous institutional and regulatory framework arguably impedes the sustainable development of PPPs in China. Neither concession nor PPP is explicitly regulated by a national law. The main government procurement legislation, namely the Tendering Law and Government Procurement Law and their respective implementing regulations, is silent on PPPs. Instead, various ministries, especially Ministry of Finance (MoF) and National Development and Reform Commission (NDRC, the former State Planning Commission) issued numerous ministerial decrees (low in legal hierarchy in comparison with laws) with little coordination and often competing agenda. Due to the segregated institutional framework, the guidance issued at the central level is often inconsistent and has caused confusion in practice. For example, MoF and NDRC issued separate standardised PPP contract and has developed mutually exclusive PPP project libraries.

Furthermore, the demarcation line between certain key legal norms, namely concession, PPP and 'government procurement of services', has not been clearly drawn up. With each term defined broad enough to cover others and the power for its interpretation held by different ministries, the segregated institutional framework inevitably resulted in competing and overlapping legislative initiatives. For example, NDRC initially proposed the draft of Concession Law whilst MoF proposed the draft of PPP Law both with the view to regulating the PPP market as a whole. The State Council (the central

[4] See '2018 2nd Quarterly Report by Ministry of Finance PPP Centre', available (in Chinese) at www.cpppc.org/zh/pppjb/7191.jhtml.

[5] Speech to China PPP Forum by Dr Shamshad Akhtar, Under-Secretary-General of the United Nations & Executive Secretary of the United Nations Economic and Social Commission for Asia and the Pacific (UNESCAP), 1 November 2017, available at www.cpppc.org/en/Multilateral/5935.jhtml.

[6] See http://image.fitchemail.fitchratings.com/lib/fe9513707560047a7d/m/4/Chinese+Public+Private+Partnerships+v4.3F.pdf; 'PPPs to Drive China Infrastructure Investments: Fitch', *China Daily*, 20 February 2017, available at www.chinadaily.com.cn/business/2017-02/20/content_28269051.htm; H Lockett, 'PPPs to Drive China Infrastructure Investments: Fitch', *Financial Times*, 2 February 2017, available at www.ft.com/content/14a44049-22bf-3062-b5b2-79ebe77b0d95.

[7] See World Bank, 'PPP Reference Guide 2017', s 2 and the work cited there, available at https://ppp.worldbank.org/public-private-partnership/library/ppp-reference-guide-3-0.

[8] Asian Development Bank, *Public–Private Partnership Handbook* (2008) 14–15, available at www.adb.org/documents/public-private-partnership-ppp-handbook.

Government) had to step in following the criticism of the Premier[9] and released a draft of State Council Regulation on PPP in Infrastructure and Public Services (hereinafter 'Draft PPP Regulation') for public consultation in July 2017.[10]

From a practical perspective, there are evidences suggesting that private investors, domestic and foreign, 'have grown shy of China's PPP schemes because of their lack of returns and legal protections for private firms' at the local courts in the event of a dispute.[11] From an international perspective, the regulatory environment of PPPs in China arguably falls short of the minimum standard drawn from the guidance issued by a number of international institutions such as the UN, OECD, World Bank, ADB and EU.[12] It was observed by a World Bank working paper in 2003 that 'the underdeveloped legal system leaves many important and routine decisions to administrative authorities-often with inconsistent results'.[13] An ADB working paper in 2016 also provided a number of suggestions for China to improve the regulatory environment for PPPs albeit without a detailed assessment of the current framework.[14] The Economist Intelligence Unit (EIU)'s Infrascope 2014 sets out an index for assessing countries' readiness to carry out sustainable PPPs, and uses the index to evaluate the PPP environment in 21 countries in Asia-Pacific.[15] According to this report, while China's overall ranking was eighth in 2014, its regulatory framework was only ranked at 16, even worse than in 2011 (ranked 11th).

The existing academic literature covers various aspects of PPPs in China, such as finance, risk allocation, management, and specific sectors such as water and transportation.[16] Whilst the importance of the regulatory environment has commonly

[9] Speech by Premier Li, Keqiang, on the role of government, rule of law and departmental interests, 9 May 2016, available (in Chinese) at www.gov.cn/guowuyuan/2016-07/08/content_5089655.htm.

[10] The draft is available (in Chinese) at http://zqyj.chinalaw.gov.cn/readmore?id=1984&listType=1.

[11] J Li, 'Investors Grow Shy of China's Public–Private Projects', *South China Morning Post*, June 2016, available at www.scmp.com/business/companies/article/1963468/investors-grow-shy-chinas-public-private-projects.

[12] For example, 'OECD Basic Elements of a Law on Concession Agreements' (2003); 'UNCITRAL Legislative Guide to Privately Financed Infrastructure Projects Guide' (2001); 'UNCITRAL Model Legislative Provisions on Privately Financed Infrastructure Projects' (2003); 'United Nations Industrial Development Organization (UNIDO), Guidelines for Infrastructure Development through Build-Operate-Transfer (BOT) Projects' (1996); UNESCAP, *A Guidebook on PPP in Infrastructure* (2011). World Bank, *PPP Reference Guide* 2017; ADB, *Public–Private Partnership Handbook* (2008); European Commission, 'Guidelines for Successful Public–Private Partnerships' (2003); see also C Greve, 'International Public–Private Partnership Policies: Convergence in Themes from ASEAN, the European Union, IMF, OECD, the UN, and the World Bank', paper presented at the Fourth Annual International Public–Private Partnership (P3) Symposium, New York, USA, 14–16 September 2015, available at https://openarchive.cbs.dk/handle/10398/9196.

[13] M Bellier, and YM Zhou, 'Private Participation in Infrastructure in China: Issues and Recommendations for the Road, Water, and Power Sectors', World Bank Working Paper No 2 (2003) 11, available at https://openknowledge.worldbank.org/handle/10986/15156; License: CC BY 3.0 IGO.

[14] P Kelly, 'Preparing a Public Private Partnership Law: Observations from the International Experience', ADB East Asia Working Paper Series No 4, April 2016, available at www.adb.org/publications/preparing-ppp-law-observations-international-experience.

[15] Economist Intelligence Unit (EIU), 'Evaluating the Environment for Public Private Partnerships in Asia-Pacific: The 2014 Infrascope' (20150.

[16] For a literature review in general See Hodge, Greve and Biygautane, 'Do PPPs Work?' (2018); For China, see, eg, APC Chan, PTI Lam, DWM Chan, E Cheung and YJ Ke, 'Potential Obstacles to Successful Implementation of Public–Private Partnerships in Beijing and the Hong Kong Special Administrative Region', (2010) 26 *Journal of Management in Engineering* 30; APC Chan, PTI Lam, DWM Chan, E Cheung, and YJ Ke, 'Critical Success Factors for PPPs in Infrastructure Developments: Chinese Perspectives' (2010) 136 *Journal of Construction Engineering Management* 484.

been recognised in the broad literature found in management journals, there exists a need for a comprehensive legal analysis of China's PPP regulatory framework. The research into regulation of PPPs in China (as a BRIC country) remains high in the global research agenda.[17] Furthermore, since mid-2017, the regulation of PPPs in China has reached a new era with the central government ministries starting to step up the scrutiny and control of PPP projects initiated by local governments in the wake of widespread abuses and increased financial risk, with the State Council proposing the Draft PPP Regulation to replace other existing legislative initiatives. Therefore, this chapter will seek to provide a comprehensive and up-to-date analysis of China's regulatory environment for PPPs with a view to identifying the obstacles for development and assessing the adequacy for the new legislative proposal to address such obstacles.

To that end, section I will first provide a brief note on terminology since term PPP is notoriously difficult to define. Section II will provide an overview of the PPPs evolution in China with a special focus on instruments for regulation. Section III briefly discusses the Chinese Government procurement legal framework and its interaction with the PPP legal framework. Section IV examines the origin and implication of these legal issues as well as other obstacles such as the difficulty in choosing appropriate procuring methods, the lack of participation from private sector/the dominance of central state-owned enterprises (SOEs) in PPP market, and the unsatisfactory nature of the remedy system. As explained there, several recent Supreme People's Court rulings have demonstrated that the inconsistent interpretation of the nature of a PPP contract (as an administrative agreement or a civil contract) has led to arguably contradicting findings by the courts and left the aggrieved party with no effective legal remedy. Section V then examines the extent to which the current legislative initiative – the Draft PPP Regulation – will sufficiently address such obstacles and defects.

I. A Note on the Terminology

Despite its popularity, the term 'public–private partnership' has no precise meaning or one widely accepted definition.[18] The World Bank PPP Knowledge Lab defines a PPP as 'a long-term contract between a private party and a government entity, for providing a public asset or service, in which the private party bears significant risk and management responsibility, and remuneration is linked to performance'.[19] OECD defines PPPs in one document as 'long term contractual arrangements between the government and a private partner whereby the latter delivers and funds public services using a capital asset, sharing the associated risks'[20] and in another as 'arrangements whereby the

[17] G Hodge and C Greve, 'Contemporary Public–Private Partnership: Towards a Global Research Agenda' (2018) 34 *Financial Accountability & Management* 3, 4.

[18] For a list of PPP definitions adopted by various institutions see Kelly, 'Preparing a Public Private Partnership Law' (2016) App C.

[19] See 'What are Public Private Partnerships', available at https://ppp.worldbank.org/public-private-partnership/overview/what-are-public-private-partnerships.

[20] OECD, 'Recommendation of the Council on Principles for Public Governance of Public–Private Partnerships' (May 2012) 18, available at www.oecd.org/governance/budgeting/PPP-Recommendation.pdf.

private sector provides infrastructure assets and services that traditionally have been provided by government, such as hospitals, schools, prisons, roads, bridges, tunnels, railways, and water and sanitation plants.'[21]

For the purpose of this chapter, PPP refers to a long-term cooperative arrangement involving significant infrastructure assets linked to the public service, whereby a government entity entrusts the finance, construction, operation/maintenance/management of such assets, for a limited but long period of time (for example, 25–30 years), to a private entity whose remuneration, contingent on performance, consists in the right to exploit the assets (charges imposed on the end users of the infrastructure such as toll charges), payment made by the Government (for example, unitary charges for a new hospital), or a combination of both.[22]

The types and structures of PPP are dynamic and constantly evolving. According to the functions for which the private party is responsible, PPPs can be divided into types such as Build-Own-Operate (BOO), Design-Build-Finance-Operate (DBFO), Build-Operate-Transfer (BOT), Build-Own-Operate-Transfer (BOOT), Transfer-Operate-Transfer (TOT), Rehabilitate-Operate-Transfer (ROT), etc. According to the payment mechanism, PPPs can be divided into user-pays PPPs and government-pays PPPs. A concession, such as a toll road, bridge or tunnel, is a typical user-pays PPP, whereby the fees (or tariffs, or tolls) are charged from end users and can be supplemented by government payments, for example, complementary payments for services provided to low-income users when the tariff is capped. In government-pays PPPs, such as the Private Finance Initiative (PFI) in the UK,[23] the sole source of revenue for the private party is the Government, which pays periodic fees/unitary charges contingent upon the asset or service being available at a contractually defined quality.[24]

However, the terms used to categorise different types of PPPs also mean different things to different people in different contexts. For example, the World Bank, following the civil law tradition, views BOT and concession as separate concepts: a BOT project is a government-pays PPP and is typically used to develop a discrete, generally entirely new, asset, and a concession is a user-pays PPP granted with regard to a whole network of normally existing utilities assets. However, it does acknowledge that in common law countries such distinction is blurred which is 'confusing'.[25] The EU Commission also notes, as an example of terms 'used loosely and can be applied to situations that are

[21] OECD, 'Glossary of Statistical Terms', available at https://stats.oecd.org/glossary/detail.asp?ID=7315.

[22] See S Arrowsmith, 'Public Private Partnerships and the European Procurement Rules: EU Policies in Conflict?' (2000) 37 *Common Market Law Review* 709, 709.

[23] The PFI (launched in 1992) and its successor, PF2 (launched in 2012), are forms of PPP. 'In a PFI or PF2 deal, a private finance company – a Special Purpose Vehicle (SPV) – is set up and borrows to construct a new asset such as a school, hospital or road. The taxpayer then makes payments over the contract term (typically 25 to 30 years), which cover debt repayment, financing costs, maintenance and any other services provided.' See National Audit Office (NAO), PFI and PF2, 18 January 2018, 4, available at www.nao.org.uk/wp-content/uploads/2018/01/PFI-and-PF2.pdf; See also S Arrowsmith (ed), *Public Private Partnerships and PFI* (London, Sweet & Maxwell; looseleaf).

[24] See the general explanation in World Bank, 'PPP Reference Guide', s 6, available at https://pppknowledgelab.org/guide/sections/6-ppp-contract-types-and-terminology.

[25] See the discussion at 'Concessions, Build-Operate-Transfer (BOT), and Design-Build-Operate (DBO) Projects', available at https://ppp.worldbank.org/public–private-partnership/agreements/concessions-bots-dbos.

fundamentally different', that 'BOT can be used to describe procurements that involves private financing, as well as those that do not'.[26] In China, BOT is generally regarded as a form of concession.

Furthermore, while a contract between a public body and a state-owned enterprise (SOE) would not always be referred to as a PPP, it remains possible for a public corporation or SOE to act as the 'private' partner in PPPs, as acknowledged by the definition of PPP adopted by the EU for accounting purposes.[27] For example, it was noted that in France for a long period after World War II due to the persistence of ' the cult of the State', 'concessions were more often than not awarded to separate public entities rather than to privately held companies looking for public partners'.[28] It is noteworthy that as explained in section II, historically most PPP contracts in China have been awarded to SOEs and the concept of PPP in the Chinese context, formally launched in 2014, refers to cooperation between local government entities and 'social capital', which includes SOEs (companies with significant government ownership), private companies, and other organisations, potentially including foreign investors.

II. Evolution of the Regulation of PPPs in China

Since the reform and opening up in the 1980s,[29] PPPs in China have arguably evolved through various phases: exploration (1984–1993), pilot (1994–2001), development/upscale (2002–2007), recession/fluctuation (2008–2012), revival/expansion (2013–mid 2017) and review/rationalisation (mid 2017–).[30]

It is important to elucidate the history of PPP practice and regulation in order to identify the drivers, underlining institutional and legal framework that form the foundation for a critical analysis of existing impediments for future sustainable development of PPP in China. It should be noted at the outset that the development of PPPs in China is driven initially by attracting foreign investment, but increasingly by addressing local government debts, as well as utilising private capital to meet the need for infrastructure and public service.

[26] European Commission, 'Guidelines for Successful Public–private Partnerships' (March 2003) 17.

[27] Article 15.41 of Regulation (EU) No 549/2013 defines PPPs as 'long-term contracts between two units, whereby one unit acquires or builds an asset or set of assets, operates it for a period and then hands the asset over to a second unit. Such arrangements are usually between a private enterprise and government but other combinations are possible, *with a public corporation as either party* or a private non-profit institution as the second party' (emphasis added).

[28] Linklaters, 'PPP in France – 2006' 1, available at http://pppstandards.org/laws/France/pppfranceoct06.pdf.

[29] For accounts of the history of PPP in China, see NZ Li and O Song, 'Public–Private Partnership in Developing China: Evolution, Institutionalization and Risks' in J Leitão, E de Morais Sarmento and J Aleluia (eds), *The Emerald Handbook of Public–Private Partnerships in Developing and Emerging Economies* (Bingley, Emerald, 2017) 113; Z Cheng, Y Ke, J Lin, Z Yang and J Cai, 'Spatio-Temporal Dynamics of Public Private Partnership Projects in China' (2016) 34 *International Journal of Project Management* 1242; S Zhang, Y Gao, Z Feng and W Sun, 'PPP Application in Infrastructure Development in China: Institutional Analysis and Implications' (2015) 33 *International Journal of Project Management* 497; R Mu, M Jong and J Koppenjan, 'The Rise and Fall of Public–Private Partnerships in China: A Path-Dependent Approach' (2011) 19 *Journal of Transportation Geography* 794; Y Jin, 'History of Chinese PPPs' (2014) available (in Chinese) at http://blog.sina.com.cn/s/blog_63502ea20102uxt5.html.

[30] This division is based upon various views expressed in the literature quoted in n 29.

A. Exploration Phase (1984–1993)

One of the main objectives of the reform initiative launched by the Chinese Government in the 1980s was to attract foreign direct investment (FDI). The BOT model was introduced to serve that objective. Only a few such projects were initiated during this period by local governments without the explicit backing of the central Government or its ministries. The symbolic project for this phase was Shajiao B power plant in Shenzhen, which is regarded as the first BOT project in China. It was invested by a Hong Kong-based company (formed by a group of Japanese companies with the financial backing of the Japanese banks) in 1984, which was successfully transferred to local government in 2000 after a concession period of 15 years. It is noteworthy that the project was not based upon any legal rules, and its procurement practice has been criticised.[31]

B. Pilot Phase (1994–2001)

In order to address the 'bottleneck' created by shortage of infrastructure especially in transportation and energy, Chinese central Government has rolled out a number of pilot BOT projects since 1994 including the Laibin B power plant, Chendu No 6 Dachang water plant, Guangdong Dianbai Motorway, Wuhan Junshan Bridge and Changsha Wangcheng power project.[32] The first BOT project with a domestic private enterprise, Quanzhou Citong Bridge as the partner was also initiated in 1994. The Laibin B power plant project in Guangxi Province is the first BOT project officially approved by the state on 10 May 1995.[33] The project was approved at the State Council level with State Planning Commission (SPC, the predecessor of NDRC), Ministry of Power Industry (MoP) and State Administration for Exchange Control (SAEC) issuing support letters to back the Guangxi Provincial Government.

Certain policy guidance papers were also adopted at this stage. In January 1995, the Ministry of Foreign Trade and Economic Cooperation (MOFCOM) – predecessor of Ministry of Commerce (MoC) – adopted the 'Circular on Attracting Foreign Investment through BOT Approach'.[34] It provided that BOT projects funded by foreign capital above a certain threshold ($30 million for coastal provinces and $10 million for other provinces) need to be approved by the central government ministries with the State Planning Commission reviewing the proposal and viability report and MOFCOM

[31] S Ye and R Tiong, 'Government Support and Risk–Return Trade-Off in China's BOT Power Projects (2000) 7 *Engineering Construction & Architectural Management* 412.

[32] L Shen, RKH Lee and Z Zhang, 'Application of BOT System for Infrastructure Projects in China' (1996) 122 *Journal of Construction Engineering & Management* 319.

[33] S Wang and Y Ke, 'Case Study IV – Laibin B Power Project – the First State Approved BOT Project in China' in HW Alfen, SN Kalidindi, S Ogunlana, S Wang, MP Abednego, A Frank-Jungbecker, Y-C A Jan, Y Ke, Y Liu, LB Singh, G Zhao, *Public–Private Partnership in infrastructure development: Case Studies from Asia and Europe* (Weimar, Faculty of Civil Engineering, Chair of Construction Economics, Bauhaus-Universität, 2009) ch 5, available at www.econstor.eu/bitstream/10419/56429/1/630589232.pdf.

[34] MOFCOM, 'Circular on Attracting Foreign Investment through BOT Approach (关于以ＢＯＴ方式吸收外商投资有关问题的通知)', 16 January 1995, available (in Chinese) at www.mofcom.gov.cn/aarticle/b/f/200207/20020700031064.html.

reviewing the contract/agreement (Article 1), and that government entities shall refrain from providing any guarantee unless otherwise approved (Article 3).

Later that year, on 21 August 1995, SPC, MoP and Ministry of Transportation (MoT) adopted the 'Circular on Matters related to the Approval of Trial Foreign Invested Concession Projects' (BOT Circular) with the assistance provided by United Nations Industrial Development Organisation (UNIDO).[35] The BOT Circular was regarded as 'a turning point for foreign investment in and financing of key infrastructure projects in China' and providing 'the first legal foundation for private sector involvement and foreign capital investment in Chinese infrastructure'.[36]

The BOT Circular defines the term 'concession'[37] narrowly as referring to BOT infrastructure projects financed by foreign enterprises only (Article 1). Domestic financial institutions is prohibited from providing financial guarantees (Article 3). It also prohibits the Government from providing guarantees on minimum returns for foreign capital (Article 3).

This instrument shows that the central Government at this stage clearly viewed BOT as a means mainly to attract FDI. It also reflects a cautious approach to such pilot BOT projects with the type and size of the eligible projects restricted/capped, for example at 30–80 km for highways, and 1000 m above for bridges and urban water plants (Article 4). Open tendering is the only permitted procurement method for such pilot projects and the SPC, together with other ministries and local governments, should be in charge of the prequalification and bid evaluation (Article 6). However, in practice, due to the rigid nature of the open tendering procedure not suitable for such complex project, the procurement of Laibin B power plant has actually gone through a hybrid of open tendering and negotiated procedure. As further discussed in section IV D, the legal requirement of using open tendering remains an obstacle to this day for the development of PPP in China.

However, it is noteworthy that SPC's BOT Circular clearly disregarded the existing MOFCOM Circular. Whilst the latter contemplates the review/approval of the BOT contract should be undertaken by MOFCOM, the former provides (Article 8) that only SPC may approve the BOT agreement. It is also noted that there are contradictions (with regard to the scope of transferable 'operating rights', designated approval authorities, maximum term, re-transferability) among main regulations granting operating rights for toll roads: the Highway Law issued by the National People's Congress, the Notice of Strengthening the Administration of Transfer of Infrastructure Assets issued by the NDRC, and the Measures of Transfer of Operating Right of Highway with Compensation issued by MoT.[38] It can be argued that the incoherence of the institutional

[35] SPC, MoP and MoT, 'Notice on Matters related to the Approval of Trial Foreign Invested Concession Projects (关于试办外商投资特许权项目审批管理有关问题的通知)', 21 August 1995, available (in Chinese) at www.chinacourt.org/law/detail/1995/08/id/23330.shtml.

[36] C Arthur, 'Opening up Public Infrastructure to Private Sector Finance: UNIDO's Pioneering Role in China', UNIDO, 21 November 2017, available at www.unido.org/stories/opening-public-infrastructure-private-sector-finance-unidos-pioneering-role-china. It is also noteworthy that the initiative to enact a BOT Law (with the draft already prepared by the SPC with the help of UNIDO) was dropped due to the change of leadership.

[37] The Chinese term used in this instrument corresponding to 'concession' is '特许权' instead of '特许经营' found in later instruments.

[38] Kelly (n 14) Table 2-1.

framework and inconsistency of the regulatory framework started to emerge alongside the development of BOT projects. The regulatory framework at that time was criticised for its 'piecemeal approach to legislation and lack of clarity' that 'have created confusion for investors on answers to basic questions' such as which laws are applicable, which approving authority at the central or local level should be involved, and what that authority's scope of approval is.[39]

An unofficial data source based upon news reports recorded 91 projects during this phase.[40] The experience is mixed. While the Laibin B power plant and Chendu No 6 water plant (both involving French companies) can be regarded as success, a number of other projects failed. One of the reasons for such failure in foreign capital financed projects was that local governments, in order to attract FDI, promised fixed minimum returns for investment by foreign enterprises, which was explicitly prohibited under the BOT Circular (Article 3) mentioned above and not affordable or sustainable. The scale and severity triggered the State Council to issue a special notice to solve this problem by providing options to buy out foreign investors or covert their shares into debts.[41] The underlying reason for the behaviour of local government officials laid arguably in the fact that one of the main criteria used to assess their performance was the amount of FDI attracted and infrastructure built. This is arguably the same reason for the abuse/misuse of PPPs in later phases. It is also noteworthy the first BOT project involving domestic private enterprise, Quanzhou Citong Bridge (construction completed in 1997, 30 years' concession), ran into trouble later on as the local government decided to build more bridges in 2006 (free of toll charges) across the same river. Without the protection of a proper contract (the project was initiated based on a local government decree only), the private operator was deprived of any effective remedy.[42]

With such mixed experience, the SPC/NDRC shifted its focus from the draft of BOT Law to Tendering Law and reduced its involvement in the promotion and regulation of PPPs. However, as explained in section III, the Chinese procurement laws, namely Tendering Law (TL) 1999 and Government Procurement Law (GPL) 2002 are silent on their application to concessions or PPPs.

C. Development/Upscale Phase (2002–2007)

This period is regarded as a 'period of positive economic growth and optimism' during which 'the PPP policy idea took off internationally'.[43]

In China, the 16th National Congress of the Communist Party of China in 2002 promoted market mechanism as a key measure for the infrastructure development. Following this call, Ministry of Construction (predecessor of current Ministry of

[39] ibid at 11.
[40] Z Cheng, Y Ke, J Lin, Z Yang, Z and J Cai, 'Spatio-Temporal Dynamics of Public Private Partnership Projects in China' (2016) 34 *International Journal of Project Management* 1242, 1246.
[41] State Council Secretariat, 'Circular on Proper Handling of Projects Involving Guarantee of Fix Returns for Foreign Investors', No 43, 10 September 2002, available (in Chinese) at www.gov.cn/gongbao/content/2002/content_61783.htm.
[42] See the news report available in Chinese at www.chinahighway.com/news/2014/857446.php.
[43] Hodge, Greve and Biygautane (n 1) 1108.

Housing and Urban-Rural Development: MOHURD) took the lead and initiated the liberalisation of urban utilities market in December 2002 through an Opinion which envisaged the use of concessions in developing urban public utilities such as water supply/waste water treatment, refuse disposal and heat supply.[44] The Opinion called for the participation of both foreign capital and 'social capital' including domestic private enterprises and SOEs.

Ministry of Construction adopted Measures on Urban Utilities Concessions (the 'Urban Utilities Concessions Measure') on 19 March 2004 which entered into force on 1 May 2004.[45] The Urban Utilities Concessions Measure has a clear objective of liberalising urban utilities market which covers urban water (supply and waste water treatment), gas, heating, refuse treatment and transport (Article 1). Although it did not cite TL 1999 as its legal base, the Urban Utilities Concession Measure requires that concessionaire shall be chosen through market competition (Article 2) in particular open tendering (Article 8). However, the open tendering procedure contained in the measure has certain unique characteristics not found in the TL. For example, the Urban Utilities Concessions Measure provides that the evaluation of the bid shall be conducted through a public hearing (Article 8.3) and there should be a 20-day standstill/public notice period between the announcement of the winning bidder and the conclusion of the concession agreement (Article 8.4). Concession contracts shall not be longer than 30 years (Article 12). In 2006, MOHURD also enacted model concession agreements/contracts that define the rights and obligations of government entities and concessionaires.[46]

The Urban Utilities Concession Measure is an important milestone in the evolution of PPPs in China as it formally introduced the concept of 'concession', which is no longer restricted to BOTs, and provided the legal basis for the application of PPPs in urban utilities. However, the Measure, as with the BOT Circular, is only a Ministerial Order/Departmental Rule which does not carry the same legal force as Laws enacted by the National People's congress, or Regulations enacted by the State Council. Based on interviews with the local officials of relevant water authorities, it is argued that various measures issued by MOHURD during this period remain 'ad hoc, fragmented and diverse' and have failed to provide 'a systematic and comprehensive regulatory framework for the Chinese urban water sectors in practice', which resulted in officials having too much discretion and 'incorrect perception government role as a regulator'.[47]

Nevertheless, with renewed support from the central government and the increased demand for infrastructure development especially with regard to the forthcoming Beijing Olympic Games 2008, concessions flourished during this period including Beijing National Stadium (the 'Bird Nest') and Beijing Metro Line 4 project. It is noted that the wider use of open tendering has contributed towards reduced costs, improved

[44] MOHURD, Opinion on Acceleration of Marketization of Urban Public Utilities (关于加快市政公用行业市场化进程的意见), [2002] No 272, available (in Chinese) at www.mohurd.gov.cn/wjfb/200611/t20061101_157067.html.

[45] Chinese version available at www.mohurd.gov.cn/zcfg/jsbgz/200611/t20061101_159064.html.

[46] The Model Contract on Urban Waste Water Treatment Concessions is available (in Chinese) at www.mohurd.gov.cn/wbdt/xzzx/sfwb/p020080423811221402688.doc.

[47] Z Lijin, A Mol and F Tao Fu, 'Public–private Partnerships in China's Urban Water Sector' (2008) 41 *Environmental Management* 863, 876.

efficiency, ensured compliance with regulations and enhanced transparency.[48] On the other hand, however, it is argued that the reliance on open tendering has given rise to higher transaction costs during the tendering process and during the contract period due to the burden of extensive monitoring.[49]

D. Recession/Fluctuation Phase (2008–2012)

The financial crisis in 2008 affected both the global financial market and the development of PPP in China. The rationales of PPPs, such as the public policy discipline and private sector's efficient risk sharing are also questioned.[50]

In response to the crisis, Chinese central government launched a stimulate package worth RMB four trillion ($630,000 million), resulting in a huge amount of public funding flooded into infrastructure sector. One of the direct consequences was the attitude change of local governments towards PPP implementation, who lost the enthusiasm and passion on PPP model and turned to traditional procurement methods in many potential PPP projects, which to some extent squeezed out plenty of private capitals. It is argued that

> the seeds for the fall of PPP's popularity were largely sown in the previous phase when a host of projects in which private contractors were unable to deliver a final product at reasonable conditions and state-owned enterprises were found to replace them.[51]

As the result, SOEs absolutely dominated the PPP market given the fact that they possessed more government resources, were highly affinitive with local governments and were favoured by state-owned commercial banks.

It is also noteworthy that Local Government Finance Platforms (LGFP, also referred to as Local Government Finance Vehicle) emerged during this period. These companies, often regarded as 'shadow governments', have met the need of infrastructure finance through loans without going through the rigid tendering procedure, and avoid the restriction imposed by the local government debt ceiling. The operation of LGFPs, often illegal, arguably give rise to a 'waterbed' effect on PPPs, driving out private capital.

As for borrowers, apart from debts guaranteed by local governments, the debts incurred through financing platform companies and which shall be repaid or relieved by governments are of the largest scale. The departments and institutions of local governments are the borrowers with the largest scale of guaranteed debts. Subnational debts that are financing platform companies as well as local government departments and institutions account for approximately 66 per cent of the total.[52] In light of the

[48] Cheng, Ke, Lin, Yang, and Cai, 'Spatio-Temporal Dynamics' (2016) 1248.

[49] Mu, Jong and Koppenjan, 'The Rise and Fall of Public–Private Partnerships in China' (2011) 799.

[50] A Roberts, *The Logic of Discipline: Global Capitalism and the Architecture of Government* (Oxford, Oxford University Press, 2010).

[51] Mu, Jong, and Koppenjan (n 29) 800.

[52] S Liu, 'China's Subnational Debts: Problems and Suggestions' in S Kahkonen, and S Gooptu, *Subnational Debt Management and Restructuring: Lessons from International Experience* (Washington, World Bank, 2016) 99, available at https://openknowledge.worldbank.org/handle/10986/23668.

threat posed by high-level local government debts, the State Council issued a Notice in 2010 calling for tightened control over LGFPs[53] and MoF, together with NDRC, Bank of China and Financial Supervision Commission, issued a Circular to the same effect in 2012.[54] While these measures shut the 'back door' for local governments to fund infrastructure through illegal borrowing through LGFPs, they also provide the driver for going back to the PPP model as the need for infrastructure investment remains.

E. Revival/Expansion Phase (2013–mid 2017)

In the Third Plenary Session of the 18th Chinese Communist Party Central Committee held in November 2013, the Party, in Decisions on Major Issues Concerning Comprehensively Deepening Reforms, initiated a new phase of reform in the PRC.to further restructure the economy and foster inclusive growth by allowing the market to play the decisive role. In particular, it allows social capital, which includes the private sector and state-owned enterprises, to participate in urban infrastructure investment and operation through *concessions and other means*.[55] This policy declaration adopted at the top level provided the decisive impetus for PPPs to be a vehicle for broadening the means for infrastructure investment and urbanisation, accelerating the transformation of government functions, and improving fiscal investment and management.

Following this call, on 21 May 2014, NDRC rolled out first batch of 80 infrastructure projects open to participation by social capital (including both SOEs and private enterprises). These projects cover sectors such as transportation (for example, the Beijing Metro No 16 line), energy (for example, the West–East Gas Pipeline No 3) and communication (for example, 3G and 4G mobile networks and next generation internet) that are traditionally monopolised by SOEs. Concession was mentioned as a mode for implementation.[56]

On 23 September 2014, the MoF issued the Notice on Questions Relating to Expanding the Use of PPPs.[57] The document used, for the first time, the term PPP as a distinctive legal concept, whereas all previous measures only mentioned concessions or BOT. Whilst the English term PPP is used directly, its Chinese equivalent ('政府和社会资本合作') actually means 'cooperation between the government and social capital'. It is defined loosely as 'a long-term partnership in infrastructure and public services' where 'the social capital normally undertakes the design, construction, operation and maintenance of infrastructure and receives remuneration through fees paid by users and/or the Government'(Article 1). However, the Notice did not address the relationship

[53] State Council, 'Notice on Strengthening Control of LGFSs (国务院关于加强地方政府融资平台公司管理有关问题的通知)', 10 June 2010, available in Chinese at www.gov.cn/zwgk/2010-06/13/content_1627195.htm.

[54] MoF, NDRC, Bank of China and Financial Supervision Commission, 'Circular on Terminating Illegal Financing Behaviour of Local Governments', 24 December 2012, available (in Chinese) at http://yss.mof.gov.cn/zhengwuxinxi/zhengceguizhang/201212/t20121231_723354.html.

[55] Article 2(7), available (in Chinese) at http://sjw.gzlps.gov.cn/xxgk/djfg/201709/t20170926_1520464.html.

[56] See the report (in Chinese) at http://finance.people.com.cn/n/2014/0522/c1004-25049030.html.

[57] MoF, Notice on Questions Relating to Expanding the Use of PPPs (关于推广运用政府和社会资本合作模式有关问题的通知), 23 September 2014, available (in Chinese) at http://jrs.mof.gov.cn/zhengwuxinxi/zhengcefabu/201409/t20140924_1143760.html.

between PPPs and concessions although the definition of PPPs clearly covers user-pay PPPs, which are normally understood as concessions in a Chinese context. It also states that 'PPPs are in fact government procurement of services' (Article 1.3). This arguably laid the seed for the overlap between these legal norms, discussed below in section IV B. The Notice also introduced the 'value for money' check informed by international experience.

Since then, the State Council, NDRC and various ministries issued a series of notices and ministerial orders/rules in forms of circulars, opinions, provisions and measures to promote and regulate the application of PPP model. One of the highlights in these rules and regulations was that the central Government paid more attention to the standardisation of PPP implementation, evident from the vital guidelines by the MoF such as PPP implementation guidelines, model contracts, value for money evaluation and fiscal affordability evaluation.

However, it is noteworthy that the rivalry between MoF and NDRC over the authority to regulate public procurement (as explained below in section III) has also spread to the regulation of PPPs. The timing and scope of the measures adopted by MoF and NDRC are often overlapping and the provisions therein are sometimes inconsistent. Furthermore, NDRC and MoF have led separate legislative initiatives to enact National Law on Concession and PPPs. This is the origin of many obstacles/issues identified and discussed below in section IV.

For example, on 30 November 2014, MoF issued the Operational Guide (trial) on PPPs. On 2 December 2014, NDRC issued the Guiding Opinion on PPPs with a Model PPP Contract as an Appendix. Two days later, on 4 December 2014, MoF rolled out the first batch of 30 PPP model projects, worth a total of CNY 180 billion (about US$29.32 billion). On the same day, the MoF also announced the establishment of a PPP centre to further support the implementation of the PPP model. The NDRC Guiding Opinion emphasises risk sharing and cooperation between the Government and private entities under the PPP model and indicates a preference for the use of PPP in future urban pilot projects (Articles 2 and 3). The Guiding Opinion includes specific requirements for selecting and implementing PPP arrangements, such as a statement of the applicable scope of the project, establishment of a departmental joint review mechanism, cooperation in partner selection, standardised price management, and performance review. Under the Guiding Opinions, different PPP arrangements can be chosen based on local circumstances (Article 3). Furthermore, all local-level development and reform commissions must establish a PPP project library and report monthly to the NDRC on the progress of PPP projects in their areas (Article 5).

However, a potential conflict exists between the NDRC Guiding Opinions and the MoF Operational Guide as to whether SOEs may provide capital for a PPP. Whilst the former allows any SOE to participate in a PPP arrangement by providing capital (Article 7 of the Model Contract), the latter precludes local SOEs (especially LGFPs) from providing capital to PPP projects in the same region (Article 2).

The main regulatory instruments during this period include:[58]

- 21 September 2014, State Council, Opinions of the State Council on Strengthening the Management of Local Government Debt.

[58] ADB, PPP Monitor 2017, at 305–06 for instruments adopted until September 2016.

- 23 September 2014, MoF, Notice on Questions Relating to Expanding the Use of PPPs.
- 16 November 2014, State Council, Guiding Opinions on the Innovative Investment Mechanism and Encouraging Social Investment in Key Sectors.
- 29 November 2014, MoF, Circular on Issuing the Operational Guidance on the Modes of Cooperation by Governments and Social Capital (for trial implementation).
- 30 November 2014, MoF, Circular on Issues concerning the Implementation of the Demonstration Projects of Public–Private Partnership.
- December 2014, NDRC, Guiding Opinions of the National Development and Reform Commission on Launching the Cooperation between Governments and Social Capitals.
- 30 December 2014, MoF, Notice on Regulating Government and Social Capital Cooperation Contract Management and Guidelines on PPP Contracts (for trial implementation) (MOF PPP Contract Guidelines).
- 31 December 2014, MoF, Measures for Administration of Government Procurement in PPP Projects.
- 31 December 2014, MoF, Circular on Issuing the Interim Measures for the Administration of Government Procurement through Competitive Dialogue.
- 10 March 2015, NDRC, MoF, Circular of the National Development and Reform Commission and the China Development Bank on Promoting the Support of Development Financing for Public Private Partnerships and Related Work.
- 7 April 2015, MoF, Guidance on Financial Affordability Assessment of PPP Projects.
- 21 April 2015, NDRC, MoF, Circular on Using Government Investment to Support Social Investment Projects.
- 19 May 2015, MoF, NDRC, People's Bank of China, Guidelines on Promoting PPP in Public Service.
- 1 June 2015, NDRC, MoF, MOHURD, Ministry of Water Resources, People's Bank of China, Measures for the Administration of Concessions for Infrastructure and Public Utilities. This measure is to replace the Urban Utilities Concession Measure 2004 adopted by MOHURD alone. However, it is odd to regulate concessions in specific whereas all other instruments regulate PPPs.
- 25 June 2015, MoF, Circular on Further Implementing the Demonstration Work relating to Public–Private Partnership Projects.
- July 2015, NDRC, Circular on Measures Implementing Administrative Measures for the Franchising of Infrastructure and Public Utilities.
- 8 December 2015, MoF, Notice on Implementing the Policy of Replacing Subsidies with Reward.
- 18 December 2015, MoF, Circular on Issuing PPP Value for Money Assessment Guidelines (for trial implementation).
- 18 December 2015, MoF, Notice on Regulating the Operation of PPP Information Platform.

- 10 August 2016, NDRC, Notice on Implementation of PPP in Traditional Infrastructure.
- 24 September 2016, MoF, Notice on Measures for Financial Administration of PPP Projects (Cai Jin [2016] No 92), which includes seven chapters and 40 Articles and provides that financial departments at all levels shall, jointly with other departments concerned, make a comprehensive arrangement of the financial funds, national assets and other public assets and public resources so as to cooperate with the social capital in PPP projects on an equal and mutually beneficial basis. The measures also provide specific provisions on recognition and demonstration of projects, government procurement, budgetary revenues and expenditures, performance management, asset-liability management, information disclosure as well as supervision and inspection.
- On 11 October 2016, the MoF issued the Notice on Promoting the Work of Public–private Partnership in the Field of Public Services (Cai Jin [2016] No 90), which provides that financial departments at all levels shall further promote the application of PPP in the fields of public services, including the fields of energy, transportation, municipal works, agriculture, forestry, water conservancy, environmental protection, affordable housing, medical and health services, elderly care services, education, culture, sports and tourism.
- On 24 October 2016, the General Office of the MOF issued a document which solicits advice on the Guidelines for Value for Money Assessment in Public–private Partnership (Revised Edition Draft for Opinion) (Cai Ban Jin [2016] No 118), which proposes numerous amendments to the former Guidelines for Value for Money Assessment issued in December 2015. Among others, amendments and improvements concerning the principle and method of quantitative analysis have been made in the new edition.
- On 24 October 2016, the NDRC issued the Notice on Issuing the Guiding Rules for Implementing Public–private Partnership Projects in Traditional Infrastructure Fields (Fa Gai Tou Zi [2016] No 2231), which includes six chapters and 25 Articles, providing the operation progress of PPP projects in the traditional infrastructure field. In addition, the traditional fields of infrastructure, to which the guidance applies, includes the fields of energy, transportation, water conservation, environmental protection, agriculture, forestry and major municipal works.
- On 21 December 2016, the General Office of the NDRC issued the Administration Measures on Public–private Partnership (PPP) Project Library in the Traditional Fields of Infrastructure (Trial) including four chapters and 16 Articles, which combines the operating requirements of the online approving and supervising platform of the investment projects and further normalises the operating progress of PPP projects in the traditional infrastructure field. This document applies to the PPP project databases established by the Development and Reform Departments at all levels.
- Also, on 21 December 2016, the NDRC and the China Securities Regulatory Commission (CSRC) jointly issued the Notice on Relevant Work of Promoting the

Asset Securitisation of Public–private Partnership (PPP) Projects in the Traditional Infrastructures Field (Fa Gai Tou Zi [2016] No 2698), vigorously promoting and supporting securitisation of PPP projects on the agenda. According to this Notice, the NDRC shall select, support and guide appropriate PPP projects, based on recommendations by provincial Development and Reform Commissions at the beginning of 2017, aiming at issuing PPP project securitisation products as early as possible, summarising experiences while communicating and promoting such practice.

Besides publishing rules, both MoF and NDRC continue to promote PPP projects by expanding PPP project libraries through compilation of different batches of model projects. In May 2015, NDRC released a project library containing 1,043 local government PPP projects, with a total investment of CNY 1.97 trillion (around $320 billion).[59] In total, the PRC's local governments had announced around 2,000 planned PPPs by mid-2015. In September 2015, MoF announced a second batch of 206 model PPPs with a total investment of CNY 0.66 trillion (around $100 billion). However, the PPP projects libraries promoted by the MoF and NDRC are mutually exclusive for no other reason but institutional rivalry. The local governments are left to wonder which library to register their projects with.

It is also noteworthy that controlling the debt accumulated by local government continues to play a decisive role in the boom of PPPs in this period. The State Council issued the Opinion on Strengthening the Management of Local Government Debt which explicitly prohibits local government from obtaining finance through LGFPs thus circumventing the debt ceiling, but provides for possibilities of issuing local government bonds and promotes the use of PPPs as an alternative funding channel (Article 2(3)).[60] The Budget Law, entered into force on 1 January 2015, also explicitly prohibits, in Article 14, local governments from providing guarantees for the debt of any legal and natural person (including LGFPs). These rules essentially 'push' the local governments towards the use of PPPs. Although a number of gateway checks, such as feasibility, value for money, fiscal affordability, have been put in place by various ministerial rules mentioned above, these checks are performed at the local level and susceptible to influence from local politicians that have a clear preference to the PPP projects to be cleared.

Despite the vast number of rules adopted in the previous phase, it can be argued that the coherence, consistency and clarity of the PPPs regulatory environment in China have not been substantially improved. This is mainly because the rules adopted by various ministries, especially MoF and NDRC, do not coordinate in a coherent manner and local governments tend to ignore the ministerial/departmental rules as they lack sufficient legal force. Coupled with a strong incentive for local governments to use PPPs as the primary means for infrastructure investment, it is inevitable that widespread abuse has been found in this booming period of PPPs.

[59] National Development and Reform Commission, PPP Project Library, available at www.ndrc.gov.cn/xwzx/xwfb/201505/t20150525_693168.html.

[60] State Council, Opinion on Strengthening the Management of Local Government Debt (国务院关于加强地方政府性债务管理的意见), available (in Chinese) at www.gov.cn/zhengce/content/2014-10/02/content_9111.htm.

Although the MoF provides that PPPs related payment payable by a given government (government-pay PPPs and viability gap funding for user-pay PPPs) cannot exceed 10 per cent of its annual budget, a lot of local governments have breached that ceiling or disguised PPPs as government procurement of services projects that are not subject to such a ceiling. A number of projects included in the PPP libraries of MoF do not have a viable source of finance. According to a study conducted by the Chinese Academy of Fiscal Sciences, up to the end of 2017, PPP projects in the MoF library included 50 per cent government-pays, 40 per cent with viability gap funding, and only 10 per cent user-pays projects.[61] It is also worrisome that certain underdeveloped provinces with mounting debts and low credit ratings registered more PPP projects than developed provinces. For example, it is reported that Guizhou Province had a debt-to-asset ratio of 189 per cent at the end of 2015 and an annual income of CNY 156.1 billion, but has 1746 PPP projects registered in MoF library worth CNY 1.5547 trillion until the end of 2016.[62] Furthermore, SOEs, as the main partner/financier of PPPs, have also accumulated significant amount of debts that are ultimately attributable to the state especially because SOEs do not need to report on their balance sheet PPPs in the project company of which they do not hold a majority share. All of these have significantly increased systematic fiscal and financial risks.

F. Review/Rationalisation Phase (mid 2017–)

The turning point came in July 2017 during the Chinese Communist Party Central Committee Meeting on Financial Matters. This meeting recognised the danger posed by systematic fiscal and financial risks and called for immediate actions towards deleveraging of local governments and SOEs.[63]

The MoF started to clean up its project library by issuing the Notice on Rationalizing the Management of PPP Project Library on 10 November 2017.[64] It tightened the admission of new PPP projects by excluding: (i) projects not suitable for PPP mode (for example, commercial exploration of land not involving public services, or construction/work projects without operational elements); (ii) those that fail gateway checks, such as value for money and fiscal affordability tests; and (iii) those without a payment scheme based upon performance (the performance of construction phase shall account for at least 30 per cent) (Article 2). The Notice also provides for the cleaning up of inadequate existing PPP projects such as those with inappropriate gateway checks, promising fixed returns or shares purchase-back and exceeding the 10 per cent annual budget ceiling (Article 4). It is reported that until the end of March 2018, 1160 PPP projects worth

[61] Chinese Academy of Fiscal Sciences, 'Report on Local Economy and Financial Operation in 2017' 17, available (in Chinese) at http://crifs.org.cn/index.php?m=content&c=index&a=show&catid=24&id=847.

[62] Chinese Academy of Fiscal Sciences, 'Fiscal Risks Caused by Irregular Operation of PPPs' (1 June 2017), available (in Chinese) at www.crifs.org.cn/index.php?m=content&c=index&a=show&catid=23&id=401.

[63] See the news report available in Chinese at https://finance.ifeng.com/a/20170716/15532710_0.shtml.

[64] MoF, Notice on Rationalizing the Management of PPP Project Library (关于规范政府和社会资本合作综合信息平台项目库管理的通知), 10 November 2017, available (in Chinese) at http://jrs.mof.gov.cn/zhengwuxinxi/zhengcefabu/201711/t20171116_2751258.html.

CNY 1.2 trillion have been removed from the MoF Library.[65] In the second quarter of 2018, a further 856 projects worth CNY 956.9 billion have been removed.[66] Whilst these figures show the success of this cleaning-up operation, it also demonstrates the extent and severity of the issues, especially those related to the regulatory environment, that have given rise to such abuse at the first place.

The MoF also tightened the control over the investment into PPP projects made by state-owned banks/financial enterprises as they normally prefer to grant loans to local governments and SOEs and indirectly contributed to rise of systematic financial and fiscal risk and the leveraging problem.[67] It provides that state banks shall not issue loans to local governments as the capital for PPP projects (Article 1); the finance provided to PPP project companies shall be conditional upon the legality of the project, as in having passed the value for money and fiscal viability tests (Article 9) and not having guaranteed fixed returns; such banks shall refrain from requiring or accepting guarantees made by local governments (Article 2).

On the other hand, the State Assets Supervision and Administration Commission (SASAC) tightened the control over the involvement in PPPs of SOEs affiliated to the central Government by issuing the Notice on Strengthening the Risk Control over Central SOEs' PPPs Operation on 17 November 2017.[68] It provides that accumulated investment into PPPs shall, in principle, not exceed 50 per cent of asset of a SOE group, any subsidiary with 85 per cent debt ratio or reporting loss for two consecutive years shall refrain from participating PPP projects alone, and SOEs other than financial/investment enterprises must not act as only a financier for PPP projects (Article 3). It also calls for SOEs to establish independent books reporting those PPPs in which they only hold minority shares (Article 4).

Another milestone of the current phase is that the State Council replaced the competing legislative initiatives led by NDRC and MoF with a move to draft State Council Regulation on PPPs. NDRC initially proposed the draft of 'Concession Law' whilst MoF proposed the draft of 'PPP Law' both with the view to regulating the PPP market as a whole. In July 2017, the State Council stepped in following the criticism of the Premier[69] and released a draft of State Council Regulation on PPP in Infrastructure and Public Services ('Draft PPP Regulation') for public consultation.[70] Section 6 will examine the extent to which the Draft PPP Regulation will address the issues regarding regulatory environment for PPPs identified in section IV.

[65] See 2018 1st Quarterly Report by MoF PPP Centre, available (in Chinese) at www.cpppc.org/zh/pppjb/6795.jhtml.

[66] See 2018 2nd Quarterly Report by MoF PPP Centre, available (in Chinese) at www.cpppc.org/zh/pppjb/7191.jhtml.

[67] MoF, Notice on Regulating Certain Investment by Financial Enterprises to Local Governments and SOEs (关于规范金融企业对地方政府和国有企业投融资行为有关问题的通知), 11 June 2018, available (in Chinese) at http://jrs.mof.gov.cn/zhengwuxinxi/zhengcejiedu/201803/t20180330_2857299.html.

[68] SASAC, Notice on Strengthening the Risk Control over Central SOEs' PPPs Operation (关于加强中央企业PPP业务风险管控的通知), 17 November 2017, available (in Chinese) at www.sasac.gov.cn/n2588035/n2588320/n2588335/index.html.

[69] Speech by Premier Li, Keqiang, on the role of government, rule of law and departmental interests, 9 May 2016, available (in Chinese) at www.gov.cn/guowuyuan/2016-07/08/content_5089655.htm.

[70] The draft is available (in Chinese) at http://zqyj.chinalaw.gov.cn/readmore?id=1984&listType=1.

III. Chinese Government Procurement Reform

A. Reform and Adoption of TL and GPL

Public procurement (purchasing goods, services and works in a competitive market) did not exist in pre-reform centrally planned Chinese economy (1949–1978). The needs of public entities to provide essential services were met by goods, services and works allocated to them under fixed terms through the central plan. After the launching of economic reform in 1978, central planning started to give way to market forces. The total number of commodity groups administered by the State Planning Commission under compulsory plans was reduced from more than 120 in 1979 to 60 in 1992.[71] In the mid-1980s, state manufacturing enterprises were allowed to freely use capacity in excess of planned output to produce directly for the market. This created inter-enterprise market relations and product markets.[72] Against this background, public procurement soon emerged and a tendering system was introduced. Certain procurement of public entities, especially procurement of construction works using public funds and procurement of mechanical and electrical equipment by state enterprises, have been subject to tendering requirements ever since.

Public procurement regulations in China have consequently boomed in the last three decades. Hundreds of regulatory documents, including two national laws,[73] numerous State Council Regulations, ministerial decrees and provincial or sub-provincial legislative acts have been promulgated. However, the competition – instead of coordination – of various procurement rules underpins the evolution of the Chinese legal framework for public procurement.

As history shows, MOFCOM started regulating international tendering of electronic and mechanic equipment (open to both domestic and foreign suppliers) to identify suitable domestic substitutes in the late 1980s and still today controls the procurement of imported electronic and mechanical products by government agencies and SOEs.

It is noteworthy that Chinese public procurement was regulated at the beginning in a way that focused mainly on tendering procedures rather than the whole concept of government procurement. The first public procurement legislation drafted by the National Development and Reform Commission (NDRC, then State Planning Commission) and enacted by the NPC in 1999 was titled Tendering Law (TL), which applies to tendering activities of *both public and private* sectors, and lacks many features of modern public procurement legislation such as a clear definition of public procurement, does not provide for procurement methods other than open and selective tendering procedures, and does not have a supplier review mechanism.

From the mid-1990s, MoF and its local branches initiated a new wave of government procurement reform as a part of the budgetary reform. Significant improvement of this new initiative, such as using widely accepted public procurement concepts, terms and

[71] D Perkins, 'Completing China's Move to the Market' (1994) 8 *Journal of Economic Perspectives* 23, 29.

[72] YP Huang and R Duncan, 'How Successful Were China's State Sector Reforms?' (1997) 24 *Journal of Comparative Economics* 65, 68–69.

[73] The Tendering Law (TL) enacted on 30 August 1999 and entered into force on 1 January 2000; and the Government Procurement Law (GPL) enacted on 29 June 2002 and entered into force on 1 January 2003.

techniques, could easily be identified. However, the 'fruit' of this new initiative – China's Government Procurement Law (GPL), enacted in 2002 – is not as comprehensive as expected.

It can be argued that the conflicts of procurement regulations at various levels are inevitable given this fragmented institutional framework. The MoF as the 'bookkeeper', the NDRC as the 'investor' and 'planner' and the MOFCOM as the 'trader' for the state are all building their own 'fortress of regulation' on public procurement. On the side, other line ministries such as the Ministry of Housing and Urban Rural Construction, MIIT, the Ministry of Transportation, the Ministry of Water Resources and the General Administration of Civil Aviation are in charge of supervising tendering activities within their respective fields and acting as review bodies for supplier challenges.

They, especially NDRC and MoF, often concurrently enact competing rules on tendering proceedings, evaluation expert databases, approved procuring agencies, designated media, publicity, review procedure and so on. This has caused not only duplication and waste of resources, but also inconsistency which jeopardises legal certainty in China's evolving legal framework on public procurement.

It is not fair to say that the central Government, in particular the State Council, has been ignorant of this problem. The State Council issued an Opinion on Further Regulating Tendering Activities on 12 July 2004.[74] On that basis, the Interim Measure on Inter-Ministerial Coordination Mechanism on Tendering Proceedings ('Interim Measure on Coordination Mechanism') that entered into force on 1 September 2005 has established an inter-ministerial coordination mechanism. The main duties of this coordination mechanism include: i) analysing the status of tendering regulations and discussing possible solutions for regulating tendering activities involving multiple government organs; ii) coordinating conflicts between different government departments regarding the administrative supervision of tendering; iii) exchange of information; iv) *coordinating the promulgation of tendering regulations by different departments*; v) communicating of the enforcement of tendering rules; and vi) joint survey and research.[75]

On the one hand, it is encouraging to see that all 'major players' in public procurement regulation, namely NDRC, MoF and MOFCOM, are covered by this mechanism with the NDRC playing the leading role, and coordinating the coverage of different regulations has been identified as one of the main objectives. On the other hand, it is doubtful whether the scheduled liaison meeting every six months and summit every year[76] will make any real difference to the current situation.

B. The Tension between GPL and TL on Coverage

Due to the failure to absorb the TL in the legislative process, the GPL provided a narrow definition of 'government procurement' which refers to 'procurement of construction works, goods and services listed in certain catalogues or above certain threshold

[74] State Council Secretariat [2004] No 56.
[75] ibid, Art 4.
[76] ibid, Arts 6 and 10.

(as promulgated annually by authorities at provincial level or above) by government agencies at all levels, public institutions and social organizations using fiscal funds'.[77] Key factors of this definition are the nature of the procuring entity (government departments, institutions and social organisations under budget control such as public hospitals, state schools and universities, cultural organisations, state-owned news agencies, sports organisations and scientific research institutes) and the source of the fund. Procurement of SOEs, commonly regarded as public procurement, and subject to existing regulations including the TL, is not within the scope of 'government procurement' defined by the GPL.

There has been a tension between GPL and TL which is manifested, in particular, on the issue of coverage.[78] The TL in principle applies to 'all tendering proceedings [open and selective tendering] within the territory of the People's Republic of China', be it public procurement or private procurement.[79] The TL also requires that procurement of certain works/construction projects and procurement of related services (such as ground exploration, design and monitoring) and related goods (important materials and equipment) incidental to such construction projects must be conducted through tendering proceedings.[80]

These construction projects include: i) projects that concern public interests or security, such as large infrastructure and public utilities; ii) projects funded wholly or partly by state-owned or state-borrowed capital; and iii) projects funded by loans or aids from international organisations or foreign governments. Procurement of these construction projects and that of associated services and goods may be regarded as the mandatory scope of application of the TL although other procurements where tendering proceedings are conducted may also apply the TL on a voluntary basis.

Furthermore, MOFCOM has a longstanding stake in regulating procurement of mechanical and electrical products by any entity. Procurement of mechanical and electrical products by government agencies, public institutions and SOEs has been required to go through domestic tendering before applying for import licence since 1985. The initial intention is to ensure that there will be no domestic substitute for the imported mechanical and electronic equipment.[81] However, since 1992, the objective of the tendering regulation has been changed to: procurement of mechanical and electrical equipment has been required to go through international competitive tendering with a view not only to encouraging domestic suppliers to compete with foreign firms but also, and mainly, to take advantage of the better value offered by the international market.[82]

MOFCOM, over the last three decades, has enacted a number of regulations to ensure competitive tendering is open to international suppliers in procurement of mechanical

[77] Article 2 of the GPL.

[78] See P Wang, 'China's Evolving Legal Framework on Public Procurement' (2004) 13 *Public Procurement Law Review* 285.

[79] Article 2 of the TL.

[80] Article 3 of the TL.

[81] J Tian, 'Public Procurement in China: The Way Forward' (2001) 10 *Public Procurement Law Review* 207, 208.

[82] News release of the Ministry of Commerce, available at www.mofcom.gov.cn/aarticle/ bb/200508/ 20050800276713.html.

and electrical equipment. The latest version is the Implementing Measures on International Tendering in Procurement of Mechanical and Electronic Products (hereinafter, the 'Tendering Regulation on M&E Products'), which was enacted by the Ministry of Commerce on 21 February 2014 and entered into force on 1 April of that year.[83]

Citing TL and IRTL as its legal basis, it provides in Article 2 that 'the regulation applies to all international tendering proceedings in procurement of mechanical and electronic products conducted in the territory of China'. Article 6 further provides the scope of mechanical and electronic products procurement subject to mandatory international tendering requirements which includes international procurement of mechanical and electronic products in: i) projects that concern public interests or security, such as large infrastructure and *public utilities*; ii) projects invested wholly or partly by state-owned or state-borrowed capital; iii) projects funded by loans or aids from international organisations or foreign governments; and iv) government procurement projects. The Tendering Regulation on M&E Products also contains a chapter on publication/transparency and one on bid challenge.[84]

It is clear that TL and its implementing regulations' approach to defining coverage is led by the nature of the projects instead of the characteristics of the procuring entity.

The TL covering all tendering proceedings and the GPL covering government procurement overlap when government procurement of construction works, goods and services is conducted through tendering proceedings. The GPL tried to address this clash with only one simple sentence. GPL Article 4 provides that 'the Tendering Law shall apply to tendering proceedings in government procurement of construction works'.

This provision could arguably imply that: i) the TL does not apply to tendering proceedings in government procurement of goods and services; and ii) the TL does not even apply to government procurement of works in which procurement methods other than open and selective tendering are used. This provision of the GPL has substantially altered the scope of application of the TL.[85]

Furthermore, there are other ambiguities regarding the demarcation line between these two laws. First of all, it is not entirely clear from GPL whether government procurement of goods (materials and equipment) and services closely related to a construction project should be covered by the TL or the GPL, although the definition of goods and construction provided in the GPL suggests that it should apply.[86] Secondly, it is not clear

[83] MOFCOM, Implementing Measure on International Tendering in Procurement of Mechanical and Electronic Products ('Tendering Regulation on M&E products'). This regulation was enacted by MOFCOM on 21 February. 2014 and entered into force on 1 April, repealing the previous measure adopted in 2004. Available at www.mofcom.gov.cn/article/fgsjk/201402/20140202649869.shtml.

[84] ibid.

[85] It is argued that although the doctrine of *lex posterior derogat priori* has been established in legal interpretation by the Legislation Law effective on 1 July 2000 (Art 83), it remains hard to reconcile the limitation conferred by the GPL with the directly conflicting provision of the TL (namely that the Tendering Law is applicable to '*all tendering activities* within the territory of People's Republic of China'). An amendment of the Tendering Law itself might be necessary.

[86] It is defined in Art 2 of the Government Procurement Law that 'Goods refers to all forms and kinds of objects, including *materials*, fuel, *equipment*, products […] Article 2 also provides that construction refers to all work associated with construction, reconstruction, extension, decoration, demolition and repair or renovation of a building or structure.'

whether government procurement of construction through tendering proceedings is completely outside of the realm of the GPL or it still applies to such procurement with respect to issues other than tendering procedure such as 'buy national' policy and other secondary policies, rules on publicity, challenge and review mechanism.

C. State Council Implementing Regulations of TL and GPL: Clarification at Last?

Drafting work of State Council implementing regulations for TL and GPL started at around the same time. Implementing Regulation for the TL (IRTL) and the Implementing Regulation for the GPL (IRGPL) sit at the third level of the legal hierarchy laid down by the Legislation Law and once adopted will replace the ministerial regulations. Therefore, State Council implementing regulations have the potential to address the tension identified above between national laws and ministerial regulations.

The drafts were published by the State Council Legislation Office respectively on 29 September 2009 and on 11 January 2010 to solicit public opinions.[87] IRTL finally won the race and was adopted on 20 December 2011 and entered into force on 1 February 2012.[88] IRGPL was adopted on 30 January 2015 and entered into force on 1 March 2015.

The need to coordinate two dimensions of Chinese procurement law has been explicitly recognised by the note of State Council Legislation Office accompanying both drafts.[89] Certain provisions have been included to address the division of scope of coverage between TL and GPL. For example, IRTL Article 4 provides that financial departments shall be responsible for supervising government procurement of works through tendering including the pursuing of governmental (secondary) policies in such procurement. IRTL Article 84 provides that government procurement of goods and services through tendering shall be subject to government procurement laws and administrative regulations (namely GPL and IRGPL). IRGPL Article 7 provides that government procurement of works and related goods and services through (open and selective) tendering shall be subject to TL, government procurement of works using procurement methods other than tendering procedures shall be subject to GPL and IRGPL, and government procurement of works (regardless whether tendering is involved) shall implement governmental policy objectives (including 'buy national').[90]

However, the fundamental problem with regard to current Chinese procurement legal framework is the lack of rationale for delineating scope of coverage of TL and GPL on the basis of both the type of procurement contract and the procurement method used. Although the EU introduced public sector supplies directive, works directive and services directive gradually and separately due to historical reasons, the EU has quickly merged them into a single instrument for the benefit of simplification

[87] The Chinese version of IRGPL is available at www.gov.cn/zhengce/content/2015-02/27/content_9504.htm.

[88] The Chinese version of IRTL is available at www.gov.cn/zwgk/2011-12/29/content_2033184.html.

[89] ibid.

[90] IRGPL Art 7 differs from previous drafts where works-related goods were not expressly mentioned.

and clarity. In the process of that reform in late 1990s, the view was taken in many quarters that the 'traditional' Directives (on supplies, works and services) should be consolidated in order to iron out inconsistencies and make them easier to understand.[91] It can be argued that China has the same, if not more urgent, need for such consolidation.

Furthermore, it is submitted that dividing the scope of procurement legal instruments by reference to the procuring method used (whether tendering is involved) is unjustifiable. Complex construction projects might require dialogue between the procuring entity and potential contractors, which renders open/selective tendering, even though initially used, eventually unsuitable. While government agencies and public bodies may take advantage of Article 7 of IRGPL mentioned above by choosing flexible procurement methods such as competitive dialogue or competitive negotiation, SOEs whose procurement is subject to TL, in theory, do not have such option and may find it difficult to achieve value for money. However, in practice, as noted in the previous report produced by the author, Chinese SOEs often have separate rules on tendering and that on procurement of goods and services.

D. Procurement Methods and Organisation

TL provides for only open and selective tendering and prohibits any negotiation. GPL provides for, in addition to open and selective tendering, competitive negotiation, single source procurement, request for quotation, or any other method approved by MoF.[92] However, other popular procurement methods, such as framework agreement procurement (including both multiple suppliers and single supplier framework) and electronic reverse auction, albeit widely used by government agencies and SOEs, are not mentioned at all in GPL, TL or IRTL. For example, Beijing municipal government announced on 10 October 2011 that for 2012, any procurement valued above one million yuan shall be conducted through open tendering unless otherwise permitted, and those below the threshold may be purchased through framework agreement.[93]

While early draft of IRGPL mentions framework agreement and electronic reverse auctions briefly without providing substantial guidance, it is disappointing to see that instead of clarifying further, reference to these methods that are frequently used in practice has been removed altogether in the final version.

On 4 February 2013, NDRC, together with the Ministry of Supervision, the Ministry of Housing and Urban Rural Construction, MIIT, the Ministry of Transportation, the Ministry of Railway, the Ministry of Water Resources and MOFCOM (without the involvement of MoF), adopted Measures on Electronic Tendering.[94] While it focuses

[91] EU Commission Communication, 'Public Procurement in Europe', Brussels, 11 March 1998, COM(98) 143, at section 2.1.3.

[92] GPL Arts 26, 27, 29, 30, 31 and 32.

[93] Financial Bureau of Beijing Municipal Government, Notice on Procurement Thresholds and Catalogue for 2012, No 2182, 10 October 2011, available (in Chinese) at www.caigou2003.com/theory/list/20111017/list_200951.html.

[94] Available at /www.ndrc.gov.cn/zcfb/zcfbl/2013ling/W020130220338847842812.pdf.

on interoperability of various platforms, it remains silent on electronic procurement methods such as electronic reverse auction and e-catalogue. While neither GPL nor TL mentioned electronic procurement explicitly, there is also a growing concern that electronic government procurement (E-GP) and 'e-tendering' will be artificially severed and subject to different specific regulations and inconsistent technical standards.[95]

Open tendering is the preferred procedure under TL and GPL. Any deviation from open tendering needs to be justified and *ex ante* approved by relevant authorities. Under the GPL, contracts above certain threshold (as set by the centralised purchasing agency for the central Government and each provincial government) are subject to open tendering by default. Therefore, it is not surprising to see that according to the official data, the procurement via open tendering accounts for the lion's share of Chinese government procurement with the proportion for framework procurement not even reported.

Another important feature is that expert panels (so-called bid valuation committees, negotiation groups or quotation soliciting groups), consisting of experts randomly appointed from the official registry/database, are widely used to evaluate the bids, conduct competitive negotiation or seek quotation, and decide the winning contractor on behalf of the procuring entity, especially in tendering procedures. The discretion of the procuring entity/agency is greatly limited by the rigid requirement to follow the expert panel's recommendation (albeit with the possibility for the procuring entity to ask the panel to reconsider).

E. Remedies and Enforcement

The remedies and enforcement in Chinese procurement rules initially rely heavily on centralised enforcement by administrative supervisory bodies. The supplier review system (also called the 'domestic review' or 'bid challenge' system), which can be an effective mechanism for securing compliance with government procurement rules due to its deterrent and corrective effects, has gained increasing attention over the years.[96]

While TL provides in detail legal liabilities such as disciplinary and administrative sanctions, it is almost silent on the supplier review thus entrust the main responsibility to detect such infringement to administrative supervisory bodies.[97] The TL Article 65 simply states that bidders and other parties with interests who consider that the tendering activities are not in conformity with the relevant TL provision shall have the right to lodge an objection with the contracting party or to complain to the relevant administrative supervision department without providing any detailed rules.

The GPL, in contrast, in addition to relying on administrative measures for enforcement of government procurement rules,[98] provides detailed rules on supplier review

[95] See P Wang, 'Development of Electronic Government Procurement in China: A Case Study Prepared for the Asian Development Bank', October 2011, available at www.adb.org/sites/default/files/projdocs/2011/43149-012-reg-tacr-05.pdf.

[96] See X Zhang, 'Supplier Review as a Mechanism for Securing Compliance with Government Procurement Rules: A Critical Perspective' (2007) 5 *Public Procurement Law Review* 325.

[97] See the TL, Arts 49-64.

[98] The GPL provides more detailed rules on administrative supervision and legal liabilities than the TL in chapters 7 and 8.

in Articles 51–58 establishing a system similar to the review system recommended in the UNCITRAL Model Law on Procurement of Goods, Construction and Services. In Articles 51–58, the GPL briefly provides for rules on forum for review, standing and procedures as well as remedies available to aggrieved suppliers.

However, because it is not clear from the GPL and the TL whether the GPL's rules on supplier review apply to complaints arising from government procurement of works regulated by the TL, the NDRC and other central government departments,[99] based on the TL Article 65, issued the Measures on the Handling of Complaints on Tendering Proceedings in Construction Projects on 21 June 2004.[100] This ministerial regulation provides detailed rules on general principles of handling complaints, forum for review, procedural rules on filing of complaints and handling of complaints, decision-making and legal liabilities. One month later, the MoF, based on the GPL, adopted the Measures on the Handling of Complaints of the Government Procurement Suppliers on 11 August 2004.[101] The timing of the introduction of these ministerial regulations indicates that little efforts have been made to achieve harmonisation and the fragmentation of national laws (GPL and TL) has profound impact on the construction of the whole public procurement legal framework.

Although now both ministerial regulations are to the large extent succeeded by and codified in IRTL and IRGPL.[102] Certain inconsistencies regarding, inter alia, scope of coverage, forum for review and legal standing remain.

i. Scope of Coverage

Review rules under GPL arguably apply to complaints arising from i) government procurement of general goods and services through any procurement method,[103] ii) government procurement of works *not* through tendering and iii) government procurement of works-related goods and services *not* through tendering.

The review rules under TL and its implementing regulations usually apply to complaints regarding government procurement of works through tendering. As far as complaints arising from government procurement of works-related goods and services through tendering are concerned, it is unclear whether the GPL and its implementing regulations or the TL and its implementing regulations shall apply.

In addition, however, complaints arising from government procurement of mechanical and electrical goods *through international tendering* shall be dealt with according to the provisions on challenge contained in the Implementing Measures on International

[99] They are the Ministry of Construction, the Ministry of Railways, the Ministry of Communications, the Ministry of Information Industry, the Ministry of Water Resources and the General Administration of Civil Aviation of China.

[100] Effective on 1 August 2004.

[101] Effective on 11 September 2004.

[102] See IRTL Arts 57–61; IRGPL Arts 64–83.

[103] However, complaints arising from government procurement of mechanical and electrical goods *through international tendering* may be dealt with according to the provisions on challenge contained in the Implementing Measures on International Tendering in Procurement of Mechanical and Electronic Products issued by the Ministry of Commerce on 1 November 2004; see also Zhang, 'Supplier Review' (2007) ch 7.

Tendering in Procurement of Mechanical and Electronic Products issued by MOFCOM on 1 November 2004.

It is fair to say that the current system does not provide a clear demarcation between different set of review rules. In practice, it is difficult for the aggrieved suppliers and the procuring entities to ascertain which set of rules should apply. This difficulty in the past was addressed to the certain extent by, oddly as it may sound, the fragmented institutional framework for conducting procurement process. NDRC and MoF, as well as MOFCOM, have established their own centralised purchasing agencies at central and local level handling works tendering, government procurement, and international tendering of mechanical and electronic products respectively. These centres will normally apply the rules of their respective founding body.

ii. *Forum for Review*

The supplier review mechanisms currently provided in all the rules mentioned above share the common characteristic of multi-tiered system which may include the following stages:

- procuring entity review (handled by the procuring entity itself or its agent);[104]
- administrative review (handled by the competent administrative review body);
- administrative reconsideration (handled by a higher administrative body or other organs empowered by law to reconsider the administrative review body's decision); and
- administrative litigation (bringing the case before the administrative division of the court).

It should be pointed out that in China, so far as supplier review is concerned, the main review body is the designated administrative review body which has the powers to stay the procurement process and even to set aside concluded contract. There is arguably no real alternative to the above-mentioned tiered system such as bringing civil action under contract law or seeking judicial review of procuring entities' decisions.

This is because, first of all, although current laws and regulations regard government procurement contracts as *civil contracts*, they are silent about whether aggrieved suppliers can lodge a civil litigation directly against the procuring entity before the civil branch of the courts. Therefore, in practice, civil courts often refuse to accept such a case on the ground that no contract has been formed yet so the dispute over government procurement activities should be treated as an administrative case and accordingly should be first handled by the competent administrative review body and then be adjudicated by the administrative divisions of the court under the Administrative Litigation Law.

Secondly, despite the presumption of certain civil judges, procurement decisions of government agencies, let alone those of SOEs, are not regarded as 'administrative acts' that could be challenged directly before the administrative division of the

[104] This is a compulsory stage under IRTL (Art 60) and IRGPL (Art 52).

People's Courts.[105] Judicial review of decisions of public bodies as an important legal concept in common law jurisdictions cannot be equated with the Chinese administrative law norm of 'administrative litigation'. Furthermore, there is no consensus among common law jurisdictions regarding whether public procurement decisions should be subject to judicial review.[106]

Even though the case eventually reaches the administrative chambers of courts following the tiered system (likely to be long after the conclusion of the procurement process), the administrative division of the court can only review the decision of the administrative review body or administrative reconsideration body on points of law but not the substance, which means that it must exercise deference to the decision of the procuring entity in question. With the court arguably deprived of the power to issue effective interim measures, to set aside concluded contracts or to award adequate damages, it is difficult to see any incentive for aggrieved suppliers to engage in the judicial process.

Therefore, it is submitted that the role of Chinese judiciary in interpreting and developing Chinese public procurement rules is rather limited. Chinese courts have no tradition of teleological approach to interpretation often employed by the CJEU or awarding punitive damages in judicial review of procurement cases. This is in contrast with the EU practice, especially the important role of CJEU in shaping the procurement jurisprudence.

More problematic is the jurisdiction of different designated administrative review bodies. The co-existence of overlapping national procurement rules including that of remedies makes jurisdictional conflicts among review bodies almost inevitable. On the one hand, GPL designates the financial departments at all levels as the competent authority for supervising government procurement and handling supplier review (Article 13).[107] On the other hand, under the TL and its implementing regulations, numerous ministries have been designated as administrative review bodies for tendering activities falling under their respective sectors and prerogatives.[108] For example,

[105] Chinese Taipei takes a similar point of view. See *Taiwan Yutong Information Technology Limited v Taiwan Highway Authority and Yuantong Limited*, Taiwan Supreme Administrative Court [2006] 01239.

[106] On the other hand, the Privy Council ruled in 1994 in the context of fraud but not procurement that in New Zealand: 'a state enterprise is a public body; … The defendant [a state enterprise] carries on its business in the interest of the public. Decisions made in the public interest by the defendant, a corporate body established by statute, may adversely affect the rights and liabilities of private individuals without affording them any redress. Their Lordships take the view that in these circumstances the decisions of the defendant are amenable in principle to judicial review both under the Act of 1972 as amended and under the common law.' *Mercury Energy Limited v Electricity Corporation of New Zealand Limited* (1994) 1 WLR 521. On the other hand, the jurisprudence in certain common law jurisdictions is not conclusive regarding public procurement decisions, for example, for Caribbean jurisdictions. See KT Hudson-Phillips, 'Judicial Review and Public Procurement in Trinidad and Tobago', paper presented at the Caribbean Public Procurement (Law and Practice) Conference, 19 March 2008, available at www.academia.edu/1108544/Judicial_Review_of_Government_Procurement.

[107] The MoF is responsible for handling suppliers' complaints in government procurement activities under the central budget projects; and the financial departments of the local governments above the county level are responsible for dealing with suppliers' complaints in government procurement activities under the budget projects at the same level.

[108] IRTL, Art 5. See also the Opinions on the Division of Duties and Obligations among Relevant Organs of the State Council in Conducting Administrative Supervision upon Tendering Activities prepared by the NDRC and issued by the State Council on 3 May 2000.

the NDRC is entrusted to supervise tendering activities in major national construction projects and complaints about tendering activities in house construction and auxiliary installation projects should be handled by the Ministry of Construction and its successor, MOHURD. MOFCOM is responsible for dealing with complaints about international tendering/procurement of mechanical and electronic equipment.

Overlaps or conflicts of jurisdiction among these ministries seem inevitable. For example, complaints arising from a major high-speed railway project might fall simultaneously under the jurisdiction of the NDRC (as a major national infrastructure project), the National Railway Bureau (as a railway project) and MOFCOM (if import of mechanical or electronic equipment is involved).

There is also a real possibility that all ministries capable of hearing the complaint decline to take on the case, arguing others should handle it and leaving the aggrieved supplier in a legal 'black hole'. This happened in *Modern Wo'er*, the leading Chinese case on government procurement.[109] This case is associated with procurement by the Ministry of Health of portable blood gas analysers as part of a major national project – construction of a Public Health Rescue and Medical Treatment System – managed by the NDRC and the Ministry of Health in November 2004. The firm that tendered the lowest price was not awarded the contract. When it subsequently sought administrative review by NDRC and MoF, it was refused admission, both of them arguing the other should handle the complaint. When the court eventually handed down a judgment in December 2006 in accordance with the Administrative Litigation Law, it could only require MoF to accept the complaint and make a decision.

With a view to addressing such conflicts or failure to act, IRTL simply provides in Article 61 that 'when any bidder or party having interests files complaints regarding the *same* issue with two or more competent administrative review bodies, the complaint shall be handled by the administrative review body which received the complaint first' (emphasis added). On the other hand, IRGPL chose to stay silent on this important issue although its early draft contains a provision (deleted from the final version) stating that 'financial departments *may* terminate the administrative review procedure if any other government department has initiated procedures with regard to the same subject matter' (emphasis added).[110]

IRTL provision arguably gives rise to or even encourages forum shopping. It is not clear what will happen if multiple complaints are lodged by different bidders with regard

[109] *Beijing Modern Wo'er Trading Co.Ltd v Ministry of Finance of the People's Republic of China*, No 1 Intermediate People's Court of Beijing Municipality, First Level Administration Division Decisions No 432 and 433 (2005). See also D Mitterhoff, 'Beijing Court Orders Ministry of Finance to Rule on Supplier's Complaints, But Skirts Broader Issues of Schism in China's Procurement Supervision' (2006) 3 *International Government Contractor* 98.

[110] This provision was criticised by the author in 2013 in the report presented to MoF, which seems to have produced effect. The argument is that under such a provision, it is not clear what will happen if the financial department in question declined to exercise the discretion (as indicated by the use of 'may' instead of 'shall'). Even if the financial department is more than happy to relinquish its jurisdiction in favour of any other administrative department to reduce its workload as MoF has done in *Modern Wo'er* case mentioned above, such referral is arguably illegal since Art 13 of the GPL explicitly designates the financial departments as the competent authority for handling supplier review in the context of government procurement. See P Wang, CH Bovis and X Tu, 'A Comparative Analysis of Utilities Procurement in the EU and China', a report prepared for EU–China Trade Project II (2013).

to different aspects of the same procurement process. There is no procedural rule with regard to time limits, transfer of document or communication in such case referral.

IV. Obstacles Impeding Sustainable Development of PPPs in China

There are a number of obstacles that have the potential to impede the healthy and sustainable development of PPPs in China. As explained above in sections II and III, the main government procurement legislation, namely the Tendering Law and the Government Procurement Law and their respective implementing regulations, is silent on PPPs. Instead, various ministries, especially MoF and NDRC, issued numerous ministerial decrees (low in legal hierarchy in comparison with laws) with little coordination and often competing agenda. Due to the segregated institutional framework, the guidance issued at the central level is often inconsistent and has caused confusion in practice. Furthermore, the demarcation line between certain key legal norms, namely concession, PPP and 'government procurement of services', has not been clearly drawn up. With each term defined broadly enough to cover others and the authority for its interpretation held by different ministries, the segregated institutional framework inevitably resulted in competing and overlapping legislative initiatives.

There is also difficulty for local government procuring officials to choose the appropriate procuring method, especially whether the use of open tendering procedure is mandatory. The lack of participation from private sector/the dominance of central SOEs in the PPP market has caused serious market concentration and accumulation of risks for central SOEs.

The remedy system for PPP contracts is also unsatisfactory. A number of recent Supreme People's Court rulings demonstrate that the inconsistent interpretation of the nature of a PPP contract (as an administrative agreement or a civil contract) has led to arguably contradicting findings by the court and left the aggrieved party with no effective legal remedy. This section seeks to identify these issues using international experience and guidance as benchmarks where appropriate.

A. Segregated Institutional Framework and Fragmented Legal Framework

International experiences indicate that the success of PPPs relies on sound PPP institutional and regulatory frameworks that 'promote sound project selection, fair and competitive procurement, effective delivery of public services, and the ultimate success and sustainability of PPP programs'.[111] Although there is no single template for how PPPs are regulated, it is suggested that regulation of PPPs may over the time 're-integrate with normal public investment and infrastructure planning, procurement,

[111] See World Bank, PPP Reference Guide 2017, s 2 and the work cited there, available at ppp.worldbank.org/public–private-partnership/library/ppp-reference-guide-3-0.

and fiscal management processes' facing the same standards in order to prevent PPPs from being used to circumvent rules and checks.[112] The OECD's recommendation on public governance of PPPs also suggest guiding principles including establishing a clear, predictable and legitimate institutional framework supported by competent and well-resourced authorities, grounding the selection of PPPs in value for money, using the budget process transparently to minimise fiscal risks and ensuring the integrity of the procurement process, and careful evaluation of new and existing regulations.[113]

In China, as the evolution of the legal framework for both government procurement and PPP demonstrated, there are numerous state and local organs involved in regulating public procurement and PPPs. The reason for the fragmented legal framework is arguably the segregated and incoherent institutional framework. As history shows, NDRC is in charge of TL, while MoF is the guardian of GPL. NDRC launched the first batch of BOT projects and took charge of Concession legislation, while MoF adopted the first genuine PPP guidelines. It can be argued that the MoF as the 'bookkeeper', the NDRC as the 'investor' and 'planner' for the state are all building their own 'fortress of regulation' on public procurement and PPPs. On the side, other line ministries such as the Ministry of Housing and the Urban Rural Construction, MIIT, the Ministry of Transportation, the Ministry of Water Resources and the General Administration of Civil Aviation are in charge of supervising tendering activities (including the PPP projects) within their respective fields and acting as review bodies for supplier challenges.

As we have seen above, they, especially NDRC and MoF, often concurrently enact competing rules on tendering proceedings, evaluation expert databases, approved procuring agencies, designated media, publicity, review procedure and so on. This has caused not only duplication and waste of resources, but also inconsistency which jeopardises legal certainty. In this sense, the Chinese Government does not have the same benefit of the UK Government which has Infrastructure UK affiliated to the Treasury.

As explained in section III A, the inter-ministerial coordination mechanism established in 2005 has done little to really coordinate the competing regulatory activities of the 'major players' in public procurement. The evolution of the PPP regulation since 2013 explained above in section I E has indeed demonstrated that the coordination mechanism is clearly not fulfilling its purpose.

The most recent attempt made by the State Council to divide the competence between NDRC and MoF in July 2016 was to confer regulatory power with regard to PPPs involving traditional infrastructure upon NDRC, and that with regard to PPPs involving public services upon MoF.[114] However, such division is only reflected in the title of subsequent measures adopted by NDRC and MoF respectively, namely August 2016 NDRC Notice on Implementation of PPP in Traditional Infrastructure and October 2016 MoF Notice on Promoting PPP in Public Services. The substantial coverage of these two Notices remains overlapping: the NDRC Notice covers energy, transportation, water resources, environmental protection, agriculture, forestry, urban utilities and related sectors; the MoF Notice covers all sectors mentioned above

[112] ibid.

[113] OECD, Recommendation of the Council on Principles for Public Governance of Public–private Partnerships, May 2012, at A.3, available at www.oecd.org/governance/budgeting/PPP-Recommendation.pdf.

[114] See the news report at http://finance.sina.com.cn/roll/2016-10-13/doc-ifxwvpqh7320167.shtml.

and in addition, affordable housing, medical care, elderly care, education, technology, culture, sport and tourism. With due respect, it is irrational and impossible to distinguish PPPs based upon a distinction between infrastructure and public service since such a distinction simply does not exist. The construction, rehabilitation and maintenance of infrastructure is the means-to-an-end provision of public service. It probably makes more sense to divide PPPs into user-pays PPPs such as concessions and government-pays PPPs and confer regulatory power accordingly. However, that is not plausible either as under the current rules (for example, 2015 Infrastructure and Public Utilities Concession Measure), the concept of concession covers not only use-pays PPPs but also government-pays PPPs.

B. Overlapping Legal Norms

As explained above in section I, there are no universally accepted definitions for key terms such as 'concession', 'PPP' or 'outsourcing'. Different countries/jurisdictions give different meanings to those legal norms. However, it is necessary for a national legal framework to draw a clear demarcation line between these key norms in order to safeguard legal certainty. Unfortunately, that has not been achieved so far in China.

i. PPP v Concession

The 2015 Infrastructure and Public Utilities Concession Measure Article 3 defines 'concession' as follows:

> [T]he government, through competitive methods, authorises domestic and foreign legal persons or other organisations to invest, construct and operate certain infrastructure and public utilities for a certain period with a view to the provision of public goods or services and receiving payment, in accordance with rights, obligations and risk sharing as provided in the agreement.

It is important to point out that this definition, unlike those under the EU Directive and other international instruments such as the World Bank guidance, does not specify how: i) the concessionaire shall be remunerated, for the most part, by the right to exploit the underlying assets, such as through payments by the users; and ii) significant commercial risks shall be transferred to the concessionaire, including demand risk. These two defining features are arguably the key distinction between conventional public procurement and concessions. An arrangement is not a concession if the terms of the contract remove or substantially limit any element of risk for the provider. For example, if an agreement were to provide a guaranteed reasonable level of income from the procuring entity if the user fees were insufficient, this might not be a service concession.[115]

Therefore, it can be argued that the concept of concession in the Chinese context goes beyond user-pays PPPs and includes government-pays PPPs as well. This view is contemplated by the Deputy Director of NDRC's Legal Department who, in a speech

[115] Case C-382/05, *Commission v Italy* [2007] ECR I-6657 (Italian waste-processing contract); and Case C-437/07, *Commission v Italy* ECJ judgment of 13 November 2008.

delivered in July 2016, stated that 'the mode of payment under a concession includes user-pays, government pays and other modes such as viability gap funding'.[116]

On the other hand, 2014 MoF PPP Guidance provides that:

> PPP is a long-term cooperation relationship between the government and social capital in the field of infrastructure and public services. The social capital is entrusted with the design, construction, operation and maintenance of infrastructure and reasonably remunerated through payment by users or the government and the government is in charge of price and quality supervision in order to maximise public interests.[117]

While this definition is to a large extent in line with various definitions found in the international instruments, it overlaps significantly with the term 'concession' as defined in the 2015 Infrastructure and Public Utilities Concession Measure.

It seems that the NDRC seeks to retain its authority in the development and approval of infrastructure projects by construing broadly the concept of concession with a view to replacing the term PPP. This is arguably against the common approach adopted in other jurisdictions such as the EU. Such deliberate ambiguity, due to the incoherent institutional framework, has resulted in competing legislative initiatives and duplicated requirement for administrative approval by different authorities. It is ironic to note that even the NDRC is not consistent itself as the NDRC adopted a measure in October 2016 which states that 'PPP includes concessions and government procurement of services' seemingly restricting the scope of concession.[118]

NDRC initially proposed the draft of 'Concession Law' whilst MoF proposed the draft of 'PPP Law' both included in the government legislative agenda and with the view to regulating the PPP market as a whole. The State Council had to step in following the criticism of the Premier,[119] who stated that rule of law should prevail over departmental interests, and the Legislative Department of the State Council should take the lead instead. The draft PPP Regulation was released for public consultation in July 2017.[120] However, as explained below in section V, the Draft PPP Regulation failed to clarify the demarcation line between concession and PPP as it does not mention the term 'concession' at all.

ii. PPP v Government Procurement of Services

In September 2013, the State Council Secretariat issued an Opinion encouraging government procurement services from private enterprises and civil society organisations in

[116] Zhang, Yefeng, Deputy Director of NDRC's Legal Department, 'Infrastructure and Public Utilities Development Forum', July 2016, Beijing, keynote speech, available (in Chinese) at www.douban.com/note/573659739/. The term 'viability gap funding' is explained in E Farquharson, C Torres de Mästle, ER Yescombe and J Encinas, 'How to Engage with the Private Sector in Public–private Partnerships in Emerging Markets' (World Bank, 2011) 66–67.

[117] Article 1 of MoF 2014 PPP Guidance, MoF, Notice on Questions Relating to Expanding the Use of PPPs (关于推广运用政府和社会资本合作模式有关问题的通知), 23 September 2014, available (in Chinese) at http://jrs.mof.gov.cn/zhengwuxinxi/zhengcefabu/201409/t20140924_1143760.html.

[118] Article 3 of NDRC Notice on Issuing the Guiding Rules for Implementing Public–private Partnership Projects in Traditional Infrastructure Fields, adopted on 24 October 2016, available in Chinese at www.ndrc.gov.cn/zcfb/zcfbtz/201610/t20161027_824138.html.

[119] Speech by Premier Li, Keqiang, on the role of government, rule of law and departmental interests, 9 May 2016, available (in Chinese) at www.gov.cn/guowuyuan/2016-07/08/content_5089655.htm

[120] The draft is available in Chinese at http://zqyj.chinalaw.gov.cn/readmore?id=1984&listType=1.

the area of education, employment, social security, medical care, housing, culture and sport, disabled care.[121] The MoF adopted the Interim Measure on Government Procurement of Services in December 2014.[122] The term 'government procurement of services' is defined in Article 2 as 'the government entrusts the provision of certain public services for which it is responsible, in accordance with certain procedure and market competition, to social force and institutions and makes payment according to the contract'.

In the absence of any prohibition on deferred payment, this definition is certainly broad enough to cover government-pay PPPs. To make it more confusing, MoF September 2014 PPP Guidance actually states in Article I:3 that 'PPP is, in essence, government procurement of services'. It is not clear whether any internal coordination has been done by different departments of the MoF. Government procurement of service in Chinese context is arguably a form of contracting out and clearly subject to the regulation of GPL. The rationale for distinctive regulation of such procurement is unclear. Government-pay PPPs could also be regarded falling into the scope of government procurement therefore subject to the regulation of GPL.

In practice, there has been widespread abuse by local governments seeking to categorise government-pay PPPs as government procurement of services contracts.[123] The reasons for such behaviour are arguably threefold: i) the approval of government-pay PPPs is subject to rigid value-for-money and fiscal affordability assessment; ii) single source procurement can be used more easily with regard to government procurement of services; and iii) the commitment towards PPPs is capped at 10 per cent of annual expenditure.

Such abuse has prompted the MoF to issue a special Notice in May 2017[124] and to draft a new Measure on Government Procurement of Services with a view to preventing circumvention, which was released for public consultation on 26 June 2018.[125] It is encouraging to see that the draft limits the contract period to no more than three years and excludes those contracts involving works (or combination of works and services).

C. Issues with SOEs as Partners in PPPs

For a project to be regarded as PPP by the World Bank and included in its PPI database, a minimum 20 per cent of private participation is required.[126] One of the objectives

[121] State Council Secretariat, Guiding Opinion on Government Procurement of Services from Social Forces, 26 Sep. 2013, available in Chinese at www.gov.cn/zwgk/2013-09/30/content_2498186.htm.

[122] MoF, Interim Measure on Government Procurement of Services (政府营买服务管理办法（暂行), 15 December 2014, available in Chinese at http://zhs.mof.gov.cn/zhengwuxinxi/zhengcefabu/201501/t20150104_1175300.html.

[123] MoF Staff Policy Comment, 'Government Procurement of Services and PPP are different', available in Chinese at www.ccgp.gov.cn/ppp/llyj/201704/t20170417_8122646.htm.

[124] MoF, Notice on Prohibition of Illegal Financing Behaviour by Local Governments under the Name of Government Procurement of Services (关于坚决制止地方以政府营买服务名义违法违规融资的通知) [2017] No 87, May 2017, available in Chinese at http://yss.mof.gov.cn/zhengwuxinxi/zhengceguizhang/201706/t20170602_2614514.html.

[125] MoF, Notice on the public consultation of Drafting Measure on Government Procurement of Services, 26 June 2018, available in Chinese at http://tfs.mof.gov.cn/zhengwuxinxi/zhengcefabu/201806/t20180626_2939688.html.

[126] World Bank, PPI Database Methodology 2015, available at https://ppi.worldbank.org/methodology/ppi-methodology.

and benefits of PPPs is to expose SOEs and government to competition provided by private enterprises, but the involvement of SOEs as the counterparty may undermine such competition as private enterprises will be deterred. It is argued that there is no effective allocation of risk when SOEs are the partner in PPPs since, ultimately, the risks of both the partner and government are retained by the state.[127]

However, as explained in section II E, SOEs are included in the concept of 'social capital' referring to the counterparty to the Government in PPPs and have indeed become the main partner for local governments. It is reported that SOEs took the lion's share (74 per cent) of 1,401 PPP projects (CNY 2.35 trillion) procured in 2016.[128] As of 29 November 2017, 53.31 per cent of all PPP projects worth CNY 6.2993 trillion have been awarded to SOEs. It is also noteworthy that the largest six central SOEs operating in the construction sector that have easy access to the capital market have recently taken 45 per cent of the PPPs market over three years.[129] With local governments mainly relying on SOEs for low-profit undertakings financed by state-owned banks, PPPs, as explained above in section II F, have given rise to significant systematic financial and fiscal risk and been subject to various measures adopted by MoF and SASAC since mid-2017 with a clear objective of deleveraging of SOEs.

The reasons for the dominance of SOEs in PPP market are arguably more practical than regulatory. Firstly, the low return rate of around five to eight per cent make PPP projects less attractive to private firms. Secondly, SOEs are perceived by local governments and state-owned banks to be more stable partners due to their state ownership and capacity to absorb losses in the event of project failures. Thirdly, SOEs are not tough negotiators in the procurement process and less sensitive about shouldering more risks.[130] Last but not least, due to the widespread presence of SOEs in construction and utilities sectors, they may actually provide value for money despite state ownership.

In fact, existing PPP regulations strongly promote the involvement of private enterprises. For example, 2013 Decisions on Major Issues Concerning Comprehensively Deepening Reforms put a special emphasis on allowing private enterprises to become concessionaries.[131] The 2014 MoF PPP Operational Guide precludes local SOEs from providing capital to PPP projects in the same region (Article 2). Moreover, MoF, in its Notices on Model PPP projects, has consistently provided that 'private capital shall be preferred under equivalent circumstances'.[132] However, it is apparent that these regulatory measures have made little differences in practice. The weak regulatory environment as a whole does not provide sufficient confidence to private enterprises to commit to long-term contracts with local governments that often fail to honour such contracts after the change of leadership. It is suggested by the UK Treasury in a report

[127] P Kelly, 'Preparing a Public Private Partnership Law: Observations From the International Experience', ADB East Asia Working Paper Series No 4, April 2016, 19–20, available at www.adb.org/publications/preparing-ppp-law-observations-international-experience.

[128] See the unofficial report at based on statistics provided by MoF and provincial websites: www.sohu.com/a/124765400_480400.

[129] See www.sasac.gov.cn//n2588025/n2588139/c8297412/content.html.

[130] C Changand and S Chen, 'Transitional Public–Private Partnership Model in China: Contracting with Little Recourse to Contracts.' (2016) 142 *Journal of Construction Engineering and Management*.

[131] Article 2(8), available (in Chinese) at http://sjw.gzlps.gov.cn/xxgk/djfg/201709/t20170926_1520464.html.

[132] See www.cpppc.org/zh/zyxmqd/4127.jhtml.

prepared for China that 'contracts between a public body and a SOE could reflect some PPP principles, but are perhaps best regarded as transitional structures on the journey toward more market-based relationships and achieving fully-fledged PPPs between public and private bodies'.[133]

D. Difficulty in Choosing the Appropriate Procuring Method

There is a strong argument that open tendering is not suitable for the procurement of PPPs. Open tendering is designed to work under clear and predetermined specifications often lacking in PPPs with only the need/output is defined; open tendering requires the Government to set specific design criteria, limiting the ability of private bidders to propose alternative and innovative approaches, which is one of the main benefits of PPPs; open tendering generally prohibits informal communication between the public and private sectors, whereas communication is the cornerstone of a successful PPP and must start as early as possible in the project planning process.[134] The 2011 UNCITRAL Model Law on Public Procurement offers a wider range of procurement methods, including, in particular, one method provided in its Article 49 ('request for proposals with dialogue') that was developed on the basis of the selection procedures recommended in chapter III ('Selection of the concessionaire') of the PFIP Legislative Guide. Request for proposals with dialogue is considered to be the adequate procurement method for both user-pay and government-pay PPPs.[135]

In China, the procurement of PPPs such as BOT projects and concessions were subject to open tendering during early phases. This is mainly because the Tendering Law, as explained in section III, requires infrastructure projects funded by public finance or involving public interest shall be procured through open or restricted tendering. Since NDRC is both the approving authority of infrastructure investment projects and the 'guardian' of the Tendering Law, it is not surprising that open tendering was regarded as the 'standard' procurement method for concessions and BOT projects. For example, the Highway Law adopted in 2005 and amended in 2017 requires that highway construction projects shall be procured through competitive tendering (Article 23).

However, in practice, due to the inadequacy of open tendering for procuring PPPs, local governments have tried to circumvent the requirement by using open tendering to select the partner then engaging in negotiation with it. This is evident in the procurement of Laibin B power plant project in Guangxi Province.[136]

[133] United Kingdom HM Treasury, 'Supporting the Development of PPPs in the People's Republic of China: An International Perspective', March 2015, 10, available at https://assets.publishing.service.gov.uk/government/uploads/system/uploads/attachment_data/file/438892/IUK_Report_1_Chinese_PPP_Enabling_Environment__executive__FINAL.pdf. However, section 5 of the report (Review of China's PPP Frameworks) was intentionally omitted.

[134] E Bennett, S James and P Grohmann, 'Joint Venture Public–private Partnerships for Urban Environmental Services, Report on United Nations Development Programme (UNDP)/PPPUE's Project Development Facility (PDF) (1995–1999)' (2000) 30–31, available at, www.ucl.ac.uk/dpu-projects/drivers_urb_change/urb_infrastructure/pdf_public_private_services/UNDP_PPPUE_Joint%20Venture_2.pdf.

[135] UNCITRAL, 'Public–private partnerships (PPPs): Proposed Updates to the UNCITRAL Legislative Guide on Privately Financed Infrastructure Project – Note by the Secretariat', A/CN.9/939, 6 April 2017.

[136] Wang and Ke, 'Case Study IV' (2009) ch 5.

On 31 December 2014, MoF adopted two ministerial rules regulating the procurement of PPP projects: Measures for Administration of Government Procurement in PPP Projects and Interim Measures for the Administration of Government Procurement through Competitive Dialogue. These measures provide a new procurement method-competitive dialogue. It is similar to the request for proposals with dialogue method in UNCITRAL Model Law and competitive dialogue in EU Public Contract Directive 2014 (Article 30).[137] In comparison with competitive negotiation procedure provided in the GPL, the competitive dialogue shifts from using lowest price as the main award criterion to using a scoring system where price may account for 30–60 per cent for goods or 10–30 per cent for services procurement. NDRC in subsequent Guidelines on PPP (for example, 2015 MoF, NDRC, People's Bank of China, Guidelines on Promoting PPP in Public Service) also acknowledged the possibility of using competitive dialogue to procure PPP projects.

However, it is argued that the extent to which competitive dialogue can be legally used to procure PPPs remains unclear. Article 3 of the MoF 2014 Competitive Dialogue Measure provides that competitive dialogue can be used in, inter alia, government procurement of services and procurement of construction projects 'other than those subject to mandatory tendering as required by the Tendering Law and its implementing regulation'. It can be argued that neither of these conditions may justify the use of competitive dialogue procedure in PPP procurement. Firstly it is problematic and undesirable to regard PPPs as government procurement of services given the abuse occurred in practice discussed above in section II F and the measures adopted by MoF mentioned in section IV B 2. Secondly, PPP is not a typical construction project since it normally involves both the construction of infrastructure (works element) and the operation and maintenance of the resulted works (service element), thus a mixed contract. Furthermore, even if PPPs can be regarded as construction projects (eg the value of works exceeds the value of service component), they are likely to be subject to mandatory tendering as required by the Tendering Law since PPPs often involves public interest associated with provision of public service through construction or managing infrastructure.

Furthermore, the competitive dialogue method only allows 10 days for potential tenders to respond to the call for dialogue. This is longer than three-day provided for competitive negotiation, but arguably remains insufficient. Last but not least, as explained below in section V D, despite the draft State Council PPP Regulation allowing the use of both tendering and competitive dialogue as competitive procuring methods, the most recent NDRC PPP measure adopted in June 2019 stipulates open tendering as the preferred procuring method for PPPs, which indicates the lack of consensus among the regulators.

E. Difficulty in Obtaining Effective Legal Remedy

It is difficult for the counterparty to the Government in PPPs to obtain effective legal remedy in China. Such difficulty is caused first of all by the uncertainty as to whether

[137] See S Arrowsmith and S Treumer (eds), *Competitive Dialogue in EU Procurement* (Cambridge, Cambridge University Press, 2012).

a PPP contract (including a BOT or concession agreement) shall be regarded as a civil contract or an administrative agreement/contract that are subject to mutually exclusive jurisdictions of the civil or administrative division of the courts respectively and secondly by the uncertainty as to whether arbitration is available due to the restrictive provision in the Arbitration Law precluding the use of arbitration in disputes arising from an administrative agreement.

Early case law of the Supreme People's Court suggests that the court was not entirely consistent in deciding the nature of a PPP contract. In the case of *Tian Rui Ltd v Hetian City Government*, the 2nd Civil Chamber of the Supreme People's Court ruled that a 20-year concession contract of gas supply, which had been unilaterally cancelled by Hetian City, was an administrative contract. The court stated that the concession contract was concluded by Hetian City Government in accordance with its public authority of granting concession rights. Even though the plaintiff entered into the concession contract with a view to seeking profit, and the contract provided for rights and obligations of both parties, the subject matter related to construction and provision of public goods and services and the Government enjoyed special status in the contractual relationship given its role in the grant of concession and subsequent supervision. Therefore the cancellation of the concession amounted to an administrative behaviour on the part of Hetian City.[138] However, in another case, *Beijing Beifang Dianlian Ltd. v. Wulumuqi City Transportation Bureau*, the 2nd Civil Chamber of the Supreme People's Court ruled that the dispute related to the sum of compensation arising from mutually agreed termination of a highway BOT project should be heard as a civil dispute.[139]

In April 2015, the Supreme People's Court adopted the Interpretation on Several Issues concerning the Application of the Administrative Litigation Law which entered into force on 1 May 2015. It provides in Article 11 that agreements having content on Administrative Law rights and obligations negotiated and concluded between administrative organs and citizens, legal persons or other organisations for the purpose of realising public interest or administrative management goals, are 'administrative agreements' and administrative suits regarding concession agreements shall be admitted. It can be argued that other PPP contracts, by analogy, shall be treated as administrative agreements as well.

However, subsequent case law indicates that the nature of PPP/concession contracts remains unclear. In the case *Xinling Highway Ltd v Huixian City Government*, the 1st Civil Chamber of the Supreme Court found that a highway BOT contract was in fact a civil contract. The finding was based upon the facts that the project does not provide free public services to the public (charging tolls); the BOT agreement was a consensus between two autonomous equal parties. The Court held that provisions regarding administrative review, approval and grant of concession rights were mere component part of the contract and should not be used to determine the nature of the agreement.[140]

[138] Supreme People's Court (2nd Civil Chamber), No 12, ruling of 7 July 2014, available (in Chinese) at www.court.gov.cn/wenshu/xiangqing-5951.html.

[139] Supreme People's Court (2nd Civil Chamber), No 40, ruling of 25 July 2014, available (in Chinese) at www.court.gov.cn/wenshu/xiangqing-4160.html.

[140] This case is discussed by H Sun, 'The Public–private Partnerships Law Review – China', April 2018, available at https://thelawreviews.co.uk/edition/the-public-private-partnerships-law-review-edition-4/1168039/china.

It can be argued that this ruling clearly contradicts the reasoning adopted in *Tian Rui Ltd v Hetian City Government* discussed above and the spirit of the 2015 Interpretation.

In the case *Zhonghuan TianChuan Water Ltd v Chihu Town Government*,[141] the Supreme Court held on 30 December 2015 that disputes related to certain public interest safeguard provision of a waste water treatment concession contract should be regarded as administrative litigation. In this case, the plaintiff refused to carry out waste water treatment since the quality of those water was lower than agreed standard despite numerous complaints. The defendant then invoking the public safety and environmental protection safeguard provision of the contract, took over the facility and subsequently terminated the contract. The plaintiff initiated both administrative and civil litigation in parallel. The administrative suit was first rejected by the local court but accepted by higher Intermediate Court. However, the plaintiff failed to obtain administrative remedy as no illegality could be established with regard to the administrative actions (taking over the facility and termination of the concession) of the defendant and the administrative court does not have the authority to grant contractual compensation. On the other hand, whilst the civil court has the authority to grant contractual remedies, the civil suit was ruled to be inadmissible as the provision relied up by the defendant is clearly administrative in nature. At the end, the plaintiff (a SOE affiliated to the Chinese Academy of Environmental Science) was left with no effective means to recoup its investment. This case is an astonishing example of how the uncertainty in law and jurisprudence may deprive PPP's social capital partners of effective legal redress.

A survey of 40 practitioners in Hong Kong shows that arbitration is the most popular method, after negotiation, for resolving disputes in international construction projects in China.[142] A number of model PPP contracts issued by various ministries provide for the possibility of using arbitration to resolve disputes. However, the Arbitration Law Article 3 provides that disputes involving contractual and other property rights may be resolved through arbitration and administrative disputes shall not be subject to arbitration. The ambiguity with regard to the nature of PPP contracts arguably also render the use of arbitration in PPP disputes uncertain.

V. Appraisal of the Draft PPP Regulation

In light of the defects of the PPP regulatory environment identified above, it is important to assess the extent to which these issues will be effectively addressed by the current legislative initiative, namely the Draft State Council PPP Regulation. The development of PPPs has reached an important crossroad. On the one hand, PPPs seem to have lost the favour of top leadership given the widespread abuse and heightened financial and fiscal risk. PPPs were mentioned in the Annual State Council Government Work Report to the National People's Congress from 2015 to 2017, but not mentioned at all in the

[141] Supreme Court (2015) Civil Appeal No 3013.

[142] EHW Chan and HCH Suen, 'Dispute Resolution Management for International Construction Projects in China' (2005) 43 *Management Decision* 589.

2018 report. On the other hand, PPPs remain a useful tool for China to meet the need for infrastructure investment and public service reform. However, the true potential of PPPs can only be realised if the regulatory environment can be improved significantly to generate confidence of private and foreign investors and to provide much needed coherent, consistent and clear regulatory framework. This is not an easy task faced by the Draft PPP Regulation, which is due to be enacted by the end of 2018.

A. Sufficient Legal Force and Coordination with Existing Laws and Regulations?

At the outset, it is noteworthy that the Draft PPP Regulation is a State Council Regulation that needs to be approved by the Standing Committee of the National People's Congress. However, it does not carry the same legal force as national laws enacted by the National People's Congress itself. On the other hand, the draft 'Concession Law' by NDRC and the draft 'PPP Law' by MoF, replaced by the Draft PPP Regulation, are both designed to be national laws ranked higher than State Council Regulations in legal hierarchy.

This means the draft PPP Regulation is incapable of addressing inconsistencies found in other national laws undermining the coherent and consistent regulation of PPPs. For example, it cannot preclude the application of GPL to certain government-pay PPPs or that of TL to PPPs involving construction of infrastructure serving public interests. Similar coordination with other existing laws such as Guarantee Law, Property Law (regarding transfer of existing assets to PPPs), Land Law (the requirement for public land use right to be auctioned) and Arbitration Law will also be difficult.

It is also noteworthy that the Draft PPP Regulation makes no attempt to evaluate, consolidate or repeal existing Laws, numerous ministerial/departmental rules, guidance and local government regulatory measures. No periodic review of such measures or different versions of standard/model PPP contracts has been suggested.

B. Integration of Institutional Framework?

Article 7 of the Draft PPP Regulation provides that ministries are responsible for guiding and supervising PPPs 'within scope of their respective duties', jointly adopting administrative measures where multiple areas are involved, and coordinating in resolving major issues through a PPP Coordination Mechanism to be established by the State Council.

It can be argued that the Draft PPP Regulation has made insufficient effort in clarify the duties and authorities of the ministries involved in PPPs. As discussed above in sections III and IV A, the State Council has tried in the past to rely on inter-ministerial coordination mechanism to resolve regulatory conflicts between NDRC and MoF. That did not work before and will not work for PPPs regulation either. The current division of duty between NDRC and MoF in July 2016 is arguably unclear and misleading at the best as discussed above in section IV A.

The need for a coherent institutional framework is paramount as explained above in the absence of which a clear and sound regulatory environment cannot be created.

Rather than relying on the good intention of the ministries, it is submitted that a central unit providing gateway checks, maintenance of a unified project library and policy guidance as soft law measures shall be created using staff from NDRC, MoF and other ministries. The recent institutional reform, which created the State Administration for Market Regulation integrating the functions of competition regulation previously held by NDRC and other ministries, provides a good precedent in this regard.[143]

C. Harmonisation of Legal Norms?

The overlap between concession and PPP is arguably the most significant defect of the current legal framework as explained above in section IV B i. The definition of PPPs provided in Article 2 states that PPPs means activities where the Government selects, through competitive methods, the social capital which, upon reaching agreements with the Government laying down both parties' rights and obligations, provides investment, construction, operation of infrastructure and public service projects, and receives reasonable remuneration through payment made by users, the Government or government subsidies. This PPP's definition is clearly broad enough to cover the definition of 'concessions' found in the 2015 concession measure.

However, the Draft PPP Regulation did not mention at all the term 'concession'. Nor does it not attempt to clarify the extent to which government-pay PPPs may be regarded as government procurement.

D. Clarification of the Appropriate Procurement Method?

Article 13 of the Draft PPP Regulation provides that the government implementing institution shall select the social capital through 'competitive methods such as tendering, competitive negotiation etc' and that 'provisions on selection methods, applicable to certain infrastructure and public service projects contained in other laws or administrative regulations, shall be applied'.

This provision arguably means a national law such as the Highway Law which requires tendering for toll road projects will continue to apply. It is absurd that competitive negotiation method, instead of competitive dialogue, has been mentioned explicitly. As discussed above in section IV D, neither tendering nor competitive negotiation (as defined in IRGPL and MoF 2014 Measure on Non-Tendering Procurement Methods) is suitable for the procurement of PPPs. The former leaves no room for more efficient and innovative solutions that may emerge through negotiations, and the latter relies heavily on lowest price as the award criterion, potentially undermining the quality of the infrastructure and service provided.

This provision does not define the term 'tendering' or 'competitive negotiation', nor does it make any reference to other regulation where the definition of these terms can be found. Although the provision is general enough to allow for the use of 'other

[143] See the reform plan at http://samr.saic.gov.cn/jg/zjzz.

competitive procurement methods', it does not provide any useful guidance at all as to important legal questions such as i) whether tendering refers to open and selective tendering only or also covers two stage tendering, ii) whether all competitive methods can be used without the need to meet any specific conditions, and iii) whether non-competitive procurement method, namely single source procurement, can no longer be used in any circumstances.

In this context it is noteworthy that in its most recent PPP measure adopted in July 2019, the NDRC states that 'open tendering shall be the main method used to select the social capital'.[144] This provision clearly reflects the entrenched view of the NDRC with regard to the appropriate procurement method for PPPs, but is not necessarily in line with the Draft PPP Regulation nor the practical needs of PPP projects as explained in section IV D above.

E. Effective Legal Remedy in the Event of Disputes?

Articles 38 and 40 of the Draft PPP Regulation provides that disputes about the performance of the agreement may be resolved through negotiation, arbitration or litigation before the court. Article 41 further provides that the with regard to specific administrative acts by the relevant government department related to the execution, supervision and administration of the project, social capital may provide statement, complain and request for administrative reconsideration or initiate administrative litigation.

The draft PPP Regulation has arguably taken the view that some disputes arising from the context of PPPs are civil in nature, such as those related to the performance of the contract, and therefore may be resolved through arbitration or civil litigation, while others are administrative in nature, arising from administrative acts relating to execution, supervision, and administration of the project. However, it is difficult in practice to ascertain whether certain act of a local government is civil or administrative in nature. As demonstrated by the Supreme Court's case law discussed above in section IV E, a local government's request to purchase back the concession right once construction of the infrastructure is completed may be regarded as giving rise to either an administrative (as in the *Tianrui v Hetian City* case) or civil (as in the *Xinling Highway v Huixian City* case) dispute by the judiciary.

With regard to early termination of the project, thè draft PPP Regulation provides in Article 27 that any project can be terminated in the event of i) force majeure, ii) serious breach of the agreement by the social capital causing harm to public interest, and iii) appropriation of the project assets in accordance with the law (whereas the social capital is entitled to reasonable compensation). It is unclear whether the social capital is also entitled to compensation in the event of serious breach harming public interest. It certainly seems disproportionate a penalty to appropriate all investment made by the social capital as demonstrated in the *Zhonghuan Tianchuan v Chihu City* case discussed above in section IV E.

[144] NDRC, Notice on Strengthening Investment and Construction of PPP Projects in accordance with Regulation (关于依法依规加强PPP项目投资和建设管理的通知), 21 June 2019, Art 8, available in Chinese at http://tzs.ndrc.gov.cn/tzgz/201907/t20190701_940617.html.

To sum up, the draft PPP Regulation (with 49 Articles in total) resembles a patchwork rather than well-thought-through legislation. Although it may provide a Regulation ranked higher in legal hierarchy, it arguably lacks the details and essential elements to address existing defects of the PPP regulatory environment.

VI. Conclusion

After more than 30 years of development, China has become one of the most important PPPs markets in the world. However, since mid-2017, the need for sound regulation of PPPs has become paramount in light of widespread abuse and increased fiscal and financial risks.

It is argued that the regulation of PPP in China is beset with uncertainty arguably caused by segregated institutional framework, incoherent legal framework, ambiguous and overlapping legal norms, inconsistent provisions and contradictory jurisprudence. It is argued that the draft PPP Regulation does not fully resolve the identified issues since it does not have the same legal status as a national law; does not mention 'concession' at all (thus failing to clarify the fate of existing concession measures); does not clarify the application of other national laws such as those on land management, state assets, property and arbitration; and does not contain detailed provision on the choice or operation of procurement methods. For such a long-term cooperation contract as PPP which plays a vital role in the delivery of infrastructure and public service, the need for legal certainty is paramount but has not yet been met. It is submitted that the regulation of PPPs in China continues to search for coherence, consistency and legal certainty.

INDEX

Note: Alphabetical arrangement is word-by-word, where a group of letters followed by a space is filed before the same group of letters followed by a letter, eg 'capital markets will appear before 'capitalism'. In determining alphabetical arrangement, initial articles and prepositions are ignored.